Organizational Behavior

Securing Competitive Advantage

Third Edition

John A. Wagner III
John R. Hollenbeck

both of
Michigan State University

Prentice Hall
Upper Saddle River, New Jersey 07458

Editor-in-Chief: Natalie Anderson
Editorial Assistant: Dawn Marie Reisner
Marketing Manager: Stephanie Johnson
Associate Managing Editor: David Salierno
Production Coordinator: Ivy Azoff
Managing Editor: Dee Josephson
Manufacturing Buyer: Kenneth J. Clinton
Manufacturing Supervisor: Arnold Vila
Manufacturing Manager: Vincent Scelta
Electronic Artist: Steven Frim
Electronic Art Supervisor: Warren Fischbach
Senior Production Manager: Lorraine Patsco
Senior Designer: Ann France
Design Director: Patricia Wosczyk
Composition/Project Management: Carlisle Publishers Services
Interior Design: Meryl Levavi
Cover Design: Ginidir Marshall
Cover Art: Doug Chezem/Mendola Artists

Copyright © 1998, 1995, 1992 by Prentice-Hall, Inc.
A Simon & Schuster Company
Upper Saddle River, New Jersey 07458

Wagner, John A., 1952-
    Organizational behavior : securing competitive advantage / John A.
  Wagner III, John R. Hollenbeck. — 3rd ed.
      p. cm.
    Rev. ed. of: Management of organizational behavior. 2nd ed. c1995.
    Includes bibliographical references and index.
    ISBN 0-13-859810-X
    1. Organizational behavior. 2. Organizational behavior—Case
studies. I. Hollenbeck, John R. II. Wagner, John A.
Management of organizational behavior. III. Title.
HD58.7.W24   1998
658.3—dc21   97-14578
                                 CIP

Prentice-Hall International (UK) Limited, London
Prentice-Hall of Australia Pty. Limited, Sydney
Prentice-Hall Canada, Inc., Toronto
Prentice-Hall Hispanoamericana, S.A., Mexico
Prentice-Hall of India Private Limited, New Delhi
Prentice-Hall of Japan, Inc., Tokyo
Simon & Schuster Asia Pte. Ltd., Singapore
Editora Prentice-Hall do Brasil, Ltda., Rio de Janeiro

Printed in the United States of America

10   9   8   7   6   5   4   3   2   1

To Mary Jane, Allison, Jillian, and John Andrew Kirby Wagner

■

To Patty, Jennifer, Marie, Tim, and Jeff Hollenbeck

■ Brief Contents

v

■ Contents

■ Preface

In today's business environment, competition arises when other organizations seek to do what your company does, only better. Advantage is gained when you can do something your competitors find difficult to duplicate. Competitive advantage is further secured when competitors cannot duplicate your company's special ability at all.

We contend—based on solid research evidence—that an especially strong source of competitive advantage lies in the people who comprise your firm. One of the most effective ways to secure competitive advantage is to make the best of the knowledge, skills, and other human assets possessed by your company's employees. No other firm has the same people as yours. For this reason, no other company can duplicate the range of products and services requiring the particular capabilities of the members of your firm. Managing organizational behavior is thus essential to the process of securing competitive advantage. This statement is the central theme of our book.

Why did we decide to write a textbook? Over the years, we have taught courses on management and organizational behavior, and we've talked with others who have taught similar courses throughout the world. In our experiences and conversations, we've noticed a recurring lament: Although the management of organizational behavior is a topic whose importance should be evident, students often don't take courses on organizational behavior all that seriously. One typical student reaction is to argue that organizational behavior is little more than common sense. Another is to suggest that management and organizational behavior are "soft" subjects, lacking much in the way of hard facts and figures. A third is to claim that organizational behavior is nothing but theory and research, and not at all about anything real or practical.

All three of these reactions are mistaken. Nonetheless, in trying to determine the reason for their existence, we've found that they *are* reasonably accurate reflections of the way that organizational behavior is treated in many of today's textbooks. In some instances textbook authors have avoided depthy coverage. In others they have failed to build in any sense of challenge. In yet others they have resisted making the connection between theory and practice. All of these failings have had the effect of driving down the substance and factuality of textbooks. All have contributed to the false perception that organizational behavior is simplistic and of little use.

Despite this trend, we know through personal experience that students *do* have the ability to excel when challenged to learn something meaningful. We know that properly presented materials can motivate exceptional student performance. Thus we have set out to develop a textbook that requires students to think and take seriously what it has to say. This challenge, we believe, is the key to reversing the all-too-prevalent tendency to underestimate the importance of understanding how to manage organizational behavior.

New to the Third Edition

Current demands from instructors and students are for more concise textbooks. For this reason, in preparing the third edition we've condensed our presentation from the 19 chapters of previous editions to 15 shorter chapters. In addition, cases and exercises included in the first two editions now appear in a separate book. By making these changes, we've reduced the length of our textbook by nearly half without diluting its contents.

As in earlier editions, our writing during the process of revision was guided by two primary goals: first, to cover the field of organizational behavior thoroughly and accurately, and second, to offer you, the student, solid guidance in using the theories and concepts that we discuss. With these two objectives before us, we created a set of tools that will help you acquire the skills and expertise you'll need to be an effective manager in the complex world of work. In particular, as you read our book you'll find a wealth of examples of real people and familiar companies. These examples are included to help make the text's theories and concepts more concrete and memorable. Important points are highlighted in figures and tables that summarize chapter contents. Each chapter also includes end-of-chapter review questions and an implementation guide. Bold faced terms in each chapter are defined in a glossary of terms that follows chapter 15. These features are designed to help you study and apply what you've learned while reading our book.

We have improved our coverage of several important subjects and added discussions of topics that have emerged since we wrote the second edition. Included for the first time are sections on meso organizational behavior (Chapter 1), legal and political perspectives on diversity (Chapter 2), high performance work systems (Chapter 3), workplace violence (Chapter 5), the quality perspective on work design (Chapter 6), equity in interpersonal relations (Chapter 7), and team decision making effectiveness (Chapter 8). Carried over from prior editions are cutting-edge discussions of creativity and innovation (Chapter 3), flexible manufacturing technologies (Chapter 6), postbureaucratic structures (Chapter 11), and maturational contingencies (Chapter 12).

Redesigned chapters on organizational behavior and competitive advantage (Chapter 1), perception, decision making, and creativity (Chapter 3), power, conflict, and negotiation (Chapter 10), and culture, change and organization development (Chapter 13) integrate material covered less succinctly in previous editions. Now appearing in the final part of our book are chapters on international organizational behavior (Chapter 14) and thinking critically about organizational behavior (Chapter 15) that can be read at any time, enabling instructors and students to fit learning experiences to personal needs and course requirements. Finally, every chapter now includes a box on "Securing Competitive Advantage" that emphasizes the usefulness and importance of organizational behavior while providing thematic consistency throughout our book.

An Invitation

By reading this book you are committing yourself to learn how to manage organizational behavior. We can't think of anything more important for you to understand. In return for this commitment, we extend a special invitation to you, our newest student. We want to know how you like our book and how you feel about the field of organizational behavior. We encourage you to contact us with your ideas, especially your suggestions for making improvements to future editions of our book. Please write to us at:

Michigan State University
Eli Broad Graduate School of Management
Department of Management
East Lansing, Michigan 48824-1121

Acknowledgments

This book has been influenced by the ideas and suggestions of many people. First, we would like to thank the many reviewers who commented on parts of the first edition: Murray R. Baruch, University of Iowa; Hrach Bedrosian, New York University; Robert A. Bolda, University of Michigan-Dearborn; Robert Bontempo, Columbia University; Joel Brockner, Columbia University; Donald Conlon, University of Delaware; Jeannette Davy, Arizona State University; Gerald R. Ferris, University of Illinois; Douglas M. Fox, Western Connecticut State University; Terry L. Gaston, Southern Oregon State College; Barrie Gibbs, Simon Fraser University; Stephen G. Green, Purdue University; James L. Hall, Santa Clara University; Nell Hartley, Robert Morris College; Diane Hoadley, University of South Dakota; Russell E. Johannesson, Temple University; Ralph Katerberg, University of Cincinnati; Kenneth A. Kovach, George Mason University; Charles Kuehl, University of Missouri, St. Louis; Vicki LaFarge, Bentley College; Edwin A. Locke, University of Maryland; Gail H. McKee, Roanoke College; Howard E. Mitchell, Wharton School, University of Pennsylvania; Linda L. Neider, University of Miami; Aaron Nurick, Bentley College; Daniel Ondrack, University of Toronto; Christine Pearson, University of Southern California; Gary N. Powell, University of Connecticut; Gerald L. Rose, University of Iowa; Joseph G. Rosse, University of Colorado, Boulder; Carol Sales, Brock University, Ontario; Mel E. Schnake, Valdosta State College; Ronald R. Sims, College of William and Mary; Randall G. Sleeth; Lucian Spataro, Ohio University; F. M. Teagarden, Dakota State University; Roger Volkema, American University; Deborah L. Wells, Creighton University; Gary L. Whaley, Norfolk State University; David G. Williams, West Virginia University; and Wayne M. Wormley, Drexel University.

Second, we would like to acknowledge the group of reviewers who commented on drafts as we prepared the second edition: James Senson, Moorhead St. University; Dennis Dossett, University of Missouri-St. Louis; John Sawyer, University of Delaware; Gerald Schoenfeld, James Madison University; Anne O'Leary–Kelly, Texas A&M University; Debra Arvanites, Villanova; Tony Buono,

Bentley College; Susan Straus, Carnegie Mellon University; Carol Carnevale, SUNY Binghamton; John Wanous, Ohio State University; Pracheta Mukherjee, Slippery Rock University; Carol Sales, Brock University; Karen Maher, University of Missouri-St. Louis; David Alexander, Angelo St.; Joan Finegan, University of Western Ohio; Charles A. White, Edison Community College; Afsaneh Nahavandi, Arizona State University; Jane Russell, California State; Charles Woodruff, Winthrop University; and Richard Sebastian, St. Cloud University.

For the third edition, we would like to acknowledge the following group of reviewers:

> Paul Fadil—Valdosta State University
>
> John P. Howell—New Mexico State University
>
> Gail E. Sype—Saginaw Valley State University
>
> Ann O'Leary-Kelly—University of Dayton
>
> Mel Schnake—Valdosta State University
>
> Gary Oddou—San Jose State University

Finally, we owe special thanks to our families, who put up with our occasional absences and our constant preoccupation with the task of writing the three editions of this book. Without their support and understanding the book would not exist.

About the Authors

John A. Wagner, III is Professor and Chair of the Department of Management in the Eli Broad College of Business and Graduate School of Managment at Michigan State University. Professor Wagner received his Ph.D. in Business Administration from the University of Illinois at Urbana-Champaign in 1982. He has taught undergraduate and graduate courses in management, organizational behavior, and organization theory.

Professor Wagner is a member of the review boards of *Administrative Science Quarterly* and the *Academy of Management Review,* and is Editor of *Advances in Qualitative Organization Research.* He is a member of the Academy of Management and the Decision Sciences Institute. In 1989 Professor Wagner was co-recipient of the Scholarly Achievement Award conferred by the Human Resources Division of the Academy of Management. In 1993 he received the Research Methods Division's Walter de Gruyter Best Paper Award.

Professor Wagner's research is in the fields of organizational behavior and organization theory. His publications have examined the efficacy of participatory decision making, the effects of individualism-collectivism on cooperation and performance, the effects of size on the performance of groups and organizations, and the long-term effects of incentive payment on group productivity.

John R. Hollenbeck received his Ph.D. in Management and Organizational Behavior from New York University in 1984. He is currently Professor of Management in the Eli Broad College of Business and Graduate School of Management at Michigan State University, where he teaches organizational behavior, human resource management, and organizational research methods at both the undergradute and graduate levels.

Professor Hollenbeck was the first recipient, in 1992, of the Ernest J. McCormick Award for Early Contributions to the field of Industrial and Organizational Psychology, and was a Teacher-Scholar Award winner in 1987 at Michigan State University. He is a Fellow of the American Psychological Association and has served on the editorial boards of journals including the *Journal of Applied Psychology, Academy of Management Journal, Organizational Behavior and Human Decision Processes,* and the *Journal of Management.* Professor Hollenbeck is currently Editor of *Personnel Psychology.*

Professor Hollenbeck has published in the areas of organizational behavior and human resource management. His current research focuses on self-regulation theories of work motivation, employee separation and acquisition processes, and team decision making and performance.

Chapter One

Organizational Behavior and Competitive Advantage

In today's world of business, creating and sustaining competitive advantage can mean the difference between the life and death of an organization. Take Harley-Davidson, the Milwaukee-based producer of heavyweight motorcycles. Near bankruptcy in 1985, the company now controls more than one-fifth of all U.S. sales. Despite this successful turnaround, Chief Executive Officer Richard F. Teerlink faces the daunting task of increasing production to meet strong demand, or watching Japanese rivals Honda, Kawasaki, and Yamaha steal customers with Harley look-alikes.[1] New design and production facilities should help, but the company's workforce must also become more productive if erosion of market share is to be avoided.

---

[1] R. A. Melcher, "Tune-up Time for Harley," *Business Week,* April 8, 1996, pp. 90–94.

Imagine yourself in a position like that of Harley's Teerlink. What should you do to boost the performance of your employees? Suppose that initial assessments confirm that weak productivity is due to poor employee motivation, and your boss tells you to solve this problem. Your future with the company—and possibly the future of the company itself—depends on whether you can find a way to improve employee motivation. To help you decide what to do, you call in four highly recommended management consultants.

After analyzing your company's situation, the first consultant states that many of today's jobs are so simple, monotonous, and uninteresting that they depress employee motivation. Workers become so bored and resentful that productivity falls off. The consultant recommends that you redesign your firm's jobs, making them more complex, stimulating, and fulfilling.

▪ **1**

Consultant number two performs her own assessment of your company. As she reviews her findings, she agrees that monotonous work can reduce employee motivation. She says, however, that the absence of clear, challenging goals is an even greater threat to motivation and productivity. She goes on to say that such goals provide performance targets that draw attention to the work to be done and focus employee effort on successful performance. The second consultant advises that you solve your company's productivity problem by implementing a program of formal goal setting.

Next, the third consultant conducts an investigation and concedes that both job design and goal setting can improve employee motivation. She suggests, however, that you consider a contingent payment program instead. She explains that contingent payment means paying employees according to their performance instead of giving them fixed salaries or hourly wages. For instance, salespeople may be paid commissions based on their sales, production employees may be paid piece-rate wages according to their productivity, and executives may be paid bonuses according to their firm's profitability. The consultant points out that contingent payment programs change the way wages are *distributed* but not necessarily the *amount* of wages paid to the workforce as a whole.

Finally, the fourth consultant examines your situation and agrees that any of the three approaches might work but describes another technique that is often used to deal with motivational problems—allowing employees to participate in decision making. He suggests that participation gives employees a sense of belongingness or ownership that energizes productivity, and he recites an impressive list of companies—among them, General Motors, IBM, and General Electric—that have recently established participatory programs.

Later, alone in your office, you consider the four consultants' reports and conclude that you should probably recommend all four alternatives—just in case one or two of the consultants are wrong. However, you also realize that your company can afford the time and money needed to implement only one of the alternatives. What should you do? Which alternative do you choose?

According to a comprehensive review of research comparing the effectiveness of these alternatives, if you chose the first one, job redesign, productivity would probably rise by about 9 percent.[1] An increase of this size would save your job, keep your company in business, and probably earn you the company president's eternal gratitude. If you chose the second alternative, goal setting, productivity would probably increase by around 16 percent.[2] This outcome would save your job and your company, and might even put you in the running for a promotion. If you chose the third alternative, contingent payment, productivity could be expected to increase by approximately 30 percent.[3] A gain of this amount would ensure you an executive position with the company until retirement.

But what about the fourth alternative, employee participation in decision making? How might this approach affect productivity where low performance is attributable to poor motivation? Knowing that managers are choosing participatory programs at an increasing rate to solve motivation problems, you might think that this alternative should work at least as well as the other three. Surprisingly, however, participation usually has virtually no effect on productivity problems caused by poor motivation. Despite the fourth consultant's suggestion, participation is likely to improve motivation and performance only when combined with one or more of the other three alternatives.[4] If you chose participation, you and the other members of your firm might soon be looking for new jobs. Your choice might even cost your company its existence.

How realistic is this story? Is the predicament it portrays an everyday problem? Experts in the United States and Canada have pointed to many other instances, besides our example of Harley-Davidson, of low organizational productivity, and they have often identified "people problems" as an important cause of these situations.[5] Solving these problems is critical to securing an advantage in today's competitive environment. Knowing which solutions to choose and how to implement them differentiates between those organizations that succeed and those that do not.

More generally, competitive success is based on the ability to produce some product or service that is perceived as valuable by some group of consumers, and to do so in a way that no one else can duplicate.[6] At first glance, there appear to be many ways to accomplish this feat. Upon closer examination, however, most of these alternatives fail to measure up. For example, companies that rely on technology as a source of competitive advantage soon learn that other companies have access to the same technology and therefore can copy successful equipment and processes. Companies that attempt to sustain advantage by creating protected or regulated local markets find that no market can be completely shielded from aggressive international competition. Companies that rely on sheer size and control over vast resources discover that largeness makes it difficult to individualize and tailor products or services, thus limiting attempts to capture the business of today's capricious customers.

Knowing this, many experts now consider an organization's employees to be the foremost source of sustainable competitive advantage. If your company employs the best people and is able to hold on to them, it has a source of competitive advantage not easily duplicated by other firms. If your company also has the know-how to properly manage its employees, it has a competitive edge that can be sustained and even strengthened over time.[7]

The know-how needed to solve motivational productivity problems like those at Harley-Davidson and similar companies can be obtained from the field of organizational behavior. Without this knowledge, managers have no conceptual basis for accepting any one consultant's advice or for choosing one particular way to solve people problems instead of another. With it, managers have the guidance needed to make the most appropriate choices and secure the greatest competitive gain. The management of people through the application of knowledge from the field of organizational behavior is thus a primary means through which competitive advantage can be created and sustained. This basic principle is the central theme of our book.

Defining Organizational Behavior

Organizational behavior (OB) is a field of study aimed at predicting, explaining, understanding, and changing human behavior as it occurs in organizations. Underlying this definition of organizational behavior are three important considerations:

1. Organizational behavior focuses on observable behaviors, such as talking with coworkers, running equipment, or preparing a report. However, it also deals with internal actions, such as thinking, perceiving, and deciding, that accompany visible actions.
2. Organizational behavior studies the behavior of people both as individuals and as members of larger social units.
3. Organizational behavior also analyzes the "behavior" of these larger social units—groups and organizations—per se. Neither groups nor organizations behave in the same sense that people do. Nevertheless, some events occur in social units that cannot be explained as resulting solely from individual behaviors. These events must be understood in terms of group or organizational processes.

Organizational behavior thus defined traces its origins to the late 1940s, when researchers in psychology, sociology, political science, economics, and other social sciences sought to develop a comprehensive body of organizational research.[8] Despite the intentions of its founders, however, the field of organizational behavior has resisted unification. It is now divided into three fairly distinct subfields, each with its own social science underpinnings: micro organizational behavior, deriving from psychology and behavioral research; meso organizational behavior, originating in social psychology and interactionist sociology; and macro organizational behavior, arising from economics, structural sociology, cultural anthropology, and political science.

Micro Organizational Behavior

Micro organizational behavior is concerned mainly with the behaviors of individuals working alone.[9] Three subfields of psychology were the principal contributors to the beginnings of micro organizational behavior. *Experimental psychology* provided theories of learning, motivation, perception, and stress. *Clinical psychology* furnished models of personality and human development. *Industrial psychology* offered theories of employee selection, workplace attitudes, and performance assessment. Because of its heritage, micro organizational behavior has a distinctly psychological orientation. Among the questions it examines are the following: What effects do differences in ability have on employee productivity? How do employees develop perceptions of their workplace? What motivates employees to perform their jobs? Why do some employees feel satisfied with their work whereas others experience work as stressful?

Meso Organizational Behavior

Meso organizational behavior is a middle ground, bridging the other two sub-fields of organizational behavior.[10] It focuses primarily on understanding the behaviors of people working together in teams and groups. In addition to sharing origins with the other organizational behavior subfields, meso organizational behavior grew out of research in the fields of *communication, social psychology,* and *interactionist sociology,* which provided theories on such topics as socialization, leadership, and group dynamics. Meso organizational behavior seeks answers to questions including the following: What forms of socialization encourage coworkers to cooperate? How can the productivity of a group be improved? What mix of skills among team members increases team performance? How can managers determine which prospective leader will be the most effective?

Macro Organizational Behavior

Macro organizational behavior focuses on understanding the behaviors of entire organizations. The origins of macro organizational behavior can be traced to four principal disciplines. *Sociology* provided theories of structure, social status, and institutional relations. *Political science* offered theories of power, conflict, bargaining, and control. *Anthropology* contributed theories of symbolism, cultural influence, and comparative analysis. And *economics* furnished theories of competition and efficiency. Research on macro organizational behavior considers questions such as the following: How is power acquired and retained? How can conflicts be resolved? What mechanisms can be used to coordinate work activities? Why do we have different forms of organizational structure? How should an organization be structured in order to best cope with surrounding circumstances?[11]

Management Origins

Besides originating in the modern social sciences, the three subfields of organizational behavior are also grounded in an older tradition of research on and thinking about management in organizations. Awareness of this tradition is thus an important part of understanding organizational behavior and the management problems it seeks to resolve. As evidence of the tradition's longevity and significance, consider the following:

1. As early as 3000 B.C., the Sumerians formulated missions and goals for government and commercial enterprises.
2. Between 3000 and 1000 B.C., the Egyptians successfully organized the efforts of thousands of workers to build the pyramids.
3. Between 800 B.C. and about A.D. 300, the Romans perfected the use of hierarchical authority.
4. Between A.D. 450 and the late 1400s, Venetian merchants developed commercial laws and invented double-entry bookkeeping.

5. In the early 1500s, at the request of an Italian prince, Niccolo Machiavelli prepared an analysis of power that is still widely read.
6. At about the same time, the Catholic Church perfected a governance structure built upon the use of standardized procedures.

Management theories and practices leading to today's organizational behavior did not begin to emerge, however, until the industrial revolution of the 1700s and 1800s. Inventions like James Watt's steam engine and Eli Whitney's cotton gin created new forms of mass production that made existing modes of administration obsolete. Mass-assembly operations, which accelerated the pace of production dramatically and required the employment of large numbers of workers, overwhelmed the small administrative staffs then employed by most companies. In addition, expertise was now needed to maintain production equipment and coordinate manufacturing jobs, and managers had little time to develop this expertise themselves. The field of industrial engineering, which arose from the need to invent and improve workplace machinery, began to address the selection, instruction, and coordination of industrial employees. Toward the end of the industrial revolution, managers and engineers throughout North America and Europe focused on developing general theories of management.

1890–1940: The Scientific Management Perspective

Theories about organizations and the people and groups within them initially took the form of *management principles* intended to provide managers with advice about managing their firms. Most of these principles were written by practicing managers or others closely associated with the management profession. Among the first principles to be widely read were those of the **scientific management perspective.**

All principles of scientific management reflected the idea that through proper management an organization could achieve profitability and long-term survival in the competitive world of business. Theorists sharing the scientific management perspective devoted their attention to describing proper management and determining the best way to achieve it.

Frederick W. Taylor. The founder of scientific management, Frederick W. Taylor (1856–1915), developed his principles of scientific management as he rose from laborer to chief engineer at the Midvale Steel Works in Philadelphia, Pennsylvania. Shown in Table 1-1, these principles focused on increasing the efficiency of the workplace by differentiating managers from nonsupervisory workers and systematizing the jobs of both.

According to Taylor, the profitability of an organization could be ensured only by finding the "one best way" to perform each job. Managers could teach workers this technique and use a system of rewards and punishments to encourage its use. An example of this approach is found in Taylor's work to improve the productivity of coal shovelers at the Bethlehem Steel Company. As he observed these workers, Taylor discovered that a shovel load of coal could range from 4 to 30 pounds depending on the density of the coal being carried. By experimenting

Table 1-1 ■ Frederick W. Taylor's Principles of Scientific Management

1. *Assign all responsibility for the organization of work to managers rather than workers.* Managers should do all the thinking related to the planning and design of work, leaving workers the task of carrying it out.

2. *Use scientific methods to determine the one best way of performing each task.* Managers should design each worker's job accordingly, specifying a set of standard methods for completing the task in the right way.

3. *Select the person most suited to each job to perform that job.* Managers should match the abilities of each worker to the demands of each job.

4. *Train the worker to perform the job correctly.* Managers should train workers in how to use the standard methods devised for their jobs.

5. *Monitor work performance to ensure that specified work procedures are followed correctly and that appropriate results are achieved.* Managers should exercise the control necessary to guarantee that workers under their supervision always perform their jobs in the one best way.

6. *Provide further support by planning work assignments and eliminating interruptions.* Managers can help their workers continue to produce at a high level by shielding them from things that interfere with job performance.

Source: Based on F. W. Taylor, *The Principles of Scientific Management* (New York: Norton, 1911), pp. 34–40.

with a group of workers, Taylor discovered that shovelers could move the most coal in a day without suffering undue fatigue if each load of coal weighed 21 pounds. He then developed a variety of different shovels, each of which would hold approximately 21 pounds of coal of a particular density. After Taylor taught workers how to use these shovels, each shoveler's daily yield rose from 16 tons to 59. At the same time, the average wage per worker increased from $1.15 to $1.88 per day. Bethlehem Steel was able to reduce the number of shovelers in its yard from more than 500 to about 150, saving the firm nearly $80,000 per year.

Taylor's ideas influenced management around the world. In the United States, Taylor's principles had such a dramatic effect on management that in 1912 he was called to testify before a special committee of the House of Representatives. Union employees and employers all objected to Taylor's idea that employers and employees should share the economic gains of scientific management and wanted Congress to do something about it. Nevertheless, with the newspaper publicity he gained from his congressional appearance, Taylor found even wider support for his ideas and was soon joined in his work by other specialists.

Other Contributors.   The husband-and-wife team of Frank (1868–1924) and Lillian (1878–1972) Gilbreth followed Taylor in pursuing the one best way to perform any job. The Gilbreths are probably best known for their invention of *motion study,* a procedure in which jobs are reduced to their most basic movements. A sample listing of these basic movements, each of which is called a *therblig* (*Gilbreth* spelled backward without inverting the *th*), is shown in Table 1-2. The Gilbreths also invented the microchronometer, a clock with a hand capable of measuring time to 1/2,000 of a second. Using this instrument, analysts could precisely determine the time required by each of the movements needed to perform a job.

Table 1-2 ■ Therblig Motions			
Search	Transport loaded	Disassemble	Transport empty
Find	Position	Inspect	Rest to relieve fatigue
Select	Assemble	Pre-position	Other unavoidable delay
Grasp	Use	Release load	Avoidable delay
Plan			

Another contributor to scientific management, Henry Gantt (1861–1919) developed a task-and-bonus wage plan that paid workers a bonus in addition to their regular wages if they completed their work in an assigned amount of time. Gantt's plan also provided bonuses for supervisors, determined by the number of subordinates who met deadlines.[12] Gantt also invented the Gantt chart, a bar chart used by managers to compare actual with planned performance.[13] Present-day scheduling methods such as the program evaluation and review technique (PERT) are based on this invention.

Harrington Emerson (1853–1931), a third contributor to scientific management, applied his own list of 12 principles to the railroad industry in the early 1900s.[14] Among Emerson's principles were recommendations to establish clear objectives, seek advice from competent individuals, manage with justice and fairness, standardize procedures, reduce waste, and reward workers for efficiency. Late in his life, Emerson became interested in the selection and training of employees, stressing the importance of explaining scientific management to workers during their initial training. Emerson reasoned that sound management practices could succeed only if understood by every member of the firm.

1900–1950: The Administrative Principles Perspective

At about the same time that Taylor and his colleagues were formulating their principles of scientific management, another group was involved in developing the **administrative principles perspective.** In contrast to scientific management's emphasis on reducing the costs of production activities, this second perspective's focus was on increasing the efficiency of administrative procedures.

Henri Fayol. Considered the father of modern management thought, Henri Fayol (1841–1925) developed his principles of administration in the early 1900s while serving as chief executive of a French mining and metallurgy firm, Commentry-Fourchambault-Decazeville, also known as Comambault. Fayol identified what he believed to be the four essential functions of management: *planning* future activities and performance objectives, *organizing* the resources of the organization to allow the pursuit of plans already made, *coordinating* the workforce in the direction of this pursuit, and *controlling* overall efforts by comparing actual outcomes with planned objectives.[15] He also formulated the 14 principles shown in Table 1-3 to help administrators perform their jobs.

Table 1-3 ■ Fayol's 14 Principles of Management

PRINCIPLE	DESCRIPTION
Division of work	A firm's work should be divided into specialized, simplified tasks. Matching task demands with workforce skills and abilities will improve productivity. The management of work should be separated from its performance.
Authority	Authority is the right to give orders and the responsibility to accept the consequences of using authority. No one should possess one without the other.
Discipline	Discipline is performing a task with obedience and dedication. It can be expected only when a firm's managers and subordinates agree on the specific tasks that subordinates will perform.
Unity of command	Each subordinate should receive orders from only one hierarchical superior. The confusion of having two or more superiors would undermine authority, discipline, order, and stability.
Unity of direction	Each group of activities directed toward the same objective should have only one manager and only one plan.
Individual versus general interests	The interests of individuals and those of the whole organization must be treated with equal respect. Neither can be allowed to supersede the other.
Remuneration of personnel	The pay received by employees must be fair and satisfactory to both them and the firm. Pay should be in proportion to personal performance, but employees' general welfare must not be threatened by unfair incentive payment schemes.
Centralization	Centralization is the retention of authority by managers. It should be used when managers desire greater control. Decentralization should be used, however, if subordinates' opinions, counsel, and experience are needed.
Scalar chain	The scalar chain is a hierarchical string extending from the uppermost manager to the lowest subordinate. The line of authority follows this chain and is the proper route for organizational communications.
Order	Order, or "everything in its place," should be instilled whenever possible because it reduces wasted materials and efforts. Jobs should be designed and staffed with order in mind.
Equity	Equity means enforcing established rules with a sense of fair play, kindliness, and justice. Equity should be guaranteed by management, because it increases members' loyalty, devotion, and satisfaction.
Stability of tenure	Properly selected employees should be given the time needed to learn and adjust to their jobs. The absence of such stability undermines organizational performance.
Initiative	Members should be allowed the opportunity to think for themselves because this improves the distribution of information and adds to the organization's pool of talent.
Esprit de corps	Managers should harmonize the interests of members by resisting the urge to split up successful teams. They should rely on face-to-face communication to detect and correct misunderstandings immediately.

Fayol believed the number of management principles that might help improve an organization's operation to be virtually limitless. He considered his principles to be flexible and adaptable, labeling them principles, rather than laws or rules,

in order to avoid any idea of rigidity, as there is nothing rigid or absolute in [management] matters; everything is a question of degree. The same principle is hardly ever applied twice in exactly the same way, because we have to allow for different and changing circumstances, for human beings who are equally different and changeable, and for many other variable elements. The principles, too, are flexible, and can be adapted to meet every need; it is just a question of knowing how to use them.[16]

For Fayol, management was more than mechanical rule following. It required that managers exercise intuition and engage in skillful behavior in deciding how, when, and why to put management principles into action.

Max Weber. Max Weber (1864–1920) was a German sociologist who, although neither a manager nor management consultant, had a major effect on 20th-century management thought and practice. Like Fayol, Weber was interested in the efficiency of different kinds of administrative arrangements. To figure out what makes organizations efficient, Weber analyzed the Egyptian empire, the Prussian army, the Roman Catholic Church, and other large organizations that had functioned efficiently over long periods of time. Based on these analyses, Weber developed his model of **bureaucracy,** an idealized description of an efficient organization that is summarized in Table 1-4. Weber's bureaucratic model provides for both the differentiation (through the division of labor and task specialization) and the integration (by the hierarchy of authority and written rules and regulations) necessary to accomplish a specific job. Weber believed that any organization with bureaucratic characteristics would be efficient. He also noted, though, that work in a bureaucracy could become so simple and undemanding that employees might grow dissatisfied and, as a result, become less productive.[17]

Table 1-4 ■ Features of Bureaucratic Organizations	
FEATURE	**DESCRIPTION**
Selection and promotion	Expertise is the primary criterion. Friendship criteria or other favoritism is explicitly rejected.
Hierarchy of authority	Superiors have the authority to direct subordinates' actions. They are responsible for ensuring that these actions are in the bureaucracy's best interests.
Rules and regulations	Unchanging regulations provide the bureaucracy's members with consistent, impartial guidance.
Division of labor	Work is divided into tasks that can be performed by the bureaucracy's members in an efficient, productive manner.
Written documentation	Records provide consistency and a basis for evaluation of bureaucratic procedures.
Separate ownership	Members cannot gain unfair or undeserved advantage through ownership.

Source: Based on information presented in H. H. Gerth and C. W. Mills, trans., *From Max Weber: Essays in Sociology* (New York: Oxford University Press, 1946).

Other Contributors.   A number of other management experts also contributed to the administrative principles perspective. One of them, James Mooney (1884–1957), was vice president and director of General Motors and president of General Motors Overseas Corporation during the late 1920s when he created his principles of organization.[18] Mooney's *coordinative principle* highlighted the importance of organizing the tasks and functions in a firm into a coordinated whole. He defined coordination as the orderly arrangement of group effort to provide unity of action in the pursuit of a common mission. Mooney's *scalar principle* identified the importance of scalar or hierarchical chains of superiors and subordinates as a means of integrating the work of different employees. Mooney's *functional principle* stressed the importance of functional divisions, such as marketing, manufacturing, and accounting. He noted how work in each functional area both differs from and interlocks with the work of other areas, and how the success of the larger firm thus requires coordination and scalar links among its different functional areas.

Lyndall Urwick (1891–1983), another writer who contributed to the administrative principles perspective, was a British military officer and director of the International Management Institute in Geneva, Switzerland. Urwick made his mark by consolidating the ideas of Fayol and Mooney with those of Taylor.[19] From Taylor, Urwick adopted the idea that systematic, rigorous investigation should inform and support the management of employees. Urwick also used Fayol's 14 principles to guide managerial planning and control and Mooney's 3 principles of organization to structure his discussion of organizing. Urwick's synthesis thus bridged Taylor's scientific management and the administrative principles approach, and integrated the work of others within the framework of the four functions of management identified by Fayol.

Finally, Mary Parker Follett (1868–1933), who became interested in industrial management in the 1920s, was among the first proponents of what became known as *industrial democracy*. In her writings on administrative principles, Follett proposed that all employees should have ownership interests in their company, to promote cooperation and attention to the company's overall mission and goals.[20] In many respects, Follett's work foreshadowed the human relations perspective, described next.

1930–1970: The Human Relations Perspective

Although followers of both the scientific management and administrative principles perspectives advocated the scientific study of management, they rarely evaluated their ideas in any formal way. This omission was corrected in the mid-1920s when university researchers began to use scientific methods to test existing management thought.

The Hawthorne Studies.   The *Hawthorne studies,* performed beginning in 1924 at Western Electric's Hawthorne plant near Chicago, Illinois, were among the earliest attempts to use scientific techniques to examine human behavior at work.[21] As summarized in Table 1-5, a three-stage series of experiments assessed the

Table 1-5 ■ The Hawthorne Studies

EXPERIMENT	MAJOR CHANGES	RESULTS
Stage I		
Illumination study	Lighting conditions	Increased productivity at nearly all levels of illumination
Stage II		
First relay-assembly test	Job simplification, shorter work hours, rest breaks, friendly supervision, incentive pay	30 percent productivity improvement
Second relay-assembly test	Incentive pay	12 percent productivity improvement
Mica-splitting test	Shorter work hours, rest breaks, friendly supervision	15 percent productivity improvement
Stage III		
Interview program	—	Discovery of presence of informal productivity norms
Bank-wiring-room test	Incentive pay	Emergence of productivity norms

effects of varying physical conditions and management practices on workplace efficiency. The first experiment tested the effects of workplace lighting on productivity, and produced the unexpected findings that changes in lighting had little effect but that changes in social conditions seemed to explain significant increases in group productivity. Additional experiments led the researchers to conclude that social factors—in particular, workers' desires to satisfy needs for companionship and support at work—explained the results observed across all the Hawthorne studies.

Later reanalyses of data from the Hawthorne experiments not only found weaknesses in the studies' methods and techniques but also suggested that changes in incentive pay, the tasks being performed, rest periods, and working hours led to the productivity improvements attributed by researchers to the effects of social factors.[22] Nonetheless, the Hawthorne studies raised serious questions about the efficiency-oriented focus of the scientific management and administrative principles perspectives. In so doing, they stimulated debate about the importance of human satisfaction and personal development at work. The **human relations perspective** on management thought grew out of this debate, directing attention away from improving efficiency and toward increasing employee growth, development, and satisfaction.[23]

Douglas McGregor. Douglas McGregor (1906–1964) played a key role in making the aforementioned redirection happen, through his efforts at sharpening the philosophical contrast between the human relations approach and the scientific management and administrative principles perspectives.[24] McGregor used the term **Theory X** to describe the key assumptions about human nature shown in the top half of Table 1-6. McGregor suggested that theorists and managers holding these assumptions would describe management as follows:

1. Managers are responsible for organizing the elements of productive enterprise—money, materials, equipment, people—solely in the interest of economic efficiency.
2. The manager's function is to motivate workers, direct their efforts, control their actions, and modify their behavior to fit the organization's needs.
3. Without such active intervention by managers, people would be passive about or even resistant to organizational needs; workers must be persuaded, rewarded, and punished for the good of the organization.[25]

According to McGregor, the scientific management and administrative principles perspectives promoted a "hard" version of Theory X. Both favored overcoming employees' resistance to organizational needs with strict discipline and economic rewards or sanctions. McGregor added that a "soft" version of Theory X seemed to underlie the Hawthorne studies. The Hawthorne researchers appeared to regard satisfaction and social relations mainly as rewards to employees who followed orders.

Table 1-6 ■ Theory X and Theory Y Assumptions

THEORY X ASSUMPTIONS

1. The average human being has an inherent dislike of work and will avoid it if possible.
2. Because they dislike work, most people must be coerced, controlled, directed, or threatened with punishment before they will put forth effort toward the achievement of organizational objectives.
3. The average human being prefers to be directed, wishes to avoid responsibility, has relatively little ambition, and wants security above all.

THEORY Y ASSUMPTIONS

1. Expending physical and mental effort at work is as natural as play and rest. The average human being does not inherently dislike work.
2. External control and the threat of punishment are not the only means to direct effort toward organizational objectives. People will exercise self-direction and self-control in the service of objectives to which they feel committed.
3. Commitment to objectives is a function of the rewards associated with their achievement. The most significant rewards—the satisfaction of ego and self-actualization needs—can be direct products of effort directed toward organizational objectives.
4. Avoidance of responsibility, lack of ambition, and emphasis on security are not inherent human characteristics. Under proper conditions, the average human being learns not only to accept but to seek responsibility.
5. Imagination, ingenuity, creativity, and the ability to use these qualities to solve organizational problems are widely distributed among people.

Source: Based on information presented in D. McGregor, *The Human Side of Enterprise* (New York: McGraw-Hill, 1960), pp. 33–34, 47–48.

Theory Y, a contrasting philosophy of management that McGregor attributed to theorists, researchers, and managers holding the human relations perspective, is based on the second set of assumptions shown in Table 1-6. McGregor indicated that individuals holding Theory Y assumptions would view the task of management as follows:

1. Managers are responsible for organizing the elements of productive enterprise —money, materials, equipment, people—in the interest of economic ends.
2. Because people are motivated to perform, have potential for development, can assume responsibility, and are willing to work toward organizational goals, managers are responsible for enabling people to recognize and develop these basic capacities.
3. The essential task of management is to arrange organizational conditions and methods of operation so that working toward organizational objectives is also the best way for people to achieve their own personal goals.[26]

Unlike Theory X managers, who try to control their employees, Theory Y managers try to help employees learn how to manage themselves.

Other Contributors.   Other management theorists, including Abraham Maslow and Frederick Herzberg, embraced the point of view embodied in McGregor's Theory Y and speculated about ways in which personal autonomy and group participation might encourage employee growth, development, and satisfaction. The works of these contributors also served as benchmark theories during the early development of research on micro and meso organizational behavior, as described later in this book.

1960–Present: The Open Systems Perspective

With the emergence in the 1960s of the **open systems perspective,** human relations concerns with employee satisfaction and development broadened to include a focus on organizational growth and survival. According to the open systems perspective, every organization is a *system*—a unified structure of interrelated subsystems—and it is *open,* or subject to the influence of the surrounding environment. Together, these two ideas form the basic tenet of the open systems approach: Organizations whose subsystems can cope with the surrounding environment can continue to do business, whereas organizations whose subsystems cannot cope do not survive.

Katz and Kahn.   In one of the founding works of the open systems perspective, Daniel Katz and Robert Kahn identified the process shown in Figure 1-1 as essential to organizational growth and survival.[27] This process consists of the following sequence of events:

1. Every organization imports *inputs,* such as raw materials, production equipment, human resources, and technical know-how, from the surrounding en-

vironment. For instance, Shell Oil Company hires employees and, from sources around the world, acquires unrefined oil, refinery equipment, and knowledge about how to refine petroleum products.

2. Some of these inputs are used to transform other inputs during a process of *throughput*. At Shell, employees use refinery equipment and their own know-how to transform unrefined oil into petroleum products like gasoline, kerosene, and diesel fuel.

3. The transformed resources are exported as *outputs*—saleable goods or services—to the environment. Petroleum products from Shell's refineries are loaded into tankers and transported to service stations throughout North America.

4. Outputs are exchanged for new inputs, and the cycle repeats. Shell sells its products and uses the resulting revenues to pay its employees and purchase additional oil, equipment, and know-how.

According to Katz and Kahn, organizations continue to survive and grow only as long as they import more material and energy from the environment than they expend in producing the outputs exported back to the environment. *Information inputs* that signal how the environment and organization are functioning can help determine whether the organization will continue to survive; *negative feedback* indicates potential failure and the need to change the way things are being done.

Emery and Trist. In Katz and Kahn's model, the environment surrounding an organization is both the origin of needed resources and the recipient of transformed products. Accordingly, organizational survival depends on sensing environments and adjusting to their demands. Describing environments and the demands they make so as to improve this sensing and adjustment was the goal of Fred Emery and Eric Trist, two other theorists of the open systems perspective.[28]

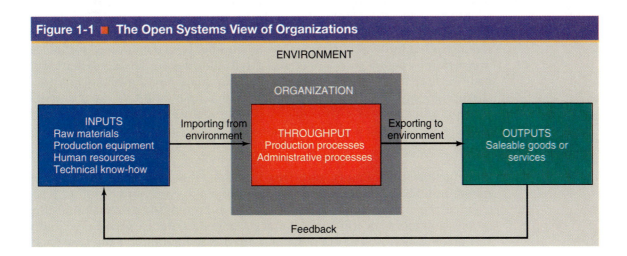

Figure 1-1 ■ The Open Systems View of Organizations

ENVIRONMENT

ORGANIZATION

INPUTS
Raw materials
Production equipment
Human resources
Technical know-how

Importing from environment

THROUGHPUT
Production processes
Administrative processes

Exporting to environment

OUTPUTS
Saleable goods or services

Feedback

After noting that every organization's environment is itself composed of a collection of more or less interconnected organizations—supplier companies, competitors, and customer firms—Emery and Trist proposed four basic kinds of environments. The first kind, which they labeled *placid random environments,* are loosely interconnected and relatively unchanging. Organizations in such environments operate independently of each other, and one firm's decision to change the way it does business has little effect on the other firms. The organizations are usually small, for example, landscape maintenance companies, construction firms, and industrial job shops, and can usually ignore each other and still stay in business by catering to local customers.

Placid clustered environments are more tightly interconnected. Here firms are grouped together into stable industries. Environments of this sort require organizations to cope with the actions of a *market*—a fairly constant group of suppliers, competitors, and customers. For this reason, firms in these environments develop strategic moves and countermoves in response to competitors' actions. Grocery stores in the same geographic region often do business in this type of environment, using coupon discounts, in-store specials, and similar promotions to lure customers away from each other.

Disturbed reactive environments are as tightly interconnected as placid clustered environments, but are considerably less stable. Changes that occur in the environment itself have forceful effects on every organization. For instance, new competitors from overseas, increasing automation, and changing consumer tastes in the U.S. automobile market revolutionized the domestic auto industry in the 1970s and 1980s. General Motors, Ford, and Chrysler had to change their way of doing business. A fourth long-time manufacturer, American Motors, failed to change quickly enough and ceased to exist. In such circumstances, organizations must respond not only to competitors' actions but also to changes in the environment itself. Due to their unpredictability, it is very difficult to plan how to respond to these changes.

Turbulent fields are extremely complex and changeful. In such an environment, companies operate in multiple markets. Public and governmental actions can alter the nature of an industry virtually overnight. Technologies advance at lightning speed. Finally, the amount of information needed to stay abreast of industrial trends is overwhelming. It is virtually impossible for organizations facing such uncertainty to do business in any consistent way. Instead, they must remain flexible, ready to adapt themselves to whatever circumstances unfold. Today's computer and communications industries exemplify this sort of environment. Technological change and corporate mergers are creating and destroying entire categories of companies at ever-increasing rates.

Other Contributors. Emery and Trist indicated that organizations must respond in different ways to different environmental conditions. Tighter environmental interconnections require greater awareness of environmental conditions, and more sweeping environmental changes require greater flexibility and adaptability. Other open systems theorists, including Paul Lawrence,

Robert Duncan, and Jay Galbraith, have similarly stressed the need for organizations to adjust to their environments. Their ideas form the basis of mainline models of macro organizational behavior and are described in later chapters of this book.

Contemporary Issues

Together, management theory and the social sciences form the foundation of the field of organizational behavior. This field and its three constituent subfields offer valuable information, insights, and advice to managers facing the challenge of understanding and reacting to a broad range of contemporary management issues.

Workforce diversity is one such issue. Within the societal cultures of the United States and Canada, subcultural differences once ignored by many managers are now requiring greater attention and sensitivity. Historically, the North American workforce has been made up largely of white males. However, demographic forecasts indicate that by the year 2000, only about 15 percent of business new-hires in the United States will be white men. Instead, most will be women or African-American, Hispanic, or Asian men.[29] Thus, it is becoming—and will continue to be—even more important for managers to know about and be ready to respond to individual differences in abilities, personalities, and motives. Knowledge about the workplace consequences of these differences, drawn from the subfield of micro organizational behavior, can provide managers with help in this regard.

Another issue concerns the growth of empowerment and teamwork in the workplace. Management is becoming less of a process of top-down command and control, in which managers have all the power and nonmanagerial employees have little say in what they do.[30] For various reasons, organizations are now experimenting with greater amounts of *empowerment*—the delegation to nonmanagers of the authority to make significant decisions on their jobs. Often, empowerment is accomplished by grouping employees into teams, then giving teams responsibility for self-management activities such as hiring, firing, and training members, setting production targets, and assessing output quality. Guidance from meso organizational behavior can help managers establish realistic expectations about the implementation difficulties and probable effects of team-based empowerment.

Corporate reengineering and total quality management are also a source of significant challenge. Emphasis in today's business world is shifting from the mass production of low-cost, interchangeable commodities to the production of high-quality goods and services, made in limited runs and geared to meet the specific demands of individuals or small groups of consumers. This shift requires greater flexibility than has ever been required before and necessitates that quality receive greater emphasis than it has in the past. Companies are reacting by implementing programs in total quality management that call for restructuring or reengineering the ways in which work is divided into jobs and then coordinated among employees.[31] Implementations of this sort benefit from insights derived from macro organizational behavior.

Finally, globalization is an issue that is changing the way business is conducted, and it promises to continue to do so at an accelerating pace.[32] In the future, fewer firms throughout the world will limit their operations to a single national or cultural region. Instead, multinationalism or even statelessness will become more the norm. As a result, managers will need to develop increased sensitivity to international cultural differences. All three subfields of organizational behavior have valuable advice to offer managers confronted with the challenge of managing global organizational behavior.

Overview of This Book

Our focus in this book is on providing conceptual frameworks that will prove helpful in the future as you seek to understand and manage behaviors in organizations. In enriching the know-how available to you for your use as a manager of people, the contents of this and the following chapters will enable you to respond effectively to contemporary problems and issues like those just described. In the process, what you learn from this book will serve as a valuable source of competitive advantage for you and your firm (see below).

Our book is organized in five parts. Part 1 consists of this introductory chapter, which gives an overview of the field of organizational behavior, describes its subfields and origins, and notes several emerging issues that will require knowledge about organizational behavior and its subfields. Part 2, on micro organizational behavior, consists of four chapters on diversity and individual differences, decision making and creativity, motivation and work performance, and satisfaction and stress at work. Chapters in this part of our book will provide you with OB information useful for managing people as individuals in organizations. In Part 3, on meso organizational behavior, four chapters deal with work design, socialization and other interpersonal processes, group and team effectiveness, and leadership in groups and organizations. These chapters contain the basic information you will need to manage interpersonal relations and group dynamics in organizations. Part 4, on macro organizational behavior, is made up of four chapters on the topics of power and conflict, organization structure, organizational design, and culture and organizational development. Information in these chapters will help you as you deal with organization-level issues and manage related processes and procedures. Finally, Part 5 is composed of two chapters on topics that span the three subfields of organizational behavior. One of these chapters is on international organizational behavior, and the other is on research methods and critical thinking in management and organizational behavior. Both provide information that will help you keep up with current and future developments in OB theory and research.

Organizational Behavior and the Bottom Line

In terms of bottom-line return on investment (ROI), Southwest Airlines has been one of the top-performing firms over the last 25 years. In fact, between 1972 and 1992, its ROI was over 21,000! What explains this success? It is not Southwest's technology, because the Boeing 737s that make up its fleet are widely available and utilized by competing airlines. Nor is it a matter of being in a desirable industry, because the airlines industry is one racked by massive competition, few barriers to entry, tight government (Federal Aviation Administration) restrictions, and numerous bankruptcies. Finally, the company's success cannot be attributed to size and economies of scale, because Southwest controls a mere 2.6 percent of the U.S. passenger market.[1]

Rather, the competitive advantage that Southwest has over other airlines lies in what it accomplishes with its people.[2] Relative to that of its competition, the Southwest Airlines workforce is more motivated, more productive, and more stable. How does this translate into competitive advantage? In terms of objective statistics, Southwest has fewer employees per aircraft and flies more miles per employee than any other airline.[3] In addition, whereas other airlines take an average of 45 minutes to prepare arriving planes for departure, Southwest turns around 80 percent of its flights in less than 15 minutes. This gives the firm a huge advantage in equipment utilization, despite its having the same equipment as everyone else. Moreover, in terms of service quality, Southwest has won the airlines "triple crown" (best on time, fewest lost bags, and fewest complaints) nine times, whereas no other competitor has achieved the same feat even once. Customers are intensely loyal as a result.

Although Southwest Airlines may be an extreme example of how "people management" know-how translates into higher ROI, the link between how firms manage their employees and their financial performance has been well established in many studies of firm performance. One study of close to 500 firms found that those that used many of the management practices described in this book enjoyed an advantage of $19,000 per employee in market value over their competitors.[4] Another study of nearly 100 small, entrepreneurial companies found that those that engaged in state-of-the-art management practices had survival rates that were over 20 percent higher than those of their competitors.[5] Yet another study of 34 retail stores showed that those using an innovative contingent payment structure generated over $1 million more in sales than traditionally managed units.[6] When it comes to the bottom line, then, there is no substitute for obtaining, motivating, and retaining the best people. Indeed, until science invents a means of cloning human beings, OB management may be the only source of sustainable competitive advantage that cannot be purchased, stolen, or copied by your competitors.

[1] B. O'Brian, "Southwest Airlines Is a Rare Carrier: It Still Makes Money," *The Wall Street Journal,* October 22, 1992, p. A1.

[2] J. Pfeffer, "Producing Sustainable Competitive Advantage through the Effective Management of People," *Academy of Management Executive* 9 (1995), pp. 55–69.

[3] J. C. Quick, "Crafting an Organizational Culture: Herb's Hand at Southwest Airlines," *Organizational Dynamics* 21 (1992), pp. 40–59.

[4] M. A. Huselid, "The Impact of Human Resource Management Practices on Turnover, Productivity, and Corporate Financial Performance," *Academy of Management Journal* 38 (1995), pp. 635–72.

[5] T. M. Wellbourne and A. O. Andrews, "Predicting the Performance of Initial Public Offerings: Should Human Resource Management Be in the Equation?" *Academy of Management Journal* 39 (1995), pp. 891–919.

[6] R. D. Banker, S. Lee, G. Potter, and D. Srinivasan, "Contextual Analysis of Performance Impacts of Outcome-Based Incentive Compensation," *Academy of Management Journal* 39 (1995), pp. 920–48.

SUMMARY

Organizational behavior is a field of research that helps predict, explain, and enable understanding of behaviors in organizations. Organizational behavior's three subfields, *micro organizational behavior, meso organizational behavior,* and *macro organizational behavior,* reflect differences among the social science disciplines that contributed to the founding of the broader field of organizational behavior. Micro organizational behavior is concerned primarily with the behaviors of people as individuals. Meso organizational behavior focuses on the activities of people in groups and teams. Macro organizational behavior addresses the behaviors of organizations as entities.

In addition to its social science origins, organizational behavior is also founded on research and practice shaped by four perspectives on management. One of these, the *scientific management perspective,* has concentrated on increasing the efficiency of job behaviors and production processes. Another, the *administrative principles perspective,* has focused instead on enhancing the efficiency of the administrative procedures used to manage organizations and their employees. The third, the *human relations perspective,* has put the emphasis on nurturing the growth and satisfaction of organization members. Finally, the *open systems perspective* has highlighted the importance of coping with the surrounding environment.

Current and emerging issues in such areas as workforce diversity, teamwork, quality reengineering, and business globalization stand as important reasons why managers should know about the field of organizational behavior and make use of its information. Applied effectively, OB know-how can be a valuable source of competitive advantage for managers and their companies.

Review Questions

1. What is the field of organizational behavior? What kinds of behavior does it examine? Why does it include examination of the behaviors of groups and organizations?
2. What are the three subfields of organizational behavior? What is the focus of each? Why have they developed separately? Why is it important for you to know about all of them?
3. What must a company do to secure a competitive advantage over other firms? How can knowledge about organizational behavior help the company gain this advantage?
4. What is the central idea underlying work in the scientific management perspective? What advice would an expert on this perspective give managers? Give an example of the kind of change experts in scientific management might recommend if they were asked to improve the efficiency of your class.
5. How does the administrative principles perspective differ from the scientific management perspective? What is a management principle? How does it differ from a law or rule? What is a bureaucracy? Give an example of an organization that is extremely bureaucratic. Of an organization that is not very bureaucratic.

6. What does the human relations perspective focus attention on? According to Douglas McGregor, what sort of viewpoint do members of this perspective have on management? The Hawthorne researchers differed from members of the human relations perspective in what important respect?

7. What are the two key ideas underlying the open systems perspective? What central tenet do they support? Explain the cycle of events described by Katz and Kahn. According to your explanation, why is it important for managers to be able to diagnose environmental conditions and adapt their organizations to environmental changes as they occur?

8. For each of the emerging issues identified at the end of the chapter, which perspective or perspectives of management thought would probably provide the most useful guidance? Why?

ENDNOTES

1. E. A. Locke, D. B. Feren, V. M. McCaleb, K. N. Shaw, and A. T. Denny, "The Relative Effectiveness of Four Methods of Motivating Employee Performance," in *Changes in Working Life*, K. D. Duncan, M. M. Gruneberg, and D. Wallis, eds. (Chichester, England: John Wiley, 1980), pp. 363–88.

2. Ibid.

3. Locke et al., "The Relative Effectiveness"; see also J. A. Wagner III, P. A. Rubin, and T. J. Callahan, "Incentive Payment and Nonmanagerial Productivity: An Interrupted Time Series Analysis of Magnitude and Trend," *Organizational Behavior and Human Decision Processes* 42 (1988), pp. 47–74.

4. Locke et al., "The Relative Effectiveness"; J. A. Wagner III and R. Z. Gooding, "Shared Influence and Organizational Behavior: A Meta-Analysis of Situational Variables Expected to Moderate Participation-Outcome Relationships," *Academy of Management Journal* 30 (1987), pp. 524–41; and J. A. Wagner III, "On Beating Dead Horses, Reconsidering Reconsiderations, and Ending Disputes: Further Thoughts about a Recent Study of Research on Participation," *Academy of Management Review* 20 (1995), pp. 506–9.

5. N. Jonas, "No Pain, No Gain: How America Can Grow Again," *Business Week*, April 20, 1987, pp. 68–69; W. J. Hampton, "Why Image Counts: A Tale of Two Industries," *Business Week*, June 8, 1987, pp. 138–40; J. A. Byrne, "How the Best Get Better," *Business Week*, September 14, 1987, pp. 98–99; B. Nussbaum, "Needed: Human Capital," *Business Week*, September 19, 1988, pp. 100–23; C. Farrell and J. Hoerr, "ESOPs: Are They Good for You?" *Business Week*, May 15, 1989, pp. 116–23; and W.

Trueman, "Alternative Visions," *Canadian Business*, March 1991, pp. 28–33.

6. J. Barney, "Strategic Market Factors: Expectation, Luck, and Business Strategy," *Management Science* 32 (1986), pp. 1231–41; and I. Dierickx and K. Cool, "Asset Stock Accumulation and Sustainability of Competitive Advantage," *Management Science* 35 (1989), pp. 1504–11.

7. J. Pfeffer, "Producing Sustainable Competitive Advantage through the Effective Management of People," *Academy of Management Executive* 9 (1995), pp. 55–69; and P. M. Wright and G. C. McMahan, "Theoretical Perspectives for Strategic Human Resources Management," *Journal of Management* 18 (1992), pp. 295–320.

8. L. L. Greiner, "A Recent History of Organizational Behavior," in *Organizational Behavior*, S. Kerr, ed. (Columbus, OH: Grid Publishing, 1979), pp. 3–14.

9. L. L. Cummings, "Toward Organizational Behavior," *Academy of Management Review* 3 (1978), pp. 90–98.

10. R. House, D. M. Rousseau, and M. Thomas-Hunt, "The Meso Paradigm: A Framework for the Integration of Micro and Macro Organizational Behavior," in *Research in Organizational Behavior* 17, L. L. Cummings and B. M. Staw, eds. (Greenwich, CT: JAI Press, 1995), pp. 71–114.

11. R. H. Miles, *Macro Organizational Behavior* (Santa Monica, CA: Goodyear, 1980); and R. L. Daft and R. M. Steers, *Organizations: A Micro/Macro Approach* (Glenview, IL: Scott, Foresman, 1986).

12. H. L. Gantt, "A Bonus System of Rewarding Labor," *ASME Transactions* 23 (1901), pp. 341–72; and *Work, Wages, and Profits* (New York: Engineering Magazine Company, 1910), pp. 18–29.

13. H. L. Gantt, *Organizing for Work* (New York: Harcourt, Brace, & Howe, 1919), pp. 74–97.

14. H. Emerson, *The Twelve Principles of Efficiency* (New York: Engineering Magazine Company, 1912), pp. 359–67.

15. H. Fayol, *General and Industrial Management*, trans. C. Storrs (London: Sir Isaac Pitman & Sons, 1949), pp. 19–43.

16. H. Fayol, *Industrial and General Administration*, trans. J. A. Coubrough (Geneva, Switzerland: International Management Institute, 1930), p. 19.

17. H. H. Gerth and C. W. Mills, trans., *From Max Weber: Essays in Sociology* (New York: Oxford University Press, 1946); N. P. Mouzelis, *Organization and Bureaucracy: An Analysis of Modern Theories* (Chicago: Aldine, 1967); and T. Parsons, trans., *Max Weber: The Theory of Social and Economic Organization* (New York: Free Press, 1947).

18. J. D. Mooney and A. C. Redev, *Onward Industry: The Principles of Organization and Their Significance to Modern Industry* (New York: Harper & Brothers, 1931); revised and published as J. D. Mooney, *The Principles of Organization* (New York: Harper & Brothers, 1947).

19. L. Urwick, *The Elements of Administration* (New York: Harper & Brothers, 1944).

20. H. C. Metcalf and L. Urwick, eds., *Dynamic Administration: The Collected Papers of Mary Parker Follett* (New York: Harper & Row, 1940); see also J. Garwood, "A Review of Dynamic Administration: The Collected Papers of Mary Parker Follet," *New Management* 2 (1984), pp. 61–62.

21. A. Carey, "The Hawthorne Studies: A Radical Criticism," *American Sociological Review* 33 (1967), pp. 403–16.

22. Carey, "The Hawthorne Studies"; R. H. Franke and J. D. Kaul, "The Hawthorne Experiments: First Statistical Interpretation," *American Sociological Review* 43 (1978), pp. 623–43; and A. J. M. Sykes, "Economic Interests and the Hawthorne Researchers," *Human Relations* 18 (1965), pp. 253–63.

23. Examples from the body of research stimulated by the Hawthorne studies include L. Coch and J. R. P. French Jr., "Overcoming Resistance to Change," *Human Relations* 1 (1948), pp. 512–33; L. Berkowitz, "Group Standards, Cohesiveness, and Productivity," *Human Relations* 7 (1954), pp. 509–14; and S. E. Seashore, *Group Cohesiveness in the Industrial Work Group* (Ann Arbor: University of Michigan Survey Research Center, 1954).

24. D. McGregor, "The Human Side of Enterprise," *Management Review* 56 (1957), pp. 22–28, 88–92; and D. McGregor, *The Human Side of Enterprise* (New York: McGraw-Hill, 1960).

25. Adapted from McGregor, "The Human Side of Enterprise," p. 23.

26. Adapted from McGregor, "The Human Side of Enterprise," pp. 88–89.

27. D. Katz and R. L. Kahn, *The Social Psychology of Organizations* (New York: Wiley, 1966).

28. F. E. Emery and E. Trist, "The Causal Texture of Organizational Environments," *Human Relations* 18 (1965), pp. 21–32; and *Towards a Social Ecology* (London: Plenum, 1973).

29. C. Hymowitz, "A Day in the Life of Tomorrow's Manager," *The Wall Street Journal*, March 20, 1989, p. B1; and J. Dreyfus, "Get Ready for the New Workforce," *Fortune*, April 23, 1990, p. 12.

30. G. E. Ledford Jr. and E. E. Lawler III, "Research on Employee Participation: Beating a Dead Horse," *Academy of Management Review* 19 (1994), pp. 633–36.

31. M. Hammer and J. Champy, *Reengineering the Corporation: A Manifesto for Business Revolution* (New York: Harper Business, 1993); D. Greising, "Quality: How to Make It Pay," *Business Week*, August 8, 1994, pp. 54–59; and J. W. Dean Jr. and D. E. Bowen, "Management Theory and Total Quality: Improving Research and Practice through Theory Development," *Academy of Management Review* 19 (1994), pp. 392–418.

32. L. Nakarmi, M. DiCicco, G. Edmondson, A. Cortese, and D. Menaker, "Global Hot Spots," *Business Week*, September 25, 1995, pp. 116–26; and B. Vlasic and Z. Schiller, "Did Whirlpool Spin Too Far Too Fast?" *Business Week*, June 24, 1996, pp. 134–36.

Chapter Two
Managing Diversity and Individual Differences

The fires that drove the industrial age were fueled by coal, oil, and natural resources, and wars between nations were fought over who would control such assets. As we move into the 21st century, the fuel that drives the new information age is mental ability and knowledge, and today's high-tech companies are waging a war over who will control this valuable resource. Moreover, just as is the case with natural resources, valuable human resources are located all over the globe, and thus these wars are being fought increasingly on foreign turf.

In the aerospace industry, for example, executive David Williams notes that "every major space contractor who wants to be cost effective and competitive has to be thinking about relations with Russian partners."[1] Indeed, there are now alliances between small Russian firms and many large Western corporations within this industry, including Rockwell, McDonnel Douglas, Boeing, Pratt and Whitney, and Rolls-Royce. The mathematical and technical ability of Russian scientists and technicians is astounding those who staff Western companies. The fact that all this talent can be had at bargain prices (many Russian Ph.D.s work for less than $5,000 a year) creates a virtual treasure, often scattered and hidden throughout regions (e.g., Novosibirsk and Yekatarinburg) that Americans can barely pronounce the names of, let alone find. In other industries, such as software development, engineering, and pharmaceuticals, high-ability–low-cost talent is being mined increasingly in India, Taiwan, Singapore, China, and Korea.

Although there have been failed legislative attempts aimed at curtailing this inevitable flow of human ability across borders, the real barrier to effectively integrating this talent deals with cultural differences between people, manifested in different personalities and working styles.[2] Many of the companies that tap global talent create cross-functional work teams (often virtual teams linked via technology), and the keys to developing new drugs often depend as much on group chemistry as on pharmaceutical knowledge. McDonnel Douglas's southern

California managers often grow impatient with what they perceive as a lack of conscientiousness among Russian workers. As one manager notes, "World practice is that we agree on a price, and if they run over, it's their problem. . . . But in Russia, if they run out of money, they just stop working."

Being able to overcome these types of individual differences is thus a critical skill for today's modern manager. The information age is creating an enormous shift in the global economy, and as Texas Instruments' William Glickman notes, "If American firms are going to compete successfully in the years ahead, they must look everywhere for those with the best ability . . . there is no place for parochialism in today's world."[3]

[1]C. Mellow, "Brain Rush: Why Western Business Is Investing in Russia and R & D," *Fortune,* June 10, 1996, pp. 83–84.
[2]R. Horn, "Give Me Your Huddled. . . . High Tech Ph.D.s: Are High Skilled Foreigners Displacing U.S. Workers?" *Business Week,* November 6, 1995, pp. 161–62.
[3]S. Greengard, "Gain the Edge in the Knowledge Race," *Personnel Journal,* August 1996, pp. 52–56.

Managers who fail to manage diversity successfully inevitably fall into one of two traps. On the one hand, they may have a persistent tendency to assume that people are all basically alike. This belief that the whole world is "just like me" has been referred to as the **mirror image fallacy;** it is attractive because it makes the world seem much easier to comprehend. For example, if owners of a firm believe that everyone in their company shares their abilities, interests, beliefs, and values, they will consider it an easy task to organize their employees and encourage them to pursue a common goal. Because the mirror image fallacy *is* a fallacy, however, the owners will soon find that the myriad differences among the people they employ will make their task far from easy.

On the other hand, some managers fail because they hold prejudicial stereotypes about people based upon sex or membership in a racial, ethnic, or age group. Indeed, there is a certain irony in the fact that many diversity training seminars, in their attempt to dispel the mirror image fallacy, go too far and imply that all women or all Asians or all African Americans differ from white males in one consistent manner or another. In most dimensions of ability and personality, there is wide variation within groups (among Hispanics or the disabled, for example), and these differences are often much more important than the sometimes trivial differences between groups (say, between Hispanics and African Americans). Managers who fail to pay attention to differences between people *within these groups* inevitably do damage to their employees, their companies, and their own careers.

Ralph Waldo Emerson once wrote that "the wise man shows his wisdom in separation, in gradation, and his scale of creatures and of merits is as wide as nature. . . . The foolish have no range in their scale, but suppose that every man is as every other man." That statement captures the essence of this chapter. We will familiarize you with some of the major occupationally relevant dimensions in which human beings vary and the means by which information on these dimensions can be used to secure competitive advantage for your organization.

In the first section of this chapter, we will lay out three ways in which information about individual differences can be used to generate value added and competitive advantage. We will then describe how to understand the critical dimensions in which people vary (three dealing with physical abilities, four dealing with cognitive abilities, and five dealing with personality differences). Although these are hardly the *only* ways in which people vary (indeed, later chapters will explore others), they serve as a useful starting point. Next we will integrate this information into a model that shows how individual differences in ability and personality combine to affect job performance. Finally, in the last section, we will revisit the issue of demographic and cultural diversity and explain how the model can be used to develop an appreciation of differences along these lines in a way that promotes neither the mirror image fallacy nor prejudicial stereotypes.

Capitalizing on Individual Differences

Even the most tolerant manager might sometimes wish that individual differences would just go away. If all supervisors, colleagues, and subordinates were alike, managing would be a much easier task. However, because individual differences are not likely to disappear, organizations that wish to be successful must try to capitalize on differences in a way that advances their competitiveness. Indeed, research on how firms gain sustainable competitive advantage consistently identifies selectivity in hiring and an emphasis on training as two central characteristics.[1]

Figure 2-1 shows that we can derive benefit from individual differences in organizational behavior through selection, training, and reengineering.

Selection

Through selection and placement programs we can assess people and jobs, and then try to match up the two in a way that maximizes the fit between the abilities and traits of the individual and the abilities and traits required by the job.

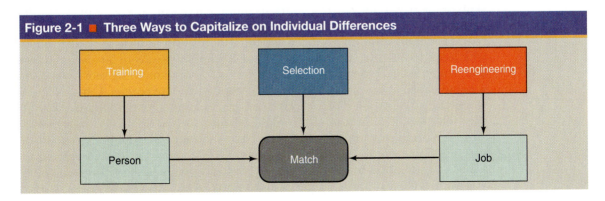

Figure 2-1 ■ Three Ways to Capitalize on Individual Differences

Training → Person

Selection → Match

Reengineering → Job

This type of matching allows us to take advantage of individual differences without changing either the person or the job. **Selection** is the process of choosing some applicants and rejecting others.

Effective selection is especially critical when teamed up with certain business strategies. For example, part of 3M's competitive advantage derives from the firm's business strategy of growing talent and innovation within the organization. At the same time, the last thing 3M wants is to have valuable people leave the company, taking 3M ideas or secrets with them. Thus, 3M's goal is to create a company of long-service employees. Therefore, as Richard Listad, a manager at 3M notes, "When you promote from within the way we do, you want to make sure that you're recruiting high-quality people."

To make sure that the organization will have a reliable pool of talent on which to draw, 3M has established a close tie with a small number of targeted midwestern universities. By forming long-term relationships with the schools, 3M gets to know the people (faculty) who are in a good position to know the people (students) whom they are likely to hire. This, along with an expansive internship program that gives 3M direct experience working with soon-to-be graduates, helps to ensure that any hiring decision will turn out to be a good one for both 3M and the applicant. The overall result of these efforts is that 3M has an annual attrition rate of less than 3 percent among salaried staff—highly in line with its chosen strategy for competing in its industry.[2]

Training

A second way to benefit from knowledge of individual differences is to train people in order to make up for any job-related deficiencies in their current profile of traits or abilities. There are now shortages of labor for some U.S. industries that are due not so much to any scarcity of workers as to the skill levels of those who are available. Even during the recession of the early 1990s, when unemployment was high, many employers had difficulty finding applicants with the right levels of skills. According to surveys conducted by the National Association of Manufacturers, five of six applicants for manufacturing jobs were rejected because of gaps between their skills and what the jobs required.[3] Of those rejected, two out of five were rejected specifically for lack of basic proficiency in reading and arithmetic.

Some organizations have responded to this crisis by trying to upgrade the skills of the new, highly diverse entrants into the labor pool. The Aetna Institute for Corporate Education, founded by the Aetna Life and Casualty Corporation, is a $42 million response to this problem. The institute is housed in a building with hotel rooms and 56 classrooms where a full-time faculty of 60 teaches up to 400 "students" each day. It is the centerpiece of Aetna's ongoing reorganization scheme aimed at keeping the company competitive. The core of Aetna's plan is to rewrite all of its job descriptions to emphasize general competencies rather than job-specific skills. Individual employees are assessed on these competencies and then assigned to the institute to master whatever skills they lack. The institute also helps employees develop competencies needed for upper-level jobs as part of a promotion-from-within policy.[4] Similar, smaller-scale efforts are being waged by GTE, Motorola, Exxon, and Adolph Coors.[5]

Training efforts can also be directed at changing people's personality styles. For example, at Chemical Bank, many accountants with excellent technical skills cannot be promoted to managerial levels because of their weaknesses in dealing with other people. As one manager notes, when the bank values an asset one way and the client another, a lack of agreeableness on the part of the accountant can make "discussions more contentious than they need to be." Accountants also struggle sometimes when placed in cross-functional teams. Training programs aimed at enhancing their skills in getting along with others help to reduce these problems. When armed with both technical skills and interpersonal skills, the bank officers find that not only are they able to make the right decisions, but they are able to facilitate the implementation of these decisions as well.[6]

The interchangeability between selecting for an attribute and training for an attribute can be seen in a recent study of 210 resort hotel employees. In this study, high levels of performance were found in employees who were high in conscientiousness or who had attended a training program that was aimed at increasing their level of self-directed leadership. Thus, one could either take advantage of existing differences in people's levels of conscientiousness or, instead, through training, change the level of conscientiousness and still get positive results. Performance in contexts where neither selective hiring nor training took place, however, was very low.[7]

Reengineering

Assessing individual differences is critical for training purposes because the intent of training is to change the person. We can also assess individual differences and then respond to any mismatch between person and job by changing the *job*, or reengineering work processes. Modifying jobs to better accommodate the abilities and traits of workers has become even more important given the passage of the Americans with Disabilities Act (ADA) of 1990. This act requires that employers make "reasonable accommodations" in an effort to employ the disabled. These accommodations often mean deleting or changing a job requirement, or moving the requirement to a different job, so that the lack of a particular ability no longer disqualifies some disabled worker from being considered.[8]

A good example of this can be seen at Samsonite Corporation in Denver, where many jobs have been changed so that they can be performed by deaf persons. The accommodations made are often very simple (in the production area, there are lights on forklifts rather than the traditional beepers to alert people to the presence of a moving vehicle), and yet they are effective in eliminating the need for an ability that some people might not have. As another example, Nordstrom's, working in conjunction with the United Cerebral Palsy Association, is attempting to isolate all the tasks in its job descriptions that can be performed by someone with cerebral palsy. These tasks (like sorting hangers) are then removed from the job, freeing up the original worker to do other things, and given to a worker who has cerebral palsy. The program provides Nordstrom's with a means of incorporating persons with disabilities into the workforce in a meaningful and productive way.[9] Successful managers strive to put each worker in a position that best taps that worker's own talents, often informally shifting, or trading, tasks between two people working under the same job title.[10] This type of informal job redesign allows the manager to take advantage of each person's unique blend of strengths and weaknesses. Of course, accommodating the different abilities and traits of different workers need not be limited to meeting the legislative requirement of ADA.

Conclusion

In a perfect world, all managers would be working with people who had all strengths and no weaknesses. In the real world, however, they rarely get this opportunity. Therefore, the next best thing is for managers to become aware of the strengths and weaknesses of different people, and then through selection, training, or reengineering, create a situation that plays to their people's strengths and leans away from their weaknesses. Given all the dimensions in which people might differ, what are the most critical for a manager to focus upon? In the next two sections of this chapter we will lay out a framework that attempts to answer this question by isolating three physical abilities, four cognitive abilities, and five personality traits.

Diversity in Abilities

Three Dimensions of Physical Ability

Edwin Fleishman was one of the first researchers to systematically analyze the structure of human physical abilities, and much of the research on this topic in the last 30 years represents a refinement and extension of his early work.[11] Recent emphasis has moved slightly, however, from evaluating physical fitness to predicting job performance. Occupation-oriented studies, taken together with what is known from human physiology, provide us with a solid foundation for understanding the structure of physical performance, and this structure is outlined in Table 2-1.[12]

Physical ability is made up of *three* major dimensions: (1) muscular strength, (2) cardiovascular endurance, and (3) movement quality. Each of these is defined in Table 2-1. Muscular strength comes in three slightly different varieties (tension, power, and endurance), and the same is true for quality of movement (flexibility, balance, and coordination).

Although a thorough analysis of a job is needed to determine whether it requires a particular physical capacity, in general the abilities listed in Table 2-1 are most frequently needed in jobs of two types: those in the protective services, such as municipal police, fire, and prison-corrections departments; and those in construction and other physically demanding industries.

If police, fire, or correctional personnel lack the necessary physical abilities, they or the persons they seek to protect may be injured.[13] Testing for the kinds of physical abilities listed in Table 2-1 is much more common now than in the

1. Muscular strength
   - Ability to exert muscular force against objects in terms of pushing, pulling, lifting, carrying, or lowering them (muscular tension)
   - Exerting muscular force in quick bursts (muscular power)
   - Exerting muscular force continuously over time while resisting fatigue (muscular endurance)
2. Cardiovascular endurance
   - Ability to sustain physical activity that results in increased heart rates for a long period
3. Movement quality
   - Ability to flex and extend body limbs to work in awkward or contorted positions (flexibility)
   - Ability to maintain the body in a stable position and resist forces that cause loss of stability (balance)
   - Ability to sequence movement of the fingers, arms, legs, or body to result in skilled action (coordination)

Source: J. Hogan, "Structure of Physical Performance in Occupational Tasks," *Journal of Applied Psychology* 76 (1991), pp. 495–507.

past, when height and weight criteria substituted for specific abilities. Because height and weight measures are considered to discriminate unfairly against women and the members of some minority groups, they are rarely used today.

Physical ability tests are also used to select employees for work such as construction, where jobs require physical strength and agility. Such tests can predict not only the level of job performance but the risk of job-related injuries. Research has shown that the incidence of lower-back injury can be predicted by tests of physical strength.[14] This is a significant finding, because back-related disability claims have been rising at 14 times the rate of the population over the last 10 years. Because employers are increasingly picking up the bill for employees' medical costs (and because lower-back pain is such a widespread and often recurring affliction), tests that predict health problems for a job applicant are extremely cost effective. General Dynamics Corporation's electric boat unit has actually developed specific physical examinations designed to screen out individuals at risk for back-pain problems.

Four Dimensions of Cognitive Ability

Although mental abilities are not one-dimensional, we do generally find positive relationships between people's performance scores on different kinds of mental tests. Thus, scores across different types of tests are often summed and treated as an index of general intelligence. Specialists substitute the term **general cognitive ability** for *intelligence* because the former term is more precise, and because it stirs up less controversy over such issues as the role of genetic factors in mental ability. The term *intelligence* is used imprecisely in the lay community,

Table 2-2 ■ The Four Dimensions of Cognitive Ability

1. Verbal ability
   - The ability to understand and effectively use written and spoken language
2. Quantitative ability
   - The ability to quickly and accurately solve arithmetic problems of all kinds, including addition, subtraction, multiplication, and division, as well as applying mathematical rules
3. Reasoning ability
   - The ability to think inductively and deductively in order to invent solutions to novel problems
4. Spatial ability
   - The ability to accurately detect the spatial arrangement of objects with respect to one's own body

Source: J. C. Nunnally, *Psychometric Theory* (New York: McGraw-Hill, 1978), pp. 59–61.

where the high social value placed on "intelligence" complicates discussions of things like age, sex, and racial differences.

In addition to this characteristic of general cognitive ability, however, there are also several different facets of mental ability, and some of these facets are sufficiently unique that they are worth assessing in their own right. Because certain specific jobs require more of one type of mental ability than others, we may want to select out data on this particular type of ability.

We will focus our attention on four primary facets of cognitive, or mental, ability that stand out in terms of both their generality and their usefulness as predictors of performance in the real world.[15] Table 2-2 lists and defines these abilities, and Figure 2-2 displays sample test items that assess each ability.

The first two dimensions are probably the most familiar to you. **Verbal ability** reflects the degree to which a person can understand and use written and spoken language. **Quantitative ability** reflects the person's ability to perform all kinds of arithmetic problems. This includes not only the four major functions of addition, subtraction, multiplication, and division, but also square root and rounding procedures, and the multiplication of positive and negative values.

Although a high school education should ensure that job applicants have at least minimal levels of these skills, many employers who engage in testing find that this is not always the case. For example, Prudential Life Insurance found that many of the applicants they tested, although they held high school diplomas, were performing at the third-grade level in math and reading proficiency. Because these deficiencies were found disproportionately within various minority groups, and because Prudential could hardly afford to hire people with such minimal skills, the company went into the business of remedial education. As the result of a precedent-setting agreement with the U.S. Department of Labor, the company spent $3 million to offer 260 hours of classroom training to some of the people it had rejected for jobs. The goal of this program was quite modest: to bring people who had completed the 12th-grade up to a 9th-grade level of competency in math and reading.[16]

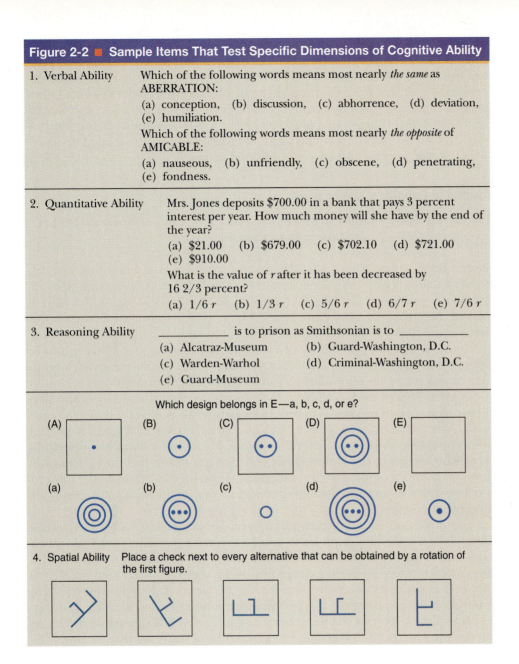

Figure 2-2 ■ Sample Items That Test Specific Dimensions of Cognitive Ability

1. Verbal Ability   Which of the following words means most nearly *the same* as ABERRATION:

(a) conception,   (b) discussion,   (c) abhorrence,   (d) deviation, (e) humiliation.

Which of the following words means most nearly *the opposite* of AMICABLE:

(a) nauseous,   (b) unfriendly,   (c) obscene,   (d) penetrating, (e) fondness.

2. Quantitative Ability   Mrs. Jones deposits $700.00 in a bank that pays 3 percent interest per year. How much money will she have by the end of the year?

(a) $21.00   (b) $679.00   (c) $702.10   (d) $721.00 (e) $910.00

What is the value of r after it has been decreased by 16 2/3 percent?

(a) $1/6\, r$ (b) $1/3\, r$ (c) $5/6\, r$ (d) $6/7\, r$ (e) $7/6\, r$

3. Reasoning Ability   _____ is to prison as Smithsonian is to _____

(a) Alcatraz-Museum   (b) Guard-Washington, D.C.

(c) Warden-Warhol   (d) Criminal-Washington, D.C.

(e) Guard-Museum

Which design belongs in E—a, b, c, d, or e?

4. Spatial Ability   Place a check next to every alternative that can be obtained by a rotation of the first figure.

A different kind of analytical skill is associated with the third dimension of mental ability. **Reasoning ability** is the ability to invent solutions to many different types of problems. Although items tapping reasoning sometimes employ numbers, they should not be confused with simple measures of quantitative ability. At the heart of a reasoning problem is the need to invent a solution or grasp a principle, not make computations.

Finally, the last dimension of mental ability we will examine is **spatial ability,** which reflects a person's ability to imagine how an object would look if its position in space were changed. It also reflects the ability to make an accurate determination of the spatial arrangement of objects with respect to one's own body. Such an ability is important, for example, to an airplane pilot, who should be able to detect changes in a plane's position just by looking at changes in the horizon seen through the cockpit window. Spatial ability is also related to career success for engineers, physical scientists, and artists.[17]

Validity of Cognitive Ability Tests

The usefulness of cognitive ability tests in predicting task performance has been investigated in both academic and organizational contexts.

General Tests.   In academic settings, researchers have found high correlations between scores on tests like the Scholastic Aptitude Test (SAT) and first-year college grade point average, or GPA (correlations in the .50s), as well as overall rank in class (correlations in the .60s).[18] These tests are more predictive for students in the physical sciences or math than for those in the humanities or social sciences. They are less predictive of success in graduate school (correlations in the .30s) because most applicants for graduate school score relatively high in mental ability and therefore form a somewhat homogeneous group.

A great deal of evidence suggests that general cognitive ability is also predictive of success in the world of work.[19] Research has shown that in virtually any job in which planning, judgment, and memory are used in day-to-day performance, individuals high in general cognitive ability will generally outperform those who are low in this ability. Other research has shown that the relationship between general cognitive ability and job performance increases as the job gets more complex in terms of decision making, planning, problem solving, and analyzing information.[20]

General cognitive ability is important even for jobs not characterized by such complexity if these jobs require the person to learn something new. Individuals high in general cognitive ability will learn the job more quickly than others. In low-complexity jobs, experience over time often wipes out this initial difference between high- and low-ability individuals, as Figure 2-3 demonstrates.[21] As months on the job increase, the performance differences attributable to differences in ability decrease. Thus, general cognitive ability is important in two respects. It relates both to learning the job and to performing the job when the job requires the person to deal continually with new situations.

Specific Tests.   For certain jobs, tests of specific mental ability can add significantly to the predictive power of tests of general intelligence.[22] For example, spatial visualization is critical for draftspersons and individuals in technical positions, and it is an important component of positions that require mechanical skills, such as machinist, forklift operator, and warehouse worker. Verbal ability and reasoning are critical to success in executive, administrative, and professional positions. Quantitative ability is important for positions such as accoun-

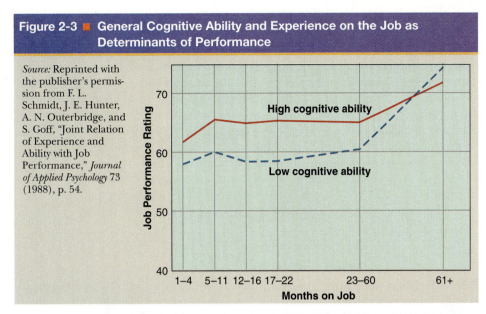

Figure 2-3 ■ General Cognitive Ability and Experience on the Job as Determinants of Performance

Source: Reprinted with the publisher's permission from F. L. Schmidt, J. E. Hunter, A. N. Outerbridge, and S. Goff, "Joint Relation of Experience and Ability with Job Performance," *Journal of Applied Psychology* 73 (1988), p. 54.

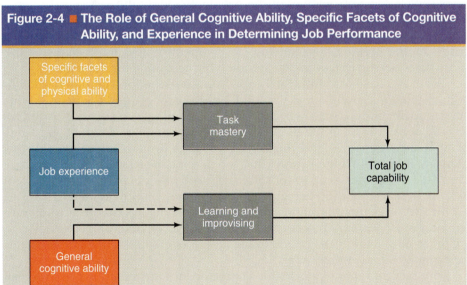

Figure 2-4 ■ The Role of General Cognitive Ability, Specific Facets of Cognitive Ability, and Experience in Determining Job Performance

tant, payroll clerk, and salesperson, and in many types of supervisory jobs. Whereas the use of general mental ability tests is applicable to a wide variety of jobs, the use of specific mental ability tests is more job specific.

Figure 2-4 illustrates how various kinds of ability combine to affect task performance. General cognitive ability influences both how fast the person can learn the job and how readily the person can adapt to changing circumstances when on the job. The more complex the job in terms of decision making, planning, and judgment, the more learning and improvising the job requires. With complex jobs, a great deal of job experience is only beneficial if it is accompanied by general cognitive ability, which helps one benefit from experience (hence the dotted line between "Job experience" and "Learning and improvising"). In simple jobs, the key is mastering a few specific tasks, and general cognitive ability is less important. Moreover, with simple jobs, experience on the job can often substitute for a lack of general or specific cognitive ability (hence the solid line between "Job experience" and "Task mastery").[23] Whereas general cognitive ability will almost always be relevant, the importance of specific abilities can be determined only by a detailed job analysis. Together, task mastery and the ability to learn and improvise on the job create the individual's total job capability.

Diversity in Personality

Whereas *abilities* are things an individual can do, *personality* is what a person is like. At a time when companies are increasingly competing on the basis of quality of service, the personalities of the people providing the service have never been more important. These customer-contact people make up one of the fastest-growing segments of the U.S. workforce, and they are the front line in the battle among organizations striving for competitive advantage. Many of the more successful firms take great care when hiring people for these jobs.

For example, at Marriott Hotels, applicants respond to a computerized, self-administered questionnaire as part of the hiring process, and the items on this survey tap dimensions such as conscientiousness and agreeableness. Marriott rejects 90 percent of all would-be guest service associates, based upon these kinds of tests and interviews, and this selectivity raises the level of service quality. Manager Richard Bell-Irvine notes that "when someone leaves, it messes up your employee teams, messes up your productivity, and messes up the service you provide." Whereas close to 50 percent of Marriott's new employees used to leave after the first three months on the job, this sort of testing has cut the attrition rate to closer to 10 percent. Another Marriott manager, Chris Kerbow, notes, "We're willing to be patient. It's so critical to the success of the hotels that our associates be committed and enthusiastic."[24]

The fact that many personality characteristics are described in everyday language—for example, aggressiveness, sociability, and impulsiveness—is both good news and bad news for the study of organizational behavior. It is good news because most people can readily perceive individual differences in these qualities and can see how such variations might affect particular situations. It is bad news because terms adopted from everyday language are usually not very precise. This can create considerable difficulty in understanding, communicating, and using information obtained from scientific measures of personality. In the next sections of this chapter, we will focus on five specific characteristics of personality and some of the existing evidence for the usefulness of measuring these characteristics in organizational contexts.

Table 2-3 ■ The Five Dimensions of Personality

1. Extroversion
   - Sociable, gregarious, assertive, talkative, expressive
2. Emotional adjustment
   - Emotionally stable, nondepressed, secure, content
3. Agreeableness
   - Courteous, trusting, good natured, tolerant, cooperative, forgiving
4. Conscientiousness
   - Dependable, organized, persevering, thorough, achievement oriented
5. Inquisitiveness
   - Curious, imaginative, artistic, sensitive, broad minded, playful

Source: M. R. Barrick and M. K. Mount, "The Big Five Personality Dimensions and Job Performance: A Meta-Analysis." *Personnel Psychology* 44 (1991), pp. 1–26.

Five Dimensions of Personality

Given the vast number of personality characteristics that are described in the scientific literature, we need some type of classification scheme in order to understand both the characteristics themselves and their interrelationships. Fortunately, just as there was a great deal of research on the dimensionality of physical and mental abilities, there is also a vast literature that has helped clarify the structure of human personality traits. Indeed, most of the current personality literature, especially that which applies to organizational behavior, focuses on "the Big Five" dimensions of personality.[25] We refer to these five major dimensions as (1) **extroversion,** (2) **emotional adjustment,** (3) **agreeableness,** (4) **conscientiousness,** and (5) **inquisitiveness.** Table 2-3 lists each of these with a corresponding set of adjectives.[26]

Many companies, including General Motors, American Cyanamid, J. C. Penney, and Westinghouse, rely heavily on personality assessment programs in evaluating and promoting employees. Many other firms use such programs as screens for initial hiring. For example, American Multi Cinema (AMC), the third largest theater chain in America, looks for individuals with "kinetic energy, emotional maturity, and the ability to deal with large numbers of people in a fairly chaotic situation."[27] Despite its widespread acceptance in industry, however, the use of personality measures in the explanation and prediction of human behavior has been criticized on several counts.

The most significant criticism deals with the validity of these measures for actually predicting future job success. Although it is possible to find reliable, commercially available measures of each of the traits shown in Table 2-3, the level of evidence for their validity and generalizability has traditionally been low.[28] Conscientiousness is the only dimension of personality that displays any validity as a predictor of success across a number of different job categories.[29] Indeed, not only is conscientiousness a valid predictor of job performance, it is also a predictor of employee theft[30] and white-collar crime.[31] Extroversion is relevant to a few types of jobs, like sales and management jobs, but the level of predictability

Emotional Adjustment and Negligent Hiring

John Padilla wanted to be a security guard, and he formally applied for positions with several companies in New York State. One company, OSC Security, rejected Padilla's application, but another, HSC Security, hired him. Padilla's first assignment was at Carle Place High School in Long Island, where two weeks after being hired, he fired 16 shots from a nine-millimeter gun into a car parked outside the school for no apparent reason. Two students were killed and three others were seriously wounded.

Had HSC Security bothered to check, they would have discovered that Padilla had a history of mental illness and was on probation for two separate weapons charges. When lawyers for the families of the slain students uncovered this information, HSC Security was finished as an organization. HSC's major competitor, OSC Security, on the other hand, is still operating and thriving. As OSC manager Brian Church notes, "Obviously, it's worth spending all the money we do on screening because we nixed John right away."[1] In fact, OSC rejected Padilla based on a $50 criminal records check that took less than 24 hours to obtain.

Although one might hope that OSC was the norm and HSC was the outlier in terms of business practice, the fact is that only 20 percent of organizations check the criminal records of those they hire.[2] The stakes in this game of Russian roulette are quite high. Under the legal doctrine of "negligent hiring," an employer can be held responsible for criminal acts perpetrated by employees. Thus, a Florida company was hit with a $2.5 million judgment after an employee—who had a criminal record that was never checked—returned to a home after a delivery and attacked the home owner. Similarly, McDonald's Corporation paid out over $200,000 to the family of a three-year-old who was assaulted by an employee who had a previous conviction for child molestation.[3]

Of course, the monetary damages in these cases are only the tip of the iceberg in terms of harm caused. The damage such an incident causes in terms of public relations and consumer trust may never be undone, especially in a competitive environment in which others stand ready to take your business. As one manager at a Florida hospital notes, "If this happens even once, it can be so damaging to your organization that you may have to close."[4]

[1]R. Behar, "Thugs in Uniform," *Time,* March 9, 1992, pp. 46–47.
[2]S. Greenguard, "Are You Well Armed to Screen Applicants?" *Personnel Journal,* December 1995, pp. 84–95.
[3]P. Dunn, "Pre-employment Referencing Aids Your Bottom Line," *Personnel Journal,* February 1995, pp. 68–75.
[4]S. R. Miller, "More Background Checks in Store for Health Care Workers," *South Florida Business Journal,* August 11, 1995, p. B2.

is low[32] and contingent upon other factors like the amount of freedom inherent in the job.[33] The low level of criterion validity of personality measures is particularly noticeable when we compare these measures with tests of cognitive or physical abilities needed to perform a particular function.

Making Personality Tests Work

Although the validity of personality tests may never match that seen with ability tests, there are concrete steps organizations can take to more successfully capitalize on individual differences in personality. For example, keeping a focus on just the Big Five traits helps in several ways. The nature of the traits themselves gives some clues as to how and why they might affect job performance. Figure 2-5 shows a way to understand the effect of personality on job performance. Certain traits like extroversion and agreeableness are probably important be-

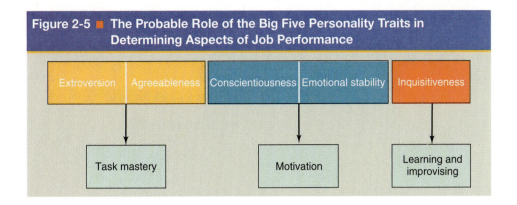

Figure 2-5 ■ The Probable Role of the Big Five Personality Traits in Determining Aspects of Job Performance

Extroversion	Agreeableness	Conscientiousness	Emotional stability	Inquisitiveness

Task mastery

Motivation

Learning and improvising

cause they relate to specific skill requirements associated with some organizational tasks (public speaking or dealing with customers). For example, selling life insurance requires a great deal of interpersonal skill and dealing with rejection. Thus, it is not surprising that when Metropolitan Life Insurance tested its applicants, it found that those who were high in extroversion generated 37 percent higher sales than those who were low. This large gain in productivity relative to the inexpensive nature of the type of test involved gives Metropolitan a competitive advantage relative to firms that do little or no selective screening on the personality dimension of extroversion.[34]

Other characteristics like conscientiousness and emotional adjustment are probably important because they affect someone's motivation to focus and excel at work. Because performance is a function of both motivation and ability, the predictive value of personality traits that affect motivation (like conscientiousness and emotional stability) might be enhanced by testing for these traits only after someone has been successfully screened on an ability test. An individual may have a great deal of conscientiousness, but if the person lacks ability, all the motivation in the world will not turn that person into an effective performer.

For example, in a study of 203 workers at Weyerhauser, researchers found that there was little relationship between conscientiousness on the one hand and supervisory ratings of performance on the other. However, as shown in Figure 2-6, for workers who were high in cognitive ability, there was a strong positive relationship between this aspect of personality and performance.[35] Thus, conscientiousness, in the absence of ability, is not really much of an asset.

This type of interaction between measurable ability and a personality trait has also been found with the characteristic of emotional stability. That is, in a sample of insurance sales personnel, research found that salespeople who were not very skilled made low commissions (over a six-month period) regardless of whether their emotional stability was low or high. For the salespeople who were extremely skilled, however, emotional adjustment made a big difference. High-ability people with low emotional adjustment made no more in sales commissions than the low-ability salespeople did. On the other hand, high-ability people who were also high in emotional adjustment earned nearly twice as much in commissions as others.[36] Emotional adjustment is also an important predictor

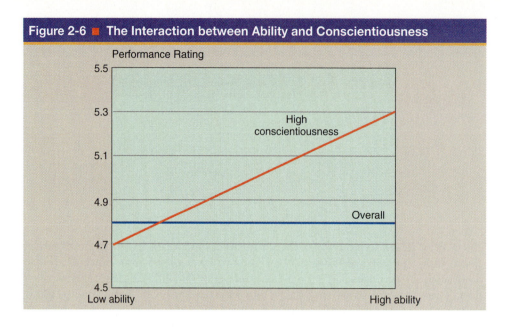

Figure 2-6 ■ The Interaction between Ability and Conscientiousness

Performance Rating

5.5

5.3

High
conscientiousness

5.1

4.9

Overall

4.7

4.5

Low ability   High ability

of the motivation to engage in deviant acts on the job. As the Securing Competitive Advantage box illustrates, making just one wrong decision with an employee on this dimension may be the difference between staying competitive and going out of business.

Finally, returning to Figure 2-5, note that a trait like inquisitiveness is probably important because it promotes learning about the job. Individuals high in this trait like to tinker and experiment with new situations, and in doing so, they often uncover new and better ways of accomplishing tasks and dealing with others.

A Model of How Individual Differences Affect Job Performance

Figure 2-7, which combines and expands on Figures 2-4 and 2-5, summarizes what we have discussed in this chapter. The diagram shows that performance levels are a function of one's motivation and total job capability. When both motivation and capability are high, performance will be high. An individual's total job capability is a function of general job knowledge and specific job skills. Specific job skills are primarily a function of specific facets of mental and physical ability, as well as certain personality traits like extroversion and agreeableness. General job knowledge, on the other hand, is a product of general cognitive ability and personality traits like inquisitiveness, both of which promote on-the-job improvisation and learning. For jobs that are low in complexity, general cognitive ability is less important. As the figure shows, for such jobs, job experience becomes a more important influence on job knowledge. Finally, an in-

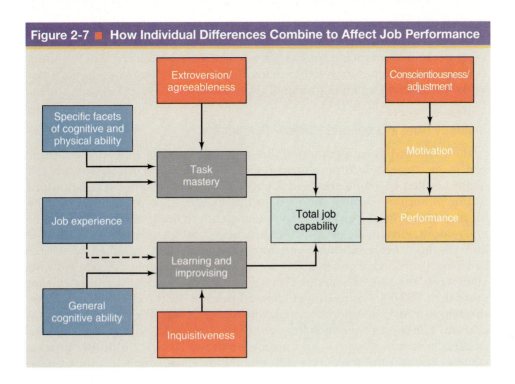

Figure 2-7 ■ How Individual Differences Combine to Affect Job Performance

dividual's motivation on the job is a function of personality traits like conscientiousness (which promotes effort, endurance, and commitment) and emotional stability (which eliminates distractions and helps keep the effort focused).

Diversity in Demographic and Cultural Characteristics

Recent changes in the labor supply have heightened managers' awareness of individual differences. However, most of this awareness has focused not so much on differences in physical abilities, cognitive abilities, or personality traits, as on diversity related to demographic and cultural characteristics.

Much of the current concern about managing diversity can be traced to demographic studies indicating that by the year 2000, 60 percent of new entrants into the labor pool will be women, minorities, or immigrants. This number has forced companies that were once staffed predominantly by white males to rethink their policies.[37] Interest in managing diversity can also be traced to the increased globalization of many corporations that are rapidly expanding operations to foreign locales. For example, at Pepsi-Cola International, a new international management institute helps employees learn skills and absorb cultural information so that they can be more effective in their assignments outside North America.[38] Many feel that North American managers are not nearly so sensitive to differences among people as are their Asian or European counterparts, who have been playing in the international field for years. Finally, demographic studies also indicate that on average, the workforce is getting older; hence, managing workers of advancing age has also become a major concern. These kinds of demographic changes have led to many changes in the way organizations view workforce diversity and integration of the workplace.

Diversity from a Legal and Political Perspective

In the 1970s and 80s integration of the workforce was driven by legal concerns, and many organizations developed policies in order to ward off lawsuits that might be filed based on the Civil Rights Act of 1964 or other legislation protecting minorities, women, the aged, or the disabled. The political strength behind such civil rights legislation has waned greatly in the 1990s, however, for several reasons. First, many of the affirmative action programs instituted in the 70s and 80s have achieved some measure of success. The number of African Americans enrolled in colleges and universities has increased 500 percent since 1965. Over the last 25 years, the share of African-American families earning more than $50,000 has risen from 8 to 20 percent. In the last five years alone, the ranks of African-American managers and professionals have increased 30 percent. The pay received by college-educated African-American men employed as executives, administrators, and professionals was 86 percent of that given to white peers, and the remaining difference in pay was largely attributed to seniority differences. Indeed, college-educated African-American women actually earned 10 percent more than comparable white women.[39]

Second, whereas existing affirmative action programs have failed to completely wipe out discrimination or all the differences between races in outcomes, the perception is that these programs no longer target the groups who need the most support. There is a growing core of poor inner city African-American youths who are most often the victims of the international competitive forces that are driving down wages and employment levels for low-skilled workers. Manufacturing jobs that used to support this group are increasingly moving overseas, and the types of benefits that come out of affirmative action programs currently in place benefit affluent, middle-class African Americans, rather than this group, which more desperately needs the support.[40]

Third, the simple black-white dichotomy that drove the early civil rights initiatives fails to capture the multiethnic and multipolar environment that is modern America. For example, in California, non-Hispanic whites comprise just 57 percent of the population. Hispanics are the second largest group (26 percent), followed by Asians (9 percent), and then African Americans (7 percent). If one adds to this the 146 different nationalities of people living in this state, and then recognizes that women, the disabled, and all people over 40 are protected by various forms of legislation, then one can see that over 85 percent of Californians can claim to be part of a protected class.[41] When protected-group status gets distributed so widely, it loses much of its political impact.

In addition to, and perhaps because of, the three reasons just listed, the 1990s have also seen an increase in backlash against the current affirmative action programs, which are seen by white males as giving preferential treatment to other groups at their expense.[42] This backlash is particularly strong among younger, Generation X whites who grew up having no experience with the segregation that drove early civil rights initiatives. The tolerance that many older white workers had for race-based remedial programs, partially fueled by guilt and direct experience, simply does not exist among younger people who grew up in less segregated schools and neighborhoods.

Diversity as a Source of Competitive Advantage

It is ironic that despite the previously noted changes in perceptions and political climate, in business organizations, the desire to integrate and diversify the workforce has never been stronger. Rather than being motivated by a sense of social justice or fear of litigation, however, today's affirmative action programs are part of a larger competitive strategy. As Mark Jennings, a top-level executive at Gannett News, notes, "Diversity is important in every company, and certainly in the news and information business. A diverse workforce is more innovative and creative. The whole point of this is getting a competitive edge from the people that work for you."[43] This same theme is echoed by IBM chief executive officer (CEO) Louis Gerstner, who notes that "our marketplace is made up of all races, religions, and sexual orientations, and therefore it is vital to our financial success that our workforce also be diverse.[44]

Cosmetics manufacturer Maybelline provides a dramatic example of how to use diversity as a means of leveraging competitive advantage. Minority women in the firm were the first to recognize that there was an untapped market for cosmetics developed specifically for women of darker skin hues. This discovery led to the 1990 launch of the Shades of You line of products aimed specifically at minority women. Thanks to the early recognition of this untapped market, Maybelline now enjoys a 35 percent share of a market that is worth $100 million a year and still growing.[45] Similarly, Pat Nichols, the district manager for Du Pont Chemicals Ag-Products Division, notes that "there is a vital need to develop different foods for different cultures and companies need a diverse workforce to do that.[46] To attract such a labor force, Du Pont runs an aggressive college recruiting campaign aimed directly at women and minorities, who have historically shown little interest in agricultural careers. In a similar outreach effort, Gaylord Container Corporation, in conjunction with the Los Angeles County Health Department, has created a program to help low-income inner city youths overcome barriers to employment. The program provides practical work experience, interpersonal communication training, and a mentor to help participants make the transition into the working world.[47]

Successfully creating a diverse workforce can also enhance the firm's bottom line via financial markets. The financial literature on capital budgeting indicates that valuable investments increase a firm's stock price. A recent study suggests that being recognized for success in the area of diversity management is viewed by financial markets as just such an investment. That is, researchers examined the stock price of firms that won the U.S. Department of Labor's Exemplary Efforts Award for Affirmative Action Programs and compared these to the stock prices of a sample of control firms matched for size and industry. This study also

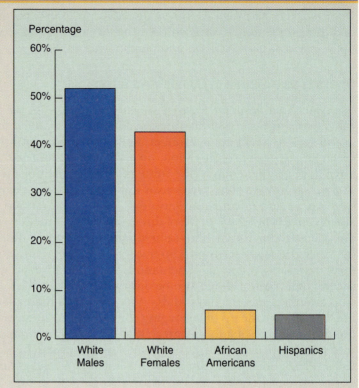

Figure 2-8 ■ Percentage of Executive and Managerial Jobs Held by Various Subgroups

Source: Based on data from M. Galen, "Diversity: Beyond the Numbers Game," *Business Week,* August 14, 1995, pp. 60–61.

examined the stock prices of firms that were publically cited for discriminatory practices. The results of this study showed that the stock prices for award-winning firms went up relative to those of control firms after the announcement of the award, whereas the stock price for firms that were cited for violations went down.[48] Clearly, the financial markets react negatively to firms that seem to be struggling in their attempts to manage a diverse workforce.

Firms that value diversity also need to work hard to ensure that they can retain members of these groups, once hired. Turnover rates among minorities at the managerial level are often two to three times those among white males, and this is often attributable to a perceived lack of opportunities for promotion. Indeed, Figure 2-8 shows the disparity in upper-level jobs for varying groups. Lawrence Perlman, CEO of Ceridian Corporation of Minneapolis, states that "the combination of women and people of color dropping out is really discouraging . . . it just isn't good business." To prevent this exodus, Ceridian has set diversity goals for promotions and career-enhancing experiences, and similar steps are being taken at Polaroid, Ameritech, Texaco, and Dow Chemical.[49]

Other companies provide training programs to help with this problem. For example, Corning found that between 1980 and 1987, African-American and female professionals left the company at roughly twice the rate of white men. A diversity training program for managers helped reduce attrition rates for both groups. Avon encourages employees to organize into African-American, Hispanic, and Asian networks by granting these groups official recognition and providing a senior mentor to act as an advisor to the group. The cosmetics company once had a similar network for women but disbanded it after the program achieved its objective (today women hold 79 percent of the management positions at Avon). Avon's chief of human resources told a reporter, "My objective is to create an organization where people don't feel a need for a black network, a Hispanic network, or an Asian network, just as women decided they didn't need their network."[50]

Retaining minority representation is also enhanced by programs that promote mentoring relationships between new minority employees and more established organization members. In fact, one recent study suggests that the real key in such programs is linking up women and minority members with white male mentors. The benefits that accrue to the new worker from these cross-race and cross-gender pairings seem to be much larger than those that accrue to women and minorities that have mentors with the same demographic characteristics.[51]

Of course, over and above all these factors, for diversity programs to be successful, they must receive top managerial support. Indeed, a recent study involving close to 800 managers pointed to this as the single most important factor in predicting the success of these programs. The second most critical factor deals with the ability of the organization to channel this top-level enthusiasm down through the hierarchy. The best way to ensure this spread of enthusiasm is to formally praise and reward middle- and lower-level managers for creating, maintaining, and profiting from diversity.[52] For managers of operating units at Colgate Palmolive the link between measurement and achievement is created by annual pay raises determined through the company's Executive Incentive Compensation Plan. Similar programs can be found at Corning and at Quaker Oats, where the ability to manage diversity is one of the major factors considered during the annual performance review of managers. In fact, recent surveys indicate that 53 percent of the Fortune 500 companies have initiated incentives for executives to enhance their skills in this area.[53]

Although people most often think of the characteristics of race and sex when it comes to workforce diversity issues, one of the more sweeping demographic forces that many organizations are attempting to come to grips with is the aging of the workforce. The majority of the 76 million baby boomers born between 1946 and 1960 are now, or will soon be, 50 years of age. Because of the baby bust that existed between 1965 and 1976, many have predicted that organizations will be facing major labor shortages. Some firms are turning this situation to their own competitive advantage by hiring and retraining older workers.

For example, McDonald's Corporation now struggles to find the young workers that once dominated the ranks of its employees. It therefore initiated its ReHIREment Program, which attempts to entice older individuals to work in its restaurants. As part of the program, McDonald's developed specific recruiting materials for this older generation. Whereas the recruiting brochures for young candidates emphasize the learning opportunities and long-term career benefits of McDonald's jobs, the brochures in the ReHIREment Program stress the scheduling flexibility and the fact that part-time earnings do not threaten Social Security earnings.[54]

Of course, attracting older workers is just one part of the problem. In addition to this, the organization must strive to ensure that existing stereotypes on the part of other workers do not destroy any chance that the older worker may have to contribute to the company. A substantial amount of data from scientific studies refutes many of the negative stereotypes that surround perceptions of older workers.[55] Organizations that hire older workers need to dispel these myths. The Home Shopping Network (HSN), the cable network based in Clearwater, Florida, has a program similar to that used at McDonald's. Located in an area well populated by retirees, HSN uses older workers on a part-time basis to answer telephones and take orders for merchandise advertised on its shows. It also maintains a sensitivity program for its managers that gives them valid information about what is fact and fiction in the area of aging and job performance.[56]

When these kinds of sensitivity training programs work well, they are able to dispel the mirror image fallacy and at the same time avoid fostering prejudicial stereotypes about various groups. They achieve their success by helping managers focus on individuals as individuals, each one of whom can be thought of as a unique constellation of physical abilities, cognitive abilities, and personality traits. Each personal profile on these abilities and traits is different from all others, and these differences transcend differences in sex, race, age, or culture.

SUMMARY

This chapter has shown that individuals differ in a number of dimensions; successfully taking advantage of this fact is essential to the effective control of organizational behavior. Individuals may differ in three primary aspects of physical ability, *muscular strength, endurance,* and *movement quality,* and there are many job situations in which people who lack the necessary physical abilities perform poorly and put themselves and others at risk for injuries. *General cognitive ability* is another characteristic in which individuals differ and one that has important implications for a much wider variety of jobs. Indeed, this characteristic is relevant for any job that requires planning and complex decision making on a daily basis. General cognitive ability also relates to both learning the job and adapting to new situations. Four specific facets of cognitive ability are *verbal ability, quantitative ability, reasoning ability,* and *spatial skills.* These specific abilities, like general cognitive ability, affect performance on certain types of jobs.

Individuals also differ in personality characteristics. These differences in traits like *extroversion, agreeableness, emotional adjustment, conscientiousness,* and *inquisitiveness* often translate into job performance differences. Changes in the demographic composition of the labor force have forced many organizations to cast aside stereotypes about different groups of people, and progressive organizations are finding ways of converting workforce diversity into a source of sustainable competitive advantage.

Review Questions

1. Do you think the mirror image fallacy is more likely to affect our assessments of others' abilities or our assessments of their personalities? Are there particular dimensions of ability or classes of personality characteristics that are especially susceptible to this kind of mistaken perception? Explain your answer.
2. Think of someone you know who was highly successful in his or her chosen field. What were the important personal characteristics that led to this person's success? Now think of what would have happened if this person had chosen a different line of work. Do you think the person would have been successful no matter what he or she ventured into, or can you imagine lines of work for which the person was poorly suited? How does your answer to this question relate to the selection-versus-placement distinction?
3. Imagine someone who is turned down for a job because of (*a*) performance on a paper-and-pencil cognitive ability test, (*b*) an interviewer's assessment of the person's intelligence and conscientiousness, or (*c*) responses to a personality inventory. What reactions would you expect from this person in each case? Explain your answer.
4. We know of a firm that hands out several different kinds of tests to prospective employees but never actually scores them before making employment decisions. What message is indirectly being sent to applicants by firms that employ rigorous selection testing, and how might the intention to send such a message explain this company's behavior?
5. Some nations such as Japan have federally controlled education, which results in educational standardization. Such nations also promote a clear hierarchy of primary schools, secondary schools, and universities, arranged in order of their prestige and quality. Other nations, including the United States, leave control over education to state and local authorities. How might this difference in educational policies lead to different employer needs in the area of personnel testing?

Implementation Guide

In managing individual differences and their effects on organizational behavior, it may help to ask the following diagnostic questions:

1. Are there any special features of this job that call for high levels of specific physical abilities? Does the jobholder possess these abilities?
2. Are there any features of this job that require specific facets of mental ability? Does the jobholder possess these abilities?
3. How much general cognitive ability does the jobholder have? How will this influence the speed with which he or she will learn the job?
4. How much improvising will the person have to do on this job? Does the jobholder have enough general cognitive ability to adapt to changing circumstances?
5. If the jobholder lacks general cognitive ability, does he or she have sufficient work experience to make up for this deficiency?

6. How complex is the job? If it is highly complex, does the jobholder have enough cognitive ability to handle this complexity?

7. Are there any features of this job that require certain types of personality traits like agreeableness or extroversion? Does the holder of this job possess those traits?

8. What motives seem to drive this person, and is he or she likely to be conscientious on the job?

9. Does the job call for developing innovative approaches, and is the jobholder likely to have the inquisitiveness needed to try new and different ways to approach the work?

10. Are there any signs of emotional maladjustments that may be hindering this person's ability to concentrate his or her effort on the task?

11. What is the relationship between the person's typical and maximum level of performance?

12. How do we know what abilities and personality characteristics this jobholder possesses? How should we go about measuring these if we are unsure?

ENDNOTES

1. J. Pfeffer, "Producing Sustainable Competitive Advantage through the Effective Management of People," *Academy of Management Executive* 9 (1995), pp. 55–72; J. T. Delaney and M. A. Huselid, "The Impact of Human Resource Management Practices on Perceptions of Organizational Performance," *Academy of Management Journal* 39 (1996), pp. 949–69; M. A. Huselid, "The Impact of Human Resource Management Practices on Turnover, Productivity, and Corporate Financial Performance," *Academy of Management Journal* 38 (1995), pp. 635–72; J. B. Arthur, "Effects of Human Resource Management Systems on Manufacturing Performance and Turnover," *Academy of Management Journal* 38 (1994), pp. 670–87; A. A. Lado and M. C. Wilson, "Human Resource Systems and Sustained Competitive Advantage," *Academy of Management Review* 19 (1994), pp. 699–727.

2. D. Anfuso, "3M's Staffing Strategy Promotes Productivity and Pride," *Personnel Journal*, February 1995, pp. 28–34.

3. W. Johnston, "The Coming Labor Shortage," *Journal of Labor Research* 13 (1992), pp. 5–10.

4. A. Durity, "A Critical Role for Corporate Education," *Personnel* 68 (1992), pp. 5–6.

5. T. Segal, "When Johnny's Whole Family Can't Read," *Business Week*, July 22, 1992, pp. 68–70.

6. A. Farnham, "Are You Smart Enough to Keep Your Job?" *Fortune*, January 15, 1996, pp. 35–48.

7. G. L. Stewart, K. P. Carson, and R. L. Cardy, "The Joint Effects of Conscientiousness and Self-Leadership Training on Employee Self-Directed Behavior in a Service Setting," *Personnel Psychology* 49 (1996), pp. 143–64.

8. B. McKee, "What You Must Do for the Disabled," *Nations Business*, December 1991, pp. 37–39.

9. N. L. Breuer, "Resources Can Relieve ADA Fears," *Personnel Journal*, September 1993, pp. 131–34.

10. J. J. Laabs, "Individuals with Disabilities Augment Marriott's Work Force," *Personnel Journal*, September 1994, pp. 46–50.

11. E. A. Fleishman, *The Structure and Measurement of Physical Fitness* (Englewood Cliffs, NJ: Prentice Hall, 1964).

12. J. Hogan, "Structure of Physical Performance in Occupational Tasks," *Journal of Applied Psychology* 76 (1991), pp. 495–507.

13. R. D. Arvey, T. E. Landon, S. M. Nutting, and S. E. Maxwell, "Development of Physical Ability Tests for Police Officers: A Construct Validation Approach," *Journal of Applied Psychology* 77 (1992), pp. 996–1009.

14. D. B. Chaffin, "Human Strength Capability and Low Back Pain," *Journal of Occupational Medicine* 16 (1974), pp. 248–54.

15. J. C. Nunnally, *Psychometric Theory* (New York: McGraw-Hill, 1978).

16. "School Days at Prudential High," *Time*, September 3, 1985, p. 60.

17. L. G. Humphreys, D. Lubinski, and G. Yao, "Utility in Predicting Group Membership and the Role of Spatial Visualization in Becoming an Engineer, Physical Scientist, or Artist," *Journal of Applied Psychology* 78 (1993), pp. 250–61.

18. A. R. Jenson, *Bias in Mental Testing* (New York: Free Press, 1980), p. 313.

19. J. E. Hunter, "Cognitive Ability, Cognitive Aptitudes, Job Knowledge, and Job Performance," *Journal of Vocational Behavior* 29 (1986), pp. 340–62.

20. R. L. Gutenberg, R. D. Arvey, H. G. Osburn, and R. P. Jeanneret, "Moderating Effects of Decision-Making/Information Processing Dimensions on Test Validities," *Journal of Applied Psychology* 68 (1983), pp. 600–08.

21. F. L. Schmidt, J. E. Hunter, A. N. Outerbridge, and S. Goff, "Joint Relation of Experience and Ability with Job Performance: Test of Three Hypotheses," *Journal of Applied Psychology* 73 (1988), pp. 46–57.

22. G. K. Bennett, H. G. Seashore, and A. G. Wesman, *Administrator's Handbook for the Differential Aptitude Test,* Psychological Corporation (San Antonio, TX: Harcourt, Brace, Jovanovich, 1982), p. 55.

23. L. S. Gottfredson, "Societal Consequences of the g Factor in Employment," *Journal of Vocational Behavior* 29 (1986), pp. 379–411.

24. R. Henkoff, "Finding, Training and Keeping the Best Service Workers, *Fortune,* October 3, 1994, pp. 110–22.

25. L. M. Hough, N. K. Eaton, M. D. Dunnette, J. D. Camp, and R. A. McCloy, "Criterion-Related Validities of Personality Constructs and the Effect of Response Distortion on Those Validities," *Journal of Applied Psychology* 75 (1990), pp. 467–76.

26. M. R. Barrick and M. K. Mount, "The Big Five Personality Dimensions and Job Performance: A Meta-Analysis," *Personnel Psychology* 44 (1991), pp. 1–26.

27. "Can You Pass the Job Test?" *Newsweek,* May 5, 1986, pp. 46–51.

28. R. M. Guion and R. F. Gottier, "Validity of Personality Measures in Personnel Selection," *Personnel Psychology* 18 (1965), pp. 135–64; and F. J. Landy, *The Psychology of Work Behavior,* 4th ed. (New York: Free Press, 1985), p. 186.

29. J. J. McHenry, L. M. Hough, J. L. Toquam, M. A. Hanson, and S. Ashworth, "Project A Results: The Relationship between Predictor and Criterion Domains," *Personnel Psychology* 43 (1990), pp. 335–55.

30. H. J. Bernardin and D. K. Cooke, "Validity of an Honesty Test in Predicting Theft among Convenience Store Employees," *Academy of Management Journal* 36 (1993), pp. 1097–108.

31. J. M. Collins and F. L. Schmidt, "Personality, Integrity, and White-Collar Crime: A Construct Validity Study," *Personnel Psychology* 46 (1993), pp. 295–311.

32. R. P. Tett, D. N. Jackson, and M. Rothstein, "Personality Measures as Predictors of Job Performance: A Meta-Analytic Review," *Personnel Psychology* 44 (1991), pp. 703–42.

33. M. B. Barrick and M. K. Mount, "Autonomy as a Moderator of the Relationships between the Big Five Personality Dimensions and Job Performance," *Journal of Applied Psychology* 78 (1993), pp. 111–18.

34. Farnham, "Are You Smart Enough?"

35. P. M. Wright, K. M. Kacmer, G. C. McMahan, and K. Deleeuw, "P = f(M × A): Cognitive Ability as a Moderator of the Relationship between Personality and Job Performance," *Journal of Management* 21 (1995), pp. 1129–39.

36. Hollenbeck et al., "An Empirical Note on the Interaction of Personality and Aptitude."

37. Johnston, "The Coming Labor Shortage."

38. Durity, "A Critical Role."

39. C. Farrell, "Is Black Progress Set to Stall?" *Business Week,* November 6, 1995, pp. 71–73.

40. D. Anfuso, "Diversity Keeps Newspaper Up with the Times, *Personnel Journal,* July 1995, pp. 30–32.

41. J. P. Pinkerton, "Why Affirmative Action Won't Die," *Fortune,* November 13, 1995, pp. 191–98.

42. M. E. Heilman, W. F. McCullough, and D. Gilbert, "The Other Side of Affirmative Action: Reactions of Non-beneficiaries to Sex-Based Preferential Selection," *Journal of Applied Psychology,* 81 (1996), pp. 346–57.

43. G. Flynn, "Do You Have the Right Approach to Diversity?" *Personnel Journal,* October 1995, pp. 68–75.

44. F. Rice, "How to Make Diversity Pay," *Fortune,* August 8, 1994, pp. 78–86.

45. C. M. Solomon, "What You Need to Know about Affirmative Action," *Personnel Journal,* August 1995, pp. 57–67.

46. R. Thompson, "More Diversity in Agriculture: A Hard Row," *The Wall Street Journal,* September 19, 1995, p. B1.

47. S. Peters, "*Personnel Journal* Announces Grant Recipients," *Personnel Journal,* October 1993, pp. 34–37.

48. P. Wright, S. P. Ferris, J. S. Hiller, and M. Kroll, "Competitiveness through Management of Diversity: Effects on Stock Price Evaluation," *Academy of Management Journal* 38 (1995), pp. 272–87.

49. M. Galen, "Diversity: Beyond the Numbers Game," *Business Week,* August 14, 1995, pp. 60–61.

50. J. Dreyfus, "Get Ready for the New Workforce," *Fortune,* April 23, 1990, p. 12.

51. G. F. Dreher and T. H. Cox, "Race, Gender, and Opportunity: A Study of Compensation Attainment and the Establishment of Mentoring Relationships," *Journal of Applied Psychology* 81 (1996), pp. 297–308.

52. S. Rynes and B. Rosen, "A Field Survey of Factors

Affecting the Adoption and Perceived Success of Diversity Training," *Personnel Psychology* 48 (1995), pp. 247–70.

53. J. Laabs, "Interest in Diversity Training Continues to Grow," *Personnel Journal,* October 1993, p. 18.

54. C. M. Solomon, "Unlock the Potential of Older Workers," *Personnel Journal,* October 1995, pp. 56–66.

55. B. J. Avolio, B. J. Waldman, and D. A. McDaniel, "Age and Work Experience in Non-managerial Jobs: The Effects of Experience and Occupational Type," *Journal of Applied Psychology* 33 (1990), pp. 407–22; and M. C. Healy, M. Lehman, and M. A. McDaniel, "Age and Voluntary Turnover: A Quantitative Review," *Personnel Psychology* 48 (1995), pp. 335–45.

56. Farnham, "Are You Smart Enough?"

Chapter Three

Perception, Decision Making, and Creativity

It was a chance meeting on the streets of Manhattan between three men who have a large stake in the future of the telecommunications industry. Raymond Smith, the CEO of Bell Atlantic, and Ivan Seidenberg, CEO of Nynex, were walking to the first meeting to discuss the merger of those two companies. Time Warner's chairman, Jerry Levin, ran into them while he was walking to a meeting on the potential takeover of Turner Broadcasting. The three swapped stories and then went their separate ways continuing to plot their mutually exclusive visions of the future, while surrounded by millions of ordinary consumers who would ultimately decide whose vision was most viable.

For Raymond Smith, this moment illustrates a basic, almost a defining, truth about modern management. In Smith's words, "Leadership in the late 20th century is all about making decisions in the midst of complexity."[1] To survive in this dynamic environment, Bell Atlantic has created a flexible, action-oriented decision-making structure that allows its managers to analyze, adjust, and change direction, without losing sight of their overall mission.

The Bell Atlantic decision-making structure is built around three central principles. The first principle involves developing accurate perceptions—both of oneself and of one's competitors. Bell Atlantic forms teams of managers who play the role of devil's advocate—challenging and questioning the beliefs and assumptions around which business strategies are formed. The company also forms teams of managers who play the role of major competitors, and it has them plan the strategies they would use to destroy Bell Atlantic.[2]

The second principle involves choosing decision options that will be correct no matter what the future holds. To do this, teams of managers are brought together and asked to map out the future. In doing this, they assign probabilities to various future developments and outcomes, and then identify strategies that Bell Atlantic could use that would be effective in a wide variety of different possible futures.

■ **49**

Finally, the third principle involves looking for creative and innovative decision options; as Smith tells his people, don't just play the game, change the rules. Whereas much of traditional business planning is based on reacting to environmental forces, Bell Atlantic stresses the need to proactively shape the environment. For example, it was once illegal for telephone companies to own the content of transmissions sent over their networks. Instead of just accepting this constraint as one of the rules of the game, Bell Atlantic sued the government, claiming that this was a violation of First Amendment rights. After winning this case, Bell Atlantic could directly challenge cable operators, and in doing so, changed the competitive landscape for telephone companies forever.[3]

[1]R. Smith, "Business as a War Game: A Report from the Battlefront," *Fortune,* September 30, 1996, pp. 190–93.

[2]K. Egolf and D. Pappalardo, "Catching Up to Ray Smith: Bell Atlantic's CEO Talks about Competition and His Not-So-Secret Weapon," *Telephony,* June 24, 1996, pp. 21–24.

[3]B. Jones, "The Telephone's Second Chance," *Economist* 340 (1996), p. 88.

Perception is the process by which individuals select, organize, store, and retrieve information. Decision making is the process whereby this perceived information is used to evaluate and choose among various courses of action. Research shows that how organizations make decisions has a large impact on financial performance and survivability, and this is particularly true in complex and dynamic environments.[1] Moreover, as our opening vignette illustrates, one key to effective decision making is that decision makers have accurate perceptions of themselves, their organization, their competitors, and their markets. In addition to having accurate perceptions of the present conditions, decision makers also need to have the ability to envision the future, and thus generate options that are innovative and creative.[2]

These three topics, perception, decision making, and creativity, will be examined in this chapter. Our first major section explores the process of human perception and discusses the keys to developing accurate beliefs about oneself and one's environment. Translating these accurate beliefs into decisions that are rational—or at least satisfactory—is taken up in the second major section. Finally, going beyond the traditional decision options to uncover new and innovative alternatives is taken up in our third major section, on creativity. As Ray Smith, the protagonist in our opening vignette notes, the emerging business environment "requires a different kind of corporate manager: flexible, rigorous, and highly tolerant of ambiguity—one who can revisit decisions constantly and reverse course, even at the risk of personal embarrassment and exposure." We hope that the material presented in this chapter will help the reader become just such a manager.

Figure 3-1 provides an overview of the processes of perception and decision making, and it will serve as a good road map for the next two major sections of this chapter. Specifically, we start at the left with the environment in which the individual is embedded. The perceptual process is the process by which some portion of the information that exists in that environment is processed by the in-

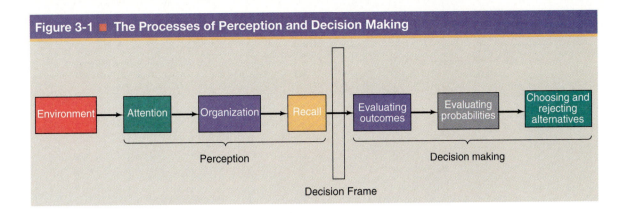

Figure 3-1 ■ The Processes of Perception and Decision Making

dividual for use in decision making. The process of perception is broken down into three stages, attention, organization, and recall, and the boxes in the figure get smaller as we move from left to right to indicate that some information is lost at each stage. At the end of the perceptual process, we say that the decision is "framed," and by this we simply mean that the decision maker has finished the process of collecting and rejecting information. At this point, the decision-making process begins, and the information is evaluated in terms of what outcomes may result from various decisions and what odds are associated with various outcomes. The combined assessment of outcomes and probabilities is used to choose alternatives that are most likely to lead to good outcomes, and to reject alternatives that are unlikely to lead to good outcomes or likely to lead to bad outcomes. We will explore each of these substages of the perception and decision-making processes more closely in the sections that follow.

Perceptual Processes

We human beings have five senses through which we experience the world around us: sight, hearing, touch, smell, and taste. Most of us "trust our senses," but sometimes this blind faith can lead us to believe that our perceptions are a perfect reflection of reality. People react to what they perceive, and their perceptions do not always reflect objective reality. This is a major problem because as the difference between perceived and objective reality increases, so too does the opportunity for misunderstanding, frustration, and conflict.

You can begin to appreciate the vast possibilities for perceptual distortion by considering some well-known illusions shown in Figure 3-2. Obviously, if we can misperceive something as objective as size, shape, or length, there is an even greater chance of our misperceiving something more subjective like the intentions or thoughts of other people. For example, the data displayed in Table 3-1 show differences between managers and subordinates in their perceptions of the manager's behavior. These kinds of perceptual differences within a work group can only lead to trouble and frustration for both the manager and all the people

Figure 3-2 ■ Four Common Perceptual Illusions

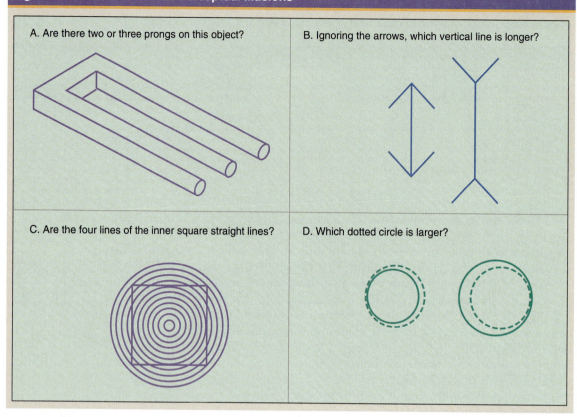

A. Are there two or three prongs on this object?

B. Ignoring the arrows, which vertical line is longer?

C. Are the four lines of the inner square straight lines?

D. Which dotted circle is larger?

Table 3-1 ■ Supervisors' and Subordinates' Views of Supervisors' Praise for Good Work

FORM OF RECOGNITION	FREQUENCY WITH WHICH SUPERVISORS SAY THEY GIVE RECOGNITION "VERY OFTEN"	FREQUENCY WITH WHICH EMPLOYEES SAY SUPERVISORS GIVE RECOGNITION "VERY OFTEN"
"A pat on the back"	82%	13%
Sincere and thorough praise	80	14
Training for a better job	64	9
Special privileges	52	14
More interesting work	51	5
Added responsibility	48	10

Source: Adapted from R. Likert, *New Patterns in Management* (New York: McGraw-Hill, 1961), p. 71.

with whom that manager works. By enhancing your understanding of the perception process, you can avoid ever being in a situation in which your perceptions are as out of touch with reality as those reported for the managers in Table 3-1.

Attention

At any given moment in time, our five senses are bombarded with information of all sorts. In the **attention stage,** most of this available information is filtered so that some enters the system and some does not. This is obviously a critical stage in the process because any piece of information that is ignored at this stage can never figure into our decision making. For this reason, it is a good idea to appreciate how characteristics of the perceiver affect how attention is directed.

For instance, the perceiver's expectations of an object will often affect the evaluation of that object. One reason for this is that our attention is more easily drawn to objects that confirm our expectations. A good example can be seen in Eden and Shani's study of tank crews in the Israeli army.[3] In this study, the researchers told one set of tank commanders that test data indicated that some members of the crews assigned to them had exceptional ability. The tank commanders were also told that some of the soldiers assigned to them were, according to the tests, only average. In reality, the soldiers were assigned to commanders randomly so that the two test groups were equally able. Nevertheless, when asked later to rate the performance of their men, the commanders reported that the performance of the "exceptional" soldiers was better than the performance of soldiers who were said to be "average." The researchers explained their findings by noting that the commanders "naturally lavished more attention on individuals for whom they harbored more positive expectancies." This effect seems to be particularly pronounced among male leaders.[4]

The effects of needs and interests on perceptions can also be seen in the area of race relations at work. For example, research by Madelein Heilman has shown that affirmative action programs designed to help advance minorities often cause misperceptions on the part of all involved. Heilman found that nonminorities who feel that their interests are not served by such programs discount the accomplishments of minorities who take advantage of such programs.[5] Other important differences in perceptions expressed by African Americans and whites are shown in Table 3-2. As you can see, there are marked differences in the way these two subgroups perceived and judged current opportunities for African Americans in the United States. These differences are probably best explained by the fact that each group was attending to different things. Given these differences in perceptual input, it is not surprising that the two sides came to markedly different judgments with respect to questions 4 and 5 in the table. Working out these kinds of perceptual differences may be essential before true progress can be made in race relations on and off the job.

Table 3-2 ■ Differences in the Views of African Americans and White Americans on Opportunities for African Americans		
PERCEPTUAL DIFFERENCES	**AFRICAN AMERICANS**	**WHITES**
Do African Americans have the same opportunities as whites?		
1. In housing?		
Yes	22%	48%
No	75	47
2. In education?		
Yes	38	73
No	59	24
3. In employment?		
Yes	26	59
No	71	37
Judgmental Differences		
4. Should colleges admit some students whose records would not normally qualify them for admission?		
Yes	33	15
5. Should businesses set a goal of hiring a minimum number of African American employees?		
Yes	62	32

Source: Adapted from R. Johnson, "Attitudes in Black and White," *Time,* February 2, 1987, p. 37.

Organization

Even though much information is automatically filtered out at the attention stage, the remaining information is still too abundant and too complex to be easily understood and stored. Because human perceivers can process only a few bits of information at a time, in the **organization stage** we further simplify and organize incoming sensory data. One method is to "chunk" several discrete pieces of information into a single piece of information that can be processed more easily.

To see how effective this kind of chunking can be, imagine your reaction if someone were to ask you to memorize a string of 40 numbers. You might very well doubt your capacity to memorize this many numbers regardless of how much time you were given. Your doubts are probably misplaced, however, because if asked, you could probably write down (*a*) your social security number, (*b*) your telephone number with area code, (*c*) your license plate number, (*d*) the month, date, and year of your birth, (*e*) your current zip code, and (*f*) your height and weight. You might say, "Well, yes, but these are only six numbers," but note that (*a*) has 9 digits, (*b*) has 10, (*c*) and (*d*) have 6, and (*e*) and (*f*) probably have 5; this comes to a grand total of over 40 digits! The fact that we think of these as 6 numbers rather than 40 shows how we mentally chunk things together. In fact, using this chunking process, we can memorize many more than 40 numbers (think of all the telephone numbers, zip codes, birthdays, and so on that you can recall), and this attests to the efficiency of this type of organizing process.

When we do this kind of chunking with nonnumerical information, we refer to the chunks as schemas. **Schemas** are cognitive structures that group discrete bits of perceptual information in an organized fashion.[6] The two types of schemas particularly important to understanding the processing of social-interpersonal information are scripts and prototypes.

Schemas that involve sequences of actions are called **scripts** for the very good reason that they resemble the material from movies or plays. Clearly, numerous events in organizations can be conceived of as having scripts, such as "taking a client to lunch," "preparing a written report," or "disciplining a subordinate." Each of these involves sequences of behavior, and thus when we tell someone to take a client to lunch, that request is actually a request to engage in hundreds of sequenced behaviors. Whereas this is clearly an efficient way of communicating, we must also recognize that not everyone shares the exact same specific behaviors for any one script. For example, in some organizations there may be informal norms against drinking alcohol at business lunches, but a new employee told to "take a client to lunch" may not be aware of this specific part of the script. Thus, although the kind of simplification that is granted by using scripts is vital for efficient information processing, we should not lose sight of the fact that, by referring to scripts, we may be adding things that never took place or deleting things that did happen. Clarifying these scripts is essential if perceptual accuracy is the goal.

Just as there are schemas for simplifying descriptions of events, there are also schemas for simplifying the description of people. **Prototypes** are schemas that enable us to chunk information about people's characteristics. For example, if one manager asked another what a new employee was like, the person might report that the new-hire was spirited, exuberant, outgoing, boisterous, and warm. The first manager might then say, "You mean she's an extrovert." Here again we see multiple bits of information chunked into one word that is meant to carry a detailed description of a person. Like scripts, however, prototypes sometimes carry excess baggage and thus may not reflect the person accurately—especially if two people have different beliefs about the meaning of a word like *extrovert*.

In the area of organizational behavior, the leader prototype is an important one. Most managers want others to perceive them as leaders. What characteristics are likely to cause people to categorize someone in this way? According to research conducted by Robert Lord, the leader prototype is made up of the 12 characteristics shown in Table 3-3, where they are listed in descending order of importance. People who exhibit a majority of these characteristics will be seen as leaders. Moreover, people generally assume that anyone who is a leader must have these characteristics.

Not all prototypes are useful. A *stereotype* is a widely held generalization about a group of people. Often it is a prototype organized around a person's race, sex, age, ethnic origin, socioeconomic group, or other sociocultural characteristics; for example, there might be stereotypes of African Americans, women, the elderly,

Table 3-3 ■ Major Characteristics of the "Leader" Prototype (in descending order of importance)		
1. Intelligent	5. Aggressive	9. Decisive
2. Outgoing	6. Determined	10. Dedicated
3. Understanding	7. Industrious	11. Educated
4. Articulate	8. Caring	12. Well dressed

Source: Adapted from R. G. Lord, R. J. Foti, and D. DeVader, "A Test of Leadership Categorization Theory: Internal Structure, Information Processing, and Leadership Perceptions," *Organizational Behavior and Human Performance* 34 (1984), pp. 343–78.

Hispanic Americans, blue-collar workers, or homosexuals. In one study, business students displayed a clear stereotype of the elderly.[7] Among other things, students described this group as being less creative, less able to do physically demanding work, and less able to change or be innovative. These perceptions led the students to make other negative judgments about elderly workers. For instance, they expressed the belief that these workers would be less likely than younger workers to benefit from training and development. Given the increasing age of our national workforce, such stereotypes need to be reconsidered.

In other cases, stereotypes might be based on gender, and people might actually be punished for not living up to widely shared stereotypes. For example, despite the fact that she had won a $34 million government contract, Ann B. Hopkins was not promoted to partner in the prestigious accounting firm of Price Waterhouse. Male colleagues criticized Hopkins for being "too macho" and suggested that she needed "a course at charm school."[8] The U.S. Supreme Court found this type of sex stereotyping a violation of the Civil Rights Act and awarded Hopkins a large settlement.

Recall

After information is organized, it then must be stored in memory for later retrieval. Just as raw information is sometimes lost in the process of being organized into scripts and prototypes, information can also be lost in the storage and retrieval process. To see how this can create illusions and decision-making errors, consider the following problem: In a typical passage of English prose, does the letter *k* occur more often as the first or the third letter in a word? Twice as many people confronted with this problem choose first as choose third, although the fact is that *k* appears in the third spot almost twice as often as in the first. This phenomenon can be explained in terms of the **availability bias,** which is the tendency of people to judge the likelihood that something will happen by the ease with which they can call examples to mind. Most people assume that *k* is more common at the beginning of words simply because we store words in memory by their first letter—not by their third. Thus, it is easier to retrieve and remember words beginning with *k* than words that have *k* as their third letter.

You can see the availability bias at work in the way people think about death, illness, and disasters. In general, people vastly overestimate the numbers of deaths caused by vividly imaginable events like airplane crashes and underestimate deaths caused by illnesses like emphysema or heart disease. Deaths caused by sudden disasters are more easily called to mind because they are so vivid and so public, often making the first page of newspapers across the country. Death caused by illness, on the other hand, is generally private and thus less likely to be recalled.

Companies that employ risky technologies, such as nuclear power plants, must deal with the availability bias continuously. Ironically, some things they do to allay people's fears actually make things worse. For example, going over disaster scenarios and detailing what would be done in case of a nuclear accident actually makes residents of a nearby community more fearful. Indeed, research shows that the more detail is presented, the more vivid the picture becomes, the greater the probability of a disaster appears, and the more strongly people resist having such a plant in their community.[9]

Reducing Perceptual Problems

Clearly there are many ways in which a human observer can fail to accurately portray the environment. Fortunately, there are also many well-known steps one can take to avoid these problems. First, one way to improve accuracy in perception is to increase the frequency of observations. That is, we can increase the observer's exposure to whatever needs to be observed. By making more observations, an observer can gather more information and thus heighten the accuracy of perceptions.[10]

Second, in addition to increasing the number of observations, it is also useful to ensure the representativeness of the information by taking care in how and when we observe. That is, the manner in which observations are obtained should also be considered. If we obtain observations by random sampling, we increase the probability that these observations will be accurate. If a supervisor observes a group of workers only at a given time on a given day or only when problems develop, the observations may not truly reflect what is happening in this group. In addition, because the very process of observing people can cause them to alter their behavior (and thus destroy representativeness), it is also important to make observations as unobtrusively as possible.

The opportunity to observe employee work behaviors frequently, randomly, and unobtrusively has increased rapidly with technological developments in the field of surveillance. In fact, this opportunity has increased so dramatically that some are beginning to raise ethical issues with regard to monitoring practices. DuPont now uses hidden long-distance cameras to monitor its loading docks. At Delta Airlines, computers track which salespeople write the most reservations. At Management Recruiters in Chicago, supervisors surreptitiously watch computerized schedules to see which interviewers talk to the most job candidates. Supervisors at the Internal Revenue Service (IRS) can tap into telephone conversations between IRS agents and taxpayers calling for information. The increased use of computerized employee monitoring has been a product of two forces. First, there has always been a need to observe employees' work behaviors, and recent developments in surveillance technology have simply made this easier and less obtrusive. The second force has been the increasing number of court cases dealing with "negligent hiring" in which employers have been held liable for the mistakes or crimes of employees. These developments have led to a serious erosion of employee rights to privacy. Finding the proper balance between these rights and the right and responsibility of employers to monitor workers will be a difficult process.[11]

Third, in addition to obtaining a large number of representative observations from one source, we can also improve the accuracy of perceptions by getting observations from different people and different perspectives. This is especially valuable when it comes to self-perceptions of upper-level managers. The need for accurate self-perceptions among personnel at the upper levels has led to the increased use of 360-degree feedback programs to overcome problems in this area; such programs are discussed in the Securing Competitive Advantage box.

Fourth, because observers have a tendency to ignore information that is inconsistent with their expectations, it is often good advice to actively seek information that is inconsistent with, or that contradicts, one's current beliefs. For example, in the vignette that opened this chapter, we saw how Bell Atlantic appoints teams of managers to play the role of devil's advocate in organizational decision making. These subsets of people are explicitly assigned the role of challenging and disputing the key assumptions on which decisions are being based. People are often reluctant to take on this role on their own because they want to be seen as a "team player" rather than a "heretic." Thus, by explicitly saying that someone's role on the team is to be a heretic, the company sees to it that the role is carried out and nobody gets alienated from the team.

Because the main problem at the organization stage is oversimplification of information, a fifth way to increase perceptual accuracy is to ensure the accuracy of scripts and prototypes. Given the limited information-processing skills that human beings have, it is unrealistic to expect people to completely give up the use of schemas. It is a good idea, on the other hand, to elaborate on prototypes and stereotypes, that is, to make people aware of the prototypes and stereotypes they hold of other people. It is also a good idea to get observers to abandon particular prototypes or scripts that seem to lead them astray, and perhaps to replace these with other scripts and prototypes that will be accurate but still helpful in simplifying data. Actively searching for disconfirming prototype information is particularly useful in this regard.

When people must work with social groups that differ from their own, a sixth method for increasing perceptual accuracy is to increase observers' exposure to different social groups in an effort to help the observers develop more accurate prototypes. Research shows that experts in all kinds of domains differ from novices not because they ignore prototypes but because they develop more complex, detailed prototypes that are more accurate.[12] As people develop experience with people and situations that were once unfamiliar to them, their processes of organization become more complex and better able to reflect the underlying reality.

For example, Park Kwang Moo, a 28-year-old employee of Samsung Company, spent a year in Russia living, eating, and drinking with the people there in an effort to help his organization learn what would be needed to expand into this mar-

360-Degree Feedback Helps Keep Perceptions and Reality in Line

Kim Jeffrey had been the CEO of Nestle's Perrier operations for only 18 months, but he knew that if things did not change soon, he might have to relinquish this post. The company was growing and maturing, but Jeffrey was not getting the kind of input he needed from his managers. In a complex and dynamic environment, it is not possible for the CEO to know every detail of the organization's operations. Thus Jeffrey, like all CEO's, needed frank and honest opinions from the managers of his functional units to plan and make decisions regarding the company's future. Having been promoted from within the company, Jeffrey had worked with all the other managers before, and he knew they were competent—he simply could not understand why they no longer seemed willing to offer opinions and recommendations.

Fortunately, Jeffrey took part in a 360-degree feedback session, and what he learned from this experience may have saved the company as well as his own career. In a typical performance appraisal system, managers being evaluated get feedback only from their supervisors. In a 360-degree feedback session, however, a manager receives anonymous feedback from a full circle of observers, including peers, subordinates, and sometimes even sources external to the organization (customers or suppliers). Many companies are now using this sort of multirater assessment to support new organizational strategies that rely on teamwork and employee empowerment rather than on traditional command-and-control types of bureaucracies.[1] Research shows that this type of all-around assessment is especially needed for poorly performing managers who are often afraid to seek feedback[2] and for upper-level managers whose sometimes inflated self-opinions rarely get challenged.[3]

This was exactly the case for Jeffrey, who learned that his elevation from manager to CEO had made him a far more frightening figure among his managers than he had been before. His temper and occasional confrontations with other managers had been tolerable when he was just the head of sales and marketing, but were terrifying when he had the ultimate authority to fire anybody. Some managers said they were so intimidated that they were afraid to come to him with problems or innovative ideas. Jeffrey was shocked by these results. "I thought I was seen as a regular guy. I didn't realize the impact of my words on people. I was mad at myself when I heard."[4] As a result of this feedback, Jeffrey developed a more supportive, team-focused management style. Now, a staff that was once cautious and dormant works aggressively to add value to the company's product line, and helps the firm compete in an important and expanding market.

[1] J. Huey, "The Leadership Industry," *Fortune,* February 21, 1994, pp. 54–56.
[2] J. W. Smither, M. London, N. L. Vasilopolous, R. R. Reilly, R. E. Millsap, and N. Salvemini, "An Examination of the Effects of an Upward Feedback Program over Time," *Personnel Psychology* 48 (1995), pp. 1–34.
[3] M. London and J. W. Smither, "Can Multi-Source Feedback Change Perceptions of Goal Accomplishment, Self-Evaluations, and Performance-Related Outcomes? Theory-Based Applications and Directions for Research," *Personnel Psychology* 48 (1995), pp. 803–39.
[4] B. O'Reilly, "360 Degree Feedback Can Change Your Life," *Fortune,* October 17, 1994, pp. 93–100.

ket. He says he learned how bribes smooth the way for obtaining everything from airplane tickets to gasoline. He also learned what it was like to stand in line for 10 hours waiting for a flight that never took off—and at that moment, he notes, "I felt strength in their misery, I felt like a Russian."[13] As part of the same program, Samsung sent out 400 other young executives with similar assignments in Europe, Australia, Africa, and the United States. Despite an average cost of $80,000 per executive, Samsung believes that the program will more than pay for itself. In the long run, programs such as this allow the firm to perceive things in the same way that those within the market they wish to enter perceive things.

In terms of our overall model shown in Figure 3-1, at the end of the process of perception, the decision has been framed. That is, we have now collected and rejected various pieces of information to arrive at the final set of information that will be used in arriving at the final decision. We next need to discuss how we will further process this information to arrive at a choice to accept one course of action and to reject all other alternatives. There are two general models for understanding the decision-making process: the rational model and the administrative model. Each of these will be explored in the following pages.

The Rational Decision-Making Model

The rational decision-making model is sometimes referred to as the rational-economic model, due to its ties to classic theories of economic behavior. As originally developed, the rational decision-making model included a primary assumption of **economic rationality,** or the notion that people attempt to maximize their individual *economic* outcomes. The system of values consistent with this assumption assesses outcomes according to their current or prospective monetary worth. Values of this type are used in business situations whenever managers weigh alternatives in terms of profitability or loss.

The next major step in the rational decision-making model, after assessing outcomes, is to choose one of the alternatives and implement it as the preferred solution, or decision. This choice is determined through a process of **utility maximization** in which the alternative with the highest expected worth is chosen as the preferred alternative. The expected worth of a particular alternative is the sum of the expected values of the costs and benefits of all the outcomes associated with that alternative.

It would be convenient to think that observers could use this information in a rational way to come to their final decisions, but this is not always the case. Earlier we used perceptual illusions to show that perception is not nearly as straightforward as it seems. Here we will use what we might call decision-making illusions to show some of the things that can go wrong in this process.[14]

Evaluating Outcomes.   As a prelude to this discussion, read the paragraph in Table 3-4 and decide what strategy you would choose if you were the sales executive faced with the situation described. If you perceive that strategy 1 is the best approach, that is, saving the 200 accounts for sure, you are not alone. In fact, research with managers and nonmanagers alike shows that people perceive this choice as being preferable to strategy 2 by a margin of roughly three to one.

Now turn to a similar decision situation, shown in Table 3-5, and decide which strategy you judge preferable under these circumstances. If this time you perceive strategy 2 as best, again you are not alone. Research shows that this choice is preferred roughly four to one over strategy 1.[15]

The surprising thing about these results, however, is that the problems described are virtually identical. Read the paragraphs in Tables 3-4 and 3-5 once

Table 3-4 ■ Two Strategies for Handling an Environmental Threat

The development of a new technology by a competitor threatens the viability of your organization because it may mean the loss of 600 accounts. You have two available strategies to counter this new technology. Your advisors make it clear that if you choose strategy 200 accounts will be saved. If you choose strategy 2, there is a one-third chance that 600 accounts will be saved and a two-thirds chance that none will be saved.

Which strategy will you choose?

Source: Adapted from A. Tversky and D. Kahneman, "The Framing of Decisions and the Psychology of Choice," *Science* 211 (1981), pp. 453–58.

Table 3-5 ■ Two More Strategies for Handling an Environmental Threat

The development of a new technology by a competitor threatens the viability of your organization because it may mean the loss of 600 accounts. You have two available strategies to counter this new technology. Your advisors make it clear that if you choose strategy 400 accounts will be lost. If you choose strategy 2, there is a one-third chance that no accounts will be lost and a two-thirds chance that all will be lost.

Which strategy will you choose?

Source: Adapted from A. Tversky and D. Kahneman, "The Framing of Decisions and the Psychology of Choice," *Science* 211 (1981), pp. 453–58.

more. You can see that strategy 1 is the same in both tables. The only difference is that in Table 3-4 it is expressed in terms of accounts *saved* (200 out of 600), whereas in Table 3-5 it is expressed in terms of accounts *lost* (400 out of 600). Clearly, if 200 are saved, 400 are lost, and vice versa. Why is strategy 1 preferred when the situation is described as it is in Table 3-4 and strategy 2 preferred when the situation is outlined as in Table 3-5?

Research indicates that, in general, people have a slight preference for sure outcomes over risky ones. Studies also show, however, that people hate losing, and this **loss aversion bias** affects their decision making even more strongly than their preference for nonrisky situations. When given a choice between a sure gain and a risky gain, most people will take the sure thing and avoid the risk. When given a choice between a sure loss and a risky loss, however, most people will avoid the sure loss and take a chance on not losing anything.[16]

We can see this preference for risk over loss in many real-world situations. For example, in the early 1980s, oil companies like Shell Oil and Amoco Oil found themselves faced with the increasing costs of managing credit card accounts. To make up for the added cost of managing these accounts, the firms began to charge customers differentially depending on whether they paid cash for gasoline or used their credit cards. Initially, some companies described the extra charge for using a card as a "credit surcharge" (a sure loss for the customer). Their customers were outraged. Other companies advertised a "discount for cash" (a sure gain), and their customers thought this was great! Needless to say, nobody talks about credit surcharges anymore, and everyone offers discounts for cash.

Table 3-6 ■ Identifying a Hit-and-Run Driver
A cab is involved in a hit-and-run accident.
Two taxicab companies serve the city. The Green Company operates 85 percent of the cabs, and the Blue Company operates the remaining 15 percent.
A witness describes the hit-and-run cab as blue. When the court tests the witness's reliability under circumstances similar to those on the night of the accident, the witness correctly identifies the color of a cab 80 percent of the time and misidentifies it 20 percent of the time.
Which cab company was most probably involved in the hit-and-run accident?

Source: Adapted from A. Tversky and D. Kahneman, "The Framing of Decisions and the Psychology of Choice," *Science* 211 (1981), pp. 453–58.

Evaluating Probabilities. Irrationality can also enter into the decision-making process as the result of errors in evaluating the probabilities associated with various outcomes. For example, consider the decision-making problem described in Table 3-6. Most people confronting this problem conclude that the hit-and-run driver was in the blue cab. In fact, however, the odds are much better that the cab was green.

That is, if there were 100 cabs in the city, 85 would be green and 15 would be blue. This is the base rate, that is, the initial probability given no other piece of information. Operating on the premise, as established in Table 3-6, that the witness (who provides an additional piece of information over and above that determining the base rate) would be right 80 percent of the time, let us see what would happen in each possible scenario. If the cab in the accident was actually a Blue, the witness would identify it correctly as a Blue 12 times ($.80 \times 15 = 12$) and would incorrectly identify it as a Green 3 times ($.20 \times 15 = 3$). If the car was a Green, however, the witness would correctly identify it as a Green 68 times ($.80 \times 85 = 68$) and misidentify it as a Blue 17 times ($.20 \times 85 = 17$). Thus, the odds are much greater that the witness's identification of the cab as a Blue was a misidentification of a green cab (which happens 17 out of 100 times) than that it was a correct identification of a blue cab (which happens only 12 out of 100 times).

The reason why virtually everyone who approaches this problem naively gets it wrong is that we put too much weight on the evidence provided by the witness and not enough weight on the evidence provided by the base rate. This is what is meant by the term **base rate bias.** People tend to ignore the background information in this sort of case and to feel that they are dealing with something unique. In this example, decision makers will discount the evidence of how few cars are actually blue, and instead put more confidence in human judgment about the color of the car. Ignoring the base rate leads to misplaced confidence in judgments.

The problem of misplaced confidence is particularly pronounced when more than one probabilistic event is involved. As you might guess, this is more often than not the case in actual business ventures. Suppose, for example, that a house builder contracts to have a house completed by the end of the year.

Assume further that the chances of accomplishing four specific tasks in time to meet this deadline are as follows:

TASK	PROBABILITY
Get permits	Excellent (90%)
Get financing	Very good (80%)
Get materials	Excellent (90%)
Get subcontractors to complete their work	Very good (80 %)

Reviewing these data, our builder might well conclude that there is a good to excellent chance that the project can be completed in the time specified in the contract. In fact, the odds that this will happen are only about 50-50. Multiplying the four probabilities together ($.9 \times .8 \times .9 \times .8 = .52$) gives us just over 50 percent, which is hardly a good to excellent chance. The axiom known as Murphy's Law states that anything that can go wrong will go wrong. This may be a tad pessimistic, but in a long series of probabilistic events, the odds are quite good that one event will go wrong, and sometimes it takes just one mishap to destroy an entire venture. Any business executive who is putting together a deal in which the ultimate outcome depends on a series of discrete events, none of which are sure things, must keep this fact in mind.

Dynamic Influences.   The rational model assumes that each decision is made independently of other decisions, that is, each decision is examined on its own merits in terms of outcomes and probabilities. However, here, too, irrationality can creep into the process because in reality people often see decisions as being related, and past decisions "reach forward" and affect future decisions in irrational ways.

For example, imagine the following scenario. You are on the ground floor of a building and have two minutes to get to a job interview on the fourth floor. You can either take the elevator, which can whisk you to the fourth floor in a matter of seconds, or you can take the stairs, which can get you to your destination in a few minutes. The elevator is the obvious choice, except that this is a 20-story building, and you don't know where the elevator is at the moment. You push the button, and nothing happens. You could immediately take to the stairs, but you decide to wait. After a few seconds you again look at the stairs and consider giving up on the elevator. But you believe the elevator will surely arrive the moment you head up the stairs, so you continue to wait. Still no elevator appears, and you realize that you probably should have taken the stairs in the first place. By now, however, if you are going to have a chance of arriving on time you must continue to wait for the elevator. On the other hand, being a little late is better than being quite late. You reconsider the stairs. You conclude, "What the heck, I've waited this long. What's a little more time?" and you continue to wait. The elevator does not appear, and in a fit of disgust, you rush to the stairs. As you are sprinting up the four flights, you are thinking up excuses for being late and wondering, "Was that the elevator I just heard?"

If you can imagine your frustration in this situation, you have a feel for another problem in arriving at judgments called **escalation of commitment**. Escalation of commitment is a process in which people invest more and more heavily in an apparently losing course of action in order to justify their earlier decisions. Usually the investments that are made once this process gets started are disproportionate to any gain that could conceivably be realized.

Even in the face of evidence that costs are actually outstripping benefits, a decision maker may feel many different kinds of pressure to continue to act in accord with a particular decision.[17] For psychological reasons, the decision maker may not want to appear inconsistent by changing course; that is, the person may not want to admit that a mistake was made earlier. Moreover, particularly where feedback is ambiguous or complex, perceptual distortions like the expectation effect can make the picture appear more hopeful than is really the case. Because we cannot make perfect predictions regarding future outcomes, there is always the hope that staying the course will pay off. What is more, we may have been rewarded in past situations for sticking it out. Although rare, such experiences are usually quite memorable (recall the availability bias). The action of giving up when it is appropriate is often not rewarded, at least in the short run, and thus this experience is something people like to forget. Finally, we sometimes throw out cost-benefit analyses altogether and develop a win-at-any-cost mentality. The quest to prove ourselves takes over, and obsession overcomes better judgment.

Factors Limiting Rational Decision-Making Models. As the decision-making illusions we have illustrated show, the complexity of real-world decision situations often makes rationality impossible. Herbert A. Simon, a cognitive scientist and Nobel laureate in economics, has remarked that "the capacity of the human mind for formulating and solving complex problems is very small compared with the size of the problems whose solution is required for objectively rational behavior in the real world."[18] Simon's comment on the limits of human intelligence is not so much a condemnation of human beings as it is an acknowledgment of the complexity of the environment in which human beings must operate. Indeed, according to Simon and to others who have followed his lead, the complexity of the real world will often overwhelm the decision maker at each step of the rational decision-making process, making complete rationality impossible to achieve.

One obstacle that may undermine the rational decision-making model is the fact that rational models work only if there is general agreement on the definitions of problems, decisions, and decision-making goals that are framed at the outset. Especially in large organizations, such consensus is difficult to achieve. Different individuals, work groups, and departments are likely to rank different outcomes in different ways. Indeed, in large, complex organizations the only problem definitions likely to be widely shared are those so vague as to be almost meaningless.[19] For example, Table 3-7 shows a generic formula that seems to be the source of most organizations' "vision statements."[20] Whereas such vision statements may be easy to agree with, they provide little in the way of guidance for day-to-day decision making.[21]

Table 3-7 ■ **Generic Corporate Vision Generator**

To generate your corporate vision, just circle one entry in each set of brackets.
TO BE A [premier, leading, growing, world-class] COMPANY THAT PROVIDES [innovative, cost-effective, diversified, high-quality] [products, services, products and services] TO [create shareholder value, serve the global marketplace, delight our customers, satisfy our stakeholders] IN THE RAPIDLY CHANGING [information solution, business solution, financial solution, consumer solution] INDUSTRY

In the day-to-day operation of the firm, broad-sweeping, general statements are worthless, and in the absence of other guidelines, if there are disagreements among members about specific objectives, there is no way to proceed in any rational manner. Instead, the political processes of bargaining and compromise are commonly used to reach decisions when there is a lack of consensus. Politics, bargaining, and compromise replace analytical processes in which people try to maximize their gains by the use of rational, calculative techniques.

Another problem with the rational decision-making model is that it is impossible to generate an exhaustive list of alternatives and then select the most promising one. Managers often cannot anticipate what actions will lead to what consequences. Because, as Simon points out, most real-world decisions are characterized by uncertainty, managers cannot even speculate on the odds. Under these conditions, they cannot compute expected values, and thus there is no common measure with which to compare various alternatives. This problem is especially common with nonprogrammed decisions, that is, decisions that are called for only infrequently. In making these kinds of decisions, no one ever develops enough experience to easily assess the odds associated with any alternative.[22]

It is also important to realize that managers are not free to choose among all the choices they may generate. The term **bounded discretion,** first suggested by Simon, refers to the fact that the list of alternatives that any decision maker generates is restricted by social, legal, and moral norms. As Figure 3-3 indicates, the discretionary area within which acceptable choices can be made is bounded on many sides. The boundaries between each of these sets of limitations and the discretionary area are not clear-cut, and as a result, decision makers do not always know whether an alternative is in or out of bounds.

Finally, the rational decision-making model assumes that the implemented alternative can be evaluated by checking actual outcomes against initial intentions. In many contexts, this assumption simply does not hold. Most business situations are complex, and many factors other than the chosen alternative can determine which outcomes are ultimately obtained. Thus, what may be the right choice may not invariably lead to the desired outcome. Such decision-making contexts, in which the link between actions and outcomes is tenuous and hard to predict, are sometimes called noisy environments. Decision makers in noisy environments often place too much value on what happens in any given instance. This can lead them to assign too much importance to their own actions in bringing about observed results and thus may inhibit their ability to learn from experience.

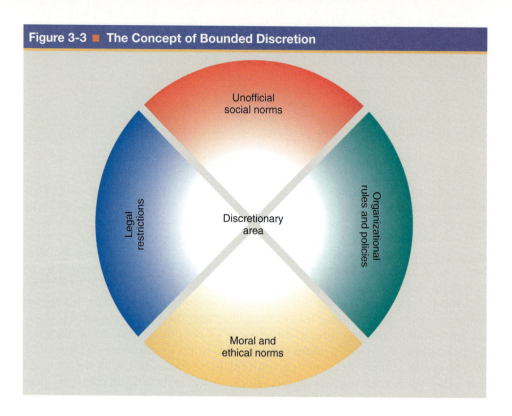

Figure 3-3 ■ The Concept of Bounded Discretion

Unofficial social norms

Organizational rules and policies

Discretionary area

Legal restrictions

Moral and ethical norms

In noisy environments, we can make sense of action-outcome links only by making many observations of the same outcomes after the same actions. If one makes the same decision numerous times, noisy influences factor themselves out, and the true nature of the action-outcome link becomes clearer. Unfortunately, most decision makers in noisy environments fail to stick with one action long enough to sort out the effects of the chosen action on the outcome from the effects of random influences. This lack of consistency in decision making makes people move from one action to another without ever learning much about the action-outcome link associated with any one specific action.[23]

Thus, there are a limited number of places where the rational decision-making model can provide helpful guidance. The model may be useful in suggesting how to structure routine decision making where everyone agrees on the desired outcomes and the best methods for attaining those outcomes, and when there are few outcomes and alternatives to consider. But because of the various factors that render the rational decision-making model less useful in many contexts, alternatives to the model have been suggested.

The Administrative Decision-Making Model

One of the most influential alternatives to the rational decision-making model is Herbert Simon's administrative decision-making model, shown in Figure 3-4. Simon's goal in developing this model was to paint a more realistic picture of

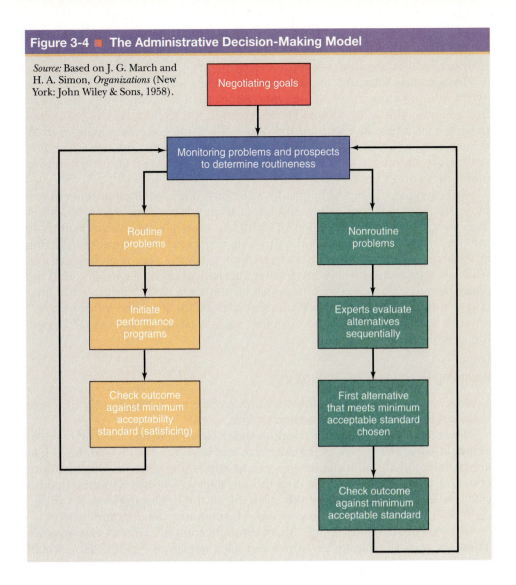

Figure 3-4 ■ The Administrative Decision-Making Model

Source: Based on J. G. March and H. A. Simon, *Organizations* (New York: John Wiley & Sons, 1958).

Negotiating goals

Monitoring problems and prospects to determine routineness

Routine problems

Nonroutine problems

Initiate performance programs

Experts evaluate alternatives sequentially

Check outcome against minimum acceptability standard (satisficing)

First alternative that meets minimum acceptable standard chosen

Check outcome against minimum acceptable standard

the way managers make most decisions.[24] According to Simon, the rational decision-making model may be useful in outlining what managers *should* do, but the administrative model provides a better picture of what effective managers *actually* do when strict rationality is impossible. Simon's model differs from the rational model in several important ways.

One difference has to do with satisficing versus optimizing. According to Simon, *optimal* solutions require that the decision arrived at be better than all other possible alternatives. For all the reasons we have discussed, such optimality is simply not possible most of the time. So instead of striving for this impossible goal, organizations try to find **satisficing** solutions to the problems they confront. Satisficing means settling for the first alternative that seems to meet some minimum level of acceptability. Needless to say, it is much easier to achieve this goal than to try for an optimal solution; indeed, Simon evokes the comparison between finding *a* needle in a haystack (satisficing) and finding the *biggest, sharpest* needle in the haystack (optimizing).

In searching for satisficing solutions, managers further simplify the process by considering alternatives sequentially rather than simultaneously. Instead of first generating a list of all possible alternatives and then comparing and contrasting each alternative with all the others, decision makers evaluate each alternative one at a time in light of the criteria for a satisficing outcome. The first satisfactory alternative a decision maker identifies is chosen, and the manager moves on to other problems.

For example, a firm needing to downsize by reducing its total number of employees is faced with over a dozen means of accomplishing this objective. Rather than trying to compare the expected results for every possible means with those for every other possible means, the firm's managers may just consider initiating an early retirement program. If management puts such a program in place and it achieves the desired results, no further alternatives need be considered. If the plan does not work, some other reasonable alternative, like a hiring freeze, may also be implemented. And if this course of action fails, it may be followed by yet another attempt to achieve the objective, such as laying employees off according to seniority.

Reducing Decision-Making Errors

Given what we know about limits to rationality, we can identify many different means of reducing errors in decision making.

First, the main problem inherent in the decision-making biases we have examined (loss aversion bias, availability bias, and base rate bias) is that the judges are oversimplifying information processing and taking decision-making shortcuts. One good means of eliminating this problem is to provide decision makers with decision aids that will force them to ask all the right questions, get all the right information, and then process this information in all the right ways.

An excellent way of doing this is through computerized expert systems. These systems are typically developed by asking a team of experts, "How would you go about making such a decision?" and then recording every piece of information they ask for, as well as how they process it. These interviews are then turned into a computer program that performs the same function for a relatively naive decision maker, who is prompted to ask the right questions by the program itself. The use of these kinds of expert systems in organizations is expanding almost as fast as computer technology itself, and although they will never replace the human decision maker, they may play an important role in helping people overcome built-in judgment biases.

Even though we can develop expert systems that help simplify more routine decision making, uncertainty in the environment makes it impossible to develop perfectly detailed scripts that will be applicable everywhere. At the highest level of any field, there is still a need for **discretion,** or individual authority, to be granted to decision makers. Thus, organizations also need to develop specialized areas of expertise that can be managed by one or more specialized staff members. The range of discretion of such experts tends to be limited to tightly defined areas, and experts are developed who become the decision makers or internal consultants for different subareas. The advantage of using experts in decision making is that people with special expertise in an area can devise more accurate and more detailed scripts.

In this way, complexity can be handled by being broken up into discrete, manageable chunks—jobs that can be handled by individuals working alone. The occupant of an individual job typically focuses on one very narrow area of organizational problem solving.

As we noted in our discussion of the perceptual process, if we break up jobs into small parts, we reduce the burden on any one individual. But then we must integrate each person's contribution with everyone else's. Chunking does not change the fact that organization members are interdependent, and it is unrealistic to think that one expert can operate unaffected by others or that one set of programs can be activated independently of others. In integrating groups, the complexity of planning is greatly simplified by **loosely coupling** the different parts, that is, weakening the effect that one subgroup has on another so that each can plan and operate almost as if the other were not there. For example, a production department's work is greatly facilitated by having steady operations, that is, operations that do not fluctuate a great deal over time. Yet the sales department may be subject to wild swings in consumer demand that need to be met quickly. These two departments can make decisions more easily if inventories can serve as buffers. By letting products accumulate in inventories, the production department can go on operating (for a while at least) as if there were a steady demand for the product, even if sales are down. Later, when demand exceeds production capacity, the sales group can sell out of the existing inventory without making rush demands on the production department.

With respect to dynamic influences on decision making, one means of trying to minimize judgment errors caused by escalating commitment is to develop separate project development and project evaluation teams. Because the evaluation team is not likely to have the same feeling of ownership as the development team, many of the forces that lead to feelings of psychological entrapment are eliminated. It is also a good idea to initially set up goals, timetables, and reevaluation parameters that will spell out under what conditions a project will be terminated. Setting these parameters prior to starting the project makes later judgments more rational and coldly calculated. Once a project is begun, sunk costs may entice us to inappropriately reevaluate the level of loss we are willing to risk.

Creativity in Decision Making

One elusive quality essential to all decision making is creativity. We will define creative decisions as choices that are new and unusual but effective. Neither the rational nor the administrative decision-making process gets at the issue of how to produce creative decisions, nor does guarding against errors in decision making necessarily guarantee that creativity will result. Indeed, there are aspects of

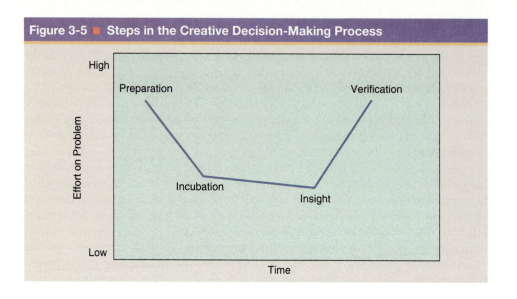

Figure 3-5 ■ Steps in the Creative Decision-Making Process

everything we have discussed in this chapter that make the generation of creative solutions to problems less, rather than more, likely. For example, strictly following the demands of expert systems will rarely result in innovation.[25] In this last section of the chapter, we will emphasize the creativity process and how organizations can enhance creativity by selecting appropriate people or by managing in the appropriate fashion.

The Creative Process

Studies of people engaged in the creative process or of the decision-making processes of people who are famous for their creativity suggest that a discernible pattern of events leads up to most innovative solutions. Most creative episodes can be broken down into the four distinct stages shown in Figure 3-5: preparation, incubation, insight, and verification.

Contrary to what most people think, creative solutions to problems rarely come out of the blue.[26] More often than not, innovations are first sparked by a problem or perceived need. For example, despite having a Ph.D. from the California Institute of Technology, Henry Yuen struggled with programming his videocassette recorder (VCR). During one of these struggles, Yuen realized that telephones would never have become so popular if one had to type in a name, address, city, and state every time one needed to make a call. Why not develop a system for programming VCRs that was more like dialing a telephone? he thought. Along with Daniel Kwoh, Yuen invented a computer program that generated unique code numbers for television programs. This software is at the core of the new VCR Plus technology, and today the numbers generated by their program appear beside each listing in every *TV Guide* and television section of the newspaper.[27]

Because creative decision making is in this way like other decision-making processes,[28] it should not surprise you to learn that **preparation,** the first stage in the creative process, requires assembling materials. Preparation is characterized by plain, old-fashioned hard work. In attempting to solve the problem, creative people immerse themselves in existing solutions to the problem, usually to the point of saturation.

The second stage, **incubation,** differs greatly from steps in other decision-making models. Rather than coming to a decision immediately after assembling and evaluating relevant material, creative decision makers enter a period during which they seem not to expend any effort on the problem. Sometimes out of frustration or sheer exhaustion, they give up working on the problem temporarily and turn to other things.

After a person spends some time in the incubation stage, the solution to the problem typically manifests itself in a flash of inspiration, or **insight.** Usually, the person is engaged in some other task when this insight comes. For example, Howard Wright invented a whistle that would work under water. After making up three or four for his skin-diving friends, Wright gave up on his invention because he never could figure out any large-scale market where it could be sold (since few people need to whistle while under water). Then several years later, while being trained in emergency procedures on a cruise ship, Wright looked down at the whistle he had been issued and remarked that it would never work once it got wet. At that moment Wright recognized for the first time that his invention was not so much an underwater whistle as it was an all-weather whistle. Wright analyzed the market for whistles and found that the U.S. Army and Air Force alone purchased close to 500,000 whistles a year. Wright tracked down purchasing agents for the services, and they all reported that they would be very interested in a new all-weather whistle. Today, Wright's company, the All-Weather Safety Whistle Co., produces 10,000 whistles a week that retail for $5.95 and can be found in the L. L. Bean catalog.[29]

The fourth stage of the creative decision-making process is **solution verification.** Here the solution formulated in the insight stage is tested more rigorously to determine its usefulness for solving the problem. This stage in creative decision making is very much like the rational decision-making model's stage of evaluation. Typically, the verification process takes a lot of time. In fact, it resembles the preparation stage in the amount of hard work it requires. This is primarily because people resist change, particularly if they have a lot invested in traditional ideas and methods. They have to be convinced, and this is rarely possible without independent verification of the new approach.

Creative People

Certain characteristics of individuals seem to be associated with creative endeavors. First, there seems to be a modest relationship between creativity, general cognitive ability, and the specific capacities of reasoning and deduction. Most research indicates that some minimum threshold of intelligence seems to be necessary for creative work; however, once we get above that minimum threshold, general intelligence becomes less critical and hard work is probably more important.

It appears that such personal characteristics as interests, attitudes, and motivation are more important than intelligence in distinguishing creative people from the general population. One common characteristic of creative people is that they set high goals for themselves, which may make them dissatisfied with the status quo and current solutions to problems.[30] High levels of aspiration may also explain why creative people often do not seem to feel any particular loyalty to an employer and are instead highly mobile, moving from company to company.[31] Like most valued commodities, creative talent is highly sought after. Thus, it is often hard for a company to hold on to its creative people.

It has also been suggested that the creative person is persistent and has a high energy level.[32] These characteristics are probably particularly useful in the stages of preparation and verification, which demand hard work for long periods of time. Persistent people will stick with something despite obstacles and setbacks, and people with a lot of energy can continue to work hard for long periods. Both of these qualities may help creative people to assemble more relevant information and to test their ideas more exhaustively.

Finally, *age* seems to be related to creativity. In a seminal study of people recognized for their creativity, one consistent finding was that regardless of the field in which the person worked (the fields studied included mathematics, physics, biology, chemistry, medicine, music, painting, and sculpture), creativity peaked between the ages of 30 and 40.[33]

Creativity-Inducing Situations

Selecting people who have characteristics that seem to be related to creativity is not the only option organizations have for increasing innovativeness.[34] Providing specific and difficult goals and firm deadlines actually seems to stimulate creative achievement. Perhaps one reason is that these kinds of constraints limit the use of traditional alternatives.[35] Some firms even set goals for creativity. For example, 3M Company has set a goal that 35 percent of its total revenues should come from new products developed in the past four years. Currently 3M insists that nearly 70 percent of its annual $12 billion in sales comes from ideas that originated in the workforce.[36] Of course, focusing people on coming up with innovative techniques, as opposed to cranking out products with the existing technologies, sometimes comes at the expense of short-term productivity.[37] For example, returning to 3M, one of the company's rules is that all employees should devote 15 percent of their time to reading and learning about recent developments that have nothing to do with their primary project.[38]

In setting goals for creativity, how these goals are framed is also important, in terms of whether one sets goals for incremental improvements or major revolutions. For example, John Pepper, CEO of Procter and Gamble (P&G), has recently argued that too much of P&G's money and scientific talent has been wasted on coming up with minor improvements of existing products based on focus groups and consumer surveys. Tide detergent, for example, has been "new and improved" over 60 times. Most of these improvements are not even improvements so much as minor tailorings of products to specific market segments. Pepper notes that "if we spend our time working on small modifications to something, we won't have time to work on big new stuff." Pepper is interested in coming up with a smaller number of big-ticket innovations with a greater upside for growth. One such project is P&G's patented Olestra, a chemical ingredient that looks, tastes, and fries like a fat, without the calories of a fat.[39]

Certain characteristics of what is called the organizational culture (see Chapter 13) may also be related to creativity. First, the degree to which organizations recognize and reward creativity is of paramount importance.[40] Although you might think otherwise, many organizations, unfortunately, place more emphasis on following existing written rules and procedures than on experimenting with new procedures.

A culture that wishes to promote creativity must ensure not only that innovativeness is reinforced but that experimentation leading to failure is not punished. Executives like James Burke, CEO of Johnson and Johnson, attempt to create a climate in which the risks of innovation are minimized. Burke, in fact, has gone so far as to tell his employees, "We won't grow unless you take risks. . . . Any successful company is riddled with failures. There's just no other way to do it."[41] Although they need not reward every failure, companies that want to encourage innovation might consider giving an award for "the best failed experiment." Recognition of this sort would drive home the point that the organization values risk taking and trying new approaches more than it fears mistakes. Supportive leadership that does not overcontrol employees seems to be a key factor in translating creative talent into innovative products.[42]

Because much creativity comes out of collaborative efforts of different individuals, organizations should promote internal diversity and exposure among organizational members. If all the people in a group have the same interests, experiences, strengths, and weaknesses, they will be less likely to generate new ideas than if they are of divergent backgrounds and capabilities. For example, Lockheed's "Skunk Works" research and development (R&D) subsidiary, famous for several aerospace technological breakthroughs (U-2 "Blackbird" spy planes and the F117A Stealth fighter plane), specializes in a team approach to production. Each team is headed by a manager with wide latitude in recruiting in-house specialists from an array of scientific and engineering backgrounds. The teams are isolated from Lockheed's sprawling bureaucracy but are allowed to have direct contact with their "customer" (the U.S. Department of Defense). In a time of shrinking defense budgets, the Skunks Work plant is still one of Lockheed's most profitable units, and this can only be achieved by continuously pushing the envelope of technological innovation.

Finally, exposing people to varying kinds of experiences, such as foreign assignments, professional development seminars, or extended leaves, may help shake up overly routine decision-making processes. The notion that difference and variety encourage creative thinking receives some support from the finding that organizations that emphasize external recruiting seem to be more innovative than firms that promote from within.[43] This does not mean that organizations should completely abandon promote-from-within policies. However, there is real value in mixing new and long-tenured employees to foster a climate of creativity.

SUMMARY

A thorough understanding of the perceptual process by which people encode and make sense out of the complex world around them is critical to those who would manage organizational behavior. The very existence of perceptual illusions documents the fact that what we perceive is not always a very close approximation to objective reality. In the attention stage, we select a small subset of all the information that is available to our five senses for processing. The degree to which any stimulus attracts our attention is a complex function of characteristics of the object and of ourselves. In the organization stage, information is simplified. We convert complex behavioral sequences into scripts and represent people by prototypes. A number of biases, including stereotyping can creep into this complex process. In the decision-making stage, we use the information processed in the prior stages to come up with an evaluation of an object, person, or event. This evaluation, once made, affects our decisions, behaviors, and subsequent perceptions.

Review Questions

1. List a set of traits that would make up the prototype for a yuppie, a hippie, an absent-minded professor, and a card-carrying member of the American Civil Liberties Union. Recalling Chapter 2, would you say that your list is dominated by abilities or personality characteristics? What kinds of abilities or personality characteristics are most heavily represented? What does this tell you about how prototypes are developed and in what ways they are most likely to be accurate?

2. Sometimes a given behavioral episode in an organization—for example, a fight among coworkers, a botched work assignment, or an ineffective meeting—can be organized perceptually along the lines of either a script or a prototype. How might the choice of schema affect what occurs later in the process of interpretation or judgment?

3. Escalation of commitment to a failing course of action has been widely researched, and it is easy to call to mind many examples of this kind of mistake. The flip side of this mistake, however, is giving up too soon, which has not been studied much and for which it is hard to think of examples. Why can we not recall such events? How might researchers in this area be victims of availability bias?

4. Compare and contrast the decision-making processes associated with rational decision making, administrative decision making, and creative decision making. At what points do these three descriptions of decision making diverge most? What implications does this have for decision makers who try to follow one of these models when they should be following another?

5. Suppose that managerial jobs can be distinguished by the kinds of decision processes required. In other words, some jobs call for rational decision making, others require administrative decision-making processes, and still others require creative decision processes. If you were a recruiter, what personal characteristics would you look for in staffing each of these three kinds of positions? Do you think

it would be possible to find one individual who would be equally adept at all three kinds of processes? If so, what characteristics would this person display?

Implementation Guide

The following questions are designed to help you diagnose problems with perception, decision making, and creativity you may encounter now or in the future.

1. On whose perceptions do you rely to describe and diagnose organizational problems? How might the choice of this person affect the description and diagnosis provided?
2. What kinds of expectations do you have for persons or objects that you need to evaluate? How might these expectations affect your judgment?
3. What are some of the major events in your organization that you think of in terms of scripts? How might your version of these scripts differ from others' views?
4. What are some of the major prototypes that exist for persons in the organization? How accurate are these prototypes?
5. What stereotypes do you hold of persons from particular social groups in the organization? Are these stereotypes accurate?
6. Do you keep external records of important past events, or do you rely exclusively on your own memory for such important information?
7. Do you take the point of view of a judge or of a coach when evaluating others? How might each of these views affect your judgments?
8. How are your present judgments influenced by judgments that you or others have made in the past?
9. Which of the many ways to manage perceptual problems and increase perceptual accuracy are most practical for the organization?
10. Does the organization have clear goals and objectives so that analytical solutions can be developed? Or is the organization characterized by a lack of goal consensus, thus requiring a bargaining solution?
11. When deciding on a course of action, does the organization tend to rely more on past practice or on experimentation?
12. Does the organization employ experts? Does it use them successfully, through loose coupling, and integrate them with other members of its own staff?

ENDNOTES

1. J. W. Dean and M. P. Sharfman, "Does Decision Process Matter? A Study of Strategic Decision-Making Effectiveness," *Academy of Management Journal* 39 (1996), pp. 368–96.
2. R. L. Priem, A. M. Rasheed, and A. G. Kotulic, "Rationality in Strategic Decision Processes, Environmental Dynamism and Firm Performance,"

Journal of Management 21 (1995), pp. 913–29.
3. D. Eden and A. B. Shani, "Pygmalion Goes to Boot Camp: Expectancy, Leadership and Trainee Performance," *Journal of Applied Psychology* 67 (1982), pp. 194–99.
4. T. Dvir, D. Eden, and M. L. Banjo, "Self-Fulfilling Prophecies and Gender: Can Women Be Pygmalion

and Galatea?" *Journal of Applied Psychology* 80 (1995), pp. 253–70.

5. M. C. Heilman, C. J. Block, and J. A. Lucas, "Presumed Incompetent: Stigmatization and Affirmative Action Efforts," *Journal of Applied Psychology* 77 (1992), pp. 536–44.

6. U. Neisser, *Cognition and Reality* (San Francisco: W. H. Freeman, 1976), p. 112.

7. B. Rosen and T. H. Jerdee, "The Influence of Age Stereotypes on Managerial Decisions," *Journal of Applied Psychology* 61 (1976), pp. 428–32.

8. Ibid.

9. P. Slovic, B. Fischoff, and S. C. Lichtenstein, "Cognitive Processes and Societal Risk Taking," in *ORI Research Bulletin* (Eugene: Oregon Research Institute, 1974), pp. 16–76.

10. W. C. Borman, "Exploring the Upper Limits of Reliability and Validity of Performance Ratings," *Journal of Applied Psychology* 63 (1978), pp. 135–44.

11. J. Rothfeder, M. Galen, and L. Driscoll, "Is Your Boss Spying on You? High Tech Snooping in the Electronic Sweatshop," *Business Week,* January 15, 1990, pp. 74–75.

12. L. T. DeFong and C. J. Ferguson-Hessler, "Information Processing Differences in Experts and Novices," *Journal of Applied Social Psychology* 21 (1987), pp. 19–27.

13. L. Rhee, "Korea's Biggest Firm Teaches Junior Exec Strange Foreign Ways," *The Wall Street Journal,* December 30, 1992, pp. A1, A4.

14. A. Tversky and D. Kahneman, "The Framing of Decisions and the Psychology of Choice," *Science* 211 (1981), pp. 453–58.

15. Ibid.

16. K. J. Dunegan, "Framing, Cognitive Modes and Image Theory: Toward an Understanding of a Glass Half Full," *Journal of Applied Psychology* 78 (1993), pp. 491–503.

17. B. M. Staw and J. Ross, "Behavior in Escalation Situations," in *Research in Organizational Behavior,* B. M. Staw and L. L. Cummings, eds. (Greenwich, CT: JAI Press, 1987), pp. 12–47.

18. J. G. March and H. A. Simon, *Organizations* (New York: John Wiley, 1958), p. 10.

19. T. A. Stewert, "Why Value Statements Don't Work," *Fortune,* June 10, 1996, pp. 137–38.

20. T. A. Stewert, "A Refreshing Change: Vision Statements That Make Sense," *Fortune,* September 30, 1996, pp. 195–96.

21. T. A. Stewert, "Company Values That Add Value," *Fortune,* July 8, 1996, pp. 145–47.

22. H. Simon, *The New Science of Management Decision* (New York: Harper & Row, 1960).

23. B. Brehmer, "Response Consistency in Probabilistic Inference Tasks," *Organizational Behavior and Human Performance* 22 (1978), pp. 103–15.

24. March and Simon, *Organizations,* pp. 10–12.

25. T. S. Kuhn, *The Structure of Scientific Revolutions* (Chicago: University of Chicago Press, 1962), pp. 22–39.

26. J. V. Anderson, "Weirder than Fiction: The Reality and Myths of Creativity," *Academy of Management Executive* 6 (November 1992), pp. 40–47.

27. L. Armstrong, "The Geniuses Who Made VCRs Simple Enough for a 50-Year-Old," *Business Week,* December 31, 1990, p. 54.

28. D. G. Marquis, "The Anatomy of Successful Innovations," *Managing Advancing Technology* 1 (1972), pp. 34–48.

29. F. Meeks, "Whistle Blower," *Forbes,* April 12, 1993, p. 104.

30. D. W. MacKinnon, "Assessing Creative Persons," *Journal of Creative Behavior* 1 (1967), pp. 303–4.

31. T. Rotundi, "Organizational Identification: Issues and Implications," *Organizational Behavior and Human Performance* 13 (1975), pp. 95–109.

32. E. Randsepp, "Are You a Creative Manager?" *Management Review* 58 (1978), pp. 15–16.

33. H. C. Lehman, *Age and Achievement* (Princeton, NJ: Princeton University Press, 1953), pp. 50–61.

34. R. W. Woodman, J. E. Sawyer, and R. W. Griffin, "Toward a Theory of Organizational Creativity," *Academy of Management Review* 18 (1993), pp. 293–321.

35. G. Zaltman, R. Duncan, and J. Holbek, *Innovations and Organizations* (New York: John Wiley, 1969), p. 191.

36. T. Curry, J. E. Gallagher, and W. McWhirter, "Let's Get Crazy," *Time,* June 11, 1990, pp. 41–42.

37. C. E. Shalley, "Effects of Coaction, Expected Evaluation, and Goal Setting on Creativity and Productivity," *Academy of Management Journal* 38 (1995), pp. 483–503.

38. T. A. Stewert, "3M Fights Back," *Fortune,* February 5, 1996, pp. 94–96.

39. R. Henkoff, "P&G: New and Improved," *Fortune,* October 14, 1996, pp. 151–56.

40. H. A. Shepard, "Innovation-Resisting and Innovation-Producing Organizations," *Journal of Business* 40 (1967), pp. 470–77.

41. W. Guzzardi, "The National Business Hall of Fame," *Fortune,* Feb. 1, 1990, pp. 17–29.

42. G. R. Oldham and A. Cummings, "Employee Creativity: Personal and Contextual Factors at Work," *Academy of Management Journal* 39 (1996), pp. 607–34.

43. B. Schneider and N. Schmitt, Staffing Organizations (Glenview, IL: Scott, Foresman, 1986), p. 71.

Chapter Four

Motivation and High Performance Work Systems

In the 1980s, U.S. businesses invested over $1 trillion in computer hardware and software. Despite this unprecedented level of investment in technology, however, business productivity rose, on average, by slightly less than 1 percent a year during that decade.[1] In the 1990s, however, the best firms started to realize that changes in technological systems can lead to productivity gains only when they are linked to changes in how organizational behavior is managed. The most competitively successful organizations are now creating "high-performance work systems" that attempt to marry new technologies with new motivational systems.[2]

MBNA, a company that produces Visa and MasterCard charge cards, provides an excellent example of how to link organizational strategy, technological advances, and motivational systems to maximize competitive advantage. MBNA's strategy is to market credit cards to "affinity groups," that is, groups with strong loyalties. Thus, it produces cards that incorporate anything from the Dallas Cowboys logo to personal pet photos (for Ralston Purina). Members of these affinity groups are lucrative customers, with incomes 20 percent above the national average and carryover balances close to $2,000 above the industry average. Not surprisingly, however, these high-profile customers also demand high levels of service, and above all, they hate to wait.

To make sure that service is provided, MBNA relies heavily on an integrated system of technology and incentives. For example, one goal the company has is to make sure that 98.5 percent of phone calls get picked up in less than two rings. The firm measures this electronically, and at any moment on any given day, it is possible to get a reading that shows, for example, that employees are achieving "two-ring pickup" 98.4 percent of the time and that this is 1.2 percent higher than average, a 1 percent falloff from the previous day, and 0.1 percent shy of the goal. Results for this and 14 other goals (e.g., processing a request to increase a credit line in 15 minutes or less) are then posted daily on 60 scoreboards at MBNA facilities around the country.

Incentives are then wrapped around these electronic measures. For example, every day that the 98.5 percent standard is met, money is thrown into an employee pool. Money from this pool is then handed out at regular intervals—as much as $1,000 per employee, depending on the percentage of times the employee has met the goal. Similar incentives are tied to the other 14 goals. The effect on employees is evident according to manager Janine Marrone, who notes that "if you're an MBNA employee and go to a restaurant and hear a phone ring more than twice, it drives you nuts—you have to stop yourself from going behind the counter and answering it."[3] The effect on MBNA in competitive financial markets is also pretty evident. Between 1991 and 1996, MBNA common stock climbed by over 600 percent.

[1]M. Magnet, "The Productivity Payoff Arrives," *Fortune,* June 27, 1994, pp. 79–84.
[2]M. A. Huselid, "The Impact of Human Resource Management Practices on Turnover, Productivity and Corporate Financial Performance," *Academy of Management Journal* 38 (1995), pp. 635–72.
[3]J. Martin, "Are You as Good as You Think You Are?" *Fortune,* September 30, 1996, pp. 142–52.

One of the basic goals of all managers is to motivate employees to perform at their highest level. There are many different theories of work **motivation,** most of which share some common elements. Indeed, the importance of goals, feedback, and incentives for directing and managing people has been known for centuries.[1] What is new in the area of work motivation, however, is the degree to which modern technologies allow one to apply what has long been known.

For example, managers at C. R. England, a trucking company, always knew they wanted to link employee pay to employee performance. The problem they had, however, was that the distance between managers and the workforce was so great that it was hard to measure performance in a reliable fashion. With the advent of new sensor technology, however, this company found that it was able to use state-of-the-art computer processors to drive home financial results. Use of automatic sensors has allowed managers at the company to measure everything from cargo temperature to the speed with which invoices are processed. Every employee then gets a customized performance report each week based on objective indicators. Performance on these dimensions is then used to calculate weekly bonuses that are prominently incorporated into paychecks. As a result of this tight alignment of employee goals with firm goals, C. R. England has grown sevenfold in seven years, while increasing revenues per truck by 25 percent over the same period.[2]

C. R. England is an example of a company that knew what to do motivationally, but needed new technology in order to put this knowledge into place. In other companies, the new technology is in place, but no benefits can be realized without corresponding changes in the motivational system. For example, a large medical supply company that introduced flexible, automated machinery into its production plants waited years for some productivity benefit that never materialized. When disappointed top managers investigated this problem, they found out that the employees and line managers were using the new machinery as if it were the old equipment, taking no advantage of its flexibility. The reason for this was that the organization's pay scheme rewarded the workers for high output and minimal machine downtime. Programming changes into the automated equipment meant downtime and loss of output, and therefore the workers avoided this at all costs.[3]

The term *high-performance work system* is often used to describe the fusion of well-established theories of motivation with new technologies. In this chapter we will describe some of the major theories of motivation that underly these systems. We will then go over the many different options organizations have for linking pay to performance through high-performance work systems.

A Model of Motivation and Performance

Expectancy Theory

The model of motivation developed in this chapter is an elaboration of Vroom's **expectancy theory,** particularly as it was extended by Porter and Lawler and supplemented by several other theories.[4] Expectancy theory is a broad theory of motivation that attempts to explain the determinants of workplace attitudes and behaviors.[5] The three major concepts underlying expectancy theory are those of valence, instrumentality, and expectancy. Sometimes the first letters of these words are used to form the term *VIE theory*.

Valence.   The concept of **valence** is based on the assumption that at any given time, a person prefers certain outcomes to others. Valence is a measure of the attraction a given outcome holds for an individual, or the satisfaction the person anticipates receiving from a particular outcome.

Outcomes can have positive, negative, or zero valence. An outcome is said to have positive valence when a person would rather attain it than not. When a person is indifferent about attaining an outcome, that outcome is assigned a valence of zero. If a person prefers *not* to attain the outcome, the outcome is said to have a negative valence. For example, in our opening story, the financial bonus at MBNA that is tied to answering the telephone after no more than two rings has a positive valence for employees of this company.

It is important to distinguish between valence and value. *Valence* refers to *anticipated* satisfaction. *Value* represents the *actual* satisfaction a person experiences from attaining a desired outcome. With experience, someone might discover that there can be quite a discrepancy between the anticipated satisfaction from an outcome (i.e., its valence) and the actual satisfaction that it provides (i.e., its value).[6]

Instrumentality.   **Instrumentality** is a person's belief about the relationship between performing an action and experiencing an outcome. This belief is sometimes referred to as a *performance-outcome expectation*. Determining people's instrumentalities is important because their desire to perform a particular action is likely to be strong only when both valence and instrumentality are perceived as being acceptably high. Thus, we need to know more than the satisfaction an individual expects as the consequence of attaining a particular outcome. We also need to know what the person believes must be done in order to obtain that outcome. Thus, the key to the success of the financial bonus that MBNA attaches to answering the phone in two rings is establishing the contingency between accomplishing the goal and getting the valued bonus.

Expectancy.   The third element of expectancy theory is the concept for which the theory is named: **expectancy.** Expectancies are beliefs regarding the link between making an effort and actually performing well. Whereas knowledge about valences and instrumentalities tells us what an individual *wants to do,* we cannot know what the individual will *try to do* without knowing the person's expectancies. According to Vroom, "Whenever an individual chooses between alternatives which involve uncertain outcomes, it seems clear that his behavior is affected not only by his preferences among these outcomes, but also by the degree to which he believes these outcomes to be probable."[7]

Conclusion.   Returning to our running example, recall that the goal at MBNA was to answer the phone within two rings 98.5 percent of the time. If this goal was pushed up, so that obtaining the bonus required two-ring pickup 100 percent of the time, many employees would feel that the goal was impossible. If there is no expectation that the goal can be reached, motivation is low, even where valences and instumentalities are high.

Expectancy theory thus defines motivation in terms of desire and effort, whereby the achievement of desired outcomes results from the interaction of valences, instrumentalities, and expectancies. Desire comes about only when both valence and instrumentality are high, and effort comes about only when all three are high.

Supplemental Theories

There are two primary reasons why, in order to build our model, we need to supplement expectancy theory with other motivation theories. First, a number of other theories deal in much more detail with certain specific components of motivation. Therefore, they help to elaborate on expectancy theory. As you will see, need theories provide important insights into how valences are developed and how they can change over time. Learning theories explain how perceptions of instrumentality come into being. Self-efficacy theory describes the origin of effort-performance expectancies, as well as the ways in which they are maintained. Second, we need to extend expectancy theory to explain outcomes other than desire and effort. To predict performance, expectancy theory needs information about human ability, goals, and strategies. Thus, along with expectancy theory, our model will also incorporate ideas from the need, learning, self-efficacy, and goal-setting theories.

Overview of the Model

The model of motivation we will build in this chapter consists of *five components* put together in *four steps* to explain *three outcomes*. One of our components (abilities) has already been explained in Chapter 2 and will be only briefly touched on here. Three of the remaining four are valence, instrumentality, and expectancy. These have already been defined, but we will elaborate on each, using need, learning, and self-efficacy theories. The final component is accuracy of role perceptions, particularly as this is described via goal-setting theory.

The model's four steps are the key places where components combine to influence outcomes. These steps build on each other progressively. For example, as we have already suggested, the components of valence and instrumentality combine to determine desire to perform. Desire to perform then combines with another component, expectancy, to determine effort.

The three outcomes of interest to us are desire, effort, and performance. Figure 4-1 presents our model of motivation and performance graphically. As you can see, the five components are shown as circles, the three outcomes are shown as rectangles, and the four steps in which these are combined are indicated by

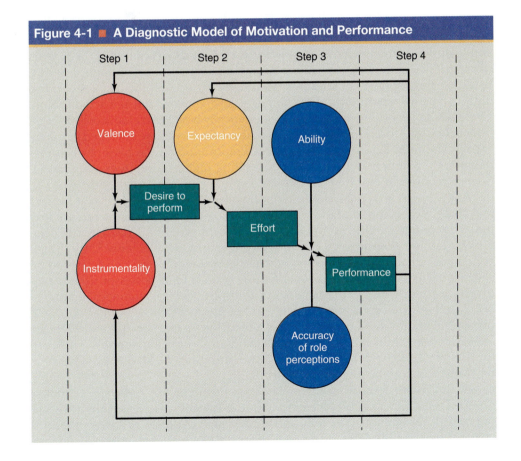

Figure 4-1 ■ A Diagnostic Model of Motivation and Performance

vertical lines. In line with expectancy theory, the first two steps of the model suggest that valence and instrumentality combine to influence desire to perform, and desire and expectancy combine to determine effort. In the third step, effort combines with ability and accuracy of role perceptions to influence performance.

You should not be concerned at this point if you do not understand all the linkages and components in this model, because it is merely a road map for where we will be going in the remainder of this chapter. Placing it here, however, will help you keep the big picture in focus as we get into more detailed descriptions of specific theories and aspects of motivation. In fact, you may want to refer again to this figure after reading each subsection that follows, to see how each subsection relates to the overall model we will be building.

Valence: Need Theories

As you know, people differ greatly in their personal preferences. One person may decide to be a missionary, and another, a stockbroker, and each may be quite satisfied with the choice. How do valences originate, and why do they differ among people? Need theories are especially helpful in understanding valences.

Maslow's Need Hierarchy. Abraham Maslow was a clinical psychologist and a pioneer in the development of *need theories*. Little existed in the way of empirical, scientific studies of motivation in Maslow's day. He based his own theory on 25 years of experience in treating individuals in varying degrees of psychological health. Based on this experience, **Maslow's need theory** proposed the existence of five distinct types of needs: physiological, safety, love, esteem, and self-actualization. These needs, according to Maslow, are genetically based and characteristic of all human beings. Moreover, Maslow argued, these five needs are arranged in the hierarchy shown in Figure 4-2 and influence motivation on the basis of need **prepotency.** Prepotency means that needs residing higher in the hierarchy can influence motivation only if needs that are lower are already largely satisfied.

At the lowest level of Maslow's hierarchy are *physiological needs* such as hunger and thirst. According to Maslow, these physiological needs possess the greatest initial prepotency.[8] On the other hand, once physiological needs have been mostly gratified, they no longer serve as strong motivating elements. Under these conditions, second-level *safety needs* increase in strength. Safety needs have to do with acquiring objects and relationships that protect their possessor from future threats, especially threats to the person's ability to satisfy physiological needs.

If both physiological and safety needs are mostly fulfilled, *love needs* become prepotent. Maslow used the term *love* in a broad sense to refer to preferences for affection from others as well as a sense of community or belongingness. The need for friends, family, and colleagues falls within this category. Maslow classified sexual desires among the physiological needs.

At the fourth level of needs in Maslow's hierarchy are *esteem needs*. Maslow grouped two distinct kinds of esteem within this category. Social esteem consists of the respect, recognition, attention, and appreciation of others. Self-esteem reflects an individual's own feelings of personal adequacy. Consequently, esteem needs can be satisfied partly from sources outside an individual and partly from sources within.

Figure 4-2 ■ **Maslow's Needs Hierarchy**

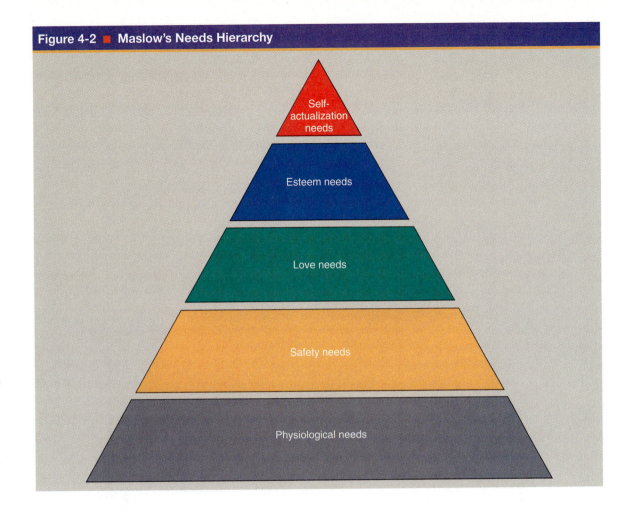

The last set of needs, at the top of Maslow's hierarchy, is *self-actualization needs.* Maslow felt that if all needs beneath self-actualization were fulfilled, a person could be considered generally satisfied. He also suggested that "since in our society, basically satisfied people are the exception, we do not know much about self-actualization, either experimentally or clinically." For this reason, perhaps, Maslow failed to define this category of needs precisely. In general, these needs seem to involve the desire individuals have to realize their full potential. In Maslow's words, self-actualization "might be phrased as the desire to become more and more what one is, to become everything that one is capable of becoming."[9]

Unlike all the other needs identified by Maslow, self-actualization needs can never be fully satisfied. Hence, the picture of human motivation drawn by Maslow is one of constant striving as well as constant deprivation of one sort or another.

Perhaps because of its simplicity, Maslow's theory has been widely accepted by managers and management educators. Maslow failed, however, to provide researchers with clear-cut measures of his concepts, and his theory has not received

Table 4-1 ■ Some of Murray's Manifest Needs	
Achievement	To do one's best, to be successful, to accomplish tasks requiring skill and effort, to be a recognized authority, to accomplish something important, to do a difficult job well
Deference	To get suggestions from others, to find out what others think, to follow instructions and do what is expected, to praise others, to accept leadership of others, to conform to custom
Order	To keep things neat and orderly, to make advance plans, to organize details of work, to have things arranged so they run smoothly without change
Autonomy	To be able to come and go as desired, to say what one thinks about things, to be independent of others in making decisions, to do things without regard for what others may think
Affiliation	To be loyal to friends, to participate in friendly groups, to form strong attachments, to share things with friends, to write letters to friends, to make as many friends as possible
Dominance	To argue for one's point of view, to be a leader in groups to which one belongs, to persuade and influence others, to supervise and direct the actions of others
Nurturance	To help friends when they are in trouble, to treat others with kindness and sympathy, to forgive others and do favors for them, to show affection and have others confide in one
Change	To do new and different things, to travel, to meet new people, to have novelty and change in daily routine, to try new and different jobs, to participate in new fads and fashions
Endurance	To keep at a job until it is finished, to work hard at a task, to work at a single job before taking on others, to stick to a problem even though no apparent progress is being made
Aggression	To attack contrary points of view, to tell others off, to get revenge for insults, to blame others when things go wrong, to criticize others publically, to read accounts of violence

Source: Based on H. A. Murray, *Explorations in Personality* (New York: Oxford University Press, 1938), pp. 152–205.

much empirical support.[10] It is of interest to us primarily because of its place in history as one of the earliest motivation models, and as a precursor to more modern theories of motivation.

Murray's Theory of Manifest Needs.   Henry Murray's *theory of manifest needs* defines needs as recurrent concerns for particular goals or end states.[11] Each need is made up of two components. The first deals with the object toward which the need is directed (e.g., achievement or autonomy). The second describes the intensity or strength of the need for that particular object (e.g., strong versus weak). Murray proposed over 20 needs, several of which are described in Table 4-1.

Because Murray's needs are not arranged in any hierarchical fashion, the theory has considerable flexibility. Unlike Maslow, Murray held that an individual could be motivated by more than one need at a time, and he also suggested that at times, needs could conflict with each other. Also, unlike Maslow, who viewed needs as innate and genetically determined, Murray regarded needs as learned.

Murray's original work on need theories was extended and expanded upon by others. Most notably, David McClelland developed a theory of motivation that focuses particularly on the need for achievement, which he called nAch.[12]

According to McClelland, people can be characterized as either high or low in need for achievement, or nAch. Those who are high in nAch prefer situations in which they have the opportunity to take personal responsibility. They also prefer to receive personal credit for the consequences of their actions and clear and unambiguous feedback about personal performance.

Task difficulty is another characteristic evaluated by high-nAch individuals. According to McClelland, such people prefer tasks of intermediate difficulty—for which the probability of success is close to 50-50—to tasks that are too easy or too difficult. Situations that have a future orientation or permit the development of novel or innovative solutions are attractive to achievement-oriented people. The key to workplace motivation for McClelland is to find high-nAch individuals (or raise the levels of low-nAch individuals through training) and expose them to situations conducive to fulfilling the need for achievement.

Instrumentality: Learning Theories

The understanding of valence contributed by need theories provides us with only one piece of the motivation puzzle—what human beings want. In order to understand behavior, we need to know not just what people want, but what they believe will lead to the attainment of what they want. These beliefs are referred to as *instrumentalities* in expectancy theory. Learning theories help clarify how relationships between behaviors and rewards come to be perceived. They also provide information that allows us to estimate the character, permanence, and strength of these relationships.

The notion that human beings generally behave to maximize pleasure and minimize pain was first formulated by the ancient Greek philosophers and captured in the concept of **hedonism.** This concept is part of virtually all modern theories of motivation. It is especially conspicuous in learning theories, all of which attempt to explain behavior in terms of the associations people form between performing some behavior and experiencing some outcome. We will look at two types of learning theories: operant learning and social learning.

Operant Learning.   **Operant Learning theory** proposes that a person engages in a specific behavior because that behavior has been reinforced by a specific outcome. For example, in the case of **positive reinforcement,** employees at MBNA might strive to process a credit application in less than 15 minutes because they know that in the past, when they have accomplished this, they have won a financial bonus. Indeed, operant learning got its name from the fact that in this type of learning the person must perform some operation in order to receive the reinforcing outcome.

Extinction is a second form of reinforcement. In extinction, a response is weakened because it is no longer paired with some positive reinforcer.

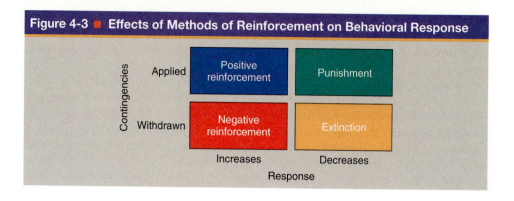

Figure 4-3 ■ Effects of Methods of Reinforcement on Behavioral Response

Indeed, one problem with reinforcement systems is that they often focus attention so exclusively on the reinforced behavior that other, nonreinforced behaviors become extinguished. For example, in attempting to fill a credit application faster, an employee may sacrifice quality (and perhaps issue credit to a poor risk) if there is no reinforcement for making good decisions as well as fast ones.

Negative reinforcement and punishment are two other types of reinforcement that can be used to influence behavior. In **negative reinforcement,** the likelihood that a person will engage in a particular behavior is increased because the behavior is followed by the removal of something the person dislikes. In **punishment,** the likelihood of a given behavior is decreased because it is followed by something that the person dislikes. The distinctions among positive reinforcement, extinction, negative reinforcement, and punishment are shown in Figure 4-3. This figure illustrates reinforcement theory's ability to both promote and inhibit behaviors, as well as its ability to predict the effects of both positive and negative rewards.

Managers in organizations sometimes contend that they cannot make use of reinforcement theory because they do not have enough resources to give positive reinforcement. For example, they cannot always raise salaries or award bonuses as they might like. What Figure 4-3 makes clear is that positive reinforcement is only one of a number of ways to increase the frequency of a desired behavior. Managers can also employ negative reinforcement to increase a response. They can find something about the job that people do not like and, when employees engage in desired behaviors, remove it. For example, a sales manager who wants to increase sales and who knows that salespeople hate to complete paperwork associated with their job might offer to shift the responsibility for completing paperwork to others if the salespeople increase their productivity. The sales force's enthusiasm for selling might increase noticeably as a result.

Moreover, money is not the only potential motivator. A recent survey of worker attitudes suggested that "time banks" ranked first among all nontraditional benefits (e.g., flextime, compressed workweeks, and on-site day care) among workers. Time banks allow employees to combine vacation days, holidays, and sick days into a pool to use as they please, no questions asked. For example, at Universal Health Services, manager Eileen Bove notes that "the company likes the plan because employees are now more apt to schedule their time off, instead of just calling in sick at the last minute, and the employees like the plan because it gives them privacy and control and eliminates game-playing.[13]

Recognition is another type of nonfinancial reward that can be used to motivate people. For example, General Electric has a Quick Thanks program that lets an employee nominate any colleague to receive a $25 gift certificate good at area restaurants and stores in appreciation for a job well done. The nominating employee hands out the reward to the deserving coworker. Although the financial bonus itself is very small, the peer recognition embodied in the award is highly significant.[14]

Operant learning is especially good for reinforcing simple or well-learned responses. In some cases, however, we may want to encourage a complex behavior that might not occur on its own. In this instance, the process of **shaping** can be helpful. Shaping consists of rewarding successive approximations to a desired behavior, so that "getting close counts." For example, it is virtually impossible for someone who has never played golf to pick up a club and execute a perfect drive the first time. Left alone to try and try again with no instruction, a novice golfer is unlikely ever to exhibit the correct behavior. In shaping, rather than waiting for the correct behavior to occur on its own, we begin by rewarding close approximations. Then, over time, rewards are held back until the person gets closer and closer to the right behavior. Thus, a golf instructor might at first reward a novice golfer for holding the club with the right grip. To obtain a second reward, the novice may be required not only to display the correct grip but to stand at the right distance from the ball. To obtain additional rewards, the novice may have to do both these things *and* perform the appropriate backswing, and so on. In this way, simple initial behaviors are shaped into a complex desired behavior.

Social Learning. **Social learning theory,** as proposed by Albert Bandura, is a theory of observational learning that holds that most people learn behaviors by observing others and then *modeling* the behaviors they perceive to be effective. Such observational learning contrasts markedly with the process of learning through direct reinforcement, and it is much better for explaining how people learn complex behavioral sequences.

For example, suppose a worker observes a colleague who, after giving bad news to the manager, is punished. Strict reinforcement theory would suggest that when confronted with the same task, the observing worker will be neither more nor less prone to be the bearer of bad tidings because that worker has not personally been the recipient of reinforcement. Social learning theory suggests otherwise, however. Despite the fact that a worker may never have directly experienced the fate of the colleague, the worker will nonetheless learn by observation that this manager "shoots the messenger." The person will probably conclude that the best response in such situations is to keep quiet. Even though the manager would probably never agree that problems should be covered up, this may be precisely the message sent by such behavior.

Besides its focus on learning by observation, social learning theory proposes that people can reinforce or punish their own behaviors; that is, they can engage in *self-reinforcement*. According to Bandura, a self-reinforcing event occurs when (1) tangible rewards are readily available for the taking, (2) people deny themselves free access to those rewards, and (3) they allow themselves to acquire the rewards only after achieving difficult self-set goals.[15] Consider the behavior of many novelists. Once alone and seated at their typewriters, a considerable number of authors refuse to take a break until they have written a certain number of pages. Obviously, these people can get up and leave anytime they wish. However, they deny themselves the reward of a rest until they have accomplished their self-set goal.[16] Research has indicated that self-reinforcement can be used to help people stop smoking, to overcome drug addiction, to cure obesity, to improve study habits, to enhance scholastic achievement, and to reduce absenteeism.[17]

Step 1: Desire to Perform

Valence and instrumentality are the first two parts of our model of motivation. As shown in Figure 4-4, these two concepts combine to influence the desire to perform. People will be motivated to perform at a high level so long as they perceive that receiving high-valence outcomes is contingent upon strong personal performance. Our understanding of the process depicted in Figure 4-4 is based in part on need theories, which help explain what outcomes individuals will perceive as having a positive valence. In addition, because reinforcement theories explain how people learn about contingencies, they also provide insight into the process that makes people want to perform.

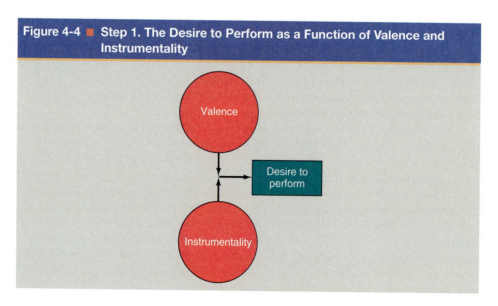

Figure 4-4 ■ Step 1. The Desire to Perform as a Function of Valence and Instrumentality

Expectancy: Self-Efficacy Theory

Self-Efficacy and Behavior.   Although actually part of Bandura's social learning theory, **self-efficacy** is an important topic in its own right.[18] The term *self-efficacy* refers to the judgments people make about their ability to execute courses of action required to deal with prospective situations. People high in self-efficacy feel they can master, or have mastered, some specific task. Self-efficacy determines how much effort people will expend and how long they will persist in the face of obstacles or aversive experiences. When beset with difficulties, people who entertain serious doubts about their capabilities slacken their efforts or give up altogether, whereas those who have a strong sense of efficacy exert greater effort to master the challenges.[19]

Sources of Self-Efficacy.   Given the effect that feelings of self-efficacy can have on behavior, it is important to know where these feelings come from. In his research, Bandura identified four different sources of self-efficacy beliefs. First, self-efficacy can be based on a person's *past accomplishments*. Past instances of successful behavior increase personal feelings of self-efficacy, especially when the successes seem attributable to unchanging factors such as personal ability or a manageable level of task difficulty.[20]

The link between self-efficacy theory and social learning theory is made clear in Bandura's second source of self-efficacy beliefs: *observation of others*. Merely watching someone else perform successfully on a task may increase an individual's sense of self-efficacy with respect to the same task. It is important to note that characteristics of the observer and model can influence the effects of observation on feelings of self-efficacy. For instance, the observer must judge the model to be both credible and similar to the observer (in terms of personal characteristics like ability and experience) if observation is to influence efficacy perceptions.

A third source of self-efficacy is *verbal persuasion*. Attempts to convince people that they can master a behavior will, under some circumstances, increase their perceptions of self-efficacy. The characteristics of the source and the target of the communication, however, can affect the influence that persuasion has on self-efficacy perceptions. Again, people who are perceived as credible and trustworthy are most able to influence others' self-efficacy perceptions through verbal persuasion.

Logical verification is another source of self-efficacy perceptions. Through logical verification, people can generate perceptions of self-efficacy at a new task if they can perceive a logical relationship between the new task and a task they have already mastered. Suppose, for example, that a highly competent secretary is worried about mastering a new word processing program. If the secretary can be convinced that the word processor is nothing more than a glorified typewriter, then the secretary's sense of self-efficacy may increase.

Step 2: Effort

In step 1 we stated that the desire to perform is influenced by both valence and instrumentality. Now we can state that effort is a function of desire to perform and expectancy. In other words, the level of effort a person will put forth is determined by three components of our model: valence, instrumentality, and expectancy.

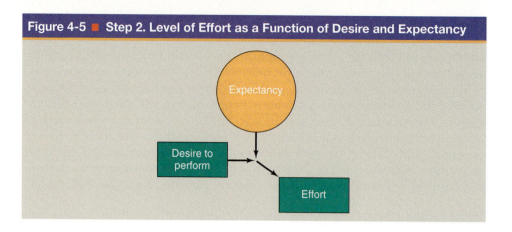

Self-efficacy theory is particularly useful as an explanation of how expectancies are formed and how they can be changed. However, as Figure 4-5 suggests, a person's beliefs do not translate into motivation unless the person truly desires to excel. Similarly, simply wanting to excel will not bring about high levels of effort unless the person has some belief that it is possible to do so.

Accuracy of Role Perceptions: Goal-Setting Theory

Role perceptions are people's beliefs about what they are supposed to be accomplishing on the job and how. When these beliefs are accurate, people facing a task know what needs to be done, how much needs to be done, and who will have the responsibility to do it. Role perception accuracy of this sort guarantees that the energy devoted to task accomplishment will be directed toward the right activities and outcomes. At the same time, it decreases the amount of energy wasted on unimportant goals and activities. **Goal-setting theory** can help us understand how to enhance the accuracy of role perceptions.

Important Goal Attributes. Employees are often told, "Do your best." This axiom is a standard instruction intended to guide job performance in everyday situations. Yet, research has consistently demonstrated that vague instructions like this can actually undermine personal performance. In contrast, over 100 studies have provided evidence supporting the assertion that performance is enhanced by goals that are both *specific and difficult*.[21] As you can see from Table 4-2, setting specific goals has improved performance in a wide variety of jobs. Goal setting is even more effective when teamed with feedback so that progress can be monitored. Finally, specific and difficult goals are especially effective when placed in a continuous improvement cycle in which future goals are reasonable increments on past goals.[22]

Specific and difficult goals seem to promote greater effort and to enhance persistence. They are also likely to encourage people to develop effective task

Table 4-2 ■ Jobholders Who Have Improved Performance in Goal-Setting Programs	
Telephone servicepersons	Loggers
Baggage handlers	Marine recruits
Typists	Union bargaining representatives
Salespersons	Bank managers
Truck loaders	Assembly line workers
College students	Animal trappers
Sewing machine operators	Maintenance technicians
Engineering researchers	Dockworkers
Scientists	Die casters

strategies. Their primary virtue, however, is that they direct attention to specific desired results, clarifying both what is important and what level of performance is needed. Indeed, sometimes goals direct people's attention so well that they forget about performing other important activities that are not captured in the goal itself.[23]

Goal Commitment and Participation.   Another factor that affects performance is the extent to which a person feels committed to a goal. Specific and difficult goals lead to increased performance only when there is high **goal commitment.** The requirement that people be committed to goals means that goals must be set carefully, because when they are too difficult, they are typically met with less commitment. People may view a goal that is set too high as impossible and reject it altogether.

Fortunately, research has examined several ways to increase commitment to difficult goals. One important factor is the degree to which the goals are public rather than private. In one study, students for whom difficult goals for GPA were made public (posted on bulletin boards) showed higher levels of commitment to those goals relative to students whose goals were private. This study also found a significant positive relationship between need for achievement and goal commitment. Moreover, the positive relationship between need for achievement and goal commitment was especially strong when the goals were set by the students themselves, as opposed to being assigned by an outside party. Figure 4-6 depicts the relationship between goal origin, need for achievement, and goal commitment.[24]

This complex relationship is typical of the results of research that deals with goal origin. Common sense might make one think that participation in the goal-setting process would invariably enhance performance and commitment. This commonsense notion has not held up well in scientific studies, however. Many contemporary studies have failed to find significant differences between participative goal-setting groups and assigned-goal groups in terms of either goal commitment or performance. Generally speaking, studies that have found positive effects resulting from participation have been able to do so only within limited

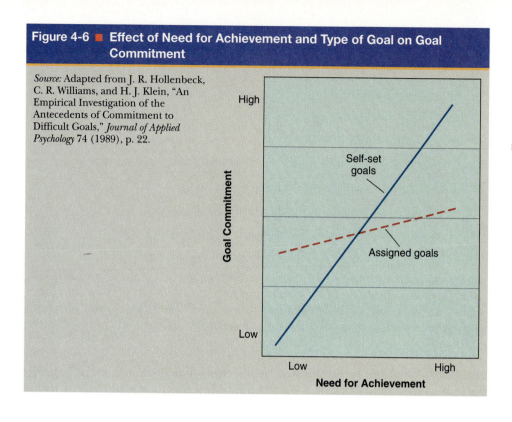

Figure 4-6 ■ Effect of Need for Achievement and Type of Goal on Goal Commitment

Source: Adapted from J. R. Hollenbeck, C. R. Williams, and H. J. Klein, "An Empirical Investigation of the Antecedents of Commitment to Difficult Goals," *Journal of Applied Psychology* 74 (1989), p. 22.

Goal Commitment

High

Self-set goals

Assigned goals

Low

Low   High

Need for Achievement

subsamples of workers or situations.[25] Thus, although commitment is important in enhancing the effect of goals on performance, participation does not always guarantee commitment.

Goals and Strategies. As Table 4-2 shows, goal setting has been used to increase performance on a variety of jobs. Yet most of the early research on goal setting consisted of studies that focused attention on relatively simple tasks. More recent research has extended goal-setting theory into more complex task domains. In these situations, however, the links between goals, effort, and performance are not so direct. A review of these studies indicates that although goals have positive effects on all tasks, the magnitude of the effect is stronger for simple tasks than for complex tasks.[26] Figure 4-7 shows how the effect of goal difficulty on performance decreases as task complexity increases.

For complex tasks, the *task strategies,* or plans of action, that people devise have a big impact on the outcome of their efforts. This impact can obscure and in some rare cases even wipe out the effects of goal setting. Research on goal setting and task strategies suggests that whereas setting specific and difficult goals may lead to increased strategy development, there is no guarantee that the resulting strategies will always be effective.[27] Moreover, because developing strategies consumes time that might otherwise be devoted to task performance, there may be situations in which goals actually hinder performance.[28]

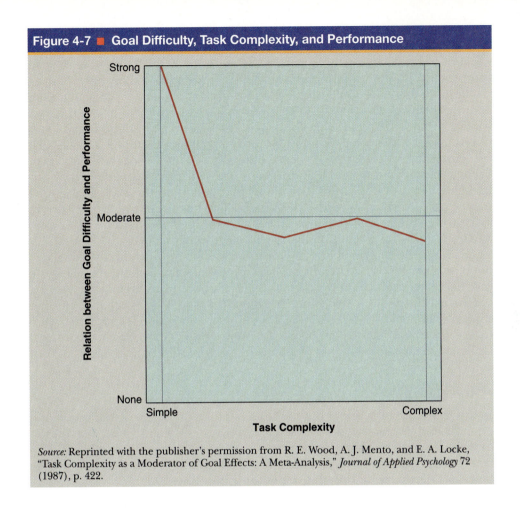

Figure 4-7 ■ Goal Difficulty, Task Complexity, and Performance

Source: Reprinted with the publisher's permission from R. E. Wood, A. J. Mento, and E. A. Locke, "Task Complexity as a Moderator of Goal Effects: A Meta-Analysis," *Journal of Applied Psychology* 72 (1987), p. 422.

Conclusion.   Although research on performance strategies has yielded findings that complicate the results of other goal-setting studies, this research is helpful in delineating the specific role-clarifying effect of goals. In simple tasks, where the *means* to perform a task are clear, specific and difficult goals lead to higher performance because they clarify the *ends* toward which task performance should be directed. In complex tasks, however, the means are not clear. Individuals performing such tasks do not know how to go about them in the best way, so merely clarifying the ends sought is unlikely to enhance performance.

Ability and Experience Revisited: Nonmotivational Determinants of Performance

Although we have focused primarily on motivation in this chapter, task performance is also contingent upon the abilities of the performer. We discussed abilities at great length in Chapter 2, so here we will focus only on how individual differences interact with goal setting and task strategies. Three things are worth noting with respect to nonmotivational determinants of performance. First, it should be obvious that people lacking the requisite abilities cannot perform a complex task even under the most favorable goal-related circumstances.

Second, there are some subtle relationships among goal setting, attention, and cognitive capacity that affect task performance. Recall that one of the ways in which goal setting affects performance is by directing attention to the kinds of results that are desired. Kanfer and Ackerman have developed a model that recognizes that different people have different amounts of cognitive ability to bring to bear on a task, and that this limits how much they can attend to at any one time.[29] Because it diverts attention from the task to the goal, goal setting may be particularly damaging to people who have low levels of ability or who are still learning the task. Such people need to devote all their attention to the task, and goal setting for them is unlikely to enhance performance.

Finally, individuals high in ability are more likely to develop effective strategies. For one thing, people with strong reasoning and deductive ability can often figure out effective strategies prior to working on the task. Second, individuals high in cognitive ability learn more quickly and are therefore more likely to deduce effective strategies through trial and error.[30] Thus, although motivation is critical to performance, the lessons learned in Chapter 2 about the importance of ability should not be forgotten. For all but the simplest tasks, there is no substitute for ability.

Step 3: Performance

In this third step of building our overall model, we can see how motivation and other factors combine to determine performance (see Figure 4-8). Specifically, performance will be high when a person (1) puts forth significant effort, (2) directs this effort toward the right outcomes, and (3) has the ability to execute the behaviors necessary for bringing about those outcomes.

Experience and Cyclical Effects

The fourth and final step needed to complete our model deals with the links that make the model dynamic over time. Let's look back at Figure 4-1, which shows three arrows that head back left. First, there is a feedback loop going from performance back to valence. Recall that valence, as a construct, deals with *anticipated* satisfaction, not realized satisfaction. The feedback loop allows for the possibility that an outcome a person receives for performing some task might not bring much real satisfaction when it is actually received. Valence for such an outcome would then decrease relative to what it had been at an earlier time.

Another link goes back from performance to instrumentality. This loop implies that the outcomes received for performing at some level at one time will affect the person's perceived instrumentalities at later times. If high performance is not followed by any reward, extinction of the performance response could take place, lowering the perceived instrumentality of high performance.

Finally, there is also an arrow going back from performance to expectancy. This affirms the fact that expectancies and self-efficacy are based at least partially

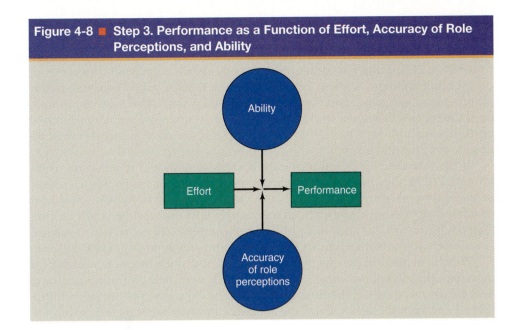

Figure 4-8 ■ Step 3. Performance as a Function of Effort, Accuracy of Role Perceptions, and Ability

on prior performance. All else being equal, successful performance strengthens self-efficacy and leads to high expectancies. Failing at a task, however, generally leads to lower levels of self-efficacy.

These three dynamic links in our model of motivation create the possibility that motivation can change over time. For example, Figure 4-1 suggests that even highly motivated persons might lose motivation for any of three reasons. First, those starting out with high expectancies might discover during job performance that they cannot perform nearly as well as they had thought. Decreased self-efficacy would reduce expectancy perceptions, and lower motivation would probably result. Second, people might discover that performing well on a job does not lead to the desirable outcomes they had expected. Motivation could diminish as projected instrumentalities failed to materialize. Third, experience with the rewards received for performing a job might lead someone to discover faults with initial valences. That is, rewards expected to yield satisfaction might not do so.

High-Performance Work Systems

In theoretical terms, one of the least controversial statements one can make about paying workers is that it is important to tie pay to job performance. Therefore, the firm may want to pay a high performer in a job category more than a low performer within the same job category. However, the actual implementation of programs to bring about such a relationship is often quite difficult. To get a feel for this difficulty, consider the following issues that arise when we try to pay for performance.

Should pay increases be based on outcomes that occur at the individual level (i.e., performance of individual workers) or the group level (i.e., performance of different teams) or the organizational level (performance of the entire business)? By determining pay at the individual level, the organization may create competition among coworkers and destroy team morale. A problem with determining pay at the group and organizational levels is that individuals may have a hard time seeing how their own performance relates to group or organizational performance and outcomes. In expectancy theory terms, these kinds of conditions lower instrumentality.

If the firm decides to stay at the individual level, should it set up the rules for payment in advance (e.g., telling workers that they will receive $5 per widget produced)? This sounds like a good idea, but the firm will be unable to forecast its labor costs (i.e., it cannot anticipate exactly how many widgets will be produced). Moreover, because the price of the product sold or service rendered cannot be known in advance, the firm will also be unable to anticipate revenue.

If the firm waits till the end of the year to see how much money is available for merit pay, people will not know in advance exactly how their performance relates to their pay. Moreover, if the firm, like most firms, engages in pay secrecy to protect people's privacy, how can anyone actually know how fair the merit system is?

If the firm decides to keep incentives at an organizational level, should the incentives be based on cost savings and distributed yearly, or on profits and distributed on a deferred basis? The calculations and accounting procedures required by cost savings plans are enormous and complex, but such plans allow rewards to be distributed quickly. Profit-sharing plans are much easier to handle from an accounting perspective. But because their rewards are distributed on a deferred basis, they are less motivating than cost savings plans.

Asking all these questions illustrates the complexity inherent in putting into practice the seemingly simple theoretical concept of paying for performance. Covering all the complexities of these issues is well beyond the scope of this chapter. However, we will examine the distinguishing features of four different kinds of pay-for-performance programs: merit-based plans, incentive plans, cost savings plans, and profit-sharing plans.

Merit Pay and Incentive Systems

Individual pay-for-performance plans base pay, at least partially, on the accomplishments of individual workers. There are two types of individual programs, those based on merit and those based on incentives.

Merit-based pay plans are by far the easiest to administer and control. In these programs, performance is assessed at the end of the fiscal year via subjective ratings of employees made by supervisors. Also at the end of the year, a fixed sum of money is allocated to wage increases. This sum is distributed to individuals in amounts proportional to their performance ratings.

In designing merit-based programs, there are three major considerations. First, what will the average performer receive? Many firms try to make sure that average performers are at least able to keep up with inflation. As a result, the midpoint of the rating scales used is often tied to the yearly consumer price index (CPI).

Second, what will a poor performer receive? Companies rarely decrease an employee's wages; however, raises that fail to cover the CPI are actually wage decreases in terms of buying power. Is it in the best interest of the firm to allow the wage increases of poor performers to slip below the inflation level? If so, how much damage does the firm wish to inflict on low performers? How replaceable are these people if they are prompted to leave the firm?

Finally, how much will high performers receive? Will high performers at the top of a pay grade receive the same raise as those at the bottom of a higher wage grade? Paying for performance could cause top performers in a job lower in the hierarchy to surpass (through yearly raises) low performers in upper-level jobs over time. Indeed, in order to prevent this type of compression, many companies have turned to the practice of broad banding. Broad banding simply means reducing the number of hierarchical distinctions between jobs. For example, General Electric has tried to move away from length of service and rank as pay determinants. In order to do this they have cut the levels of salary grades from 29 to 6. This gives people more opportunity to get a raise without a promotion.[31]

Although the performance ratings that determine merit pay have traditionally come from supervisors, this is starting to change. In the service sector of the economy, high-performance work systems have eliminated the "middle man" (the supervisor). These companies tie merit pay raises directly to customer service ratings obtained from surveys. For example, at GTE, customer ratings are weighted 35 percent in annual merit pay decisions for certain managerial groups.[32]

In general, although many organizations rely partially on merit systems, throughout the first half of the 1990s raises went down while other forms of pay for performance went up (as shown in Figure 4-9). Some of these other forms of pay involve incentive systems.

Incentive systems differ from merit systems in two ways. First, incentive programs stipulate the rules by which payment will be made in advance, so that the worker can calculate exactly how much money will be earned if a certain level of performance is achieved. Second, rewards in an incentive program are based on objective measures of performance.

In simple *piecework plans,* a standard of productivity per time interval is set, and any productivity beyond that standard is rewarded with a set amount per unit. This type of plan is easy for the worker to understand, and it creates an obvious performance-outcome expectancy. On the other hand, the standard must often be adjusted. If the standard is initially set too low, labor costs can get out of hand. If it is set too high, workers will reject it when they find that even though they are trying harder, the standard cannot be reached. If the standard is flexible, gradual increases in the standard may be viewed as a manipulative management trick, and decreases will cause some workers to try to manipulate the system by lowering output. Furthermore, without built-in safeguards, these programs also lead workers to achieve quantity at the price of quality or ethical violations.[33]

For example, the government actually has regulations that put a ceiling on the percentage of salary that can be paid out in the form of commissions in the insurance agency (55 percent). This ceiling has been established to prevent the practice of "churning," which in the insurance industry means selling unsophisticated

Figure 4-9 ■ Changes in Salary Raises and Pay-for-Performance Bonuses over Time

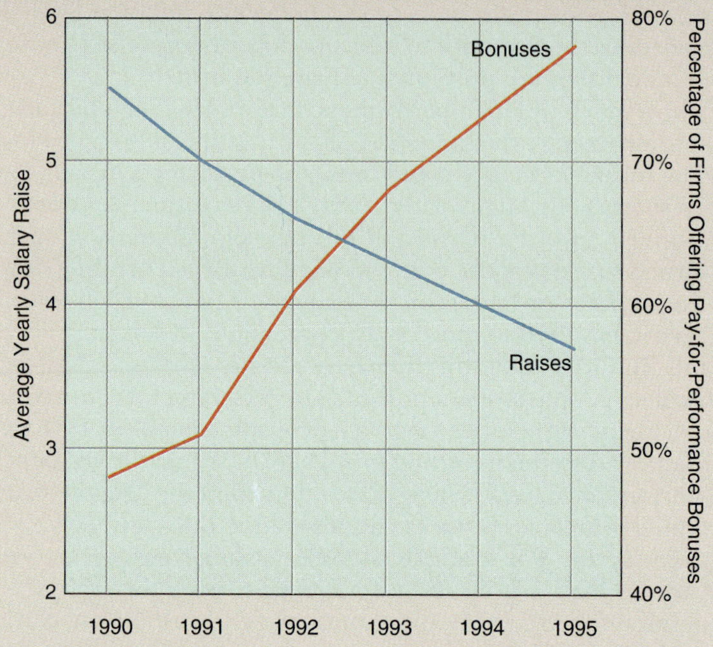

Source: S. Tully, "Are You Being Paid Enough," *Fortune,* June 26, 1995, pp. 66–74. © 1995 Time Inc. All rights reserved.

customers insurance policies that they do not need, financed with cash value drained out of their existing coverage. Insurers are lobbying to end these restrictions because they find themselves increasingly in competition with non–insurance companies (e.g., brokerage houses) when it comes to helping people plan for retirement. These restrictions on how to pay employees hinder the ability of the insurance companies to compete with the unregulated non–insurance companies, which shows the important link between motivational systems and competitive advantage.[34]

In addition to creating ethical difficulties, individual-based incentives can also hinder cooperation within the organization. That is, individuals get so focused on their own specific goals and rewards that they lose their concern for the overall health of the organization or their coworkers. For example, Lantech, a small manufacturer of packaging material in Louisville, had a bonus-type incentive system built around cost containment. The competition within the organization to get the bonus grew heated, and each person tried to assign costs to others. At one point, the competition got so petty that one of the managers tried to pass off the cost of his toilet paper to a different division. Pat Lancaster, CEO at Lantech, noted that "by the early 1990s I was spending 95 percent of my time on conflict resolution instead of on how to serve our customers."[35] To eliminate these types of problems, Lantech, like many other organizations, has rejected individual-based plans, and instead focuses in on organization-level plans, such as those discussed next.

Profit-Sharing, Stock Option, and Cost Savings Plans

Whereas merit plans and incentive plans tie pay to performance at the individual level, profit-sharing and cost savings plans tie pay to performance at a broader level. As the name suggests, **profit-sharing plans** distribute organizational profits to employees. According to recent estimates, 20 percent of U.S. firms have such plans in place, and these plans are becoming increasingly popular. Cash distribution plans provide full payment soon after profits have been determined (annually or quarterly). To reap tax advantages, however, most plans—indeed, as many as 80 percent—provide deferred payments.[36] In these plans, current profits accumulate in employee accounts, and a cash payment is made only when a worker becomes disabled, leaves the firm, retires, or dies. Of course, not all the firm's profits are redistributed. Research suggests that the percentage of profits distributed may range from a low of 14 percent to a high of 33 percent.[37]

In addition to profit-sharing plans, a growing number of organizations now offer lower-level employees company-sponsored stock option plans. Stock options were once solely the province of the corporate elite, but many companies including Merck, DuPont, PepsiCo, Toys "R" Us, and Wendy's, have now begun to initiate such programs for lower-level workers. Unlike piece-rate incentive systems that often make the employee lose sight of the big picture, stock option plans attempt to create perceptions of instrumentality between the company's overall performance and the individual's economic well-being.

A typical stock option plan works like this. First, an anniversary date is established and the price of the company's stock on that day is recorded. A waiting period then ensues, and this can last anywhere from one year (at DuPont) to five years (at Merck). At the end of the waiting period, the employee has the option to purchase the company's stock at the old value regardless of the current value. If the current value of the stock has increased, then the employee can "cash out" (sell the stock) at that point or hold on to the stock even longer. If the current value of the stock is less than the old value, the employee simply does not exercise the option (thus, there is no risk of losing money). There is always some limit on the number of options any one person can accumulate (PepsiCo workers can only purchase stock up to an amount equal to 10 percent of their pay, and Merck imposes a cap of 100 shares per employee).

One problem with both profit-sharing plans and stock option plans is that employees often find it hard to see the connection between their activities and their company's profits. When multiple businesses are involved, people may find it even harder to see the link between their efforts and corporate profits. Thus, the day-to-day motivational value of these kinds of programs may be questionable. Would a worker who might otherwise quit work an hour early really stop this practice for fear of what it might do to the company's stock price?

For this reason, some firms adopt **cost savings plans** that pay workers bonuses out of the money the company has saved as a result of the efficient performance of its workers. Workers often have more control over the costs of doing business than over profits. Thus, it is easier for them to see the connection between their own work and cost reduction.

One type of cost savings plan, called the *Scanlon Plan,* is designed to reduce labor costs. Incentives are calculated as a function of labor costs relative to the sales value of production (SVP). SVP is the revenue that would be obtained from sales of all the goods or services produced in a time unit. Say that in one year, $100,000 worth of labor is needed to generate $500,000 in goods and services. In the next year, however, let's say that the same amount of goods and services can be produced with $70,000 worth of labor. A portion of the $30,000 saved is then distributed to the workers. A typical practice is to return 50 percent of such savings to the workers, retain 25 percent for the firm, and place 25 percent in a fund to cover future years in which a "negative bonus" might occur.

Conclusion

We have sampled only a few of the many pay-for-performance programs currently in use, and as the Securing Competitive Advantage box highlights, there is no limit to the complexity of some of these programs. You should, however, have some feel for the kinds of issues raised by such programs. Figure 4-10 provides guidance on choosing a suitable plan. It tells you under what circumstances an individual or a group plan is appropriate and in what situations specific individual or group plans are most effective.

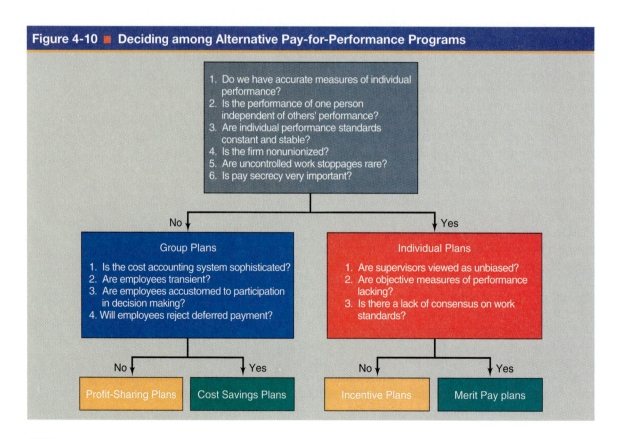

Figure 4-10 ■ Deciding among Alternative Pay-for-Performance Programs

1. Do we have accurate measures of individual performance?
2. Is the performance of one person independent of others' performance?
3. Are individual performance standards constant and stable?
4. Is the firm nonunionized?
5. Are uncontrolled work stoppages rare?
6. Is pay secrecy very important?

No → Group Plans

1. Is the cost accounting system sophisticated?
2. Are employees transient?
3. Are employees accustomed to participation in decision making?
4. Will employees reject deferred payment?

No → Profit-Sharing Plans
Yes → Cost Savings Plans

Yes → Individual Plans

1. Are supervisors viewed as unbiased?
2. Are objective measures of performance lacking?
3. Is there a lack of consensus on work standards?

No → Incentive Plans
Yes → Merit Pay plans

Economic Value Added: Business Basics for Employees in High-Performance Work Systems

As most (though probably not all) Master of Business Administration (MBA) Finance majors could tell you, economic value added (EVA) is calculated as posttax operating profit reduced by cost of capital multiplied by the operating unit's investment. This index gauges whether a business is earning more than its true cost of capital, and it gives top-level managers a clearer idea of whether they are creating or destroying shareholder wealth. Indeed, in the late 1990s this indicator is being increasingly used as *the measure* of organizational effectiveness.

Thus, when organizations decide to link employees' pay to firm performance, setting goals and establishing rewards in EVA terms is a logical choice. The only problem with this is that outside the finance department, few employees appreciate EVA and how it is affected by workers' behaviors. To eliminate this roadblock, more and more companies are aggressively educating their workforce in financial basics. Once EVA and similar concepts are understood by the workforce, goals and worker in-

centives can be based on EVA performance, thus aligning the interests and perceptions of managers, workers, and shareholders.

For example, Honeywell's commercial avionics division developed a course called Business Basics to provide general information on business objectives, as well as specific information on how to calculate working capital and, of course, EVA. The training program focused on these three specific concepts because they are all used to determine employee bonuses. This training is comprised of two parts. First, a generic lesson explains the three concepts in general and shows employees how each is used to calculate their bonus. However, the training also includes a second, job-specific component that helps employees learn how their individual jobs can contribute to EVA.

Two years into the program, it seems to be doing what it is supposed to do—focus employees on bottom-line business objectives. According to manager Donald Schwanz, "The employees see a distinct tie between what they do

and the health of the business in general, and they're making better decisions as a result."[1] In 1994, the first full year the program was in place, goals for profit and EVA were exceeded by 10 percent. In 1995, the workforce reached all its goals and employees received 3.5 percent of their salaries in the form of EVA bonuses—an average of $1,225 per employee.

Eli Lilly has a similar program that bases worker incentives on EVA, but its program focuses more on long-term success. In order to prevent a manager from focusing on one-time, short-term gains in EVA, Lilly's program creates a bank. One portion of the bonus is paid out right away, but the rest rolls into a "bank" and cannot be accessed by managers for three years. As Randall Tobias, CEO of Eli Lilly, notes, "EVA really makes you align your thinking with shareholder value. From the end of June 1994 when we first adopted the EVA program to today [September of 1996], the share price for Eli Lilly has gone up 105 percent. That's what really matters."[2]

[1] S. Caudron, "How Pay Launched Performance," *Personnel Journal,* September 1996, pp. 70–76.
[2] E. M. Davies, "Eli Lilly Is Making Shareholders Rich by Linking Pay to EVA," *Fortune,* September 9, 1996, pp. 173–74.

SUMMARY

Our model of *motivation* and *performance* is based on *expectancy theory* and incorporates concepts from four other theories of motivation: *need theory, learning theory, self-efficacy theory,* and *goal-setting theory.* The model focuses on explaining three outcomes. The first, desire to perform, is a function of *valences* and *instrumentalities.* A person's desire to perform well will be high when rewards are associated with high performance. The second outcome, *effort,* is a function of desire to perform and *expectancy.* Effort will be forthcoming only when individuals want to perform well and when they believe they can do so. The third outcome, performance, is a function of effort, *accurate role perceptions,* and *ability.* Performance will be high only when individuals with the requisite abilities and knowledge of desired goals and strategies put forth their best effort. The dynamic nature of the motivation process is revealed in the way present levels of performance affect future levels of valence, instrumentality, and expectancy. The complexity of the motivational process can be seen in high-performance work systems and the many issues that need to be considered when one attempts to "pay for performance."

Review Questions

1. Recent research suggests that individual needs may be determined more by genetic factors than previously thought. Take each of the need theories described in this chapter and discuss whether this new evidence supports, contradicts, or is irrelevant to that theory.
2. Specific, difficult goals have been suggested to enhance performance, but researchers have also shown that performance will be high only when expectancies are high. We might think that as goals became increasingly difficult, expectations for accomplishing them would decrease. Can you resolve this apparent contradiction between goal-setting theory and expectancy theory?
3. Analyst Daniel Shore once called motivation researchers "servants of power" because their research was often used to manipulate lower-level workers. Is trying to motivate people necessarily exploitative? Are there any conditions under which providing external motivation might be exploitative? Which theories of motivation do you feel are exploitative? Which ones are not?
4. Imagine two different pharmaceutical companies that employ the same job categories yet differ in their business strategy. One is trying to increase market share through innovation (developing new and better drugs). The other sticks to established products and tries to increase market share by lowering costs. Why might the two firms wind up with dramatically different pay-for-performance programs? What types of program might be most and least suitable for each of the organizations?

Implementation Guide

When you are trying to diagnose a situation in which motivation may be a problem, the following questions can help guide your inquiry:

1. What are the most important needs of the person I am trying to motivate?
2. What contingencies has this person learned over the course of his or her reinforcement history?

3. How can I make the receipt of outcomes that have positive valence for this person contingent upon performing at a high level?

4. What outcomes that have negative valence for this person can I remove, contingent upon performance at a high level?

5. Does the person I am trying to motivate believe that he or she can perform well? If not, what can I do to increase the person's self-efficacy perceptions?

6. Does the person I am trying to motivate actually have the ability to accomplish the tasks that he or she is attempting to perform?

7. Does the person I am trying to motivate have specific, difficult performance goals in mind?

8. Is the person I am trying to motivate committed to goals?

9. Does the person I am trying to motivate know the best strategies for accomplishing these goals?

10. If the person I am trying to motivate was initially higher in motivation than he or she is at present, which of the three feedback loops in the diagnostic model might account for the loss in motivation?

11. How does the firm reward employees for their performance? If it uses pay as a reward, is a merit or an incentive plan most appropriate?

12. How does the organization reward people for organizational performance? If it uses pay, would a cost savings or a profit-sharing approach be most appropriate?

ENDNOTES

1. J. T. Austin and J. B. Vancouver, "Goal Constructs in Psychology: Structure, Process and Content," *Psychological Bulletin* 129 (1996), pp. 338–75.

2. S. Sherman, "You Can Have It All," *Fortune,* March 4, 1996, pp. 193–94.

3. M. Magnet, "The Productivity Payoff Arrives," *Fortune,* June 27, 1994, pp. 79–84.

4. V. H. Vroom, *Work and Motivation* (New York: John Wiley, 1964), pp. 55–71; and L. W. Porter and E. E. Lawler, *Managerial Attitudes and Performance* (Homewood, IL: Richard D. Irwin, 1968), pp. 107–39.

5. T. R. Mitchell, "Expectancy Models of Job Satisfaction, Occupational Choice, and Effort: A Theoretical, Methodological, and Empirical Appraisal," *Psychological Bulletin* 81 (1974), pp. 1053–77.

6. Vroom, *Work and Motivation,* p. 27.

7. Ibid., p. 17.

8. A. H. Maslow, "A Theory of Human Motivation," *Psychological Reports* 50 (1943), pp. 370–96.

9. Ibid.

10. M. A. Wahba and L. G. Bridwell, "Maslow Reconsidered: A Review of Research on the Need Hierarchy," *Organizational Behavior and Human Performance* 15 (1976), pp. 121–40.

11. H. A. Murray, *Explorations in Personality* (New York: Oxford University Press, 1938).

12. D. C. McClelland, *The Achieving Society* (Princeton, NJ: Van Nostrand Press, 1963).

13. E. J. Pollock, "Workers Want More Money, but They Also Want to Control Their Own Time," *The Wall Street Journal,* November 28, 1995, p. B12.

14. S. Kerr, "Risky Business: The New Pay Game," *Fortune,* July 22, 1996, pp. 94–95.

15. A. Bandura, "Self-Reinforcement: Theoretical and Methodological Considerations," *Behaviorism* 4 (1976), pp. 135–55.

16. I. Wallace, "Self-Control Techniques of Famous Novelists," *Journal of Applied Behavioral Analysis* 10 (1977), pp. 515–25.

17. F. H. Kanfer and J. S. Phillips, *Learning Foundations of Behavior Therapy* (New York: John Wiley, 1970), p. 59; F. H. Kanfer, "Self-Regulation: Research, Issues, and Speculation," in *Behavior Modification in Clinical Psychology,* C. Neuringer and J. Michael, eds. (New York: Appleton-Century-Crofts, 1974), pp. 178–220; M. J. Mahoney, N. G. Moura, and T. C. Wade, "The Relative Efficacy of Self-Reward, Self-Punishment, and Self-Monitoring Techniques for Weight Loss," *Journal of Consulting and Clinical*

Psychology 40 (1973), pp. 404–7; C. S. Richards, "When Self-Control Fails: Selective Bibliography of Research on the Maintenance Problems in Self-Control Treatment Programs," *JSAS: Catalog of Selected Documents in Psychology* 8 (1976), pp. 67–68; E. L. Glynn, "Classroom Applications of Self-Determined Reinforcement," *Journal of Applied Behavioral Analysis* 3 (1970), pp. 123–30; and C. A. Frayne and G. P. Latham, "Application of Social Learning Theory to Employee Self-Management of Attendance," *Journal of Applied Psychology* 72 (1987), pp. 387–92.

18. A. Bandura, "Self-Efficacy Mechanism in Human Behavior," *American Psychologist* 37 (1982), pp. 122–47.

19. Ibid.

20. J. E. Mathieu, J. W. Martinau, and S. I. Tannenbaum, "Individual and Situational Influences on the Development of Self-Efficacy: Implications for Training Effectiveness," *Personnel Psychology* 46 (1993), pp. 125–47.

21. E. A. Locke, "Toward a Theory of Task Motivation and Incentives," *Organizational Behavior and Human Performance* 3 (1968), p. 145.

22. J. M. Phillips, J. R. Hollenbeck, and D. R. Ilgen, "Prevalence and Prediction of Positive Discrepancy Creation: Examining a Discrepancy between Two Self-Regulation Theories," *Journal of Applied Psychology* 81 (1996), pp. 498–511.

23. P. M. Wright, J. M. George, S. R. Farnsworth, and G. C. McMahan, "Productivity and Extra-Role Behavior: The Effects of Goals and Incentives on Spontaneous Helping," *Journal of Applied Psychology* 78 (1993), pp. 374–81.

24. J. R. Hollenbeck, C. R. Williams, and H. J. Klein, "An Empirical Examination of Antecedents of Commitment to Difficult Goals," *Journal of Applied Psychology* 74 (1989), pp. 18–25.

25. G. P. Latham, M. Erez, and E. A. Locke, "Resolving Scientific Disputes through the Joint Design of Crucial Experiments by the Antagonists: Application to the Erez-Latham Dispute Regarding Participation in Goal Setting," *Journal of Applied Psychology* 73 (1987), pp. 753–72.

26. R. E. Wood, E. A. Locke, and A. J. Mento, "Task Complexity as a Moderator of Goal Effects: A Meta-Analysis," *Journal of Applied Psychology* 72 (1987), pp. 416–25.

27. P. C. Earley and B. C. Perry, "Work Plan Availability and Performance: An Assessment of Task Strategy Priming on Subsequent Task Completion," *Organizational Behavior and Human Decision Processes* 39 (1987), pp. 279–302; and P. C. Earley, P. Wajnaroski, and W. Prest, "Task Planning and Energy Expended: Exploration of How Goals Influence Performance," *Journal of Applied Psychology* 72 (1987), pp. 107–14.

28. P. C. Earley, T. Connolly, and G. Ekegren, "Goals, Strategy Development and Task Performance: Some Limits on the Efficacy of Goal Setting," *Journal of Applied Psychology* 74 (1989), pp. 24–33.

29. R. Kanfer and P. L. Ackerman, "Motivation and Cognitive Abilities: An Integrative/Aptitude-Treatment Interaction Approach to Skill Acquisition," *Journal of Applied Psychology* 74 (1989), pp. 657–90.

30. J. Shapiro, "Goal Setting, Cognitive Ability, and Task Strategy" (master's thesis, Michigan State University, 1990), p. 79.

31. S. Kerr, "Risky Business."

32. S. Phillips, A. Dunkin, J. B. Treece, and K. H. Hammonds, "King Customer: At Companies That Listen Hard and Respond Fast, Bottom Lines Thrive," *Business Week,* March 12, 1990, pp. 88–94.

33. C. W. Hamner, "How to Ruin Motivation with Pay," *Compensation Review* 21 (1975), pp. 88–98.

34. L. Scism, "Insurers Study Ways of Paying Sales Personnel," *The Wall Street Journal,* November 3, 1995, p. A7.

35. P. Nulty, "Incentive Pay Can Be Crippling," *Fortune,* November 13, 1995, p. 235.

36. Bureau of National Affairs, "Incentive Pay Schemes Seen as a Result of Economic Employee Relation Change," *BNA Daily Report,* October 9, 1984, p. 1.

37. R. McCaffery, *Managing the Employee Benefits Process* (New York: AMACOM, 1983), p. 17.

Chapter Five
Satisfaction and Stress in the Workplace

Every executive recognizes the need for satisfied and loyal customers. If the firm is publically held, it is also safe to assume that every executive appreciates the need to have satisfied and loyal investors. Customers and investors provide the financial resources that allow the organization to survive. Not every executive understands the need to generate satisfaction and loyalty among employees, however; yet the fact is that retention rates among employees are strongly related to retention rates among both customers[1] and investors.[2] Because executives at many organizations have been slow to pick up on this linkage, this provides yet another area in which one firm can gain a competitive advantage over others in the market. That is, the best firms are able to convert employee satisfaction and loyalty, on the one hand, into customer and investor satisfaction and loyalty on the other.

For example, sales agents at State Farm Insurance stay with the company, on average, 18 to 20 years. This is two to three times the average tenure in this industry. This kind of tenure allows the average State Farm agent to better learn the job and to develop long-term customer relations that cannot be matched by competitors who may lose half of their sales staff each year. State Farm also draws benefits from this experienced staff by systematically surveying its agents to get their views about where customer satisfaction is high, where it is low, and what can be done to improve service.[3] The result in terms of the bottom line is that State Farm agents achieve 40 percent higher sales per agent as compared to the competition. In addition, as an indicator of quality of service, the retention rates among State Farm customers exceed 95 percent. USAA, a company that sells financial services primarily to military personnel, is another firm that achieves 95 percent retention rates among both employees and customers, resulting in one of the highest annual-earnings-per-employee ratios in the industry.[4]

Firms that take advantage of the employee retention–customer retention link are still in the minority, however. The massive restructurings and downsizing efforts of the 1990s have left many organizations filled with dissatisfied, stressed, and insecure workers who are ready to leave their current job for a new opportunity at a moment's notice. Recognizing this, some firms are working hard to rebuild lost loyalty. For example, at Monsanto's Searle division, the company is expanding its efforts to help employees cope with stress via seminars and training brochures. Monsanto is also trying to promote satisfaction and retention of employees by opening up two personal development centers. At these centers, employees are able to discuss current problems relating to their jobs, as well as future career prospects, with counselors and upper-level management. "Five years ago, management's attitude was very much one that employees are disposable," notes Monsanto manager Sophia Capelli. "The company now recognizes people as a critical renewable asset."[5]

[1] M. J. Schmit and S. P. Allscheid, "Employee Attitudes and Customer Satisfaction: Making Theoretical and Empirical Connections," *Personnel Psychology* 48 (1995), pp. 521–36.
[2] F. Reichheld, *The Loyalty Effect* (Cambridge, MA: Harvard Business School Press).
[3] B. Schneider, S. D. Ashworth, A. C. Higgs, and L. Carr, "Design, Validity and Use of Strategically-Focused Employee Attitude Surveys," *Personnel Psychology* 49 (1996), pp. 695–705.
[4] M. Loeb, "Wouldn't It Be Good to Work for the Good Guys?" *Fortune,* October 14, 1996, pp. 223–24.
[5] J. B. White and J. S. Lublin, "Some Companies Try to Rebuild Loyalty," *The Wall Street Journal,* September 26, 1996, pp. B1–B7.

Most organizations are not in the "job satisfaction business." Thus, it is sometimes difficult to make managers see the importance of understanding and enhancing employees' attitudes and feelings about their work. Employee dissatisfaction and stress have several important effects on the organization that cannot be overlooked, however, including their contributing to high health care costs, turnover, absenteeism, and workplace violence. Indeed, given the newly recognized link between employee retention and the retention of customers and investors, employee attitudes have to be considered critical even to managers who are only interested in financial profits. It is still true, however, that some managers who would not think of ignoring their physical equipment and resources give little thought to their human resources, and the consequences can be disastrous in terms of competing in the marketplace.

This chapter focuses on key emotions that affect people in the workplace. We will start by defining job satisfaction and job stress. Then, to underline the importance of job satisfaction, we will examine the consequences of dissatisfaction and stress, both in human terms and in terms of financial loss. Next, we will review the major sources of dissatisfaction and stress in work environments. We will end the chapter with a discussion of methods for managing dissatisfaction and stress in the workplace.

Defining Satisfaction and Stress

Satisfaction

Job satisfaction is "a pleasurable feeling that results from the perception that one's job fulfills or allows for the fulfillment of one's important job values."[1] There are three key components of our definition of job satisfaction: values, importance of values, and perception.

First, job satisfaction is a function of values. In a review of the topic, Edwin Locke defined values in terms of "what a person consciously or unconsciously desires to obtain."[2] Locke distinguished between values and needs, suggesting that needs are best thought of as "objective requirements" of the body that are essential for maintaining life, such as the needs for oxygen and for water. Values, on the other hand, are "subjective requirements" that exist in the person's mind.

The second component of job satisfaction is importance. People differ not only in the values they hold, but in the importance they place on those values, and these differences are critical in determining their degree of job satisfaction. One person may value job security above all else. Another may be most concerned with the opportunity to travel. Yet another person may be most interested in doing work that is fun or that helps others. Although the first person may be satisfied by long-term employment, the other two may find little satisfaction in a permanent employment relationship.

The last important component of our definition of job satisfaction is perception. Satisfaction is based on our perception of the present situation in terms of our values. Remember that perceptions may not be completely accurate reflections of objective reality. When they are not, we must look at the individual's perception of the situation—not the actual situation—to understand personal reactions.

Most attempts to measure worker satisfaction rely on self-reports. Some measures, like the Job Descriptive Index (JDI), emphasize aspects of work, such as pay, work itself, supervision, and coworkers. Other measures, like the Faces Scale, emphasize overall satisfaction. Table 5-1 shows several items from these two measures. The JDI and the Faces Scale are useful measures for the manager who wants to assess the satisfaction of employees. They are easy to use across the board because the JDI requires minimal reading skills and the Faces Scale requires none. The tests' reliability and validity have been supported by many studies.[3] Because there is a wealth of data on the use of these measures, it is easy to compare results in one firm with results in another.

Stress

Stress is an unpleasant emotional state that results when people are uncertain of their capacity to resolve a perceived challenge to an important value.[4] As in the case of satisfaction, it is easier to understand the nature of stress if this definition is broken into three key components.

Table 5-1 ■ Examples of Items Taken from Various Measures of Organizational Attitudes

Job Satisfaction From the Job Descriptive Index

PAY	WORK ITSELF	SUPERVISION	COWORKERS
Income adequate for personal expenses	Fascinating	Hard to please	Slow
Satisfactory pay levels	Boring	Asks my advice	Talk too much
Less than I deserve	Routine	Annoying	Unpleasant
Underpaid	Challenging	Quick tempered	Loyal
Income provides for luxuries	Endless	Stubborn	Smart

Job Satisfaction From the Faces Scale

Consider all aspects of your job. Circle the face which best describes your feelings about your job in general.

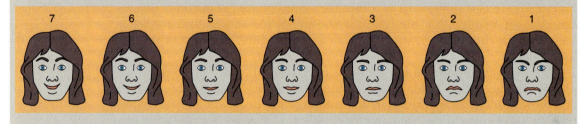

This female faces scale was created by R. B. Dunham and J. B. Herman and published in the *Journal of Applied Psychology* 60 (1975), pp. 629–31. Reprinted with permission of the publisher.

One component, perceived challenge, emphasizes that stress arises from the interaction between people and their perception of the environment (not necessarily reality). For example, unfounded rumors about a factory closing will create stress among employees, even if no real threat exists.

The second component of the definition, important value, is critical for the same reason it is critical to our definition of satisfaction. Unless a challenge threatens some important value, it will not cause stress. So, for example, the rumored plant closing may not create stress for a worker who is about to retire anyway.

Finally, the third component, uncertainty of resolution, emphasizes that the person interprets the situation in terms of the perceived probability of successfully coping with the challenge.[5] Obviously, if people perceive that they can cope easily with the challenge, no stress is experienced. You might be surprised to learn, however, that experienced stress is also low if the person is overwhelmed by the challenge and sees no possible chance that it can be resolved. Stress is actually highest when the perceived difficulty of the challenge closely matches the person's perceived capacity to meet the demand. The reason is that as the difficulty level and the ability level get closer and closer, the outcome becomes increasingly uncertain. It is this uncertainty about meeting the challenge that creates the stress, not the fear of a negative outcome.

The body's physiological reaction to this type of threat is a process that probably once had great survival value. When a threat is perceived, the body produces chemicals that cause blood pressure to rise and that divert blood from the skin and digestive organs to the muscles. Blood fats are then released to provide a

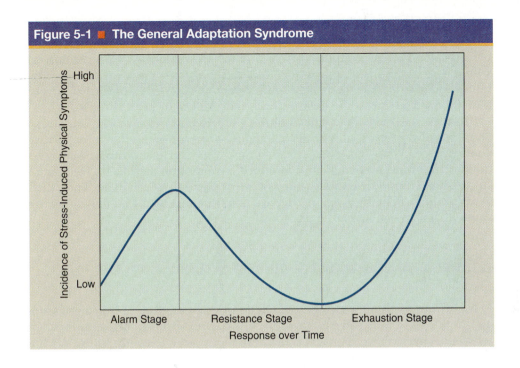

Figure 5-1 ■ The General Adaptation Syndrome

Incidence of Stress-Induced Physical Symptoms

High

Low

Alarm Stage · Resistance Stage · Exhaustion Stage

Response over Time

burst of energy and to enhance blood clotting in case of injury. When the threat facing the individual is prolonged over time, other changes begin that prepare the body for a long battle. The body begins to conserve resources by retaining water and salts. Extra gastric acid is produced to increase the efficiency of digestion in the absence of blood (which has been diverted away from internal organs).[6] Ages ago, these changes were probably adaptive, in the sense that they readied the person either to physically fight or to flee some threat.[7] Unfortunately, these same physiological changes occur today in response to threats regardless of whether the increased physical capacity they produce is adaptive. For example, workers who hold jobs with many demands over which they have little control are three times more likely to suffer from high blood pressure than other workers. However, the increased physical capacity purchased with high blood pressure is not going to help these workers cope with the demands they face.[8]

Hans Selye, a prominent physician and researcher, developed the theory of the **general adaptation syndrome** to explain the relationship between stress and such physical-physiological symptoms. According to Selye, the body's reaction to chronic stress occurs in three stages (see Figure 5-1).

In the alarm stage, the person identifies the threat. Whether this threat is physical (a threat of bodily injury) or psychological (the threat of losing one's job), the physiological changes described previously ensue. In the resistance stage, the person becomes resilient to the pressures created by the original threat. All the symptoms that occurred in the alarm stage disappear, even though the stressor itself is still in place. Resistance seems to be accomplished through increased levels of hormones secreted by the pituitary gland and the adrenal cortex.

If exposure to the threatening stressor continues, the person reaches the exhaustion stage. Pituitary gland and adrenal cortex activity slows down, and the person can no longer adapt to the continuing stress. Many of the physiological symptoms that originally appeared in the alarm stage now reappear. If stress continues unabated, individuals may suffer **burnout,** and this can lead to severe physical damage, including death via coronary failure or heart disease.[9]

Interestingly, a challenge need not be perceived as negative to create stress. Stress can also be associated with challenges or opportunities that have positive consequences. This kind of stress is sometimes referred to as **eustress.** Managers notified that they are being considered for a promotion are likely to feel more stressed than they did before learning of the opportunity. Even if they know that, at worst, they will be right where they are now, the possibility of failing to secure a potential gain can invoke stress.

Organizational Costs of Dissatisfaction and Stress

Our previous section focused on the effects of stress in terms of human physiology. In this section we will examine the costs of stress from an organizational effectiveness perspective. The fact is that, even if we were to coldly ignore the human costs, there are important financial reasons for monitoring and managing the stress levels of employees.

Health Care Costs

As we have seen, work-related stress can have a large impact on workers' health and well-being. A fact of current organizational life is that employing organizations bear much of the cost for employee health care.[10] Although wages have risen over the last 30 years, the spiraling costs of medical fees and hospital room and board have caused the cost of patient insurance to increase by three times as much as wages.[11]

Besides paying for general health insurance, employers are increasingly finding themselves held liable for specific incidents of stress-related illness. The Occupational Safety and Health Act (OSHA) of 1970 and many state laws hold employing organizations accountable "for all diseases arising out of and in the course of employment."[12] A study conducted at Boeing Company found that dissatisfied employees were more than twice as likely to file back-injury claims as were satisfied workers.[13] Back injury is the most common and expensive type of disability claim, costing the nation $30 billion annually. Similarly, research has shown a strong link between stress and mental disorders, and thus it was possible for an overworked advertising executive who was the victim of a nervous breakdown to successfully sue his employer.[14] Indeed, stress-induced mental disorders are the fastest-rising category of occupational disease, and the number of lawsuits involving organizations and allegedly stress-damaged employees is increasing at a rapid rate. In the U.S. federal government workforce, for example, claims for emotional illness rose by more than 500 percent between 1980 and 1995.[15]

Absenteeism and Turnover

Dissatisfaction and stress do more than create direct costs for organizations in terms of health care programs. They also are the source of indirect costs, most notably in the form of absenteeism and turnover. Dissatisfaction is one of the major reasons for absenteeism, a very costly organizational problem. Surveys estimate that a single unscheduled absence costs an average organization over $650 a day, and that absenteeism rates across the U.S. economy increased by close to 15 percent between 1992 and 1995.[16]

Dissatisfaction also triggers organizational turnover, and replacing workers who leave the organization voluntarily is also a costly undertaking.[17] One high-tech company, Hewlett-Packard, estimates that the cost of replacing one middle-level manager is $40,000.[18] Moreover, replacement costs are not the only issue. If people who leave an organization are better performers than those who stay, turnover lowers the productivity of the remaining workforce.[19] This kind of "negative employee flow" has the most noticeable effects in the case of complex jobs that take a long time to learn.[20] When people leave these jobs, companies lose the investment they have made in employee development. In the worst cases, disgruntled, experienced employees take jobs with competitors. A company's investment in employee development is not only lost, but actually winds up as a bonus for a competing firm that gains access to a lot of knowledge of the original firm's operations.

Low Organizational Commitment

Dissatisfaction is also a major cause of declining **organizational commitment.** Organizational commitment is the degree to which people identify with the organization that employs them. Commitment implies a willingness to put forth a great deal of effort on the organization's behalf and an intention to stay with the organization for a long time. Sample items from the most frequently used measure of organizational commitment are shown in Table 5-2.

The subject of organizational commitment has recently been attracting a great deal of attention.[21] Many employers fear that the downsizing policies they pursued in the 1980s may have killed company loyalty in the 1990s. For example,

Table 5-2 ■ Items Measuring Organizational Commitment	
I find that my values and this organization's values are very similar.	<u>Agree</u> or Disagree
I am proud to tell others that I work for this organization.	<u>Agree</u> or Disagree
I could just as well be working for a different organization as long as the type of work was similar.	Agree or <u>Disagree</u>
This organization really inspires the very best in me in terms of job performance.	<u>Agree</u> or Disagree
It would take very little change in my present circumstances to cause me to leave this organization.	Agree or <u>Disagree</u>
I am extremely glad that I chose this organization to work for over others I was considering at the time I joined.	<u>Agree</u> or Disagree
Note: Underlined responses indicate a committed employee.	

in 1989, during one two-month period, Chrysler, Kodak, Campbell's Soup, Sears, and RJR Nabisco let a total of 13,000 workers go. Between 1980 and 1989, General Motors fired over 150,000 workers. As chief economist for the American Federation of Labor and Congress of Industrial Organizations (AFL-CIO) Rudy Oswald notes, "Workers have a right to be upset and angry. They have been bought and sold and have seen their friends and relations fired and laid off in large numbers. There is little bond between employers and workers anymore."[22]

Evidence provided by surveys of U.S. workers bolsters this claim. When asked if employees today are more loyal or less loyal to their companies than they were 10 years ago, 63 percent of respondents said less loyal, and only 22 percent said more loyal. A full 50 percent of those responding said it was likely that they would change employers in the next five years. Thus, just when U.S. businesses are trying to inculcate a new sense of worker participation and involvement, many of their employees are looking to reduce their levels of commitment and dependency.

Workplace Violence

In the years since the mid-1980s, violence in the workplace has become a major organizational problem. Workplace homicide is the fastest-growing form of murder in the United States. This is especially a problem for women, for whom workplace homicide is the leading cause of death in the workplace.[23] Moreover, whereas homicide is the most extreme example, other forms of violence are also proliferating in the workplace. Research indicates that in any one year, 2 million employees are physically attacked, 6 million are threatened with physical attack, and 16 million are the target of some form of harassment. One of the most infamous employers in this regard is the U.S. Postal Service, for which, during one 18-month period, there were 500 recorded cases of employee violence directed toward a manager, and 200 cases of violence by a manager directed at an employee.[24]

Most violence that involves organizational insiders is triggered by extreme levels of dissatisfaction and stress being experienced by the attacker.[25] In order to come to grips with problems in this area, the U.S. Postal Service has launched an intense initiative to improve the agency's work environment. Managers and supervisors now go through a series of training sessions that deal with such issues as employee empowerment, conflict resolution, and positive reinforcement. The agency is also working with the unions to improve the grievance process and has launched a regular series of employee attitude surveys that allows the agency to measure and monitor employee satisfaction levels. Cross-functional intervention teams of employees and managers were created to step in and try to change the environment in regions where levels of dissatisfaction or stress seemed dangerously high.[26]

Sources of Dissatisfaction and Stress

Certain inherent features of organizations can cause dissatisfaction and stress. In this section, we will focus on the physical and social environment, the person, the task, and the role.

Rising From the Ashes

When one of the worst industrial fires in New England history destroyed the Malden Mills factory in Lawrence, Massachusetts, owner Aaron Feuerstein was faced with a number of options. Business analysts were divided about which he should pursue. Half felt he should pocket the insurance proceeds and walk away from an industry in which it was becoming increasingly difficult to make a profit because of low-wage offshore producers. Others felt he should remain in business, but take this opportunity to move the company out of Massachusetts and into a foreign country where wages would be lower. No one thought Feuerstein should rebuild the plant in Lawrence, and certainly no one would ever have suggested he give the 1,000 employees made jobless by the fire full pay for several months after the disaster. That is exactly what he did, however.

Although many at the time thought Feuerstein should be canonized as a saint or ridiculed as a fool, in reality the decision to rebuild in Lawrence was completely rational from an economic viewpoint and highly consistent with Malden Mills's long-term business strategy. Even in the late 1950s, when the Lawrence plant was first built, many felt that the local New England labor pool was already too expensive, and many were in the process of moving to southern states. As wages in southern states then rose over the years, textile jobs were exported to third-world nations. But as Feuerstein himself states, "Why would I go to Thailand to bring the cost lower when I might run the risk of losing the advantage I've got, which is superior quality?"[1]

Indeed, Malden Mills's business strategy has never focused on attempts to be the lowest-cost producer. Instead, the strategy has been focused on being the highest-quality producer, and this has been achieved through superior technology and skilled labor—capable, experienced textile designers, engineers, and manufacturing personnel that simply cannot be matched by overseas competitors. This strategy has been highly successful. For example, in the 1980s, when faced with a collapse in demand for artificial furs (the company's leading product at the time), the employees helped save the company by using their expertise in synthetic fibers, napping, and finishing to create a series of lightweight, thermal, resilient, wool-like fabrics under the brand names Polarfleece and Polartec. The quality of these fabrics, along with Malden Mills's ability to engineer to order, made the company a favorite among upscale retailers like Land's End, Eddie Bauer, L. L. Bean, and Patagonia.

Overall, in terms of business performance, Malden Mills more than tripled its revenues (in constant dollars) between 1985 and 1996, whereas the increase in revenues across all U.S. firms for the same time period was only 1 percent. Moreover, while most U.S. manufacturers were downsizing and laying off personnel, Malden Mills actually doubled employment levels. This expansion of the labor force occurred despite the introduction of labor-saving technologies. The trick to this feat is that Malden Mills keeps growing fast enough to give new jobs to the people technology displaces.[2] This is facilitated, of course, by having highly skilled and experienced personnel that are easily retrained, and this is enhanced by a 95 percent employee retention rate. At Malden Mills, the relationship between loyal employees and loyal customers is well understood, and once this is appreciated, it is also easy to understand the decision to rebuild in Lawrence.

[1]T. Teal, "Not a Fool, Not a Saint," *Fortune,* November 11, 1996, pp. 201–4.
[2]D. Anfuso, "Strategies to Stop the Layoffs," *Personnel Journal,* June 1996, pp. 65–69.

Physical and Social Environment

A wealth of documented evidence shows that some physical features of the workplace can stimulate negative emotional reactions in workers. For example, studies have shown that extremes in temperatures can affect job attitudes, as well as performance and decision making.[27] Research has also shown that there are different optimal lighting levels for different tasks, and perceived darkness has been found to correlate significantly with job dissatisfaction.[28] Moreover, research shows that physical features of the work environment such as cleanliness, outdoor settings, and health hazards play a very important role in determining the way people perceive their tasks.[29]

Recent research has also focused on some very subtle characteristics of the physical environment. Researchers have coined the term *sick-building syndrome* to refer to physical structures whose indoor air is contaminated by invisible pollutants. Sometimes problems like these get so bad that workers take matters into their own hands. In June 1988, 70 workers picketed the headquarters of the Environmental Protection Agency in Washington, charging that the air inside the building was so contaminated that it caused burning eyes, fatigue, dizziness, and breathing difficulty. In California, one worker won $600,000 in a lawsuit that claimed that formaldehyde fumes in a new office building had caused him to lose consciousness and suffer permanent brain damage.[30]

In terms of the social environment, supervisors and coworkers serve as the two primary sources of satisfaction or frustration for the employee. The employee may be satisfied with a supervisor or coworkers because they help the employee attain some valued outcome. Such an attitude is referred to as **functional attraction.** A person may also be attracted to others because of similarities in values, attitudes, or philosophy. This type of attraction is referred to as **entity attraction.** The fact that we can make such a distinction is made evident by cases in which people say that they like their manager as a supervisor but not as a person. The greatest degree of satisfaction with supervisors and coworkers will be found where both kinds of attraction exist.[31]

Social support is the active provision of sympathy and caring. Many researchers have suggested that social support from supervisors and coworkers can buffer employees from stress. The notion behind **buffering** is illustrated in Figure 5-2, where, as you can see, the presence of people who are supportive is shown to lower the incidence of stress-related symptoms under conditions of high stress. Evidence for this effect has come largely from research in medical contexts that shows that recovery from and rehabilitation after illness proceed better when the patient is surrounded by caring friends and family.[32]

The concept of buffering is somewhat controversial, however. For example, although one study showed that student nurses who received social support were much better able to perform their jobs in the face of stress than nurses who received little support,[33] a second study found just the opposite. Despite conflicting evidence regarding social support as a buffer, it is clear that social support is an independent predictor of stress and dissatisfaction. That is, holding the type of stressor constant, people receiving support are less stressed.

The behavior setting is where the physical and social aspects of work converge. Two important and interrelated aspects of the behavior setting are **social density** and **privacy.** Social density is a measure of crowding. It is calculated by dividing the number of people in a given area by the number of square feet in that area. Privacy, on the other hand, is the freedom to work without observation or unnecessary interruption. Research with clerical workers has shown that job satisfaction decreases as social density increases.[34] Social density is a partic-

Figure 5-2 ■ How Social Support May Buffer Stress

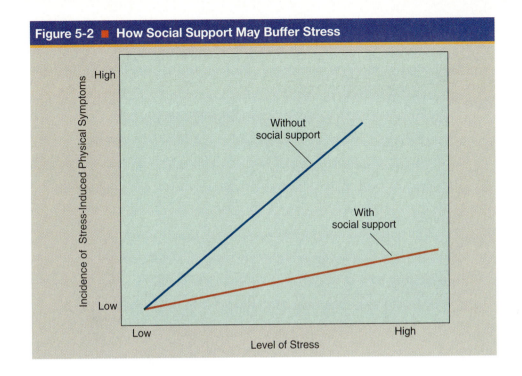

ular problem when it is compounded by lack of privacy (for example, when work stations are not enclosed by walls or partitions).[35] Research has uncovered the fact that turnover runs exceptionally high when workers are both crowded and deprived of privacy.[36] Privacy is also related to performance in jobs requiring concentration or creativity, and office designs are increasingly being engineered to meet the needs of workers in these types of jobs.[37]

Personal Dispositions

Because both stress and dissatisfaction ultimately reside within a person, it is not surprising that many who have studied these outcomes have focused on individual differences. The term **negative affectivity** describes a dispositional dimension of subjective distress that includes such unpleasant mood states as anger, contempt, disgust, guilt, fear, and nervousness.[38] Table 5-3 shows items that are used to assess individual differences on aspects of negative affectivity.

People who are generally high in negative affectivity tend to focus on both their own negative qualities and those of others. Such people are also likely to experience significantly higher levels of distress than are individuals who are low on this dimension. Being familiar with the concept of negative affectivity is important because this concept highlights the fact that some people bring stress and dissatisfaction with them to work.[39] They may be relatively dissatisfied regardless of what steps are taken by the organization or the manager.[40]

Table 5-3 ■ Items from a Measure of Negative Affectivity

This scale consists of a number of words that describe different feelings and emotions. Please indicate to what extent you have the following feelings _____.*

Read each item in the second and third columns and then write the number from the scale in the first column that corresponds to your answer in the space next to that word.

1 Very slightly or not at all	_____ interested	_____ irritable
	_____ distressed	_____ alert
	_____ excited	_____ ashamed
2 A little	_____ upset	_____ inspired
	_____ strong	_____ nervous
3 Moderately	_____ guilty	_____ determined
	_____ scared	_____ attentive
4 Quite a bit	_____ hostile	_____ jittery
	_____ enthusiastic	_____ active
5 Extremely	_____ proud	_____ afraid

*By filling in the blank with such instructions as "at this moment," "today," or "generally," we can use this scale to measure feeling states at particular times or over different time periods.

Although the origins of negative affectivity are not completely known, research on identical twins who had been separated at birth and reared apart suggests that these origins may have a genetic component.[41] One study examined 34 pairs of such twins and assessed general job satisfaction as well as satisfaction with intrinsic and extrinsic aspects of their jobs. Surprisingly, there was a significant correlation between twin pairs' ratings on general satisfaction and intrinsic satisfaction. Despite the fact that the twins had been reared apart and were working in different jobs, the work attitudes they expressed were very similar.

A second critical individual-difference variable is the Type A behavior pattern.[42] People with Type A personality are characterized as being aggressive and competitive, as setting high standards for themselves and others, and as putting themselves under constant time pressure.[43] Type Bs, on the other hand, are free of such feelings of urgency. The unrealistic expectations of the impatient, ambitious, and overly aggressive Type A person make this person particularly susceptible to dissatisfaction and stress. This susceptibility may also account for the Type A person's higher risk of developing coronary heart disease, which is twice that of the Type B person.

Stress can also originate from one-time events that occur outside work. Some events affect the stress levels that employees bring to the job. Table 5-4 presents a list of various life-change events that are sources of stress, with a scale value of 100 representing the most stressful event and 11 the least stressful. In one of the original studies using this scale, people with scores between 0 and 150 usually reported good health in the year that followed. People who scored over 300, however, had a 70 percent greater chance of contracting a major illness the following year.[44]

Table 5-4 ■ The Stress-Inducing Impact of Some Work-Related and Non-Work-Related Events

LIFE EVENT	SCALE VALUE	LIFE EVENT	SCALE VALUE
Death of spouse	100	Change in responsibilities at work	29
Divorce	73	Son or daughter leaving home	29
Marital separation	65	Trouble with in-laws	29
Jail term	63	Outstanding personal achievement	28
Death of a close family member	63	Spouse begins or stops work	26
Major personal injury or illness	53	Begin or end school	26
Marriage	50	Change in living conditions	25
Fired from work	47	Revision of personal habits	24
Marital reconciliation	45	Trouble with boss	23
Retirement	45	Change in work hours or conditions	20
Major change in health of family member	44	Change in schools	20
Pregnancy	40	Change in recreation	19
Sex difficulties	39	Change in church activities	19
Gain of a new family member	39	Change in social activities	18
Business readjustment	39	Change in sleeping habits	16
Change in financial state	38	Change in number of family get-togethers	15
Death of a close friend	37	Change in eating habits	15
Change to a different line of work	36	Vacation	13
Change in number of arguments with spouse	35	Christmas	12
Assuming a large mortgage	31	Minor violations of the law	11
Foreclosure of mortgage or loan	30		

Source: Reprinted with the publisher's permission from L. O. Ruch and T. H. Holmes, "Scaling of Life Changes: Comparison of Direct and Indirect Methods." *Journal of Psychosomatic Research* 14 (June 1971), p. 213.

Organizational Tasks

Although we cannot entirely discount the influence of dispositional traits and nonwork experiences, nothing predicts a person's level of workplace satisfaction or stress better than the nature of the work itself.[45] Table 5-5 shows a list of some of the most and least stressful jobs. Innumerable aspects of tasks have been linked to dissatisfaction and stress. In general, the key factors that determine satisfaction and stress are task complexity, physical strain, and task meaningfulness.

Task Complexity. Although in extreme cases tasks can get overly complex, in general, research shows a positive relationship between task complexity and satisfaction.[46] The boredom generated by simple, repetitive jobs that are not mentally challenging leads to frustration for many workers. This frustration in turn manifests itself in the form of dissatisfaction, stress, and, ultimately, tardiness,

Table 5-5 ■ Jobs Characterized as High and Low in Stress	
HIGH-STRESS JOBS	**LOW-STRESS JOBS**
Manager	Farm laborer
Supervisor	Craft worker
Nurse	Stock handler
Waitress	College professor
Air traffic controller	Heavy-equipment operator

absenteeism, and turnover.[47] In some cases, the boredom in these kinds of jobs can be alleviated by external interventions. For example, research suggests that for some simple jobs, allowing employees to use personal stereos increases both performance and satisfaction.[48]

Boredom created by lack of task complexity can also hinder performance on certain types of jobs. For example, airport security personnel, air traffic controllers, operators in nuclear power stations, medical technicians, and inspectors on production floors are all employed in a class of jobs that require vigilance. Workers on these jobs must continually monitor equipment and be prepared to respond to critical events. However, because such events are so rare, these jobs are exceedingly boring, and boredom results in poor concentration.[49] Ultimately, this inattention results in performance breakdowns of often serious dimensions. For example, in 1985, TWA flight 847 from Athens to Rome was hijacked and forced to land in Beirut, beginning an ordeal that lasted 17 days. The hijackers had been able to pass a dozen hand grenades and handguns through airport security. This performance lapse was attributed by experts to a breakdown in vigilance on the part of security personnel, who up until that day had never personally encountered a smuggling incident.

Interestingly, there is research indicating that for tasks requiring vigilance, what are often considered to be disabilities can actually enhance performance. Certain basic research has shown that blind subjects do better than sighted people on auditory vigilance tasks, and that deaf people do better than hearing subjects on visual vigilance tasks. Judging from these results, businesses might serve themselves well by hiring disabled individuals for jobs that entail particular types of vigilance.[50]

Physical Strain. Another important determinant of work satisfaction is how much physical exertion the job involves.[51] This factor is sometimes overlooked in the present age of technology, in which much of the physical strain associated with jobs has been removed by automation. Indeed, the very fact that technology continues to advance highlights the degree to which physical strain is universally considered to be an undesirable work characteristic. Many jobs, however, can still be characterized as physically demanding.

Task Meaningfulness. Finally, it is also important for the worker to believe that the work has value. The Peace Corps recruits applicants by describing its work as "the toughest job you'll ever love." Similar recruiting advertisements for

Catholic priests note that "the pay is low but the rewards are infinite." Indeed, there are over one million volunteer workers in the United States alone who perform their jobs almost exclusively because of the meaning attached to the work.

Organization Roles

The person and the social environment converge in the form of an organization role. The person's role in the organization can be defined as the total set of expectations of the person held by both the person and others who make up the social environment.[52] These expectations of behavior include all the formal aspects of the job as well as the informal expectations of coworkers, supervisors, clients, and customers. They have a great impact on how the person responds to the work. Three of the most heavily researched aspects of roles are **role ambiguity, role conflict,** and **role scope.**

Role Ambiguity. Role ambiguity is uncertainty, or lack of clarity, surrounding expectations about the person's role in the organization. It is an indication that the person in the role does not have enough information about what is expected. Role ambiguity can also stem from a lack of information about the rewards for performing well and the punishments for failing. For example, imagine that you were in a class in which an instructor assigned a term paper but neglected to tell you (1) what topics were pertinent, (2) how long the paper should be, (3) when it was due, (4) how it would be evaluated, and (5) how much it was worth toward the final course grade. Would you feel stress under these circumstances?

Role Conflict. Role conflict is the recognition of incompatible or contradictory demands that face the person who occupies a role. Role conflict can occur in many different forms. Intersender role conflict occurs when two or more people in the social environment convey mutually exclusive expectations. For example, a middle manager may find that upper management wants severe reprimands for worker absenteeism but that the workers themselves expect consideration of their needs and personal problems.

Intrasender role conflict occurs when one person in the social environment holds two competing expectations. A research assistant for a magazine editor may be asked to write a brief but detailed summary of a complex and lengthy article from another source. In trying to accomplish this task, the assistant may experience considerable distress over what to include and what to leave out of the summary.

A third form of role conflict is called interrole conflict. Most of us occupy multiple roles, and the expectations for our different roles may conflict. A parent who has a business trip scheduled during a daughter's first piano recital is likely to feel torn between the demands of two roles.

Role Scope. Role scope refers to the absolute number of expectations that exist for the person occupying a role. In role overload, too many expectations or demands are placed on the role occupant, and in role underload we have the opposite problem. Because researchers have focused primarily on jobs with high role scope, they have tended to look at the negative consequences of jobs that are too challenging. Jobs that are too high in role scope also demand a tremendous amount of time from incumbents.

When this time is demanded from hourly employees, it often creates conflict. For example, the United Food and Commercial Workers Union has used disputes over "off-the-clock" work at Food Lion stores to organize a class action suit against the chain. Because Food Lion's primary competitive advantage over other stores is in its low labor costs (roughly half the industry's average), this represents a direct threat to Food Lion's corporate strategy.[53]

Conclusion. The items shown in Table 5-6 are useful for assessing the problems that people experience with regard to their roles on the job. This is an important first step. Getting rid of the sources of stress or finding ways to cope with stress is the next task, and as we will see, it is often a challenging one.

Table 5-6 ■ Some Items That Measure Role Problems

Role Conflict

1. Having to work under conflicting guidelines
2. Having to work with two or more groups of people who expect different things from you
3. Having conflicting demands from people at work
4. Not knowing exactly what your responsibilities are
5. Having to do things you feel should be done differently
6. Being uncertain about how much authority you have

Role Ambiguity

7. Not knowing how you must perform to do your work well
8. Being uncertain whether you have divided your time properly between the work you have to do
9. Doing work where you can't always be certain what's expected of you
10. Doing work where it's hard to get all the necessary information, resources, or materials
11. Feeling that you don't have all the necessary skills to do your job well

Role Underload

12. Working on tasks that could be done by someone less qualified
13. Doing work that is repetitive or boring
14. Working on things you feel are not absolutely necessary or helpful

Role Overload

15. Working under continuous time pressure
16. Working hard to meet deadlines

Source: Reprinted with the publisher's permission from T. J. Newton and A. Keenan, "Role Stress Reexamined: An Investigation of Role Stress Predictors." *Organizational Behavior and Human Decision Processes* 40 (1987), p. 356.

Eliminating and Coping with Dissatisfaction and Stress

Because the costs associated with employee dissatisfaction and stress can be high, identifying these problems should be a major part of the job description of every manager. Once a problem is identified, interventions should be directed at the source of the stress. If it is impossible to eliminate the stressor for some reason, then the manager should at least help the employee manage and cope with stress. In the next three subsections of this chapter we will discuss how to identify and then eliminate or manage dissatisfaction and stress in the workplace.

Identifying Symptoms of Dissatisfaction and Stress

In some cases, employees themselves report problems of dissatisfaction or stress. Often, however, employees are afraid to admit that they cannot overcome some problem associated with their work. Other workers dissatisfied with some facet of their job may not speak out because they want to avoid sounding like chronic complainers. Finally, the attitudes of some workers may have gotten so bad that they see reporting dissatisfaction as a waste of time. For these reasons, it is critical for managers to monitor the kinds of physiological, cognitive, and behavioral responses we discussed earlier for clues to underlying levels of dissatisfaction and stress.

Any firm that is serious about enhancing employee attitudes needs to conduct satisfaction surveys on a regular basis in order to monitor trends and changes in this area. In any case, a systematic, ongoing program of survey research should be a prominent part of any human resource strategy for a number of reasons. First, it allows the company to monitor trends over time. Second, it provides a means of empirically assessing the impact of changes in policy (e.g., introduction of a new performance appraisal system) or personnel (e.g., introduction of a new CEO) on worker attitudes. Third, when these surveys incorporate standardized scales like the JDI discussed earlier, they often allow the company to compare itself with others in the same industry along these dimensions.

Conducting an organizational opinion survey is not something that should be taken lightly, however, because such surveys often raise expectations. It is critical that the organization conducting the survey be ready to act on the results. For example, at Doctors Hospital in Manteca, California, a survey of employee opinions revealed dissatisfaction (defined as an "unfavorable" rating by at least 35 percent of the employees) in several areas. When these results were fed back to employees, each problem area description was accompanied by a corresponding action plan that allowed people to see how the organization intended to address the problem. And, what is most important, the hospital followed through on these intentions. For example, in the area of career development, the survey indicated that even though the hospital reimbursed 100 percent of employee expenses for tuition, because it did so at the end of the semester, the inability to have the money up front had prevented many from using this benefit. Now, tuition is provided up front, along with loans to help defray other non-tuition costs associated with taking a class (e.g., child care expenses). Thus, what was once a source of dissatisfaction for employees is now a plus, and this program helped win Doctors Hospital the 1994 Society of Human Resources Creative Application Award.[54]

While a firm is in the process of using employee surveys to monitor employee satisfaction, research shows that in the case of service organizations, it is also a good idea to use employee surveys to monitor employees' perception of customer satisfaction. Frontline employees of service organizations have a great deal of information on what makes customers satisfied or dissatisfied, and organizations that tap this resource consistently outperform other firms when it comes to customer satisfaction ratings.[55]

In addition to closely observing employees and conducting surveys, it is also a good idea for managers to be aware of well-known sources of dissatisfaction and stress. As we will see in the next subsection, many of these sources have been documented empirically by organizational researchers.

Given the huge direct and indirect costs associated with dissatisfaction and stress in organizations, it is not surprising that a great many ways of dealing with stress have been proposed. The specific approaches we will discuss are organized according to whether they attempt to eliminate stress and dissatisfaction at the source or instead deal with the physiological and behavioral symptoms associated with stress. Clearly, interventions aimed at the source are preferable to those aimed only at symptoms. Because it is not always possible to eliminate stressors, however, research on symptom-based approaches is valuable.

Changing the Source of Dissatisfaction and Stress

Because the nature of the task has such a strong influence on dissatisfaction and stress, some of the most effective means of reducing negative reactions to work focus on the task. Job enrichment methods include many techniques designed to add complexity and meaning to a person's work. As the term *enrichment* suggests, this kind of intervention is directed at jobs that are boring because of their repetitive nature or low scope. Although enrichment is not universally successful in bringing about improved employee reactions to work, it can be very useful. We will have more to say about this topic in Chapter 6.

Role problems rank right behind job problems in creating distress. The role analysis technique is designed to clarify role expectations for a jobholder by improving communication between the person and supervisors, coworkers, subordinates, and perhaps even customers. In role analysis, both jobholder and those who work with the jobholder are asked to write down their expectations. These people are then gathered together to review their lists. All expectations are written down so that ambiguities can be removed and conflicts identified. Where there are conflicts, the group as a whole tries to decide how these conflicts should be resolved. When this kind of analysis is done throughout an organization, instances of overload and underload may be discovered, and role requirements may be traded off, so that more balanced roles can be developed.

Skills training is a means of trying to help the employee change what is dissatisfying or stressful. For example, training in time management and goal prioritization has been successful in reducing managers' physiological stress symptoms such as rapid pulse rate and high blood pressure.[56] Subjects in one study first decided on their most important work values. They were then taught how to pinpoint goals, how to identify roadblocks to successful goal accomplishment, and how to seek the collaboration of coworkers in achieving these goals.

Other research points to the importance of good job skills in overcoming stress. The greater job incumbents' ability to predict, understand, and control events occurring on the job, the less stress they experience. Moreover, being able to understand and control these events weakens the effect of perceived stress on job satisfaction.[57] Results from studies in this area are being applied around the globe. For example, Jerry Lee, managing director of Texas Instruments' Malaysian operation, notes, "The key to employee loyalty lies not in offering higher wages or better amenities, but in giving workers more control over their jobs."[58]

A person's ability to handle dissatisfying or stressful work experiences is also enhanced when there is an opportunity to air problems and grievances.[59] The formal opportunity to complain to the organization about one's work situation has been referred to as **voice.**[60] Having voice provides employees with an active, constructive outlet for their work frustrations.[61] Research with nurses shows that the provision of such voice mechanisms as grievance procedures, employee attitude surveys, and question-and-answer sessions between employees and management leads to better worker attitudes and less turnover.[62]

One step beyond voicing opinions is the chance to take action or make decisions based on one's opinions. Participation in decision making (PDM) gives workers the opportunity to provide input into important organizational decisions that involve their work. In a field experiment that randomly assigned subjects to PDM and non-PDM conditions, Susan Jackson found that PDM in the form of bimonthly information-sharing meetings among nursing staff and nursing supervisors resulted in reduced role conflict and ambiguity. In turn, there was less emotional stress and absenteeism, and fewer nurses resigned. Figure 5-3 depicts the process suggested by this study.

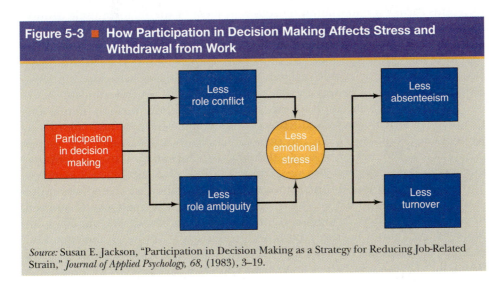

Figure 5-3 ■ How Participation in Decision Making Affects Stress and Withdrawal from Work

Participation in decision making

Less role conflict

Less role ambiguity

Less emotional stress

Less absenteeism

Less turnover

Source: Susan E. Jackson, "Participation in Decision Making as a Strategy for Reducing Job-Related Strain," *Journal of Applied Psychology, 68,* (1983), 3–19.

Managing Symptoms of Dissatisfaction and Stress

In some situations, neither roles, tasks, nor individual capacities can be altered sufficiently to reduce dissatisfaction and stress. Here, interventions have to be aimed at the symptoms of stress. Although not as desirable as eliminating the stressors themselves, eliminating the symptoms is better than nothing. Some interventions that fall into this category focus exclusively on physiological reactions to stress.

Physical conditioning, particularly in the form of aerobic exercise, helps make a person more resistant to the physiological changes, such as high blood pressure, that accompany stress reactions. CTI, a Knoxville-based manufacturer of medical equipment, and Southwestern Bell are but two of the many companies that hold aerobic exercise classes for their employees. Other firms organize group hikes and cross-country ski trips. Tenneco, a diversified manufacturing company, even provides its employees, free of charge, with a gym that occupies 25,000 square feet. Here employees can find basketball and racquetball courts, a workout area, a glass-enclosed running track with piped-in music, and $200,000 worth of exercise and body-building equipment. Tenneco chairman James Ketelsen feels that the $3 million it takes to run the center is well worth it. He comments, "Our testing process discovered problems that could have been fatal. I'm sure we've saved some lives. How do you put a value on that?"[63]

Research strongly supports the fact that this kind of program can be successful in reducing stress-related symptoms.[64] Other programs not only focus on encouraging positive behaviors like exercise but also aim at discouraging negative behaviors that make the person less resistant to stress, like smoking or overeating.[65] Research shows that both of these factors are significantly associated with sickness and absenteeism and increase the impact of existing stressors on absenteeism and stress reactions.[66]

Another approach to treating stress symptoms is to employ relaxation techniques. When a person is under a severe amount of stress (as when preparing for a fight-or-flight response), many of the body's muscles tighten. Relaxation programs focus on eliminating tenseness in most of the major muscle groups, including those in the hand, forearm, back, neck, face, foot, and ankle. Relaxing all these major muscle groups lowers blood pressure and pulse rate and reduces other physiological stress manifestations. One experiment that dealt with relaxation therapy in a social service agency found that subjects who were randomly assigned to such therapy reported less anxiety than did control subjects.[67]

Some forms of relaxation therapy, such as meditation, include mental concentration as well as tension reduction. In one popular form of meditation, transcendental meditation (TM), the person sits comfortably, relaxing all muscle groups, concentrating on a single thought, and repeating a special sound (a mantra) for 20 minutes. George Bennett, CEO of Symetrix, a Lexington, Massachusetts, consulting firm, signed up his organization for a meditation program when he noticed that many of his employees seemed overly stressed. According to Bennett, "There's no question that employees who meditate are more relaxed, and some are even more productive."[68] Although anecdotal evidence like this should be taken lightly, there is evidence from organizational research that TM can reduce heart rate, blood pressure, and oxygen consumption.[69]

It was once thought that people had no voluntary control over physiological responses. **Biofeedback** machines that allow people to monitor their own physiological reactions have changed all that.[70] Indeed, with the right feedback, some people can learn to control brain waves, muscle tension, heart rate, and even body temperature. Biofeedback training teaches people to recognize when these physiological reactions are taking place, as well as how to lower the levels of these symptoms when under stress. A biofeedback program set up by Equitable Life Insurance, for example, led to an 80 percent reduction in visits to the company's health center for stress-related problems.[71]

Because, as we have seen, a supportive environment can reduce stress, many organizations encourage team sports both at work and in off-hours. The hope behind softball and bowling leagues is that group cohesiveness and support for individual group members will be increased through socializing and team effort. Although management certainly cannot ensure that every stressed employee will develop friends hips, it can make it easier for employees to interact.

Other means of coping with stress that cannot be eliminated at the source focus on allowing the person time away from the stressful environment. Although a person may not feel capable of handling the stress or putting up with the dissatisfying aspects of a particular job indefinitely, it is often possible for that person to do so temporarily. Many employers use **job rotation,** that is, moving workers from one job to another temporarily, in an effort to give workers a break from stress. Air traffic controllers at Chicago's O'Hare airport are restricted to 90-minute work periods for just this reason.

Job rotation in more conventional organizations can do even more than simply spread out the stressful aspects of a particular job. It can also increase the complexity of the work and provide valuable cross-training in jobs, so that any one person eventually comes to understand many different tasks. For example, at Rhino Foods, a producer of frozen desserts, employees spend up to five hours a week in positions that have no relationship to their own job description. This allows employees to familiarize themselves with a variety of functions within the company, and helps develop a more knowledgeable and flexible workforce.[72]

Finally, if the negative aspects of a job cannot be changed, managers should be up front with prospective jobholders about the nature of the work. Many companies are hesitant to admit to the undesirable aspects of a job when trying to recruit workers, for fear that nobody will take the job. Fooling a person into taking a job that the person would not otherwise be interested in, however, is not good for the company or the person. The ultimate result is increased turnover. Realistic job previews (RJPs) lower expectations and are likely to attract workers whose values will more closely match the actual job situation. RJPs are especially important for applicants who lack work experience.[73] When people who have been prepared by the use of RJPs do go on the job and begin to experience its negative aspects, they are more likely to downplay them, noting, "I knew the job was like this when I took it." Although RJPs have not been 100 percent effective, there is some evidence that they can reduce subsequent turnover (especially through audiovisual presentations).[74]

SUMMARY

Among the great variety of attitudes and emotions generated in the workplace, the most important are job satisfaction and occupational stress. Job satisfaction is a pleasurable emotional state resulting from the perception that a job helps one attain valued outcomes. Occupational stress, an unpleasant emotional state, comes from perceived uncertainty about one's ability to meet the demands of a job. There are multiple responses to stress, including physiological responses, behavioral responses, and cognitive reactions. These stress reactions have important consequences for organizations, particularly in terms of the financial costs of health care, absenteeism, turnover, low organizational commitment, and workplace violence. There are several sources from which dissatisfaction and stress originate: the physical and social environment, the person, the organizational task, and the organization role. A number of different intervention programs are aimed at eliminating the stress-inducing event, enabling the person to avoid or cope with the stressor, or, failing these efforts, eliminating the symptoms of stress. Some of the intervention techniques are job enrichment, skills training, biofeedback, job rotation, and the use of realistic job previews.

Review Questions

1. Recall from Chapter 1 some of the many roles a manager must play. Which of these roles do you think create the most stress, and which are probably the least stressful? From which role do you think most managers derive their greatest satisfaction? Compare your answers to these three questions and speculate on the relationship between satisfaction and stress for managerial employees.
2. Organizational turnover is generally considered to be a negative outcome, and many organizations spend a great deal of time, money, and effort on trying to reduce turnover. Can you think of any situations in which an increase in turnover might be just what an organization needs? What are some steps organizations might take to enhance functional types of turnover? Do you think mass firings of ineffective workers are likely to enhance overall organization effectiveness, or do you think that they would have deleterious effects on the firm's ability to recruit the most desirable applicants?
3. Characteristics like negative affectivity and the Type A behavior pattern are associated with aversive emotional states including dissatisfaction and stress. Do you think these tendencies are learned or genetically determined? If these tendencies are learned, then from a reinforcement theory perspective, what reinforcers might sustain the behaviors associated with them?
4. If off-the-job stress begins to spill over and create on-the-job problems, what do you think are the rights and responsibilities of managers in helping employees overcome these problems? If employees are engaged in unhealthy off-the-job behavior patterns such as smoking, overeating, or alcohol abuse, what are the rights

and responsibilities of the employer in attempting to change these behaviors? Is this an invasion of privacy? Or is it simply a prudent step taken to protect the firm's financial well-being?

Implementation Guide

In evaluating an organization to determine where and when dissatisfaction and stress may be problems and how to go about resolving these problems, the following diagnostic questions may prove a useful start.

1. Why might the organization be concerned about dissatisfaction and stress? What costly health-related or behavioral problems linked to stress are evident?
2. Are the values that the organization expects its members to uphold consistent with the members' own values and needs?
3. Are any aspects of the physical environment (e.g., noise, darkness, and hazards) causing stress among organizational members?
4. Are any aspects of the social environment (e.g., hostile coworkers or supervisors) causing stress among organizational members?
5. Are any aspects of the behavioral settings (such as crowding or lack of privacy) causing stress among organizational members?
6. Do certain characteristics of organization members (e.g., negative affectivity or the Type A behavior pattern) contribute to stress problems at work?
7. How can the jobs that need to be performed by organization members be described in terms of complexity, meaning, and physical demand? How might characteristics of the jobs relate to dissatisfaction and stress?
8. How clear are the role expectations that are being sent to various organization members? How might the ambiguity of some expectations relate to stress?
9. Is the organization most interested in eliminating the sources of stress, or is it willing (or forced) to deal only with stress-related symptoms?
10. How can overly simple jobs in the organization be enriched? How can jobs characterized by too many conflicting role requirements be simplified?
11. Do employees have outlets for registering complaints? Do they have any influence in decisions that affect how they conduct their jobs?
12. What other types of programs would be most useful in handling stress-related physiological symptoms that arise in this organization?

ENDNOTES

1. E. A. Locke, "The Nature and Causes of Job Dissatisfaction," in *Handbook of Industrial-Organizational Psychology*, M. D. Dunnette, ed. (Chicago: Rand McNally, 1976), pp. 901–69.
2. Ibid.
3. S. M. Johnson, P. C. Smith, and C. M. Tucker, "Response Format of the Job Descriptive Index: Assessment of Reliability and Validity by the Multitrait-Multimethod Matrix," *Journal of Applied Psychology* 67 (1982), pp. 550–5.
4. J. E. McGrath, "Stress in Organizations," in *Handbook of Industrial and Organizational Psychology*, M. D. Dunnette, ed. (Chicago: Rand McNally, 1977), pp. 1310–67.

5. J. R. Edwards, "An Examination of Competing Versions of the Person-Environment Fit Approach to Stress," *Academy of Management Journal* 39 (1996), pp. 292–339.

6. D. Foley, "How to Avoid 'The Perfect Day for a Heart Attack,' " *Prevention,* September 6, 1986, pp. 54–58.

7. D. H. Funkenstein, "The Physiology of Fear and Anger," *Scientific American* 192 (1955), pp. 74–80.

8. R. Winslow, "Study Uncovers New Evidence Linking Strain on the Job and High Blood Pressure," *The Wall Street Journal,* April 11, 1990, p. B18.

9. H. J. Freudenberger, "Staff Burnout," *Journal of Social Issues* 30 (1974), pp. 159–64.

10. U.S. Department of Labor, *Employee Benefits 1985* (Washington, DC: U.S. Chamber of Commerce, 1984).

11. D. W. Belcher and T. J. Atchison, *Compensation Administration* (Englewood Cliffs, NJ: Prentice Hall, 1987), p. 57.

12. *Analysis of Workers' Compensation Laws* (Washington, DC: U.S. Chamber of Commerce, 1985), p. 3.

13. O. Port, "Does Job Satisfaction Prevent Back Injuries?" *Business Week,* April 1, 1991, p. 82.

14. R. Poe, "Does Your Job Make You Sick?" *Across the Board* 9 (1987), pp. 34–43.

15. N. Seppa, "Growing Toll of Job Stress Hikes Compensation Claims," *APA Monitor,* October 1996, pp. 13–14.

16. B. Jones, "Absenteeism on the Rise for the Fourth Straight Year," *Personnel Journal,* December 1995, p. 21.

17. T. W. Lee, T. R. Mitchell, L. Wise, and S. Fireman, "An Unfolding Model of Voluntary Employee Turnover," *Academy of Management Journal* 39 (1996), pp. 5–36.

18. W. R. Wilhelm, "Helping Workers to Self-Manage Their Careers," *Personnel Administrator* 28 (1983), pp. 83–89.

19. D. A. Harrison, M. Virick, and S. William, "Working without a Net: Time, Performance, and Turnover under Maximally Contingent Rewards," *Journal of Applied Psychology* 81 (1996), pp. 331–45.

20. J. W. Boudreau and C. J. Berger, "Decision-Theoretic Utility Analysis Applied to Employee Separations and Acquisitions," *Journal of Applied Psychology* 70 (1985), pp. 581–619.

21. J. J. Laabs, "Employee Commitment: New Employment Rules," *Personnel Journal,* August 1996, pp. 58–68.

22. Ibid.

23. A. Q. Nomani, "Women Likelier to Face Violence in the Workplace," *The Wall Street Journal,* October 31, 1995, p. A16.

24. O. M. Kurland, "Workplace Violence," *Risk Management* 40 (1993), pp. 76–77.

25. A. M. O'Leary-Kelly, R. W. Griffen, and D. J. Glew, "Organization-Motivated Aggression: A Research Framework," *Academy of Management Review* 21 (1996), pp. 225–53.

26. D. Anfuso, "The Postal Service Delivers a Violence Prevention Program," *Personnel Journal,* October 1994, p. 69.

27. E. Van de Vliert and N. W. Van Yperen, "Why Cross-Material Differences in Role Overload? Don't Overlook Ambient Temperature!" *Academy of Management Journal* 39 (1996), pp. 986–1004.

28. G. B. Meese, M. I. Lewis, D. P. Wyon, and R. Kok, "A Laboratory Study of the Effects of Thermal Stress on the Performance of Factory Workers," *Ergonomics* 27 (1982), pp. 19–43; H. D. Ellis, "The Effect of Cold on Performance of Serial Choice Reaction Time and Various Discrete Tasks," *Human Factors* 24 (1982), pp. 589–98; D. G. Hayward, "Psychological Factors in the Use of Light and Lighting in Buildings," in *Designing for Human Behavior: Architecture and the Behavioral Sciences,* J. Lang, C. Burnette, W. Moleski, and D. Vachon, eds. (Stroudsburg, PA: Dowden, Hutchinson, and Ross, 1974), pp. 120–29; and G. R. Oldham and N. L. Rotchford, "Relationships between Office Characteristics and Employee Reactions: A Study of the Physical Environment," *Administrative Science Quarterly* 28 (1983), pp. 542–56.

29. E. F. Stone and H. G. Gueutal, "An Empirical Derivation of the Dimensions along Which Characteristics of Jobs Are Perceived," *Academy of Management Journal* 28 (1985), pp. 376–96.

30. A. Toufexis, "Got That Stuffy, Run-Down Feeling," *Time,* June 6, 1988, p. 36.

31. B. M. Meglino, E. C. Ravlin, and C. L. Adkins, "A Work Values Approach to Corporate Culture: A Field Test of the Value Congruence Process and Its Relationship to Individual Outcomes," *Journal of Applied Psychology* 74 (1989), pp. 424–33.

32. R. E. Mitchell, A. G. Billings, and R. M. Moos, "Social Support and Well-Being: Implications for Prevention Programs," *Journal of Primary Prevention* (1982), pp. 77–98.

33. K. R. Parkes, "Occupational Stress among Student Nurses: A Natural Experiment," *Journal of Applied Psychology* 67 (1982), pp. 784–96.

34. R. I. Sutton and A. Rafaeli, "Characteristics of Work Stations as Potential Occupational Stressors," *Academy of Management Journal* 30 (1987), pp. 260–76.

35. S. Greengard, "Privacy: Entitlement or Illusion?" *Personnel Journal,* May 1996, pp. 74–88.

36. G. R. Oldham and Y. Fried, "Employee Reactions to Workspace Characteristics," *Journal of Applied Psychology* 72 (1987), pp. 75–84.

37. R. B. Lieber, "Cool Offices," *Personnel Journal,* December 1996, pp. 204–10.

38. D. Watson, L. A. Clark, and A. Tellegen, "Development and Validation of Brief Measures of Positive and Negative Affect: The PANAS Scales," *Journal of Personality and Social Psychology* 54 (1988), pp. 1063–70.

39. M. J. Burke, A. P. Brief, and J. M. George, "The Role of Negative Affectivity in Understanding Relations between Self-Reports of Stressors and Strains: A Comment on the Applied Psychological Literature," *Journal of Applied Psychology* 78 (1993), pp. 402–12.

40. B. M. Staw, N. E. Bell, and J. A. Clausen, "The Dispositional Approach to Job Attitudes: A Lifetime Longitudinal Test," *Administrative Science Quarterly* 31 (1986), pp. 56–78.

41. R. D. Arvey, T. J. Bouchard, N. L. Segal, and L. M. Abraham, "Job Satisfaction: Genetic and Environmental Components," *Journal of Applied Psychology* 74 (1989), pp. 187–93.

42. J. H. Howard, D. A. Cunningham, and P. A. Rechnitzer, "Health Patterns Associated with Type A Behavior: A Managerial Population," *Journal of Human Stress* 2 (1976), pp. 24–31.

43. K. A. Mathews, "Psychological Perspectives on the Type A Behavior Pattern," *Psychological Bulletin* 91 (1982), pp. 293–323.

44. T. H. Holmes and R. H. Rahe, "The Social Readjustment Rating Scale," *Journal of Psychosomatic Research* 40 (1967), pp. 213–18; D. V. Perkins, "The Assessment of Stress Using Life Change Scales," in *Handbook of Stress,* L. Goldberger and S. Breznitz, eds. (New York: Free Press, 1982), pp. 320–31; and S. C. Kobasa, "Stressful Life Events, Personality, and Health: An Inquiry into Hardiness," *Journal of Personality and Social Psychology* 35 (1983), pp. 1–11.

45. B. A. Gerhart, "How Important Are Dispositional Factors as Determinants of Job Satisfaction? Implications for Job Design and Other Personnel Programs," *Journal of Applied Psychology* 72 (1987), pp. 493–502.

46. M. A. Campion and C. L. McClelland, "Follow-Up and Extension of the Interdisciplinary Costs and Benefits of Enlarged Jobs," *Journal of Applied Psychology* 78 (1993), pp. 339–51.

47. L. W. Porter and R. M. Steers, "Organizational, Work and Personal Factors in Employee Absenteeism and Turnover," *Psychological Bulletin* 80 (1973), pp. 151–76.

48. G. R. Oldham, A. Cummings, L. J. Mischel, J. M. Schmidtke, and J. Zhou, "Listen While You Work? Quasi-experimental Relations between Personal-Stereo Headset Use and Employee Work Responses," *Journal of Applied Psychology* 80 (1995), pp. 547–64.

49. J. R. Hollenbeck, D. R. Ilgen, D. B. Tuttle, and D. J. Sego, "Team Performance in Monitoring Tasks: An Examination of Decision Errors in Contexts Requiring Sustained Attention," *Journal of Applied Psychology* 80 (1995), pp. 685–96.

50. J. S. Warm and W. N. Dember, "Awake at the Switch," *Psychology Today,* April 1986, pp. 46–50.

51. Locke, "The Nature and Causes."

52. S. E. Jackson and R. S. Schuler, "A Meta-Analysis and Conceptual Critique of Research on Role Ambiguity and Role Conflict in Work Settings," *Organizational Behavior and Human Decision Processes* 36 (1987), pp. 16–78.

53. W. Konrad, "Much More Than Just a Day's Work—For Just a Day's Pay?" *Business Week,* September 23, 1991, p. 40.

54. T. Gray, "A Hospital Takes Action on Employee Survey," *Personnel Journal,* March 1995, pp. 74–77.

55. B. Schneider, S. D. Ashworth, A. C. Higgs, and L. Carr, "Design, Validity and Use of Strategically-Focused Employee Attitude Surveys," *Personnel Psychology* 49 (1996), pp. 695–705.

56. N. S. Bruning and D. R. Frew, "Effects of Exercise, Relaxation, and Management Skills Training on Physiological Stress Indicators: A Field Experiment," *Journal of Applied Psychology* 72 (1987), pp. 515–21.

57. L. E. Tetrick and J. M. LaRocco, "Understanding, Prediction and Control as Moderators of the Relationship between Perceived Stress, Satisfaction and Psychological Well-Being," *Journal of Applied Psychology* 72 (1987), pp. 538–48.

58. K. Park, "A New Frontier: U.S. Electronics Firm Expands in Asia," *Far Eastern Economic Review* 41 (1992), pp. 75–93.

59. L. E. Parker, "When to Fix It and When to Leave: Relationships among Perceived Control, Self-Efficacy, Dissent, and Exit," *Journal of Applied Psychology* 78 (1993), pp. 949–59.

60. A. O. Hirshman, *Exit, Voice, and Loyalty* (Cambridge, MA: Harvard University Press, 1970), p. 51.

61. D. Farrell, "Exit, Voice, Loyalty and Neglect as Responses to Job Dissatisfaction: A Multidimensional Scaling Study," *Academy of Management Journal* 26 (1983), pp. 596–607.

62. D. G. Spencer, "Employee Voice and Employee Retention," *Academy of Management Journal* 29 (1986), pp. 488–502.

63. M. Freudenheim, "Assessing the Corporate Fitness Craze," *New York Times,* March 18, 1990, p. D1.

64. Bruning and Frew, "Effects of Exercise."

65. K. D. Brownell, A. J. Stunkard, and P. E. McKeon, "Weight Reduction at the Worksite: A Promise Partially Fulfilled," *American Journal of Psychiatry* 142 (1985), pp. 47–52.

66. K. R. Parkes, "Relative Weight, Smoking and Mental Health as Predictors of Sickness and Absence from Work," *Journal of Applied Psychology* 72 (1987), pp. 275–86.

67. D. C. Ganster, B. T. Mayes, W. F. Sime, and G. D. Tharp, "Managing Organizational Stress: A Field Experiment," *Journal of Applied Psychology* 67 (1982), pp. 533–42.

68. A. Dunkin, "Meditation, the New Balm for Corporate Stress," *Business Week,* May 10, 1993, pp. 86–87.

69. D. Kuna, "Meditation at Work," *Vocational Guidance Quarterly* 12 (1975), pp. 342–46.

70. N. E. Miller, "Learning of Visceral and Glandular Responses," *Science* 163 (1969), pp. 1271–78.

71. J. S. Manuso, "Executive Stress Management," *Personnel Administrator* 24 (1979), pp. 23–26.

72. G. Flynn, "Rhino Foods Is a Workplace of the Future Now," *Personnel Journal,* January 1996, p. 64.

73. B. M. Meglino, A. S. DeNisi, and E. C. Ravlin, "Effects of Previous Job Exposure and Subsequent Job Status on the Functioning of a Realistic Job Preview," *Personnel Psychology* 46 (1993), pp. 803–22.

74. S. L. Premack and J. P. Wanous, "A Meta-Analysis of Realistic Job Preview Experiments," *Journal of Applied Psychology* 70 (1985), pp. 706–19.

Chapter Six

Efficiency, Empowerment, and Quality in Work Design

> **I** stand in one spot, about a two- or three-feet area, all night. . . . We do about thirty-two [welding] jobs per car, per unit. Forty-eight units an hour, eight hours a day. Thirty-two times forty-eight times eight. Figure it out. That's how many times I push that button. . . . You dream, you think of things you've done. I drift back continuously to when I was a kid and what me and my brothers did. . . . You're nothing more than a machine. They give better care to that machine than they will to you. They'll have more respect, give more attention to that machine. . . . Somehow you get the feeling that the machine is better than you are.[1]
>
> The other day when I was proofreading [insurance policy] endorsements I noticed some guy had insured his store for $165,000 against vandalism and $5,000 against fire. Now that's bound to be a mistake. They probably got it backwards. . . . I was just about to show it to [my supervisor] when I figured, wait a minute! I'm not supposed to read these forms. I'm just supposed to check one column against another. And they do check. . . . They don't explain this stuff to me. I'm not supposed to understand it. I'm just supposed to check one column against the other. . . . If they're gonna give me a robot's job to do, I'm gonna do it like a robot! Anyway, it just lowers my production record to get up and point out someone else's error.[2]

---

[1] S. Terkel, *Working* (New York: Avon Books, 1972), pp. 221–23.
[2] B. Garson, *All the Livelong Day: The Meaning and Demeaning of Routine Work* (New York: Penguin Books, 1977), p. 171.

In every organization, difficult work is broken into smaller tasks. This **division of labor** enables organized groups of people to accomplish tasks that would be beyond their physical or mental capacities as individuals. Few people can build a car by themselves, but companies like Ford, Chrysler, and General Motors turn out thousands of cars each year by dividing car building into simple assembly line jobs. Likewise, insurance policies cannot be underwritten by individuals working alone, but companies like Allstate, State Farm, and Prudential succeed by breaking down policy preparation into a number of less complicated clerical tasks.

Entered into mindfully, the division of labor can lead to the creation of jobs that contribute to satisfaction, success, and significant competitive advantage. Sometimes, however, it leads to the creation of jobs that are monotonous and unchallenging, like the welding and proofreading jobs just described. Why do managers intentionally design jobs that are so unappealing? What do they expect to gain by simplifying work so drastically? What can be done to counteract the negative effects of oversimplified work—effects like the welder's detached daydreaming or the proofreader's alienation? Can oversimplification be avoided altogether?

We will find answers to these questions in this chapter as we examine theories and methods of **work design,** the formal process of dividing an organization's total stock of work into tasks and jobs its members can perform. We will begin by overviewing one approach to work design, the efficiency perspective, that originated in the work on scientific management described in Chapter 1. Today this approach is widely used to economize on the costs of production activities. Next we will turn our attention to a second approach, the empowerment perspective, that arose largely in reaction to problems with the efficiency perspective. It is based on ideas about human motivation and satisfaction like those discussed in Chapters 4 and 5, and it highlights the importance of designing jobs that encourage employee growth and fulfillment. We will conclude by describing an emerging approach, the quality perspective, that combines key elements of the efficiency and empowerment perspectives. A primary focus of this new perspective, which originated in the total quality management movement, is on improving innovation and quality through the use of self-managed teams and advanced production technologies.

The Efficiency Perspective

To achieve *efficiency,* companies minimize the resources consumed in providing a product or service. The **efficiency perspective** on work design is thus concerned with creating jobs that conserve time, human energy, raw materials, and other productive resources. It is the heart of **industrial engineering,** a field of engineering that focuses on maximizing the efficiency of the methods, facilities, and materials used to produce commercial products. Methods engineering and work measurement are two areas of industrial engineering that have had especially noticeable effects on the division of labor in modern organizations.

Methods Engineering

Methods engineering, an area of industrial engineering that originated in Frederick Winslow Taylor's work on scientific management, attempts to improve the methods used to perform work. It incorporates two related endeavors—process engineering and human factors engineering.

Process engineering studies the sequence of tasks required to produce a particular product or service and examines the way these tasks fit together into an integrated job. It also analyzes tasks to see which should be performed by human beings and which by machines, and tries to determine how workers can perform their jobs most efficiently. Process engineers examine the product or service to be produced and decide what function, if any, human beings should serve in its production. They also determine the need for some employees to serve as managers, to direct and control the flow of work, and they differentiate the resulting managerial jobs from those of nonmanagerial workers. Process engineers specify the procedures for employees to follow, the equipment they should use, and the physical layout of offices, workstations, and materials-storage facilities.

Consider the job of selling women's shoes. The process chart in Figure 6-1 depicts the job as originally performed. The large circles in the figure denote operations completed at a fixed location. The small circles indicate instances in which the jobholder moves toward an object or changes the location of an object. As shown in Figure 6-1, before job redesign, clerks regularly performed 19 different work activities and walked a distance of 870 feet to complete a sale in which the customer decided to try on nine styles of shoes, one at a time.

To redesign this job, process engineers analyzed the salesperson's movements and actions, guided by questions like the following:

1. Should all the work activities now included in the job actually be in this one job?
2. Does the jobholder currently perform some of the work activities in the job in a random fashion when order and consistency might promote greater efficiency?
3. Can some of the work activities be batched, that is, performed in groups for several transactions, rather than separately for each one?
4. Can instructions for managing work activities be standardized?
5. Does the layout of the workplace (including equipment and supplies) facilitate the completion of work activities?
6. Is the time and effort consumed by a particular work activity so great that the activity should be broken into a sequence of smaller activities?
7. Can some of these smaller work activities be eliminated by physical rearrangement of the workplace or by the use of different equipment (calculators rather than adding machines, word processors instead of typewriters)?
8. If some of the smaller work activities were performed in a different sequence, could any of them be eliminated or combined?
9. Could overall productivity be increased by the redistribution of work activities among a group of workers?[1]

Figure 6-2 shows the same job after the completion of process engineering. Once implemented, the new method reduced the job of selling women's shoes by 13 activities and saved clerks 480 feet of walking.

Figure 6-1 ■ Process Chart of Selling Women's Shoes, Original Method

BASIC CHART FORM

Type of chart_____Proc–cht pers_____

Original ☒ Proposed ☐   Chart by _____J.D._____

Subject charted _____Selling women's shoes (shoe clerk)_____

Date charted _____7/22_____   Department _____Women's shoes_____

DISTANCE	SYMBOL	EXPLANATION
30'	○	To seated customer
	●	Sit, greet, make style inquiry
60'	○	To stock storage
	●	Select style, size
60'	○	Return to customer
	①	Sit, fit, discuss (5% sales here)
60'	○	To stock storage
	●	Select alternative style, size
60'	○	Return to customer
	②	Sit, fit, discuss (10% leave)
60'	○	To stock storage
	●	Select alternative style, size
60'	○	Return to customer
	③	Sit, fit, discuss
60'	○	To stock storage
	●	Select alternative style, size
60'	○	Return to customer
	④	Sit, fit, discuss (90% of sales here)
60'	○	To stock storage for #5 to #9
		(5% sales–rest. leave)

Source: Reprinted with the publisher's permission from M. E. Mundel and D. L. Danner, *Motion and Time Study: Improving Productivity,* 7th ed. (Englewood Cliffs, NJ: Prentice Hall, 1994), p. 228.

Figure 6-2 ■ **Process Chart of Selling Women's Shoes, Improved Method**

BASIC CHART FORM

Type of chart_____Proc–cht pers_____

Original ☐ Proposed ☒   Chart by _____J.D._____

Subject charted_____Selling women's shoes (shoe clerk)_____

Date charted _____7/23_____   Department _____Women's shoes_____

DISTANCE	SYMBOL	EXPLANATION
30'	○	To seated customer
	⬤	Sit, greet, make style inquiry
60'	○	To stock storage
	⬤	Select style + alternative, size
60'	○	Return to customer
	(1+2)	Sit, fit, discuss (10% sales here)
60'	○	To stock storage (10% leave)
	⬤	Select two alternative styles, size
60'	○	Return to customer
	(3+4)	Sit, fit, discuss (85% of sales here)
60'	○	To stock storage
	(5–9)	Select five alternative styles, size
60'	○	Return to customer
		(5% sales–rest leave)

SUMMARY AND RECAPITULATION

	ORIG	PROPOSED	SAVING
⬤	19*	6	13
○	15*	7	8
Dist	870'*	390'	480'

*Includes 5th through 9th style

Source: Reprinted with the publisher's permission from M. E. Mundel and D. L. Danner, *Motion and Time Study: Improving Productivity,* 7th ed. (Englewood Cliffs, NJ: Prentice Hall, 1994), p. 230.

Table 6-1 ■ Areas of Study in Human Factors Engineering

AREA OF STUDY	EXAMPLES
Physical aspects of the user-machine interface	Size, shape, color, texture, and method of operation of displays and controls for such things as cars, home appliances, and industrial and commercial equipment
Cognitive aspects of the user-machine interface	Understanding of instructions and other information; style of dialogue between computer and user
Workplace design and workspace layout	Layout of offices, factories, home kitchens, and other places in which people work; detailed relationships between furniture and equipment and between different equipment components
Physical environment	Effects of climate, noise and vibration, illumination, and chemical or biological contaminants on human performance and health

Source: Adapted with the publisher's permission from I. A. R. Galer, *Applied Ergonomics Handbook* (London: Butterworth, 1987), p. 6.

In contrast to process engineers who focus on improving work processes, experts in **human factors engineering,** sometimes called **ergonomics,** design machines and work environments so that they match human capacities and limitations. Table 6-1 lists some of the guiding concerns of human factors engineering.

When people make mistakes at work, human factors engineers ask if the equipment being used is partially to blame for these mistakes. Are mistakes made when certain kinds of equipment are used rather than others? Is it possible to redesign equipment so as to minimize or even eliminate human error? More often than not, the effects of human fallibility and carelessness can be substantially decreased by minimizing error-provoking features of jobs and equipment. For example, shape-coded controls like those shown in Figure 6-3 are used to reduce aircraft accidents caused by reaching for the wrong control. To help pilots differentiate among control levers without looking at them, designers of these levers followed two general rules: (1) the shape of a control should suggest its purpose, and (2) the shape should be distinguishable even when gloves are worn.

Work Measurement

Besides designing job methods, industrial engineers sometimes also examine the motions and time required to complete each job. Such work can be traced to Taylor's principles of scientific management, but is more directly the product of research by Frank and Lillian Gilbreth, who set out to find the "one best way" to do any job. In the course of this pursuit, the Gilbreths developed motion study, a procedure that reduces jobs to their most basic movements. As noted in Chapter 1, each of these basic movements is called a therblig (a near reversal of *Gilbreth*)

Figure 6-3 ■ Shape Coding to Reduce Pilot Errors

Source: Adapted from C. T. Morgan, J. S. Cook, A. Chapanis, and M. W. Lund, *Human Engineering Guide to Equipment Design* (New York: McGraw-Hill, 1963), p. 25.

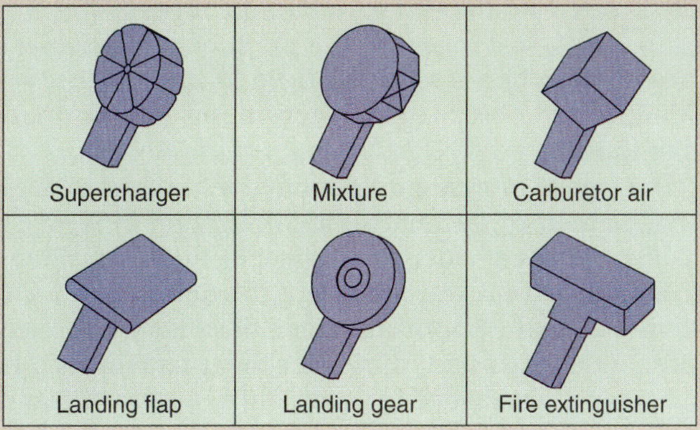

Supercharger Mixture Carburetor air

Landing flap Landing gear Fire extinguisher

and consists of motions such as "search," "grasp," and "assemble." The Gilbreths also developed procedures to specify in advance the time that should be required by each of the movements needed to perform a job. These procedures gave rise to **work measurement,** an area of industrial engineering concerned with measuring the amount of work accomplished and developing standards for performing work of an acceptable quantity and quality. Work measurement includes micromotion analysis, memomotion analysis, and time study procedures.

In **micromotion analysis,** industrial engineers analyze the hand and body movements required to do a job. This technique is a direct descendant of the motion study methods devised by the Gilbreths, whose therbligs continue to be used in current micromotion procedures. Industrial engineers usually conduct micromotion analysis by viewing a slowed-down videotape of a person performing a job. They analyze the movements performed in the task and try to improve efficiency by applying principles like the following:

1. Try to have both hands doing the same thing at the same time or to balance the work of the two hands.
2. Try to avoid using the hands simply for holding. Use specialized jigs, vises, or clamps instead.
3. Keep all work inside a work area bounded by the worker's reach.
4. Relieve the hands of work wherever possible.
5. Eliminate as many therbligs or as much of a therblig as possible and combine therbligs when possible.
6. Arrange therbligs in the most convenient order. Each therblig should flow smoothly into the next.
7. Standardize the method of performing the job in the manner that promotes the quickest learning.[2]

As suggested by these principles, jobs designed by means of micromotion analysis are characterized by economy of motion.

Memomotion analysis is used to analyze jobs that are less repetitive than most assembly line jobs and that have longer activity sequences. This time, the analyst uses a slow speed to videotape a person at work and then plays back the tape at normal speed. In this manner, job activities are sped up—one hour of activity may be viewed in as little as four minutes—and the analyst is able to identify and observe gross movements that normally occur over long periods of time.

The type of movements identified in this sort of analysis and some of the potential benefits of the analysis are illustrated in Figure 6-4, which shows two alternative layouts of a dentist's office. In the top diagram, a memomotion analysis has captured the travel paths of the dentist and an assistant during a typical patient visit. In the bottom diagram, the analyst has traced the travel paths of the dentist and the assistant during a similar patient visit, but after the dentist's office has been rearranged in accordance with the recommendations of the memomotion analyst. Far fewer motions are shown in the bottom diagram, and those that remain in the job require a smaller physical area.

Time study techniques measure the time consumed by job performance. In **stopwatch time analysis,** an analyst uses a stopwatch to time the sequence of motions needed to complete a job. In **standard time analysis,** the analyst matches the results of micromotion analysis with standard time charts to determine the average time that should be required to perform a job. When combined with micromotion analyses, the results of either type of time analysis can be used to create job element descriptions that identify the therblig motions required to perform a job and the length of time the job should take to complete.

Evaluating the Efficiency Perspective

In keeping with the efficiency perspective that serves as their foundation, all industrial engineering methods attempt to enhance productivity by simplifying jobs. Often, industrial engineers using these methods can improve productivity dramatically. There is, however, a danger that simplification will be carried too far, leading to the creation of oversimplified jobs like those of the welder and proofreader described at the beginning of this chapter.

Workers performing oversimplified, routine jobs often become bored, resentful, and dissatisfied, which contributes to problems with workforce absenteeism and turnover. Employees may also resort to loitering or sabotage because of the absence of challenge and interest in their work. Performance quantity and quality are likely to suffer as a consequence.[3]

Oversimplification can also have dire health consequences. According to U.S. government sources, well over 50 percent of all workplace illnesses are attributable to the adverse effects of repetitive stress caused by doing routine jobs again and again. Repetitive stress injuries (RSIs) accounted for 117,000 instances of job-related illness in 1989, and for another 185,000 reported cases in 1990. Workers' compensation claims and other expenses related to these injuries cost U.S. employers as much as $20 billion a year, according to

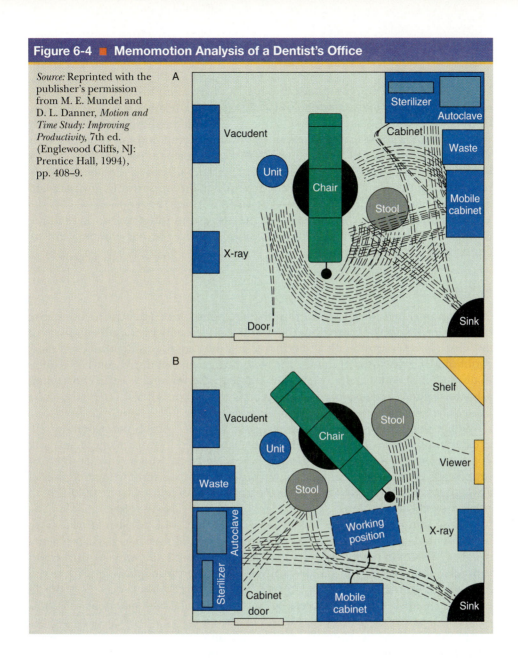

Figure 6-4 ■ **Memomotion Analysis of a Dentist's Office**

Source: Reprinted with the publisher's permission from M. E. Mundel and D. L. Danner, *Motion and Time Study: Improving Productivity,* 7th ed. (Englewood Cliffs, NJ: Prentice Hall, 1994), pp. 408–9.

estimates made by insurer Aetna Life and Casualty. As a result, businesses like Chrysler Corporation have begun to rotate workers among tasks to break up repetition over the course of each working day. Chrysler has also re-designed many jobs and developed special tools to reduce or eliminate repet-itive stress.[4]

The Empowerment Perspective

What can be done to counteract the effects of oversimplification, or to make sure that jobs are not oversimplified to begin with? The answer to this question, offered initially by Lillian Gilbreth, is that jobs should be designed in such a way that performing them creates feelings of fulfillment and empowerment in their holders.[5] This idea is the central tenet of the **empowerment perspective** on work design, which suggests that fitting the characteristics of jobs to the needs and interests of the people who perform them provides the opportunity for personal growth, development, and satisfaction at work.[6] Among the methods of work design developed with the empowerment perspective in mind are horizontal job enlargement, vertical job enrichment, comprehensive job enrichment, and sociotechnical enrichment.

Horizontal Enlargement

To counteract oversimplification, managers sometimes attempt to boost the complexity of work by increasing the number of task activities a job entails. This approach is based on the idea that increasing **job range,** or the number of tasks a jobholder performs, will reduce the repetitive nature of the job and thus eliminate worker boredom.[7] Increasing job range in this manner is called **horizontal job enlargement** because the resulting job is created out of tasks from the same horizontal "slice" of an organization's hierarchy.

Some horizontal job enlargement programs rely on **job extension,** an approach in which several simplified jobs are combined to form a single new job. For example, the job of our insurance company clerk, which consists solely of proofreading, might be extended by the addition of filing and telephone-answering tasks. Similarly, the welder's job might be extended by the addition of other assembly operations.

Organizations as diverse as Maytag, AT&T, and the U.S. Civil Service have implemented job extension in one form or another. However, especially when a number of simple, readily mastered tasks are combined, it is easy for workers to view job extension as giving them more of the same routine, boring work to do. Although initial tests seemed promising, most research has suggested that job extension rarely succeeds in reversing oversimplification to an extent sufficient to strengthen employee motivation and satisfaction.[8]

In **job rotation,** workers are rotated among several jobs in a structured, predefined manner. Rotation of this sort creates horizontal enlargement without combining or otherwise redesigning a firm's jobs. For instance, a supermarket employee might run a checkout lane for a specific period of time and then, switching jobs with another employee, restock shelves for another set period of time. As workers rotate, they perform a wider variety of tasks than they would if limited to a single job. Again, however, critics have observed that job rotation often achieves little more than having people perform several boring, routine jobs rather than one. As a result, although companies including Ford Motor Company and Western Electric have tried job rotation, it has generally failed to improve worker motivation or satisfaction (although it can be useful in correcting the RSI problems mentioned earlier).[9]

Vertical Enrichment

The failure of horizontal job enlargement to counteract oversimplification has led managers to try other approaches instead. Many such trials involve attempts to increase **job depth,** that is, the amount of discretion a jobholder has in choosing job activities and outcomes. This approach, called **vertical job enrichment,** is based on the work of Frederick Herzberg, an industrial psychologist who studied the causes of employee satisfaction and dissatisfaction at work.[10]

Herzberg, who began his research in the mid-1950s, started out by interviewing 200 engineers and accountants in nine companies, asking them to describe incidents at work that had made them feel "exceptionally good" or "exceptionally bad" about their jobs. From these interviews, Herzberg concluded that satisfaction, or feeling good, and dissatisfaction, or feeling bad, should be thought of as independent concepts, not opposites on a single continuum as traditional views had held. What this suggests is that a person might feel more satisfied with a job without feeling less dissatisfied, more dissatisfied without feeling less satisfied, and so forth.

As he dug further into his interview data, Herzberg also found that certain characteristics of the work situation seemed to affect employee satisfaction. Other work characteristics appeared to be associated with employee dissatisfaction. **Motivator factors,** such as achievement or recognition, increased satisfaction. Their absence produced a lack of satisfaction, but not active dissatisfaction. On the other hand, **hygiene factors,** such as company policy or employees' relationships with their supervisors, often led to serious dissatisfaction, but rarely contributed to a gain in satisfaction.

Armed with this distinction, Herzberg then noticed that only the motivator factors identified in his research seemed able to increase the incentive to work. Hygiene factors, he said, could help to maintain motivation, but would more often contribute to a decrease in motivation. As indicated in Figure 6-5, many of Herzberg's hygiene factors are the very same job characteristics emphasized by the efficiency perspective on work design. In fact, Herzberg contended that following the principles advocated by Taylor, the Gilbreths, and later specialists in industrial engineering would create oversimplified jobs that could only dissatisfy and demotivate workers. This led him to suggest that managers should pay less attention to things like working conditions and salary, and instead should design jobs that incorporate opportunities for growth, achievement, and recognition.

Over the years, many critics have attacked Herzberg's ideas.[11] Among the most serious criticisms are the following:

1. The *critical-incident technique* that Herzberg used, in which he asked people to recall earlier feelings and experiences, is a questionable research method subject to errors in perception or memory and to subconscious biases. Thus, the validity of his conclusions is open to question.

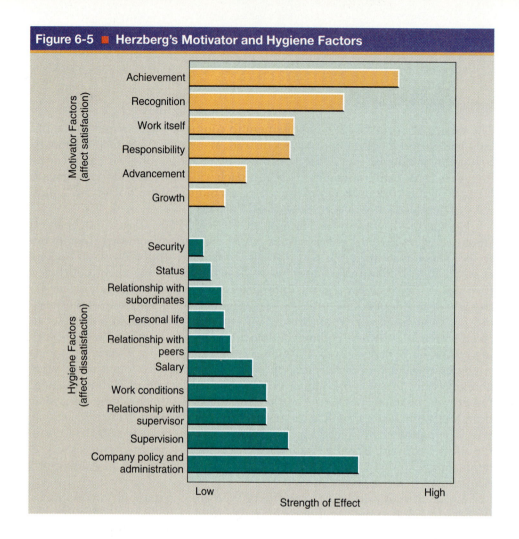

Figure 6-5 ■ Herzberg's Motivator and Hygiene Factors

2. Herzberg's interviewees, engineers and accountants, were all members of professional, white-collar occupational groups and male (few women were engineers or accountants in Herzberg's day). Women, minorities, and members of other occupational groups, such as salespeople or industrial laborers, might choose to answer Herzberg's questions differently.

3. Other studies have failed to replicate Herzberg's results. These failures cast grave doubts on the merits of Herzberg's findings.

4. Work design programs based on Herzberg's model almost always fail to stimulate workforce satisfaction of lasting significance.

Because of questions about its validity, Herzberg's two-factor theory is not considered to be a useful guide for managerial actions.[12] Nonetheless, it is widely known among managers and continues to stimulate interest in questions

Figure 6-6 ■ The Hackman-Oldham Job Characteristics Model

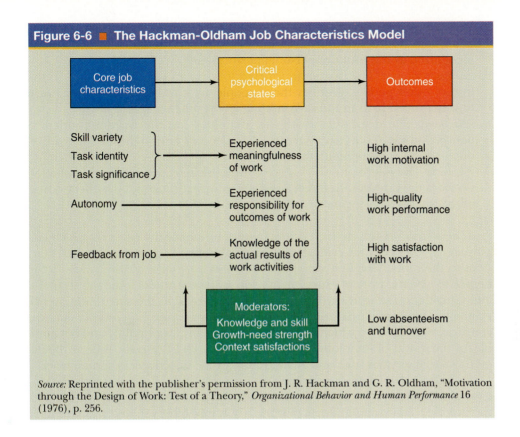

Source: Reprinted with the publisher's permission from J. R. Hackman and G. R. Oldham, "Motivation through the Design of Work: Test of a Theory," *Organizational Behavior and Human Performance* 16 (1976), p. 256.

of motivation, satisfaction, and work design. In addition, it has influenced more recent ideas about work design by highlighting the importance of designing jobs that satisfy *higher-order* desires for growth, achievement, and recognition.

Comprehensive Enrichment

Although neither the horizontal loading of job enlargement nor the vertical loading of Herzberg's job enrichment is able to counteract oversimplification when used separately, **comprehensive job enrichment** programs that combine both horizontal and vertical improvements are usually quite successful in stimulating motivation and satisfaction. Many such programs are based on the model of work design developed by J. Richard Hackman and Greg Oldham, shown in Figure 6-6.[13]

According to Hackman and Oldham, jobs that are likely to motivate performance and contribute to employee satisfaction exhibit high amounts of the following five **core job characteristics:**

1. *Skill variety.* The degree to which a jobholder must carry out a variety of different activities and use a number of different personal skills in performing the job.

2. *Task identity.* The degree to which performing a job results in the completion of a whole and identifiable piece of work and a visible outcome that can be recognized as the result of personal performance.
3. *Task significance.* The degree to which a job has a significant impact on the lives of other people, whether those people are coworkers in the same firm or other individuals in the surrounding environment.
4. *Autonomy.* The degree to which the jobholder has the freedom, independence, and discretion necessary to schedule work and to decide what procedures to use in carrying it out.
5. *Feedback.* The degree to which performing the activities required by the job provides the worker with direct and clear information about the effectiveness of the worker's performance.

These five core job characteristics, in turn, influence the extent to which employees experience three **critical psychological states,** or personal, internal reactions to their jobs. The first state, *experienced meaningfulness of work,* refers to the degree to which a worker experiences a job as having an outcome that is useful and valuable to the worker, the company, and people in the surrounding environment. The second psychological state, *experienced responsibility for work outcomes,* concerns the degree to which workers feel personally accountable and responsible for the results of their jobs. The third state, *knowledge of results,* reflects the degree to which workers maintain an awareness of the effectiveness of their work.[14]

As indicated in Figure 6-6, each job characteristic influences one particular psychological state. Specifically, skill variety, task identity, and task significance affect the experienced meaningfulness of work. Thus, jobholders should perceive their jobs as being meaningful if they must use a variety of activities and skills to produce an identifiable piece of work that influences the lives of others. Autonomy, on the other hand, influences the jobholder's experienced responsibility for work outcomes. Therefore, workers who have the discretion to determine work procedures and outcomes should feel responsible for the results of their work. Finally, feedback determines whether a worker will have knowledge of the results of work. Through information about performance effectiveness that comes from the job itself, jobholders can maintain an awareness of how they are performing.

According to the Hackman-Oldham model, if workers experience all three states at once, four kinds of work and personal outcomes are likely to result. First, such workers will tend to view their jobs as interesting, challenging, and important, and may be motivated to perform those jobs simply because they are so stimulating, challenging, and enjoyable. *High internal work motivation,* or being "turned on" to job performance by its personal consequences, is thus one possible outcome. Second, experiencing the three critical psychological states and the internal, or intrinsic, motivation they arouse can encourage *high-quality work performance* (and sometimes greater production quantity).[15] Third, workers who experience the three psychological states do so because their work allows them opportunities for personal learning, growth, and development. As indicated in Chapter 5, such opportunities generally promote *high satisfaction with work.* Fourth, work that stimulates all three psychological states also tends to promote *lower absenteeism and turnover.*

The Hackman-Oldham model proposes several moderating factors that determine whether the five core job characteristics will indeed trigger the three psychological states and lead to the four outcomes just described. The first of these moderators is the worker's *knowledge and skill*. To succeed on a job with high levels of the five core job characteristics, a worker must have the knowledge and skill required to perform the job successfully. People who cannot perform a job because they lack the necessary knowledge or skill will only feel frustrated by their failure. The motivational aims of job enrichment will thus be thwarted.

Growth-need strength, the strength of a worker's need for personal growth, is a second factor that moderates the operation of the Hackman-Oldham model. Workers who have strong growth needs are attracted to enriched work because it offers the opportunity for growth. However, workers whose need for growth is weak are likely to feel overburdened by the opportunities offered them. Therefore, they will try to avoid enriched work and will not derive personal benefit if required to perform it.

Finally, certain *context satisfactions* can influence the Hackman-Oldham model's applicability. Hackman and Oldham identified several such context satisfactions—satisfaction with pay, with job security, with coworkers, and with supervisors. Workers who feel exploited and dissatisfied because they are poorly paid, who feel insecure about their jobs, or who have abusive coworkers or unfair supervision are likely to view job enrichment as just one more type of exploitation. Context dissatisfaction can thus negate the expected benefits of Hackman-Oldham job enrichment.

Managers have a number of options available, should they attempt to counteract oversimplification through comprehensive enrichment. To enhance skill variety and task identity, they can *combine* oversimplified jobs to form enlarged modules of work. For example, the production of a toaster could be redesigned so that the entire appliance is constructed by a single employee working alone rather than by a dozen people working on an assembly line. Managers can form *natural units of work* by clustering similar tasks into logical or inherently meaningful groups. For instance, a data entry clerk who formerly selected work orders randomly from a stack might be given sole responsibility for the work orders of an entire department or division. This intervention is aimed at strengthening task identity and task significance for the clerk.

In an effort to increase task variety, autonomy, and feedback, a firm can give workers the responsibility for *establishing and managing client relationships*. At John Deere and Company, assembly line workers take stints as traveling salespersons, getting to know their customers' needs and complaints (see box). To increase autonomy, a firm can design managerial duties into a particular job through *vertical loading*. Finally, to increase feedback, the firm can open *feedback channels* by adding to a job such things as quality-control responsibilities and computerized feedback mechanisms.

Sociotechnical Enrichment

The Hackman-Oldham model focuses on designing individualized units of work, each performed by a single employee. Therefore, it is not appropriate for jobs that must be performed by closely interacting groups of workers. To

The Importance of Work Design

It was the early 1990s, and John Deere and Company, headquartered in Moline, Illinois, faced the one-two punch of weakening demand for the firm's farm equipment and intensifying challenge from international competitors. What did chief executive Hans W. Becherer do? One of his first actions was to ask a group of assembly line workers to retrain as salespersons and travel across North America explaining Deere's new products to dealers and farmers. The retrained workers, with their intimate knowledge of the company's equipment and production processes, made a powerful marketing team. John Soliz, an early participant, reported, "I developed new skills. I got to know the customer." After slumping by 11 percent prior to the new program, company sales climbed by 35 percent in a single year. Deere's management attributed this gain to the sort of

teamwork and partnering represented by Soliz's experiences in the field.[1]

At about the same time, General Motors Corporation's Saginaw, Michigan, steering-column plant was on the block—a victim of the effects of numbingly repetitive jobs and the cheaper costs of outside suppliers. Marathon talks led plant managers and the United Auto Workers local union to agree to slash job classifications from 160 to 12 and form teams around specific steering products. Once formed, teams began to plan everything from production techniques to vacation schedules. Productivity rose by 14 percent, and quality defects fell by 58 percent. What had been a losing proposition was on its way to becoming a star performer in GM's Delphi components division. Delphi's chief, J. T. Battenberg III, planned to use lessons learned at

Saginaw to enrich work and turn around operations in the division's other plants.[2]

Both at Deere and the Saginaw plant, changes in the division of labor—and in the design of work—proved to be essential elements of efforts to overcome prior failure and secure competitive advantage. More generally, companies that ignore problems stemming from faulty work design, such as lower quality, higher production costs, depressed workforce motivation, and greater employee absenteeism and turnover, risk losing out to more vigilant competitors who keep up with developments in work design and use this knowledge to continually upgrade production tasks and procedures. In contrast, firms that look at work design as a source of competitive advantage are far more likely to succeed in the short run and remain viable far into the future.

---

[1]K. Kelly, "The New Soul of John Deere," *Business Week,* January 31, 1994, pp. 64–66.
[2]B. Vlasic, "The Saginaw Solution," *Business Week,* July 15, 1996, pp. 78–79.

counteract the negative effects of oversimplified *group* work, managers can instead make use of the **sociotechnical enrichment** approach.

Sociotechnical enrichment originated in the early 1950s when researchers from England's Tavistock Institute set out to correct faults in the processes used to mine coal in Great Britain.[16] Historically, coal had been mined by teams of miners working closely with each other to pool efforts, coordinate activities, and cope with the physical threats of mining. However, with the advent of powered coal-digging equipment in the 1930s and 1940s, coal mining changed drastically. Teams were split up, and miners often found themselves working alone along the long walls of exposed coal created by the equipment. Mining, normally a hazardous, physically demanding occupation anyway, grew even more unbearable as the result of changes stimulated by the new technology. Miners expressed their dissatisfaction with these circumstances through disobedience, absence, and occasional violence.

The Tavistock researchers soon concluded that the roots of the miners' dissatisfaction lay in the loss of the social interaction that mining teams had provided and that had made the dangerous, demanding job of mining more tolerable. It appeared to the researchers that technology had been allowed to supersede important social factors and that performance in the mine could be improved only if this situation were redressed. Indeed, after small teams were formed to operate and provide support for clusters of powered equipment, production rose substantially. This finding, along with similar results at other research sites, led the Tavistock researchers to make the general suggestion that workforce productivity could be hurt when either social or technical factors alone were allowed to shape work processes. They further suggested that job designs that balanced social and technological factors—*sociotechnical designs*—would encourage both performance and satisfaction in the workplace. In other words, employees should work in groups that allow them to talk with each other about their work as they do it. These work groups should include the people whose frequent interaction is required by the production technology being used. For instance, salespeople, register clerks, and stock clerks who must often interact with each other to serve customers in a department store should be grouped together to facilitate communication about work. Salespeople and clerks from other departments should not be included in the group because they do not share job-related interdependencies with the group's members.

In the course of performing their research, the Tavistock sociotechnical researchers identified the following psychological requirements as being critical to worker motivation and satisfaction:

1. The content of each job must be reasonably demanding or challenging and provide some variety, although not necessarily novelty.
2. Performing the job must have perceivable, desirable consequences. Workers should be able to identify the products of their efforts.
3. Workers should be able to see how the lives of other people are affected by the production processes they use and the things they produce.
4. Workers must have decision-making authority in some areas.
5. Workers must be able to learn from the job and go on learning. This implies appropriate performance standards and adequate feedback.
6. Workers need the opportunity to give and receive help and to have their work recognized by others in the workplace.[17]

This list of required job characteristics was developed independently of the work of Hackman and Oldham. Nonetheless, items one through five of the Tavistock list correspond with the five core job characteristics of the Hackman-Oldham model. Only item six of the Tavistock list diverges, and it reflects the emphasis placed by sociotechnical enrichment on the importance of satisfying social needs at work.

Contemporary sociotechnical designs normally create **semiautonomous groups.** These groups are subject to the management direction needed to ensure adherence to organizational policies, but are otherwise responsible for managing group activities. Within each such group

> individuals must move about within the group spontaneously and without being ordered to do so, because it is necessary to the efficient functioning of the [group]. . . . If we observe the group in action, we will see movements of individuals between different jobs. When an especially heavy load materializes at one work station and another is clear for the moment, we will see the person at the latter spontaneously move to help out at the former. . . . It is a natural and continuous give and take within a group of people, the object being to attain an established production target. . . . The group members are not merely carrying out a certain number of tasks. They are also working together, on a continuing basis, to coordinate different tasks, bearing responsibility, and taking whatever measures are necessary to cope with the work of the entire unit.[18]

As they work together in this manner, the members of a semiautonomous group are able to (1) rotate in and out of tasks to enhance skill variety; (2) work together on a group product that is a whole, identifiable piece of work; (3) influence the lives of other members of the group and the lives of those who consume the group's output; (4) decide as a group who will belong to the group and what tasks group members will perform; (5) obtain feedback from group members about task performance; and (6) count on the help and support of other group members if it is needed. Therefore, the work of semiautonomous groups is rich in the psychological requirements for enhancing workforce motivation and satisfaction identified by sociotechnical researchers.

Figure 6-7 contrasts a traditional assembly line with semiautonomous groups. As the figure shows, the decision to adopt sociotechnical design principles has important implications for shop floor operations. In both panels of the figure, workers are assembling truck engines. In panel A, each worker performs a simplified job that consists of taking a part from a storage bin and attaching it to a partially completed truck engine as the engine moves along a conveyor. In panel B, however, workers are grouped into semiautonomous groups, each of which removes a bare engine block from a conveyor loop, assembles a complete truck engine from parts in surrounding storage bins, and returns the finished engine to the conveyor loop for transportation to other truck assembly operations. As is suggested by this example, sociotechnical job designs normally eliminate traditional assembly line operations.

Evaluating the Empowerment Perspective

In keeping with the empowerment perspective that serves as their foundation, all enlargement and enrichment techniques are aimed at designing jobs that satisfy the needs and interests of their holders. Methods that consist solely of horizontal enlargement or vertical enrichment have largely failed to achieve this goal. However, methods of work design that incorporate *both* horizontal enlargement and vertical enrichment have proven effective in stimulating workforce motivation and satisfaction in a wide variety of situations.[19]

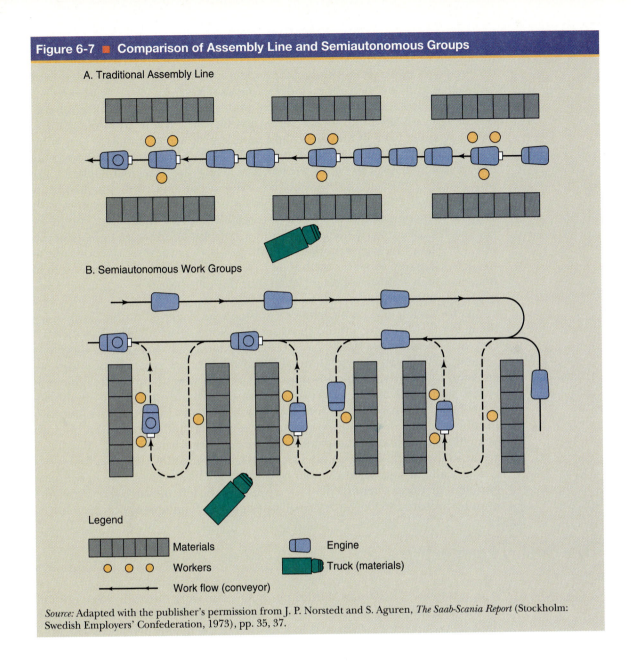

Figure 6-7 ■ **Comparison of Assembly Line and Semiautonomous Groups**

A. Traditional Assembly Line

B. Semiautonomous Work Groups

Legend

	Materials
	Engine
○ ○ ○	Workers
	Truck (materials)
←———————←	Work flow (conveyor)

Source: Adapted with the publisher's permission from J. P. Norstedt and S. Aguren, *The Saab-Scania Report* (Stockholm: Swedish Employers' Confederation, 1973), pp. 35, 37.

Research on the Hackman-Oldham model has sometimes failed to verify the existence of five distinct job characteristics.[20] It is also unclear whether the characteristics are truly objective, stable job characteristics or instead the product of subjective, changing worker opinions.[21] Some researchers have even questioned whether job characteristics like those identified by Hackman and Oldham truly influence motivation and satisfaction. These researchers suggest instead that employees' feelings about themselves and their work might be affected more by the opinions of others in the surrounding social context.[22] We will return to this idea when we talk about *social information processing* in Chapter 13. Finally, some disagreement exists as to whether the moderators identified by Hackman and Oldham actually influence the model's applicability.[23]

Nonetheless, the Hackman-Oldham model has served as the basis for successful work design programs at Texas Instruments, AT&T, Motorola, Xerox, and many other firms of similar size and reputation. Such programs are not without their drawbacks. In particular, they are usually incompatible with assembly line production processes. To enrich jobs using the Hackman-Oldham approach, a firm must almost always abandon the sort of simplified, repetitive tasks that serve as the foundation of assembly lines. Consequently, companies with substantial investments in modernized assembly lines are often reluctant to try Hackman-Oldham enrichment. In addition, because some 5 to 15 percent of the workforce lacks the necessary skills, growth needs, or context satisfactions, those workers are likely to be "overstretched" by enriched work. Therefore, a firm must maintain a cluster of unenriched jobs if it wants to avoid displacing a significant number of its employees.

As for sociotechnical enrichment, this approach started out in Europe, influencing the design of jobs in firms such as Norsk Hydro, Volvo, Saab-Scania, and the Orrefors Glass Works. Now, U.S. companies including Xerox, Cummins Engine, IBM, Polaroid, and General Electric have also experimented with sociotechnical job design, and investigation has shown that virtually the same outcomes stimulated by the Hackman-Oldham method are produced by the sociotechnical approach.[24] Sociotechnical job designs do not always improve productivity, nor do they always reduce absenteeism and turnover, but they *do* strengthen motivation, satisfaction, and similar workplace attitudes.[25] Finally, as is true for programs based on the Hackman-Oldham model, experience suggests that a small but significant number of workers are likely to resist sociotechnical enrichment. Consequently, either a few jobs must be left unchanged or managers must be prepared to deal with a small but significant amount of overstretching.

The Quality Perspective

Within the last two decades, a third perspective on work design has emerged in North America as researchers and managers have sought new ways to improve the quality of products and services. Founders of the **quality perspective** include W. Edwards Deming, Philip B. Crosby, and Joseph M. Juran, three U.S. quality experts who have inspired widespread adoption of an approach known as total quality management (TQM).[26] TQM is guided by an overarching emphasis on making *continuous* improvements in quality throughout the process of planning objectives, organizing work, designing products, undertaking production, and monitoring results.[27] Reflecting this emphasis, TQM advocates recommend the use of self-management, teamwork, and advanced technology to stimulate innovation and flexibility, so that companies can produce high-quality products and be responsive to changing customer demands.[28] As part of the TQM movement, quality circles, self-managed teams, and automation and robotics have been introduced throughout North America and have had significant effects on the way work is now designed.

Quality Circles

Quality circles (QCs) are small groups of employees, ranging in size from about 3 to 30 members, who meet on company time to identify and resolve job-related problems. Although usually thought of as a Japanese management technique, QCs were actually invented in the United States and exported to Japan by Deming and Juran during the Allied occupation that followed World War II.[29] In North America, companies such as Lockheed, Westinghouse, Eastman Kodak, Procter and Gamble, General Motors, Ford, and Chrysler have implemented QCs in an attempt to achieve the following:

- Reduce assembly errors and enhance product quality
- Inspire more effective teamwork and cooperation in everyday work groups
- Promote a greater sense of job involvement and commitment
- Increase employee motivation
- Create greater decision-making capacity
- Substitute problem prevention for problem solving
- Improve communication in and between work groups
- Develop harmonious relations between management and employees
- Promote leadership development among nonmanagerial employees[30]

Ordinarily, QC membership is voluntary and stable over time. The amount of time spent on QC activities can range from an hour a month to a few hours every week. Topics of discussion can include quality control, cost reduction, improvement of production techniques, production planning, and even long-term product design.[31] Over the course of many meetings, the activities of a typical QC proceed through a series of steps:

1. Initially, members of the QC raise issues about their work and workplace in a group discussion coordinated by their supervisor or a specially trained facilitator. Often, the facilitator is an internal change agent with expertise in organization development (see Chapter 13).
2. QC members next examine their concerns and look for ways to collapse or integrate them into specific projects. For instance, concerns about production speed and raw-material quality may be grouped together in a production methods project. Concerns about workplace safety and worker health may be put into a work environment project.
3. Members perform initial analyses of their QC's projects using various group decision-making techniques and tools, including data gathering, graphs, checklists, or charts.
4. QC members then reach consensus decisions about the feasibility and importance of different projects, deciding which ones to abandon and which ones to pursue.

5. Representatives from the QC make a presentation or recommendation to management that summarizes the work of their group.
6. Management reviews the recommendation and makes a decision. Often, the decision is that QC members will have the opportunity to implement their own recommendation and assess the success of that implementation.[32]

Many companies that suffer the negative consequences of job oversimplification are unable or unwilling to modify production equipment or methods to the extent required by the Hackman-Oldham and sociotechnical models. In some of these firms, managers are trying to use QCs to counteract the negative effects of overzealous job specialization and simplification. QCs fight oversimplification by giving employees the opportunity to participate in the management of their jobs, and they do not require the modification of existing work technologies. For example, employees who work on an assembly line for 39 hours each week might meet as a QC group during the last hour to evaluate the assembly line's performance and prepare for the following week's work. They might also meet in an extended session once a month to discuss more complicated issues and resolve more difficult problems. These monthly sessions offer an opportunity for QC members to engage in more managerial activity, group autonomy, and information exchange than the regular QC meetings allow. To the extent that QC meetings focus workers' attention on the outputs of the whole assembly line, they may also reinforce task identity and task significance.

Self-Managing Teams

Self-managing teams take the general orientation of QCs a step further, grouping employees together into *permanent* teams and empowering each team with the authority to manage itself.[33] Such teams are similar to the semiautonomous groups investigated in Tavistock's sociotechnical research, except that self-managing teams have even greater autonomy.[34] This difference is attributable to the recent emergence of computer networks, which grant self-managing teams the ability to interact with one another and exchange information about company goals, job assignments, and ongoing production progress without the aid of a hierarchy of managers.[35]

Among the management responsibilities allotted each self-managing team is that of continually assessing the work of the team and redesigning the jobs of the team's members. To enable teams to fulfill this responsibility, management trains team members in how to design jobs and assess performance quality and efficiency. Of the techniques taught to team members, many are the kinds of industrial engineering procedures described earlier in this chapter. For example, at the Freudenberg-NOX auto parts factory in Ligonier, Indiana, teams of production employees are given goals to boost capacity, increase productivity, reduce work-in-process, and raise quality. In a process that chief executive Joseph C. Day calls process GROWTTH (Get Rid of Waste through Team Harmony), each team must then come up with ways of improving existing operations to meet its goals. A member of one such team described how the team worked together to analyze the job of casting rubber engine mounts:

> After a morning training session, we grab our stopwatches and white lab coats emblazoned with the GROWTTH logo and head onto the floor. Towering above us are five three-story-tall presses, which melt 100-foot-long strips of natural rubber, inject part of the 235°F molten mass into a series of 4-inch-by-4-inch molds, and quickly cure it. . . . As we watch, the long strip of rubber being fed into the press breaks. As we time every step, the machine operator sprints up a short stepladder, reloads the rubber, hustles through several other tasks, then waits for the press to open again. When we reconvene in our conference room, we agree that the workers, who finish their tasks in about 13 minutes, are not the problem. The bottleneck is the 18-minute machine cycle. . . . Can we shorten the cure time from 14 minutes to 12 minutes without affecting quality? By the next day [we have our] answer: Yes.[36]

As is suggested by this example, in many TQM programs, the members of self-managing teams analyze each of the team's jobs by performing stopwatch time studies, micromotion analyses, equipment assessments, or similar investigations in order to find ways to improve each job's efficiency. Jobs found to be inefficient are either done away with or redesigned by the team. Newly designed jobs are then retested, assessed, and, if proven successful, adopted throughout the plant.

Based on the Japanese process of *kaizen* (continuous improvement), team efforts at Freudenberg-NOX have enabled the firm to keep up with demands from customers Ford Motor and Chrysler for price cuts of 6 percent or more a year. The use of self-managing teams will also help the company double its sales by the year 2000 to $1 billion, without adding additional employees.[37] At the same time, team self-management affords employees like those at Freudenberg-NOX a degree of autonomy they would not otherwise have and enables them to seek out social satisfaction at work. Thus, jobs in self-managing teams are substantially enriched relative to the kinds of work that team members might otherwise perform.

Automation and Robotics

Automation is a third approach available to managers who seek to improve quality. Like other TQM approaches, it also has implications for the design of jobs. For years, automation in the form of assembly line manufacturing created many of the most oversimplified, demotivating, dissatisfying jobs in industry. Today, however, with the invention of automated technologies that can totally replace people in production processes, automation is sometimes used instead to eliminate repetitive, physically demanding, mistake-prone work.[38] Frequently found in such situations are **industrial robots,** or machines that can be programmed to repeat the same sequence of movements over and over again with extreme precision. Robots have been introduced throughout the automotive industry, where they have taken over various painting and parts installation jobs. In fact, the welding job described at the beginning of this chapter is currently performed by robots on many North American auto-assembly lines. Robots have also moved from the factory floor to the operating room, performing such functions as precision hip replacement and cancerous tumor irradiation.[39]

Computer-integrated manufacturing in the form of *flexible manufacturing cells* is another type of automated technology introduced in the name of TQM, but one that focuses primary attention on adaptability instead of robotic repetitiveness. Products made in such cells include gearboxes, cylinder heads, brake components, and similar machined-metal components used in the automotive, aviation, and construction equipment industries. Companies throughout Europe, Japan, and North America are also experimenting with using flexible manufacturing cells to manufacture items out of sheet metal.[40]

Each flexible manufacturing cell consists of a collection of automated production machines that cut, shape, drill, and fasten together metal components. These machines are connected with each other by convertible conveyor grids that allow quick rerouting to accommodate changes from one product to another. It is possible, for instance, to produce a small batch of automotive door locks, then switch over to fabricate and finish a batch of crankshafts for automotive air-conditioner compressors. It is simply a matter of turning some machines on and others off, then activating those conveyors that interconnect the machines that are in use. Operations of this sort are normally computer controlled. They enable the same collection of machines to make a wide variety of products without substantial human involvement and without the need to alter the cells substantially.[41]

Workers in a flexible manufacturing cell need never touch the product being produced, nor do they perform simple, repetitive production tasks. Instead, their jobs consist of the surveillance and decision making required to initialize different cell configurations and oversee equipment operations. Often, a cell's workforce forms a self-managing team to accommodate the sizeable amount of coordination that must occur to manage occasional crises and keep production flowing smoothly. Under such circumstances, employees in a flexible manufacturing cell have enriched jobs that allow them to exercise expertise in teamwork, problem solving, and self-management.[42]

Evaluating the Quality Perspective

In many respects, the quality perspective is a hybrid of the efficiency and empowerment perspectives on work design. For instance, quality circles are a means of allowing employees at least modest satisfaction under conditions in which work processes are shaped mainly by concerns about productive efficiency. Self-managed teams enable their members to satisfy needs for social and growth-oriented outcomes, partly by requiring them to work together to apply many of the work design methods of the efficiency perspective. Automation, perhaps the peak of mechanical efficiency, releases employees from jobs devoid of satisfying elements.

What effects does this "middle ground" approach have on performance and satisfaction in the workplace? Research evidence seems to suggest that QCs have little effect on productivity but can enhance feelings of satisfaction and involvement significantly.[43] The magnitude of such effects is usually smaller than that of results produced by job enrichment programs based on the Hackman-Oldham model or the Tavistock sociotechnical model. This is understandable, however, because workers who participate in QCs must still perform unenriched jobs during most of the time spent at work.

Evidence concerning the job enrichment effects of self-managing groups is more sparse. Extrapolation from research on semiautonomous groups and QCs suggests that self-management should improve team members' satisfaction and perhaps performance, and anecdotal accounts seem to support this suggestion.[44] However, research on the efficacy of using self-managing teams as a means of job enrichment has yet to provide conclusive results.

Research on the work design effects of automation is similarly lacking. At its core, automation represents a return to the efficiency perspective of industrial engineering. Some jobs resist enrichment, and it is more effective to turn them over to machines than to attempt to convert them into interesting, enjoyable work. Among the old jobs that remain, or the new ones created by adoption of innovation, the danger exists that human satisfaction may be ignored. However, research seems to suggest that employees in flexible manufacturing cells *do* show signs of increased motivation, increased satisfaction, and improved performance if the tasks they perform allow greater autonomy than was available before the introduction of automation.[45]

In sum, relevant evidence seems supportive of the conclusion that work design implementations stimulated by the quality perspective may have positive effects on workforce motivation, satisfaction, and productivity. Nonetheless, this evidence is far from conclusive, suggesting that additional information is needed before the true benefits of TQM and the quality perspective can be determined.[46]

SUMMARY

Contemporary work design began with Frederick Taylor, Frank and Lillian Gilbreth, and other experts whose work on *industrial engineering* served as the beginning of the *efficiency perspective* on work design. Within this perspective, *methods engineering* attempts to improve the methods used to perform work, and *work measurement* examines the motions and time required to complete each job.

A second approach to work design began when Frederick Herzberg differentiated between *motivator* and *hygiene factors* and joined other specialists in introducing early models of *horizontal job enlargement* and *vertical job enrichment*. The *empowerment perspective* emerged as work progressed on *comprehensive* and on *sociotechnical job enrichment*.

Due to recent developments in *total quality management*, a *quality perspective* has emerged in which the process of work design is now influenced by *quality circles*, *self-managing teams*, and *automation*. Incorporated into this third perspective are elements of both the efficiency and empowerment perspectives that preceded its development.

Review Questions

1. Explain how following Taylor's principles of scientific management can simplify the jobs in an organization. What are some of the positive effects of this simplification? What negative effects might occur?

2. What do the fields of process engineering and human factors engineering share in common? How do they differ from one another? Are they more likely to enhance satisfaction or efficiency? Why?

3. What effects do motion and time studies have on the design of jobs? What type of work measurement would you use to analyze the job of installing engines on an automobile assembly line? What type would you use to analyze the job of sorting and shelving library books? Why?

4. Why do horizontal job enlargement programs like job extension and job rotation often fail to stimulate employee satisfaction?

5. How do work design programs based on the Hackman-Oldham job characteristics model differ from programs based on Herzberg's motivator-hygiene model? Of the two types of programs, which are most likely to lead to significant improvements in employee motivation and satisfaction?

6. In what ways is the sociotechnical model of work design similar to the Hackman-Oldham model? In what ways do the two models differ? Which would you use if you were designing the job of a postal carrier? Which would you use to design the job of a surgical team?

7. How does the quality perspective differ from the efficiency and empowerment perspectives? What similarities does it share with each of the two alternatives?

8. Within the quality perspective are included quality circles, self-managed teams, and automation. Which of these approaches would you use to enrich jobs on a newly built assembly line? Which would you use to redesign jobs that resist all attempts at enrichment?

Implementation Guide

The large number of different work design methods available today invites confusion, requiring managers to consider carefully which of the various methods to use in solving the specific work design problems faced by their organizations. The following questions may help alleviate this confusion:

1. Does the design of the organization's current jobs seem to reflect the efficiency or the empowerment perspective? Are most jobs simplified, or have attempts been made to alter job range or depth? Does the quality perspective, and a balance between efficiency and satisfaction, seem evident?

2. If the efficiency perspective appears to be dominant, do productivity and satisfaction data support the idea that jobs have not been oversimplified? Or do faltering productivity and conspicuous dissatisfaction indicate that oversimplification may be a problem?

3. Can the firm's current technology be changed to the degree required by job enrichment methods? Are jobs mainly individualized, indicating the appropriateness of the Hackman-Oldham model of job enrichment? Or are jobs often performed by groups of people working together closely, suggesting the need for the sociotechnical approach?

4. If technological considerations prohibit job enrichment, might quality circles provide enough relief to restore motivation and satisfaction? If not, can you eliminate the troublesome jobs through automation?

5. If the empowerment perspective appears to be dominant, do productivity and satisfaction data suggest that jobs have been enriched without the creation of work that is overdemanding? Or do falling productivity and satisfaction indicate that workers are being overstretched and asked to do more than they can?

6. If you are facing an overenrichment problem, do the results of work measurement procedures suggest ways to simplify jobs enough to facilitate successful performance while still retaining opportunities for growth, achievement, and recognition? Could self-managing teams solve this problem instead?

7. If work measurement fails to reveal a remedy, can methods engineering be used to create new jobs that are both doable and capable of providing adequate enrichment? If not, can you eliminate the troublesome jobs through automation?

ENDNOTES

1. Adapted from M. E. Mundel and D. L. Danner, *Motion and Time Study: Improving Productivity,* 7th ed. (Englewood Cliffs, NJ: Prentice Hall, 1994), pp. 218–19.

2. Adapted from Mundel, *Motion and Time Study,* p. 398.

3. J. R. Hackman and G. R. Oldham, *Work Redesign* (Reading, MA: Addison-Wesley, 1980).

4. M. Galen, M. Mallory, S. Siwolop, and S. Garland, "Repetitive Stress: The Pain Has Just Begun," *Business Week,* July 13, 1992, pp. 142–46; "Repetitive Motion Disorders Lead Increase in Job Illnesses," *New York Times,* November 16, 1990, p. D7; and "Chrysler Agrees to Curtail Repetitive Tasks for Workers," *Lansing State Journal,* November 3, 1989, p. 4B.

5. L. M. Gilbreth, *The Psychology of Management* (New York: MacMillan, 1921), p. 19.

6. G. R. Salancik and J. Pfeffer, "An Examination of Need-Satisfaction Models of Job Attitudes," *Administrative Science Quarterly* 22 (1977), 427–56.

7. The classic piece on this approach to counteracting oversimplification is C. R. Walker and R. H. Guest, *The Man on the Assembly Line* (Cambridge, MA: Harvard University Press, 1952).

8. J. D. Kilbridge, "Reduced Costs through Job Enlargement: A Case," *Journal of Business* 33 (1960), pp. 357–62; J. F. Biggane and P. A. Stewart, "Job Enlargement: A Case Study," in *Design of Jobs,* L. E. Davis and J. C. Taylor, eds. (New York: Penguin, 1972), pp. 264–76; G. E. Susman, "Job Enlargement: Effects of Culture on Worker Responses," *Industrial Relations* 12 (1973), pp. 1–15; J. E. Rigdon, "Using Lateral Moves to Spur Employees," *The Wall Street Journal,* May 26, 1992, p. B1; and B. G. Posner, "Role Changes," *Inc.,* February 1990, pp. 95–98.

9. R. W. Griffin, *Task Design: An Integrative Approach* (Glenview, IL: Scott, Foresman, 1982), p. 25.

10. F. Herzberg, B. Mausner, and B. B. Snyderman, *The Motivation to Work* (New York: John Wiley, 1959).

11. For example, see R. J. House and L. A. Wigdor, "Herzberg's Dual-Factor Theory of Job Satisfaction and Motivation: A Review of the Empirical Evidence and a Criticism," *Personnel Psychology* 20 (1967), pp. 369–89; M. D. Dunnette, J. P. Campbell, and M. D. Hakel, "Factors Contributing to Job Dissatisfaction in Six Occupational Groups," *Organizational Behavior and Human Performance* 2 (1967), 146–64; J. Schneider and E. A. Locke, "A Critique of Herzberg's Classification System and a Suggested Revision," *Organizational Behavior and Human Performance* 6 (1971),

pp. 441–58; D. P. Schwab and L. L. Cummings, "Theories of Performance and Satisfaction: A Review," *Industrial Relations* 9 (1970), pp. 408–30; and R. J. Caston and R. Braito, "A Specification Issue in Job Satisfaction Research," *Sociological Perspectives* 28 (1985), pp. 175–97.

12. Griffin, *Task Design;* see also J. R. Hackman, "On the Coming Demise of Job Enrichment," in *Man and Work in Society,* E. L. Cass and F. G. Zimmer, eds. (New York: Van Nostrand, 1975), pp. 45–63.

13. J. R. Hackman and G. R. Oldham, "Motivation through the Design of Work: Test of a Theory," *Organizational Behavior and Human Performance* 16 (1976), pp. 250–79; Hackman and Oldham, *Work Redesign;* K. H. Roberts and W. H. Glick, "The Job Characteristics Approach to Task Design: A Critical Review," *Journal of Applied Psychology* 86 (1981), pp. 193–217; R. J. Aldag, S. H. Barr, and A. P. Brief, "Measurement of Perceived Task Characteristics," *Psychological Bulletin* 99 (1981), pp. 415–31; Y. Fried and G. R. Ferris, "The Validity of the Job Characteristics Model: A Review and Meta-Analysis," *Personnel Psychology* 40 (1987), pp. 287–322; and B. T. Loher, R. A. Noe, N. L. Moeller, and M. P. Fitzgerald, "A Meta-Analysis of the Relation of Job Characteristics to Job Satisfaction," *Journal of Applied Psychology* 70 (1985), pp. 280–89.

14. Hackman and Oldham, "Motivation through the Design of Work," pp. 256–57.

15. R. A. Katzell, P. Bienstock, and P. H. Faerstein, *A Guide to Worker Productivity Experiments in the United States 1971–1975* (New York: New York University Press, 1977), p. 14; E. A. Locke, D. B. Feren, V. M. McCaleb, K. N. Shaw, and A. T. Denny, "The Relative Effectiveness of Four Methods of Motivating Employee Performance," in *Changes in Working Life,* K. D. Duncan, M. M. Gruneberg, and D. Wallis, eds. (London: John Wiley, 1980), pp. 363–88; and R. E. Kopelman, "Job Redesign and Productivity: A Review of the Evidence," *National Productivity Review* 4 (1985), pp. 237–55.

16. E. L. Trist and K. W. Bamforth, "Some Social and Psychological Consequences of the Longwall Method of Coal-Getting," *Human Relations* 4 (1951), pp. 3–38.

17. Adapted from F. E. Emery and E. Thorsrud, *Democracy at Work: The Report of the Norwegian Industrial Democracy Program* (Leiden, The Netherlands: H. E. Stenfert Kroese, 1976), p. 14.

18. D. Jenkins, trans., *Job Reform in Sweden: Conclusions from 500 Shop Floor Projects* (Stockholm: Swedish Employers' Confederation, 1975), pp. 63–64.

19. Apparently, the motivational effects of Hackman-Oldham enrichment grow stronger over time, because a study by Griffin indicated that productivity increased over the course of four years. However, the same study suggested that initial improvements in satisfaction triggered by Hackman-Oldham enrichment may disappear over the same period of time. See R. W. Griffin, "Effects of Work Redesign on Employee Perceptions, Attitudes, and Behaviors: A Long-Term Investigation," *Academy of Management Journal* 34 (1991), pp. 425–35.

20. Studies that have confirmed the existence of five distinct characteristics include R. Katz, "Job Longevity as a Situational Factor in Job Satisfaction," *Administrative Science Quarterly* 23 (1978), pp. 204–23; and R. Lee and A. R. Klein, "Structure of the Job Diagnostic Survey for Public Service Organizations," *Journal of Applied Psychology* 67 (1982), pp. 515–19. Studies that have failed to reveal confirmatory evidence include R. B. Dunham, "The Measurement and Dimensionality of Job Characteristics," *Journal of Applied Psychology* 61 (1976), pp. 404–9; J. Gaines and J. M. Jermier, "Functional Exhaustion in a High Stress Organization," *Academy of Management Journal* 26 (1983), pp. 567–86; J. L. Pierce and R. B. Dunham, "The Measurement of Perceived Job Characteristics: The Job Diagnostic Survey vs. the Job Characteristics Inventory," *Academy of Management Journal* 21 (1978), pp. 123–28; and D. M. Rousseau, "Technological Differences in Job Characteristics, Job Satisfaction, and Motivation: A Synthesis of Job Design Research and Sociotechnical Systems Theory," *Organizational Behavior and Human Performance* 19 (1977), pp. 18–42.

21. Objectivity is suggested by studies such as R. W. Griffin, "A Longitudinal Investigation of Task Characteristics Relationships," *Academy of Management Journal* 42 (1981), pp. 99–113; E. F. Stone and L. W. Porter, "Job Characteristics and Job Attitudes: A Multivariate Study," *Journal of Applied Psychology* 60 (1975), pp. 57–64; and C. T. Kulik, G. R. Oldham, and P. H. Langner, "Measurement of Job Characteristics: Comparison of the Original and the Revised Job Diagnostic Survey," *Journal of Applied Psychology* 73 (1988), pp. 462–66. Other studies that seem to support the subjectivity side of the argument include A. P. Brief and R. J. Aldag, "The Job Characteristic Inventory: An Examination," *Academy of Management Journal* 21 (1978), pp. 659–70; and P. H. Birnbaum, J. L. Farh, and G. Y. Y. Wong, "The Job Characteristics Model in Hong Kong," *Journal of Applied Psychology* 71 (1986), pp. 598–605.

22. G. R. Salancik and J. Pfeffer, "A Social Information Processing Approach to Job Attitudes and Task Design," *Administrative Science Quarterly* 23 (1978), pp. 224–53.

23. A. P. Brief and R. J. Aldag, "Employee Reactions to Job Characteristics: A Constructive Replication," *Journal of Applied Psychology* 60 (1975), pp. 182–86; and H. P. Sims and A. D. Szilagyi, "Job Characteristic Relationships: Individual and Structural Moderators," *Organizational Behavior and Human Performance* 17 (1976), pp. 211–30.

24. R. E. Walton, "From Control to Commitment in the Workplace," *Harvard Business Review* 63 (1985), pp. 76–84; and J. C. Taylor and D. F. Felten, *Performance by Design: Sociotechnical Systems in North America* (Englewood Cliffs, NJ: Prentice Hall, 1993).

25. T. G. Cummings and E. S. Molloy, *Strategies for Improving Productivity and the Quality of Work Life* (New York: Praeger, 1977); W. A. Passmore, *Designing Effective Organizations: The Sociotechnical Perspective* (New York: Wiley, 1988); J. L. Cordery, W. S. Mueller, and L. M. Smith, "Attitudinal and Behavioral Effects of Autonomous Group Working: A Longitudinal Field Study," *Academy of Management Journal* 34 (1991), pp. 464–76; and C. A. Pearson, "Autonomous Work Groups: An Evaluation at an Industrial Site," *Human Relations* 45 (1992), pp. 905–36.

26. T. A. Lowe and J. M. Mazzoo, "Three Preachers, One Religion," *Quality* 25 (September 1986), pp. 32–37; see also W. E. Deming, *Out of the Crisis* (Cambridge, MA: MIT Center for Advanced Engineering Study, 1986); P. B. Crosby, *Quality Is Free* (New York: McGraw-Hill, 1979); and J. M. Juran, *Juran on Leadership for Quality* (New York: Free Press, 1989).

27. R. J. Schonberger, "Is Strategy Strategic? Impact of Total Quality Management on Strategy," *Academy of Management Executive* 6 (1992), pp. 80–87; and J. W. Dean Jr. and J. R. Evans, *Total Quality: Management, Organization, and Strategy* (St. Paul, MN: West, 1994).

28. R. Blackburn and B. Rosen, "Total Quality and Human Resources Management: Lessons Learned from Baldridge Award-Winning Companies," *Academy of Management Executive* 7 (1993), pp. 49–66.

29. W. L. Mohr and H. Mohr, *Quality Circles: Changing Images of People at Work* (Reading, MA: Addison-Wesley, 1983), p. 13.

30. D. L. Dewar, *The Quality Circle Handbook* (Red Bluff, CA: Quality Circle Institute, 1980), pp. 17–104.

31. G. R. Ferris and J. A Wagner III, "Quality Circles in the United States: A Conceptual Reevaluation," *Journal of Applied Behavioral Science* 21 (1985), pp. 155–167.

32. B. R. Lee, "Organization Development and Group Perceptions: A Study of Quality Circles" (Ph.D. diss., University of Minnesota, 1982); and M. Robson, *Quality Circles: A Practical Guide*, 2d ed. (Hants, England: Gower, 1988), pp. 47–62.

33. C. C. Manz and H. P. Sims, "Leading Workers to Lead Themselves," *Administrative Science Quarterly* 32 (1987), pp. 106–28; J. D. Orsburn, L. Moran, E. Musselwhite, and J. H. Zenger, *Self-Directed Work Teams: The New American Challenge* (Homewood, IL: Irwin, 1990); and R. S. Wellins, W. C. Byham, and J. M. Wilson, *Empowered Teams: Creating Self-Directed Work Groups That Improve Productivity* (San Francisco: Jossey-Bass, 1991).

34. J. R. Barker, "Tightening the Iron Cage: Concertive Control in Self-Managed Organizations," *Administrative Science Quarterly* 38 (1993), pp. 408–37.

35. M. Hammer and J. Champy, *Reengineering the Corporation: A Manifesto for Business Revolution* (New York: Harper Business, 1993).

36. J. B. Treece, "Improving the Soul of an Old Machine," *Business Week*, October 25, 1993, pp. 134, 136.

37. Treece, "Improving the Soul," pp. 134–36.

38. K. L. Miller, "The Factory Guru Tinkering with Toyota," *Business Week*, May 17, 1993, pp. 95–97.

39. S. Baker, "A Surgeon Whose Hands Never Shake," *Business Week*, October 4, 1993, pp. 111–14.

40. R. B. Kurtz, *Toward a New Era in U.S. Manufacturing* (Washington, DC: National Academy Press, 1986), p. 3.

41. R. Jaikumar, "Postindustrial Manufacturing," *Harvard Business Review* 44 (1986), pp. 69–76.

42. P. Senker, *Towards the Automatic Factory: The Need for Training* (New York: Springer-Verlag, 1986), pp. 27–43.

43. R. P. Steel and R. F. Lloyd, "Cognitive, Affective, and Behavioral Outcomes of Participation in Quality Circles: Conceptual and Empirical Findings," *Journal of Applied Behavioral Science* 24 (1988), pp. 1–17; H. H. Greenbaum, I. T. Kaplan, and W. Metlay, "Evaluation of Problem Solving Groups: The Case of Quality Circle Programs," *Group and Organization Studies* 13 (1988), pp. 133–47; K. Buch and R. Spangler, "The Effects of Quality Circles on Performance and Promotions," *Human Relations* 43 (1990), pp. 573–82; and R. P. Steel, K. R. Jennings, and J. T. Lindsey, "Quality Circle Problem Solving and Common Cents: Evaluation Study Findings from a United States Federal Mint," *Journal of Applied Behavioral Science* 26 (1990), pp. 365–81.

44. Orsburn et al., *Self-Directed Work Teams;* and Wellins, Byham, and Wilson, *Empowered Teams.*

45. P. S. Adler, "Workers and Flexible Manufacturing Systems: Three Installations Compared," *Journal of Organizational Behavior* 12 (1991), pp. 447–60; but see J. W. Dean Jr. and S. A. Snell, "Integrated Manufacturing and Job Design: Moderating Effects of Organizational Inertia," *Academy of Management Journal* 34 (1991), pp. 776–804.

46. J. W. Dean Jr. and D. E. Bowen, "Management Theory and Total Quality: Improving Research and Theory through Theory Development," *Academy of Management Review* 19 (1994), pp. 392–419; and R. Reed, D. J. Lemak, and J. C. Montgomery, "Beyond Process: TQM Content and Firm Performance," *Academy of Management Review* 21 (1996), pp. 173–202.

Chapter Seven
Interdependence and Role Relationships

"**Y**ou can trust your car to the man who wears the star" was Texaco's slogan. But, if you were an employee of this company, could you trust Texaco with your career? If you were a member of a minority group, the answer to this question appeared to be no. On November 4, 1996, the *New York Times* published excerpts from a secret tape recording made of an all-white, all-male group of executives discussing a discrimination lawsuit filed by African-American middle managers regarding promotions. In this discussion dealing with the diversification of upper-level management, one executive noted, "You know how black jelly beans agree." Another executive then responded, "That's funny, all the black jelly beans seem to be glued to the bottom of the bag."[1] These and other racially incendiary comments on the tape led to a public outrage that devastated Texaco's competitive position in labor markets, financial markets, and consumer markets.

In terms of labor markets, 11 days after the content of the tapes was published in the *Times,* Texaco agreed to settle the discrimination suit that was discussed in the tapes by paying out $176 million. The company also had to surrender power regarding all personnel decisions involving new-hires and minorities to a task force of outsiders. In terms of financial markets, Texaco's stock plummeted from $104 to $94 the day after the story. Many investors simply moved their capital from this energy gas company to others in the same industry (e.g., Atlantic Richfield's stock soared the following week), giving a direct boost to Texaco's competitors. Many large cities and states even threatened to divest their vast portfolios of Texaco stock—a move that would have threatened the very existence of the company.[2] Finally, in relation to consumer markets, Jesse Jackson led a highly successful boycott of Texaco gas stations. Virtually all business from members of minority groups stopped (which by itself represented a 10 percent drop in revenue). Even worse, however, was the loss of revenue from nonminority consumers who honored the boycott. For many of these consumers, gas was a commodity, and few were willing to cross threatening picket lines when there were usually competing gas stations across the street.[3]

Perhaps the most remarkable aspect of the Texaco case was the apparent inability of the company to learn from past experience. In 1991, Texaco had paid a record $17.7 million in compensatory and punitive damages to Janella Sue Martin, who sued for sex discrimination after the company denied her a long-promised promotion and gave the job to a man instead. Together, the two suits paint a picture of a group of people who simply cannot be trusted to deal fairly in their relationships with employees. And if a company cannot be trusted with its own employees, why should consumers or shareholders expect to fare any better in their relationships with the company? Texaco CEO Peter Bijur noted, "Unfortunately, there is bigotry in society and Texaco mirrors society . . . I can't do much about society, but I certainly can do something about Texaco."[4] With that, he set about trying to restore the relationships damaged by this incident.

---

[1]J. E. White, "Texaco's White-Collar Bigots," *Time,* November 18, 1996, pp. 31–32.
[2]M. Brush, "Texaco's Stock Suffers on Negative News," *Money Daily,* November 12, 1996, p. 3.
[3]K. H. Hammonds, "Texaco Was Just the Beginning," *Business Week,* December 16, 1996, pp. 34–35.
[4]T. Smart, "Texaco: Lessons from a Crisis in Progress," *Business Week,* December 2, 1996, p. 44.

Our last chapter dealt with jobs and how these can be designed to enhance the fit between tasks on the one hand and individual people on the other. Jobs and the individuals that hold these jobs do not exist in a vacuum, however. Rather, in organizations, jobs and individuals are linked to each other, and much of the competitive success of an organization can be traced to how well the relationships between jobs and individuals are managed. Thus, managers need to know about various factors that affect people as they work *together.* We begin by identifying several different patterns of *interdependence* that develop among people and connect them as they work with one another. Next we note that people occupy specific roles in the networks of interdependence they share with others, and we examine the socialization processes through which individuals learn about the roles they are expected to fill. We will also examine the process of communication, which is the glue that holds role occupants together. We conclude the chapter by examining equity theory as a framework for judging and enhancing the quality of relationships between individuals and organizations in terms of fairness. When the quality of relationships is high, organizations are rewarded with trust and well-coordinated efforts. As Texaco discovered, however, when this trust is violated through acts of unfairness, the damage often spills over from relationships with employees to relationships with shareholders and customers—severely detracting from the organization's ability to compete.

Interaction and Patterns of Interdependence

People in organizations share a rich variety of interconnections. Their work may require them to associate with each other as a regular part of job performance. They may band together to share resources, such as access to valuable equipment or financial resources, even when their work does not require direct contact with each other. People may talk informally with one another and share ideas as they form opinions about their work and workplace. Connections like these make interpersonal relations a very important aspect of organizational life. Among individuals and groups, such connections take the form of patterns, or networks, of interdependence.

Types of Interdependence

In the workplace, interdependence typically takes one of the four forms diagrammed in Figure 7-1: pooled, sequential, reciprocal, or comprehensive.

Pooled Interdependence. **Pooled interdependence,** as shown in Figure 7-1A, occurs among people who draw resources from a shared pool but have little else in common. Resources pooled together in such interdependence might include money, equipment, raw materials, information, or expertise. As the simplest form of interdependence, pooled interdependence requires little or no interpersonal interaction. In a company like Metropolitan Life Insurance, individual data entry specialists draw off a common pool of work that needs to be entered into the firm's computers. Each data entry person works alone to perform the task of entering information. Little interaction with other employees is required by the task itself.

Sequential Interdependence. **Sequential interdependence,** shown in Figure 7-1B, is a chain of one-way interactions in which people depend on those who precede them. People earlier in the chain, however, are independent of those who follow them. Thus, sequentially interdependent relationships are said to be *asymmetric,* meaning that the people involved depend on others who do not depend on them. Employees at Steelcase who work on an assembly line manufacturing office furniture are connected by sequential interdependence. Workers earlier

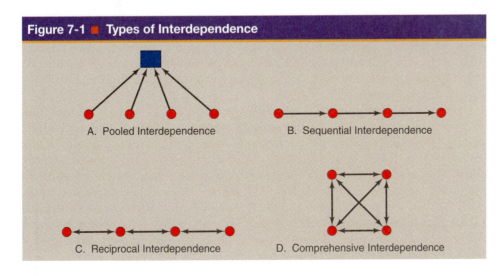

Figure 7-1 ■ Types of Interdependence

A. Pooled Interdependence

B. Sequential Interdependence

C. Reciprocal Interdependence

D. Comprehensive Interdependence

in the line produce partial assemblies that workers later in the line complete. By its nature, sequential interdependence prevents people at the end of the chain from performing their jobs unless people at the head of the chain have performed theirs. People at the head of the chain, however, can complete their tasks no matter what people at the other end do.

Sequential interdependence usually involves some form of direct interaction. For example, people on an assembly line sometimes talk with each other to pass on information about work coming down the line. Although sequential interdependence is more complex than pooled interdependence, its one-way asymmetry makes it less complex than the types of interdependence we discuss next.

Reciprocal Interdependence.

In **reciprocal interdependence,** shown in Figure 7-1C, a network of two-way relationships ties a collection of people together. A good example of this kind of interdependence is found in the relationship between a sales force and a clerical staff. Sales representatives rely on clerks to complete invoices and process credit card receipts, and clerks depend on salespeople to generate sales. Reciprocal interdependence also occurs among the members of a hospital staff. Doctors depend on nurses to check patients periodically, administer medications, and report alarming symptoms. Nurses depend on doctors to prescribe medications and to specify what symptoms to look for.

Reciprocal interdependence always involves direct interaction of one sort or another, such as face-to-face communication, telephone conversations, or written instructions. As a result, people who are reciprocally interdependent are more tightly interconnected than are individuals who are interconnected by either pooled or sequential interdependence. In addition, reciprocal interdependence is significantly more complex than either pooled or sequential interdependence. It incorporates symmetric, two-way interactions in which people depend on the people who depend on them.

Comprehensive Interdependence.

Comprehensive interdependence, depicted in Figure 7-1D, develops in a tight network of reciprocal interdependence. What makes comprehensive interdependence the most complex form of interdependence is that everyone involved is reciprocally interdependent with one another. As in reciprocal interdependence, people who depend on each other interact directly. In comprehensive interdependence, however, interactions tend to be more frequent, more intense, and of greater duration than those in any other type of interdependence.

For example, in the brand management groups that oversee the development of new products at firms like Colgate-Palmolive and Procter and Gamble, product designers, market researchers, production engineers, and sales representatives are linked by a completely connected network of two-way relationships. The product designers interact with the market researchers, production engineers, and sales representatives. The market researchers also interact with both the production engineers and the sales staff, who in turn interact with each other. Similarly, the teams of engineers and scientists who design National Aeronautics and Space Administration (NASA) spacecraft and satellites are linked by comprehensive interdependence.

Implications of Interdependence

The type of interdependence that connects people together in interpersonal relationships has several important managerial implications. First, there is a greater potential for conflict as the interdependence grows in complexity, from pooled to comprehensive. Sharing a greater number of interconnections and being more tightly connected increases the likelihood that differences in opinions, goals, or outcomes will be noticed and disputed. Second, the loss of individuals due to turnover has more of an influence as interdependence becomes more intense. One person's departure requires that few interactions be rebuilt under conditions of pooled or sequential interdependence, but in instances of reciprocal or comprehensive interdependence, many more relationships must be redeveloped if a new individual is brought in. In some situations characterized by extreme interdependence, the loss of even a single person can make everyone else perform below par. Third, comprehensive interdependence can stimulate greater flexibility and can enable groups of people to adapt more quickly to changing environments than can less complex forms of interdependence. However, as will be discussed more fully in the next chapter, this flexibility requires that greater attention be paid to maintaining continued interdependence, and it can thus contribute to *process loss* and reduced productivity. Fourth, the type of interdependence also has implications for the design of motivational systems. Group-level goals and group-level feedback are associated with high performance for those confronting sequential, reciprocal, or comprehensive interdependence, but individual-level goals and performance feedback work best for people connected via pooled interdependence.[1]

Roles and Socialization

As interdependent people associate with one another and gain experience with interpersonal relations, they come to expect others to behave in particular ways. Instructors expect students to complete reading assignments before coming to class, and students, in turn, expect that the tests instructors administer will be based on the same reading assignments. When either of these expectations is violated, strain in the relationship will be evident. As another example, upper-level managers expect middle-level managers to put the company's interests ahead of their own personal career interests. At the same time, as we saw in the story that opened this chapter, middle-level managers expect promotion decisions made by upper-level managers to be based on merit and experience rather than racial or sexual prejudices. As we saw, when these expectations were violated, a whole host of problems arose.

Expectations such as these, and the behaviors they presuppose, make up the **roles** that individuals occupy in interpersonal relations.[2] We introduced the concept of work-related roles in Chapter 5, as a source of dissatisfaction and stress. In this chapter we will elaborate on the concept of role, using it as a framework for understanding how interpersonal relationships develop and sometimes break down.

Table 7-1 ■ Elements of Work Roles	
ESTABLISHED TASK ELEMENTS	**EMERGENT TASK ELEMENTS**
1. Created by managers or specialists, independently of the role incumbent	1. Created by everyone who has a stake in how the role is performed, including the role incumbent
2. Characterized by elements that are objective, that are formally documented, and about which there is considerable consensus	2. Characterized by elements that are subjective, not formally documented, and open to negotiation
3. Static and relatively constant	3. Constantly changing and developing

As indicated in Table 7-1, the behavioral expectations that make up work-related roles can include formal **established task elements** that are generally determined by a company's management, as well as many other informal **emergent task elements** that evolve over time as interpersonal relations develop and mature.[3]

The established task elements are those parts of a role that arise because the role occupant is expected to perform a particular *job,* and the design of jobs was the focus of our last chapter. A job is a formal position and often comes with a written statement of the tasks it entails. Such written statements are called *job descriptions* and are generally prepared by managers or by specialists with expertise in job analysis and description. When such descriptions exist, there is usually a fair amount of agreement at the outset as to what constitutes the established task elements of a role.

Because job descriptions are prepared before the fact by people who do not actually perform the job, they are often incomplete. Moreover, typical job descriptions do not take account of job incumbents' personal characteristics or of the complex and dynamic environments in which jobs must be performed. Thus, as a person begins to do a job, it often becomes clear that tasks left out of the written job description need to be performed for the role to be successfully fulfilled. These added-on tasks are the **emergent task elements.** For instance, secretarial workers are increasingly being called on to perform a variety of duties other than typing, filing, and answering telephones. As business has grown more complex and executives' time has become more precious, some secretaries have expanded their roles. "Today's executive secretaries have started to assume many of the burdens of middle management," according to Nancy Shuman, vice president of a New York placement firm called Career Blazers. Kay Kilpatrick, assistant to Richard Smith, chairperson of Harcourt General, finds herself doing tasks that were never part of her job description. She runs the firm's employee matching gift program and charitable corporate gift program. She also evaluates stock portfolios and handles distributions from various trusts.[4]

As you can see from Figure 7-2, established and emergent task elements can combine in different ways. At one extreme is the *bureaucratic prototype,* shown in Figure 7-2A, in which the role occupant performs few duties other than those

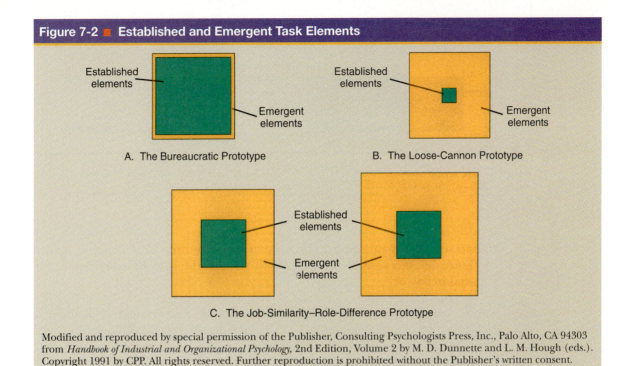

Figure 7-2 ■ Established and Emergent Task Elements

Established
elements

Emergent
elements

A. The Bureaucratic Prototype

Established
elements

Emergent
elements

B. The Loose-Cannon Prototype

Established
elements

Emergent
elements

C. The Job-Similarity–Role-Difference Prototype

written in the job description. Many low-level jobs in automated, assembly line factories are of this type. At the other extreme is the *loose-cannon prototype*, depicted in Figure 7-2B, in which the few established elements are greatly outnumbered by emergent elements. Between these extremes, Figure 7-2C shows the *job-similarity–role-difference prototype*. In this kind of role, although two individuals have the same job, special characteristics of the incumbents lead to the development of many emergent elements in one job but few in the other. On a football team, for example, an outside linebacker has established duties to contain the outside run and cover running backs in passing situations. A rookie linebacker will typically perform just those duties. An eight-year veteran, because of his experience, may have an expanded role with many emergent elements, such as serving as a team leader, calling defensive formations, and making decisions about whether to accept or decline penalties. As Figure 7-2 suggests, a work role often includes a great deal more than the formally prescribed job. It is important that managers identify and reward individuals who are performing expanded roles, if such performance leads to increases in desirable behaviors.

Role Taking and Role Making

Organizations are structured in terms of role behaviors, not in terms of the unique acts of specific individuals, and because of this, they are able to remain stable despite persistent turnover of personnel. Thus, roles are of crucial

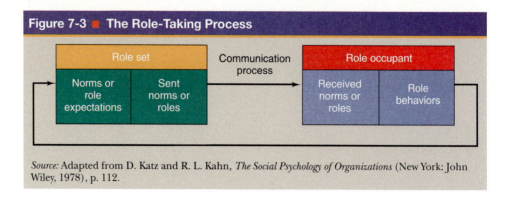

Figure 7-3 ■ The Role-Taking Process

Role set — Norms or role expectations — Sent norms or roles → Communication process → Role occupant — Received norms or roles — Role behaviors

Source: Adapted from D. Katz and R. L. Kahn, *The Social Psychology of Organizations* (New York: John Wiley, 1978), p. 112.

importance to organizations. The process by which they are developed, shown in Figure 7-3, is a central concern for those with the job of managing organizational behavior.

Norms. As indicated in Figure 7-3, the expectations that make up roles and give shape to interpersonal relations are called **norms.** In a classroom setting, norms exist that direct students to sit down and wait for the instructor to begin the day's activities. Norms may also direct students to participate in class discussions and exercises and to contribute to group case discussions. Without such norms, each class meeting would require the instructor to reestablish basic rules of behavior and an agenda for the day. As a result, there would be much less time for the learning activities on the day's agenda.

In organizations, there are norms for both the formal requirements of the job, or its established task elements, and its generally agreed-upon informal rules, or emergent task elements.[5] Either type of norm may evolve out of a number of sources.[6] Sometimes *precedents* that are established in early exchanges simply persist over time and become norms. For example, students take certain seats on the first day of class, and even though the instructor establishes no formal seating arrangement, they tend, over time, to keep the same seats. Norms may also be *carryovers* from other situations. In such instances, people may generalize from what they have done in the past in other, similar situations. A person may stand when called on to make a presentation at a meeting because that person was required to stand in prior meetings. Sometimes norms reflect *explicit statements from others.* A part-time summer worker, for instance, may be told by more experienced workers to "slow down and save some work for tomorrow." Finally, some *critical historical event* may influence norms. Suppose, for example, that a secretary leaks important company secrets to a competitor. In response to this incident, a norm may evolve that requires all sensitive information to be typed by managers, not given to the secretarial staff for typing.

Out of these sources, two different types of norms develop in all work situations. Adherence to the first type of norms, **pivotal norms,** is an absolute requirement if interpersonal relations are to persist and work is to continue to be performed without major interruption. Failure to adopt such norms threatens

Table 7-2 ■ Norms and Individual Adjustment			
		Pivotal norms	
		ACCEPT	**REJECT**
Peripheral	**ACCEPT**	Conformity	Subversive rebellion
Norms	**REJECT**	Creative individualism	Open revolution

Source: E. H. Schein, *Organization Psychology*, 3d ed. (Englewood Cliffs, NJ: Prentice Hall, 1980), p. 100. Reprinted with permission of the publisher.

the survival of existing interpersonal relations and continued interdependence.[7] For example, the members of management teams are typically required to heed norms favoring free enterprise, capitalism, and the pursuit of profits. In a company like Levi Strauss, groups of managers must adhere to pivotal norms stressing product quality and durability.

In contrast, adherence to the second type of norms, **peripheral norms,** is desirable but not essential. For instance, business schools often have dress codes that favor suits or jackets. As long as faculty members adhere to pivotal norms, they can violate one or more peripheral norms—and, for example, wear jeans and sweaters—without being ousted from their jobs. Although such violations can threaten the basic character of interpersonal relations, they do not jeopardize the continued existence of those relations.

Whether interdependent individuals adopt pivotal and peripheral norms has important consequences for their behaviors and performance as members of groups and organizations. As Table 7-2 indicates, *individual adjustment,* or the acceptance or rejection of these norms, leads to four basic behavior patterns: conformity, subversive rebellion, open revolution, and creative individualism.

When role occupants choose to accept both pivotal and peripheral norms, the resulting **conformity** is marked by a tendency to try to fit in with others in a loyal but uncreative way. People who conform to all norms are caretakers of the past. So long as tasks remain unchanged and the work situation remains stable, conformity can facilitate productivity and performance. However, it can endanger long-term survival if tasks or the surrounding situation changes significantly.

When individuals accept peripheral norms but reject pivotal ones, the result is **subversive rebellion.** People conceal their rejection of norms that are critical to the survival of existing interpersonal relations by acting in accordance with less important ones. This outward show of conformity may make it possible for rebellious members to continue occupying important roles. If their number is large, however, their failure to adhere to important pivotal norms may jeopardize the survival of ongoing interpersonal relations.

Open revolution may break out if role occupants choose to reject both pivotal and peripheral norms. If only a few individuals revolt, they may be pressured to conform or asked to leave. However, interpersonal relations dominated by open revolution may simply fall apart.

Finally, in **creative individualism,** individuals accept pivotal norms but reject peripheral ones. This ensures continued productivity and survival. It also opens the door to the individual creativity needed to develop new ways of doing things. Creative individualism is, therefore, especially desirable when dealing with change in tasks or work situations. It gives individuals the freedom to invent new responses to changing conditions.

The Role Set.　A **role set** is a collection of people who interact with a role occupant and serve as the source of the norms that influence the role occupant's behaviors (see Figure 7-3). A typical role set includes such people as an employee's supervisor and subordinates, other members of the employee's functional unit, and members of adjacent functional units that share tasks, clients, or customers with the employee. Members of the role set communicate norms to the role occupant in *role-sending messages*.

Some of these messages are informational and tell the role occupant what is going on. Others are attempts to influence role occupants in one way or the other (e.g., by letting role occupants know what punishments will follow if they disregard norms). Some of these messages may be directed toward accomplishing organizational objectives. Others may be unrelated to, or even contrary to, official requirements.

As long as the role occupant complies with these expectations, role senders will attend to their own jobs. However, if the role occupant starts to deviate from expectations, the role senders, their expectations, and their means of enforcing compliance will become quite visible. The part-time summer worker who fails to heed the warnings of more experienced personnel may soon become the victim of derision, practical jokes, or isolation. Indeed, recent research shows that peers can be the most accurate and discriminating source in terms of monitoring norm-related activity.[8]

The Role Occupant.　Although it is through the *sent role* that the members of the organization communicate the dos and don'ts associated with a role, it is the *received* role that has the most immediate influence on the behavior of the **role occupant.** As we will discuss later in this chapter, a number of factors that influence the process of communication can distort a message or cause it to be misunderstood. But even when messages are communicated effectively, senders' role expectations often fail to be met by role occupants. Several types of role conflict that we discussed in Chapter 5 can prevent a role receiver from meeting the expectations of a sender.

First of all, *intersender role conflict* may place competing, mutually exclusive demands on the role occupant. A person who meets one sender's expectations may violate the expectations of another. In addition, the role occupant may experience *person-role conflict* and have some ideas about how the role should be performed that conflict with role sender demands. Finally, *interrole conflict* caused by occupying two roles at once (e.g., being a manager and a parent) can create stress both at home and at work.

The Role Episode.　A single iteration of the role expectation–sent role–received role–role behavior sequence is called a *role episode*. As Figure 7-3 shows, the role-taking process is cyclical. The way the role occupant conforms to the expectations of role senders on a particular occasion will affect the expectations held by role senders at a later point in time.

A role message that leads a role occupant to engage in expected behaviors reinforces the expectations included in the message. If, however, a message is met with a defensive refusal to conform to expectations, role senders may find it necessary to modify their expectations. If the role occupant conforms partially when placed under a little pressure, the pressure may be increased in the next cycle. If the role occupant is obviously overwhelmed by the role, the role senders may agree to "lay off" until the person has developed a little further. Thus, role making and taking is a process characterized not by unilateral demands and forced acceptance, but instead by flexibility and give-and-take negotiation.

The Communication Process

In Figure 7-3, we drew a straight line between the sent role and the received role to denote the **communication** of a message between members of the role set and the role occupant. A more detailed representation of the process of communication breaks it into three general stages: encoding information into a message, transmitting the message via some medium, and decoding information from the received message.[9] Because problems can develop at any one of these stages, it is important to understand what happens at each stage, and how this might translate into barriers to effective communication.

Encoding the Message.   **Encoding** is the process by which a communicator's abstract idea is translated into the symbols of language and thus into a message that can be transmitted to someone else. The idea is subjective and known only to the communicator. Because it employs a common system of symbols, the message can be understood by other people who know the communicator's language.

Communication Media.   The *medium* is the carrier of the message; it exists outside the communicator and can be perceived by everyone. We can further characterize media by the human senses they use: oral speech, which uses hearing; written documentation, which uses vision or touch (Braille); and nonverbal communication, which may use at least four of the five basic senses.

Nowhere is technology having a greater impact on the workplace than in the area of communication media.[10] Fax machines, electronic mail (E-mail), and cellular phones decrease the need for travel among executives and professional workers, and also make these individuals more efficient when they must travel. The menu of options in terms of finding the best medium for each message has never been larger or more varied.[11] Many of these new media choices, such as E-mail, are so new that their advantages and disadvantages have not been well documented.[12]

New wireless technology is also being increasingly employed by service personnel and repair workers. For example, all copy machine repair workers at Pitney Bowes carry wireless data terminals that allow them to tap into a database while on remote repair jobs. The database tells the workers the location of their next assignment and provides information about the make and model of the machine used there, the date and nature of its last service, and the person to see upon arrival. If parts need to be ordered, employees can put in the request from their remote location, drastically reducing delivery times. Pitney Bowes figures that the system has improved productivity by 15 percent and raised customer satisfaction at the same time.[13]

Oral communication relies predominantly on the sense of hearing; its symbols are based on sounds and consist of spoken language. Face-to-face conversations, meetings, and telephone calls are the most commonly used forms of communication in organizations. As much as 75 percent of a manager's time is devoted to meetings and telephone calls,[14] and a major advantage of this media is that oral communications are fast. One can encode information quickly, and the feedback cycle is rapid. If receivers are unclear about the message, they can immediately ask for clarification. Presenting a proposal orally, for example, provides much more opportunity for resolving questions than does preparing a written report. Oral messages are generally efficient in the handling of the day-to-day problems that arise in groups and organizations.

Sometimes *written communication* is preferred over oral communication. Although written messages are more slowly encoded, they allow the communicator to use more precise language. A sentence in a labor contract, for example, can be rewritten many times to make certain that everyone involved knows exactly what it means. The aim is to minimize the possibility of any future confusion or argument over interpretation. Written materials also provide a hard copy of the communication that can be stored and retrieved for later purposes. For example, a supervisor may write a formal memo to an employee informing her that she has been late for work 10 of the last 11 days and if she does not begin coming in on time she will be fired. If the behavior continues, the supervisor has documentary evidence that the employee received fair warning.

Decoding the Message.   To complete the communication process, the message sent must be subjected to **decoding,** a process in which the message is translated in the mind of the receiver. When all works well, the resulting idea or mental image corresponds closely to the sender's idea or mental image. Unfortunately, however, there is no shortage of things that can go wrong and make communication ineffective. The term **noise** refers to the factors that can distort a message. Noise can occur at any stage of the process.

Another communication problem may lie in the selection of the medium for a message. Suppose you write a memo giving a coworker information about the date and time of an important meeting and a clear outline of the meeting agenda. You leave the memo in your coworker's mailbox. Unfortunately, your coworker, who is a sales representative, does not come into the office that day to collect her mail, so no communication takes place. A telephone call might have avoided this problem. Some executives seem to be feeling a growing need to communicate quickly with others, which explains the skyrocketing popularity of electronic telephone pagers.

Barriers to Effective Communication.   A variety of organizational, interpersonal, and individual factors can hinder communication within groups or organizations. The nature of the physical space occupied by jobholders inevitably affects patterns of communication. If an organization wants to promote the development of interpersonal relations, for example, it must place people in close physical proximity. People who work closely together have more opportunities to interact and are more likely to form lasting relationships than people who are physically distant. Apparently, whether you are a clerk, a college professor, or a member of a bomber crew, the nearer you work to other people, the more often you will communicate with them.[15]

Whether the purpose of the communication is to inform or to persuade, the *credibility* of the source will largely determine whether the message is internalized by the role occupant. Credibility refers to the degree to which the information provided by the source is believable, and it is a function of three factors. The first is expertise, or the source's knowledge of the topic at hand. The second is trustworthiness, or the degree to which the recipient believes the communicator has no hidden motives. The third is consistency between words and actions. Credibility is low whenever the source of the communication is either unknowledgeable, untrustworthy, or acting in a way that contradicts the spoken message. For example, in 1994, Walter Shipley, CEO of Chemical Bank, noted, "We are very fortunate in having bright, highly motivated men and women . . . our employees' interests have never been more in line with our shareholders' interests." Chase Manhattan CEO Thomas Lebrecque echoed these sentiments for his own employees, noting that same year, "Our people are among the best in their fields, the most motivated and committed." In 1995, however, when Chemical Bank and Chase Manhattan merged, 12,000 of these "bright, motivated, and committed" employees were summarily terminated.[16] The degree to which those employees who remain in the merged firm are likely to find any credibility in management's pronouncements on the value of their human resources is open to question.

A *power imbalance* between a role sender and a role occupant can also impede communication. For example, *upward communication* flows from people low in the organizational hierarchy to people above them. Because people at upper levels of the hierarchy have a great deal of power to reward and punish employees at lower levels, the latter are sometimes inhibited in their upward communication. Insecure lower-level workers may have a tendency to forget about losses and exaggerate gains when reporting information upward, leaving those at upper levels with a distorted sense of reality. Similarly, lower-level employees who are unsure about how to do their jobs may be reluctant to ask for assistance, fearing that they will appear less than knowledgeable.[17] Here too, upper-level managers may get a distorted view of the competencies of those who serve under them. The top executives at some organizations are struggling to find ways around this problem. At Pillsbury, for example, CEO Paul Walsh initiated an InTouch program whereby any employee could call up a number and register an anonymous complaint, problem, or idea, which would be automatically transcribed and then sent to Walsh's office. The system more than paid for itself in the first few months by uncovering scores of inefficiencies and identifying many small problems while they were still small.[18]

Finally, distortion can also occur because of **jargon.** Jargon is an informal language shared by long-tenured, central members of units. Within a small closed group, jargon can be extremely useful. It maximizes information exchange with a minimum use of time and symbols by taking advantage of the shared training and experience of its users. On the other hand, because jargon is likely to confuse anyone lacking the same training and experience, it can be a barrier to communication with new members or between diffferent groups. Often, technical specialists get to the point where they use jargon unconsciously and indeed have a hard time expressing themselves in any other terms. This can become a permanent disability, greatly reducing people's career opportunities outside their own small groups.

Socialization

Closely related to the process of making and taking roles is **socialization,** a procedure through which people acquire the social knowledge and skills necessary to correctly assume roles in a group or an organization.[19] Socialization is the process of "learning the ropes" and entails much more than simply learning the technical requirements associated with one's job. It also deals with learning about the group or organization, its values, its culture, its past history, and its potential, and where the role occupant fits in.

Socialization occurs anytime an individual moves along any of three organizational dimensions: functional, hierarchical, or inclusionary.[20] The *functional* dimension reflects differences in the various tasks performed by members of a group or an organization. Figure 7-4A shows the typical functional groupings of a conventional business organization: marketing, production, accounting, human resources, research and development, and finance. Similarly, the functional groupings common to many universities are shown in Figure 7-4B. They include the schools of business, social sciences, arts and letters, medicine, engineering, and law. The roles performed in each of these groupings are quite distinct because the jobholders are concentrating on different aspects of the organization's overall mission.

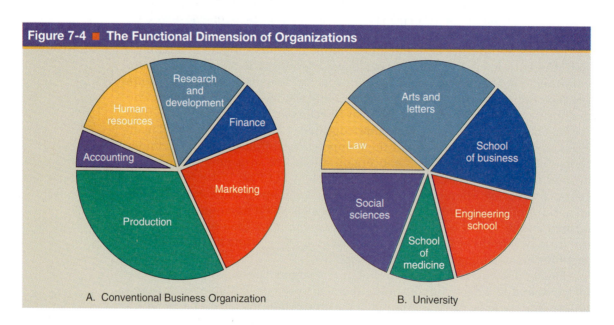

Figure 7-4 ■ The Functional Dimension of Organizations

A. Conventional Business Organization

B. University

The second, *hierarchical,* dimension concerns the distribution of rank and authority in a group or an organization. As you will recall from Chapter 1, a hierarchy establishes who is officially responsible for the actions of whom. In traditional organizations, this dimension takes the shape of a pyramid in which the highest ranks are occupied by fewer people. The roles performed by people higher in the pyramid differ from the roles of individuals lower in the pyramid largely in that the former have greater authority and power. In a highly centralized organization like an army, this triangle is often rather steep, as depicted in Figure 7-5A. However, in a more decentralized organization, fewer levels of authority exist and the hierarchical pyramid looks flatter. As indicated in Figure 7-5B, city police departments

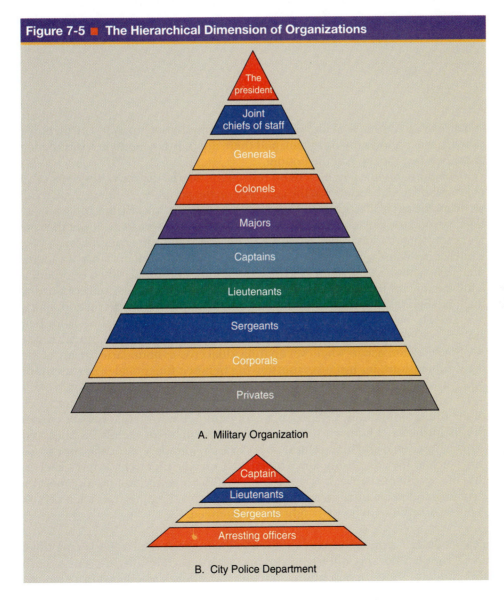

Figure 7-5 ■ The Hierarchical Dimension of Organizations

The president
Joint chiefs of staff
Generals
Colonels
Majors
Captains
Lieutenants
Sergeants
Corporals
Privates

A. Military Organization

Captain
Lieutenants
Sergeants
Arresting officers

B. City Police Department

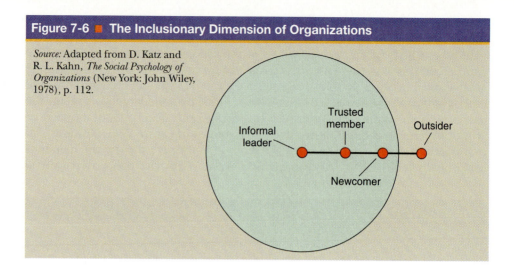

Figure 7-6 ■ The Inclusionary Dimension of Organizations

Source: Adapted from D. Katz and R. L. Kahn, *The Social Psychology of Organizations* (New York: John Wiley, 1978), p. 112.

usually have fewer levels of hierarchy than the army. Most employees are arresting officers, the highest rank is captain, and there are only two genuine levels of hierarchy between the top and the bottom.

The third, *inclusionary,* dimension reflects the degree to which employees of an organization find themselves at the center or on the periphery of things. As you can see from the circular diagram in Figure 7-6, a person may move from being an outsider, beyond the organization's periphery, to being an informal leader, at the center of the organization. A job applicant, or outsider, joins the organization and becomes a newcomer, just inside the periphery. To move further along the radial dimension shown in the figure, the newcomer must become accepted by others as a full member of the organization. One can accomplish this move only by proving that one shares the same assumptions as others about what is important and what is not. Usually, newcomers must first be tested—formally or informally—as to their abilities, motives, and values before being granted inclusionary rights and privileges.

Socialization occurs whenever an individual crosses boundaries in any of the three dimensions, for instance, transferring between functional departments or being promoted to a position of higher authority. However, socialization is likely to be particularly intense when a person is crossing boundaries in two or three of the dimensions at once. When a person joins a new firm, that person crosses the inclusionary boundary, moving from nonmember to member status, and crosses functional and hierarchical boundaries by joining a particular functional unit, such as the advertising department, at a specific hierarchical level, such as that of account executive. It is at this time that the organization has the most instructing and persuading to accomplish. This is also the time at which a person is most susceptible to being taught and influenced.

Desired Goals.   Although instructing individuals about their roles is part of all socialization programs, different firms may seek to accomplish different goals in this process. Some organizations may pursue a **role custodianship** response.

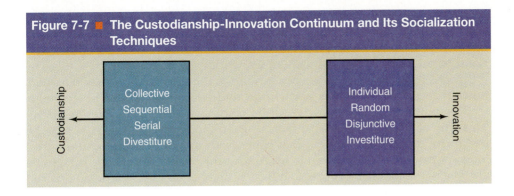

Figure 7-7 ■ The Custodianship-Innovation Continuum and Its Socialization Techniques

Here recipients of socialization take a caretaker's stance toward their roles. They do not question the status quo but instead conform to it. A popular expression in the U.S. Marine Corps, paraphrased from Tennyson's "Charge of the Light Brigade," is "Ours is not to question why; ours is but to do or die."

When an organization hopes instead that recipients of socialization will change either the way their roles are performed or the ends sought through role performance, it may have as a goal **role innovation.** For example, businesses that live and die by identifying changes in consumer needs, such as Colgate-Palmolive or Procter and Gamble, may find it especially desirable to encourage market researchers to come up with innovative ways of identifying new products and measuring consumer reactions. The continued existence of computer companies like DEC, IBM, and Compaq is also extremely dependent on innovation and creativity.[21]

Socialization Strategies.   Firms can use any of several strategies in socializing new members, each of which has different effects. As shown in Figure 7-7, we can classify these strategies along four critical dimensions to help provide an understanding of their likely consequences: collective-individual, sequential-random, serial-disjunctive, and divestiture-investiture. The first alternative in each of these pairs is used to bring about a custodianship response from the new member. The second alternative of each pair leads the recipient toward role innovation.

In *collective socialization,* recipients are put in groups to go through socialization experiences together. This method is characteristic of army boot camps, fraternities, sororities, and management training courses. In collective processes, much of the socialization is accomplished by the recruits themselves. For example, Marine Corps recruits may abuse each other verbally or even physically in a way that the formal institution never could. However, in *individual socialization,* new members are taken one at a time and put through unique experiences. This treatment is characteristic of apprenticeship programs or on-the-job learning. It has much more variable results than collective socialization, and its success depends a great deal on the qualities of the individual recruit.

In the second dimension of socialization, the alternative of *sequential socialization* takes new members through a set sequence of discrete and identifiable steps leading to the target role. A physician's training, for example, includes several observable steps: the undergraduate premed program, medical school, an internship, and a residency. A person must complete all these before taking specialist board examinations. Usually, in sequential processes, each stage builds on the prior stage. The algebra teacher socializing the student to the world of math notes that geometry will be easy if one understands algebra. The geometry teacher notes that trigonometry will be painless if one appreciates geometry. This type of presentation helps recruits keep focused on the current stage. It minimizes the discouragement that comes with the knowledge that they are a long way from where they need to be. At the other end of the second dimension are *random socialization* processes, in which there is no apparent logic or structure to learning experiences. In this type of socialization, the steps of the process are unknown, ambiguous, or continually changing. Training for a general manager, for example, tends to be much less rigorously specified than that for a medical professional. Some managers rise from lower ranks, some come from other organizations, and some come straight from business school programs.

Socialization strategies also differ along a third dimension that concerns the amount of help and guidance provided to new members as they learn their roles. In *serial socialization,* experienced members of the organization teach individuals about the roles they are about to assume. These experienced members become role models or mentors for the new members. Observing these role models and discussing issues with them are the primary means by which newcomers gather information.[22] In police departments, for example, rookies are assigned as partners to veteran officers. Some observers have suggested that this practice creates a remarkable degree of intergenerational stability in the behaviors of police officers. This method of socialization also allows recruits to see into the future, that is, to get a glimpse of what their role will be like in several years. This can be good or bad, depending upon the person doing the socialization, and thus organizations need to take great care in assigning mentors to new members. In *disjunctive socialization,* on the other hand, new members must learn by themselves how to handle a new role. For example, the first woman to become a partner in a conservative law firm may find few people, if any, who have faced her unique problems. She may be completely on her own in coping with them. Disjunctive socialization is sometimes brought on by organizations who "clean house," that is, sweep out all the older members of the organization and replace them with new personnel. Such a shake-up makes it necessary for almost all employees of the firm to relearn their roles. Typically the organization hopes that the result will bring more creativity in problem solving, since individuals who might have taught others the established way of doing things are no longer around.

The fourth dimension of socialization deals with the degree to which a socialization process confirms or denies the value of an individual's personal identity. *Divestiture socialization* ignores or denies the value of the individual's personal characteristics. The organization in this case wants to tear new members down to nothing and then rebuild them as completely new and different individuals. Some organizations require either explicitly or implicitly that recruits sever old relationships, undergo intense harassment from experienced members, and engage for long periods of time in doing the dirty work of the trade (work that is associated with low pay and low status). As described in the Securing Competitive Advantage box, some organizations may even force each new member to take on a new name. The organization promotes these ordeals in the belief that those who emerge from them will lose their sense of personal identity and become strongly committed to the organization's mission and objectives. In contrast, *investiture socialization* affirms the value to the organization of the recruit's particular personal characteristics. The organization says, in effect, "We like you just the way you are." This type of socialization implies that rather than wanting to change the new member, the firm hopes that the recruit will change the organization. Under these conditions, the organization may try to make the recruit's transition process as smooth and painless as possible.

Designing Socialization Programs. The strategy chosen in designing a socialization program depends on the goals of that program. If the goal is to bring about a custodianship response, a group or an organization is best served by a strategy that is collective, sequential, and serial and involves divestiture. Such a strategy will ensure that every socialization recipient starts with the same "clean slate" and receives the same experiences in the same order. If the goal is to promote innovation, a group or organization is better served by just the opposite strategy, which provides a unique and individualized program for each recipient and places value on each recipient's particular personality, characteristics, and style.[23]

Quality of Interpersonal Role Relationships

Given the importance of role relationships within organizations, it is critical to have a framework whereby the quality of these relationships can be judged and enhanced. **Equity theory** is a theory of social exchange that describes the process by which people determine whether they have received fair treatment in their relationships, and we will examine this theory in detail in this last section of the chapter.

Equity and Social Comparisons

As shown in Figure 7-8, equity theory holds that people make judgments about relational fairness by forming a ratio of their perceived investments (or inputs, I) and perceived rewards (or outcomes, O). They then compare this ratio to a similar ratio reflecting the perceived costs and benefits of some other person. Equity theory does not require that outcomes or inputs be equal for equity to

Figure 7-8 ■ Algebraic Expression of How People Make Equity Comparisons

$$\frac{I \text{ person}}{O \text{ person}} = \frac{I \text{ reference person}}{O \text{ reference person}}$$

Legio Patria Nostra

It was a cold, rainy October night in Sarajevo in October 1993. Bosnian refugees were running for their lives from Serbian forces when a 14-year-old boy was shot. Without hesitation, Bruno Chaumont leaped out from the protected wooded area he was in and crawled through 40 yards of muddy open field under heavy gunfire to reach the child. Chaumont dressed the boy's wounds, hoisted the boy on his back, and then crawled back to the protection of the trees. Chaumont was not related to the boy, nor was he a part of the Bosnian defense force—he was not even a member of the United Nations (UN) peacekeeping force. This act of heroism could only be credited to a member of the French foreign legion.

Many business organizations complain about their inability to integrate people of different nationalities into a common organizational culture, as well as their inability to get their members to function effectively in international locales. Some of these firms might learn a lesson from the French foreign legion, whose motto—*Legio patria nostra*—means "The legion is our homeland." This organization has a 150-year history of competitive excellence in an industry in which success is measured in life and death rather than dollars and cents. Much of the success of this organization can

be attributed to its socialization practices, which are clearly aimed at instilling a custodianship response in new members.

The socialization task confronting the foreign legion is formidable. Recruits come from over 100 different countries and need to be assembled into a cohesive unit, the members of which are willing to risk their lives for strangers. Far from being the "cream of the crop," most applicants to the foreign legion are fugitive criminals, ex-convicts, dishonorably discharged members of regular armies, ex-mercenaries, and other men running from their past for one reason or another. The foreign legion is probably the only employer in the world that does not request any formal proof of identification before hiring. Indeed, the first step of the socialization program is to assign new names and nationalities to all recruits. Along with their former identities, most recruits must also say good-bye to their native tongue, because multilingualism is not appreciated. There is one official language in this organization: French.

New recruits are then whisked off to train in exotic locales—the jungles of French Guiana or the deserts of Chad—far from their homes, families, and friends. This training includes many of the task-specific fighting skills that one would imagine, but the standards for proficiency are much higher

than those of North Atlantic Treaty Organization (NATO) armies. Many individuals cannot stand up to the hardships of this training and drop out, leaving only a small core of the most committed members. In addition to receiving this technical training, however, legionnaires are also steeped in the historical culture and tradition of the foreign legion. Recruits are taken through the foreign legion's museum, where they hear stories like that of Jean Danou, who lost his hand and then his life in Mexico in 1863, when he and two dozen legionnaires successfully defended a position against 2,000 foes. Current-day recruits get to see Danou's mummified hand, which symbolizes the tradition of courage and discipline that is still expected to be upheld by all recruits.

Although few businesses would want to emulate all the socialization tactics practiced by the foreign legion, there are lessons to be learned here for organizations whose socialization goals involve instilling change in recruits. Changing recruits into conforming organizational members requires replacing old identities and behavior patterns with new identities and behavior patterns. The organization does not achieve this by making everything as easy as possible for the new member. Rather, it instills change by disconnecting new members from their pasts, and challenging them to a new future.

[1]F. Coleman, "Colonial Grunts No Longer," *U.S. News and World Reports,* November 1, 1993, pp. 74–76.
[2]D. Porch, *The French Foreign Legion: A Complete History of a Legendary Fighting Force* (New York: Harper Collins, 1991).

Table 7-3 ■ Inputs and Outcomes in Equity Theory

INPUTS	OUTCOMES
Education	Pay
Intelligence	Satisfying supervision
Experience	Seniority benefits
Training	Fringe benefits
Skill	Status symbols
Social status	Job perquisites
Job effort	Working conditions
Personal appearance	
Health	
Possession of tools	

exist. Those receiving fewer desirable outcomes than someone else may still feel fairly treated if they see themselves as contributing fewer inputs than the other person. The key to achieving perceived fairness despite unequal outcomes is that the methods used to translate inputs into outcomes must be seen as fair—a concept referred to as *procedural justice.* So, for example, the highest scorer on a professional basketball team may be paid more than a player who sits on the bench, but most people would still feel that the team's management is treating both players fairly because of differences in their inputs. A number of possible inputs and outcomes that might be incorporated into equity comparisons in work organizations are listed in Table 7-3.

Equity theory provides a simple framework for understanding how people decide whether or not they are being treated fairly in their relationships. Yet, even with this simple framework, it is difficult to achieve widespread perceptions of equity in organizations for two reasons. First, equity judgments are based on individual perceptions of inputs and outcomes, and perceptions of the same inputs or outcomes may differ markedly from one person to the next. For instance, some CEOs might perceive that their inputs justify a multimillion-dollar salary, whereas the general public might perceive the situation differently. Second, it is difficult to predict who will be chosen as the reference person, and thus any change in policy that is targeted to one group may, in an unforeseen way, spill over and create perceived inequity in another group. For example, in the late 1980s many organizations put in place "family-friendly policies" that enhanced the benefits package and time-off provisions for working parents. By the mid-1990s, however, organizations were seeing a backlash from single workers without children who felt such policies were unfair. As one worker noted, "It's downright discriminatory for an employer to offer more or better benefits because you have children."[24]

Responses to Inequity

Perceptions of inequity create unpleasant emotions. When people feel they are receiving a greater share of outcomes than they deserve, they may feel guilty. Perceiving oneself as coming up short in the equity comparison results in anger, which is a much stronger emotion than guilt. Whether the emotion is guilt or anger, the tension associated with inequity motivates the person to do something to reduce the inequity, and this response can manifest itself in different ways. First, the individual might *alter personal inputs*. For example, one study found that in a decision-making team, if team members perceived that their opinions were not being given any weight, they stopped contributing to the group's discussion.[25] A second response to inequity is to try to *alter personal outcomes*. Individuals who feel they are relatively underpaid according to the market may demand raises and threaten to leave or strike.

A third way of responding to inequity is to use what is called *cognitive distortion*, that is, rationalizing the results of one's comparisons. For example, people can distort their perceptions of outcomes. In one equity theory study, people who were underpaid for a particular task justified this underpayment by stating that the task they were working on was more enjoyable than the task performed by people who were overpaid—even though their tasks were identical. Yet another means of eliminating inequity via cognitive distortion is to change the reference person. A salesperson who brings in less revenue than others in the department may claim, "You can't compare me with them because I have a different territory." By making this statement the salesperson seeks to disqualify peers as reference persons.

A fourth way to restore equity is to take some action that will *change the behavior of the reference person*. Workers who in the eyes of their peers perform too well on piece-rate systems often earn the derogatory title of "rate buster." Research has shown that if name calling of this sort fails to constrain personal productivity, more direct tactics may be invoked. In one study, for instance, researchers coined the term "binging" to refer to a practice in which workers periodically punched suspected rate busters in the arm until they reduced their level of effort. Finally, if all else fails, a person can secure equity by *leaving an inequitable situation* altogether. Turnover and absenteeism are common means of dealing with perceptions of unfairness in the workplace.

Managing Inequitable Situations

In a perfect world, managers would be able to ensure that every employee felt equitably treated at all times. However, given the wide variety of inputs and outputs that any one employee might consider relevant, as well as the wide variety of reference people that might be called into comparison, there will inevitably be situations in which the manager is confronted with employees who are angry and feel they have been treated unfairly. When this happens, the first step of the manager should be to see if the actual source of the inequity can be changed. That is, can the manager increase the outcomes the aggrieved individual receives (e.g., raise pay) or decrease the inputs that the aggrieved individual has to contribute (e.g. reduce responsibilities)?

If for some reason true change cannot be initiated, the manager's second step might be to change the aggrieved persons' perceptions of the situation, getting them to focus on outcomes they may not be aware of (e.g., the added chances of being promoted given those added responsibilities) or inputs they take for granted (e.g., the fact that they are never asked to travel or work weekends). The manager can also try to change the reference person being utilized by the aggrieved individual to someone even worse off (e.g., noting how many people with similar jobs have been laid off).

As a last resort, if a manager cannot change either the conditions or the perceptions of the angry individual, the manager may be left with only excuses and apologies. With an excuse, the manager basically admits that the person was treated unfairly, but implies that the problem was beyond the manager's control. For example, returning to our opening story in this chapter, CEO Peter Bijur admitted that few African Americans occupied upper-level ranks at Texaco, but noted that "there were only nine petroleum engineering minority graduates that came out of all engineering schools in the U.S.—only nine."[26]

With an apology, the manager is admitting both harm and responsibility, but shows remorse and denies that the inequity is truly representative of the past and future of the relationship. A successful apology is usually accompanied by some form of compensation that, at least symbolically, restores equity in the relationship. As we saw with Texaco, this type of compensation can often be costly, and thus, treating people fairly in the first place is far preferable to trying to make up for past injustices.

SUMMARY

In this chapter we have discussed the three key ingredients of all interpersonal relations: interdependence, roles, and communication. Different types of interdependence form among people who are joined together in interpersonal relations. *Pooled interdependence* is the simplest form of interdependence; increasingly more complex forms are *sequential, reciprocal,* and *comprehensive interdependence*. *Roles* form among interdependent individuals to guide their behaviors as they interact with one another. These roles capture the expectations that members of a *role set* have for the person occupying a given work role. Roles can be differentiated along *functional, hierarchical,* and *inclusionary* dimensions. *Socialization* is the process through which individuals learn about their roles. Depending upon the goal of socialization, different communicators, using different tactics, may be required to strengthen *custodianship* or *innovation* expectations. Just as socialized roles are the building blocks of interpersonal relations, *communication* is the cement that holds these blocks together. Communication involves the encoding, transmission, and decoding of information sent from one person to another via any one of a number of media. Equity theory is a theoretical framework that is useful for understanding how people judge the fairness of their relationships, and this theory provides a great deal of practical guidance in terms of managing perceptions of fairness.

Review Questions

1. Of the four types of interdependence discussed in this chapter, which type do you think is most adversely affected by turnover among organizational members? Which type of interdependence is most adversely affected by turnover in group leadership? How might the nature of the turnover process affect the kind of interdependence one builds into groups?

2. Socialization refers to the effect that the group or organization has on the individual. We noted that this effect tends to be greatest when the individual is moving through more than one dimension at a time (e.g., functional and hierarchical). In contrast, when is the individual most likely to have the greatest effect on the organization? (Are there honeymoon periods? Do lame ducks have any influence?) How might your answer depend on the tactics of socialization employed when the individual is brought into the group or organization to begin with?

3. What role do ceremonies play in the socialization process of someone crossing an important organizational boundary? Looking at the three kinds of boundaries a person can traverse, where would you say ceremonies are most frequently encountered, and why? What role do ceremonies play in the motivation of group members who are not crossing a boundary but are merely observers at the affair?

4. In communication, it has been said that "the medium is the message." What are the factors that one should consider when choosing a medium for one's communication? Some of the greatest leaders of all time actually wrote very little. What might explain why people who are perceived as strong leaders avoid leaving a paper trail? When might writing be used to enhance leadership?

Implementation Guide

When you are confronting problems of communication or socialization, or attempting to deal with difficulties that arise in interpersonal relations, the following questions may prove useful.

1. What type of interdependence unites people in the system of interpersonal relations you are analyzing? What sorts of problems might this interdependence cause?

2. What important components of the work roles of interdependent individuals are not part of their job descriptions? Are they consistent with formal job requirements?

3. What are some of the important functional, hierarchical, and inclusionary dimensions in the group or organization? Do current problems seem attributable to recent passage across boundaries on one or more of these dimensions?

4. For a particular individual, who are the members of the relevant role set? What are their expectations for the role occupant? How do they communicate these expectations to the occupant?

5. What are the occupant's own expectations? How do these expectations compare with those of the role set? What should be done about any discrepancies?

6. Do group members demonstrate the adherence to pivotal norms necessary for group or organizational survival? If the group or organization must cope with a changing work situation, is there evidence that it can adapt by selectively ignoring peripheral norms?

7. Is custodianship or innovation the goal of socialization processes? How should the socialization program be designed to promote this goal?

8. What means of communication (oral, written, or nonverbal) are used in order to accomplish the goals of the group or organization? Do these seem to be the best choice? Why?

9. How do individuals perceive each other's influence and credibility? How do these perceptions affect the communications they exchange with one another?

10. What are some of the major values, beliefs, and frames of reference of the individuals involved in interpersonal relations? How might these affect their interpretation of communications received from others?

11. What are the major inputs that people give this organization, what outcomes do they receive in return for these inputs, and how does this compare with the situations of their peers in terms of fairness?

12. Are people angry about how they are being treated, and can this be managed by changing inputs, outcomes, perceptions, or reference persons or is it excusable for some other reason?

ENDNOTES

1. R. Wageman, "Interdependence and Group Effectiveness," *Administrative Science Quarterly* 40 (1995), pp. 145–79.

2. B. J. Biddle, *Role Theory: Expectations, Identities and Behaviors* (New York: Academic Press, 1979), p. 20.

3. D. R. Ilgen and J. R. Hollenbeck, "The Structure of Work: Job Design and Roles," in *Handbook of Industrial Organizational Psychology*, M. Dunnette, ed. (Houston: Consulting Psychologist Press, 1993), pp. 165–207.

4. D. Fanning, "Calling on Secretaries to Fill In the Gaps," *New York Times,* March 11, 1990, p. A12.

5. J. R. Hackman, "Toward Understanding the Role of Tasks in Behavioral Research," *Acta Psychologica* 31 (1979), pp. 97–128.

6. D. C. Feldman, "The Development and Enforcement of Group Norms," *Academy of Management Review* 9 (1984), pp. 47–53.

7. E. H. Schein, *Organizational Psychology,* 3d ed. (Englewood Cliffs, NJ: Prentice Hall, 1980), p. 99.

8. C. Shannon and W. Weaver, *The Mathematical Theory of Communication* (Urbana: University of Illinois Press, 1948), p. 17.

9. Ibid.

10. S. Kiesler and L. Sproull, "Group Decision Making and Communication Technology," *Organizational Behavior and Human Decision Processes* 52 (1992), pp. 96–123.

11. J. Webster and L. K. Trevino, "Rational and Social Theories of Communication Media Choices: Two Policy-Capturing Studies," *Academy of Management Journal* 38 (1995), pp. 1544–72.

12. S. P. Weisband, S. K. Schneider, and T. Connolly, "Computer-Mediated Communication and Social Information: Status Salience and Status Differences," *Academy of Management Journal* 38 (1995), pp. 1124–51.

13. B. Ziegler, "Going Wireless," *Business Week,* April 5, 1993, pp. 56–60.

14. H. Mintzberg, *The Nature of Managerial Work* (New York: Harper & Row, 1973), p. 22.

15. J. T. Gullahorn, "District and Friendship as Factors in the Gross Interaction Matrix," *Sociometry* 15 (1952), pp. 123–34.

16. T. A. Stewart, "Watch What We Did, Not What We Said," *Fortune,* April 15, 1996, pp. 140–41.

17. A. S. Tsui, "A Role Set Analysis of Managerial Reputation," *Organizational Behavior and Human Decision Processes* 34 (1984), pp. 64–96.

18. T. Petzinger, "Two Executives Cook Up Way to

Make Pillsbury Listen," *The Wall Street Journal,* September 27, 1996, p. B1.

19. J. Van Maanen and E. H. Schein, "Toward a Theory of Organizational Socialization," in *Research in Organizational Behavior,* B. Staw and L. L. Cummings, eds. (Greenwich, CT: JAI Press, 1979), pp. 209–64.

20. Schein, *Organizational Psychology,* pp. 111–33.

21. J. W. Verity, "Deconstructing the Computer Industry," *Business Week,* November 23, 1992, pp. 90–100.

22. C. Ostroff and S. W. J. Kozlowski, "Organizational Socialization as a Learning Process: The Role of Information Acquisition," *Personnel Psychology* 45 (1992), pp. 849–74.

23. B. E. Ashforth and A. M. Saks, "Socialization Tactics: Longitudinal Effects on Newcomer Adjustment," *Academy of Management Journal* 39 (1996), pp. 149–78.

24. G. Flynn, "Backlash: Why Single Employees Are Angry," *Personnel Journal,* September, 1996, pp. 58–69.

25. M. A. Korsgaard, D. M. Schweiger, and H. J. Sapienza, "Building Commitment, Attachment, and Trust in Strategic Decision-Making Teams: The Role of Procedural Justice," *Academy of Management Journal* 38 (1995), pp. 60–84.

26. T. Smart, "Texaco: Lessons from a Crisis in Progress," *Business Week,* December 2, 1996, p. 44.

Chapter Eight

Group Dynamics and Team Effectiveness

3M, the Minnesota Mining and Manufacturing Company, headquartered in St. Paul, Minnesota, had long been known for securing competitive advantage through new-product innovation. During the second half of the 1980s, the firm had seen sales rise by 60 percent as it introduced such wildly successful products as surgical staples and Post-It notes. By 1993, however, 3M's new-product development had slowed to a trickle and sales growth had fallen to a sluggish 2 percent. Against this backdrop, chief executive L. D. "Desi" DeSimone vowed to reinvigorate product development and slash the time required to introduce new products by half, to less than three years on average.

To accomplish this ambitious goal, DeSimone first encouraged closer teamwork among researchers and marketers who had previously worked independently on product design and market introduction. Next, he ordered teams to scour 3M's research libraries for existing materials that might be adapted to developing customer needs. Out of this effort grew a special film for laptop computer screens that enhances brightness while conserving energy. The film, made of microscopic reflective prisms, had originally been developed in the mid-1980s for decorative signs on buildings. Thanks to this single innovation, the battery life of laptops made by Compaq and Apple has been extended from about 2 1/2 hours to over 4.

Now that product developers work directly with marketers, 3M's scientists know more about the firm's customers, and its sales force has ready access to the company's vast storehouse of materials and technologies. New-product development time is down considerably, bordering on the three-year target set by DeSimone, and such innovative products as Never Rust Wool Soap Pads, manufactured from recycled plastic bottles and marketed against Clorox Company's S.O.S. brand, are propelling sales growth to something on the order of 6 percent. Although this rate is not as dramatic as the growth rate of earlier times, it appears to be strong enough to move the company back to the forefront in newly emerging international markets.[1]

[1]K. Kelly, "The Drought Is Over at 3M," *Business Week,* November 7, 1994, pp. 140–41; and T. A. Stewart and M. Warner, "3M Fights Back," *Fortune,* February 5, 1996, pp. 94–99.

Besides 3M, companies as well known and diverse as Hewlett-Packard, General Electric, and Mattel have also begun using groups and teams to increase competitiveness.[1] Throughout North America, managers and nonmanagers work together in teams to make decisions about what products to produce, which raw materials to purchase, and what production processes to use. Groups of skilled production employees staff modern flexible manufacturing facilities that can customize products to the unique needs of different customer groups. Researchers, engineers, and marketers work in cross-functional teams to accelerate the processes of product development and introduction.

In light of the trend toward use of groups and team-based technologies, today's managers must be especially good at encouraging teamwork and productivity in groups of employees. In this chapter, we discuss the management of group and team performance. We begin by examining how groups are formally constituted in organizations, and by exploring the processes within groups that give rise to a sense of group identity and purpose. After laying this groundwork, we identify several critical factors that can influence group productivity, and we discuss how to manage these factors in order to enhance group performance. We conclude by describing the special challenges in managing teams—groups whose members must work together closely despite significant differences in the information, jobs, or skills they possess—and discussing how individual, social, and organizational factors act together to shape team effectiveness.

Formation and Development of Groups

A *group* is a collection of two or more persons who interact with one another in such a way that each person influences and is influenced by the others.[2] The members of a group draw important psychological distinctions between themselves and people who are not group members. Generally, they

- Define themselves as members
- Are defined by others as members
- Identify with one another
- Engage in frequent interaction
- Participate in a system of interlocking roles
- Share common norms
- Pursue shared, interdependent goals
- Feel that their membership in the group is rewarding

- Have a collective perception of unity
- Stick together in any confrontation with other groups or other individuals[3]

These distinctions provide the group with boundaries and a sense of permanence. They lend the group a distinct identity and separate it from other people and other groups.[4] They also contribute to **group effectiveness,** the ultimate aim of group activities. A group is effective when it satisfies three important criteria:

1. *Production output.* The product of the group's work must meet or exceed standards of quantity and quality defined by the organization. *Group productivity* is a measure of this product.
2. *Member satisfaction.* Membership in the group must provide people with short-term satisfaction and facilitate their long-term growth and development. If it does not, members will leave and the group will cease to exist.
3. *Capacity for continued cooperation.* The interpersonal processes the group uses to complete a task should maintain or enhance members' capacity to work together. Groups that don't cooperate cannot remain viable.[5]

An effective group is thus able to satisfy immediate demands for performance and member satisfaction while making provisions for long-term survival. Whether a group is able to achieve these often conflicting goals depends on the closely related processes of group formation and group development.

Group Formation

In most organizations, groups are formed according to similarities either in what people do or in what they make.[6] To illustrate these two contrasting approaches to **group formation,** imagine a company that makes wooden desks, bookshelves, and chairs. To produce each of these products, four basic activities are required. A receiver must unpack and stock the raw materials required for the product. A fabricator must shape and assemble the raw materials into a partially completed product. A finisher must complete the assembly operation by painting and packaging the product. A shipper must dispatch the finished products to the organization's customers. Also imagine that the company's manufacturing workforce consists of 12 employees organized into three assembly lines consisting of 4 employees each, with 1 employee on each line performing each of the four basic work activities.

What must be decided is whether to group the 12 employees by the tasks they perform, which is called **functional grouping,** or by the flow of work from initiation to completion, which is called **work flow grouping.** Each of these alternatives offers significant advantages and disadvantages.

Consider first what functional grouping, or grouping by the means of production, can offer the firm. The upper panel of Figure 8-1 shows how performers of the four tasks from each assembly line can be grouped together so that the four resulting work groups consist of people with the same sets of abilities, knowledge, and skills: the receivers, the fabricators, the finishers, and the shippers form four *functional* work groups.

Figure 8-1 ■ **Group Formation by Function or Work Flow**

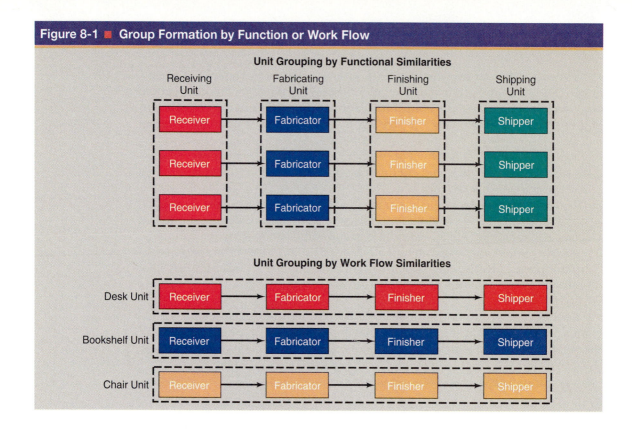

Functional work groups help integrate and coordinate employees who perform similar tasks. Employees in such groups can exchange information about task procedures, sharpening their knowledge and skills. They can also help each other out when necessary. This sort of cooperation can greatly enhance productivity.

In addition, functional grouping can allow the organization to take advantage of other cost savings. Suppose that receivers for all three of the assembly lines in Figure 8-1 need only five hours per day to complete their work and are idle for the remaining three hours. If receiving is handled in a single work group, the firm can economize by employing two receivers instead of three. In a full eight-hour day, these two people should be able to complete the group's work (3 workers × 5 hours each = 15 hours; 2 workers × 8 hours each = 16 hours), minimizing idle time and improving the firm's economic efficiency. The third receiver can be moved elsewhere in the company to perform a more productive job, and the company can derive substantial benefit from improved efficiency in the use of human resources.

On the negative side, functional grouping separates people performing different tasks along the same flow of work. This differentiation can encourage slowdowns that block the flow, reducing productivity. For instance, suppose the finisher on the desk assembly line has nothing to do and wants the desk fabricator to speed up in order to provide more work. Because of functional grouping, the two people are in different groups, and there is no simple way for them to communicate with each other directly. Instead, the desk finisher must rely on hierarchical communication linkages between the fabricating and finishing groups. The finisher must tell the supervisor of the finishing group about the problem. The finishing supervisor must notify the superintendent overseeing all manufacturing operations. The manufacturing superintendent must talk with the supervisor of the fabricating group. Finally, the fabricating supervisor must tell the desk fabricator to work faster. Meanwhile, productivity suffers because of the absence of direct communication along the flow of work.

Now consider what happens if work groups are created on the basis of work flow. In our furniture company, a different flow of work is associated with each of the firm's three product lines—desks, bookshelves, and chairs. The lower panel of Figure 8-1 illustrates the results of choosing the approach of grouping on the basis of work flow.

The primary strengths of work flow grouping grow out of the fact that it integrates all the activities required to manufacture a product or provide a service. Each separate work flow is completely enclosed within a single group. If employees who fill different functions along the assembly line need to coordinate with each other to maintain the flow of work, they can do so without difficulty. In an organization grouped by work flow similarities, work tends to flow smoothly.

Because of its encouragement of work flow integration, work flow grouping also enhances organizational adaptability. Operations on any of the firm's three assembly lines can be halted without affecting the rest of the company. Suppose, for example, that the desk assembly line in the company is shut down because of poor sales. To simulate this situation, cover the upper assembly line in the bottom panel of Figure 8-1 with a piece of paper. You can see that neither of the remaining two groups will be affected in any major way. Work on the bookcase and chair lines can continue without interruption. Under functional grouping, however, the firm would not have the same degree of flexibility. If you cover the upper assembly line in the top panel of Figure 8-1, you will note that all four of the groups created by functional grouping would be affected if desk production were interrupted. Complete reorganization would be required by any long-term disturbance.

Despite its strengths, work flow grouping does not permit the scale economies of functional grouping. With work flow grouping, people who perform the same function cannot help or substitute for one another. In addition, at times they will inevitably duplicate one another's work, adding to the firm's overall costs. Companies like General Electric have long struggled to reduce the costs of maintaining multiple sales forces—one for financial services, one for military contracts, one for consumer electronics, and so on. Moreover, it becomes very difficult for people who perform the same task to trade information about such things as more efficient work procedures and ways to improve task skills. So, just as functional grouping does not allow the adaptability of work flow grouping, work flow grouping does not produce the economic efficiency of functional grouping.

Group Development

In most organizations, choices between functional and work flow grouping are made by managers who are responsible for deciding whether efficiency or adaptability is of greater importance. Group formation is thus a process of determining the formal, established characteristics of groups.

How do the members of a group, once formed into a group, develop a sense of identity and purpose? A second process, that of group development, is the means through which such informal aspects emerge. As groups develop, members modify formally prescribed group tasks, clarify personal roles, and negotiate group norms. Research indicates that these developmental processes tend to advance through the four stages shown in Figure 8-2: initiation, differentiation, integration, and maturity.[7]

The first stage of group development, **initiation,** is one of uncertainty and anxiety. New or potential members focus on getting to know each other's personal views and abilities.[8] In the beginning they are likely to discuss neutral topics like the weather and local news that have little bearing on the group's purpose. As they gain familiarity and begin to feel more comfortable, members turn to discussing general work issues and each person's probable relationship to the formally prescribed task of the group. Attention now concentrates on determining which behaviors should be considered appropriate and what sorts of contributions people should be expected to make to the group. As ideas are exchanged and discussed, people who have the option may decide whether to join or leave the group. Members may also try to choose someone to act as their leader.

When a group enters the second stage of development, **differentiation,** conflicts are likely to erupt as members try to reach agreement on the purpose, goals, and objectives of the group. Strong differences of opinion may also emerge as members try to achieve consensus on exactly how they will accomplish the group's formally prescribed task. Sorting out who will do what—and when,

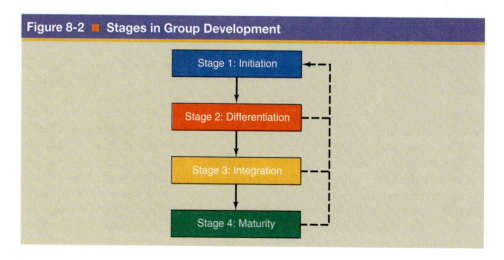

Figure 8-2 ■ Stages in Group Development

Stage 1: Initiation

Stage 2: Differentiation

Stage 3: Integration

Stage 4: Maturity

where, why, and how—and what reward members will receive for their performance often proves to be extremely difficult. Sometimes disagreements about members' roles in the group become violent enough to threaten the group's very existence. If successful, however, differentiation creates a structure of roles and norms that allows the group to accomplish missions its members could not accomplish alone.

Having weathered the differentiation stage, group members must resolve conflicts over other crucial issues in the third, **integration,** stage of group development. Integration focuses on reestablishing the central purpose of the group in light of the structure of roles developed during differentiation. The task of the group may come to be defined in informal terms that modify the group's formal purpose and reflect the experience and opinions of group members. Reaching a consensus about the group's purpose helps develop a sense of group identity among members and promotes cohesiveness within the group. It also provides the foundation for the development of additional rules, norms, and procedures to help coordinate interactions among members and facilitate the pursuit of group goals.

In the final stage of group development, **maturity,** members fulfill their roles and work toward attaining group goals. Many of the agreements reached about goals, roles, and norms may take on formal significance, being adopted by management and documented in writing. Formalizing these agreements helps to ensure that people joining the group at this stage will understand the group's purpose and way of functioning.

Even at this late stage a group may be confronted with new tasks or new requirements for performance. Changes in the group's environment or in its members may make it necessary to return to an earlier stage and resume the development process. Group development is thus a dynamic, continuous process in which informal understandings support or sometimes displace the formal characteristics of the group and its task.

Not every group passes through all four of the stages just described in a predictable, stepwise manner. Moreover, the process of passing between stages may be more erratic than smooth.[9] Nonetheless, together with the process of group formation, group development is the means through which groups come into existence and become organized.

Group Productivity

Are people necessarily more productive when working in groups than when working alone? Based on the growing prevalence of groups and teams in organizations, it seems that the answer to this question should be an unqualified yes.[10] However, a large body of research indicates that groups of individuals working together are sometimes less productive than the same number of people working alone.[11] Often this falloff in productivity can be avoided if managers work to reduce the negative effects of various obstacles to group productivity.

Obstacles to Group Productivity

Adding more people to a group increases the human resources that the group can put to productive use. Thus, as depicted in Figure 8-3, the *theoretical* productivity of a group should rise in direct proportion to the size of the group. However, after an initial rise, the group's *actual* productivity falls as its size continues to increase. The difference between what a group actually produces and what it might theoretically produce is known as **process loss.**[12] It is caused by a variety of obstacles to group productivity, the most influential of which are production blocking, group-maintenance activities, and social loafing.

Production blocking occurs when people get in each other's way as they try to perform a group task,[13] for example, when one member of a moving-van crew carries a chair through a doorway and another member waits to carry a box of clothing through the same doorway. Similarly, in a classroom discussion, one student's comments will be blocked if others talk at the same time. Such interruptions can cause the student to forget important ideas. The result is process loss.

In order for a group to continue to function effectively, its members must fulfill the requirements of several **group-maintenance roles.** Each of these roles helps to ensure the group's continued existence by building and preserving strong interpersonal relations among its members. The roles include *encouragers,* people who enhance feelings of warmth and solidarity within the group by

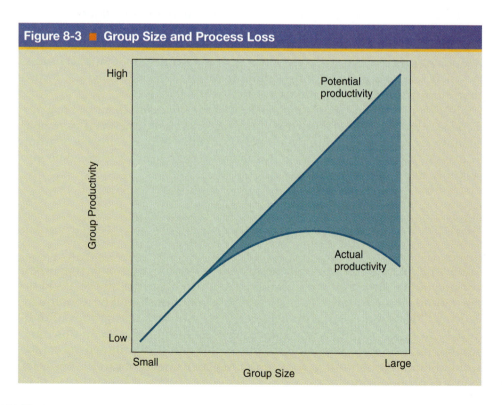

Figure 8-3 ■ Group Size and Process Loss

High

Potential
productivity

Group Productivity

Actual
productivity

Low

Small

Large

Group Size

praising, agreeing with, and accepting the ideas of others; *harmonizers,* who attempt to minimize the negative effects of conflicts among the group's members by resolving disagreements fairly, quickly, and openly and relieving interpersonal tension; and *standard setters,* who raise questions about group goals and goal attainment and set achievement standards with which group members can evaluate their performance.[14]

Although group-maintenance activities support and facilitate a group's continued functioning, they can also interfere with productive activity. For instance, members of a management team who are in conflict about a proposal must spend time not only on improving the proposal but also on harmonizing among themselves. Thus, group-maintenance activities have both positive and negative aspects. Without them, a group's existence may be seriously threatened. But, by diverting valuable time and effort, maintenance activities reduce a group's productivity and thus contribute to process loss.

Process loss can also be caused by **social loafing,** the result of the choice made by some members of a group to take advantage of others by doing less work, working more slowly, or in other ways decreasing their own contributions to group productivity.[15] According to economists, social loafing—also called *free riding*—makes sense from a loafer's perspective if the rewards the group receives for productivity are shared more or less equally among all group members.[16] A loafer can get the same rewards that everyone else gets but without having to expend the same personal effort.

Unless someone else in the group takes up the slack, the effect of even one person's loafing may be to lower the entire group's productivity. Consider a team of accountants performing an audit. If one takes a long lunch and misses an afternoon of counting inventory items, the others may be able to compensate by finishing their own work early and completing the inventory count themselves. However, if the other team members are so busy that they cannot take the time to count the inventory, the count will not be completed and process loss will occur.

Increasing Group Productivity

Managers can do a number of things to maintain or improve group productivity. These include adjusting the sizes of groups, enhancing group motivation, promoting group cohesion and norms that favor high productivity, and strengthening communication within groups.

Group Size.   Decreasing group size can have a positive effect on productivity. On average, people working in smaller groups are more productive than people in larger groups.[17] As suggested by Figure 8-4, this relationship can be traced to the effect of several factors—physical constraints, social distractions, coordination requirements, behavioral masking, and diffusion of responsibility.

To begin with, small groups simply have fewer members to get in each other's way. Clearly, production blocking caused by physical crowding is less likely to occur in small groups than in large ones. The effects of *physical constraints* are, therefore, weaker in small groups. In addition, group size influences productivity by affecting the amount of *social distraction* people experience when

Figure 8-4 ■ How Group Size Affects Group Productivity

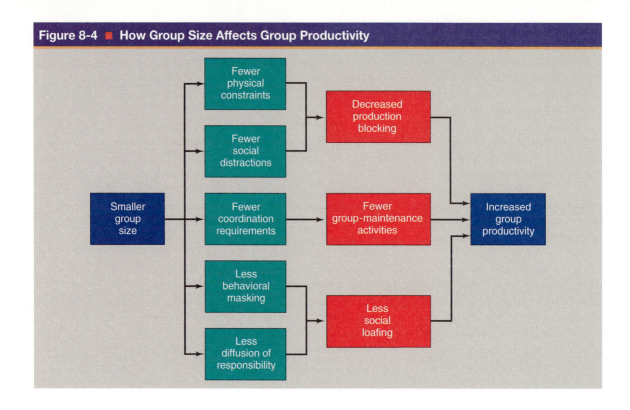

they work in a group. The smaller the group, the less likely it is that group members will distract one another and interrupt behavioral sequences that are important to the task. Production blocking traceable to distractions caused by others is, therefore, less likely to occur in small groups than in large ones.

Smaller groups also have lower *coordination requirements*. The fewer members a group has, the fewer the interdependencies that must be formed and maintained. In small groups, managers and group members need not devote a lot of time, energy, and other resources to group maintenance. As a result, they have more time for productive work.

Group size is also related to the incidence of *behavioral masking*. The behaviors of a group member may be masked or hidden by the simple presence of other members.[18] The smaller the group, the easier it is to observe each member's behavior, and this visibility affects the frequency of social loafing.[19] If loafers can be easily detected, they can also be easily expelled from the group and lose their share of group rewards. In such a setting, the role of social loafer is unattractive.[20]

Finally, group size influences the *diffusion of responsibility,* the sense that responsibility is shared broadly rather than shouldered personally. In general, the larger the group, the more likely it is that people will feel they share the responsibility for group tasks with others. Diffusion of responsibility tends to encourage social loafing because it provides a ready excuse for loafing. In a large group, productivity can be seen as someone else's responsibility. In a small group, however, each person is more apt to feel personally responsible for group performance and effectiveness.

Member Motivation. Member motivation is another important factor that affects group productivity and that can be managed to avoid or minimize process loss. As was indicated in Chapter 4, motivation is a crucial determinant of individual achievement, and it is just as crucial in determining the achievement of a group. Group members must be sufficiently motivated to reach the highest level of group productivity that their abilities permit. Just as goals and rewards can strengthen the motivation of individuals, they can also enhance motivation in groups.

As is true for research on individuals, studies of group performance have substantiated that setting specific, difficult group goals has a strong positive effect on group productivity. In one early study, members of groups with clear, specific goals were compared with members of groups whose goals were vague and ambiguous. The members of groups with specific goals were more attracted to their groups' tasks and conformed more to their groups' expectations. These factors enhanced group performance.[21] In another study of goal setting, researchers examined the effects of goal difficulty by comparing the outcomes of 149 United Way campaigns over a four-year period. Communities that set higher goals had better results than those that set lower goals.[22]

Other research has also shown that group goals have strong, persistent effects on group productivity. For instance, in a study of Air Force base personnel, researchers found that instituting a group goal-setting and feedback program increased productivity by 75 percent.[23] Similarly, in a two-year study performed at Notre Dame, the university hockey team established goals for aggressive behavior. The result was an increase in the team's legal bodychecking (opponent blocking). Bodychecking increased in the first playing season by 82 percent and in the second season by 141 percent. In addition, the team posted two winning records, its first winning records in five years.[24]

Research has also begun to highlight the specific processes through which group goals influence performance. One study in which students participated in a managerial simulation found that groups with specific, difficult goals outperformed groups with vague, "do your best" goals. The groups with specific and difficult goals were better than the other groups at planning how to meet those goals.[25] Groups confronted with difficult goals also seem to put forth more effort.[26]

Rewards contingent on specific achievement also help to motivate groups. There are two fundamentally different types of group rewards. **Cooperative group rewards** are distributed *equally* among the members of a group. That is, the group is rewarded *as a group* for its successful performance, and each member receives exactly the same reward.[27] This technique does not recognize individual differences in effort or performance but instead rewards employees' efforts to coordinate their work activities and to rely on one another. As a result, the cooperative reward system ignores the possibility that some members will make greater contributions to group task performance than others. As was discussed in Chapter 4, the inequity caused by this type of reward distribution can demotivate group members who are high performers.

Under the **competitive group rewards** system, group members are rewarded for successful performance *as individuals in a group*. They receive *equitable* rewards that vary according to their individual performance. This system, which is based on the idea that high group performance requires all members to perform at their highest capacity, rewards those who do, more than those who do not. It provides a strong incentive for individual effort, and so it can enhance individual productivity. However, it can pit group members against each other in a struggle for greater personal rewards. If this happens, the cooperation and coordination needed to perform group tasks may never develop, and group performance may suffer as a result.

Which of these two approaches to rewarding performance is likely to ensure the highest group productivity? It all depends on the degree of *task interdependence*.[28] Recall from Chapter 7 that higher levels of task interdependence—sequential, reciprocal, or comprehensive—require that group members work together. For this reason, cooperative rewards, which encourage cooperation and coordination, promote group productivity when paired with high task interdependence. In contrast, lower task interdependence, either complete independence or pooled interdependence, enables the members of a group to work independently. In such a situation, competitive rewards motivate high personal performance and lead to increased group productivity.

What happens if reward systems are switched? Pairing cooperative rewards with low interdependence will encourage unnecessary cooperation, may stifle personal performance, and may also promote social loafing. A similar mismatch can occur when competitive rewards are coupled with high interdependence. In this case, conflicts and competition between group members striving to maximize their own outcomes undermine cooperation. Imagine a group of salespersons, organized by geographic region, who are all competing for a sales bonus. One salesperson may become aware of a potential sale in some other salesperson's region but not share this information for fear of losing the bonus to the other person. Figure 8-5 summarizes the relations among type of group reward, task interdependence, and group productivity.

Cohesiveness and Productivity Norms.   In addition to being motivated by the appropriate goals and rewards, group members must also know what is expected of them on the job if the group is to be productive. Group norms provide this sort of knowledge, and group cohesiveness determines whether a mix of different norms will be found in a single group. Group norms and group cohesiveness thus combine to shape the performance expectations that influence member productivity.

A group's **cohesiveness** is measured by the degree to which a group sticks together. In a cohesive group, members feel attracted to one another and to the group as a whole.[29] A variety of factors encourage group cohesiveness. Among the most important are the following:

1. *Shared personal attitudes, values, or interests.* People who share the same attitudes, values, or interests are likely to be attracted to each other.
2. *Agreement on group goals.* Shared group goals encourage members to work together. When group members participate in determining their purpose and goals, they get to know and influence each other.

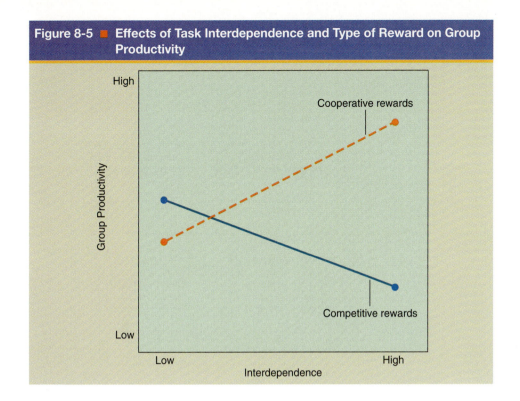

Figure 8-5 ■ Effects of Task Interdependence and Type of Reward on Group Productivity

3. *Frequent interaction.* Frequent interaction and the physical closeness it affords encourage group members to develop the mutual understanding and intimacy that characterize cohesiveness.
4. *Small group size.* Smaller groups are more likely to be cohesive than larger groups because physical proximity makes it easier for members to interact.
5. *Group rewards.* Cooperative group rewards that encourage interaction can also stimulate cohesiveness, especially when group members are performing interdependent tasks.
6. *Favorable evaluation.* Recognition given a group for effective performance can reinforce feelings of pride in group membership and group performance.
7. *External threat.* Threats to a group's well-being that originate from outside the group can strengthen the group's cohesiveness by providing a common enemy that motivates a unified response. Conflict between groups can promote cohesion within groups.
8. *Isolation.* Being cut off from other groups can reinforce members' sense of sharing a common fate, which, again, motivates a unified response.

The first six of these factors are clearly useful for building group cohesiveness. It is probably not a good idea to use intergroup conflict or isolation to encourage group cohesiveness, however, because both of these approaches discourage the cooperation between groups required to accomplish organizational goals.[30]

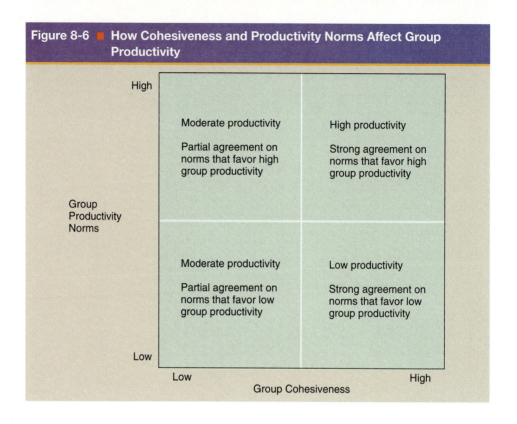

Figure 8-6 ■ How Cohesiveness and Productivity Norms Affect Group Productivity

	Low Group Cohesiveness	High Group Cohesiveness
High	Moderate productivity — Partial agreement on norms that favor high group productivity	High productivity — Strong agreement on norms that favor high group productivity
Low	Moderate productivity — Partial agreement on norms that favor low group productivity	Low productivity — Strong agreement on norms that favor low group productivity

Group Productivity Norms (vertical axis, High to Low)

Group Cohesiveness (horizontal axis, Low to High)

If a group is highly cohesive, shouldn't group productivity be high? Possibly, but not necessarily. Cohesiveness does affect the degree to which the members of a group *agree* on productivity norms, but it does not ensure that the group will adopt *high* productivity norms.[31] If a highly cohesive group has adopted norms favoring high productivity, its productivity will be high because everyone agrees that working productively is the right thing to do (see the upper right cell in Figure 8-6). In contrast, the productivity of highly cohesive groups adopting norms that favor low productivity tends to be quite low because everyone agrees that working productively is *not* the thing to do (see lower right cell in Figure 8-6).

Once group cohesiveness has been stimulated, what can be done to ensure that the group will perform productively? First, the group must be persuaded to adopt norms favoring high productivity. The material in Chapter 4, on motivation, would suggest that one means of persuasion is to reward productivity whenever it occurs. Managers can use both material rewards and praise for this purpose. At the same time, in order to avoid encouraging negative productivity norms, managers must not reward unacceptable performance or punish effective performers. Suppose, for example, that the management of an insurance company gives a group of salespeople $1,000 to split among themselves for every insurance policy a group member sells. Suppose further that the group sells more policies than expected and that the company then tightens the incentive system by reducing the group bonus to $500 per sale. The group will probably feel punished and may even decide to reduce its performance in the future.

What about the productivity of groups with low cohesiveness? As shown in both left cells in Figure 8-6, group productivity in situations of low cohesiveness fits between the two extremes described earlier because group members hold varying productivity norms. Some members of each group adopt norms that favor high productivity and work hard. Others adopt norms that favor low productivity and slack off. The aggregate result of this mix of norms is usually a low to moderate level of productivity.

Group Communication Structure.   If the members of a group cannot exchange information about their work, the group cannot function effectively. A viable **communication structure** is thus crucial to group productivity. For managers, it is important to know about the different kinds of group communication structures and to be able to implement those that encourage the greatest productivity.

In research on group communication and productivity, five structures have received considerable attention. They are the wheel, Y, chain, circle, and completely connected communication networks shown in Figure 8-7. The first three of these networks are the most centralized in that a central member can control information flows in the group. In the *wheel,* one group member can communicate with all the other members from a central hub, but the others can communicate only with the member at the hub. The *Y* is a variation on this theme. It consists of three spokes, two of which are lengthened into, in this case, two-person chains. Again, one group member serves as a central hub. A further modification produces the *chain,* in which members are linked sequentially. A member in a chain network can communicate only with the two members who are immediately adjacent to that member. Members at the ends of the chain can communicate with only one other person.

In contrast, in the decentralized circle and completely connected networks all members are equally able to send and receive messages. The *circle* allows each member to communicate with two others. The *completely connected* network puts every person in the group in touch with every other.

These five communication networks differ in the following:

- The *speed* at which information can be transmitted
- The *accuracy* with which information is transmitted
- The degree of *saturation,* which is high when information is distributed evenly in a group and low when some members have significantly more information than others
- The *satisfaction* of members with communication processes and the group in general[32]

Speed is linked directly to production quantity, and accuracy to production quality. Saturation and satisfaction are closely related to each other in that members who have access to information are also the most satisfied with group communication processes; so both factors can have indirect effects on group productivity and effectiveness.

Figure 8-7 ■ Group Communication Structures and Group Effectiveness

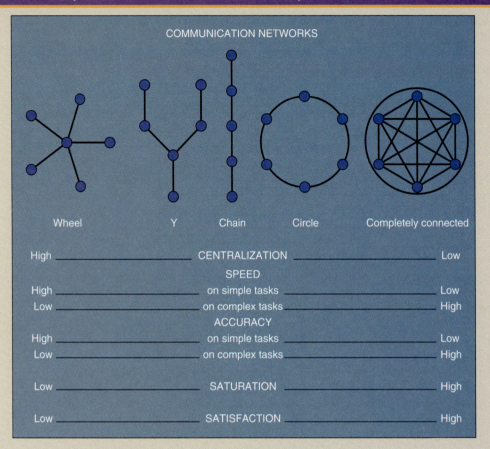

COMMUNICATION NETWORKS

Wheel | Y | Chain | Circle | Completely connected

High _____	CENTRALIZATION	_____ Low	

SPEED

| High _____ | on simple tasks | _____ Low |
| Low _____ | on complex tasks | _____ High |

ACCURACY

| High _____ | on simple tasks | _____ Low |
| Low _____ | on complex tasks | _____ High |

| Low _____ | SATURATION | _____ High |

| Low _____ | SATISFACTION | _____ High |

Source: Based on information in M. E. Shaw, *Group Dynamics: The Psychology of Small Group Behavior* (New York: McGraw-Hill, 1976), pp. 262–314.

As indicated in Figure 8-7, communication speed and accuracy in a group are influenced both by the nature of the group's communication network and by the relative complexity of the group's task. Group tasks can range in complexity from *simple* tasks that involve physical demands but little mental effort or need for communication among coworkers, to *complex* tasks that require greater mental effort, less physical exertion, and significant need for communication.[33] When a task is simple and communication networks are centralized, both speed and accuracy are higher. Centralization facilitates the minimal communication required to succeed at simple tasks. When tasks are simple and communication networks are decentralized, however, speed and accuracy are lower because more people are involved in communication than need be.

In contrast, when tasks are relatively complex, centralized communication networks lower both speed and accuracy because people serving as network hubs succumb to **information overload.** Overload and its effects are less likely in decentralized networks, because more people can get involved in processing information and share responsibilities for communication.

Both network saturation and member satisfaction are generally higher in decentralized networks. Everyone is informed and fully involved in the communication process and the task. (The only exception to this rule is that in centralized networks the one person at the hub of the network is usually very satisfied.) Task complexity does not appear to affect saturation or satisfaction in groups.

In sum, centralization increases the productivity of groups performing simple tasks that require little or no communication, but it generally reduces member satisfaction. For managers, this means that a group may perform a simple task efficiently, but because members' satisfaction is low, the group is not totally effective. In contrast, decentralization not only increases the productivity of groups performing complex tasks that require a lot of communication but also increases member satisfaction. The decentralized network is therefore an efficient *and* an effective way of organizing communication when complex tasks are at hand.

Team Effectiveness

Yet to be discussed is the performance of **teams,** a special type of group. All teams are groups, and thus team performance is influenced by all of the factors discussed so far. However, not all groups are teams, and team performance is also affected by additional factors that do not influence the productivity of other sorts of groups. In the next three sections of this chapter we will examine some of the features that make teams a special type of group, and we will discuss several keys to effective team performance.

Distinguishing Features of Teams

Teams are groups characterized by three important distinguishing features:

1. The members of teams are highly interdependent, typically being interconnected via comprehensive interdependence.
2. Teams are formed using work flow grouping, so the members of a team are responsible for performing several different functions.
3. Skills, knowledge, expertise, and information are often distributed unequally among the members of a team, because of differences in background, training, abilities, and access to resources, and all these differences are relevant to the cross-functional differences noted in point 2.

Because sports teams tend to be highly visible, and because they epitomize the differences between teams and other groups, we will illustrate some of our major points about teams by describing a football play that involved San Francisco 49ers quarterback Steve Young and wide receiver Jerry Rice. The play was designed to be a pass from Young to Rice. Rice was to start out on the right

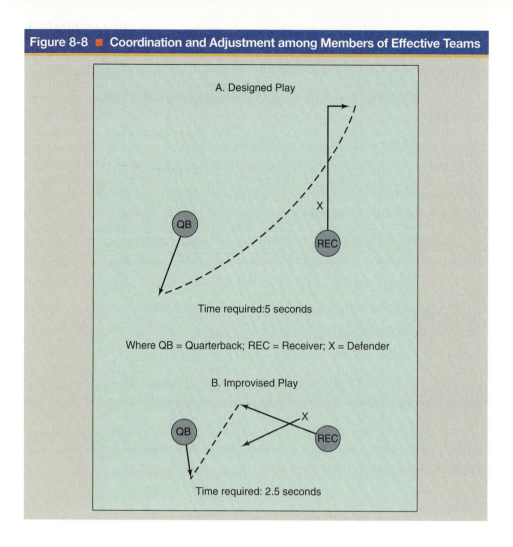

Figure 8-8 ■ Coordination and Adjustment among Members of Effective Teams

A. Designed Play

X

QB

REC

Time required:5 seconds

Where QB = Quarterback; REC = Receiver; X = Defender

B. Improvised Play

X

QB

REC

Time required: 2.5 seconds

side of the field, run 20 yards downfield, and then quickly turn back to the right sideline. Young was supposed to drop back six steps, fake a pass to the left sideline, and then turn hard and throw to the right sideline. The designed play is shown in the top half of Figure 8-8. But the moment the play started, the defensive player who was covering Rice left him and ran straight for Young (see the solid arrow in the bottom half of Figure 8-8). This surprise move on the defensive player's part spelled disaster for the planned play, which took five seconds to run properly, because Young was going to be hit by the defensive player in less than three seconds.

The moment the defensive player made his move, however, both Young and Rice—without any explicit communication—changed from the designed play to a different play. Instead of dropping back six steps and faking left (which would have taken too long), Young dropped back just three steps and looked over the middle. Instead of running 20 yards out and turning right, Rice immediately slanted toward the middle of the field (see the lines in the lower half of Figure 8-8). Two seconds into the play, Young threw the ball toward a vacant spot in the middle of the field. Three seconds into the play, Rice sprinted through that vacant spot, caught the ball while running at full speed, and ran unhindered for a touchdown. What could have been a disaster turned into triumph through successful teamwork.

The three distinguishing features of teams—high interdependence, work flow grouping, and differentiated skills and abilities—are clearly evident in this example. Young and Rice are dependent upon each other because neither one can both throw the ball and catch it. Work flow grouping is present in that each position (quarterback versus receiver) has separate responsibilities. With the exception of rare "trick plays," there are virtually no instances in which receivers throw the ball to quarterbacks. Finally, differentiated skills and abilities make the team members noninterchangeable. In other words, if Young and Rice switched positions so that Rice threw the ball and Young tried to run and catch it, there would be an immediate, substantial, and permanent drop-off in team effectiveness.

These same three characteristics are critical for distinguishing teams from other kinds of groups in work organizations. For example, Chrysler's "platform teams" are composed of designers, engineers, suppliers, manufacturing personnel, and marketing experts who all work together on a project at the same time.[34] Thus, concurrent engineering processes at Chrysler are built around such small teams of differentiated experts, and similar teams have been created in thousands of organizations over the last 10 years.[35]

These team-based structures offer two primary advantages over traditional hierarchical structures. First, they enable organizations to bring products to market faster than did previous systems in which the experts worked sequentially—with, for instance, designers handing over drawings to engineers, who would then hand over specifications to manufacturers, who would then hand a product over to marketers. With team-based structures, if the designers draw up a project that will be too difficult to produce or a problem to market, this problem is spotted early, when it is easier to rectify (see box).

A second advantage of team-based structures is that they eliminate the need for many different levels of middle management, giving workers autonomy over decisions that were previously the province of managers. Autonomy has a powerful, positive effect on workforce motivation, as indicated in Chapter 6, and reduction in the number of managers reduces administrative overhead. For both of these reasons, the use of teams can result in significant operating economies.

Keys to Team Effectiveness

The complexity of teams and team performance requires that managers know about factors that occur at many different levels of analysis. Some keys to effective team performance depend on factors associated with the *task,* so an analysis of the team's task is required.[36] Other keys to team effectiveness reside at the level of the *individual team member,* and therefore, individual contributions must also be examined. At yet a third level, effective interaction between pairs of team members—dyads—is critical for team success. Thus, it is necessary to study the

The Team that Helped Ford Build a Success

By 1992, Ford's Taurus had overtaken the Honda Accord as America's best-selling automobile. Along with its close relative, the Mercury Sable, Taurus accounted for more than 10,000 jobs at Ford—6 percent of the company's U.S. total—and 100,000 jobs at the 240 suppliers that furnished outsourced parts and services. It was no exaggeration to state that Ford's future rested on Taurus's continued success.

Yet, the Taurus was "maturing" in the marketplace, having undergone little change in styling since its 1986 introduction. Passes at designing a new model, in 1991, led at first to tame updates, causing many at Ford, among them family member William Clay Ford Jr., to advocate more extensive change. At roughly the same point in time, Richard L. Landgraff began assembling the 700-member Team Taurus to bring a new best-seller to market. Landgraff and team responded to the call for radical redesign by reinventing the Taurus from the ground up. Along the way, they also reinvented Ford's process of reinvention.

In the beginning, 150 members set up shop in the basement of Ford's Dearborn, Michigan, design center, in an area earlier nicknamed "the dungeon" by the creators of the original Taurus. Engineers handling chassis, engine, and manufacturing planning worked alongside designers, marketers, accountants, suppliers, and assembly employees to design and test the vehicle. Christopher Clements and Douglas F. Gaffka, designers of the Taurus interior and exterior, literally sat side by side to coordinate the car's total appearance. The two often exchanged drawings and critiqued each other's work, which resulted in a final design in which interior styling echoed prominent exterior features.

Meanwhile, team engineers tore apart a Toyota Camry, looking for product refinements that could be benchmarked during Taurus's redevelopment. In the process, the Taurus team learned that Japanese competitors were adding, not deleting, premium products on their cars. This led to the strategic decision to design in greater value, even if it meant increased costs and reduced profitability. Resulting changes in the car and projected pricing would cost the company about $700 per unit—or some $280 million over the 400,000 vehicles to be produced during the 1996 model year—but appeared necessary to compete in a slowing market.

As the design phase neared its end, a group of 120 factory workers from Atlanta and Chicago began building prototypes to test Taurus's ease of manufacturing. The assembly team discovered nearly 700 improvements while assembling over 200 cars. Workers from the team then returned to their home assembly plants, and later formed the core of the workforce that assembled the first Taurus models for public sale.

With its sizeable development costs and added features, the 1996 Taurus cost Ford $750 more per car to build than the 1995 model. Attempts to pass this addition on to customers were met by stiff resistance from Ford's dealers, who felt compelled to push for lower prices and rebate campaigns to counter expected price cutting by Japanese rivals. Nonetheless, after an initial period of consumer adjustment to Taurus's sweeping restyling, market signals indicated that Team Taurus's product would most likely continue to secure Ford's dominant position in the U.S. automotive market. In the words of Chairperson Alexander J. Trotman, the Taurus-Sable combination remained firmly positioned as "the 'family jewels' of the Ford car line."[1]

[1] K. Kerwin, E. H. Updike, and K. Naughton, "The Shape of a New Machine," *Business Week,* July 24, 1995, pp 60–68; and A. Taylor III, "Ford's Really Big Leap at the Future," *Fortune,* September 18, 1995, pp. 134–44.

joint performance of pairs of individuals. Finally, at the highest level of analysis, some important variables related to team effectiveness are contingent on characteristics of *the team as a whole*. For this reason, the team must also be analyzed as a distinct entity. Figure 8-9 shows these four levels arranged in a hierarchy, in which success at lower levels (e.g., the task or individual level) becomes a necessary but not a sufficient condition for success at higher levels (e.g., the dyad or team level).

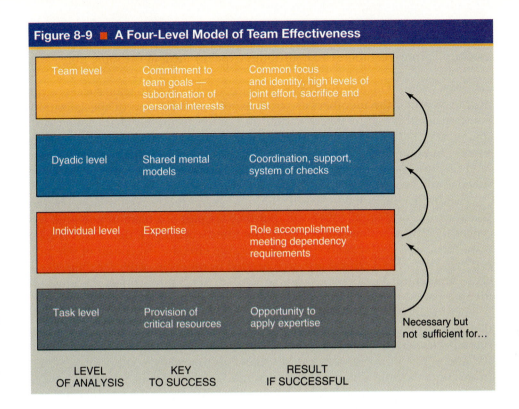

Figure 8-9 ■ A Four-Level Model of Team Effectiveness

Team level	Commitment to team goals — subordination of personal interests	Common focus and identity, high levels of joint effort, sacrifice and trust
Dyadic level	Shared mental models	Coordination, support, system of checks
Individual level	Expertise	Role accomplishment, meeting dependency requirements
Task level	Provision of critical resources	Opportunity to apply expertise

Necessary but not sufficient for...

| LEVEL OF ANALYSIS | KEY TO SUCCESS | RESULT IF SUCCESSFUL |

Task Level.   The key to team success at the task level is to ensure that all team members have the critical resources necessary to execute their specialized tasks. Needed resources include time, information, materials, and equipment. Without these resources, little else matters. If the team is not successful at this level, it is virtually certain that success will not occur at higher levels.

In the workplace, time is often the most critical resource. Organizations must make sure that team assignments are not simply "tacked on" to individuals' existing responsibilities, otherwise there will be insufficient time to successfully execute the stages of effective group development outlined earlier in this chapter. Moreover, time is especially critical when teams are composed of culturally diverse members. Culturally diverse teams tend to take a longer time to develop effective coordination strategies relative to homogeneous teams. Once such strategies are developed, however, culturally diverse teams perform just as effectively as homogeneous teams.[37]

Another resource that is becoming increasingly important to teams is computer networking technology. "Groupware" software allows teams of people to collaborate electronically, often from remote locations, and enables managers to put together teams without having to worry about geographic proximity. Groupware can also keep track of team members' schedules and distribute electronic mail. Finally, in many instances, groupware can eliminate the production blocking problems discussed earlier in this chapter, in which one person's behavior (e.g., talking) gets in the way of another person's behavior. With electronic media, all group members can contribute (type in) ideas at the same time.[38]

Individual Level. Once resources are in place, the next key to team success is the degree to which the members are truly experts in their area of specialization. Some quarterbacks can throw harder and more accurately than others, and some receivers run faster and catch more reliably than others. No amount of resources can make up for a lack of ability in these areas. Having the appropriate level of expertise in the right positions helps ensure that the team's tasks and subgoals will be accomplished.

Clearly, having individuals with the right skills, abilities, knowledge, or dispositions is critical for all jobs—whether they are part of a team or not—but it is especially critical within teams due to the interdependence that exists among team members. Under such circumstances, the effective execution of one person's role becomes a critical resource needed by others in order for them to execute their roles. The best receivers in football become worthless the moment they are paired with a weak-armed quarterback who cannot throw straight.

Because of the dependence of team members on one another, one practice that is becoming more widespread is the involvement of team members in personnel selection decisions. For instance, the I/N Tek plant in South Bend, Indiana, is one of the most advanced steel-finishing mills in the United States. In this organization, which is a joint venture between Inland Steel and Japan's Nippon Steel, job candidates interview with a human resource specialist, the prospective manager, and a representative of the team. An applicant cannot be hired unless rated acceptable by all three interviewers. This practice reinforces the idea that members must get along with each other and work together in order to succeed as a team.[39]

Dyadic Level. Provided that critical resources are in place and that individuals have the requisite abilities to accomplish their own specific tasks, the next key to effective teamwork is that the members of every *dyad* in a team have an understanding of one another's roles. The term *dyad* means "two persons," and every team of a set number of individuals can be thought of in terms of the number of "two-person teams" that are created by the overall team structure. A three-person team can be thought of as three dyads, a four-person team can be thought of as six dyads, and so on.

To work together smoothly, dyad members need to have a "shared mental model" regarding each other's needs and responsibilities.[40] Although one member may not be able to perform the task of the other, that member needs to understand the requirements and objectives of the other's task.

Recall how Steve Young and Jerry Rice both instantly abandoned the designed play the moment something unexpected happened (that is, when the player covering Rice ran at Young). Rice recognized that Young would no longer have the time needed to run the designed play and therefore ran straight across the field, minimizing the time needed to make a throw as well as the distance the ball would have to be thrown. Although Rice might not have had the knowledge and abilities to be a quarterback, he did have an understanding of what the quarterback needed from a receiver in this type of situation. Similarly, due to the speed with which the play developed, Young never had time to tell Rice what to do. He simply assumed that Rice would recognize the problem confronting the quarterback in this situation, and threw the ball to the spot he believed Rice would reach in a second or two. The fact that all this happened without any communication shows how Young and Rice shared a single mental model about what was happening, and the implications that it had for each of the two specialists. As indicated in this example, an unstated mutual understanding and appreciation of each other's role is critical to effective teamwork.

Teams made up of dyads with shared mental models show a great deal of coordination with a minimum of communication. Although it might seem that good teams should communicate more than poor teams, research on airline cockpit crews indicates just the opposite. The mutual understanding embodied by dyads in the best crews makes a lot of talk unnecessary. Typically, too much communication in these kinds of crews is a sign of a team struggling to organize and coordinate itself.[41]

Sharing mental models also has other benefits beyond coordination. First, high levels of mutual understanding create the conditions necessary for supporting and backing up other team members. If one team member knows another's responsibilities and is aware of extenuating circumstances that prohibit this person from meeting them, the first team member may fill in and help out. The mutual understanding that comes about through shared mental models also helps the team diagnose problems with a member who for one reason or another (perhaps illness or injury) is not doing what everyone else on the team has come to expect. This type of mutual understanding among team members helps provide a system of checks that is especially critical given the interdependence and specialization that characterize teams.

Team Level.   At the team level, the key to success is commitment to team goals and the subordination of personal or specialized interests. All groups have some goal or purpose, but in teams the specialization of team members creates a situation especially conducive to differentiated interests. This, combined with the comprehensive nature of independence among team members, makes succumbing to self-interest a constant threat and fatal problem. No amount of resources, individual competence, or shared mental models can overcome the problems that occur when team members place personal pursuits above the team's best interests.

A common symptom of poorly performing teams is that specialized members focus more on their specialty and their performance within that specialty than on the performance of the team. For instance, the quarterback on a losing team might care more about his own performance and statistics than the team's performance. This might lead him to engage in behaviors that enhance personal success but do not advance the interests of the team. On the pass from Young to Rice, for example, to execute the improvised play properly, each player puts himself at some personal risk. A receiver running a short route over the middle of the field (the improvised play) is much more likely to be injured than one running a long pattern heading out to the side of the field (the designed play). A quarterback who is about to be hit is much safer holding on to the ball and bracing for the hit (taking the sure loss) than waiting until the last moment and throwing the ball (and therefore being off balance when the hit is delivered). Yet, success on such a play requires that both players have the shared mental model of what needs to be done and the willingness to do it, even at the cost of being exposed to personal risk.

A shared vision of and desire for team-level success ensures that each member is willing to sacrifice personal interests for the common goal. In addition, it alleviates tendencies toward social loafing and creates an environment in which all members put forth their best efforts. A strong sense of overarching purpose also gives the team's differentiated members something shared to focus upon, thus reinforcing feelings of unity. Finally, and perhaps of most importance, once all team members are convinced that everyone shares the same desire for team-level success, a sense of trust develops that can help the team weather short-term problems or isolated failures.

Team Decision Making

Though developed for general application, the model of team effectiveness just described can also be adapted to specific circumstances and types of team performance. One specific type of performance that is critical to a large number of teams is decision making. In fact, the purpose of forming teams in the first place is often to bring more expertise to bear on a problem so that better decisions can be made.

The multilevel theory of team decision-making effectiveness, shown in Figure 8-10, is an adaptation of the general model that is useful when a decision-making team is organized as a hierarchy, with a single leader who ultimately commits the team to one decision or another and several followers who provide advice and other input about the decision to be reached. It highlights the information-processing requirements confronting such teams and isolates the most important determinants of team performance found at the decision level, the individual level, and the dyadic level. In so doing, it suggests that many of the critical determinants of team effectiveness occur at levels *below the team level*. The theory also indicates that, for each lower-level determinant, there is an analogous variable at the team level. The resulting pairs of variables, described next, are shown in the double triangle in Figure 8-10.

Decision informity resides at the decision level (similar to the task level of the general model described previously). It is the degree to which team members have accurate, relevant information about the particular decision to be made. This variable is at the decision level because a team can have a great deal of reliable information regarding some decisions but be poorly informed regarding others.

Over many decision-making opportunities, some teams are consistently better informed than others. This variation is captured by a team-level variable, analogous to decision informity, that can be referred to as **team informity.** Team

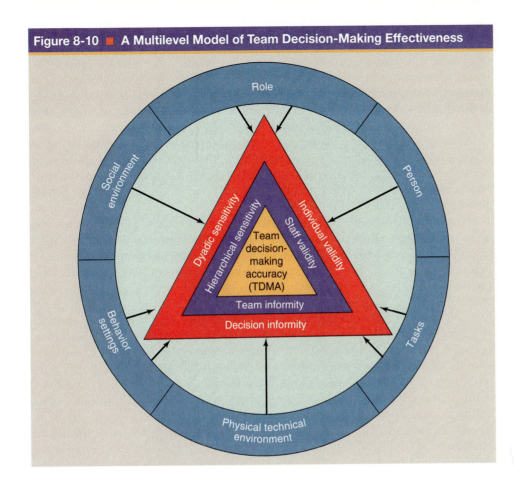

Figure 8-10 ■ A Multilevel Model of Team Decision-Making Effectiveness

informity is the average level of decision informity for a given team across many decisions. The theory behind the multilevel theory proposes that team informity is one of the core driving influences behind the accuracy of team decisions.

At the level of the individual team member, the most critical variable is *individual validity,* or the degree to which a particular team member can process available information and provide sensible input into team decision-making processes. Some individuals are able to make highly valid recommendations to their team about which decision to make, and some individuals can only make poor recommendations. This difference is one of individual validity.

The team-level analog of individual validity is **staff validity.** Some teams have, on average, better members than other teams. Staff validity is the average level of validity across all of the members of a team (the team's "staff"). The multilevel theory proposes that staff validity is another of the core influences of team-level decision accuracy.

The final core variable identified by the multilevel theory is at the dyadic level and is labeled *dyadic sensitivity.* A team with multiple members and a leader is composed of several hierarchical dyads, and it is quite possible that a team leader will be confronted from time to time with different recommendations from different team members regarding what decision the team should make. Dyadic sensitivity is the degree to which the leader accurately weighs each team member's recommendation in arriving at a team decision. This variable resides at the dyadic level, because a leader may develop an effective weighting system for one staff member but not another.

In addition, there are likely to be stable differences among teams in the average level of dyadic sensitivity. These differences are captured in a team-level variable called **hierarchical sensitivity.** Hierarchical sensitivity is then the third core, team-level variable that accounts for differences among teams in the degree of team decision-making accuracy.

The multilevel theory suggests that all other variables are "non-core variables" and proposes that their effects, if any, are transmitted through the core variables just described. So, for instance, a variable like cohesiveness is predicted to affect the accuracy of team decision making only by leading to greater hierarchical sensitivity or higher levels of team informity. Several empirical studies of the multilevel theory have supported this suggestion, indicating that the effects of variables traditionally studied in the group decision-making research (e.g., group cohesiveness, stress, familiarity, and experience) on the decision accuracy of hierarchically organized teams are mediated by the effects of the three core variables. More generally, the same research has provided support for the multilevel theory as a whole. Results have shown that hierarchically organized teams that are high on all three core characteristics are 5 to 10 times more accurate in their decision making than are teams that are low on these characteristics.[42] For managers, the implications of these findings are straightforward: Management of decision making in hierarchically organized teams requires attention to and regulation of the core variables identified in the multilevel theory of team decision-making effectiveness.

SUMMARY

Groups in organizations are formed on the basis of *functional grouping*, which favors efficiency, or *work flow grouping*, which enhances flexibility. Informal characteristics emerge during the process of *group development* as groups pass through the four stages of *initiation, differentiation, integration,* and *maturity*.

Due to *process loss*, groups in general are less productive than individuals working alone. Process loss can be traced to the effects of *production blocking, group-maintenance activities*, and *social loafing*. Factors that can be managed to reduce or eliminate the effects of process loss include group size, member motivation and group rewards, group cohesiveness and norms, and the group's communication structure.

Teams are a special type of group that are characterized by high levels of interdependence, work flow grouping, and differentiated knowledge, skills, and abilities among team members. These unique features of teams make certain factors more critical for success than is the case for other types of groups. The availability of *specialized resources, high levels of expertise* at each position, *shared mental models* for the manner in which pairs of specialists work with each other in different situations, and a *willingness to put team success ahead of personal interests* are the hallmarks of successful teamwork.

Decision making in hierarchically organized teams places special requirements on team processes and resources. Key variables that influence the accuracy of team decisions are *team informity, staff validity,* and *hierarchical sensitivity.* These are paired with lower-level origins in *decision informity, individual validity,* and *dyadic sensitivity,* respectively.

Review Questions

1. What are the three criteria of group effectiveness? Why is group effectiveness assessed in terms of all three of these criteria instead of being measured by group productivity alone?
2. Why is work flow grouping more flexible than functional grouping? If your company sold pencils, pens, and notebook paper, which type of unit grouping would provide the greatest benefit? Why?
3. What is process loss? How do production blocking and social loafing contribute to its presence? How does a group's size affect its productivity? What factors explain this relationship?
4. What influence do group goals have on member motivation? What effects do group rewards have on this motivation? What implications do your answers have for managers who must motivate individuals to perform productively in groups?
5. Explain why the statement "Highly cohesive groups are more productive than groups that are not cohesive" is not necessarily correct. What specific things might you do as a manager to ensure that high cohesion actually leads to high productivity?
6. Explain why centralized communication structures enhance the productivity of groups performing simple tasks but depress the performance of groups performing complex jobs. What sort of structure would you recommend for a group of accountants auditing the books of a large manufacturing firm? Why?
7. In the United States, television ratings make it clear that many more people are interested in watching professional football games than are interested in watching professional major-league baseball games. One major exception to this rule, however, is seen with the all-star games of these sports. Baseball's all-star game is much more popular than football's all-star game (which is not even televised by any of the three major networks). Most people believe that baseball's all-star game is exciting and filled with great plays, whereas football's all-star game is dull and filled with many major miscues on each side. Since no one could question the skills of individual players in either of these all-star games, why might one of these sports surpass the other in terms of generating effective all-star teams?
8. How does each of the three core variables identified in the multilevel theory affect decision making in hierarchically organized teams? If you were the leader of a hierarchical team prone to making poor decisions, what would you do to improve your team's decision accuracy?

Implementation Guide

Managing group effectiveness in general, and group and team productivity in particular, requires careful analysis. The following questions can help guide this analysis.

1. Was the group formed using functional grouping or work flow grouping? Does its formation seem to match its purpose in the organization? Does the group's formation seem to match the mission and purpose of the organization?
2. In what stage of development is the group? Can symptoms of ineffectiveness, such as poor productivity or member dissatisfaction, be traced to the group's current level of development?
3. Have you evidence that the group suffers from serious process loss? Is production blocking a problem? Are maintenance activities overwhelming productive resources? Is social loafing a problem?
4. Can group size be manipulated to solve productivity problems? If so, does available evidence suggest that this manipulation will enhance productivity?
5. Can productivity problems be traced to poor group member motivation? Does the group have specific and difficult individual *and* group performance goals? Are performance-contingent rewards used? Does the type of reward match the level of task interdependence?
6. Is the group cohesive? If so, do group norms support productive activities?
7. Can the group's communication structure cope with the information required to perform its task?
8. Can this group be considered a team, and if so, does it have the resources necessary to accomplish its mission?
9. Does each team member have the necessary specialized skills and abilities, and do these specialists have a shared mental model of how they should coordinate their activities?
10. Are team members committed to team goals or are team members driven by their own self-interests?
11. If the team is responsible for decision making and is organized in a hierarchy—with a leader responsible for team output—does the absence of one or more of the variables of team informity, staff validity, and hierarchical sensitivity contribute to inaccuracy?

ENDNOTES

1. J. Hoerr, "The Payoff from Teamwork: The Gains in Quality Are Substantial—So Why Isn't It Spreading Faster?" *Business Week,* July 10, 1989, pp. 56–62; E. Schine, "Mattel's Wild Race to Market," *Business Week,* February 21, 1994, pp. 62–63; K. Kerwin, E. H. Updike, and K. Naughton, "The Shape of a New Machine," *Business Week,* July 24, 1995, pp. 60–66; and S. Sherman, "Secrets of HP's 'Mud-dled' Team," *Fortune,* March 18, 1996, pp. 116–20.
2. G. C. Homans, *The Human Group* (New York: Harcourt, Brace, Jovanovich, 1950), p. 1; M. E. Shaw, *Group Dynamics: The Psychology of Small Group Behavior* (New York: McGraw-Hill, 1981), p. 8; and D. L. Gladstein, "Groups in Context: A Model of Task Group Effectiveness," *Administrative Science Quarterly* 29 (1984), pp. 499–517.

3. D. Cartwright and A. Zander, *Group Dynamics: Research and Theory* (New York: Harper & Row, 1968), pp. 46–48.

4. K. L. Bettenhausen, "Five Years of Group Research: What We Have Learned and What Needs to be Addressed," *Journal of Management* 17 (1991), pp. 345–81.

5. D. A. Nadler, J. R. Hackman, and E. E. Lawler III, *Managing Organizational Behavior* (Boston: Little, Brown, 1979), pp. 136–37.

6. H. Mintzberg, *The Structuring of Organizations* (Englewood Cliffs, NJ: Prentice Hall, 1979), pp. 108–29.

7. B. W. Tuckman, "Developmental Sequence in Small Groups," *Psychological Bulletin* 63 (1965), pp. 384–99; B. M. Bass and E. C. Ryterband, *Organizational Psychology,* 2d ed. (Boston: Allyn & Bacon, 1979), pp. 252–54; J. P. Wanous, A. E. Reichers, and S. D. Malik, "Organizational Socialization and Group Development: Toward an Integrative Perspective," *Academy of Management Review* 9 (1984), pp. 670–83; R. Albanese and D. D. Van Fleet, *Organizational Behavior: A Managerial Viewpoint* (Hinsdale, IL: Dryden, 1983), p. 259; M. F. Maples, "Group Development: Extending Tuckman's Theory," *Journal for Specialists in Group Work* 13 (1988), pp. 17–23; and J. D. Rothwell, *In Mixed Company: Small Group Communication* (Fort Worth, TX: Harcourt, Brace, Jovanovich, 1992), pp. 55–80.

8. M. Booth-Butterfield, S. Booth-Butterfield, and J. Koester, "The Function of Uncertainty Reduction in Alleviating Tension in Small Groups," *Communication Research Reports* 5 (1988), pp. 146–53.

9. K. L. Bettenhausen and J. K. Murnighan, "The Emergence of Norms in Competitive Decision-Making Groups," *Administrative Science Quarterly* 30 (1985), pp. 350–72; C. J. Gersick, "Time and Transition in Work Teams: Toward a New Model of Group Development," *Academy of Management Journal* 31 (1988), pp. 9–41; "Marking Time: Predictable Transitions in Task Groups," *Academy of Management Journal* 32 (1989), pp. 274–309; K. L. Bettenhausen and J. K. Murnighan, "The Development of an Intragroup Norm and the Effects of Interpersonal and Structural Changes," *Administrative Science Quarterly* 36 (1991), pp. 20–35; and E. Romanelli and M. L. Tushman, "Organizational Transformation as Punctuated Equilibrium: An Empirical Test," *Academy of Management Journal* 37 (1994), pp. 1141–66.

10. For a discussion of several of the assumptions underlying this belief, see G. R. Ferris and J. A. Wagner III, "Quality Circles in the United States: A Conceptual Reevaluation," *Journal of Applied Behavioral Science* 21 (1985), pp. 155–67.

11. G. W. Hill, "Group versus Individual Performance: Are N + 1 Heads Better Than One?" *Psychological Bulletin* 9 (1982), pp. 517–39; Shaw, *Group Dynamics,* p. 78; and P. B. Smith, *Groups within Organizations* (London: Harper & Row, 1973), p. 17.

12. I. D. Steiner, *Group Processes and Productivity* (New York: Academic Press, 1972). We use the term *process loss* somewhat more broadly than Steiner, applying it to all decrements in group productivity.

13. M. Diehl and W. Stroebe, "Productivity Loss in Brainstorming Groups: Toward the Solution of a Riddle," *Journal of Personality and Social Psychology* 53 (1987), pp. 497–509.

14. K. Benne and P. Sheats, "Functional Roles of Group Members," *Journal of Social Issues* 2 (1948), pp. 42–47.

15. B. Latané, K. Williams, and S. Harkins, "Many Hands Make Light Work: The Causes and Consequences of Social Loafing," *Journal of Personality and Social Psychology* 37 (1979), pp. 822–32; A. Shepperd, "Productivity Loss in Performance Groups: A Motivation Analysis," *Psychological Bulletin* 113 (1993), pp. 67–81; S. J. Karau and K. D. Williams, "Social Loafing: A Meta-Analytic Review and Theoretical Integration," *Journal of Personality and Social Psychology* 64 (1993), pp. 681–706; and D. R. Comer, "A Model of Social Loafing in Real Work Groups," *Human Relations* 48 (1995), pp. 64–67.

16. M. Olson, *The Logic of Collective Action* (Cambridge, MA: Harvard University Press, 1965), p. 11. See also R. Albanese and D. D. Van Fleet, "Rational Behavior in Groups: The Free-Riding Tendency," *Academy of Management Review* 10 (1985), pp. 244–55.

17. R. Z. Gooding and J. A. Wagner III, "A Meta-Analytic Review of the Relationship between Size and Performance: The Productivity and Efficiency of Organizations and Their Subunits," *Administrative Science Quarterly* 30 (1985), pp. 462–81.

18. J. A. Fleishman, "Collective Action as Helping Behavior: Effects of Responsibility Diffusion on Contributions to a Public Good," *Journal of Personality and Social Psychology* 38 (1980), pp. 629–37; and G. R. Jones, "Task Visibility, Free Riding, and Shirking: Explaining the Effect of Structure and Technology on Employee Behavior," *Academy of Management Review* 9 (1984), pp. 684–95.

19. K. Williams, S. Harkins, and B. Latané, "Identifiability as a Deterrent to Social Loafing: Two Cheering Experiments," *Journal of Personality and Social Psychology* 40 (1981), pp. 303–11.

20. J. George, "Extrinsic and Intrinsic Origins of Perceived Social Loafing in Organizations," *Academy of Management Journal* 35 (1992), pp. 191–202.

21. B. H. Raven and J. Reitsema, "The Effects of Varied Clarity of Group Goals and Group Path on the Individual and His Relation to the Group," *Human Relations* 10 (1957), pp. 29–44.

22. A. Zander and T. Newcomb, "Group Level of Aspiration in United Fund Campaigns," *Journal of Personality and Social Psychology* 6 (1967), pp. 157–62.

23. R. D. Pritchard, S. D. Jones, P. L. Roth, J. Stuebing, and S. E. Ekeberg, "Effects of Group Feedback, Goal Setting, and Incentives on Organizational Productivity," *Journal of Applied Psychology* 73 (1988), pp. 337–58.

24. D. C. Anderson, C. R. Crowell, M. Doman, and G. S. Howard, "Performance Posting, Goal Setting, and Activity-Contingent Praise as Applied to a College Hockey Team," *Journal of Applied Psychology* 73 (1988), pp. 87–95.

25. K. G. Smith, E. A. Locke, and D. Berry, "Goal Setting, Planning and Organizational Performance: An Experimental Simulation," *Organizational Behavior and Human Decision Processes* 46 (1990), pp. 118–34.

26. L. R. Weingart, "Impact of Group Goals, Task Component Complexity, Effort, and Planning on Group Performance," *Journal of Applied Psychology* 77 (1992), pp. 682–93; see also A. M. O'Leary-Kelly, J. J. Martocchio, and D. D. Frink, "A Review of the Influence of Group Goals on Group Performance," *Academy of Management Journal* 37 (1994), pp. 1285–301; D. J. Mesch, J. L. Farh, and P. M. Podsakoff, "Effects of Feedback Sign on Group Goal Setting, Strategies, and Performance," *Group and Organization Management* 19 (1994), pp. 309–33; and D. F. Crown and J. G. Rosse, "Yours, Mine, and Ours: Facilitating Group Productivity through the Integration of Individual and Group Goals," *Organizational Behavior and Human Decision Processes* 64 (1995), pp. 138–50.

27. M. Deutsch, *The Resolution of Conflict: Constructive and Destructive Processes* (New Haven, CT: Yale University Press, 1973), p. 325.

28. L. K. Miller and R. L. Hamblin, "Interdependence, Differential Rewarding, and Productivity," *American Sociological Review* 28 (1963), pp. 768–78; R. Slavin, "Classroom Reward Structure: Analytical and Practical Review," *Review of Educational Research* 47 (1977), pp. 633–50; J. A Wagner III, P. A. Rubin, and T. J. Callahan, "Incentive Payment and Nonmanagerial Productivity: An Interrupted Time Series Analysis of Magnitude and Trend," *Organizational Behavior and Human Decision Processes* 42 (1988), pp. 47–74; and R. Wageman, "Interdependence and Group Effectiveness," *Administrative Science Quarterly* 40 (1995), pp. 145–80.

29. Shaw, *Group Dynamics,* p. 197; D. Cartwright, "The Nature of Group Cohesiveness," in *Group Dynamics,* D. Cartwright and A. Zander, eds., 3d ed., (New York: Harper & Row, 1968), pp. 91–109; L. Festinger, S. Schachter, and K. Back, *Social Pressures in Informal Groups* (New York: Harper & Row, 1950), p. 164; L. Libo, *Measuring Group Cohesiveness* (Ann Arbor: University of Michigan Press, 1953), p. 1; I. Summers, T. Coffelt, and R. E. Horton, "Work Group Cohesion," *Psychological Reports* 63 (1988), pp. 627–36; and J. Keyton and J. Springston, "Redefining Cohesiveness in Groups," *Small Group Research* 21 (1990), pp. 234–54.

30. L. R. Weingart, R. J. Bennett, and J. M. Brett, "The Impact of Consideration of Issues and Motivational Orientation on Group Negotiation Process and Outcome," *Journal of Applied Psychology* 78 (1993), pp. 504–17.

31. L. Berkowitz, "Group Standards, Cohesiveness, and Productivity," *Human Relations* 7 (1954), pp. 509–19; S. Schachter, N. Ellertson, D. McBride, and D. Gregory, "An Experimental Study of Cohesiveness and Productivity," *Human Relations* 4 (1951), pp. 229–38; S. E. Seashore, *Group Cohesiveness in the Industrial Work Group* (Ann Arbor, MI: Survey Research Center, Institute for Social Research, 1954), p. 80; B. Mullen and C. Copper, "The Relation between Group Cohesiveness and Performance: An Integration," *Psychological Bulletin* 116 (1994), pp. 210–27; see also J. R. Hackman, "Group Influences on Individuals in Organizations," in *Handbook of Industrial and Organizational Psychology,* M. D. Dunnette and L. M. Hough, eds., 2d ed. (Palo Alto, CA: Consulting Psychologists Press, 1992), pp. 199–267.

32. A. Bavelas and D. Barrett, "An Experimental Approach to Organizational Communication," *Personnel* 27 (1951), pp. 366–71.

33. J. A. Wagner III and R. Z. Gooding, "Shared Influence and Organizational Behavior: A Meta-Analysis of Situational Factors Expected to Moderate Participation-Outcome Relationships," *Academy of Management Journal* 30 (1987), pp. 524–41.

34. J. B. Treece, "Does Chrysler Finally Have the Jeep That It Needs?" *Business Week,* January 20, 1992, pp. 21–22.

35. J. A. Byrne, "Why Several Heads Are Better Than One," *Business Week,* September 11, 1993, pp. 45–46.

36. M. A. Campion, G. J. Medsker, and A. C. Higgs, "Relations between Work Group Characteristics and Effectiveness: Implications for Designing Effective Work Groups, *Personnel Psychology* 46 (1993), pp. 823–50.

37. W. E. Watson, K. Kumar, and L. K. Michaelson, "Cultural Diversity's Impact on Interaction Process and Performance: Comparing Homogeneous and Diverse Task Groups," *Academy of Management Journal* 36 (1993), pp. 590–602.

38. R. B. Gallupe, A. R. Dennis, W. H. Cooper, J. S. Valacich, L. M. Bastianutti, and J. F. Nunamaker, "Electronic Brainstorming and Group Size," *Academy of Management Journal* 35 (1992), pp. 350–69.

39. M. Levinson, "When Workers Do the Hiring," *Newsweek,* June 21, 1993, p. 48.

40. P. Senge, "The Leader's New Work: Building Learning Organizations," *Sloan Management Review* 32 (1990), pp. 7–23; and P. Senge, *The Fifth Discipline: The Art and Practice of the Learning Organization* (New York: Doubleday/Currency, 1990).

41. J. Orasanu and E. Salas, "Team Decision Making in Complex Environments," in *Decision-Making in Action: Models and Methods*, G. Klein, J. Orasanu, R. Calderwood, and C. Szambok, eds., (Wildwood, NJ: Ablex Publishing Corporation, 1993), pp. 31–55.

42. J. R. Hollenbeck, D. R. Ilgen, D. J. Sego, J. Hedlund, D. A. Major, and J. Phillips, "The Multi-level Theory of Team Decision-Making: Decision Performance in Teams Incorporating Distributed Expertise," *Journal of Applied Psychology* 81 (1995), pp. 292–316.

Chapter Nine

Leadership of Groups and Organizations

In the early 1990s, no company experienced more internal strife and dissension than United Airlines. The flight attendants had bitter relations with the pilots, because of what they perceived as unequal treatment. The pilots in turn had bitter relations with the mechanics, because each side blamed the other for the poor condition of many of their aged aircraft. The unionized mechanics, who worked outside in all conditions, had nothing but contempt for the office managers who worked inside lavish company headquarters. Indeed, the only thing that united these groups was the perception that the company's leader, Stephen M. Wolf, could not be trusted to do what was best for any of them. As one employee stated, "This is the kind of place where management thinks they are way up there, and the rest of us are way down here. They want to make sure the shareholders get what they want, but they don't care much about the employees."[1]

As might be expected, these kinds of dysfunctional internal dynamics severely detracted from the firm's ability to compete in a deregulated market.[2] In particular, the company was being ravaged by Southwest Airlines, whose fun-loving and popular CEO, Herb Kelleher, had created just the opposite corporate culture (see box in Chapter 1). United competed directly with Southwest in 20 percent of its markets, but the cost of flying one passenger one mile for United during these years was close to 10 cents, versus 7 cents for Southwest. When you are flying as many passengers as many miles as these companies do, this difference adds up, and United piled up huge losses during this period—$332 million in 1991, $1 billion in 1992, and $50 million in 1993. In 1994, in an act of desperation, United shareholders awarded various employee groups 55 percent of the company's stock, in return for $4.9 million in wage concessions. Also as part of the deal, the new "owners" demanded the removal of Wolf.

The new leader selected to turn United around was Gerald Greenwald. Although he had no experience in the airline industry, as one United pilot noted,

"He has a track record for employee relations, and this trust thing is the key to the whole future." These words turned out to be prophetic. In a little over two years, Greenwald had led United through one of the most dramatic turnarounds in U.S. business history. By 1996, operating margins were up, costs were down, labor grievances had almost vanished, and the company's stock price had doubled. The doubling of the stock price was especially significant because all employees were also shareholders.

From the outset, Greenwald's leadership style was one of consensus building and egalitarianism. He showed up at his first shareholders' meeting wearing a "Proud Owner" button and preaching worker empowerment. A no-layoff commitment was made to every employee, and four seats on United's board of directors were awarded to employee representatives. Policies that alienated employees (like mandatory weigh-ins and weight rules for flight attendants) were revoked, and the company started really listening to employees. In fact, the 1996 decision not to merge with USAir was based largely on employee input sought out via open chats on the company's E-mail system. According to Greenwald, the days of adversarial labor-management relations are over because

> the inefficiencies such wrangling causes make it that much more difficult for U.S. companies to compete in the world. . . . If we keep our heads down and continue to build a record of improving profits, if we continue to make decisions for the benefit of passengers, Wall Street will almost certainly reward us with a higher stock price.[3]

---

[1]K. Labich, "Will United Fly?" *Fortune,* August 22, 1994, pp. 70–77.
[2]R. Hagberg, "Rambos in Pinstripes: Why So Many CEOs Are Lousy Leaders," *Fortune,* June 24, 1996, p. 147.
[3]K. Labich, "When Workers Really Count," *Fortune,* October 14, 1996, pp. 212–13.

As we noted in Chapter 8, few important tasks or goals can be accomplished by one person working alone. Indeed, this is the main reason why there are so many organizations in our society. However, few groups or organizations can accomplish much without the help of a single individual acting as a leader. Leadership is the force that energizes and directs groups. Given the centrality of leadership to the behavior of people in groups and to organizational achievement, it is important that we understand how leaders emerge and what qualities make them effective. In this chapter, we will focus on this topic and show how leadership is a complex function of the leader, followers, and situations.

A large number of theories exist about leadership. It would be difficult to try to explain them all without leaving you more confused about the topic than when we started. However, ignoring important approaches in order to simplify our discussion might give you a false impression regarding the real subtlety and complexity of the leadership process. If leadership were a simple process, everyone would be a great leader. This is hardly the case.

To make it easier to learn about the many different theories of leadership that exist today, we will start this chapter by presenting a single conceptual framework, the transactional model, that encompasses all other theories. With this framework in place, we will then be able to examine additional theories and fit them into a single overall scheme. This single framework will also allow us, in the last section of the chapter, to build one integrated model of leadership that will incorporate significant features of each theory we have discussed. The resulting model will be comprehensive in reflecting the many ingredients that contribute to effective leadership. At the same time, however, the model will be concise in classifying these ingredients and showing how they can be combined and applied in different organizational situations.

Defining Leadership and the Transactional Model

Most people have a hard time expressing exactly what they mean by the word *leadership,* and the definitions offered by experts often conflict. At the same time, when asked to name strong leaders throughout history, people respond in a remarkably consistent way. Table 9-1 lists a number of people who are almost always cited as strong leaders. It should give you an idea of how difficult it is to come up with a definition of leadership that is specific enough to be useful, yet broad enough to include people who differ so greatly from each other. What traits do the people in the table have in common?

One characteristic shared among the people listed in Table 9-1 is their ability to influence others. The use of influence certainly should be paramount in any definition of leadership. Yet, would we consider a mugger who enters a subway train and induces passengers to hand over their personal belongings a leader? Most people would recognize this person's influence, but they would not consider this act one of leadership.

Instead, a leader's influence must to some degree be sanctioned by followers. In some situations a person may be compelled by others to lead, and in other situations a leader may be merely tolerated for the time being. Still, the idea that followers voluntarily surrender control over their own behavior to someone else is an integral part of any definition of leadership.

A complete definition of leadership must also describe the context in which leadership occurs and the symbolism captured in the leader. Leadership occurs in goal-oriented group contexts. However, this does not mean that moving the group toward its goal is a leader's only function. Leaders also serve an important

Table 9-1 ■ Conventional Examples of Strong Leaders	
Adolf Hitler	Martin Luther King Jr.
Mahatma Gandhi	Napoleon Bonaparte
Mao Tse-Tung	Moses
Franklin D. Roosevelt	Abraham Lincoln
Winston Churchill	Golda Meir
John F. Kennedy	Mikhail Gorbachev

symbolic function for both group members and outsiders. It is impossible for every employee to understand all that goes on in the organization. As we saw in Chapter 3, when the complexity of a stimulus exceeds a person's cognitive capacity, the person attempts to simplify the stimulus. In the organizational context, the leader provides the means for much of this simplification. The leader offers a logically compelling and emotionally satisfying focal point for people who are trying to understand the causes and consequences of organized activity. Focusing on the leader reduces organizational complexities to simple terms that people can understand and communicate.[1]

With these points in mind, the definition we will adopt is one suggested by Arthur Jago, who has defined **leadership** as the use of noncoercive and symbolic influence to direct and coordinate the activities of the members of an organized group toward the accomplishment of group objectives.[2] In defining leadership, it is important to distinguish between leadership and management. One way to do this is to recall from Mintzberg's overview of managerial roles (see Chapter 1) that the role of leader is just 1 of 10 commonly occupied by managers. Leadership, according to Mintzberg, deals explicitly with guiding and motivating employees.[3] From this point of view, leadership is one of many managerial tasks.

Edward Hollander has suggested that the leadership process is best understood as the occurrence of mutually satisfying transactions among leaders and followers within a particular situational context.[4] His model is known as the transactional model. As Figure 9-1 indicates, the locus of leadership in the transactional model is found where these three forces—leaders, followers, and situations—come together. In Hollander's view, we can understand leadership only by gaining an appreciation of the important characteristics of these three forces and the ways in which they interact.

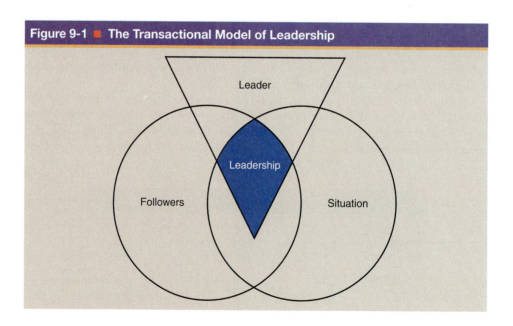

Figure 9-1 ■ The Transactional Model of Leadership

To appreciate the influence of followers on leadership, ask yourself the following questions. Could a person with Hitler's totalitarian characteristics have risen to power in the United States just after the Vietnam War, when opposing almost any government act was close to a national pastime? Could Martin Luther King Jr.'s peaceful, patient approach to civil rights have worked for Central European Muslims in their recent opposition to the Serbians—who seemed to want nothing less than to exterminate the Muslims? Can anyone establish a position of leadership with a group of intellectuals who reject the very idea that they need to be led?[5]

Turning to the characteristics of the situation, would Mahatma Gandhi's program of civil disobedience have been successful if he had been opposing the Nazis instead of the British? In 1989, could Tadeusz Mazowiecki have risen as the first non-Communist leader of Poland in 40 years if the Polish economy had not been in total shambles? These questions underline the complex nature of leadership and the contribution of the situation in making a leader successful.

Universal Approaches to Leadership

Not all theoretical approaches to leadership emphasize the three-dimensional character of the leadership process proposed by Hollander. The earliest probes into the nature of leadership focused almost exclusively on leader characteristics (rather than on followers or situations). These universal theories emphasized the traits and abilities, decision-making styles, and typical behaviors that made leaders different from nonleaders.

Leader Traits

The earliest approaches to explaining leadership held that leaders were born, not made. Sir Francis Galton argued in 1869 that the traits of great leaders were inherited. Later researchers influenced by behavioral schools of thought discarded this idea, suggesting instead that many characteristics associated with successful leadership could be learned. Studies of the physical characteristics of leaders have yielded weak but consistent relationships between a person's energy level and the ability to rise to positions of leadership.[6] Large-scale research projects involving hundreds of leaders and thousands of followers suggest that the amount of time and energy that the leader is perceived as devoting to the job is a major determinant of follower ratings of leader effectiveness.[7] Certainly, anecdotal reports also support the notion that many leaders simply work harder than average individuals. Bill Gates, founder and CEO of Microsoft, is famous for working 80 to 90 hours a week.[8] Similar workweeks have been reported for CEOs of companies like Symantec[9] and American International Group (AIG) Insurance.[10]

Weaker and less consistent results have been found for characteristics like height. Oddly, we tend to think of leaders as tall people even though many are not. Consider the leaders listed in Table 9-1. No more than half of them could have been considered tall or physically imposing people. Research on mental abilities has produced few substantial predictors of leadership quality and effectiveness, although, again, some consistent findings have been reported. General cognitive ability seems to be one of the best overall predictors of leadership ability.[11] Specific technical skills or knowledge about a group's task also show modest relationships with success in leadership.[12]

In terms of personality, there is evidence that leaders tend to exhibit the social trait of dominance. Self-esteem (or self-confidence, or self-assurance) also seems to be related to leadership across a wide variety of situations and followers.[13] These findings notwithstanding, for every personality characteristic that does appear to be related to leadership potential, skill, or effectiveness, there are probably 10 others for which no such evidence exists. It was this failure to find significant relationships between leadership and the personal traits of leaders that led researchers to explore other approaches to understanding this important concept.

Recently, however, investigators have begun to propose various neo-universal theories of leadership that, like earlier universal models, focus on a particular characteristic of the leader and exclude followers and situations. Among these are theories of **charismatic leadership,** which emphasize the ability of the leader to communicate new visions of an organization to followers.[14] Charismatic leaders, or, as they are sometimes called, transformational leaders, raise followers' awareness of the importance of group goals, often getting people to transcend their own interests.[15] They also "raise the stakes" of organizational performance by convincing subordinates of the importance of the leader's vision and the dangers of not adopting this vision (see box).[16] It is this vision that distinguishes top performers from more ordinary leaders, according to this theory.[17] Although charisma may seem hard to capture operationally, standardized measures of charisma have been developed recently, and these have been found to relate to leader effectiveness.[18]

Leader Decision-Making Styles

Whereas the research discussed previously focused on leader traits, other early research in the area of leadership focused more specifically on how leaders made decisions, and the effect this had on subordinates' rates of productivity and general satisfaction. Research in this tradition has looked at three different decision-making styles: authoritarian, democratic, and laissez-faire. **Authoritarian leaders** make virtually all decisions by themselves. The **democratic leader** works with the group to help members come to their own decisions. The **laissez-faire leader** leaves the group alone to do whatever it wants.

Results of studies on leader decision styles suggest that most groups prefer a democratic leader. In these studies, members of groups led by an authoritarian leader were either extremely submissive or extremely aggressive in interacting with each other. They were also the most likely to leave the organization. Authoritarian groups were also the most productive, but only when members were closely supervised. When left alone, these groups tended to stop working. At the time of their publication, these results were considered interesting and provocative.[19] As with the leader traits discussed earlier, however, these studies

Adding Value through Charismatic Leadership

Anyone who has ever "surfed the net" is probably familiar with Netscape Communications, one of the leaders in Internet software and World Wide Web browser services. However, in January of 1995, when CEO Jim Barksdale arrived on the scene, it was unclear whether the struggling company would stay afloat, let alone surf. At that time, Netscape was a small, talented, but chaotic group of 100 or so employees. Many of the employees were very young engineers with little business experience, who were struggling to meet product delivery deadlines. Netscape managers, facing a new and uncertain market, were bewildered about strategy and because they were afraid of running out of money, had just initiated a hiring freeze and a cutback on R&D expenses. In the words of Netscape's technical founder, Marc Andreesen, "We were like a tornado . . . we were desperate for leadership."[1]

Enter their new CEO, Jim Barksdale, who quickly exhibited all three cornerstones of charismatic leadership. First, like all charismatic leaders, Barksdale spoke in metaphors and analogies——creating messages that could be understood equally well by electrical engineers and night shift janitors. For example, he likened Netscape to a rocket and noted that "if it fails to reach escape velocity, it will crash back to earth."[2] Barksdale's first moves reinforced this takeoff analogy in that he lifted the hiring freeze, jacked up R&D spending, opened foreign offices, and broadened Netscape's target market.

Second, he created a crisis mentality by elevating in the minds of his employees the dangers faced by the firm. He stressed the threat of other small start-ups by noting the low barriers to entry in the market. He also stressed the threat posed by established giants like Microsoft, which was personified as the "Evil Empire," led by Bill Gates—the Darth Vader of the software industry. In simple words, Barksdale sent the clear message that "if we can't establish presence and brand name, we'll die."[3]

Finally, he established an action-oriented, risk-taking culture at the company that challenged everyone to reach higher standards of excellence. His Bugs Bounty program, for example, offered cash awards to outside hackers who could crack the Netscape code or find errors in Netscape programming. Many in the industry felt that outside hackers were bad enough on their own—did anyone really want to provide them with extra motivation? Yet this program was essential for both identifying problems and assuring investors that the few remaining bugs in Netscape software were going to be identified soon.[4]

Although the final chapter on Netscape and the Internet has yet to be written, it is clear that at the moment this rocket is still ascending. The Netscape stock price has quintupled since August 1995 and August 1996, and much of this can be attributed to the charismatic leadership of Jim Barksdale. In the words of one venture capitalist, "He has a great ability to convey confidence and give comfort. . . . A huge portion of what Netscape is worth is Jim Barksdale."[5]

---

[1] P. Sellers, "What Exactly Is Charisma?" *Fortune,* January 15, 1996, pp. 68–75.
[2] Ibid.
[3] J. P. Kotter, "Kill Complacency," *Fortune,* August 5, 1996, pp. 168–70.
[4] R. M. Rao, "Webmasters: Deciding the Fate of the Internet Universe," *Fortune,* April 15, 1996, p. 47.
[5] Sellers, "What Exactly Is Charisma?"

revealed only modest relationships between leader style and follower behavior. Subsequent research has indicated that democratic and participative leadership is not always the one best way for all followers. Indeed, recent research on cultural differences suggests that Russian workers perform very poorly under participative leaders.[20]

In today's project-oriented, team-driven business environment, autocratic leadership is becoming more and more rare.[21] For example, work at Hewlett-

Packard (HP) is organized around project teams that have no clear hierarchy, in which employees have no formal titles or job descriptions. Leaders of these cross-functional teams are often not the direct supervisor of any of the project members; they do not formally evaluate them or determine their average salary raises. In these types of short-term situations, leaders who want to be successful need to develop a more democratic decision style that allows diverse team members to make the most of their unique knowledge or skill.[22] One of these project teams was instrumental in cutting product delivery times from 26 days to 8 days. This type of speed gives HP a major competitive advantage, and shows how effective leadership can be converted into customer satisfaction and retention.[23] This in turn results in shareholder satisfaction and retention. In fact, since 1961, when HP's stock was publically listed, it has risen by 7,885 percent.

Leader Behaviors

A third school of early leadership research focused on the behaviors exhibited by leaders. Based upon interviews with supervisors and clerical workers at the Prudential Insurance Company, researchers concluded that there were two general classes of supervisory behavior: **employee-oriented behavior,** aimed at meeting the social and emotional needs of group members, and **job-oriented behavior,** focused on careful supervision of employees' work methods and task accomplishment.[24] Early studies indicated that work attitudes were better and productivity was higher in the groups led by supervisors who displayed employee-oriented behaviors.[25]

Another set of early studies that relied on questionnaires rather than interviews arrived at a similar conclusion about leader behavior. Analyzing workers' responses to a questionnaire by means of a sophisticated statistical procedure called factor analysis, researchers concluded that most supervisory behaviors could be assigned to either of two dimensions: **consideration** or **initiating structure.**[26] Table 9-2 shows some items from the Leader Behavior Description Questionnaire (LBDQ) that

---

Table 9-2 ■ Items Similar to Those in the Leader Behavior Description Questionnaire

Consideration Items
1. Is easy to get along with
2. Puts ideas generated by the group into operation
3. Treats everyone the same
4. Lets followers know of upcoming changes
5. Explains actions to all group members

Initiating-Structure Items
1. Tells group members what is expected
2. Promotes the use of standardized procedures
3. Makes decisions about work methods
4. Clarifies role relationship among group members
5. Sets specific goals and monitors performance closely

---

evolved out of these original studies. As you can see, the consideration dimension is very much like that of employee-oriented behavior, in that both dimensions address the individual and social needs of workers. Similarly, initiating-structure behavior is like job-oriented behavior because both concern the clarification of work processes and expectations. Rather than being mutually exclusive (i.e., if a person is high on one, that person must be low on the other), however, these two dimensions are somewhat independent (i.e., a person can be high on one, and high, medium, or low on the other). If anything, there is actually a small positive correlation between the two, in that leaders who are considerate also seem to be slightly higher on initiating structure.[27]

Based upon this early research, Blake and Mouton developed the notion of the managerial grid, republished in 1991 as the **leadership grid figure** by Blake and McCanse.[28] Blake and Mouton identified two attitudinal dimensions that captured behavioral styles. As Figure 9-2 shows, the leadership grid proposes five

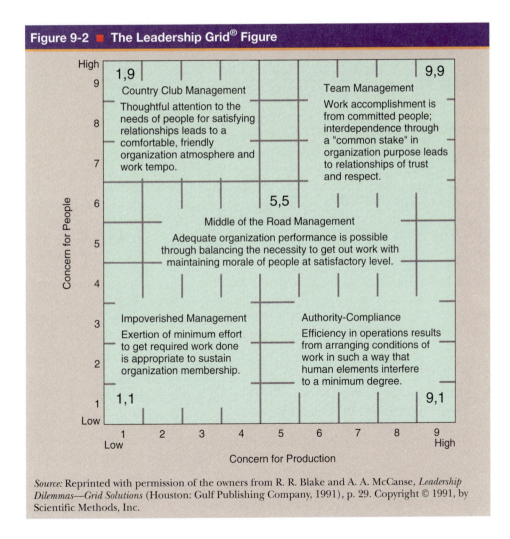

Figure 9-2 ■ The Leadership Grid® Figure

Source: Reprinted with permission of the owners from R. R. Blake and A. A. McCanse, *Leadership Dilemmas—Grid Solutions* (Houston: Gulf Publishing Company, 1991), p. 29. Copyright © 1991, by Scientific Methods, Inc.

different styles of leadership based on the interaction between concern for people and concern for production. Each of these two dimensions is measured on a scale of 1 (low) to 9 (high). Blake and Mouton explicitly stated that the 9,9 Team Management style (see the upper right-hand corner of the grid) is "the one best way" to lead (i.e., regardless of followers or situations), and they developed an elaborate training program to move managers in that direction. Managers find the program appealing because it points to two specific sets of behaviors—consideration and initiating structure—that they can engage in to enhance the attitudes and performance of their group.

Despite its appeal, however, the managerial grid approach lacks support from rigorous scientific studies. In fact, some investigators have gone so far as to label the whole 9,9 idea a myth.[29] Indeed, a good deal of research argues against the notion that there is any one best way of leading, regardless of followers and situations. The primary problem with all of the approaches we have discussed is that they specify one best way to lead (e.g., be dominant, or initiate structure, or use a democratic leadership style) regardless of the characteristics of followers and situations.

Characteristics of Followers and Situations

Vertical Dyad Linkage

One approach to leadership that emphasizes the characteristics of followers as well as those of leaders is the vertical dyad linkage (VDL) theory of leadership. A **vertical dyad** consists of two persons who are linked hierarchically, for example, a supervisor and a subordinate.[30] Most studies using measures of leader consideration or initiating structure average subordinates' ratings of leaders. However, VDL proponents argue that there is no such thing as an "average" leadership score. Instead, they insist, each supervisor-subordinate relationship is unique. A supervisor may be considerate toward one person but not toward another. Similarly, the leader may initiate structure for some workers but not for others.

For example, consider the following quote from Jimmy Johnson, who won two Super Bowls as coach of the Dallas Cowboys, when he was asked if he treated some players differently than others:

> At least I am being honest about it. Treat everybody the same? That's bull. You don't treat [All-Pro quarterback] Troy Aikman the way you treat a rookie free agent lineman. We don't have a lot of rules, but if we did, they'd basically be for the guys at the bottom of the scale.[31]

Similarly, Mickey Drexler, president of The Gap, has noted that he uses different styles of leadership for "rock star" clothing designers than he does for more "down-to-earth store managers."[32]

The importance of distinguishing dyadic from average scores has received broad research support. For example, Figure 9-3 compares the strength of the

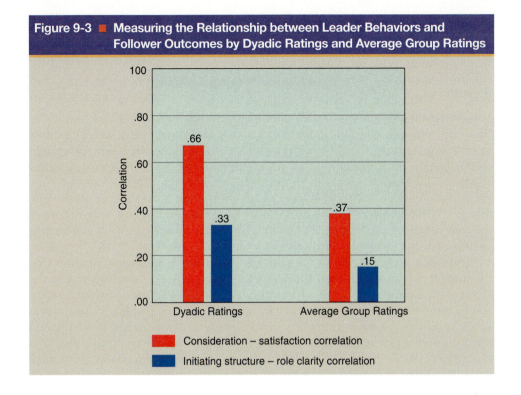

relationship between (1) leader consideration and follower satisfaction and (2) leader initiating structure and follower role clarity as measured by both dyadic scores and average scores.[33] As you can see, the relationships based on dyadic scores were much stronger than the relationships based on average scores. This suggests that leaders do behave differently with different subordinates and that these differences spill over into worker reactions.

Graen's vertical dyad linkage approach also suggests that leaders tend to classify subordinates into in-group members and out-group members. According to Graen, in-group members are willing and able to do more than the tasks outlined in a formal job description. Once they have been identified, the leader gives these people more latitude, authority, and consideration. Out-group members, on the other hand, either cannot or will not expand their roles beyond formal requirements. Leaders assign these individuals more routine tasks, give them less consideration, and communicate less often with them.[34]

Whether distinguishing among subordinates in this manner improves a leader's effectiveness depends on the leader's reasons for placing some people in the in-group and others in the out-group. Research shows that performance is not always the reason for separating members into in-groups and out-groups, and if these kinds of distinctions are based on information that is not related to performance, then this can interfere with leader effectiveness.[35] Highly competent and committed workers might differ from their supervisors but could excel if given in-group status and support. Unfortunately, the evidence suggests that in-group selections are often made capriciously. Demographic similarity and things like mutual interests outside of work have been found to predict in-group membership.[36]

Substitutes for Leadership

Substitutes-for-leadership theory is an approach that emphasizes the role of the situation in leadership. This theory argues that traditional leader behaviors such as initiating structure and consideration are often made irrelevant by certain characteristics of the situation.[37] That is, characteristics of situations can act to substitute for leader behavior. Figure 9-4 illustrates the effect of a substitute. Here, consideration leads to follower satisfaction when boring tasks must be performed. When tasks are intrinsically satisfying, however, the satisfying nature of the task substitutes for leader behavior, and leader consideration has no effect because satisfaction is already high.

Indeed, a recent review of the scientific literature on this topic suggests that the impact of many substitutes for leadership is over three times larger than the effect of leadership per se. The strongest substitutes for leadership deal with characteristics of both the task and the organization as a whole. In general, leadership tends to be neutralized in situations in which tasks are intrinsically satisfying and there is good objective feedback about task performance. Leadership is also neutralized in organizations that are highly formalized (i.e., organizations in which there are written rules and procedures for most jobs) and lacking in flexibility.[38]

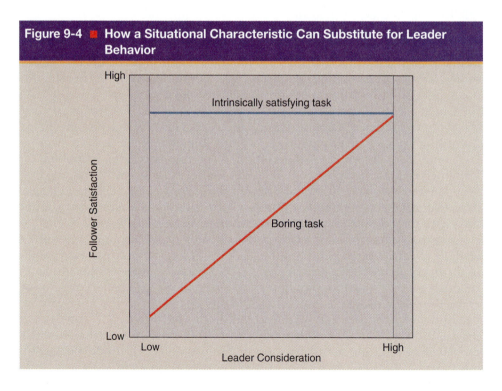

Figure 9-4 ■ How a Situational Characteristic Can Substitute for Leader Behavior

Comprehensive Theories of Leadership

Whereas the VDL and substitutes-for-leadership theories each deal with two of the three forces identified in the transactional model of leadership (leader, follower, and situation), the comprehensive leadership theories discussed in this section incorporate all three. The three comprehensive theories that we will examine differ only in that each tends to focus on a particular leader characteristic—either a personal characteristic, a behavioral orientation, or a decision style.

Fiedler's Contingency Model

Think for a moment of someone you don't like to work with. In fact, consider all the people you have ever worked with, and see who you remember as being the worst. Now rate this person on the qualities listed in the scale shown in Table 9-3.

If you described your least preferred coworker (LPC) in relatively harsh terms, then, according to Fred Fiedler, you are most likely to take a task orientation to leadership. In Fiedler's view, task-oriented leaders emphasize completing tasks successfully, even at the expense of interpersonal relations. A task-oriented leader finds it difficult to overlook the negative traits of a poorly performing subordinate. On the other hand, if you described your least preferred coworker in relatively positive terms, you are likely to take a relationship orientation to leadership. Relationship-oriented leaders, according to Fiedler, are permissive, considerate leaders who can maintain good interpersonal relationships even with workers who are not contributing to group accomplishment.

The leader's orientation toward either tasks or relationships is the central piece in the complex and controversial theory of leadership that Fiedler has proposed. Fiedler's theory is called a contingency theory of leadership because it holds that the effectiveness of a leader's orientation depends both on the leader's followers and on the situation. A leadership situation can be placed on a continuum of favorability, depending upon three factors (see Figure 9-5) described next.

Table 9-3 ■ Items Similar to Those on the Least Preferred Coworker Scale									
Agreeable									Disagreeable
	8	7	6	5	4	3	2	1	
Close minded									Open minded
	1	2	3	4	5	6	7	8	
Courteous									Rude
	8	7	6	5	4	3	2	1	
Agitated									Calm
	1	2	3	4	5	6	7	8	
Dull									Fascinating
	1	2	3	4	5	6	7	8	

Figure 9-5 ■ How Situation Favorability Is Determined by Leader-Follower Relations, Task Structure, and Position Power

Situations	Leader-Follower Relations	Task Structure	Position Power
I	Good	High	Strong
II	Good	High	Weak
III	Good	Low	Strong
IV	Good	Low	Weak
V	Poor	High	Strong
VI	Poor	High	Weak
VII	Poor	Low	Strong
VIII	Poor	Low	Weak

When a relationship-oriented leader is needed: moderately favorable
When a task-oriented leader is needed: highly favorable or highly unfavorable

☐ = Highly favorable ☐ = Moderately favorable ☐ = Highly unfavorable

Source: Reprinted with the publisher's permission from F. E. Fiedler, *A Theory of Leadership Effectiveness* (New York: McGraw-Hill, 1967), p. 29.

Leader-follower relations are good if followers trust and respect the leader. Good relations are obviously more favorable for leader effectiveness than poor relations. **Task structure** is high when a group has clear goals and clear means of achieving those goals. High task structure is more favorable for the leader than low task structure. Finally, **position power** is the ability to reward or punish subordinates for their behavior. Clearly, the more power a leader has, the more favorable the situation is from the leader's perspective.[39]

Fiedler's analysis of a number of studies that used the Least Preferred Coworker Scale suggested to him that task-oriented leaders are most effective in situations that are either extremely favorable or extremely unfavorable (I, II, III, and VIII in Figure 9-5). Relationship-oriented leaders, he found, were most successful in situations of moderate favorability (IV, V, VI, and VII in Figure 9-5). Figure 9-6 shows the results of later studies of Fiedler's model, conducted over the course of 25 years. For each of the eight situations described by the model, average correlations between a leader's LPC score and the leader's effectiveness, and the range of these correlations, are plotted.[40]

The results shown in Figure 9-6 suggest that the model works quite well at the extremes. Both the average correlation and the range of correlations between an

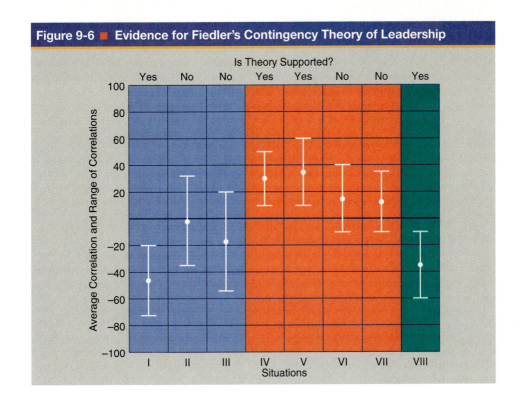

Figure 9-6 ■ Evidence for Fiedler's Contingency Theory of Leadership

LPC score and leader effectiveness are negative in situations I and VIII, as the model predicts. Similarly, in situations IV and V, the average correlation and the range of correlations are both positive, again as the model predicts. However, LPC scores fail to predict leader effectiveness in situations II, III, VI, and VII.

Leader Match Training.   One offshoot of this theory is the leader-training program called Leader Match, which attempts to translate OB theory into managerial practice. Fiedler has commented that it is easier to change almost anything in the job situation other than personality and leadership style, and this belief in the immutability of human beings is reflected in Leader Match training.[41] This self-paced, programmed text tells leaders not to change their styles but instead to try to manipulate the situation. For example, if leader-follower relations are poor, the leader may try to raise morale by giving bonuses or time off. If a task is unstructured, a leader may break it down into simpler subtasks. If position power is low, leaders may try to increase their authority by seeing that all information is channeled through the leader.[42]

Critique of Fiedler's Model.   Both the contingency theory and Leader Match training have been subject to considerable criticism. The theory has been criticized as being "too data driven." According to his critics, Fiedler started with a set of results that he tried to explain, rather than with a logical, deductive theory. Moreover, there is continuing controversy over why low-LPC leaders should be best in situations that are either extremely good or extremely bad but not in situations of moderate favorability. It is somewhat disconcerting that a theory with a history as long as Fiedler's has not yet been able to specify why its predictions turn out to be correct. The LPC measure itself has aroused controversy. Critics have questioned what the scale actually measures and how well it measures this variable.[43]

Leader Match training has been criticized for using questionable measures of performance and for failing to control for rater expectation biases and the so-called Hawthorne effect.[44] In addition, some people have noted that the classifications of situations in the Leader Match booklet are not what the original theory would predict.[45] Indeed, critics have suggested that mismatches could total 60 percent.[46] Finally, as Figure 9-6 shows, current evidence suggests that for as many as half of the situations that might be encountered, LPC scores show no consistent relationship with performance.[47]

Despite these problems, there certainly seem to be some situations (I, IV, V, and VIII) in which the theory works well. In particular, assigning task-oriented, low-LPC leaders to groups in situations of extreme favorability or unfavorability seems to be a defensible prescription.

Vroom-Yetton Decision Tree Model

The comprehensive model developed by Fiedler focused on personality characteristics of the leader. In contrast, the decision tree model of leadership originated by Victor Vroom and his colleagues emphasizes the fact that leaders achieve success through effective decision making.[48] Vroom's model recognizes four general styles of leadership decision making: authoritarian (or autocratic), consultative, delegative, and group based (or participative). These four alternatives are then broken down into seven specific decision styles. Three of these are appropriate for both individual and group decisions, two are appropriate only for decisions involving individual followers, and two are appropriate only for decisions that involve an entire group of followers (see Table 9-4).

Like all comprehensive theories of leadership, the decision tree model proposes that the most effective leadership style depends on characteristics of both the situation and the followers. Specifically, the model asks eight questions—three about the situation and five about the followers—in order to determine which of the seven leadership styles outlined in Table 9-4 is best. The decision tree presented in Figure 9-7 makes the question-and-answer process easy.[49] Responding to questions A through H will lead you to one of 18 answers, each of which identifies one or more decision styles that are appropriate for the problem you confront. To choose among two or more styles, the leader must decide whether to maximize the speed of decision making or the personal development of subordinates. Autocratic approaches favor speed, whereas consultative or group approaches favor employee growth.

Using the Decision Tree. Suppose you are a corporate vice president who has just been given the responsibility for starting up a new plant in a developing country, and you must choose a plant manager. Should it be one of your five

Table 9-4 ■ The Seven Decision Styles in the Vroom-Yetton Decision Tree Model of Leadership

For All Problems

AI   You solve the problem or make the decision yourself, using information available to you at the time.

AII   You obtain any necessary information from subordinates, then decide on the solution to the problem yourself. You may or may not tell subordinates what the problem is in getting the information from them. The role played by your subordinates in making the decision is clearly one of providing specific information that you request, rather than one of generating or evaluating solutions.

CI   You share the problem with the relevant subordinates individually, getting their ideas and suggestions without bringing them together as a group. Then *you* make the decision. This decision may or may not reflect your subordinates' influence.

For Individual Problems

GI   You share the problem with one of your subordinates, and together you analyze the problem and arrive at a mutually satisfactory solution in an atmosphere of free and open exchange of information and ideas. You both contribute to the resolution of the problem, with the relative contribution of each being dependent on knowledge rather than formal authority.

DI   You delegate the problem to one of your subordinates, providing any relevant information that you possess, but giving your subordinate responsibility for solving the problem independently. Any solution that the person reaches will receive your support.

For Group Problems

CII   You share the problem with your subordinates in a group meeting. In this meeting you obtain their ideas and suggestions. Then, *you* make the decision, which may or may not reflect your subordinates' influence.

GII   You share the problem with your subordinates as a group. Together you generate and evaluate alternatives and attempt to reach agreement (consensus) on a solution. Your role is much like that of chairperson, coordinating the discussion, keeping it focused on the problem, and making sure that the critical issues are discussed. You do not try to influence the group to adopt "your" solution and are willing to accept and implement any solution that has support of the entire group.

Note: A stands for authoritarian, C for consultative, D for delegative, and G for group based.

---

current and highly experienced plant managers? Should it be someone from outside the firm who has had experience working overseas? Should it be a citizen of the target country?

As vice president, you might move through the decision tree as follows:

Question A: Yes. Some managers may be better suited than others.
Question B: No. You, the vice president, may not know all the interests or past experience that would be relevant to the assignment.
Question C: No. This is a new problem for the company, and thus there are no clear guidelines dictating what steps to take.
Question D: Yes. Any of your current managers could find good jobs with other firms in their own country if they refused the overseas job.

Figure 9-7 ■ **The Vroom-Yetton Decision Tree Model of Leadership**

A. Is there a quality requirement such that one solution is likely to be more rational than another? (Situation)
B. Do I have sufficient information to make a high-quality decision? (Situation)
C. Is the problem structured? (Situation)
D. Is acceptance of decision by subordinates critical to effective implementation? (Followers)
E. If I were to make the decision by myself, is it reasonably certain that it would be accepted by my subordinates? (Followers)
F. Do subordinates share the organizational goals to be attained in solving this problem? (Followers)
G. Is conflict among subordinates likely in preferred solutions? (This question is irrelevant to individual problems. (Followers)
H. Do subordinates have sufficient information to make a high-quality decision? (Situation)

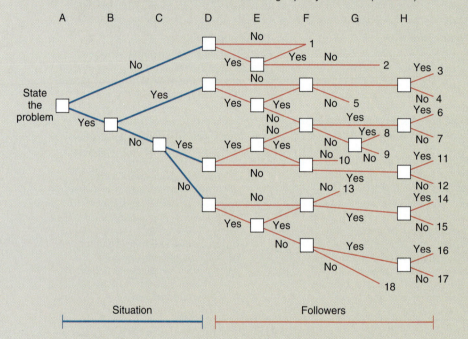

Answers and Appropriate Leadership Styles (see also Table 9-4)

Answer Number	Individual Problems	Group Problems	Answer Number	Individual Problems	Group Problems
1	AI, AII, CI, DI, GI	AI, AII, CI, CII, GII	10	AII, CI	AII, CI, CII
2	DI, GI	GII	11	AII, CI, DI, GI	AII, CI, CII, GII
3	AI, AII, CI, DI, GI	AI, AII, CI, CII, GII	12	AII, CI, GI	AII, CI, CII, GII
4	AI, AII, CI, GI	AI, AII, CI, CII, GII	13	CI	CII
5	AI, AII, CI	AI, AII, CI, CII	14	CI, DI, GI	CII, GII
6	DI, GI	GII	15	CI, GI	CII, GII
7	GI	GII	16	DI, GI	GII
8	CI, GI	CII	17	GI	GII
9	CI, GI	CI, CII	18	CI, GI	CII

Question E: No. The decision will have too large an impact on subordinates' lives.

Question F: Yes. They have been with the company a long time and are committed to the organization.

Question H: No. There are many details of the assignment that only you, the vice president, know about.

The no response to question H leads to answer 17. This answer, applied to a group problem, eliminates autocratic, delegative, and consultative styles and recommends the GII, group-based decision style.

Evidence for Validity.   Early studies of the model's usefulness asked managers to think about past decisions that had been effective or ineffective, and had them trace their decision processes back to see whether they had followed the model's prescriptions. When the managers' decision processes were consistent with the model, 68 percent of decisions were effective, compared to only 22 percent when decisions violated the model.[50] For example, Donald Fites, the CEO at Caterpillar, notes that while making sales calls in Africa, he often had pricing decisions forced upon him from headquarters that made little sense in the local market. He recognized that he "was on the scene and knew what needed to be done, but someone back at the general office would make decisions that didn't fit the situation."[51] Clearly this was a situation in which those at headquarters did not have all the necessary information (see question B), and this should have eliminated a centralized, autocratic decision style.

Research also indicates that most managers' natural decision processes seem to violate the model's prescriptions. In particular, managers tend to overuse the consultative CII style and underutilize the group-based GII style.[52] The difference between these two styles is subtle but critical; the leader retains ultimate decision-making responsibility in the first but not in the second. Giving up this ultimate responsibility is difficult for many leaders, especially those who lead once small, but now large organizations. For example, Joseph Montgomery, founder and CEO of Cannondale Corporation (a manufacturer of high-tech bicycles), notes that in the "old days, I did everything from selling to bill collecting." However, his is now a $95 million business and it is impossible to manage every detail from the top. As his marketing vice president notes, "He has to realize his own capacities and get used to delegating more authority."[53]

Path-Goal Theory

The most comprehensive theory of leadership to date and the theory that best exemplifies all the aspects of the transactional model is the path-goal theory of leadership.[54] At the core of path-goal theory is the notion that the primary purpose of the leader is to motivate followers by clarifying goals and the best paths to achieve those goals. Because motivation is essential to the leader role, this approach is based on the expectancy theory of motivation described in Chapter 4, and it emphasizes the three motivational variables that leaders may influence through their behaviors or decision styles: valences, instrumentalities, and expectancies (i.e., VIEs).

Manipulating Motivation.   The job of the leader, according to path-goal theory, is to manipulate these three factors in desirable ways. Correspondingly, the theory's proponents recommend that leaders fulfill three major roles. First, leaders need to manipulate follower valences by recognizing or arousing needs for outcomes the leader can control. Second, leaders are also responsible for manipulating follower instrumentalities by ensuring that high performance results in satisfying outcomes for followers. Third, leaders need to manipulate follower expectancies by reducing frustrating barriers to performance.[55]

A good example of the use of path-goal theory can be seen in the behavior of Rich Melman, who has developed 32 restaurants with annual revenues of $110 million. Melman has used many different tools, including equity stakes, employee training, a lucrative benefits package, and a system of promotion from within, to develop a core of workers who are both entrepreneurial and loyal. Luis Garcia started as a dishwasher in one of Melman's restaurants in 1987, and at that time he spoke no English. Melman adjusted Garcia's schedule so that he could take English classes and then promoted Garcia through a series of jobs that eventually led to his managing the very restaurant where he first washed dishes. Garcia, a loyal employee if ever there was one, notes that "if you want to become someone, Rich Melman opens the door for you."[56] This type of opportunity-creating activity is the key according to path-goal theory.

Behavioral Styles.   Path-goal theory proposes four behavioral styles that can enable leaders to manipulate the three motivational variables: directive, supportive, participative, and achievement-oriented leadership. As you can see from Table 9-5, these styles are composed of both behaviors, like initiating structure, and decision styles, like the authoritarian approach. Note that the leader's effectiveness in each case depends on follower and situation characteristics. Much like the substitutes-for-leadership approach, path-goal theory recognizes that situational characteristics may make leader behavior unnecessary or impossible.[57]

Table 9-5 ▪ The Path-Goal Theory's Four Behavioral Styles	
Directive leadership	The leader is authoritarian. Subordinates know exactly what is expected of them, and the leader gives specific directions. Subordinates do not participate in decision making.
Supportive leadership	The leader is friendly and approachable and shows a genuine concern for subordinates.
Participative leadership	The leader asks for and uses suggestions from subordinates but still makes the decisions.
Achievement-oriented leadership	The leader sets challenging goals for subordinates and shows confidence that they will attain these goals.

Evidence for Validity.   Researchers have tested small parts of the path-goal model. Some of their findings are as follows:

- Leader participative behavior results in satisfaction in situations in which the task is nonroutine, but only for followers who are nonauthoritarian.[58]
- Leader directive behavior produces high satisfaction and high performance, but only among followers who have high needs for clarity.[59]
- Leader supportive behavior results in follower satisfaction, but only in situations in which the task is highly structured.[60]
- Leader achievement-oriented behavior results in improved performance, but only when followers are committed to goals.[61]

Perhaps because the path-goal theory is so complex, no one has yet mounted a comprehensive study of the theory in which every variable is tested. The theoretical framework provided by path-goal theory, however, is an excellent one for generating, testing, and understanding the complexities of the leadership process. Moreover, its tie to the expectancy theory of motivation makes it particularly suitable for leadership as conceptualized by Mintzberg, that is, a process in which the leader is seen as a group motivator.

The Transactional Model Revisited

We started this chapter with a discussion of Hollander's theory of leadership. Hollander expressed leadership as a complex transaction involving characteristics of the leader, the followers, and the situation. These ideas provided a framework for our discussion of several theories of leadership that vary in breadth and emphasis.

The dynamic relationships among elements of these several theories as they fit together in an integrated transactional model of leadership are depicted in Figure 9-8. At the core of this model is the notion that leaders exist in order to meet the performance and satisfaction needs of individual group members. Through their abilities and personality characteristics, their behaviors, and their decision styles, leaders must affect their followers' valences, instrumentalities and expectancies. The first key to applying this model to your own leadership situation is to engage in self-assessment to learn your standing on various traits (e.g., self-confidence LPC opinions), behavioral tendencies (on dimensions like consideration and initiating structure), and decision styles (autocratic, consultative, participative, and delegative).[62] High levels of self-awareness are critical for leadership effectiveness, and levels of this characteristic can often be raised through 360-degree feedback interventions like those discussed earlier, in Chapter 3.[63]

At the same time, leaders must recognize that these phenomena are affected by a variety of follower characteristics. A trait, behavior, or decision style that works well with one group of followers is unlikely to work well with another group. Thus, the second key to applying this model to your own leadership situation is to make a critical assessment of those people who are following you, in terms of their competence and demographic composition to determine the degree of match between their characteristics and yours.

Figure 9-8 ■ The Fully-Articulated Transactional Model of Leadership

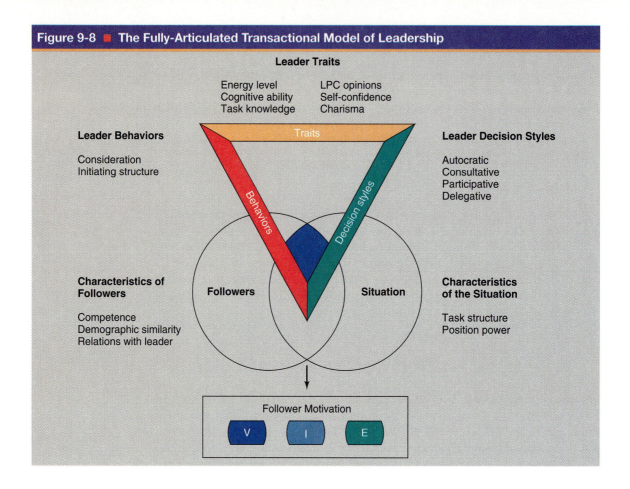

Leader Traits

Energy level   LPC opinions
Cognitive ability   Self-confidence
Task knowledge   Charisma

Leader Behaviors

Consideration
Initiating structure

Leader Decision Styles

Autocratic
Consultative
Participative
Delegative

Traits

Behaviors

Decision styles

Characteristics of Followers

Competence
Demographic similarity
Relations with leader

Followers   Situation

Characteristics of the Situation

Task structure
Position power

Follower Motivation

V   I   E

Finally, the situations in which leaders find themselves will also affect the relationship between the leader's traits, behaviors, and decision styles on the one hand, and group effectiveness on the other. Thus, the third key to applying this model is that leaders need to study the situation they are in (e.g., in terms of task structure or the leader's power to change certain conditions like the overall economy) to determine what kinds of leadership will be most effective with this specific configuration of followers and situation. Effective leadership requires careful analysis of and reaction to the three forces—leader, followers, and situation—highlighted in the transactional framework you have learned about in this chapter.

SUMMARY

A great deal of theory and research has examined the topic of *leadership*. Leadership differs from management in that leading is only one of the tasks of managerial work. The emergence and continued success of a leader is a complex function of personal characteristics, characteristics of the followers, and characteristics of the situation.

Some of the more important personal characteristics of a leader seem to be high intelligence, high energy level, and charisma. These characteristics are typically manifested in particular leader behaviors or decision styles.

The more important dimensions of leader behavior include *consideration of employee needs,* sometimes referred to as *relationship orientation* or *concern for people; initiating structure,* sometimes referred to as *task orientation* or *concern for production;* and *leader-member exchange* behaviors that separate subordinates into in-groups and out-groups.

Leaders also differ in terms of decision styles. Some *authoritarian* leaders make all decisions for their followers, whereas others take a *laissez-faire* approach and leave followers to do as they please. Still others take a *democratic* approach, working actively with followers to ensure that all group members have a chance to contribute to a decision. According to the *transactional model of leadership,* the effectiveness of these different behaviors and decision styles is contingent on characteristics of the followers and of the situation.

Followers differ along several important dimensions. They may be highly knowledgeable, mature, professional, and committed to the organization and its mission, or they may be quite the opposite. Different leadership styles will be required to work effectively with followers with different characteristics.

The situation in which the leader and followers find themselves also affects the relationship between leader characteristics, behaviors, and decision styles on the one hand, and leader effectiveness on the other. Where the leader has great *position power,* where *task structure* is high, and where *leader-follower relations* are characterized by trust and respect, one set of behaviors or decision styles may be warranted. In situations in which the opposite conditions hold, a completely different kind of leader or leader style may be needed.

Review Questions

1. Theories of leadership differ in terms of how adaptable they suggest the leader can be. Of the theories discussed in this chapter, choose two that suggest that the leader is inflexible and two that suggest that the leader is readily adaptable. Which of these two conflicting perspectives seems most likely to be true? Are leaders born or are they made?

2. Most of the early research on leadership was done with leaders who were almost exclusively white and male. Demographic research suggests that few of the new entrants into the labor force in the year 2000 will be white males. Which theories of leadership may need to be seriously reexamined because of this change? Which do you feel will generalize well to the new workforce?

3. We discussed the Least Preferred Coworker Scale in this chapter. Although no such instrument exists, what if there were a Least Preferred Leader Scale? Who would be your least preferred leader? Why? Can you think of followers other than yourself, or situations other than the one you were in, for which this person might be an excellent leader?

4. Although we can think of a few exceptions, in general, people who achieve pre-eminence as leaders in business organizations do not achieve success as political leaders. What are some characteristics of leaders, followers, or situations that would make the transition from business leadership to political leadership difficult?
5. The list of often-cited leaders in Table 9-1 clearly includes both saints and sinners. Why is it that the general moral character of the leader apparently plays no consistent role in a leader's emergence or continuation in power?

Implementation Guide

We have attempted to develop and describe a model of the leadership process that will help you diagnose organizational problems attributed to poor leadership. The following questions should help you apply the transactional model in performing diagnostic analyses.

1. Compared to other aspects of managerial work, how important to you is the specific process of leadership?
2. Which of the five components of follower motivation—valence, instrumentality, expectancy, accuracy of role perceptions, or rewards—seems most lacking in your setting?
3. What abilities related to leadership (e.g., general cognitive ability, task knowledge, and supervisory skills) do you or your managers have? How do these abilities relate to the five components of motivation?
4. What personality characteristics that are related to leadership (e.g., self-esteem and charisma) do you or your managers have? How do these characteristics relate to the five components of motivation?
5. How readily do you think your abilities and characteristics or the abilities and characteristics of your managers can be changed?
6. What leader behaviors (e.g., consideration, initiating structure, contingent rewarding and punishing) do you or your managers typically employ? How do these behaviors relate to the five components of motivation?
7. Do you and your managers tailor your behaviors to different followers?
8. How do you or your managers determine in-group versus out-group status for group members? For example, do you base your selection on competence or on demographic similarity?
9. What kinds of decision styles (autocratic, participative, or delegative) do you or your managers typically employ?
10. How should decision style be tailored to your followers? Should you fit it to their level of maturity? To their commitment to goals? To the situation?
11. What are some of the major characteristics of the followers or of the situation you confront that might substitute for leader behaviors or neutralize them?
12. How favorable is the situation for the leader in terms of task structure, position power, and leader-member relations? What can be done to make this situation more favorable?

ENDNOTES

1. J. R. Meindl and S. B. Ehrlich, "The Romance of Leadership and the Evaluation of Organizational Performance," *Academy of Management Journal* 30 (1987), pp. 91–109.
2. A. Jago, "Leadership: Perspectives in Theory and Research," *Management Sciences* 28 (1982), pp. 315–36.
3. H. Mintzberg, *The Nature of Managerial Work* (New York: Harper & Row, 1973).
4. E. P. Hollander, *Leadership Dynamics* (New York: Free Press, 1978).
5. H. Donovan, "Managing Your Intellectuals," *Fortune,* October 29, 1989, pp. 177–80.
6. G. Yukl, *Leadership in Organizations* (Englewood Cliffs, NJ: Prentice Hall, 1981), p. 71.
7. A. S. Tsui, S. J. Ashford, L. St. Clair, and K. R. Xin, "Dealing with Discrepant Expectations: Response Strategies and Managerial Effectiveness," *Academy of Management Journal* 38 (1995), pp. 1515–43.
8. R. Karlgaard, "An Interview with Bill Gates," *Forbes,* December 7, 1992, pp. 63–74.
9. K. Rebello, "This Boss Measures 6.0 on the Richter Scale," *Business Week,* April 20, 1992, pp. 96–97.
10. W. Glasgall, "Mr. Risk," *Business Week,* December 7, 1992, pp. 104–9.
11. R. M. Stodgill, *Handbook of Leadership* (New York: Free Press, 1974), p. 112.
12. R. Katz, "Skills of an Effective Administrator," *Harvard Business Review* 72 (1974), pp. 90–101.
13. Jago, "Leadership," p. 319.
14. J. M. Burns, *Leadership* (New York: Harper & Row, 1979), p. 52.
15. S. A. Kirkpatrick and E. A. Locke, "Direct and Indirect Effects of Three Core Charismatic Leadership Components on Performance and Attitudes," *Journal of Applied Psychology* 81 (1996), pp. 36–51.
16. J. J. Hater and B. M. Bass, "Superiors' Evaluations and Subordinates' Perceptions of Transformational Leadership," *Journal of Applied Psychology* 73 (1988), pp. 695–702.
17. J. M. Howell and B. J. Avolio, "Transformational Leadership, Transactional Leadership, Locus of Control, and Support for Innovation: Key Predictors of Consolidated-Business-Unit-Performance," *Journal of Applied Psychology* 78 (1993), pp. 891–902.
18. P. Bycio, R. D. Hackett, and J. S. Allen, "Further Assessments of Bass's (1985) Conceptualization of Transactional and Transformational Leadership," *Journal of Applied Psychology* 80 (1995), pp. 468–78.
19. K. Lewin, R. Lippitt, and R. K. White, "Patterns of Aggressive Behavior in Experimentally Created Social Climates," *Journal of Social Psychology* 10 (1939), pp. 271–301.
20. D. B. Welsh, F. Luthans, and S. M. Summer, "Managing Russian Factory Workers: The Impact of U.S. Based Behavioral and Participative Techniques," *Academy of Management Journal* 36 (1993), pp. 58–79.
21. T. A. Stewart, "The Corporate Jungle Spawns a New Species: The Project Manager," *Fortune,* July 10, 1996, pp. 179–81.
22. S. Sherman, "How Tomorrow's Leaders Are Learning Their Stuff," *Fortune,* November 27, 1995, pp. 90–102.
23. S. Sherman, "Secrets of HP's 'Muddled Team'," *Fortune,* March 18, 1996, pp. 116–20.
24. R. Likert, *New Patterns of Management* (New York: McGraw-Hill, 1961), p. 36.
25. N. C. Morse and E. Reimer, "The Experimental Change of a Major Organizational Variable," *Journal of Abnormal and Social Psychology* 52 (1956), pp. 120–29.
26. R. M. Stodgill and A. E. Coons, *Leader Behavior: Its Description and Measurement* (Columbus: Ohio State University, Bureau of Business Research, 1957), p. 75.
27. P. Weissenberg and M. H. Kavanaugh, "The Independence of Initiating Structure and Consideration: A Review of the Evidence," *Personnel Psychology* 25 (1972), pp. 119–30.
28. R. Blake and J. S. Mouton, *The Managerial Grid III: The Key to Leadership Excellence* (Houston: Gulf Publishing, 1985); and R. Blake and A. A. McCanse, *Leadership Dilemmas—Grid Solutions* (Houston: Gulf Publishing, 1991), pp. 21–31.
29. L. L. Larson, J. G. Hunt, and R. Osburn, "The Great Hi-Hi Leader Myth: A Lesson from Occam's Razor," *Academy of Management Journal* 19 (1976), pp. 628–41.
30. G. Graen, "Role-Making Processes within Complex Organizations," in *Handbook of Industrial/Organizational Psychology,* M. D. Dunnette, ed. (Chicago: Rand McNally, 1976), pp. 1210–59.
31. L. Weisman, "Johnson Sees That Cowboys Play Heads-Up," *USA Today,* January 21, 1994, p. 2C.
32. "The Gap: Can the Nation's Hottest Retailer Stay on Top?" *Business Week,* March 9, 1992, pp. 58–64.
33. R. Katerberg and P. Hom, "Effects of Within-Group and Between-Groups Variation in Leadership," *Journal of Applied Psychology* 66 (1981), pp. 218–23.
34. G. Graen, R. Liden, and W. Hoel, "Role of Leadership in the Employee Withdrawal Process," *Journal of Applied Psychology* 67 (1982), pp. 868–72.
35. R. C. Liden, S. J. Wayne, and D. Stilwell, "A Longitudinal Study on the Early Development of

Leader-Member Exchanges," *Journal of Applied Psychology* 78 (1993), pp. 662–74.

36. D. Duchon, S. G. Green, and T. D. Taber, "Vertical Dyad Linkage: A Longitudinal Assessment of Antecedents, Measures, and Consequences," *Journal of Applied Psychology* 71 (1986), pp. 56–60; A. S. Tsui and C. A. O'Reilly, "Beyond Simple Demographic Effects: The Importance of Relational Demography in Superior-Subordinate Dyads," *Academy of Management Journal* 32 (1989), pp. 402–23; and A. Crouch and P. Yetton, "Manager-Subordinate Dyads: Relationships among Task and Social Contract, Manager Friendliness and Subordinate Performance in Management Groups," *Organizational Behavior and Human Decision Processes* 41 (1988), pp. 65–82.

37. S. Kerr and J. M. Jermier, "Substitutes for Leadership: Their Meaning and Measurement," *Organizational Behavior and Human Decision Processes* 22 (1978), pp. 375–403.

38. P. M. Podsakoff, S. B. MacKenzie, and W. H. Bommer, "Meta-Analysis of the Relationships between Kerr and Jermier's Substitutes for Leadership and Employee Job Attitudes, Role Perceptions, and Performance," *Journal of Applied Psychology* 81 (1996), pp. 380–99.

39. F. E. Fiedler, *A Theory of Leadership Effectiveness* (New York: McGraw-Hill, 1967), pp. 120–37.

40. L. H. Peters, D. D. Hartke, and J. T. Pohlmann, "Fiedler's Contingency Theory of Leadership: An Application of the Meta-Analysis Procedures of Schmidt and Hunter," *Psychological Bulletin* 97 (1985), pp. 274–85.

41. F. E. Fiedler, "Engineering the Job to Fit the Manager," *Harvard Business Review* 43 (1965), pp. 115–22.

42. Ibid.

43. A. K. Korman, "Contingency Approaches to Leadership: An Overview," in *Contingency Approaches to Leadership,* J. G. Hunt and L. L. Larson, eds. (Carbondale: Southern Illinois Press, 1974), p. 24; and C. A. Schriesheim, B. D. Bannister, and W. H. Money, "Psychometric Properties of the LPC Scale: An Extension of Rice's Review," *Academy of Management Review* 4 (1979), pp. 287–90.

44. B. Kabanoff, "A Critique of LEADER MATCH and Its Implications for Leadership Research," *Personnel Psychology* 34 (1981), pp. 749–64.

45. A. G. Jago and J. W. Ragan, "The Trouble with LEADER MATCH Is That It Doesn't Match Fiedler's Contingency Model," *Journal of Applied Psychology* 71 (1986), pp. 555–59.

46. A. G. Jago and J. W. Ragan, "Some Assumptions Are More Troubling Than Others: Rejoinder to Chemers and Fiedler," *Journal of Applied Psychology* 71 (1986), pp. 564–65.

47. M. M. Chemers and F. E. Fiedler, "The Trouble with Assumptions: A Reply to Jago and Ragan," *Journal of Applied Psychology* 71 (1986), pp. 560–663.

48. V. H. Vroom, "Leadership," in *Handbook of Industrial/Organizational Psychology,* M. D. Dunnette, ed. (Chicago: Rand-McNally, 1976), p. 912.

49. V. H. Vroom and A. G. Jago, "Decision Making as a Social Process: Normative and Descriptive Models of Leader Behavior," *Decision Sciences* 5 (1974), pp. 743–69.

50. V. H. Vroom and P. W. Yetton, *Leadership and Decision Making* (Pittsburgh, PA: University of Pittsburgh Press, 1973), p. 12.

51. K. Kelly, "Caterpillar's Don Fites: Why He Didn't Blink," *Business Week,* August 10, 1992, pp. 56–57.

52. Vroom and Yetton, *Leadership and Decision Making,* p. 13.

53. R. Stodghill, "Joe Montgomery's Wild Ride," *Business Week,* April 19, 1992, pp. 50–51.

54. M. G. Evans, "The Effect of Supervisory Behavior on the Path-Goal Relationship," *Organizational Behavior and Human Performance* 5 (1970), pp. 277–98; and R. J. House, "A Path-Goal Theory of Leadership Effectiveness," *Administrative Science Quarterly* 16 (1971), pp. 321–38.

55. R. J. House and T. R. Mitchell, "Path-Goal Theory of Leadership," *Journal of Contemporary Business* 3 (1974), pp. 81–97.

56. L. Therrien, "Why Rich Melman Is Really Cooking," *Business Week,* November 2, 1992, pp. 127–28.

57. A. C. Filley, R. J. House, and S. Kerr, *Managerial Processes and Organizational Behavior* (Glenview, IL: Scott, Foresman, 1976), p. 91.

58. R. T. Keller, "A Test of the Path-Goal Theory of Leadership with Need for Clarity as a Moderator in Research and Development Organizations," *Journal of Applied Psychology* 74 (1989), pp. 208–12.

59. Ibid.

60. J. E. Stinson and T. W. Johnson, "A Path-Goal Theory of Leadership: A Partial Test and Suggested Refinements," *Academy of Management Journal* 18 (1975), pp. 242–52.

61. M. Erez and I. Zidon, "Effect of Goal Acceptance on the Relationship between Goal Difficulty and Performance," *Journal of Applied Psychology* 69 (1984), pp. 69–78.

62. L. E. Atwater and F. J. Yammarino, "Does Self-Other Agreement on Leadership Perceptions Moderate the Validity of Leadership and Performance Predictions?" *Personnel Psychology* 45 (1992), pp. 141–64.

63. L. Atwater, P. Roush, and A. Fischthal, "The Influence of Upward Feedback on Self- and Follower Ratings of Leadership," *Personnel Psychology* 48 (1995), pp. 35–59.

Chapter Ten

Power, Conflict, and Negotiation

J.P. Bolduc, chief executive of W. R. Grace and Company, knew that his strained relationship with octogenarian chairman J. Peter Grace Jr. was putting his job in jeopardy, but he didn't know how serious the problem was becoming. Then, on the night of February 11, 1994, Grace and his youngest son, Patrick, president of Grace Logistics Services, telephoned company director Robert C. Macauley to arrange an urgent meeting. Several hours later the two Graces told Macauley of allegations against Bolduc that included steering Grace company business to his friends and to a company on whose board he served. The elder Grace, who had preceded Bolduc as CEO, demanded that the board investigate these allegations immediately.

Bolduc countered by approaching John Cardinal O'Connor, archbishop of the archdiocese of New York, to ask him to referee the developing blowup. But Grace ignored the cardinal's request to patch things up. Bolduc next approached the board of the Boca Raton, Florida, chemical and health services giant, but was met by additional charges of sexual harassment. Thirteen months later, despite having overseen the sale of $2.1 billion worth of extraneous businesses and having triggered a 32 percent run-up in the price of the company's stock, Bolduc was forced out. His letter of resignation cited "philosophical differences" between himself and the board as the reason for his exit, but few doubted that the real cause had been his failure to realize the true power of the patrician Grace family and their loyal, financially beholden directors.[1]

---

[1] E. Lesly, "The Knights of Business," *Business Week,* May 1, 1995, pp. 42–43; E. Lesly, "Fall from Grace," *Business Week,* May 29, 1995, pp. 60–70; E. Lesly, G. DeGeorge, and P. Valdes-Dapena, "The Secret War inside Grace and Company," *Business Week,* April 17, 1995, pp. 40–41; and G. DeGeorge, E. Lesly, and L. Nathans, "A New Power Play at W. R. Grace," *Business Week,* June 19, 1995, p. 44.

Far from being the exception, W. R. Grace is only one of many companies that have experienced serious management strife during the 1990s. *Palace revolts* throughout North America have led to the ouster of top executives in such firms as American Express, Westinghouse, General Motors, Scott Paper, Micron Technology, Eli Lilly, and Apple Computer.[1] Rather than diminishing, these kinds of political processes will certainly continue to influence business organizations into the next century.

Power and conflict in firms can increase productivity and efficiency or reduce them substantially. Political processes can even determine the existence and strategic direction of entire organizations. Restructuring, often stimulated as much by internal power struggles as by external market conditions, is prompting executives to search out new strategic directions for their firms. In the process, political considerations are altering the careers of thousands of employees, both managers and nonmanagers, and creating opportunities for some, but costing many others their jobs.[2]

Understanding power and conflict is therefore critical to managerial success—and survival—in today's business organizations. For this reason, we begin Chapter 10 with a discussion of the nature, sources, and consequences of power. Next we turn our attention to the closely related topic of conflict, describing the most important bases and results of confrontation in organizations. We conclude by discussing negotiation, as well as other methods of managing power and conflict relations.

Power and Politics

If someone asked you to define *power*, how would you respond? Many people might recall master politicians like Great Britain's wartime prime minister Winston Churchill or former U.S. president Lyndon Johnson and define power as the ability to influence the behaviors of others, getting them to do things they would not otherwise do.[3] For other people, images of the less powerful might come to mind, leading them to define power as the ability to avoid others' attempts to influence one's behavior. In truth, both of these views are correct because **power** can be formally defined as the ability to influence the conduct of others and to resist unwanted influence in return.[4]

Why do people seek power over others? The work of David McClelland, a researcher interested in determining why some people succeed as managers and others do not, provides a clue.[5] McClelland deduced that people are driven to gain and use power by a need for power—which he called *nPow*—that is learned during childhood and adolescence. McClelland thus suggested that experience teaches some people to seek and use power, contributing to the development of a high nPow. Others, he said, learn to avoid the use of power and develop a low nPow as a result.

The need for power can have several different effects on the way people behave. Generally speaking, people with high nPow are competitive, aggressive, prestige conscious, action oriented, and prone to join groups. They are likely to be effective managers and leaders if, in addition to pursuing power, they also do the following:

- Use power to accomplish organizational goals instead of using it to satisfy personal interests
- Coach subordinates and use empowering, influence-sharing management techniques rather than autocratic, authoritarian methods
- Remain aware of the importance of managing interpersonal relations, but avoid developing close relationships with subordinates[6]

According to McClelland, seeking power and using it to influence others are not activities to be shunned or avoided. In fact, the processes of management and leadership *require* that power be put to appropriate use—where appropriateness depends on important ethical and political considerations, and inappropriateness can have significant personal and organizational costs (see box).

Interpersonal Sources of Power

If management and leadership require the use of power, then how do people in organizations acquire the power to influence others' behaviors? Where does a manager's power come from? In their pioneering work aimed at identifying different types of power in organizations, John French and Bertram Raven sought to answer these questions by identifying the major bases, or sources, of power in organizations.[7] The five sources and types of power they discovered are listed in Table 10-1.

The first type of power listed in the table, **reward power,** is based on the ability to allocate rewarding outcomes—either the receipt of positive things or the elimination of negative things. Praise, promotions, raises, desirable job assignments, and time off from work are rewarding outcomes that managers often control. If they can make decisions about the distribution of such rewards, managers can use them to acquire and maintain reward power. Similarly, eliminating unwanted outcomes such as unpleasant working conditions or mandatory overtime can be used to reward employees.

Table 10-1 ■ Five Types of Power and Their Sources	
TYPE OF POWER	**SOURCE OF POWER**
Reward	Control over rewarding outcomes
Coercive	Control over punishing outcomes
Legitimate	Occupation of legitimate position of authority
Referent	Attractiveness, charisma
Expert	Expertise, knowledge, talent

Source: Based on J. R. P. French Jr. and B. Raven, "The Bases of Social Power," in *Studies in Social Power,* D. Cartwright, ed. (Ann Arbor: Institute for Social Research, University of Michigan, 1959), pp. 150–65.

The Ethics of Power and Costs of Abuse

How should power holders determine whether the use of power is appropriate? One approach is to adopt the *utilitarian* perspective and judge the appropriateness of the use of power in terms of the consequences of this use. Does the use of power provide the greatest good for the greatest number of people? If the answer to this question is yes, then, according to the utilitarian perspective, power is being used appropriately.

A second perspective, derived from the theory of *moral rights,* suggests that power is used appropriately only when no one's personal rights or freedoms are sacrificed. It is certainly possible for many people to derive great satisfaction from the use of power to accomplish some purpose, so that utilitarian criteria are satisfied, and at the same time for the rights of a few individuals to

be abridged, an indication of inappropriateness according to the theory of moral rights. Power holders seeking to use their power appropriately must therefore respect the rights and interests of the minority, as well as looking after the well-being of the majority.

A third perspective, drawn from theories of *social justice,* suggests that even having respect for the rights of everyone in an organization may not be enough to fully justify the use of power. In addition, those using power must treat people equitably, making sure that people who are similar in relevant respects are treated similarly and that people who are different in relevant respects are treated differently in proportion to the differences between them. According to this perspective, power holders must also be accountable for injuries caused by their use of power

and must be prepared to provide compensation for these injuries in order for the use of power to be considered appropriate.[1]

What are some of the costs of failing to use power ethically? Consider the plight of Astra USA, a Westborough, Massachusetts, subsidiary of giant Swedish drugmaker Astra AB. According to complaints uncovered during a special investigation conducted by *Business Week,* during the 15-year tenure of CEO Lars Bildman, female employees were expected to escort male senior executives to bars and dancing clubs, and pressured to join often-inebriated managers in hotel suites for intimate late-night gatherings. Female staff members were also required to attend company parties where, according to former Astra sales representative Kimberley A. Cote, "guys were encouraged to get as

[1] G. F. Cavanagh, D. Moberg, and M. Velasquez, "The Ethics of Organizational Politics," *Academy of Management Review* 6 (1981), pp. 363–74.

Whereas reward power controls the allocation of desirable outcomes, **coercive power** is based on the distribution of undesirable outcomes—either the receipt of something negative or the removal of something positive. Coercive power exploits fear. People who control undesirable outcomes get others to conform to their wishes by threatening to penalize them in some way. To influence subordinates' behaviors, managers may resort to punishments such as public scoldings, assignment of undesirable tasks, loss of pay, or, taken to the extreme, layoffs, demotions, or dismissals.

Legitimate power is based on norms, values, and beliefs that particular individuals have the legitimate right to govern or influence others. From childhood, people learn to accept the commands of authority figures—first parents, then teachers, and finally bosses. It is this well-learned lesson that gives people with authority the power to influence other people's attitudes and behaviors. In most organizations, authority is distributed in the form of a hierarchy. People who hold positions of hierarchical authority are accorded legitimate power by virtue of the fact that they are office holders. So, the vice president of marketing at a

drunk as they could—and do whatever they could to the women. If they felt like grabbing a woman by the boob or by the ass, that was okay."

Bildman's personal abuse of power extended to include insistence on absolute adherence to other rigid, almost militaristic policies and practices. Most staff members were required to go to lunch at precisely the same time every day and had to get written permission to display anything personal in their cubicles. The company maintained a single centralized fax machine for all but the highest-ranking executives, so that Bildman could read all incoming and outgoing messages. Also mandated by Bildman were a variety of unusual rules about attire at work, including one requiring that an

Astra pin had to be worn at all company functions. People who forgot their pins were severely reprimanded in front of colleagues. Reports a former manager, "I used to carry extra pins around. The fear got so out of hand that I recall at least six times that I gave somebody an extra pin and they were literally shaken by the fact that they had lost theirs."

The costs to Astra of this abuse, already immense, are still growing. During Bildman's reign, appalled employees—both male and female—left Astra USA in droves, which cost the company millions in lost recruitment and training expenditures and curtailed productivity. Following the *Business Week* investigation, top managers including Bildman himself were forced by the Swedish

parent firm to resign in June 1996. Scandal also crossed the Atlantic Ocean to affect the parent corporation, where senior executive Anders Lönner was asked to resign for failing to report the misconduct to Swedish superiors.

Back in the United States, Astra now faces a blizzard of sexual harassment lawsuits likely to lead to immense court settlements, according to Eric J. Wallach, a New York attorney who specializes in defending companies against harassment suits. And the Equal Employment Opportunity Commission (EEOC) has launched an investigation of Astra that will most likely generate embarrassing publicity for the firm. Astra USA will not recover from the costs of abuses of power by Bildman and other company officials for years, if ever.[2]

---

[2]M. Maremont and J. A. Sasseen, "Abuse of Power: The Astonishing Tale of Sexual Harassment at Astra USA," *Business Week,* May 13, 1996, pp. 86–98; M. Maremont, "Aftershocks Are Rumbling through Astra," *Business Week,* May 20, 1996, p. 35; and M. Maremont, "Day of Reckoning at Astra," *Business Week,* July 8, 1996, p. 36.

firm like RJR-Nabisco issues orders and expects people in subordinate positions to obey them because of the clout that being a vice president affords.

Have you ever admired a teacher, a student leader, or someone else whose personality, way of interacting with other people, values, goals, or other characteristics were exceptionally attractive? If so, you probably found yourself wanting to develop and maintain a close relationship with that person. This desire can give a person **referent power** over you. Individuals you hold in such esteem are likely to influence you by their attitudes and behaviors. In time you may come to identify with a person to such an extent that you begin to think and act like the person. Referent power is also called *charismatic power.*

Famous religious leaders and political figures often develop and use referent power. Mahatma Gandhi, John F. Kennedy, Martin Luther King Jr., and Nelson Mandela have all used personal charisma to profoundly influence the thoughts and behaviors of others. Referent power can also be put to more everyday use. For instance, consider advertising's use of famous athletes and actors to help sell products. Athletic shoe manufacturers like Nike and Reebok,

Table 10-2 ■ **Three Responses to Interpersonal Power**

LEVEL	DESCRIPTION
Compliance	Conformity based on the desire to gain rewards or avoid punishment; continues as long as rewards are received or punishment is withheld.
Identification	Conformity based on the attractiveness of the influencer; continues as long as a relationship with the influencer can be maintained.
Internalization	Conformity based on the intrinsically satisfying nature of adopted attitudes or behaviors; continues as long as satisfaction continues.

Source: Based on H. C. Kelman, "Compliance, Identification, and Internalization: Three Processes of Attitude Change," *Journal of Conflict Resolution* 2 (1958), pp. 51–60.

for example, employ sports celebrities like Michael Jordan of the Chicago Bulls basketball team or Barry Sanders of the Detroit Lions football team as spokespeople in an effort to influence consumers to buy their products.[8]

Expert power is based on the possession of expertise, knowledge, and talent. People who are seen as experts in a particular area can influence others in two ways. They can provide other people with knowledge that enables or causes them to change their attitudes or behavior, or they can demand conformity to their wishes as the price of the knowledge others need. Thus, experts such as doctors, lawyers, and accountants provide advice that influences what their clients do. By expressing their own opinions, media critics shape people's attitudes about new books, movies, recordings, and television shows. Auto mechanics, plumbers, and electricians also exert a great deal of influence over customers who are not themselves talented craftspeople.

Conformity Responses

How do employees respond when managers use these different kinds of power? According to Herbert Kelman, three distinctly different types of reactions are likely to occur: compliance, identification, and internalization (see Table 10-2).[9]

Compliance ensues when people conform to the wishes or directives of others to acquire favorable outcomes for themselves in return. They adopt new attitudes and behaviors not because the latter are agreeable or personally fulfilling but because they lead to specific rewards and approval or head off specific punishments and disapproval. People are likely to continue to engage in such behaviors only as long as favorable outcomes remain contingent on conformity.

Of the different types of power identified by French and Raven, which are most likely to stimulate compliance? The answer is reward and coercive power, which are based on linking employee performance with the receipt of positive or negative outcomes. Employees who work harder because a supervisor with reward power has promised them incentive payments are displaying compliance behavior. Likewise, employees who work harder to avoid punishments administered by a supervisor with coercive power will continue doing so only while the threat of punishment remains salient.

Identification takes place when people accept the direction or influence of others because they identify with the others and seek to maintain relationships with them, not because they value or even agree with what it is they are asked to do. Referent power, discussed by French and Raven, is based on the same sort of personal attractiveness as is identification. Consequently, referent power and identification are likely to be closely linked. Charismatic leaders are able to continue influencing other people's behaviors for as long as identification continues.

Finally, through *internalization*, people may adopt others' attitudes and behaviors in order to satisfy their personal needs, or because they find those attitudes and behaviors to be congruent with their own personal values. In either case, they accept the others' influence wholeheartedly. It follows that legitimate and expert power can stimulate internalization. Both forms of power rely on personal credibility—the extent to which a person is perceived as truly possessing authority or expertise. This credibility can be used to convince people of the intrinsic importance of the attitudes and behaviors they are being asked to adopt.

In internalization, people find newly adopted attitudes and behaviors to be personally rewarding and self-reinforcing. Supervisors who can use their expertise to convince colleagues to use consultative leadership can expect the other managers to continue consulting with their subordinates long after they have withdrawn from the situation. Managers whose legitimate power lends credibility to the orders they issue can expect their subordinates to follow those orders even in the absence of rewards, punishments, or charismatic attraction.

A Model of Interpersonal Power: Assessment

French and Raven describe the different kinds of interpersonal power used in organizations, and Kelman identifies how people respond to this use. Though valuable as a tool for understanding power and its consequences, the model integrating these ideas, shown in Figure 10-1, is not entirely without fault. There is some question as to whether the five bases of power are completely independent, as proposed by French and Raven, or whether they are so closely interrelated as to be virtually indistinguishable from one another. The idea that reward, coercive, and legitimate power often derive from company policies and procedures has led some researchers to subsume these three types of power in a single category labeled **organizational power.** Because expert and referent power are based on personal expertise and charisma, respectively, they have sometimes been lumped together in the category of **personal power.**[10]

In fact, French and Raven's five bases of power may be even more closely interrelated than this two-category model suggests. In their study of two paper mills, Greene and Podsakoff found that changing just one source of managerial power affected employees' perceptions of three other types of power.[11] Initially, both paper mills used an incentive payment plan in which employees' pay was determined by supervisors' monthly performance appraisals. At one mill, the incentive plan was changed to an hourly wage system in which seniority determined an employee's rate of pay. The existing incentive plan was left in place at the other mill. The researchers found that, following this change, not only did the employees at the first mill perceive their supervisors as having significantly less

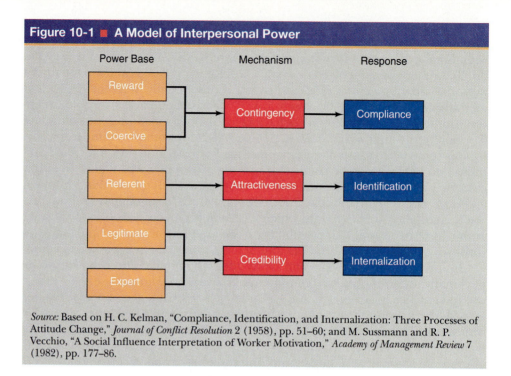

Figure 10-1 ■ **A Model of Interpersonal Power**

Power Base | Mechanism | Response

Reward
Coercive → Contingency → Compliance

Referent → Attractiveness → Identification

Legitimate
Expert → Credibility → Internalization

Source: Based on H. C. Kelman, "Compliance, Identification, and Internalization: Three Processes of Attitude Change," *Journal of Conflict Resolution* 2 (1958), pp. 51–60; and M. Sussmann and R. P. Vecchio, "A Social Influence Interpretation of Worker Motivation," *Academy of Management Review* 7 (1982), pp. 177–86.

reward power, as we might expect, but they also saw significant changes in their supervisors' punishment, legitimate, and referent power. As shown in Figure 10-2, they attributed a great deal more punishment power to their supervisors, as well as a little less referent power and substantially less legitimate power.

In contrast, employees in the second mill, where the incentive plan remained unchanged, reported no significant changes in their perceptions of their supervisors' reward, punishment, legitimate, and referent power. Because all other conditions were held constant in both mills, employees' changed perceptions in the first mill could not be attributed to other unknown factors. Instead, their perceptions of reward, coercive, legitimate, and referent power proved to be closely interrelated. This finding suggests that four of the five types of power identified by French and Raven appear to be virtually indistinguishable to interested observers.[12]

Despite this important limitation, the model formed by joining French and Raven's classification scheme with Kelman's is useful in analyzing social influence and *interpersonal* power in organizations. Managers can use the model to help predict how subordinates will conform to directives based on a particular type of power. For example, how likely is it that the use of expertise will result in long-term changes in subordinates' behavior? Because the model shown in Figure 10-1 indicates that internalization is stimulated by the use of expert power, long-term behavioral changes are quite likely to occur. Alternatively, subordinates may find the model useful as a means of understanding—and perhaps

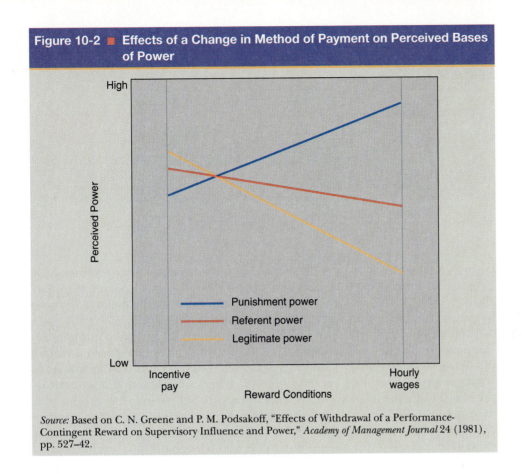

Figure 10-2 ■ Effects of a Change in Method of Payment on Perceived Bases of Power

Source: Based on C. N. Greene and P. M. Podsakoff, "Effects of Withdrawal of a Performance-Contingent Reward on Supervisory Influence and Power," *Academy of Management Journal* 24 (1981), pp. 527–42.

influencing—the behaviors of their superiors. Can you explain why employees interested in influencing their boss to make a permanent change in style of management are best advised to try using personal expertise?

Structural Sources of Power

In addition to issuing from the interpersonal sources discussed so far, power also originates in the *structure* of patterned work activities and flows of information found in every organization. Chapter 11 will examine the topic of organization structure in detail, so current discussion will be limited to those characteristics of organizations that shape power relations—uncertainty reduction, substitutability, and centrality. As is depicted in Figure 10-3, these three variables combine to form the critical contingencies model of power.[13]

Uncertainty Reduction. **Critical contingencies** are things an organization and its various parts need in order to accomplish organizational goals and continue surviving. The raw materials needed by a company to manufacture the goods it sells are critical contingencies. So, too, are the employees who make these goods, the

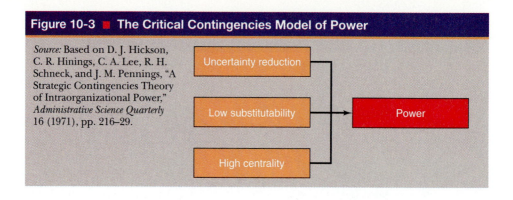

Figure 10-3 ■ The Critical Contingencies Model of Power

Source: Based on D. J. Hickson, C. R. Hinings, C. A. Lee, R. H. Schneck, and J. M. Pennings, "A Strategic Contingencies Theory of Intraorganizational Power," *Administrative Science Quarterly* 16 (1971), pp. 216–29.

Uncertainty reduction

Low substitutability

High centrality

Power

customers who buy them, and the banks that provide loans to buy inventory and equipment. Information can also be a critical contingency. Consider the financial data used by banks to decide whether to grant loans, or the mailing lists used by catalog merchandisers to locate prospective customers.

Uncertainty about the continued availability of such critical contingencies threatens organizational well-being. If a purchasing manager cannot be certain of buying raw materials at reasonable prices, the organization's ability to start or continue productive work is compromised. When a marketing department reports shifting consumer tastes, its firm's ability to sell what it has produced is threatened. Thus, as explained by Gerald Salancik and Jeffrey Pfeffer, the critical contingencies model of power is based on the principle that "those [individuals or groups] most able to cope with [their] organization's critical problems and uncertainties acquire power"[14] by trading **uncertainty reduction** for whatever they want in return.

One way to reduce uncertainty is to gain *resource control,* that is, to acquire and maintain access to those resources that are otherwise difficult to get.[15] A personnel department may be able to reduce an important source of uncertainty in an organization that has had problems attracting qualified employees if it can hire and retain a productive workforce. Similarly, a purchasing department that can negotiate discounts on raw materials can help reduce uncertainty as to whether the firm can afford to continue to produce its line of goods. Each of these departments, by delivering crucial resources and thereby reducing success-threatening uncertainty, can gain power.[16]

Information control offers another way of reducing uncertainty in organizations. Providing information about critical contingencies is particularly useful when such information can be used to predict or prevent threats to organizational operations.[17] Suppose, for example, that a telecommunication company's legal department learns of impending legislation that will restrict the company's ability to buy additional television stations unless it divests stations it already owns. By alerting management and recommending ways to form subsidiary companies to allow continued growth, the firm's legal department can eliminate a lot of uncertainty for the firm.

A third way to reduce uncertainty is to acquire *decision-making control*, that is, to have input into the initial decisions about what sorts of resources are going to be critical contingencies. At any time, events may conspire to give certain groups power over others, power that allows the former to determine the rules of the game or to decide such basic issues as what the company will produce, to whom it will market the product, and what kinds of materials, skills, and procedures are needed. Kodak's decision to concentrate on photographic products and get out of unrelated businesses was due in part to the power of executives involved in the company's photography product divisions and their desire to retain or even increase their influence over company operations.[18]

Having power can even enable those already in power to make the contingencies they manage more important to organizational well-being. Thus, marketing research departments sometimes report the results of their research using exotic statistics that cannot be easily interpreted by other managers. Management, therefore, develops additional reliance on marketing researchers as interpreters of the reports they generate. In this manner, power can be used to acquire power of even greater magnitude—"the rich get richer."[19]

Substitutability. Whether individuals or groups gain power as a result of their success at reducing uncertainty depends partly on their **substitutability.** If others can serve as substitutes and reduce the same sort of uncertainty, then individuals or departments who need help in coping with uncertainty can turn to a variety of sources and no single source is likely to acquire much power. For example, a legal department's ability to interpret laws and regulations is unlikely to yield power for the department if legal specialists working in other departments can fulfill the same function. In the presence of substitutes, other departments are able to ignore the pressures of any particular group, and so each group's ability to amass power is undermined.

However, if others cannot get help in coping with uncertainty from any but the target person or group, this person or group is clearly in a position to barter uncertainty reduction for desired outcomes. For example, a research and development group that is a company's sole source of new product ideas can threaten to reduce the flow of innovation if the firm does not provide the resources it wants. The less substitutability there is in a situation, the more likely it is that a particular person or group will be able to amass power.[20]

Centrality. The ability of a person or a group to acquire power is also affected by **centrality,** or position within the flow of work in the organization.[21] The ability to reduce uncertainty is unlikely to affect a group's power if no one outside the group knows the group has this ability and no one inside the group knows how important the ability is. Simply because few other people know of its existence, a clerical staff located on the periphery of a company is unlikely to amass much power even if its typing and filing activities bring it into direct contact with critically important information. Even when uncertainty emerges that the staff could help resolve, the staff is ignored because no one is aware of the knowledge and abilities the staff members possess.

The Critical Contingencies Model: Assessment

Despite a few criticisms of the critical contingencies model,[22] research strongly supports the model's suggestion that power is a function of uncertainty reduction, substitutability, and centrality. An analysis of British manufacturing firms in business during the first half of the 20th century confirms this idea. The analysis revealed that accounting departments dominated organizational decision making in the depression era preceding World War II because they kept costs down at a time when money was scarce.[23] Following the war, power shifted to purchasing departments as money became more readily available and strong consumer demand made access to plentiful supplies of raw materials more important. Then, during the 1950s, demand dropped so precipitously that marketing became the most important problem facing British firms. As a result and as the model predicts, marketing and sales departments that succeeded in increasing company sales gained power over important decision-making processes.

An even more intriguing piece of evidence supporting the critical contingencies model was discovered by Michel Crozier, a French sociologist who studied a government-owned tobacco company located just outside of Paris.[24] As the situation was described by Crozier, maintenance mechanics in the tobacco company sought control over their working lives by refusing to share knowledge needed to repair crucial production equipment. The mechanics memorized repair manuals and then threw them away so that no one else could refer to them. In addition, they refused to let production employees or supervisors watch as they repaired the company's machines. They also trained their replacements in a closely guarded apprenticeship process so that outsiders could not learn what they knew. Some mechanics even altered equipment so completely that the original manufacturer could not figure out how it worked. In this manner, the tobacco company's maintenance mechanics retained absolute control over the information and skill required to repair production equipment. In essence, maintenance personnel ran the production facility as a result of the information they alone possessed about its equipment.

Crozier's account of the tobacco factory mechanics illustrates the usefulness of the critical contingencies model in explaining why people who have hierarchical authority and formal power sometimes lack the influence needed to manage workplace activities. If subordinates have knowledge, skills, or abilities required to manage critical contingencies, thereby reducing troublesome uncertainties, they may gain the power to refuse to obey hierarchical superiors. Correspondingly, as long as superiors must depend on subordinates to manage such contingencies, it will be the subordinates and not the superiors who determine which orders will be followed and which will be ignored.[25]

In sum, the critical contingencies model appears to depict the structural bases of power quite accurately. Its utility for contemporary managers lies in the observation that the roots of power lie in the ability to solve crucial organizational problems. It is important for managers to know about these roots because such knowledge can help them acquire and hold on to the power needed to do their jobs.

Conflict in Organizations

Conflict—a process of opposition and confrontation that can occur in organizations between either individuals or groups—occurs when parties exercise power in the pursuit of valued goals or objectives and obstruct the progress of one or more others.[26] Key to this definition is the idea that conflict involves the use of power in confrontation, that is, disputes over clashing interests. Also important is the notion that conflict is a process—something that takes time to unfold, rather than an event that occurs in an instant and then disappears. Finally, to the extent that obstructing progress threatens effectiveness and performance, the definition implies that conflict is a problem that managers must be able to control.

Is Conflict Necessarily Bad?

Conflict might seem inherently undesirable. In fact, many of the models of organization and management discussed in Chapter 1 support this view. Classic theorists often likened organizations to machines and portrayed conflict as symptomatic of breakdown. Managers in the days of Henri Fayol and Frederick Taylor concerned themselves with discovering ways either to avoid conflict or to suppress it as quickly and forcefully as possible.

Modern theorists, however, suggest that conflict is not necessarily bad.[27] To be sure, they say, *dysfunctional* conflict—confrontation that hinders progress toward desired goals—does occur. In the 1990s, for example, protracted strikes at Bridgestone-Firestone and Caterpillar Tractor, manufacturers of tires and earth-moving equipment, left both sides with bad feelings and cost union employees millions in lost wages and benefits. But current research suggests that conflict is often *functional*, having positive effects such as the following:

1. Conflict can lessen social tensions, helping to stabilize and integrate relationships. If resolved in a way that allows the discussion and dissipation of disagreements, it can serve as a safety valve that vents pressures built up over time.
2. Conflict lets conflicting parties express rival claims and can provide the opportunity to readjust the allocation of valued resources. Resource pools may thus be consumed more effectively due to conflict-induced changes.
3. Conflict can help to maintain the level of stimulation or activation required to function innovatively. In so doing, conflict can serve as a source of motivation to seek adaptive change.
4. Conflict supplies feedback about the state of interdependencies and power distributions in an organization's structure. The distribution of power required to coordinate work activities may be more clearly apparent and readily understood as the result of conflict.
5. Conflict can help provide a sense of identity and purpose by clarifying differences and boundaries between individuals or groups. Outcomes of this sort are discussed in greater detail later in this chapter.[28]

At the very least, conflict can serve as a red flag signaling the need for change. Believing that conflict can have positive effects, contemporary managers try to manage or resolve conflict rather than avoiding or suppressing it.

Conditions That Stimulate Conflict

In order for conflict to occur, three key conditions must exist. These are interdependence, political indeterminism, and divergence.

Interdependence exists when individuals, groups, or organizations depend on each other for assistance, information, feedback, or other coordinative relations.[29] As indicated in Chapter 7, four types of interdependence—pooled, sequential, reciprocal, and comprehensive—can link parties together. Any such linkages can be sources of conflict. For example, two groups that share a pool of funds may fight over who will receive money to buy new office equipment. Similarly, employees organized along a sequential assembly process may fight about the pace of work. In the absence of interdependence, on the other hand, parties have nothing to fight about and, in fact, may not even know of each other's existence.

The emergence of conflict also requires *political indeterminism,* a state in which the political pecking order among individuals or groups is unclear and subject to question. If power relations are unambiguous and stable, and if they are accepted as valid by all, appeals to authority will replace conflict, and differences will be resolved in favor of the most powerful. Only a party whose power is uncertain will gamble on getting its way through conflict rather than by appealing to power and authority. For this reason, individuals and groups in a newly reorganized company are much more likely to engage in conflict than are parties in an organization with a stable hierarchy of authority.

Finally, in order for conflict to emerge, there must be *divergence,* or differences or disagreements that are worth fighting over.[30] For example, differences in the functions they perform may lead individuals or groups to have *varying goals.* Table 10-3 describes some differences in the goal orientations of marketing and manufacturing groups. In this example, each group's approach reflects its particular orientation—marketing's focus on customer service versus manufacturing's concern with efficient production runs. In such situations, conflicts may occur over whose goals to pursue and whose to ignore.

Individuals and groups may also have different *time orientations.* For example, tasks like making a sale to a regular customer require only short-term planning and can be initiated or altered quite easily. On the other hand, tasks like traditional assembly line manufacturing operations necessitate a longer time frame because such activities require extensive preplanning and are not easy to change once they have begun. Certain tasks, such as the strategic planning activities that plot an organization's future, may even require time frames of several decades. When differences between time orientations exist among parties in a firm, conflicts develop about which orientation should regulate task planning and performance.

Often, *resource allocations* among individuals or groups are unequal. Such differences usually stem from the fact that parties must compete with each other to

Table 10-3 ▪ Differences in Goal Orientations: Marketing and Manufacturing

GOAL FOCUS	MARKETING APPROACH	MANUFACTURING APPROACH
Product variety	Customers demand variety.	Variety causes short, often uneconomical production runs.
Capacity limits	Manufacturing capacity limits productivity.	Inaccurate sales forecasts limit productivity.
Product quality	Reasonable quality should be achievable at a cost that is affordable to customers.	Offering options that are difficult to manufacture undermines quality.
New products	New products are the firm's lifeblood.	Unnecessary design changes are costly.
Cost control	High cost undermines the firm's competitive position.	Broad variety, fast delivery, high quality, and rapid responsiveness are not possible at low cost.

Source: Based on information presented in B. S. Shapiro, "Can Marketing and Manufacturing Coexist?" *Harvard Business Review* 55, 5 (September-October 1977), pp. 104–14.

get a share of their organization's resources. When the production department gets new personal computers to help schedule weekly activities, the sales department may find itself having to do without the new computers it wants for market research. In such instances, someone wins and someone loses, which lays the groundwork for additional rounds of conflict.

Another source of conflict may be the practices used to *evaluate* and *reward* groups and their members. Consider, for example, that manufacturing groups are often rewarded for efficiency, achieved by minimizing the quantity of raw materials consumed in production activities. Sales groups, on the other hand, are more likely to be rewarded for flexibility, which sacrifices efficiency. Conflict is likely to arise in such situations as each group tries to meet its own performance criteria or tries to force others to adopt the same criteria.

In addition, *status discrepancies* invite conflict over stature and position. Although the status of a person or group is generally determined by position in the organization's hierarchy of authority—with parties higher in the hierarchy having higher status—sometimes other criteria influence status.[31] For instance, a group might argue that its status should depend on the knowledge possessed by its members or that status should be conferred on the basis of such factors as loyalty, seniority, or visibility.

Conflict can emerge in *jurisdictional disputes* when it is unclear who has responsibility for something. For example, if both the personnel and the employing departments interview a prospective employee, the two groups may get into a dispute over which has the ultimate right to offer employment and which must take the blame if mistakes are made.

Finally, individuals and groups can differ in the *values, assumptions,* and *general perceptions* that guide performance. Values held among the members of a production group that stress easy assembly differ from the values of research and development staff that favor complex product designs. These values clash, leading to conflict, whenever researchers fight for demanding product specifications that production personnel dismiss as unnecessarily complicated.

Effects of Conflict

Conflict affects relationships among people and groups in many ways. When conflict occurs between groups, several important effects can be predicted to occur within each conflicting group.[32]

First, as we noted in Chapter 8, external threats such as intergroup conflict bring about *increased group cohesiveness*. As a result, groups engaged in conflict become more attractive and important to their own members. Ongoing conflict also stimulates an *emphasis on task performance*. All efforts within each conflicting group are directed toward meeting the challenge posed by other groups, and concerns about individual members' satisfaction lose importance. A sense of urgency surrounds task performance; defeating the enemy becomes uppermost, and there is much less loafing.

In addition, when a group faces conflict, members who might otherwise resist *autocratic leadership* will often submit to such leadership when it is employed to manage the crisis, perceiving participatory decision making as being overly slow and weak for the situation at hand. Strong, authoritarian leaders often emerge as a result of this shift. A group in such circumstances is also likely to place much more emphasis on standard procedures and centralized control. As a result, it becomes characterized by *structural rigidity*. By adhering to established rules, and creating and strictly enforcing new ones, the group seeks to eliminate any conflicts that might develop among its members and ensure that it is able to succeed again and again at its task.

Besides these changes within groups, other changes often occur in relations *between* conflicting groups. Hostility often surfaces in the form of hardened *"we-they" attitudes*. Each group sees itself as virtuous and other groups as enemies. Intense dislike often accompanies these negative attitudes. As attitudes within each group become more negative, group members develop *distorted perceptions* of other groups. Negative stereotyping results, creating even greater differences between groups and further strengthening cohesiveness within each group.

In time, negative attitudes and perceptions of group members regarding other groups are likely to fuel a *decrease in communication* among conflicting groups. The isolation that results only adds to the conflict, making resolution even more difficult. At the same time, however, conflicting groups often engage in *increased surveillance* intended to provide information about the attitudes, weaknesses, and likely behaviors of other groups.

Negotiation and Restructuring

A variety of conflict management techniques have been developed to resolve conflicts and deal with the kinds of negative effects just described. In general, these techniques are of two types: bargaining and negotiation procedures that have to do with *managing divergence* among the interests of conflicting parties, and restructuring techniques that focus on *managing interdependence* between conflicting individuals and groups.

Managing Diverging Interests

Bargaining and **negotiation** are two closely associated processes that are often used to try to work out the differences in interests and concerns that generate conflict. Bargaining between conflicting parties consists of offers, counteroffers, and concessions exchanged in a search for some mutually acceptable resolution. Negotiation, in turn, is the process in which the parties decide what each will give and take in the exchange between them.[33]

In the business world, relations between management and labor are often the focus of bargaining and negotiation. However, bargaining and negotiation also occur elsewhere in organizations as people and groups try to satisfy their own desires and control the extent to which they must sacrifice in order to satisfy others. In tight economies, groups of secretaries who are dependent on the same supply budget may have to bargain with each other to see who will get new office equipment and who will have to make do with what is already available. A company's sales force may try to negotiate favorable delivery dates for their best clients by offering manufacturing personnel leeway in meeting deadlines for other customers' orders.

In deciding whose conflicting interests will be satisfied and whose will not, parties engaged in bargaining and negotiation can choose the degree to which they will assert themselves and look after their own interests. They can also decide whether they will cooperate with their adversary and put its interests ahead of their own. As Figure 10-4 shows, there are five general approaches to managing divergent interests that are characterized by different mixes of assertiveness and cooperativeness:[34]

1. *Competition* (assertive, uncooperative). This means overpowering other parties in the conflict and promoting one's own concerns at the expense of the others'. One way of doing this is by resorting to authority to satisfy one's own

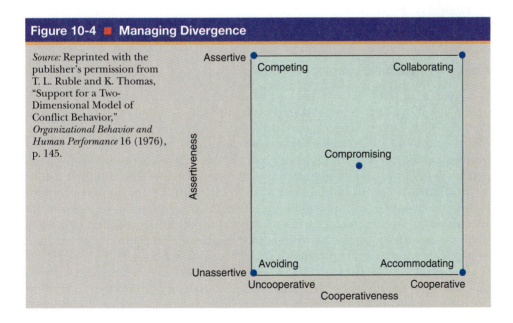

Figure 10-4 ■ Managing Divergence

Source: Reprinted with the publisher's permission from T. L. Ruble and K. Thomas, "Support for a Two-Dimensional Model of Conflict Behavior," *Organizational Behavior and Human Performance* 16 (1976), p. 145.

Assertive — Competing — Collaborating

Assertiveness

Compromising

Unassertive — Avoiding — Accommodating

Uncooperative — Cooperativeness — Cooperative

concerns. Thus, the head of a group of account executives may appeal to the director of advertising to protect the group's turf from the intrusions by other account execs.

2. *Accommodation* (unassertive, cooperative). This allows other parties to satisfy their concerns at the expense of one's own interests. In accommodation, differences are smoothed over to maintain superficial harmony. A purchasing department that fails to meet budgetary guidelines because it deliberately overspends on raw materials to satisfy the demands of production groups is trying to use accommodation to cope with conflict.

3. *Avoidance* (unassertive, uncooperative). This approach requires staying neutral at all costs or refusing to take an active role in conflict resolution procedures. The finance department that sticks its head in the sand and hopes that dissension about budgetary allocations will blow over is exhibiting avoidance.

4. *Collaboration* (assertive, cooperative). Parties who engage in this strategy attempt to satisfy everyone by working through differences and seeking solutions that result in gains for all concerned. A marketing department and a manufacturing department that meet on a regular basis to plan mutually acceptable production schedules are collaborating.

5. *Compromise* (midrange assertive, cooperative). This approach seeks partial satisfaction of everyone through exchange and sacrifice, settling for acceptable rather than optimal resolution. Contract bargaining between union representatives and management typically involves significant compromise by both sides.

As indicated in Table 10-4, the appropriateness of each of the five approaches depends on the situation surrounding the conflict and, often, the time pressure for a negotiated settlement. Beyond these general alternatives, experts on organizational development have devised an assortment of more specific techniques for conflict management that are based on structured sessions of bargaining and negotiation. Several of these techniques will be described in detail in Chapter 13, on culture and organizational development.

Managing Structural Interdependence

Because, in addition to divergence in interests, conflict requires interdependence, conflict can also be managed or resolved by a restructuring of the connections that tie conflicting parties together.[35] One way to achieve such a restructuring is to *develop superordinate goals,* identifying and pursuing a set of performance targets that conflicting parties can achieve only by working together. Sharing a common goal requires the parties to look beyond their differences and learn how to cooperate with each other. In the automobile industry, for instance, unions and management fearing plant closures have forgone adversarial relations in order to strengthen the competitiveness of their firms. For them, teamwork has replaced conflict in the pursuit of the superordinate goal of producing high-quality products for today's world markets.

Expanding the supply of critical resources is another way to restructure; it removes a major source of conflict between individuals and groups that draw from the same supply. Pools of critical resources are not easily enlarged—which is

Table 10-4 ■ When Different Styles of Managing Divergence Should Be Applied

STYLE	APPLICATION
Competing	When quick, decisive action is required, to cope with crises; on important issues when unpopular solutions, such as cost cutting or employee discipline, must be implemented; on issues vital to organizational welfare when your group is certain that its position is correct; against groups who take advantage of noncompetitive behavior
Accommodating	When your group is wrong and wants both to show reasonableness and to encourage the expression of a more appropriate view; when issues are more important to groups other than yours, to satisfy others and maintain cooperation; to build credits or bank favors for later issues; to minimize losses when your group is outmatched and losing; when harmony and stability are especially important
Avoiding	When a conflict is trivial or more important conflicts are pressing; when there is no chance that your group will satisfy its own needs; when the costs of potential disruption outweigh the benefits of resolution; to let groups cool down and gain perspective; when others can resolve the conflict more effectively
Collaborating	To find an integrative solution when conflicting concerns are too important to be compromised; when the most important objective is to learn; to combine the ideas of people with different perspectives; to gain commitment through the development of consensus; to work through conflicting feelings in individuals and between groups
Compromising	When group concerns are important but not worth the disruption caused by more assertive styles; when equally powerful groups are committed to pursuing mutually exclusive concerns; to achieve temporary or transitional settlements; to arrive at expedient resolutions under time pressure; as a backup when neither competing nor problem-solving styles are successful

Source: Adapted with permission from K. W. Thomas, "Toward Multidimensional Values in Teaching: The Example of Conflict Behaviors," *Academy of Management Review* 2 (1977), p. 487.

what makes them critical to begin with. When this method is successful, it decreases the amount of interdependence between the connected parties, who now compete less for available resources. For example, one way to eliminate interoffice conflicts over the availability of shared computers is to buy every department a network of personal computers. Some organizations, such as Ford Motor Company's casting division, purchase large quantities of used computers at reduced prices instead of a few new ones at full retail.

A third way to manage conflict by restructuring interdependence is to *clarify existing relationships* and make the political position of each party readily apparent. If it is feasible, this political clarification affects interdependence by strengthening everyone's understanding of how and why they are connected and reducing the political indeterminism that must exist for conflict to occur.

A fourth approach is to *modify existing structural relationships;* this approach makes use of a number of mechanisms that either uncouple conflicting parties or modify the structural linkage between them.[36] Two such mechanisms, the **decoupling mechanisms** of slack resources and self-contained tasks, manage conflict by eliminating the interdependence that must exist for conflict to occur. *Slack resources* help to decouple otherwise interconnected individuals and groups by creating buffers that lessen the ability of one party to affect the activities of another. Suppose one person assembles telephone handsets, and another person connects finished handsets to telephone bodies to form fully assembled units. The two employees are sequentially interdependent because the second person's ability to perform, by connecting the handsets, is contingent on the first person's ability to complete the assembly task. The second employee cannot work if the first employee stops producing. If, however, a buffer inventory is created—a supply of finished handsets—that the second worker can draw on when the first worker is not producing anything, we have at least temporarily decoupled the two individuals.

In contrast, the creation of *self-contained tasks* involves combining the work of two or more interdependent parties and assigning this work to several independent parties. If the parties are groups, it is usually the case that the self-contained groups resulting from work combination are staffed by employees drawn from each of the original interdependent groups. For example, engineering and drafting groups might have problems coordinating engineering specifications and the drawings produced by the drafting group. These two groups might be regrouped into several independent engineering-drafting groups. After such regrouping, the original two groups no longer exist. Key interdependencies that lay outside the original groups are contained within the redesigned groups and can be managed without crossing group boundaries or involving outside managers.

Sometimes concerns about minimizing inventory costs rule out the use of slack resources. Among U.S. manufacturers, for instance, the cost of carrying excessive inventory is a growing concern and has stimulated increasing interest in just-in-time (JIT) procedures. When a company uses JIT, it produces items for use only when they are needed, eliminating the cost of having unused inventory lying around. In addition, work often cannot be divided into self-contained tasks. For example, the task of producing the parts required to make a car and assembling them into a final product is so immense that many individuals and groups (in fact, many companies) must be involved. In such cases in which decoupling is not possible, existing structural relationships may be modified instead by means of various **unit-linking mechanisms.** *Network information systems* are one such mechanism, consisting of mainframe computers with remote terminals or network servers connected to personal computers that can be used to input and exchange information about organizational performance. If you have taken courses in computer science, you have probably had experience with a computer network similar to the *intranets* now used in businesses. Managers use such systems to communicate among themselves and store information for later review. These systems facilitate the transfer of large amounts of information up and down an organization's hierarchy of authority. In addition, they support lateral transfers among interdependent individuals and groups. In the process, they facilitate communication that might otherwise develop into misunderstandings and contribute to the emergence of conflict. The fact that many organizations have recently added the corporate position of chief information officer (CIO) reflects the growing use of network information systems to manage interdependent, potentially conflictful relationships.[37]

A second type of unit-linking mechanism consists of several *lateral linkage devices* that managers can use to strengthen communication between interdependent parties. For example, an employee may be assigned a *liaison position* in which that employee is responsible for seeing that communications flow directly and freely between interdependent groups. The liaison position offers an alternative to hierarchical communication channels. It reduces both the time needed to communicate between groups and the amount of information distortion likely to occur. The person occupying a liaison position has no authority to issue direct orders but serves as a neutral third party and relies on negotiation, bargaining, and persuasion. This person is called on to mediate between groups if conflict actually emerges, resolving differences and moving the groups toward voluntary intergroup coordination.[38]

The liaison position is the least costly of the lateral linkage devices. Because one person handles the task of coordination, a minimum of a firm's resources is diverted from the primary task of production. In addition, because the position has no formal authority, it is also the least disruptive of normal hierarchical relationships. However, sometimes a liaison position is not strong enough to manage interdependence relations. Managers then have the option of turning to a second type of lateral linkage device, *representative groups,* to coordinate activities among interdependent parties. Representative groups consist of people that represent the interdependent individuals or groups, who meet to coordinate interdependent activities. There are two kinds of representative groups. One, called a *task force,* is formed to complete a specific task or project and is then disbanded. Task force members can get together, talk out the differences among the parties they represent, and resolve conflicts before they are manifested. For this reason, companies like Colgate-Palmolive and Procter and Gamble form product task groups by drawing together members from advertising, marketing, manufacturing, and product research departments. Each product task group identifies consumer needs, designs new products that respond to these needs, and manages their market introduction. Once a new product is successfully launched, the product task group responsible for its introduction is dissolved, and its members return to their former jobs.

The other type of representative group is a more or less permanent one. Like the members of the task force, the members of this group, called the *standing committee,* represent interdependent parties, but they meet on a regular basis to discuss and resolve ongoing problems. No specific task is assigned to the standing committee, nor is the committee expected to disband at any particular time. An example of a standing committee is seen in a factory's Monday morning production meeting. At that meeting, representatives from production control, purchasing, quality assurance, shipping, and the company's different assembly groups overview the week's production schedule and try to anticipate problems.

Like task forces, standing committees make it possible to use face-to-face communication to manage interdependence problems and resolve differences. Despite their usefulness in this regard, both of these linkage devices are more costly than the liaison position. The reason is that through process loss, group meetings inevitably consume otherwise productive resources. In addition, because representative groups (especially task forces) are sometimes designed to operate outside of customary hierarchical channels, they can prove to be quite disruptive to normal management procedures.

When neither liaison positions nor representative groups are enough to solve intergroup conflict problems, the *integrating manager* is a third type of lateral linkage device that may be used. Like the liaison, the integrating manager mediates between interdependent parties, but unlike the liaison, the integrating manager has the formal authority to issue orders and expect obedience. This person can tell interdependent parties what to do in order to resolve conflict. Project managers at companies like Rockwell International and Lockheed fill the role of integrating manager. They oversee the progress of a project by making sure that the various planning, designing, assembling, and testing groups work together successfully.

Normally, when coordinating the efforts of groups, integrating managers issue orders only to group supervisors. Their giving orders to the employees who report to these supervisors could cause confusion if these employees felt they were being asked to report to two supervisors. Because an integrating manager disrupts normal hierarchical relationships by short-circuiting the relationship between group supervisors and their usual superior, this device is used much less often than either the liaison position or representative groups.

Once in a while, even integrating managers cannot provide the guidance needed to manage conflict through structural means. In these rare instances, a fourth type of lateral linkage device, called the *matrix organization structure,* is sometimes employed. Matrix structures are the most complicated of the mechanisms used to coordinate among groups and resolve intergroup conflicts, and are extremely costly to sustain.[39] We will discuss the matrix organization structure in greater detail in Chapter 11, on organization structure, because it is both a conflict resolution device and a specific type of structure. For now we will conclude by saying that matrix structures are appropriate only when all other intergroup mechanisms have proven ineffective.

SUMMARY

Power is the ability to influence others and to resist their influence in return. Compliance, identification, and internalization are outcomes that may result from the use of five types of interpersonal power—*reward, coercive, legitimate, referent,* and *expert.* Power also grows out of uncertainty surrounding the continued availability of *critical contingencies.* It is thus based on the ability to *reduce this uncertainty* and is enhanced by low *substitutability* and high *centrality.*

Conflict is a process of opposition and confrontation that requires the presence of interdependence, political indeterminism, and divergence. It can be managed through *bargaining* and *negotiation,* or resolved by the restructuring of interdependence relations through the use of various *decoupling* or *unit-linking mechanisms.*

Review Questions

1. Is power being exercised when a manager orders a subordinate to do something the subordinate would do even without being ordered? When a subordinate successfully refuses to follow orders? When a manager's orders are followed despite the subordinate's reluctance?
2. What is the difference between reward power and coercive power? What do these two types of power have in common? How are they similar to legitimate power? How do they differ from both expert and referent power?
3. Why must uncertainty, centrality, and low substitutability *all* be present in order for power to be acquired? Explain how a group's power might be reduced by an increase in substitutability.
4. Why is accommodation unlikely to succeed as a conflict management technique in most instances? Under what specific conditions is it most useful?
5. Why does conflict require interdependence? How does political indeterminism influence whether conflict will occur? Based on your answers to these two questions, what can managers do to resolve conflicts without attempting to reduce divergence?
6. How does an integrating manager differ from one in a liaison position? Which of the two is more likely to prove successful as a means of resolving a long-standing conflict? Given your answer, why isn't this "stronger" approach the only one of the two used in organizations?

Implementation Guide

The following questions should help you to manage the political face of organizations:

1. Do individuals and groups in the organization have the power required to function productively and interact effectively?
2. Which types of interpersonal power are currently in use? Are these types of interpersonal power likely to generate the compliance, identification, or internalization needed to energize appropriate behaviors? Might other types of interpersonal power be more effective?
3. If power inadequacies exist, are they traceable to limitations in the ability to reduce uncertainty? To high substitutability? To low centrality? What actions can be taken to correct these deficiencies?

4. Do antecedent conditions—interdependence, political indeterminism, and/or divergence—favor the emergence of conflict? Is there evidence that dysfunctional conflict is brewing? Can any of the antecedent conditions be modified to resolve the conflict before it causes harm?

5. Is there evidence of ongoing conflict? Do the dysfunctional, destructive effects of this conflict outweigh its functional benefits? Can any of the antecedent conditions be modified to resolve the conflict?

6. If divergence can be modified, which style of bargaining and negotiation best fits the conflict situation?

7. If interdependence or political indeterminism can be modified, which of the approaches to managing interdependence seems most suitable?

ENDNOTES

1. D. W. Linden and N. Rotenier, "Goodbye to Berle and Means," *Forbes,* January 3, 1994, pp. 100–103; K. Rebello, R. D. Hof, and P. Burrows, "Inside Apple's Boardroom Coup," *Business Week,* February 19, 1996, pp. 28–30; P. Burrows, "Micron's Comeback Kid," *Business Week,* May 13, 1996, pp. 70–74.

2. J. A. Byrne, W. Zeller, and S. Ticer, "Caught in the Middle: Six Managers Speak Out on Corporate Life," *Business Week,* September 12, 1988, pp. 80–88.

3. R. A. Dahl, "The Concept of Power," *Behavioral Science* 2 (1957), pp. 201–15; A. Kaplan, "Power in Perspective," in *Power and Conflict in Organizations,* R. L. Kahn and E. Boulding, eds. (London: Tavistock, 1964), pp. 11–32; and R. M. Emerson, "Power Dependence Relations," *American Sociological Review* 27 (1962), pp. 31–41.

4. V. V. McMurray, "Some Unanswered Questions on Organizational Conflict," *Organization and Administrative Sciences* 6 (1975), pp. 35–53.

5. D. C. McClelland, *Power: The Inner Experience* (New York: Irvington Publishers, 1975), pp. 3–29; and D. C. McClelland and D. H. Burnham, "Power Is the Great Motivator," *Harvard Business Review* 54 (1976), pp. 100–110.

6. McClelland and Burnham, "Power Is the Great Motivator."

7. J. R. P. French Jr. and B. Raven, "The Bases of Social Power," in *Studies in Social Power,* D. Cartwright, ed. (Ann Arbor: Institute for Social Research, University of Michigan, 1959), pp. 150–65.

8. D. Greising, L. Himelstein, Z. Schiller, and B. Bremner, "Run, Jump, and Sell," *Business Week,* July 29, 1996, pp. 36–37.

9. H. C. Kelman, "Compliance, Identification, and Internalization: Three Processes of Attitude Change," *Journal of Conflict Resolution* 2 (1958), pp. 51–60.

10. For an alternative typification based on attributional ratings, see A. Rodrigues, "Attribution and Social Influence," *Journal of Applied Social Psychology* 25 (1995), pp. 1567–77.

11. C. N. Greene and P. M. Podsakoff, "Effects of Withdrawal of a Performance-Contingent Reward on Supervisory Influence and Power," *Academy of Management Journal* 24 (1981), pp. 527–42.

12. Another criticism of our model concerns problems with the measures and methods used to study the French and Raven classification scheme. For further information about these problems and their effects on power research, see G. A. Yukl, *Leadership in Organizations* (Englewood Cliffs, NJ: Prentice Hall, 1981), pp. 38–43; and P. M. Podsakoff and C. A. Schreisheim, "Field Studies of French and Raven's Bases of Power: Critique, Reanalysis, and Suggestions for Future Research," *Psychological Bulletin* 97 (1985), pp. 387–411.

13. D. J. Hickson, C. R. Hinings, C. A. Lee, R. H. Schneck, and J. M. Pennings, "A Strategic Contingencies Theory of Intraorganizational Power," *Administrative Science Quarterly* 16 (1971), pp. 216–29; J. Pfeffer and G. R. Salancik, *The External Control of Organizations: A Resource Dependence Perspective* (New York: Harper & Row, 1978), p. 231; and J. Pfeffer, *Power in Organizations* (Marshfield, MA: Pitman, 1981), pp. 109–22.

14. G. R. Salancik and J. Pfeffer, "Who Gets Power and How They Hold on to It: A Strategic-Contingency Model of Power," *Organizational Dynamics* 5 (1977), pp. 3–4.

15. R. M. Kanter, "Power Failures in Management Circuits," *Harvard Business Review* 57 (1979), pp. 65–75.

16. R. H. Miles, *Macro Organizational Behavior* (Santa Monica, CA: Goodyear, 1980), pp. 171–72.

17. Ibid., p. 171.

18. J. W. Verity, "Kodak: Shoot the Works," *Business Week,* November 15, 1993, pp. 30–32.

19. G. R. Salancik and J. Pfeffer, "The Bases and Uses of Power in Organizational Decision Making," *Administrative Science Quarterly* 19 (1974), p. 470.

20. Hickson et al., "A Strategic Contingencies Theory," p. 227.

21. D. Krackhardt, "Assessing the Political Landscape: Structure, Cognition, and Power in Organizations," *Administrative Science Quarterly* 35 (1990), pp. 342–69; D. J. Brass and M. E. Burkhardt, "Potential Power and Power Use: An Investigation of Structure and Behavior," *Academy of Management Journal* 36 (1993), pp. 441–70; H. Ibarra, "Network Centrality, Power, and Innovation Involvement: Determinants of Technical and Administrative Roles," *Academy of Management Journal* 36 (1993), pp. 471–501; and H. Ibarra and S. B. Andrews, "Power, Social Influence, and Sense Making: Effects of Network Centrality and Proximity on Employee Perceptions," *Administrative Science Quarterly* 38 (1993), pp. 277–303.

22. W. G. Astley and E. J. Zajac, "Intraorganizational Power and Organizational Design: Reconciling Rational and Coalitional Models of Organization," *Organization Science* 2 (1991), pp. 399–411.

23. H. A. Landsberger, "A Horizontal Dimension in Bureaucracy," *Administrative Science Quarterly* 6 (1961), pp. 299–332.

24. M. Crozier, *The Bureaucratic Phenomenon* (Chicago: University of Chicago Press, 1964), pp. 153–54.

25. C. I. Barnard, *The Functions of the Executive* (Cambridge, MA: Harvard University Press, 1938), p. 163; D. Mechanic, "Sources of Power of Lower Participants in Complex Organizations," *Administrative Science Quarterly* 7 (1962), pp. 349–64; L. W. Porter, R. W. Allen, and H. L. Angle, "The Politics of Upward Influence in Organizations," in *Research in Organizational Behavior,* B. M. Staw and L. L. Cummings, eds., vol. 3 (Greenwich, CT: JAI Press, 1981), pp. 109–50; and R. S. Blackburn, "Lower Participant Power: Toward a Conceptual Integration," *Academy of Management Review* 6 (1981), pp. 127–31.

26. Miles, *Macro Organizational Behavior,* p. 122.

27. R. E. Quinn, *Beyond Rational Management: Mastering the Paradoxes and Competing Demands of High Performance* (San Francisco: Jossey-Bass, 1988), p. 2; A. C. Amason, "Distinguishing the Effects of Functional and Dysfunctional Conflict on Strategic Decision Making: Resolving a Paradox for Top Management Teams," *Academy of Management Journal* 39 (1996), pp. 123–48.

28. L. Coser, *The Functions of Social Conflict* (New York: Free Press, 1956), p. 154; Miles, *Macro Organizational Behavior,* p. 123; and J. Wall and R. R. Callister, "Conflict and Its Management," *Journal of Management* 21 (1995), pp. 515–58.

29. Miles, *Macro Organizational Behavior,* p. 131.

30. Ibid., pp. 132–38; and J. M. Ivancevich and M. T. Matteson, *Organizational Behavior and Management,* 3d ed. (Homewood, IL: Irwin, 1993), pp. 340–44.

31. D. Ulrich and J. B. Barney, "Perspectives on Organizations: Resource Dependence, Efficiency, and Population," *Academy of Management Review* 9 (1984), pp. 471–81.

32. M. Sherif and C. W. Sherif, *Groups in Harmony and Tension* (New York: Harper, 1953), pp. 229–95; A. D. Szilagyi Jr. and M. J. Wallace Jr., *Organizational Behavior and Performance,* 4th ed. (Glenview, IL: Scott, Foresman, 1987), p. 301; J. L. Gibson, J. M. Ivancevich, and J. H. Donnelly Jr., *Organizations: Behavior, Structure, Process,* 7th ed. (Homewood, IL: Irwin, 1991), pp. 308–9; and Ivancevich and Matteson, *Organizational Behavior and Management,* pp. 344–47.

33. J. Z. Rubin and B. R. Brown, *The Social Psychology of Bargaining and Negotiation* (New York: Academic Press, 1975), p. 3; and R. J. Lewicki and J. R. Litterer, *Negotiation* (Homewood, IL: Richard D. Irwin, 1985).

34. K. W. Thomas, "Conflict and Conflict Management," in *Handbook of Industrial and Organizational Psychology,* M. D. Dunnette, ed. (Chicago: Rand McNally, 1976), pp. 889–935; see also K. W. Thomas, "Toward Multidimensional Values in Teaching: The Example of Conflict Behaviors," *Academy of Management Review* 2 (1977), pp. 472–89; and K. W. Thomas, "Conflict and Conflict Management: Reflections and Update," *Journal of Organizational Behavior* 13 (1992), pp. 265–74.

35. M. Sherif, "Superordinate Goals in the Reduction of Intergroup Conflict," *American Journal of Sociology* 63 (1958), pp. 349–56; J. R. Galbraith, "Organization Design: An Information Processing View," *Interfaces* 4 (1974), pp. 28–36; and Pfeffer, *Power in Organizations.*

36. J. R. Galbraith, *Designing Complex Organizations* (Reading, MA: Addison-Wesley, 1973), pp. 14–18.

37. J. R. Galbraith, *Competing with Flexible Lateral Organizations* (Reading, MA: Addison-Wesley, 1994); T. Smart, "Jack Welch's Cyber-Czar," *Business Week,* August 5, 1996, pp. 82–83; and A. L. Sprout, "The

Internet inside Your Company," *Fortune,* November 27, 1995, pp. 161–68.

38. D. E. Conlon, P. Carnevale, and W. H. Ross, "The Influence of Third Party Power and Suggestions on Negotiation: The Surface Value of Compromise," *Journal of Applied Social Psychology* 24 (1994), pp. 1084–113.

39. L. R. Burns and D. R. Wholey, "Adoption and Abandonment of Matrix Management Programs: Effects of Organizational Characteristics and Interorganizational Networks," *Academy of Management Journal* 36 (1993), pp. 106–38.

Chapter Eleven
Structuring the Organization

Decentralizing. Divisionalizing. Downsizing. It's hard to find a major company that hasn't resorted to at least one of these "three *D*s" to streamline its structure and pump up corporate performance. Take Johnson and Johnson, the $15 billion firm known for producing everything from Band-Aids and Tylenol to artificial cornea lenses and brain surgery equipment. As early as 1930, founder's son and then-CEO Robert W. Johnson favored decentralization, believing that dispersing decision making throughout the company would result in smaller, self-contained units that would be easier to manage and quicker to react to changing market conditions. Today, J&J consists of 33 major lines of business conducted in 53 countries by 168 separately chartered companies. Included are such household names as Johnson and Johnson Consumer Products, Ortho Biotech, and McNeil, all doing business without having to worry about routine intrusions from a centralized headquarters bureaucracy. Current CEO Ralph Larsen sometimes lies awake at night, worrying that J&J's companies are too decentralized to take advantage of strengths they share. But he is also the first to argue that decentralization is the heart of Johnson and Johnson, stressing that it enables company managers to capitalize on emerging opportunities and establish themselves as dominant players before more centralized firms recognize that opportunities exist.[1]

Or consider Boeing Company, a U.S. manufacturer of jet aircraft and aerospace equipment. Historically the foremost producer in its industry, Boeing has had to adjust to worldwide fluctuations in the sales of commercial airliners and faces the prospect of competing against the likes of Toyota Motor Corporation. To cope with the present and prepare for the future, Boeing eliminated over 10,000 jobs in 1992 and another 9,300 in 1994. The 118,000 employees remaining in the smaller Boeing now participate in courses designed to encourage innovation and efficiency in every area of the company's operations.

Hierarchical, rigid management methods are giving way to flexible procedures aimed at reducing inventory costs and the time required to manufacture planes. Customers who once complained about Boeing's shrouds of secrecy are now consulted at early stages of product design, which enables the company to better meet their needs and avoid costly redesigns. Its new 777 is a best-seller, and plans are in the works for production of a super-jumbo jet, larger than the company's venerable 747, to begin sometime just after the turn of the century.[2]

[1]J. Weber, "A Big Company That Works," *Business Week,* May 14, 1992, pp. 124–32; and B. O'Reilly, "J&J Is on a Roll," *Fortune,* December 26, 1994, pp. 178–92.
[2]D. J. Yang, "Boeing's Can-Do Co-pilot," *Business Week,* September 14, 1992, p. 32; D. J. Yang and A. Rothman, "Boeing Cuts Its Altitude as the Clouds Roll In," *Business Week,* February 8, 1993, p. 25; D. J. Yang, "Reinventing Boeing: Radical Changes and Crisis," *Business Week,* March 1, 1993, pp. 60–67; A. Taylor III and J. McGowan, "Boeing: Sleepy in Seattle," *Fortune,* August 7, 1995, pp. 91–98; and A. Reinhardt, S. Browder, and P. Engardio, "Booming Boeing," *Business Week,* September 30, 1996, pp. 118–25.

Johnson and Johnson and Boeing are but two of many companies—including Scott Paper, Sunbeam, AT&T, Delta Airlines, Pepsico, and IBM—currently in the throes of major structural modification.[1] Each such instance serves as another indicator of the importance accorded to the management of organization structure. Why is structure and its management so important? First, the structure of an organization serves as the context that surrounds and influences the micro OB processes discussed in Chapters 2 through 5. Second, it also gives shape to the various groupings and meso OB processes examined in Chapters 6 through 9. Third, it is the source of many of the macro OB processes that influence efficiency, flexibility, and interaction with the surrounding environment, as indicated in Chapters 10 through 13. For all of these reasons, an organization's structure has widespread effects on behavior and productivity within the firm, and on the firm's ability to thrive in the face of competitive environmental pressures.

In order to secure competitive advantage, managers must know how to structure their organizations in different ways. They must also know about the strengths and weaknesses of the different ways of structuring. In this chapter we examine the basic elements of an organization's structure—how coordination is established along lines of interdependence, how the groups in an organization are joined together in a hierarchy, and how information and decision making are distributed among members of the organization. Using these basic elements, we then describe the different kinds of structures an organization can adopt. Thus, upon concluding this chapter, you will be able to recognize and make informed choices among alternative organization structures.

Coordination and Bureaucracy

Whether it is as well known as Boeing or as anonymous as a locally owned convenience store, every organization is characterized by a pattern of interrelated tasks essential to its efficient functioning. This identifiable **organization struc-**

ture consists of a relatively stable network of interconnections among the people and work that make up the organization.[2] Like the steel framework of a building or the skeletal system of the human body, the structure of an organization separates its different parts from each other and also helps keep those parts interconnected. In so doing, it creates and reinforces relationships of interdependence within and among groups. A firm's structure is the final means by which labor divided through job design is reintegrated into a meaningful whole. It is structure that enables people to work together, and in so doing to accomplish things beyond the abilities of unorganized individuals.

Basic Coordination Mechanisms

Achieving structural integration is an important challenge facing all managers, requiring them to make decisions about how to coordinate relationships among the interdependent people and groups they manage.[3] *Coordination* is a process in which otherwise disorderly actions are integrated so as to produce a desired result. Different parts of the human body, for example, work together to produce complex, coordinated behaviors. Your arms follow a trajectory plotted by your eyes in order to catch a ball. Your hands manipulate your car's steering wheel at the same time that your foot depresses the accelerator pedal. It would be very difficult, if not impossible, to catch the ball if you could not see it. It would be dangerous to accelerate or even to move the car if you could not control its direction.

Similarly, through coordination, the members of an organization are able to work together to accomplish shared tasks or objectives. The primary means by which organizational activities are integrated, the **basic coordination mechanisms** of mutual adjustment, direct supervision, and standardization, act as the glue that holds organizations together.[4]

Mutual adjustment is coordination accomplished through interpersonal communication processes in which coworkers who occupy positions of similar hierarchical authority share job-related information.[5] It is the simplest of the three basic coordination mechanisms, based on the exchange among coworkers of information about how a job should be done and who should do it (see box). A group of factory maintenance mechanics examining service manuals and discussing how to fix a broken conveyor belt are coordinating by means of mutual adjustment. Sales managers meeting together to discuss their company's market position are also using mutual adjustment to coordinate among themselves. Note that in both these examples, information is exchanged among people who can exercise at least partial control over the tasks they are talking about. Unless the people doing the communicating possess this control, they cannot successfully coordinate their activities with mutual adjustment.

In **direct supervision,** one person takes personal responsibility for the work of a group of others.[6] As part of this responsibility, a direct supervisor acquires the hierarchical authority to determine which tasks need to be performed, who will perform them, and how they will be linked together to produce the desired end result. A direct supervisor may then issue orders to

Mutual Adjustment on the Company Intranet

Until recently, virtually all of the mutual adjustment in an organization occurred as the result of face-to-face communication among coworkers. This has changed, however, with the advent of company *intranets*. Intranets are communication networks within organizations that are based on the technology of the Internet, the global interorganizational network that has received so much recent attention. With an intranet, employees who need to "talk" with one another to coordinate work activities can send and receive E-mail messages without ever having to get together. Workers who need information about a particular product, customer, or technology in order to determine how to perform their tasks can consult electronic bulletin boards (EBBs) located on the company intranet. In electronic "conference rooms," employees can "chat" with one another about job problems and fixes without ever having to meet face to face.

Many intranet communication features, such as E-mail and EBBs, are asynchronous, meaning that people do not have to be in the same place or work at the same time in order to talk with one another. Others, like electronic conferences or chat rooms, use real-time procedures that require participation at the same point in time but not necessarily in the same physical location. All work out of the network of computers found in a business, and require a "browser," or a software program that links together different computer protocols, thus enabling users to search the company network for needed information. Most are extensions of the larger Internet, but are protected from outside access by a "fire wall" or security shield. Intranet users can get information from the outside, but Internet users cannot gain ready access to information on the inside.

What do companies gain from mutual adjustment via an intranet? At investment banking firm Morgan Stanley, the company intranet serves as a global intercom, making it possible for traders in New York to keep up with what is going on in markets in Europe and Asia. The company also forms "teams" of employees located at offices around the world to work together on projects that require varied expertise. In this way, Morgan Stanley has become a leader in international finance.[1] Intranet links among Swedish manufacturer L. M. Ericsson's 17,000 engineers in 40 research centers located in 20 countries allow team members in Australia and England to work on the same design, then zip off the final blueprint to a factory in China. Ericsson is thus able to take advantage of mutual adjustment without having to consolidate large numbers of employees in a single facility.[2] Turner Broadcasting employees can click on an icon and watch animated clips of a cartoon-in-progress that is ultimately to be shown on the company's Cartoon Network. If they dislike what they see, they can E-mail the animators directly to vent their opinions. Only after a cartoon has survived this "internal focus group" can it move on to a public venue.[3]

As these examples indicate, geographic separation no longer impedes needed mutual adjustment. Instead of having to limit the use of mutual adjustment to the coordination of activities in close physical proximity, employees can use it to coordinate work activities separated by thousands of miles. In addition, time need not stand in the way of coordinating via mutual adjustment. E-mail messages can accomplish the coordination among employees working at different times that would otherwise require some other means. The need for hierarchy is reduced, which results in a flatter structure of empowered employees.[4]

---

[1] A. L. Sprout, "The Internet inside Your Company," *Fortune,* November 27, 1995, pp. 161–68.
[2] C. Arnst, "The Networked Corporation," *Business Week,* June 26, 1995, pp. 86–89.
[3] Sprout, "The Internet inside Your Company."
[4] G. G. Dess, A. M. A. Rasheed, K. J. McLaughlin, and R. L. Priem, "The New Corporate Architecture," *Academy of Management Executive* 9 (1995), pp. 7–20.

subordinates, check to see that these orders have been followed, and redirect subordinates as needed to fulfill additional work requirements. The owner of a grocery store is functioning as a direct supervisor when, having instructed an employee to restock the shelves, the owner finds that the clerk has completed the job and directs the clerk to help another employee change the signs advertising weekly specials. In this example, as in every instance of direct supervision, an individual with the authority to issue direct orders coordinates activities by telling subordinates what to do.

Standardization coordinates work by providing employees with stable standards and procedures that help them determine how to perform their tasks. This kind of coordination is achieved by setting standards and designing procedures before the work to be performed is actually undertaken.[7] So long as "drawing board" plans are followed and the work situation remains essentially unchanged, interdependent relationships can be reproduced again and again, and coordination can be maintained.

There are four types of standardization—standardization of work processes, or behaviors, and standardization of outputs, skills, and norms. The first of these alternatives, *work process standardization,* is also called *behavioral standardization.* It means specifying the precise behaviors or actions employees must perform to accomplish their jobs. Some of these behaviors link each job with other jobs in the organization, contributing to continued coordination of work activities. For instance, the behavioral specifications for a worker responsible for filling bottles of Snapple may include step-by-step instructions for positioning bottles for filling and placing filled bottles on a conveyor line. The behavioral specifications for the worker who is responsible for capping the bottles may include instructions for verifying that all bottles on the conveyor line have been filled and ensuring that all properly capped bottles move forward along the line to the shipping department. The two people are connected by the conveyor line and are able to work together and with others further down the line without any further coordination, as long as the line does not break down and their company continues to produce Snapple.

Output standardization is the formal designation of output targets, or performance goals. For instance, a sales representative of a publishing company might be assigned the goal of getting university English departments to purchase 1,000 copies of a new English grammar textbook within a 12-month period. Unlike employees working under behavioral standardization, people coordinated by output standardization are free to decide for themselves *how* to attain their goals. So long as employees accomplish their goals, interdependence continues unchanged, and no one needs to engage in further coordination.

Skill standardization specifies in advance the skills, knowledge, or abilities that people must have to perform a task competently. Skilled employees seldom need to communicate with each other to figure out what to do and can usually predict with reasonable accuracy what other similarly skilled employees will do on the job. Consequently, on jobs staffed by skilled employees, there may be much less need to coordinate work behaviors in other ways.

Because skill standardization is aimed at regulating characteristics of people rather than jobs, it is used most often in situations in which neither work processes nor output standards can be easily specified. For example, few experts agree on the precise behaviors that high school teachers should engage in while teaching. In addition, there is a general consensus that the output indicators for the job of teaching, such as course grades and standardized test scores, have little validity as measures of teaching success (grades can be artificially inflated, and test scores can be influenced by pretest coaching). On the other hand, almost all community school districts mandate that their teachers be certified by an agency of the state, and such certification often requires that teachers not only hold certain educational degrees but give evidence of having acquired specific knowledge and skills. Thus, all teachers hired by a school district that requires state certification should possess a more or less standardized set of job qualifications or skills.

Finally, *norm standardization* is present when the members of a group or organization share a set of beliefs about the acceptability of particular types of behavior, which leads them to behave in ways that are generally approved. At Ford Motor Company, employees accept the importance of producing high-quality automobiles, a norm that is reflected in the company's well-known slogan "Quality is job one." Ford's workers do not need to discuss the merits of this philosophy with each other or to be directed by a supervisor to produce quality products. When people accept shared norms and behave accordingly, it reduces the need to coordinate activities in other ways because it increases the likelihood that people will behave appropriately, and that they will behave the same way again and again over the course of time.

Managers charged with managing an organization's structure continually confront choices among the basic coordination mechanisms, summarized in Table 11-1. Most of the time, two or more of these mechanisms are used con-

Table 11-1 ■ Basic Coordination Mechanisms	
MECHANISM	**DEFINITION**
Mutual adjustment	The coordination of work procedures accomplished by the exchange among coworkers of information about those procedures
Direct supervision	Direction and coordination of the work of a group by one person who issues direct orders to the group's members
Standardization	Planning and implementation of standards and procedures that regulate work performance
Work process, or behavioral, standardization	Specification of sequences of task process and behaviors
Output standardization	Establishment of goals or desired end results of task performance
Skill standardization	Specification of the abilities, knowledge, and skills required by a particular task
Norm standardization	Encouragement of attitudes and beliefs that lead to desired behaviors

currently to integrate work activities among the people and groups in an organization. In such instances, one of them serves as the primary mechanism used to solve most coordination problems; the others serve as secondary mechanisms that supplement the primary mechanism, backing it up when it fails to provide enough integration.

Two factors influence choices among coordination mechanisms: the number of people whose efforts must be coordinated to ensure the successful performance of interdependent tasks, and the relative stability of the situation in which the tasks must be performed.[8] In small groups of about 12 people or fewer, coordination is often accomplished by everyone's doing what comes naturally. Employees communicate face to face, using mutual adjustment to fit individual task behaviors into the group's overall network of interdependence. No other coordination mechanisms are needed, and none are used. Family farms and specialty restaurants are sometimes organized around this type of coordination.

Suppose, however, that a group is made up of more than 12 people—as many as 20, 30, or even 40—who use mutual adjustment alone to coordinate their activities. As depicted in Figure 11-1, the number of pairings needed to link each person with everyone else rises geometrically as the number of individuals rises arithmetically—although 2 people need only 1 link, 3 people need 3, 6 people need 15, and so on. Consequently, the members of larger

Figure 11-1 ■ Group Size and Mutual Adjustment Links

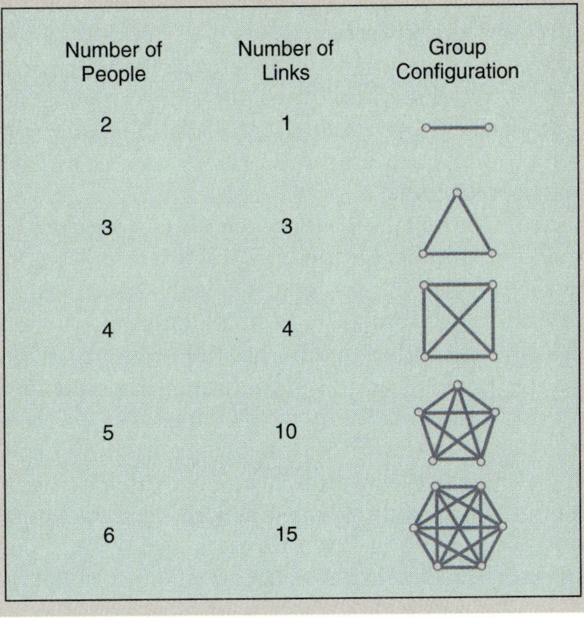

Number of People	Number of Links	Group Configuration
2	1	
3	3	
4	4	
5	10	
6	15	

groups have to consume so much time and effort communicating with each other that very little time is left for task completion. The sort of *process loss* we discussed in Chapter 8 diminishes group productivity in such instances.

For this reason, direct supervision takes the place of mutual adjustment in larger groups as the primary means of coordinating group activities. In communicating information to subordinates, the direct supervisor acts as a proxy for the group as a whole. To use an analogy, we might say that the direct supervisor functions like a switching mechanism that routes telephone messages from callers to receivers. The supervisor originates direct orders and collects performance feedback while channeling information from one interdependent group member to another. In such situations, however, mutual adjustment still continues as a supplementary coordination mechanism. When the direct supervisor is unavailable or does not know how to solve a particular problem, employees resort to communication among themselves to try to figure out what to do.

Besides clarifying how direct supervision functions as a basic coordination mechanism, the telephone-switching analogy also helps to explain the failure of direct supervision to coordinate the activities of members in even larger groups of approximately 50 or more individuals. Just as a switching mechanism can become overloaded by an avalanche of telephone calls, in successively larger groups the direct supervisor is increasingly burdened by the need to obtain information and channel it to the right people. Ultimately, the supervisor succumbs to information overload, being unable to keep up with subordinates' demands for information and coordination.

At this point, standardization replaces supervision as the primary means of coordination. Coordination by standardization can prevent information overload because it greatly reduces or eliminates the need for communication in order to have effective coordination. Workers are performing prespecified task behaviors, producing prespecified task outputs, using prespecified task skills, or conforming to prespecified workplace norms. Members of very large groups can complete complex, interdependent networks of task activities with little or no need for further coordination.

Where standardization is the primary means of coordination, direct supervision and mutual adjustment are still available for use as secondary coordination mechanisms. Direct supervision may be used to make sure that workers on an assembly line adhere to standards. Mutual adjustment may also be used on the assembly line to cope with machine breakdowns, power outages, or other temporary situations in which standard operating procedures are ineffective.

Standardization requires stability. If the conditions envisioned during the planning of a particular standardization program change, the usefulness of that program may be lost. For example, behavioral specifications that detail computerized check-in procedures are likely to be of little use to hotel registration personnel facing a long line of guests and a dead computer screen. Mutual adjustment often reemerges in such instances as the primary basic coordination device. When especially large groups or organizations face rapidly changing conditions that make standardization impossible, they rely heavily on face-to-face communication. The process loss associated with mutual ad-

Figure 11-2 ■ Continuum of Coordination Mechanisms

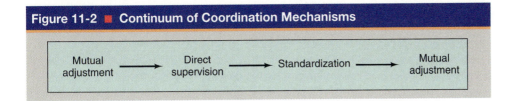

Mutual adjustment → Direct supervision → Standardization → Mutual adjustment

justment in these situations is simply tolerated as a necessary cost of staying in business.

The three means of coordination, then, form a continuum, depicted in Figure 11-2.[9] As coordination needs progress from left to right along the continuum, mechanisms to the left are not completely abandoned. At the point all the way to the right in the continuum, standardization, direct supervision, and secondary mutual adjustment are all available to supplement the mutual adjustment that serves as the primary means of coordination.

A critical trade-off exists between the *costs* of using a particular mechanism and the *flexibility* it permits. Mutual adjustment requires neither extensive preplanning nor the hierarchical differentiation of an organization's membership into superiors and subordinates. Therefore, it affords a high degree of flexibility. The links forged by mutual adjustment, however, cannot usually be banked for future use. Instead, each time mutual adjustment is used, it generates new coordination costs, which tend to be modest individually but over time add up and become quite significant. These costs generally take the form of time, effort, and similar resources that must be diverted away from task-related activities.

In contrast, the initial costs of standardization are quite high. The process of developing standards and procedures often requires the guidance of highly paid specialists, and otherwise productive resources must be diverted to this process. Yet, once designed and implemented, the program no longer consumes resources of major significance. The large initial costs of standardization can therefore be amortized, or spread over long periods of time and across long production runs. The result is an extremely low cost per incidence of coordination, making standardization less costly than mutual adjustment over the long run. As mentioned earlier, however, standardization requires that the work situation remain essentially unchanged because changing conditions would render existing standards obsolete. So it lacks the flexibility of mutual adjustment.

Direct supervision lies between the extremes of mutual adjustment and standardization in terms of flexibility. Because direct supervision presupposes a hierarchy of authority, it lacks the spontaneity and fluidity of mutual adjustment. Yet because direct supervision requires much less planning than standardization, it is more flexible than this latter option. Not surprisingly, the costs of direct supervision also fall between those of mutual adjustment and standardization. Although supervision requires fewer costly communication links than mutual adjustment, new coordination costs are generated each time a supervisory action is taken.

Table 11-2 ■ Types of Formalization

TYPES	DEFINITION
Formalization by job	Planning and documentation of the details of task performance, such as the specific steps to be taken and the sequence of those steps
Formalization by work flow	Planning and documentation of work flow standards, such as quality specifications and daily output goals
Formalization by rules	Planning and documentation of general workplace rules and procedures

Enacting Standardization

Managers who make the decision to coordinate interdependence with standardization are also making the decision to introduce structural **formalization.** Formalization is the process of planning regulations and standards that can be used to control organizational behavior. It also refers to the written documentation produced by the planning process. Formalization is thus the means of developing the written standards required to coordinate by standardization.[10]

Three types of formalization found in organizations are formalization by job, formalization by work flow, and formalization by rules (see Table 11-2). *Formalization by job* is used to set up work process standardization. It is a process of planning and documenting the sequence of steps employees must take to perform their jobs. For example, at the corporate offices of Burger King, job analysts develop procedures manuals that specify how long company employees should cook each type of food they serve, what condiments they should use to flavor it, and how they should package it for the customer.

Formalization by work flow is the process of establishing standards, or goals, for the flow of work in a firm. It provides the underpinnings for output standardization. One example would be the posted monthly sales goals that insurance sales representatives are expected to achieve. Another would be a set of standards for display screen brightness, keyboard responsiveness, and exterior appearance prepared for workers assembling notebook computers.

In *formalization by rules,* general rules and procedures are planned and documented to govern all the members of an organization regardless of the specific jobs they perform or work flows to which they contribute. For instance, everyone in an organization might be required to follow the rule that lunch breaks are to be taken between noon and 1:00 P.M. Other examples of this type of formalization can be found in the work-rules sections of collective bargaining contracts or in the policy manuals that many organizations prepare to guide employees' conduct.

In addition to using formalization, managers can also enact standardization using the processes of professionalization, training, and socialization (see Table 11-3). Each of these is meant to ensure that employees have the personal know-how to perform their jobs effectively. In *professionalization,* managers hire people to perform certain work for which useful written specifications do not ex-

Table 11-3 ■ Other Bases of Standardization

COMPLEMENT	DEFINITION
Professionalization	The use of professionally trained people whose abilities, knowledge, and skills equip them to perform work for which written specifications have not been developed
Training	Teaching an organization's employees skills needed to perform specific jobs within the organization
Socialization	Teaching new employees the norms of the organization

ist and in some cases cannot be prepared.[11] *Professionals* are people who develop work-related knowledge, skills, and abilities in training programs conducted outside the employing organization. For example, teachers learn how to teach in schools of education, and medical doctors acquire their skills in medical schools. Similarly, business professionals develop their expertise in business programs in colleges and universities. Professional skills form the basis for skill standardization. Because professionals learn the rules and standards of conduct needed to perform their jobs during the professional-training process, formalization and related process or output standardization may prove unnecessary—perhaps even reducing professionals' ability to do their jobs.

When the knowledge and skills needed to perform the work of an organization can be acquired within the organization itself, *training* may be used to teach relevant knowledge, skills, and abilities. Such training, provided by the employing organization, is purposely organization specific and often job specific. No attempt is made to teach the trainee the sort of generalized code of conduct that professionals learn. Like professionalization, however, training enables individuals to coordinate by means of skill standardization without reliance on formalization of any type.

Finally, as indicated in Chapter 7, organizations can use *socialization* to teach employees, particularly newcomers, important behavioral norms. To the extent that these norms regulate activities required to coordinate the flow of work, coordination by norm standardization can be enacted without formalized written rules and procedures. This approach is at the heart of the system of coordination used in many companies in Japan and Korea. Practices such as reciting company mottos before beginning work each day and singing company songs during social outings after work are used in Asian companies to constantly remind employees of the norms of their company and to ensure that these norms are followed.

In less apparent forms, norm standardization is also being used with increasing frequency in North American organizations. For instance, at Hewlett-Packard, employees learn the history of their company. In the process, they learn stories about the company's founders and early management that illustrate which behaviors are appropriate at Hewlett-Packard and which are not. In addition to being entertaining, these stories promote important company norms that help employees coordinate their work.

Specialization

Just as some mix of formalization, professionalization, training, and socialization precedes standardization, **specialization** usually follows it. Specialization is the way in which an organization's work is divided into individualized tasks. In some organizations, everyone performs the same sort of *generalized* tasks. In others, employees perform *specialized* tasks that differ from each other in significant ways.

The degree of specialization can be measured by the variety of activities included in the employees' jobs. The higher the degree of specialization, the narrower the scope of each job's activities.[12] Assembly line work is extremely specialized because each worker is responsible for only a small task, such as attaching the label to a bottle of liquid detergent or putting a pair of shoes into a box. At the opposite extreme, the task of being the owner and sole employee of a small company is not at all specialized because the same person is responsible for doing all the buying, bookkeeping, selling, and other tasks required to keep the company in business.

There are two distinct types of specialization—horizontal and vertical. **Horizontal specialization** refers to the way in which the work performed in each hierarchical level, or horizontal "slice," of an organization is divided into discrete, individualized jobs. At one extreme, that of *low horizontal specialization,* the work at a particular hierarchical level is distributed among workers who function as generalists. The upper panel of Figure 11-3 shows an office arrangement in which filing, typing, and telephone-answering duties are distributed equally among three generalist secretaries. All three secretarial jobs are virtually identical, and each person performing one of these jobs can readily substitute for any of the others.

At the other extreme, that of *high horizontal specialization,* the work within a hierarchical level is distributed in the form of specialist jobs. This level of specialization is shown in the lower panel of Figure 11-3, where each of three employees—a typist, a file clerk, and a receptionist who answers the phone—has entirely separate duties.

Although the same type of work can be performed in both of the situations depicted in Figure 11-3, higher horizontal specialization has the potential to produce greater productivity. First, people performing horizontally specialized

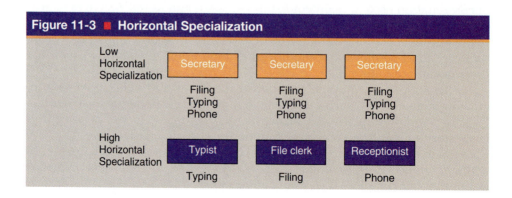

Figure 11-3 ■ Horizontal Specialization

Low Horizontal Specialization	Secretary	Secretary	Secretary
	Filing Typing Phone	Filing Typing Phone	Filing Typing Phone
High Horizontal Specialization	Typist	File clerk	Receptionist
	Typing	Filing	Phone

jobs complete the same task activities again and again. This repetition enables them to learn their jobs thoroughly and, over time, to sharpen job-related knowledge and skills. Second, high horizontal specialization substantially reduces the amount of time lost in switching from one task activity to another because highly specialized jobs consist of a limited number of different activities. Third, because it is easier to identify and analyze a smaller number of critical task activities, high horizontal specialization makes it easier to develop new methods and new equipment for any given job. It is the potential for high productivity associated with these three benefits that makes horizontal specialization attractive to managers.

However, as indicated in Chapter 6, the efficiency expected from horizontal specialization sometimes fails to materialize, due to oversimplification and related workforce dissatisfaction. In such instances, lower horizontal specialization is implemented—through job enrichment or total quality management procedures—so that, although potential efficiency will be reduced, actual productivity will increase.

The other type of specialization, **vertical specialization,** concerns the degree to which an organization is divided into hierarchical levels. As shown in Figure 11-4, the higher the degree of vertical specialization, the more layers are contained in an organization's hierarchy of authority—and the greater the separation of the management of a task from its performance. The upper panel of Figure 11-4 illustrates low vertical specialization. With only a single managerial layer, much of the actual management of the organization's tasks rests with those

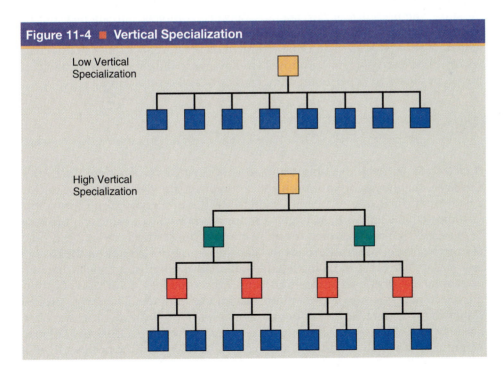

Figure 11-4 ■ Vertical Specialization

Low Vertical Specialization

High Vertical Specialization

who perform them. For instance, workers on the shop floor of a company like Whirlpool or Gaines Pet Food may design their own jobs and decide who will do what. They may also order their own raw materials, set their own work hours, and even hire and fire coworkers. In the second hierarchy shown in Figure 11-4, higher vertical specialization has produced several managerial layers. Here, hierarchical superiors, rather than the people who actually perform the work, generally handle management activities. Decision making about work methods, job assignments, hours of work, and such is taken away from shop floor employees and made the task of management.

Bureaucracy

When they occur together, standardization, formalization, and specialization form a type of structure often called *bureaucratic,* due to similarities between it and the model of bureaucracy developed by Max Weber. As indicated in Chapter 1, Weber's bureaucracy is a type of organization in which rules and regulations are used to govern member behaviors. Written documentation is also maintained to provide consistency over time. Authority is distributed in a hierarchy, in which only certain people have the ability to issue direct orders. Finally, work is divided into tasks that can be performed efficiently. These four bureaucratic characteristics correspond with standardization, formalization, vertical specialization, and horizontal specialization as just defined.

The choice to emphasize standardization as a primary means of coordination is thus the choice to create a bureaucratic organization. In contrast, the choice to place primary emphasis on other means of coordination is also the choice to minimize the presence of bureaucracy. Between complete bureaucracy and no bureaucracy lies a continuum of different structures, each based on different structural choices. We will describe several of these alternatives later in this chapter, after first discussing how groups of employees are clustered together and controlled by means of departmentation, hierarchy, and centralization.

Departmentation

Besides making decisions about how to coordinate interdependent activities, managers shaping an organization's structure must also determine how to cluster together the groups or teams produced by the process of group formation. As indicated in Chapter 8, managers can form groups of coworkers on the basis of *functional* similarities, which results in efficient but relatively inflexible groups of functional specialists. Alternatively, managers can form groups on the basis of *work flow* similarities, producing flexible but relatively inefficient teams that blur functional distinctions. Managers also apply the same logic to the job of grouping the resulting groups together into a larger organization. This larger process results in two different types of **departmentation.**[13] To illustrate these two alternatives, think of an organization that consists of the four functional areas of marketing, research, manufacturing, and accounting and the three product lines of

Figure 11-5 ■ Types of Departmentation

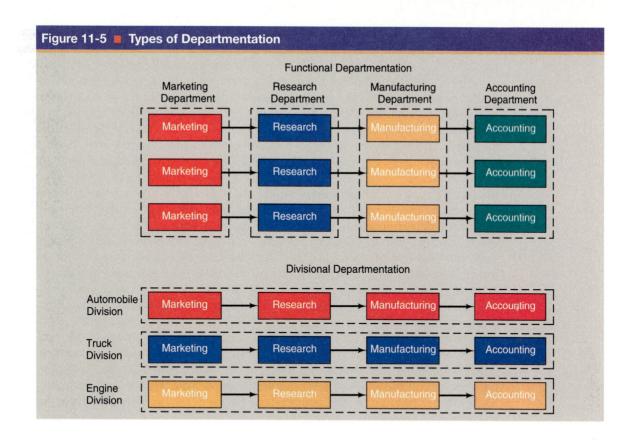

Figure 11-5 ■ Types of Departmentation

automobiles, trucks, and small gasoline engines. Figure 11-5 depicts this firm. Each box represents one of the four functions. Each of the horizontal work flows, represented by a series of arrows, is one of the three product lines. Dashed lines illustrate the alternative forms of departmentalization.

Shown in the upper diagram in Figure 11-5 is one type of departmentation, *functional departmentation.* It is the equivalent of functional grouping, but rather than forming groups of individuals, the aim is now to form groups of groups. All marketing groups are combined into a single marketing department, all research groups are combined into a single research department, and so forth. As with functional grouping, the *departments* that result from functional departmentation are economically efficient. In each department, members can trade information about their functional specialty and improve their skills. Also, managers can reduce overstaffing or duplication of effort by reassigning redundant employees elsewhere in the firm. However, changes to any of the product lines crossing a particular department require reorganization of the entire department. Thus, departments lack the flexibility to deal easily with change.

In contrast, implementation of the type of departmentation shown in the lower diagram of Figure 11-5, *divisional departmentation,* is the same as using work flow grouping at the top of the organization. Instead of being clustered into marketing, manufacturing, research, and accounting departments, the organization's activities are grouped into product *divisions*—an automobile division, a truck division, and a gasoline engine division. When an organization's clients differ more than its products, the organization's work may be grouped according to differences in the clients served. For instance, there might be a military contracts division, a wholesale distribution division, and an aftermarket parts division. In a third alternative, when an organization's operations are spread throughout the world, its parts may be geographically grouped into a North American division, an Asian division, and a European division. In any of these alternatives, the organization possesses division-by-division flexibility. Each division can tailor its response to the particular demands of its own market. For example, Ford's Lincoln-Mercury division can decide to redesign its luxury-market automobiles to be more Mercedes-like without having to worry about other Ford products and markets. Some of the economic efficiency of functional departmentation is sacrificed, however, because effort is duplicated across the organization's product lines. Lincoln-Mercury's product design studios duplicate Ford's, but the two divisions' studios cannot be consolidated without losing divisional flexibility. So as with group formation, managers making departmentation decisions must grapple with a trade-off between economy and flexibility.

By clustering related groups, departmentation of either type accentuates similarities that facilitate the management of intergroup relations. Specifically, in an organization structured around functional departmentation, groups in the same department share the same specialized knowledge, language, and ways of looking at the company's business. For instance, all the members of a marketing department share the same general marketing know-how. They talk about things like market segmentation and market share and generally agree that the best way to ensure their company's success is by appealing to customer needs. A manager charged with coordinating different groups in the marketing department can base managerial actions on this common knowledge, language, and viewpoint despite having to deal with several different groups of employees. The manager can manage the various groups using the same basic management approach.

Similarly, in an organization structured around divisional departmentation, groups in the same division share interest in the same basic line of business. Thus, all employees in the truck division of a company like General Motors or Ford are concerned about doing well in the truck industry. This commonality allows the manager of a division to treat groups performing different functions—marketing, manufacturing, research, and so on—in much the same way without having to tailor management practices to the functional specialty of each particular group.

Hierarchy and Centralization

By gathering groups together, departmentation creates clusters of groups and layers of managers having responsibility for the activities of particular clusters. Hierarchy and varying degrees of centralization can then be used to control intergroup relations.

A manager having hierarchical authority over a particular cluster of groups can use this authority to issue orders that, when followed, will help coordinate activities among those groups. For instance, the manager having hierarchical authority over all the manufacturing groups of the company depicted in the top diagram in Figure 11-5 can use that authority to smooth the flow of information among groups of manufacturing employees. Alternatively, the manager of the automobile division shown in the lower diagram in Figure 11-5 can help facilitate work flows among employees in the division. In turn, interdependencies that span different departments or divisions can be coordinated by managers higher in the organization's hierarchy. For example, problems between the manufacturing department and the marketing, research, or accounting departments shown in the upper diagram can be dealt with by the executive responsible for overseeing the various department managers. The organization can use hierarchical authority, then, to coordinate relations among groups by extending the scope of direct supervision.

The use of hierarchy to coordinate intergroup relations differs from one organization to the next as to the level of managers—top, middle, or supervisory—that will have the ultimate authority to make decisions and issue orders. Left to their own devices, top managers often favor **centralization,** the concentration of authority and decision making at the top of a firm.[14] Centralization affords top managers a high degree of certainty. Because they alone make the decisions in centralized firms, they can be sure not only that decisions are made but that they are made in accordance with their own wishes. In addition, centralization can minimize the time needed to make decisions because only a limited number of people are involved in decision-making processes.

Despite centralization's appeal to top management, **decentralization** is increasingly common in modern organizations. In decentralized organizations, authority and decision making are dispersed downward and outward in the hierarchy of managers and employees. Several factors push otherwise reluctant top managers toward its implementation. First, some decisions require top managers to consider a great deal of information. The managers may become overloaded by the task of processing all this information and therefore find it useful to involve more people in the decision-making process. Second, the move to decentralization may be stimulated by a need for flexibility. If local conditions require that different parts of an organization respond differently, managers of those organizational groups must be empowered to make their own decisions. Third, decentralization may be useful in dealing with employee motivation problems if those problems can be solved by according employees control over workplace practices and conditions. In any of these cases, the failure to decentralize can seriously undermine attempts to coordinate intergroup relations.

Types of Organization Structure

How do the structural characteristics we have discussed—coordination mechanisms, formalization (or alternatives), specialization, departmentation, and centralization—combine together to make organization structures? What

Figure 11-6 ■ **The Simple Undifferentiated Structure**

| Employee 1 | Employee 2 | Employee 3 | Employee 4 |

kinds of structures are formed as a result of different combinations of these features? The answers to these questions are found in a menu of different structures overviewed in the rest of this chapter.

Prebureaucratic Structures

As is suggested by their name, **prebureaucratic structures** lack the standardization, formalization, and pronounced specialization that are the defining characteristics of bureaucracies. They can be used successfully only in organizations so small in size and simple in purpose that mutual adjustment or direct supervision provides enough coordination to maintain interdependence.

In one type of prebureaucratic structure, the **simple undifferentiated structure,** coordination is accomplished solely by *mutual adjustment,* the process in which coworkers interact directly with one another to determine how to coordinate work among themselves. Because talking with other people is natural for most of us, mutual adjustment is easy to initiate and relatively simple to sustain. For this reason, simple undifferentiated structures can often be established and perpetuated fairly easily.

As Figure 11-6 suggests, there is no hierarchy of authority in a simple undifferentiated structure. Such a structure is nothing more than an organization of people who decide what to do by talking with each other as they work. No single individual has the authority to issue orders, and there are few if any written procedures to guide performance. A group of friends who decide to open a small restaurant, gift shop, or similar sort of business might, at the outset, adopt this type of structure for the business.

The primary strengths of simple undifferentiated structures are their simplicity and extreme flexibility. Networks of face-to-face conversations occur spontaneously and can be reconfigured almost instantly. For example, adding another member to a small classroom discussion group is likely to cause only a momentary lapse in the group's activities. A major weakness of these structures, however, is their limitation to small organizations. Suppose you were a member of an advertising firm composed of 25 or 30 people. You would find it difficult or impossible to rely on mutual adjustment alone to ensure that the firm's accounts were properly handled, because process loss would undermine the usefulness of face-to-face coordination among such a large number of individuals. So many interpersonal links would be required that valuable time and effort would be lost in the attempt to maintain some degree of organization.

Another important and related weakness is that simple undifferentiated structures cannot provide the coordination needed to accomplish complex tasks. It is unlikely, for example, that a simple undifferentiated structure of 12 people

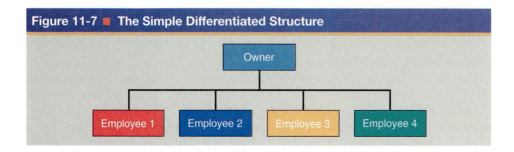

Figure 11-7 ■ The Simple Differentiated Structure

could succeed at mass-producing automobiles. Complicated work of this sort requires a more complicated form of organization structure.

In the second type of prebureaucratic structure, the **simple differentiated structure,** direct supervision replaces mutual adjustment as the primary means of coordination. Organizations with simple differentiated structures are a common part of everyday life—a family-owned grocery store or neighborhood gas station, for example. As shown in Figure 11-7, this type of structure is organized as a hierarchy with small but significant amounts of *vertical specialization* and *centralization.* One person (usually the firm's owner or the owner's management representative) retains the hierarchical authority needed to coordinate work activities by means of *direct supervision.* As a secondary mechanism, mutual adjustment is used to deal with coordination problems that direct supervision cannot resolve. For instance, while the owner of a small insurance office is at the post office getting the morning mail, clerks in the insurance office may talk among themselves to decide who will answer the telephone and who will process paperwork until the owner returns.

The simple differentiated structure can coordinate larger numbers of people than the simple undifferentiated structure. The reason is that shifting to direct supervision eliminates much of the process loss associated with reliance on mutual adjustment alone. In addition, because its decision-making powers are centralized in the hands of a single person, an organization with a simple differentiated structure can respond rapidly to changing conditions. At the same time, this structure affords a good deal of flexibility because it avoids standardization. Its weaknesses, however, are its inability to coordinate the activities of more than about 50 people, and its failure to provide the integration needed to accomplish complex tasks. It is just as unlikely that a group of people could organize themselves to produce cars by using a combination of direct supervision and mutual adjustment as it is that they might organize themselves for such a task using mutual adjustment alone. A single direct supervisor would soon be overwhelmed by the vast amount of information required to know which sort of cars to produce, what parts to order, whom to order them from, how to assemble them properly, and so forth.

Bureaucratic Structures

Prebureaucratic structures are likely to be overwhelmed by the coordination requirements of complicated tasks. Instead, standardization of processes, outputs, skills, or norms is typically required to deal with tasks of this sort. Standardization of any type greatly reduces the amount of information that must be exchanged and the number of decisions that must be made as work is being performed. It also stimulates formalization and specialization of both types, and is thus the hall-mark of **bureaucratic structures.** In such structures, direct supervision and mutual adjustment are retained as secondary mechanisms that take effect when standardization fails to meet all coordination needs. This combination of coordination mechanisms allows organizations with bureaucratic structures to integrate the variety of jobs needed to perform complicated, demanding work.

The **functional structure** is a form of bureaucratic structure adopted by organizations that are larger than the 50 or so members that can be coordinated by means of a simple differentiated structure, yet not so large that they do business in several different locations or serve a widely varying clientele. If there are locally owned banks, department stores, or manufacturing plants in your community, chances are good that they have functional structures. Such structures are characterized by four key attributes. First, as bureaucratic structures, functional structures are based on coordination by *standardization*. Since this standardization must be preceded by formalization and contributes to both vertical and horizontal specialization, all of these are also features of functional structures. Second, these structures are organized according to *functional departmentation*. That is, groups within them are clustered into departments that are named for the functions their members perform, such as marketing, manufacturing, or accounting. Third, functional structures are *centralized*. Most, if not all, important decisions are made by one or a few people at the tops of firms with functional structures—especially decisions having to do with the formation of organizational goals and objectives.

As Figure 11-8 suggests, one of the easiest ways to determine whether a particular firm has a functional structure is to examine the titles held by its vice presidents. If the firm has a bureaucratic structure and all its vice presidents have titles that indicate what their subordinates do (for example, vice president of manufacturing, vice president of marketing, and vice president of research and development), the firm has a functional structure. If, however, one or more vice presidents have other sorts of titles, for instance, vice president of the consumer finance division or vice president of European operations, the firm has one of the other types of structure to be described later.

The primary strength of the functional structure is its economic efficiency. Standardization minimizes the long-term cost of coordination. In addition, centralization makes it possible for workers to focus their attention on their work rather than having to take time out to make needed decisions. Functional structures, however, have a critical weakness. They lack flexibility. The standardization that provides so much efficiency not only takes lengthy planning and substantial documentation (formalization) to set in place, but also requires that the same standards be followed again and again. This inflexibility reduces the functional structure's ability to cope with instability or change. Functional departmentation adds to this rigidity because changes to any work flow in a company organized by functional departmentation also affect the other work flows in the organization.

A functional structure can coordinate the work of an organization effectively if the firm limits itself to one type of product, produces this product in a single

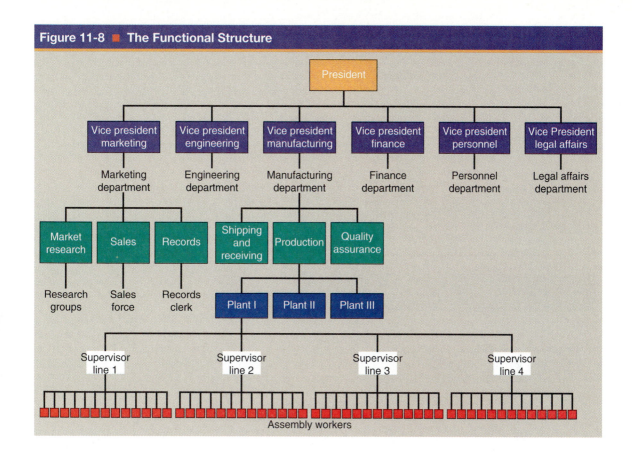

Figure 11-8 ■ The Functional Structure

geographic location, and sells to only one general type of client. Many organizations produce more than one product, however, or do business in several different locations or seek to serve a variety of clients. Such diversity of products, locations, or clients injects variety into the information a firm needs to make managerial decisions. This variety overloads the centralized decision-making processes on which the functional structure is based. In such situations, other structures are more useful.

The **divisional structure** is a second type of bureaucratic structure, and as such, it is characterized by standardization, formalization, and specialization. Unlike functional structures, however, divisional structures are moderately *decentralized*. Decision making is pushed downward one or two hierarchical layers, so a company's vice presidents and sometimes their immediate subordinates share in the process of digesting information and making key decisions. *Divisional departmentation* is another feature that distinguishes divisional structures from functional structures. Groups in divisional structures are clustered together according to similarities in products, geographic locations, or clients. For this reason, divisional structures are also sometimes called product structures, geographic structures, or market (or client) structures.

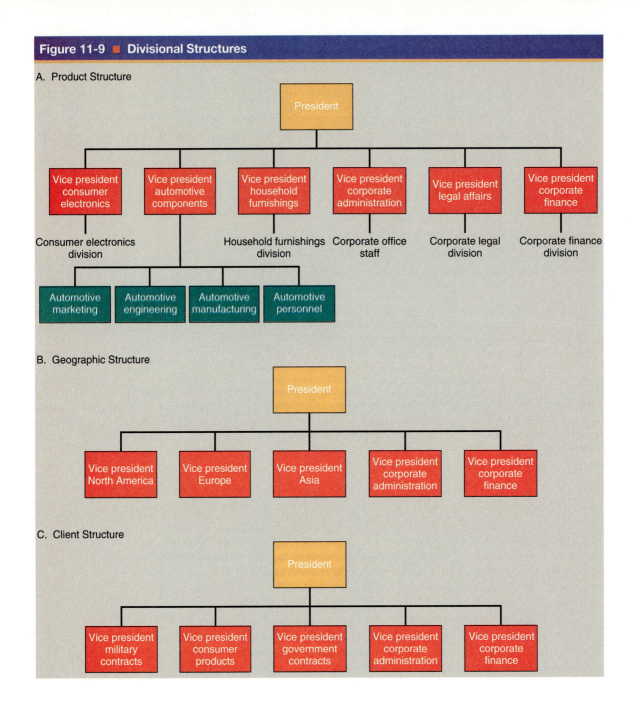

Figure 11-9 ■ Divisional Structures

A. Product Structure

President

Vice president consumer electronics

Vice president automotive components

Vice president household furnishings

Vice president corporate administration

Vice president legal affairs

Vice president corporate finance

Consumer electronics division

Household furnishings division

Corporate office staff

Corporate legal division

Corporate finance division

Automotive marketing

Automotive engineering

Automotive manufacturing

Automotive personnel

B. Geographic Structure

President

Vice president North America

Vice president Europe

Vice president Asia

Vice president corporate administration

Vice president corporate finance

C. Client Structure

President

Vice president military contracts

Vice president consumer products

Vice president government contracts

Vice president corporate administration

Vice president corporate finance

Figure 11-9 depicts several different divisional structures based on (1) product similarities, (2) geographic similarities, and (3) client similarities. Each differs from the functional structure diagrammed in Figure 11-8: in each of the structures in Figure 11-9, the vice presidential titles of *line* divisions include product, geographic, or client names. Note, however, that in these same divisional structures, vice presidents of *staff* divisions have titles incorporating what sound like functions, for example, vice president of legal affairs or vice president of corporate finance.

The divisional structure's departmentation scheme and moderate decentralization give it a degree of flexibility not found in the functional structure.[15] Each division can react to issues concerning its own product, geographic region, or client group without disturbing the operation of other divisions. It remains securely connected to the rest of the organization, however, and is not allowed to drift away from the overall organization's goals and objectives. Thus, for example, the vice president of consumer electronics, shown in the upper panel of Figure 11-9, can make decisions affecting the production and sales of clock radios and steam irons without consulting with the company's president or other vice presidents, but cannot decide to redirect the division into another line of products.

The limited degree of independence afforded the divisions in a divisional structure allows one division to stop doing business without seriously interrupting the operations of other divisions. For example, the division of TRW that fulfills NASA space contracts could discontinue doing business without affecting work in the firm's credit information division. Remember, however, that each division in a divisional structure is itself organized like a functional structure, as shown in the product structure diagrammed in Figure 11-9. As a result, a particular division cannot change products, locations, or clients without serious interruption to its own internal operations. For example, the decision at TRW to reduce reliance on military contracts would require that the division servicing such contracts be substantially reorganized.

The flexibility that is the main strength of divisional structures comes at the price of increased costs because of duplication of effort across divisions. For example, every division will have its own sales force, even though that means that salespeople from several different divisions may visit the same customer. The primary weakness of divisional structures is the fact that they are, at best, only moderately efficient.

Matrix structures, like divisional structures, are bureaucratic structures adopted by organizations that must integrate work activities having to do with a variety of products, locations, or customers. However, firms such as the Monsanto Company, Prudential Insurance, and the Chase Manhattan Bank that have matrix structures need even more flexibility than divisional structures allow.[16] They try to achieve this flexibility by reintegrating functional specialists across different product, location, or customer lines. Because matrix structures use functional and divisional departmentation simultaneously to cluster together structural groups, they are also called *simultaneous structures*.

Figure 11-10 illustrates the matrix structure of a firm that has three divisions, each of which manufactures and sells a distinct product line. Each box, or cell, in the matrix is a distinct group composed of a small hierarchy of supervisors and one or more structural groups having both functional and divisional responsibilities. For example, cell 1 in the figure is a consumer electronics marketing group composed of units that market televisions, radios, cellular telephones, and other electronic merchandise. Cell 2 is the automotive components engineering group consisting of engineering units that design automobile engines, suspensions,

Figure 11-10 ■ **The Matrix Structure**

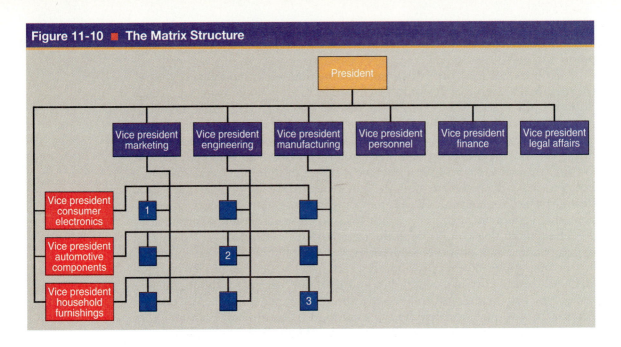

steering assemblies, and other such items. Cell 3 is a household products manufacturing group made up of facilities that produce furniture polish, floor wax, window cleaner, and other household supplies. Note that the figure also indicates that staff groups in a matrix structure are often excluded from the matrix itself. The three staff departments shown in the diagram—personnel, finance, and legal affairs—provide advice to top management but are not part of the matrix.

Mutual adjustment is the primary means of coordination within the upper layers of a matrix structure, and decision making is *decentralized* among matrix managers. Both of these characteristics enable top managers to reconfigure relationships among the cells in the matrix, promoting extreme flexibility. Because of their dual responsibilities, each matrix cell has two bosses—a functional boss and a divisional boss. This arrangement violates Fayol's principle of unity of command (see Chapter 1). Thus, mutual adjustment must also be used in the upper layer of each cell to cope with conflicting orders from above.

Beneath the upper layer of each cell, however, formalization, standardization, and specialization are used to integrate work activities. Both direct supervision and lower-level mutual adjustment serve as supplementary mechanisms that coordinate cell activities. For instance, once managers at the top of the matrix structure shown in Figure 11-10 have decided to manufacture a new kind of floor wax, formalization is used to develop new standards. Standardization is then used to coordinate activities in the units in the household products manufacturing cell that make this new product. Direct supervisors help employees learn the new standards and also work to correct deficiencies in the standards as they become apparent. In addition, employees engage in mutual adjustment to cope with problems that their supervisor cannot resolve. Thus, a matrix structure basically consists of a simple differentiated structure designed into the upper layers of a bureaucracy, including the president and vice presidents shown in Figure 11-10, plus the individuals who manage each of the cells. This simple structure injects mutual adjustment into an otherwise bureaucratic organization in order to encourage communication, coordination, and flexibility among the managers who oversee organizational operations.

The primary strength of matrix structures is their extreme flexibility. They can adjust to changes that would overwhelm other bureaucratic structures. Nonetheless, matrix structures are relatively rare, because they are extremely costly to operate. In part, this costliness stems from the proliferation of human resource expenses. In particular, matrix structures require two complete sets of vice presidents. They also incorporate the same sort of duplication of effort—multiple sales forces, for instance—that make divisional structures so expensive to operate. Moreover, because employees near the top must deal with two bosses and often conflicting orders, working in a matrix is a stressful situation. This stress can lead to absenteeism, turnover, and, ultimately, lowered productivity.[17]

More important, however, matrix structures are economically inefficient because they rely on mutual adjustment as their primary coordination mechanism, despite extremely costly levels of process loss. Matrix structuring thus represents the decision to put up with costly coordination in order to secure high flexibility. Firms that choose matrix structures and function effectively thereafter are generally those that face radical change that would destroy them if they could not easily adapt to such change. In effect, they are choosing the lesser of two evils—the inefficiency of a matrix rather than dissolution. Firms that try matrix organization but later abandon it do not face the degree of change required to justify the costs of the matrix approach.

Postbureaucratic Structures

Within the last 20 years, many organizations have grown extremely large, employing hundreds of thousands of individuals, producing a tremendous variety of goods or services, and doing business in every corner of the world. At the same time, these firms have found it necessary to be more flexible than would be allowed by even the most flexible form of bureaucracy. As a result, managers have begun to experiment with new kinds of **postbureaucratic structures.**

One form of postbureaucratic structure, the **multiunit structure,** achieves high flexibility by *deintegrating* divisions of a large organization rather than by integrating divisional elements along functional lines, as is done in a matrix structure. A multiunit structure emerges when the divisions of a divisional structure are permitted to separate themselves from the rest of the organization and develop into autonomous, self-managed business units. Each business unit is allowed to fend for itself, with little or no interference from the *holding unit* that oversees the complete firm. Companies including Ford, Xerox, and Alco Standard are currently experimenting with variations of this form of structure.[18]

Figure 11-11 shows a multiunit structure. Compared to bureaucratic structures, multiunit structures are extremely *decentralized.* Unit managers several levels below the holding unit's CEO have the authority to define their unit's purpose and formulate its mission. In the most flexible multiunit structures, the

Figure 11-11 ■ The Multiunit Structure

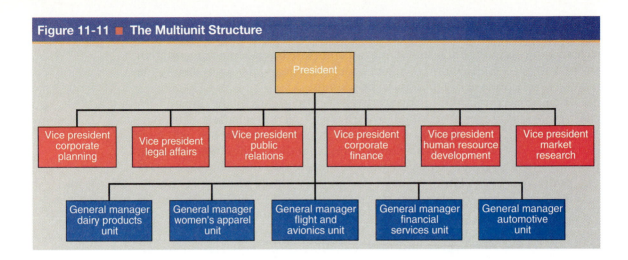

units themselves are further decentralized. Teams of nonmanagerial employees assume supervisory duties and use mutual adjustment to coordinate work activities. Computer networks tie teams together horizontally and provide the vertical information flows required to ensure unitwide coordination. In the process, computerized information processing takes the place of hierarchy and centralized decision making as an important means of coordinating interdependence among groups.

At the same time, however, routine activities are coordinated as much as possible by standardization to control the costs of process loss. Often such standardization is of skills or norms and is accomplished by training or socialization rather than through the process of formalization. To the degree that standardization is present, both vertical and horizontal specialization are also evident. All multiunit structures are organized around *divisional departmentation*. As we've already noted, however, each of a multiunit structure's "divisions" is actually a self-sufficient business concern.

A major strength of the multiunit structure is its ability to provide the coordination required to manage large or extremely large organizations, albeit in parts, without incurring the high costs of the matrix structure. In addition, the personal autonomy afforded employees in multiunit structures can be a strong source of motivation, satisfaction, and personal growth.[19] However, even multiunit structures have some degree of inefficiency, inasmuch as their divisional departmentation means substantial duplication of effort. Another drawback is that multiunit structures are not useful when strong links are needed between the different parts of an organization. For example, it is difficult to imagine organizing a hospital as a multiunit structure. Too many transfers of patients and treatment information are required among the units of a hospital to allow any of them to operate autonomously.

On the cutting edge of structural experimentation is a second type of post-bureaucratic structure, the **virtual structure.** It is a form of structure in which several organizations attain the performance capacities of a single, much larger firm while retaining extreme flexibility and significant efficiency.[20] The label *virtual structure* is taken from the term *virtual memory,* which refers to a way of making a computer act as though it has more memory capacity than it actually possesses. Similarly, virtual structure is a way of making an organization act as though it has more productive capacity than it actually controls. A structure of this type develops when a company forms temporary alliances or joint ventures with other companies to quickly exploit a business opportunity. Thus, a virtual structure is not a single organization, but is instead a temporary network of several organizations. Levi Strauss, Atlas Industrial Door, and Hewlett-Packard are some of the better-known companies currently implementing aspects of the virtual structuring approach.[21]

In virtual structures, each firm focuses on doing the thing it does best—using its core competency in design, manufacturing, marketing, or any other necessary function—and together, all the firms form a "best of everything" organization. During the period of its temporary existence, a virtual structure resembles a loosely coupled functional structure in which each "department" is an otherwise autonomous company. Connecting the various companies together is a network of computerized information-processing systems that takes the place of hierarchy in coordinating interdependent relationships among companies. Other coordination among companies is accomplished mainly by mutual adjustment.

The temporary nature of the virtual structure is the source of its flexibility, because companies can be added or subtracted as the situation warrants. The virtual structure's efficiency comes from each company's singular focus on doing what it does best. Thus, it would seem that the virtual structure overcomes the efficiency-versus-flexibility trade-offs evident in the other structures just discussed. However, at present, it is too early to tell whether virtual structures truly possess this strength, and whether managers are truly able to cope with the difficulties involved in managing the fluid interfirm relations needed to make virtual structures succeed. Nonetheless, growing interest among present-day managers ensures that the costs and benefits of virtual structuring will become apparent in the coming years.

SUMMARY

An organization's *structure* is a relatively stable network of interdependencies among the people and tasks that make up the organization. It is created and sustained by the *basic coordination mechanisms* of *mutual adjustment, direct supervision,* and *standardization,* all of which coordinate interdependent relationships among people and groups. Using standardization encourages the emergence of formalization, professionalization, training, or socialization, and *specialization.* Standardization, formalization, and specialization, if present in the same organization, create *bureaucracy.*

Structure emerges as the groups in an organization are clustered together during *departmentation* (either *functional* or *divisional*). The resulting departments or divisions are coordinated with *hierarchy* and *centralization,* in addition to the basic coordination mechanisms. Depending on the mix of coordination mechanism, departmentation, and centralization chosen by the managers of a firm, various types of *prebureaucratic, bureaucratic,* or *postbureaucratic* structures may be produced. These include the *simple undifferentiated structure,* the *simple differentiated structure,* the *functional structure,* the *divisional structure,* the *matrix structure,* the *multiunit structure,* and the *virtual structure.*

Review Questions

1. Given that an organization's structure integrates and differentiates activities in the organization, tell which of the following structural characteristics provide integration and which produce differentiation: basic coordination mechanisms, formalization, specialization, departmentation, and centralization.
2. Explain why standardization requires stability. Why is mutual adjustment so much more flexible? How does direct supervision fit between the two extremes? What mechanism or mechanisms would you use to coordinate a television-assembly group of 50 employees? Six custom jewelry makers? A dozen door-to-door magazine salespeople? Why?
3. Draw and explain a diagram showing how standardization, formalization, and specialization are interrelated. If an organization decided to institute participatory decision making, thereby replacing standardization with mutual adjustment, what effects does your diagram suggest this plan would have on other characteristics of the organization's structure?
4. Explain how professionalization, training, and socialization can complement, or supplement, formalization. Based on what you have learned in other chapters, name some additional purposes these three processes serve in organizations.
5. What kinds of departmentation can be used to cluster groups together? How do centralization and hierarchy work together to resolve coordination problems among departments or divisions?
6. What major differences exist between prebureaucratic and bureaucratic structures? Between bureaucratic structures and postbureaucratic structures? What role do managerial choices among basic coordination mechanisms play in determining which kind of structure develops in an organization?

Implementation Guide

You can use what you have learned in this chapter to identify the specific characteristics of an organization's structure and to gain insight into the strengths and weaknesses of that structure. The following questions are provided to assist you in this process.

1. Which of the three basic coordination mechanisms are used in and among the organization's groups? Which is used as the primary means of coordination,

and what does that tell you about the importance the firm accords to efficiency? To flexibility?

2. What secondary coordination mechanisms back up the primary mechanism used throughout the firm? Are activities coordinated adequately?

3. If standardization of a particular type is present, is the appropriate type of formalization or complement—professionalization, training, or socialization—also present?

4. If standardization and formalization are evident in the firm, are jobs horizontally specialized? Is vertical specialization also present? Does each type of specialization seem balanced in relation to the other?

5. Is the firm's structure based on functional or divisional departmentalization? What does that tell you about the probable balance between efficiency and flexibility in the organization? Does this balance seem correct, given the firm's business situation?

6. Across the array of structural characteristics that you have identified, does a general profile stressing efficiency emerge or does a profile stressing flexibility and adaptability appear instead?

7. What specific kind of structure does the organization possess? Does it appear to be the appropriate one, given the profile you have already identified?

ENDNOTES

1. J. A. Byrne, "The Pain of Downsizing," *Business Week*, May 9, 1994, pp. 60–61; J. Weber and P. Dwyer, "Scott Rolls Out a Risky Strategy," *Business Week*, May 22, 1995, p. 48; P. Sellers and A. Hadjian, "Pepsico's Shedding Ugly Pounds," *Fortune*, June 26, 1995 pp. 84–86; C. Arnst, "For a Pink Slip, Press 2," *Business Week*, November 27, 1995, p. 48; and D. Greising, "It Hurts So Good at Delta," *Business Week*, December 11, 1995, pp. 106–7.

2. J. G. March and H. A. Simon, *Organizations* (New York: John Wiley, 1958), p. 4; J. D. Thompson, *Organizations in Action* (New York: McGraw-Hill, 1967), p. 51; and W. R. Scott, *Organizations: Rational, Natural, and Open Systems*, 3d ed. (Englewood Cliffs, NJ: Prentice Hall, 1992), p. 15.

3. P. R. Lawrence and J. W. Lorsch, "Differentiation and Integration in Complex Organizations," *Administrative Science Quarterly* 12 (1967), pp. 1–47; and P. R. Lawrence and J. W. Lorsch, *Organization and Environment* (Homewood, IL: Irwin, 1967), p. 7.

4. Lawrence and Lorsch, "Differentiation and Integration," pp. 2–3; March and Simon, *Organizations*, p. 160; and J. R. Galbraith, *Designing Complex Organizations* (Reading, MA: Addison-Wesley, 1973), p. 4.

5. Thompson, *Organizations in Action*, p. 62.

6. H. Mintzberg, *Structuring of Organizations* (Englewood Cliffs, NJ: Prentice Hall, 1979), pp. 3–4.

7. Ibid., p. 5.

8. Ibid., pp. 7–9; and H. Mintzberg, "The Structuring of Organizations," in *The Strategy Process: Concepts, Contexts, and Cases*, J. B. Quinn, H. Mintzberg, and R. M. James, eds. (Englewood Cliffs, NJ: Prentice Hall, 1988), pp. 276–304.

9. Mintzberg, *Structuring of Organizations*, p. 7.

10. D. S. Pugh, D. J. Hickson, C. R. Hinings, and C. Turner, "Dimensions of Organization Structure," *Administrative Science Quarterly* 13 (1968), pp. 65–91; J. H. K. Inkson, D. S. Pugh, and D. J. Hickson, "Organization, Context, and Structure: An Abbreviated Replication," *Administrative Science Quarterly* 15 (1970), pp. 318–29; and J. Child, "Organization, Structure, and Strategies of Control: A Replication of the Aston Study," *Administrative Science Quarterly* 17 (1972), pp. 163–77.

11. R. H. Hall, "Professionalism and Bureaucratization," *American Sociological Review* 33 (1968), pp. 92–104; and J. Hage and M. Aiken, "Relationship of Centralization to Other Structural Properties," *Administrative Science Quarterly* 12 (1967), pp. 72–91.

12. Mintzberg, *Structuring of Organizations*, p. 69.

13. P. N. Khandwalla, *The Design of Organizations* (New York: Harcourt, Brace, Jovanovich, 1977), pp. 489–97; and A. Walker and J. Lorsch, "Organizational Choice: Product versus Function," *Harvard Business Review* 46 (1968), pp. 129–38.

14. Pugh et al., "Dimensions of Organization Structure," p. 72; Hage and Aiken, "Relationship of Centralization"; P. M. Blau, "Decentralization in Bureaucracies," in *Power in Organizations,* M. N. Zald, ed. (Nashville, TN: Vanderbilt University Press, 1970), pp. 42–81; N. M. Carter and J. B. Cullen, "A Comparison of Centralization/Decentralization of Decision Making Concepts and Measures," *Journal of Management* 10 (1984), pp. 259–68; and R. Mansfield, "Bureaucracy and Centralization: An Examination of Organizational Structure," *Administrative Science Quarterly* 18 (1973), pp. 477–78.

15. R. E. Hoskisson, C. W. L. Hill, and H. Kim, "The Multidivisional Structure: Organizational Fossil or Source of Value?" *Journal of Management* 19 (1993), pp. 269–98.

16. R. C. Ford and W. A. Randolph, "Cross Functional Structures: A Review and Integration of Matrix Organization and Project Management," *Journal of Management* 18 (1992), pp. 267–94.

17. L. R. Burns, "Matrix Management in Hospitals: Testing Theories of Matrix Structure and Development," *Administrative Science Quarterly* 34 (1989), pp. 349–68; and L. R. Burns and D. R. Wholey, "Adoption and Abandonment of Matrix Management Programs: Effects of Organizational Characteristics and Interorganizational Programs," *Academy of Management Journal* 36 (1993), pp. 106–38.

18. M. Hammer and J. Champy, *Reengineering the Corporation: A Manifesto for Business Revolution* (New York: Harper Business, 1993); S. Lubove, "How to Grow Big Yet Stay Small," *Forbes,* December 7, 1992, pp. 64–67; and M. Rothschild, "Coming Soon: Internal Markets," *Forbes ASAP,* June 7, 1993, pp. 19–21.

19. W. E. Halal, "From Hierarchy to Enterprise: Internal Markets Are the New Foundation of Management," *Academy of Management Executive* 8 (1994), pp. 69–83.

20. G. G. Dess, A. M. A. Rasheed, K. J. McLaughlin, and R. L. Priem, "The New Corporate Architecture," *Academy of Management Executive* 9 (1995), pp. 7–20.

21. W. H. Davidow and M. S. Malone, *The Virtual Corporation: Structuring and Revitalizing the Corporation for the 21st Century* (New York: Harper Collins, 1992); J. A. Byrne, R. Brandt, and O. Port, "The Virtual Corporation: The Company of the Future Will Be the Ultimate in Adaptability," *Business Week,* February 8, 1993, pp. 99–102; J. A. Byrne, "The Futurists Who Fathered the Ideas," *Business Week,* February 8, 1993, p. 103; M. Malone and W. Davidow, "Virtual Corporation," *Forbes ASAP,* December 7, 1992, pp. 102–7; J. W. Verity, "A Company That's 100% Virtual," *Business Week,* November 21, 1994, p. 85; and D. Greising, "The Virtual Olympics," *Business Week,* April 29, 1996, pp. 64–66.

Chapter Twelve

Organization Design

In 1993, American Express Financial Advisors (AEFA), headquartered in Minneapolis, Minnesota, basked in the glow of a five-year record of 21 percent annual growth in corporate earnings. Yet, turnover was sky-high—nearly 70 percent in four years—among the 8,000 financial planners who worked as independent contractors and sold the company's mutual funds, insurance, and investment certificates on commission. Without correcting this problem, AEFA stood to lose valuable clients, who could be expected to follow former AEFA planners to competitor firms, and relinquish its position as a leader in the market for financial products aimed at middle-class consumers.

AEFA responded in 1994 by restructuring corporate operations. Gone were the general sales manager and staff of regional sales managers who had overseen geographic sales regions. In their place were seven process executives, each of whom took charge of a horizontal process like client satisfaction or sales management. The 180 regional divisions beneath the executive level were collapsed into 45 clusters, now managed by group vice presidents and assigned process responsibilities like client acquisition or new planner integration.

Such radical structural change created a sense of ambiguity, and in some cases intense trauma, among AEFA employees upset about losing sales territories and unsure about where their jobs would fit within the newly reengineered company. At the same time, though, AEFA's long history of success helped its workforce accept the new organizational vision and expect continued prosperity. By the middle of 1995, goals of 95 percent client retention and 80 percent planner retention after four years, once seemingly unthinkable, now appeared within reach. Initial customer feedback showed evidence of increasing client satisfaction, and the company's financial planners expressed growing contentment with their jobs in the restructured organization.[1]

---

[1] R. Jacob and R. M. Rao, "The Struggle to Create an Organization for the 21st Century," *Fortune,* April 3, 1995, pp. 90–98.

As indicated by events at AEFA, **organization design**—the process of managing organization structure—has important implications for the competitiveness and continued survival of business organizations. Contemporary managers, whether they are maintaining existing structures or devising new ones, need to know about the different kinds of structures that exist and about the key strengths and weaknesses of each structural type. They must also be able to diagnose and react to the various factors that influence the effectiveness of each type of structure, and they must know how a particular structure matches up with their company's own business situation.

Consequently, in this chapter we present an adaptive model of organization design that provides guidance to managers engaged in structuring modern organizations. After a brief introduction to the idea of an adaptive model, we move on to a discussion of the concept of organizational effectiveness, the ultimate goal of all attempts at managing organizational structure. Then we describe several of the most influential contingency factors that govern the effectiveness of alternative structures. In the process, we identify which of the various structures described in Chapter 11 work best under each of several kinds of business conditions.

An Adaptive Model of Organization Design

Is there a single best form of organizational structure? The fact that many different kinds of structures exist suggests that no one type of structure is suitable for all organizations. Instead, each type of organization structure has unique strengths and weaknesses that make it appropriate for some situations but not for others. Structuring an organization involves making well-considered choices among various alternatives.

Organization design is the process of making these choices. In this process, managers diagnose the situation confronting their organization and select and put in place the structure that seems most appropriate. The process of organization design is consciously adaptive and is guided by the principle that the degree to which a particular type of structure will contribute to the effectiveness of an organization depends on contingency factors that impinge on the organization and shape its business (see Figure 12-1).

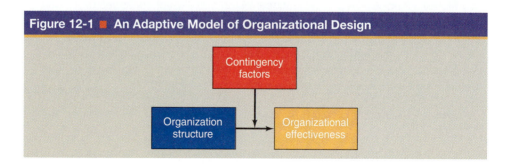

Figure 12-1 ■ An Adaptive Model of Organizational Design

Organizational Effectiveness

Organizational effectiveness, the ultimate aim of organization design, is a measure of an organization's success in achieving its goals and objectives. Goals and objectives might include targets pertaining to profitability, growth, market share, product quality, efficiency, stability, or other similar outcomes.[1] An organization that fails to accomplish its goals is ineffective because it is not fulfilling its purpose.

An effective organization must also satisfy the demands of the various **constituency groups** that provide it with the resources it needs to survive. For example, as Figure 12-2 suggests, if a company satisfies customers' demands for desirable goods or services, it will probably continue to enjoy its customers' patronage. If it satisfies its suppliers' demands for payment in a timely manner, the suppliers will probably continue to provide it with needed raw materials. If it satisfies its employees' demands for fair pay and satisfying work, it will probably be able to retain its workers and recruit new employees. If it satisfies stockholder demands for profitability, it will probably have continued access to equity funding.[2] If a firm fails to satisfy any one of these demands, however, its effectiveness will be weakened because the potential loss of needed resources, such as customers or employees, threatens its survival.

Figure 12-2 ■ Types of Constituency Groups and Their Demands

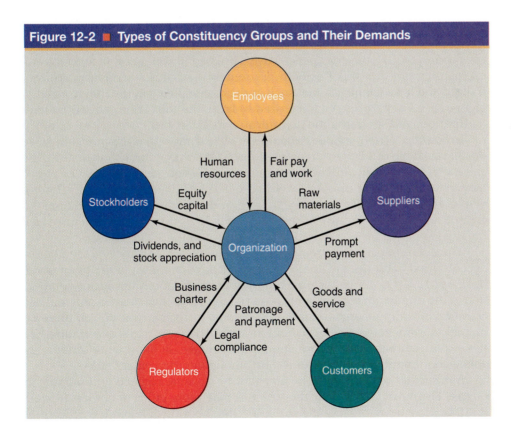

Effectiveness differs from **organizational productivity.** The concept of productivity does not take into account whether a firm is producing the right goods or services.[3] A modern company producing more glass milk bottles than ever before is certainly productive, but it is also ineffective because most milk companies now sell their products in plastic jugs. Effectiveness differs from efficiency, as well. **Organizational efficiency** means minimizing the raw materials and energy consumed by the production of goods and services. It is usually measured as the ratio of inputs consumed to units of output produced, for instance, the number of labor hours required to manufacture a bicycle.[4] Efficiency means doing the job right, whereas effectiveness means doing the right job—producing what ought to be produced in light of the goals, objectives, and constituency demands that influence a company's performance and are its reason for being.

Structural Alternatives

The extent to which an organization is effective is strongly influenced by its structure. For each firm, only one type of structure—whether simple undifferentiated, simple differentiated, functional, divisional, matrix, multiunit, or virtual—will have the greatest positive effect on its ability to attain goals and satisfy constituencies. To clarify the fundamental differences among the various types of structures, alternatives are sometimes classified along a dimension whose values range from "mechanistic" to "organic."[5]

At one extreme, purely **mechanistic structures** are machinelike. They permit workers to complete routine, narrowly defined tasks designed according to the dictates of the efficiency perspective discussed in Chapter 6 in an economical manner, but they lack flexibility. Extremely mechanistic structures are centralized and have tall hierarchies such as the one depicted in the upper panel of Figure 12-3. They are also characterized by large amounts of formalization, standardization, and specialization, as indicated in Table 12-1.

In contrast, purely **organic structures** are like living organisms in that they are flexible and able to adapt to changing external conditions. In such structures, the empowerment and quality perspectives on job design described in Chapter 6 have greater influence on the way tasks are developed and performed, allowing employees more control over their work and affording the organization increased adaptability. Because of their flexibility, however, organic structures lack the single-minded focus required to perform routine work efficiently.

The different parts of extremely organic structures are connected together by decentralized networks, in flat hierarchies like the one shown in the lower panel of Figure 12-3. The emphasis placed on horizontal relationships means a reduction in the number of vertical layers required to process information and manage activities. In addition, organizations with organic structures typically rely more on mutual adjustment than on formalization, standardization, and specialization. For this reason, computerized information networks take on importance as tools enabling coordination and communication among interdependent tasks.

A particular structure may be mechanistic in some respects and organic in others. The more mechanistic the structure, the more efficient but less flexible it will be. The more organic the structure, the more flexible but less efficient it

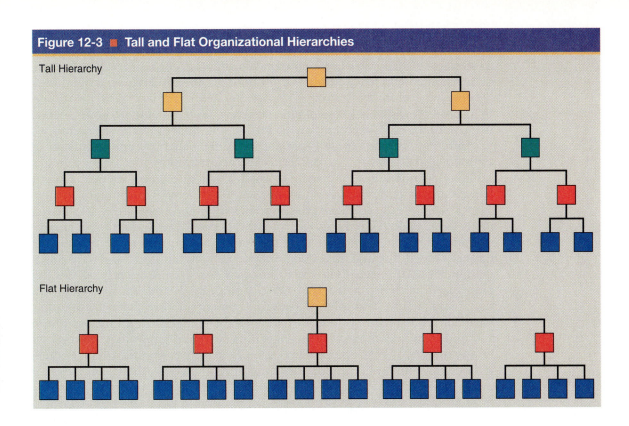

Figure 12-3 ■ Tall and Flat Organizational Hierarchies

Tall Hierarchy

Flat Hierarchy

Table 12-1 ■ Comparison of Mechanistic and Organic Structures

MECHANISTIC STRUCTURES	ORGANIC STRUCTURES
Tasks are highly specialized. It is often not clear to members how their tasks contribute to accomplishing organizational objectives.	Tasks are broad and interdependent. The relation of task performance to attainment of organizational objectives is emphasized.
Tasks remain rigidly defined unless formally altered by top management.	Tasks are continually modified and redefined by means of mutual adjustment on the part of task holders.
Specific roles (rights, duties, technical methods) are defined for each member.	Generalized roles (acceptance of the responsibility for overall task accomplishment) are defined for each member.
Control and authority relationships are structured in a vertical hierarchy.	Control and authority relationships are structured in a network of both vertical and horizontal connections.
Communication is primarily vertical, between superiors and subordinates.	Communication is both vertical and horizontal, depending on where needed information resides.
Communication is mainly in the form of instructions and decisions issued by superiors, performance feedback, and requests for decisions sent from subordinates.	Communication takes the form of information and advice.
Loyalty to the organization and obedience to superiors are insisted upon.	Commitment to organizational goals is more highly valued than is loyalty or obedience.

Source: Based in part on T. Burns and G. M. Stalker, *The Management of Innovation* (London: Tavistock Publications, 1961), pp. 120–22.

will be. These differences in efficiency and flexibility can be traced partly to the mechanisms used to coordinate work activities. As indicated in Chapter 11, standardization incorporates low long-term coordination costs and is thus the basis of mechanistic efficiency. Mutual adjustment, on the other hand, is quite flexible and is therefore the source of organic flexibility. In this regard, the distinction between mechanistic and organic structures exactly parallels the distinction made in Chapter 11 between bureaucratic and nonbureaucratic structures.

Differences in the efficiency and flexibility of mechanistic and organic structures are also attributable to differences in centralization, a characteristic that varies independently of the degree to which a structure is bureaucratic. On one hand, the greater centralization of mechanistic structures encourages efficient specialization, with centralized decision makers gaining ever-growing expertise in decision making. On the other hand, the greater decentralization of organic structures facilitates adaptive responsiveness because decentralized decision makers located throughout an organization can lead its parts in several different directions at once. IBM's recent move to decentralize itself illustrates this point. As formerly organized, IBM was so centralized that decisions about the design, manufacture, and sales of personal computers were made by the same headquarters managers who made decisions about larger mainframe computers and midsize minicomputers. The company's current organization, however, allows managers of IBM's personal computer (PC) lines to refocus PC products without consulting with other parts of the firm or affecting their operations.

Structural Contingencies

In light of the contrasting strengths and weaknesses of different types of structures, it is critically important that managers be able to identify key **structural contingency factors** that help determine whether a particular type of structure will function successfully. These factors make up the situation—both within the organization and in the surrounding environment—that managers must perceive and diagnose correctly in order to design an effective organizational structure.

Maturation Contingencies: Age and Stage of Development

Company age and stage of development are **maturation contingencies** associated with organizational growth. As organizations age and mature, they often grow out of one type of structure and into another.[6] This process can be thought of in terms of the series of developmental stages outlined in Table 12-2.

At the stage of *inception,* one person or a small group of people create an organization and identify the firm's initial purpose. As commitment to this purpose develops, initial planning and implementation bring the firm to life. If the organization proves to be successful initially, it may grow rapidly. As routines emerge, general rules may be invented to preserve customary ways of doing things. However, there is little, if any, formalized coordination. Mutual adjustment or direct supervision usually suffices. Due to these considerations, the or-

Table 12-2 ■ Stages in Organizational Maturation

STAGE	PRIMARY CHARACTERISTICS	STRUCTURAL TYPE
Inception	Determination of firm's purpose Growth of commitment Initial planning and implementation Reliance on mutual adjustment	Prebureaucratic
Formalization	Rapid growth and change Development of routine activities Division of work into functions Systematic evaluation and rewards Formal planning and goal setting Emphasis on efficiency, stability	Bureaucratic (functional)
Elaboration	Search for new opportunities Diversification, decentralization Maturation and continued growth	Bureaucratic (divisional)
Transformation	Large size, either real or virtual Flattened organization hierarchy Massive change and complexity Emphasis on flexibility	Postbureaucratic

ganization takes on one of the prebureaucratic forms of structure, either simple undifferentiated or simple differentiated, depending on the effects of other contingency factors discussed later in this chapter.

During the second developmental stage, that of *formalization,* work is divided into different functional areas, systematic evaluation and reward procedures are developed, and the organization's direction is determined through formal planning and goal setting. As the organization continues to grow, professional managers first supplement and then replace the firm's owners, becoming the day-to-day bosses who run the company, and decision making is increasingly centralized. Management emphasizes efficiency and stability, and work becomes routine as tasks are designed in accordance with the efficiency perspective on job design. In the process, formalization and standardization become the means by which coordination is developed and implemented. As a consequence, the organization's structure becomes bureaucratic, and typically functional.

To adapt to changing conditions and to pursue continued growth, a firm that has progressed to the third stage, *elaboration,* seeks out new product, location, or client opportunities. As the company's business diversifies, its centralized management loses the ability to coordinate work activities, and a need develops for decentralization and divisional departmentalization. If the firm continues to mature even further, continued growth and diversification may require yet more structural elaboration. Although the company's structure remains bureaucratic, management must consider reliance on mutual adjustment, no matter how costly, to cope with the firm's greater complexity or with its need for greater flexibility. The empowerment perspective begins to affect job design at this point, as standardization fades in importance and employees gain greater control over their work. Whether the specific type of structure possessed by the firm will be divisional or matrix depends on the effects of other contingency factors.

Finally, an organization that has advanced to the fourth developmental stage, that of *transformation,* finds itself confronted by extremes of both change and complexity in its business situation. To compete, the company enters into the process of mass customization, wherein it relies on skilled teams and advanced technologies to tailor mass-produced goods or services to the unique demands of different clientele.[7] The quality perspective on job design is fully apparent at this stage of development. Mutual adjustment and decentralization are used together as autonomous teams manage themselves and coordinate with one another by sharing information on computerized networks. The pyramidal hierarchy developed during the stages of formalization and elaboration is transformed into a flattened horizontal structure of process flows and peer relationships. These flows and relationships may be wholly contained within the organization itself, or they may extend outward and into other firms. The organization adopts a postbureaucratic structure, either multiunit or virtual, depending on the influence of additional contingency factors discussed later.

The four-stage maturation model just described suggests that as older organizations grow more complex, so do their structures and the jobs within them. It is important to note that not every organization progresses through every developmental stage. For instance, a family-owned convenience store might never grow beyond the stage of inception. Such notable companies as Apple Computer and Coca-Cola have yet to grow beyond elaboration. In addition, some companies leapfrog over one or more stages as they develop, starting out with formalization or elaboration, or moving directly from inception to transformation. Not every company starts small, nor do all firms invest in bureaucracy.

Nonetheless, the fact remains that with increasing age comes a tendency to progress from prebureaucratic structures developed during the stage of inception, to bureaucratic structures developed during formalization and elaboration, and then to postbureaucratic structures developed during transformation. As an organization advances through this sequence of stages and structures, its management faces a progression of different contingency factors. This progression is the focus of the remainder of this chapter.

Inception Contingencies

Organizations at the developmental stage of inception are typically new, small, and fairly simple in form. Thus they are most likely to have prebureaucratic structures. It follows that the organization design choice confronting managers concerns which prebureaucratic structure to adopt—simple undifferentiated or simple differentiated. Both alternatives are relatively organic, despite the ownership-related direct supervision and vertical specialization found in simple differentiated structures. Due to this general similarity, considerations regarding trade-offs between mechanistic efficiency and organic flexibility have little importance here. Instead, the choice between the two prebureaucratic structures is influenced by the contingency factors of organization size and ownership norms.

Organization Size

Organization size can be defined in terms of the number of members in an organization; the organization's volume of sales, clients, or profits; its physical capacity (e.g., a hospital's number of beds or a hotel's number of rooms); or the total financial assets it controls.[8] For present purposes, size is considered to be the number of members, or employees, within the organization, thus, the number of people whose activities must be integrated and coordinated.

Defined in this manner, the size of an organization affects the organization's structure mainly by determining which of the three coordination mechanisms—mutual adjustment, direct supervision, or standardization—is most appropriate to serve as the primary means of coordination in the organization. As indicated in Chapter 11, in extremely small organizations of 12 or fewer people, mutual adjustment alone can provide adequate coordination without incurring overwhelming process loss. However, if more than about a dozen people try to coordinate by means of mutual adjustment alone, so much process loss occurs that performance declines substantially. Thus, the activities of larger numbers of people—30, 40, or 50—are better coordinated by direct supervision, because supervision reduces the number of coordination linkages that must be maintained. In even larger organizations, direct supervision succumbs to information overload, and standardization must be implemented in its place to reduce information-processing demands and sustain coordinated efforts.

This relationship between organization size and coordination mechanism has especially strong contingency effects on choices between the two prebureaucratic structural alternatives. Simple undifferentiated structures, coordinated solely by means of mutual adjustment, can be used to effectively integrate the people and tasks that make up small organizations. Simple differentiated structures, with their reliance on direct supervision, become the necessary choice for organizations that grow in size beyond a dozen or so individuals. For managers of small organizations who must choose among alternative prebureaucratic structures, organization size influences structural choice and effectiveness through its effects on coordination.

Ownership Norms

The **ownership norms** that reside in the national culture surrounding an organization can also have significant effects on choices among prebureaucratic structures. Some national cultures, such as those in countries located throughout North America and Western Europe, favor capitalist forms of organization in which private ownership is common and owners' rights to retain profits are widely approved. In other cultures, private ownership and the personal accumulation of wealth are not as readily accepted. For instance, in Israeli kibbutzim (see Chapter 14), kibbutzniks are not supposed to claim private ownership of items other than those needed for reasons of personal health and security. Instead, ownership of kibbutz property is either disavowed or attributed to the kibbutz as a whole.[9]

Ownership norms influence choices among prebureaucratic structures by determining whether the alternative of a simple differentiated structure is even considered. If private ownership is permitted, choices can be made between simple undifferentiated and simple differentiated structures. In capitalist societies, cultural tendencies may favor the unambiguous ownership status afforded by simple differentiated structures, although nothing forbids the emergence of unowned or collectively owned simple undifferentiated structures. If, however, a society's cultural norms prohibit private ownership, then only the simple undifferentiated structure can be considered. Simple differentiated structures cannot emerge where ownership is not allowed.

Formalization and Elaboration Contingencies

As an organization grows beyond a membership of 50 people or so, simple undifferentiated structures and simple differentiated structures become overwhelmed by coordination requirements. As the primary means of coordination, mutual adjustment becomes extremely expensive, and direct supervision is bogged down by growing information-processing needs. As a consequence, standardization assumes the role of primary coordination mechanism. For this reason, organizations that have progressed beyond the stage of inception and outgrown prebureaucratic structures must consider the adoption of more bureaucratic forms of structure.

Relative to prebureaucratic structures, all bureaucratic structures are more mechanistic and, thus, more standardized and centralized. However, there are notable differences among the three types of bureaucratic structures, as well. Functional structures are the most mechanistic, due to their standardization and centralization. Divisional structures are substantially less mechanistic, because of their noticeably greater decentralization. Matrix structures are even less mechanistic, and therefore more organic, due to their reliance on mutual adjustment among the managers of matrix cells.

As a result of these differences, for managers trying to decide which bureaucratic structure to implement, the trade-off between mechanistic efficiency and organic flexibility plays a major role in shaping structural choices. In relation to this trade-off, the most influential contingency factors at the formalization and elaboration stages of development are the organization's core technology and the environment that surrounds the firm.[10]

Core Technology

An organization's **technology** consists of the knowledge, procedures, and equipment used to transform unprocessed resources into finished goods or services.[11] **Core technology** is a more specific term pertaining to the dominant technology used in performing work at the base of the organization. Core technologies are found in the automotive assembly lines at GM, Ford, and Chrysler; in the fast-food kitchens at McDonald's, Burger King, and Wendy's; in the employment and job-training offices in state and federal agencies; and in the reactor buildings where electricity is generated at nuclear power plants. This section introduces two contingency models that focus on differences in core technology, the Woodward manufacturing model and the Thompson service model. Both propose that core technology influences the effectiveness of an organization by placing certain coordination requirements on its structure, and that some of these requirements push toward mechanistic efficiency whereas others pull in the direction of organic flexibility.

Woodward's Manufacturing Technologies. Joan Woodward, a British researcher who started studying organizations in the early 1950s, was one of the first proponents of the view that an organization's technology can have tremendous impact on structural effectiveness.[12] She began her work by studying 100 British manufacturing firms, examining their organizational structures and their relative efficiency and success in the marketplace. Analyzing her data, she discovered that not all companies that had the same type of structure were equally effective. Theorizing that these differences in effectiveness might be traced to differences in core technologies, Woodward devised a classification scheme of three basic types of manufacturing technology: small-batch production, mass production, and continuous process production. When she tested her theory by reanalyzing data from the 100 firms, she found evidence to support it.

Small-batch production (also called unit production) is a technology for the manufacture of one-of-a-kind items or small quantities of goods designed to meet unique customer specifications. Such items range from specialized electronic instruments, weather satellites, and space shuttles to custom-tailored clothing and handmade leather sandals. To make this kind of product, craftspeople work alone or in small, close-knit groups. Because customer specifications often change from one order to another, it is almost impossible to predict what will be required on the next job. Thus, the work in firms using small-batch technologies varies in an unpredictable way.

It is this unpredictability that fuels the effect of small-batch technologies on organizational structures and effectiveness. Unpredictability impedes planning and therefore makes it difficult to coordinate by means of standardization. It is impossible to plan legitimate standards for use in a future that cannot be foreseen. Instead, employees must decide for themselves how to perform their jobs. When employees work alone, they are guided by their own expertise and by customer specifications. When employees work in groups, they coordinate with one another by means of mutual adjustment.

Woodward found that the role played by mutual adjustment in coordinating small-batch production was pivotal. Her research showed that among organizations using this type of technology, firms with organic structures were significantly more likely to be successful than companies with mechanistic structures. Of the three types of bureaucratic structures likely to be adopted during the developmental stages of formalization and elaboration, Woodward's findings would seem to indicate that the matrix structure, itself a massive lateral linkage mechanism, is the most suitable alternative for organizations based on small-batch technologies.

However, it is also true that the other lateral linkage mechanisms described in Chapter 10—liaison positions, representative groups, and integrating managers—can be positioned in functional and divisional structures to increase mutual adjustment and introduce greater flexibility. In this way, otherwise mechanistic structures can be made at least modestly organic. Thus, it follows that functional or divisional structures with extensive lateral linkages can also prove effective when paired with small-batch technology. As with all other technology-based decisions regarding organization structure, which one of this reduced set of structural alternatives is best suited to the needs of a particular organization becomes clearer after consideration of the environmental contingencies discussed later in this section.

In Woodward's second type of technology, *mass production* (also referred to as large-batch production), the same product is produced repeatedly, either in large batches or in long production runs. For instance, rather than producing a few copies of this book each time an order was received, Prentice Hall initially printed thousands of copies at the same time and warehoused them to fill incoming orders. Other examples of mass production range from word-processing pools in which midterm examinations are consolidated and typed in large batches, to car-manufacturing operations in which thousands of Ford Escorts are made on an assembly line that remains virtually unchanged for years at a time.

As these examples suggest, work in mass-production facilities is intentionally repetitive and remains so over the course of extended periods of time. Employees perform the same jobs over and over. They know that the work they will do tomorrow will be the same as the work done today. This stability facilitates planning and formalization. As a result, the company is likely to use standardization to reduce the long-term costs of coordination. Woodward's research revealed that mass-production firms with mechanistic structures were far more likely to be effective than those with organic structures. Functional or divisional structures are thus better able to enhance effectiveness in these firms than are more organic alternatives.

In the third type of technology identified in Woodward's research, *continuous process production,* automated equipment makes the same product in the same way for an indefinite period of time. At Phillips Petroleum, one refinery makes nothing but gasoline, another refines motor oil, and a third produces only diesel fuel. The equipment used in this type of technology is designed to produce one product and cannot readily be used for any other. There is no starting and stopping once the equipment has been installed. Machines in continuous process facilities perform the same tasks without interruption.

Of the three types of technology discussed so far, continuous process production involves the most routine work. Few changes, if any, occur in production processes even over the course of many years. Thus it seems logical to assume that organizations using continuous process production would be most effective if structured along mechanistic lines. Interestingly, however, closer examination reveals that few, if any, of the people involved in continuous process production perform routine, repetitive jobs. Machines perform these jobs instead. The people are technicians, who monitor production equipment, watching dials and gauges, checking machinery, and inspecting finished goods, and who deal with the problems that arise when this equipment fails to function properly. Although some of these problems occur again and again and can be planned for in advance, a significant number are emergencies that have never happened before and cannot be anticipated.

Some of the most critical work performed by people in continuous process production technologies is therefore highly unpredictable. As a result, standardization is not feasible. Mutual adjustment, sometimes in conjunction with direct supervision, is the dominant mode of coordination. Technicians who oversee production equipment manage unusual events by conferring with each other and devising solutions to emergencies as they arise. It is not surprising that Woodward found that firms using continuous process production technologies were most effective when structured organically. Laterally linked functional or divisional structures, or matrix structures are the most likely to encourage effectiveness for such firms.

Since Woodward's studies, advances in computers, robotics, and automation have helped create another type of manufacturing technology, *flexible cell production*. As was described in Chapter 6, in this type of production system, computer-controlled production machines in a group, or cell, are connected by a flexible network of conveyors that can be rapidly reconfigured to adapt the cell for different production tasks. This technology is used mainly to produce a wide variety of machined-metal parts such as pistons for car engines and parts for the lock on the front door of your home. Conceivably, however, it could be used to make virtually any kind of product.

As is the case in continuous process production, work in flexible cells is performed by automated equipment. The only people involved are technicians who monitor the equipment and handle problems. But whereas continuous process production facilities can make only a single product, flexible cells can make many different things. In this respect, flexible cell production resembles small-batch production. It is an efficient method of producing one-of-a-kind items or small quantities of similar items built to satisfy unique customer specifications.

Inasmuch as Woodward found mutual adjustment to be the most effective coordination mechanism for both continuous process and small-batch production technologies, an organic structure would seem most suitable for a firm using flexible cell production. Indeed, a study of 110 manufacturing firms in New Jersey revealed a significant positive relationship between organic structuring and the effectiveness of organizations with flexible cells.[13] This information updates Woodward's research, suggesting that companies employing flexible cell technologies are likely to be more effective if they adopt laterally linked functional or divisional structures, or matrix structures to coordinate work activities.

Thompson's Service Technologies. Because Woodward focused her research solely on manufacturing firms, her contingency model is applicable only to technologies used to produce tangible goods. Today, however, firms that provide services like telephone communications, appliance repair, or vacation planning make up an increasingly critical element of the U.S. economy as well as the economies of other nations. Thus, another contingency model, developed by James D. Thompson, is also quite useful because it examines technologies often employed in service organizations. These technologies, diagrammed in Figure 12-4, are mediating technology, long-linked technology, and intensive technology.[14] In this figure, rectangles represent work groups or organizations, circles represent employees, and arrows represent flows of work.

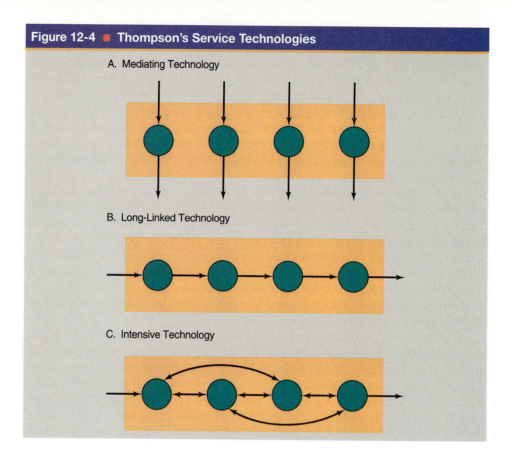

Figure 12-4 ■ Thompson's Service Technologies

A. Mediating Technology

B. Long-Linked Technology

C. Intensive Technology

A *mediating technology* provides services that link clients together. For example, banks connect depositors who have money to invest with borrowers who need loans; insurance companies enable their clients to pool risks, permitting one person's losses to be covered by joint investments; and telephone companies provide the equipment and technical assistance people need to talk with each other from separate locations.

When mediating technology is used to provide a service, employees usually serve each client individually. As shown in Figure 12-4A, bank tellers and workers in other mediating technology settings normally perform their jobs without assistance from others in their organization. Assuming adequate training, a single bank teller can handle a deposit or withdrawal without requiring help from other tellers. The single teller and other workers, however, may share equipment, such as the central computer that keeps track of all bank transactions.

Although individual employees work independently in a company using a mediating technology, many perform the same job. Coordination is needed in such firms to make sure that workers provide consistently high-quality service and offer the same basic service to each client. Thus, managers in service firms develop lists of the different types of clients their organization is likely to serve and devise a particular standard operating procedure to be followed while serving each type of client. For example, a bank teller will follow one procedure while serving a client who is making a savings account deposit, another procedure when waiting on a client who is making a loan payment, and yet a third when helping a client open a new checking account. This standardization of work processes, or behaviors, means that firms using mediating technologies are most likely to have mechanistic structures. Either functional or divisional structures are suitable for such organizations.

Thompson's second type of technology, *long-linked technology,* is analogous to Woodward's mass-production technology. Both refer to sequential chains of simplified tasks. A service sector example of this type of technology is seen in the state employment agency that requires all clients to follow the same lockstep procedures. Each client moves along an "assembly line" starting with registration and progressing through assessment, counseling, training, and placement activities. The sequential movement from one station to the next that characterizes long-linked technology is diagrammed in Figure 12-4B.

Like firms that use mass-production technology, those that use long-linked technology coordinate by means of standardization. According to Thompson, the effectiveness of a firm using long-linked technology is likely to be enhanced by mechanistic structuring. This suggests that long-linked technology is most effectively paired with functional or divisional structures.

Intensive technology, the third type of technology in Thompson's model, consists of work processes whose configuration may change as employees receive feedback from the clients they serve. The specific assortment of services to be rendered to a particular patient in a hospital, for example, depends on the symptoms the patient exhibits. A patient entering the hospital's emergency room complaining of chest pains may be rushed to a cardiac care unit. A patient with a broken arm may be shuttled to the radiology lab for an x-ray and then back to the emergency room for splinting. A third patient with uncertain symptoms may be checked into a room for further observation and testing (see Figure 12-4C).

To fit itself to the needs of each client, a firm using intensive technology must be able to reorganize itself again and again. Above all, it must have flexibility. Moreover, because the needs of future clients cannot be foretold, the work of such a firm is too unpredictable to be successfully formalized. Both the need for flexibility and unpredictability require the use of mutual adjustment as a coordinating mechanism. Thus, firms using intensive technology will be best served by laterally linked functional or divisional structures, or matrix structures.

Technological Contingencies: Integration.   The Woodward and Thompson models just described help identify which organization structure is most likely to enhance the effectiveness of a firm using a specific type of technology. As indicated in Table 12-3, standardization and mechanistic structuring generally enhance the effectiveness of firms using technologies suited to routine work—mass-production, mediating, and long-linked technologies. Mutual adjustment and organic structuring, on the other hand, promote effectiveness in firms that use technologies suited to unpredictable, often rapidly changing requirements—small-batch, continuous process, flexible cell, and intensive technologies.[15]

Table 12-3 ■ Technological Contingencies

INDUSTRY TYPE	TECHNOLOGY	STRUCTURAL CATEGORY	STRUCTURAL TYPES	EXAMPLE
Manufacturing	Small batch	Organic	Laterally linked functional or divisional, matrix	Scientific instrument fabricator
	Mass	Mechanistic	Functional, divisional	Television manufacturer
	Continuous process	Organic	Laterally linked functional or divisional, matrix	Petroleum refinery
	Flexible cell	Organic	Laterally linked functional or divisional, matrix	Auto parts supplier
Service	Mediating	Mechanistic	Functional, divisional	Bank
	Long linked	Mechanistic	Functional, divisional	Cafeteria
	Intensive	Organic	Laterally-linked functional or divisional, matrix	Hospital

The External Environment

An organization's **environment** consists of everything outside the organization. Suppliers, customers, and competitors are part of an organization's environment, as are the governmental bodies that regulate its business, the financial institutions and investors that grant it funding, and the labor market that provides it with employees. In addition, general factors such as the economic, geographic, and political conditions that impinge on the firm are part of its environment. Central to this definition is the idea that the term *environment* refers to things external to the firm.[16] The internal "environment" of a firm, more appropriately called the company's culture, is distinctly different and will be discussed in Chapter 13.

As a structural contingency factor affecting organizations in the stages of formalization and elaboration, the environment influences effectiveness by placing certain coordination and information-processing requirements on the firm (see box). Five specific environmental characteristics influencing structural effectiveness are environmental change, complexity, uncertainty, receptivity, and diversity.

Environmental Change. **Environmental change** concerns the extent to which conditions in an organization's environment change unpredictably. At one extreme, an environment is stable if it does not change at all or if it changes only in cyclical, predictable ways. An example of a stable environment is the one that surrounds many of the small firms in Amish communities throughout the midwestern United States. Amish religious beliefs require the rejection of modern conveniences, such as automobiles, televisions, and gasoline-powered farm

Enacting a Favorable Environment

Sometimes environmental coordination and information-processing requirements are as much the consequence of an organization's actions as they are the result of unchanging external forces. Consider the happy plight of Levi's, the San Francisco–based manufacturer of casual clothing. Following a 1992 study commissioned by the company that found that businesses were growing increasingly receptive to casual attire in the office, Levi's began a direct mail campaign to corporate human resource directors in which it pitched the company's Dockers brand as a fashionable yet relaxed alternative to the traditional dresses-and-suits code of attire. As a follow-up, Levi's shot a "how to dress business casual" video, which it distributed to over 7,000 companies, and began conducting fashion seminars for various corporations and trade associations in the United States and Canada.

Once dependent on the faddish market for denim jeans and accessories, Levi's is now a major player in the comparatively more stable market for office apparel. Organizations as diverse as Charles Schwab and Company, Nationwide Insurance, and The New England Employee Benefits Council have sent employees to Levi's presentations, and Levi's has built a database of attendees for use in future promotions. The company's earnings are up by more than 32 percent, in an industry that is otherwise languishing. And Dockers shops are sprouting up in regional malls and outlet centers to respond to rapidly growing demand. In the terminology of noted organization theorist Karl Weick, Levi's is "enacting" an environment that will favor the company for years to come.[1]

[1] L. Himelstein and N. Walster, "Levi's versus the Dress Code," *Business Week,* April 1, 1996, pp. 57–58; and K. Weick, *The Social Psychology of Organizing,* 2d ed. (Reading, MA: Addison-Wesley, 1979).

equipment. So Amish blacksmiths, carpenters, farmers, and livestock breeders have conducted business in much the same way for generations. Another stable environment surrounds firms that sell Christmas trees. The retail market for cut evergreen trees is predictably strong in November and December but weak at other times of the year.

At the other extreme, an environment is dynamic when it changes over time in an unpredictable manner. Because the popular style of dress changes so frequently in North America, the environment surrounding companies in the fashion industry is quite dynamic. Similarly, the environment surrounding companies in the consumer electronics industry has changed dramatically. New products, such as caller-identification telephones, Watchman televisions, and portable digital assistants (PDAs) have created entirely new markets. Older products have been redesigned to incorporate advanced computer microchips, color digital displays, infrared remote controls, and similar technological breakthroughs.

Environmental change affects the structure of an organization by influencing the predictability of the firm's work and, therefore, the method of coordination that should be used to integrate work activities.[17] Stability allows managers to complete the planning needed to formalize organizational activities. Firms operating in stable environments can use standardization as their primary coordination mechanism and will typically elect to do so to reduce long-term coordination costs. Mechanistic structures—functional or divisional—are the most likely to prove effective for such firms.

In dynamic environments, it is difficult to establish formal rules and procedures. In fact, it is useless for managers to try to plan for a future they cannot foresee. Members of an organization facing a dynamic environment must adapt to changing conditions instead of relying on inflexible, standardized operating procedures. Dynamism in the environment leaves management with little choice but to rely on mutual adjustment as a primary coordination mechanism. The organic structuring of laterally linked functional or divisional structures or of matrix structures is therefore appropriate.

Environmental Complexity.   **Environmental complexity** is the degree to which an organization's environment is complicated and therefore difficult to understand. A simple environment is composed of relatively few component parts, for example, suppliers, competitors, and types of customers. There is not much in such an environment that can affect organizational performance. A locally owned gas station does business in a relatively simple environment. It orders most of its supplies from a single petroleum distributor, does business almost exclusively with customers who want to buy gasoline or oil for their cars, and must pay attention to the competitive activities of only a fairly small number of nearby stations. On the other hand, a complex environment consists of a large number of component parts. The environments of automotive manufacturers like Chrysler are extremely complex, including an enormous number of suppliers, many different types of customers, and scores of foreign and domestic competitors.

Complexity influences structural effectiveness by affecting the amount of knowledge and information people must process to understand the environment and cope with its demands.[18] Consider an inexpensive digital watch. If you took this watch apart, you would probably not have much trouble putting it back together again, because it has very few parts—a computer chip programmed to keep time, a digital liquid crystal face, a battery, and a case. With only a few minutes of practice or simple instructions, you could quickly learn to assemble this watch. Now suppose you had the pieces of a Rolex watch spread out before you. Could you reassemble the watch? Probably not, because it is made up of hundreds of springs, screws, gears, and other parts. Learning to assemble a Rolex properly would require extensive training and a lot of practice.

Similarly, the organization facing a simple environment—one with few "parts"—can understand environmental events and meet the challenges they pose using a minimal amount of knowledge and processing little new information. A local restaurant that is losing business can determine the reason for its plight simply by telephoning a few prospective customers and asking them for their comments. However, organizations in complex environments—environments with many parts—must draw on a considerable store of knowledge and process an overwhelming amount of information to understand environmental events. To find the reason for its loss of market share at various times, Chrysler Corporation has analyzed competitors' marketing strategies and performed extensive market studies of consumer preferences. To recapture market share, Chrysler has also worked with hundreds of suppliers to increase the quality and reduce the cost of the parts used to produce its cars.[19]

Environmental complexity affects organizational structure by influencing the suitability of centralized decision making. As indicated in Chapter 11, in centralization, decision making is limited to a select group of top managers. Centralization thus minimizes the number of people available to digest information and determine its meaning. Because simple environments require little information processing, organizations operating in such environments can be centralized and function quite effectively.

However, because environmental complexity requires the ability to process and understand large amounts of information, centralized organizations in complex environments can suffer the effects of information overload. One way to cope with this information overload is to invest in computerized information systems. However, the usual net effect of such an investment is actually to *increase* the amount of environmental information known to be available, thus contributing to *additional* information overload. Another, more successful way to deal with the problem of information overload due to environmental complexity is to involve more individuals in information-processing activities. Thus, organizations like Chrysler that are attempting to cope with complex environments often decentralize decision making. That way, they include more people—more brains—in the process of digesting and interpreting information.

Environmental Uncertainty.   In addition to pointing out distinctive environmental differences, the two environmental dimensions of change and complexity also combine in the manner shown in Figure 12-5 to create yet another important environmental characteristic—**environmental uncertainty.** Uncertainty reflects the absence of information about environmental factors, activities, and events.[20] It undermines an organization's ability to manage current circumstances and plan for the future. To cope with uncertainty, organizations try to find better ways of acquiring information about the environment. This effort often involves the creation of boundary-spanning positions that can strengthen the information linkage between an organization and its environment.[21]

A **boundary spanner** is a member or unit of an organization that interacts with people or firms in the organization's environment.[22] Salespeople who have contact with customers, purchasing departments that deal with suppliers of raw materials, and top managers who represent their company to outsiders are all boundary spanners. In boundary-spanning roles, employees or units

- Monitor the environment for information that is relevant to the organization
- Serve as gatekeepers, simplifying incoming information and ensuring that it is routed to the appropriate people in the firm
- Warn the organization of environmental threats and initiate activities that protect it from them
- Represent the organization to other individuals or firms in its environment, providing them with information about the organization
- Negotiate with other organizations to acquire raw materials and sell finished goods or services
- Coordinate any other activities that require the cooperation of two or more firms.[23]

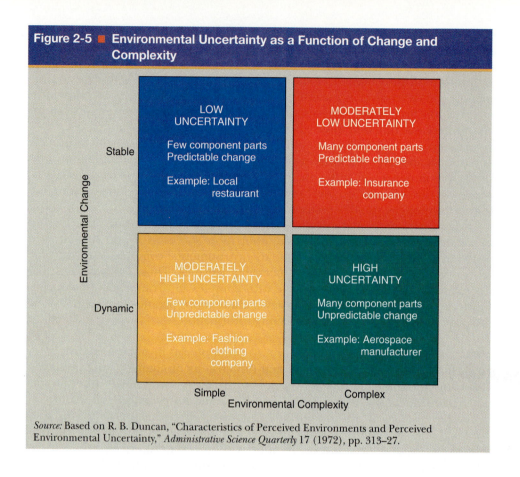

Figure 2-5 ■ **Environmental Uncertainty as a Function of Change and Complexity**

	Simple	**Complex**
Stable	**LOW UNCERTAINTY** Few component parts Predictable change Example: Local restaurant	**MODERATELY LOW UNCERTAINTY** Many component parts Predictable change Example: Insurance company
Dynamic	**MODERATELY HIGH UNCERTAINTY** Few component parts Unpredictable change Example: Fashion clothing company	**HIGH UNCERTAINTY** Many component parts Unpredictable change Example: Aerospace manufacturer

Environmental Change (vertical axis) · Environmental Complexity (horizontal axis)

Source: Based on R. B. Duncan, "Characteristics of Perceived Environments and Perceived Environmental Uncertainty," *Administrative Science Quarterly* 17 (1972), pp. 313–27.

When successful, these activities enable boundary spanners to provide their organization with information about its environment that can help make change and complexity more understandable.

Environmental Receptivity. **Environmental receptivity,** which ranges from munificent to hostile, is the degree to which an organization's environment supports the organization's progress toward fulfilling its purpose. A munificent environment is one in which a firm is able to acquire the raw materials, employees, technology, and capital resources needed to perform productively.[24] In such an environment, the firm finds a receptive market for its products. Its competitors, if any, do not threaten its existence. Regulatory bodies do not try to impede its progress. Thus, for example, the environment surrounding the McDonald's fast-food chain at the time of its founding was munificent. Few other fast-food franchises existed, labor was fairly plentiful in the post–Korean War era, and a convenience-minded middle class was emerging throughout North America.

In a hostile environment, the opposite situation occurs. An organization may have great difficulty acquiring, or may be unable to acquire, needed resources, employees, knowledge, or money. The firm's future may also be threatened by customer disinterest, intense competition, or severe regulation. For instance, the Phillip-Morris Company and other members of the tobacco industry have had to cope with extreme hostility due to widespread concerns about negative health effects of smoking. During the early 1990s, U.S. defense contractors faced similar hostility as the cold war ended and the demand for defense weaponry dropped off.[25]

Environmental hostility, though normally temporary, represents a crisis that must be dealt with quickly and effectively if the firm is to survive. An organization facing such hostility either finds a way to deal with it—for example, by substituting one raw material for another, marketing a new product, or lobbying against threatening regulations—or ceases to exist. Thus, Phillip-Morris has contributed to the campaign funds of politicians known to be against the passage of antismoking laws, and defense contractors have sought federal funds to convert to peacetime manufacturing.

To deal with the crisis of a hostile environment, firms that are normally decentralized in response to environmental complexity may centralize decision making for a limited period of time.[26] This temporary centralization facilitates crisis management. Because centralization reduces the number of people who must be consulted to make a decision, it allows the organization to respond to threatening conditions more quickly. It is important to emphasize that centralization established in response to a hostile environment should remain in effect only so long as the hostility persists. When the threat is over, a firm dealing with a complex environment will perform effectively again only if it reinstates decentralized decision making.

Environmental Diversity. **Environmental diversity** refers to the number of distinct **environmental domains** served by an organization. A firm in a uniform environment serves a single type of customer, provides a single kind of product, and conducts its business in a single geographic location. Thus, it serves only a single domain. A campus nightclub, for example, that caters to the entertainment needs of local college students operates in a uniform environment. So does a building-materials firm whose sole product is concrete, which it sells only to local contractors. In contrast, an organization in a diverse environment produces an assortment of products, serves various types of customers, or has offices or other facilities in several geographic locations. It does business in several different domains. IBM, for instance, sells computers to businesses, universities, and the general public. General Electric handles durable consumer goods, financial services, jet engines, and locomotives. Ford Motor Company markets cars in North America, South America, Europe, and Asia.

Environmental diversity affects an organization by influencing the amount of diversity that must be built into its structure.[27] In organizations with uniform environments, managers can use functional departmentation to group units together. Because firms in uniform environments face only a single domain, they must concern themselves only with information about a single kind of environment, and they need react to only a single set of environmental events. Functional departmentation, which facilitates this sort of unified information processing and response, is sufficient in such situations.

The absence of environmental diversity permits the firm to operate effectively without significant internal diversification.

In organizations with diverse environments, however, management must use divisional departmentation so as to gather work associated with each product, customer, or location into its own self-contained division. Companies in diverse environments face a number of distinct domains and must acquire information about each in order to cope with its particular demands. Divisional departmentation allows these firms to keep track of each domain separately and respond to the demands of one domain without regard for the others. If managers did not structure the firm along these lines, work on one product could get in the way of work on other products; services rendered to one type of customer could detract from services provided to other types of customers; or operations at one location could impede operations at other locations.

Environmental Contingencies: Integration.   As we have just indicated, organizational environments have five distinct characteristics—change, complexity, uncertainty, receptivity, and diversity. Diagnosing the nature of a firm's environment during the process of organization design requires that managers do five environmental analyses more or less simultaneously. The decision tree shown in Figure 12-6 can help guide this process. If you trace through the branches of this tree as you answer each of the four questions, you will be led to an organizational structure suited for the environment you are diagnosing.

Each question deals with one of the environmental characteristics just examined. Note that it is not necessary to ask a separate question about uncertainty. Because environmental uncertainty represents a combination of change and complexity, it is assessed implicitly by the answers to questions 1 and 2.

1. Is the environment stable or dynamic? The answer to this question identifies the amount of change in the environment and helps to determine whether standardization or mutual adjustment is likely to be the more effective coordination mechanism for the firm under analysis. Stable environments either do not change or change in a predictable, cyclical manner and thus allow the use of standardization. Dynamic environments change in unpredictable ways and require mutual adjustment as a result.
2. Is the environment simple or complex? Here the answer will be an assessment of environmental complexity and will indicate whether centralization or decentralization is more appropriate for the firm. Simple environments are easy to figure out and allow centralization. Complex environments require a great deal of information processing and therefore exert pressure toward decentralization.
3. Is the environment munificent or hostile? This question is relevant only if an organization has a complex environment and is thus decentralized. How it is answered gauges environmental receptivity and indicates whether temporary centralization is necessary. Munificent environments are resource rich and allow continued decentralization, but hostile environments are resource poor and stimulate crises that mandate temporary centralization.
4. Is the environment uniform or diverse? In response to this question, a manager must evaluate environmental diversity so as to determine what form of

Figure 12-6 ■ Environmental Contingencies Decision Tree

Figure 12-6 ■ Environmental Contingencies Decision Tree

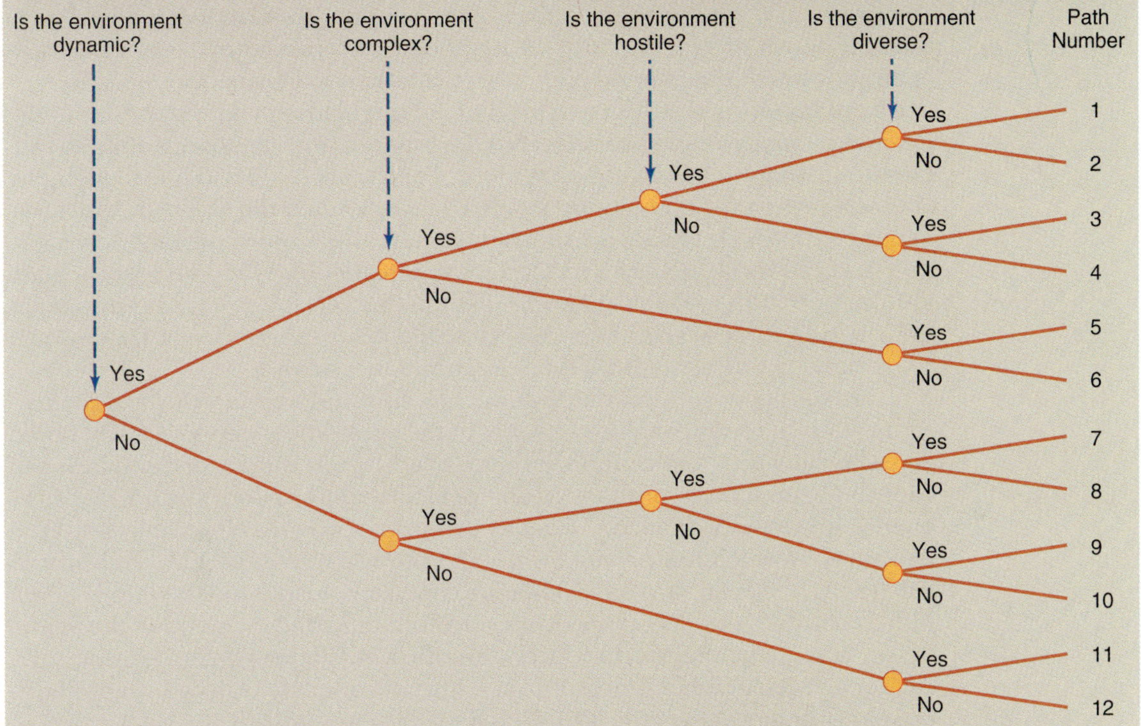

Is the environment dynamic?	Is the environment complex?	Is the environment hostile?	Is the environment diverse?	Path Number

Yes — 1
No — 2
Yes — 3
No — 4
Yes — 5
No — 6
Yes — 7
No — 8
Yes — 9
No — 10
Yes — 11
No — 12

Path Number	Structural Alternatives	Path Number	Structural Alternatives
1	Divisional with lateral linkages, or matrix; temporarily centralized; extensive boundary spanning	5	Divisional with lateral linkages
2	Functional with lateral linkages, or matrix; temporary centralization; extensive boundary spanning	6	Functional with lateral linkages
		7	Divisional; temporary centralization
3	Divisional with lateral linkages, or matrix; extensive boundary spanning	8	Functional
		9	Divisional
4	Functional with lateral linkages, or matrix; extensive boundary spanning	10	Functional
		11	Simple or divisional, depending on size
		12	Simple or functional, depending on size

departmentation to use. Environmental uniformity allows the structural uniformity of functional departmentation. Environmental diversity requires the structural diversity of divisional departmentation.

Transformation Contingencies

Transition beyond bureaucratic structuring is caused by the fact that formalization, standardization, and specialization intended to stimulate efficient performance can, in some instances, actually reduce efficiency and productivity. This reduction can occur for several reasons. For example, the very existence of bureaucratic rules can encourage the practice of following them to the letter. Some employees may interpret rules that were intended to describe minimally acceptable levels of performance as describing the maximum level of performance for which they should aim. As a result, their performance may suffer.

In addition, rigid adherence to rules and regulations can discourage initiative and creativity among workers, and the organization can lose its ability to anticipate or adapt to changing conditions. For instance, rules requiring lengthy approval reviews for even minor design changes limited the ability of U.S. firms to improve existing products or introduce new ones in the consumer electronics market of the 1980s. As a result, U.S. companies like General Electric have lost their position as major manufacturers in markets for everything from hair-curling irons to stereo receivers. Foregone flexibility can cost organizations precious markets, and sometimes even organizational survival.

Formalization and standardization can also undermine efficiency by narrowing the scope of workplace activities to the point where employees feel bored and unchallenged. Oversimplification caused by too much specialization can contribute to serious problems with workforce motivation and, as a consequence, poor performance.[28] Groups of workers may develop informal social structures in which low productivity is the norm. Employees may even turn to dangerous horseplay or costly sabotage to break up the monotony or to get even with a company they perceive as insensitive and uncaring. Sometimes the job redesign and enrichment procedures described in Chapter 6 can provide sufficient relief. But at other times, nothing short of complete restructuring will succeed in countering the effects of overspecialization.

Bureaucracy can also contribute to inefficiency because of the fact that greater horizontal specialization requires increases in vertical specialization. The more specialized each job is, in the horizontal sense, the less easily an employee working in the technological core of the company can get the view of the big picture required to coordinate with others, let alone manage the organization as a whole. One managerial level is added above specialized workers to handle coordination and management tasks. If this new level becomes so specialized that it can no longer develop and pursue organizational goals, another, then another, and yet another managerial level may be added. The end result may be a hierarchy with as many as 15 managerial levels, consisting of thousands of middle managers whose job it is to connect top management with production employees. You can see that achieving productivity through horizontal specialization can lead to significant costs in the form of management payroll expenses.

Besides inflating the management payroll, greater bureaucratic specialization can cut into efficiency by increasing the costs of management in numerous other significant ways. Vertical specialization increases the number of managers, who must then spend increasing amounts of time coordinating with each other to oversee organizational activities. Coordination costs rise as a result. Furthermore, horizontal specialization increases task interdependence because it creates networks of tasks that workers must perform together in order to accomplish the desired end result. For example, the typist, file clerk, and telephone receptionist depicted in Figure 11-3 (see Chapter 11) must cooperate closely to complete the same work that any one of the three secretaries could complete alone. Again, the costs of coordination creep upward.

Finally, specialization can also force an organization to pay for specialists who may be idle at a given moment but who are expected to be needed at some future time. These carrying costs can add up. Imagine a small hospital that must offer full-time employment to a highly skilled cardiovascular surgeon so that the surgeon will be available to perform the three or four operations per month that the hospital requires. The hospital has a choice. Either it must bear the costs of carrying an idle specialist or it must reduce the scope of the services it offers its patients.

So the formalization, standardization, and specialization of bureaucratic structures can have major drawbacks. To the degree that these drawbacks impede efficiency, bureaucracy fails to achieve its intended purpose and can become a threat to organizational success and continued well-being. Organizations facing this threat have grown beyond the developmental stages of formalization and elaboration. They find themselves entering into the next stage of organizational maturation, transformation.

Managers of organizations in the stage of transformation face the challenge of dealing with business conditions that require the resources of a large organization but the flexibility of a small one. Global competition, technological volatility, and trends toward the mass customization of products and services underlie this challenge.[29] Due to the drawbacks just mentioned, bureaucratic structures often depress organizational performance under the circumstances that characterize the transformation stage. For this reason, with entry into the stage of transformation comes the task of converting the bureaucratic structure into one of two postbureaucratic alternatives, either the multiunit structure or the virtual structure.

Both postbureaucratic structures are organic, with the virtual structure being more decentralized due to the complete absence of a single central management team. Thus, both are quite flexible. Choices between the two involve trade-offs between completing the entire process of design, production, and distribution within the confines of a single organization, in the case of the multiunit structure, and relying instead on a network of several organizations connected together by temporary alliances, in the case of the virtual structure. At this advanced stage of growth and development, choices pertaining to organization design are influenced by two contingency factors: environmental turbulence and transaction costs.

Environmental Turbulence

The term **environmental turbulence** describes both the speed and the scope of change that occurs in the environment surrounding an organization.[30] The condition of high turbulence is characterized by simultaneous, and extremely high levels of, environmental change, complexity (therefore, uncertainty), and diversity, as well as rapid technological advances that often include the use of the team-managed flexible cell technology described in Chapter 6. Such conditions, sometimes referred to as *hypercompetitive,* require flexibility beyond the limits of bureaucracy, necessitating progression to postbureaucratic structures.[31] At the other end of the spectrum, low turbulence exists when the factors of environmental change, complexity, and diversity, and rapid technological advances are not simultaneous or are less extreme in effect. The organization can achieve the flexibility required by such conditions in traditional bureaucratic structures by adding lateral linkages or opting for matrix structuring, as suggested by the technological and environmental contingency models already discussed.

By defining the degree of flexibility and adaptability an organization must have to perform effectively, the level of environmental turbulence can also act as a contingency factor that influences choices between the two postbureaucratic alternatives. It is true that relative to bureaucratic structures, multiunit structures are far more flexible. For instance, General Electric's decision to allow its different units to function as independent entities has enabled each of the company's businesses—consumer finance, jet engines and avionics, military contracting, and others—to adapt itself to its own business situation without affecting the operations of other units. However, relying on temporary associations, as in virtual structures, allows even more flexibility. Such associations in the form of short-term contracts or longer-term joint venture relationships are easier to modify and eliminate than are the interconnections among parts of a single firm.[32] For example, IBM, Apple, and Motorola combined forces to design a new computer memory chip—the PowerPC chip—and successfully introduced it to computer manufacturers throughout the world. When the project was completed, the companies disbanded joint operations, retrieved the resources they had loaned to the PowerPC project, and moved on to other activities of their own.[33] In sum, whereas high levels of turbulence push toward the adoption of multiunit structures, extremely high levels push instead toward the use of virtual structures.

Transaction Costs

Decisions about "doing it yourself" in a multiunit structure versus "contracting it out" in a virtual structure also boil down to a comparison of the costs of sustaining a single organization and maintaining a unified management hierarchy, on the one hand, and the costs of writing enforceable contracts and ensuring contractual compliance, on the other. As is suggested by economist Oliver Williamson, such **transaction costs** are a second contingency factor influencing whether managers opt for the permanence of a single organization or the transience of contractual relationships.[34] Transaction costs associated with preserving a single company or maintaining contractual relationships are especially affected by two important considerations. First, people are limited in the amount of information they can process, and greater complexity in a particular business situation creates a need for information processing that can prove overwhelming. Such complexity in a business situation makes contracting difficult because it increases feelings of uncertainty on the part of contractors. In turn, uncertainty increases the reluctance of prospective contractors to consign costly resources or commit to long-term relationships. Consider, for instance, the situation in which you are looking for an apartment to rent. Are you likely to sign a lease when you know exactly what apartment you will live in, what your monthly payments will be, and how long the lease will last? Are you likely to sign a lease for an apartment you have never seen, with monthly payments that have yet to be specified, for a period of time that may change without notice? For most people, the uncertainty of the second alternative makes it the less attractive of the two.

In contrast, creating a single organization can help in coping with human limitations in the face of complexity because it affords a sense of social stability and permanence. Containing business transactions within a single organization also allows the use of the basic coordination mechanisms previously described and makes it easier to involve many more people in decision making. All these factors help reduce the uncertainty of work relationships. People who opt for co-ops or condominiums instead of apartments are, to some extent, buying into a permanent organization. This organization provides them the greater stability of permanent ownership and unites them with other owners who share similar interests in housing quality and affordability. What might otherwise require a contract among co-owners can be taken care of through periodic meetings in which the owners get together to discuss problems and negotiate acceptable solutions.

Second, contracting is made more difficult and the transaction costs of contractual relationships are increased by the threat that one or more of the contractors will use deception and seek to profit at the expense of the others. The threat of opportunism becomes especially troublesome when few prospective contractors are available, because low substitutability affords them power that enables them to demand special treatment (see Chapter 10). Opportunism is also an issue when uncertainty hides the true intentions of contractors, blocking efforts to verify honesty. In the absence of such verification, contractors are best advised to prepare for the worst and expect deceit. Surveillance, even though costly, should be conducted to detect opportunism before it can prove destructive.

Thus, considerations of bounded rationality and complexity drive up the transaction costs of contracting. In situations in which uncertainty about the future undermines temporary relationships, the multiunit structure is favored. Likewise, concerns about opportunism increase the transaction costs of contracting and favor the multiunit structure. Thus, with reference to transaction costs, the virtual structure is preferable only when prospective contractors are able to negotiate good-faith contracts that are fair to all parties, honest in intention, and verifiable in every regard.[35]

Paths of Transition

For large organizations that have progressed through the developmental stages of formalization and elaboration, transition to a multiunit structure is a matter of forming teams and giving them autonomy by decentralizing operations and reducing middle management. Currently, Aetna Insurance is headed in this direction, implementing a reengineered structure based on concepts espoused by Michael Hammer.[36] Transition to the virtual structure is more dramatic, requiring massive downsizing and the formation of contractual relationships. General

Motors' North American Operations may be headed in this direction, because GM's management is selling off the company's parts-manufacturing facilities and relying more on outside contractors.

For small organizations that have jumped directly from inception or early formalization to transition, adoption of a multiunit structure means rapid growth through merger or internal expansion. In contrast, movement into a virtual structure requires the identification of prospective contractors and development of contractual relationships. Thus, Ron Oklewicz's TelePad, manufacturer of a handheld pen-based computer, developed its computer with GVO, an industrial design company in Palo Alto, California, and collaborated with a battery maker to design a portable power supply. Then it manufactured the computer using spare capacity at an IBM plant in Charlotte, North Carolina, and contracted with Automatic Data Processing for that firm to act as a payroll agent for its production employees.[37] By forming strategic alliances, joint ventures, or other contractual relationships with various firms, a relatively small company like TelePad can form a temporary business entity with the apparent resources of a much larger organization.

If successful, transitions that take place during the stage of transformation result in postbureaucratic structures that enable companies to act both large and small at the same time. Through mutual adjustment and decentralization, firms are able to realize extensive flexibility. Through large size, whether real or virtual, firms are able to control the scope of resources needed to accomplish complex tasks in an effective manner. Key to the success of such organizations are the information-processing networks that tie their members together. In the absence of modern computer equipment, postbureaucratic structures could not exist.

What does all this suggest for the future? If current trends are any indication, the next form of organization structure may bring about the emergence of the virtual manager. Already, managers like Will Pape, chief information officer of San Francisco's VeriFone, "commute" to work electronically, using computers and electronic mail to exchange information with headquarters and fulfill managerial duties.[38] In coming years, it is possible that "headquarters" may cease to exist entirely, and that a company may consist of a single individual managing by electronic network a collection of contractual relationships that allows the creation, production, and distribution of goods or services. This possibility suggests that the next postbureaucratic structure may be no structure at all, at least not in the traditional sense.

SUMMARY

Organization design is the process of structuring an organization so as to enhance *organizational effectiveness* in light of the *contingency factors* the firm faces. As they develop, organizations grow through the stages of *inception, formalization, elaboration,* and *transformation.*

During inception, structural effectiveness is influenced by the contingency factors of *organization size* and *ownership norms.* Managers choose between the prebureaucratic alternatives of the simple undifferentiated and simple differentiated structures.

While an organization is in the stages of formalization and elaboration, structural effectiveness becomes a function of the contingency factors of *core technology* and *external environment*. Managers of organizations at these stages choose between the bureaucratic alternatives of functional, divisional, and matrix structures.

At the stage of transformation, structural effectiveness is shaped by the contingency factors of *environmental turbulence* and *transaction costs*. Managers choose between the postbureaucratic alternatives of multiunit and virtual structures.

Review Questions

1. Name a specific business organization in your community and identify three of its most important constituency groups. What interests do each of the constituency groups expect the organization to satisfy? How does the organization's structure affect its ability to satisfy these interests? Is the company effective?

2. How do mechanistic structures differ from organic structures? Compare the strengths and weaknesses of each. Which bureaucratic structure is the most mechanistic? Why? Which bureaucratic structure is the most organic? Why?

3. How does the developmental stage of an organization affect its structure? What roles do age and size play in this process?

4. Why do organizations in the inception stage usually have prebureaucratic structures? What effects do organization size and ownership norms have on organization design at this stage?

5. In which of Woodward's and Thompson's technologies is work routine and predictable? In which of them is work nonroutine and unpredictable? What kinds of structures are most fitting for each of the two clusters of technologies you have identified? In general terms, how does the routineness and predictability of an organization's technology affect the appropriateness of different types of structure?

6. Explain why environmental change impedes an organization's ability to coordinate by means of standardization. What sort of coordination can be used instead? Why does environmental complexity push toward decentralization? Given that environmental uncertainty is a combination of change and complexity, what effects besides encouraging increased boundary spanning would you expect it to have on the way an organization is structured?

7. Why is environmental receptivity an issue only for organizations facing complex environments? Under conditions of environmental complexity, why should the centralization stimulated by hostility be eliminated as the environment becomes munificent?

8. How does the developmental stage of transformation differ from the stages of formalization and elaboration? Why does this difference push toward the adoption of a postbureaucratic form of organization structure? How do the level of environmental turbulence and transaction costs affect the process of organization design at this developmental stage?

Implementation Guide

The following questions should help you during the process of designing or re-designing an organization's structure by guiding you through the diagnosis of the contingency factors discussed in this chapter.

1. What kind of structure does the organization currently have? What is its primary means of coordination? Do the titles of its line vice presidents provide evidence of one particular form of structure?

2. Is the organization's current structure the one suggested by the firm's developmental stage and age? If the firm is young and in the inception stage, does it have a prebureaucratic structure? If it is older and in the formalization stage, does it have a bureaucratic functional structure? If it is in the elaboration stage, does it have a bureaucratic divisional or matrix structure? If it has matured, does it have a postbureaucratic structure?

3. If the firm is in the inception stage, does it have 12 or fewer members, suggesting the appropriateness of a simple undifferentiated structure? If it consists of more than 12 members, does the firm have a simple undifferentiated structure? Is the firm so large that it should progress to the formalization stage and adopt a bureaucratic structure?

4. If the organization is in the inception stage, do ownership norms play a part in determining which structure it has? If these norms have effects that conflict with the effects of size, should the organization adopt a bureaucratic structure?

5. If the organization is in the formalization or elaboration stage, is its primary purpose to manufacture a tangible product? Does it use small-batch production, continuous process production, or flexible cell production? If it uses one of these, does the organization have an organic bureaucratic structure? Is it functional or divisional with lateral linkages, or a matrix? Or does it use mass production? Does the organization have a mechanistic structure? Is it functional or divisional?

6. If the organization is in the formalization or elaboration stage, is its primary purpose instead to provide a service? Does it use intensive technology? If so, does the organization have one of the organic structures named in question 5? Or does the firm use mediating technology or long-linked technology? If it uses one of these, does the organization have one of the mechanistic structures named in question 5?

7. If the organization is in the formalization or elaboration stage, is its external environment stable or dynamic? Does the organization's primary mode of coordination match the amount of change in its environment? Is the environment simple or complex? Does the degree of decentralization in the organization's structure match the amount of complexity in the organization's environment?

8. If the organization is in the formalization or elaboration stage, is its external environment uncertain? If so, is there evidence of significant boundary-spanning activities? Is the environment munificent or hostile? If hostility exists and the environment is also complex, is the organization temporarily centralized? Is the environment uniform or diverse? Does the type of departmentalization used to structure the firm match the diversity of its environment?

9. If the organization is in the transformation stage, does environmental turbulence push in the direction of adopting a virtual structure? Do transaction costs push instead toward adoption of a multiunit structure?

10. Do the various contingencies seem to mandate the same type of structure? If not, and if there is no evidence of recent changes that might serve as an explanation for this lack of consensus, look for faulty diagnosis in one or more of your contingency analyses.

11. If the different contingencies *do* seem to point toward the same type of structure, is this structure the one the organization has now? If not, the structure recommended by your analysis should be implemented; structural redesign is needed. If, however, the current structure is the one recommended by your analysis, structural deficiencies would not be the cause of any organizational problems. If the organization *is* experiencing problems, look for individual or group-level causes instead.

ENDNOTES

1. J. L. Price, "The Study of Organizational Effectiveness," *Sociological Quarterly* 13 (1972), pp. 3–15; S. Strasser, J. D. Eveland, G. Cummings, O. L. Deniston, and J. H. Romani, "Conceptualizing the Goal and System Models of Organizational Effectiveness: Implications for Comparative Evaluative Research," *Journal of Management Studies* 18 (1981), pp. 321–40; and Y. K. Shetty, "New Look at Corporate Goals," *California Management Review* 22 (1979), pp. 71–79.

2. Constituency models of effectiveness and other examples of constituencies and their interests are discussed by P. S. Goodman, J. M. Pennings, and Associates, *New Perspectives on Organizational Effectiveness* (San Francisco: Jossey-Bass, 1977); J. A. Wagner III and B. Schneider, "Legal Regulation and the Constraint of Constituent Satisfaction," *Journal of Management Studies* 24 (1987), pp. 189–200; and R. F. Zammuto, "A Comparison of Multiple Constituency Models of Organizational Effectiveness," *Academy of Management Review* 9 (1984), pp. 606–16. Related stakeholder models are discussed in R. E. Freeman, *Strategic Management: A Stakeholder Approach* (Boston: Pitman, 1984); C. W. L. Hill and T. M. Jones, "Stakeholder-Agency Theory," *Journal of Management Studies* 29 (1992), pp. 131–54; and T. Donaldson and L. E. Preston, "A Stakeholder Theory of the Corporation: Concepts, Evidence, and Implications," *Academy of Management Review* 20 (1995), pp. 65–91.

3. R. Z. Gooding and J. A. Wagner III, "A Meta-Analytic Review of the Relationship between Size and Performance: The Productivity and Efficiency of Organizations and Their Subunits," *Administrative Science Quarterly* 30 (1985), pp. 462–81.

4. Ibid.

5. T. Burns and G. M. Stalker, *The Management of Innovation* (London: Tavistock Publications, 1961), pp. 119–22; J. A. Courtright, G. T. Fairhurst, and L. E. Rogers, "Interaction Patterns in Organic and Mechanistic Systems," *Academy of Management Journal* 32 (1989), pp. 773–802.

6. R. F. Quinn and K. Cameron, "Organizational Life Cycles and Shifting Criteria of Effectiveness: Some Preliminary Evidence," *Management Science* 29 (1983), pp. 29–34.

7. S. M. Davis, *Future Perfect* (Reading, MA: Addison-Wesley, 1987); and B. J. Pine II, *Mass Customization: The New Frontier in Business Competition* (Boston: Harvard University Press, 1993).

8. J. R. Kimberly, "Organizational Size and the Structuralist Perspective: A Review, Critique, and Proposal," *Administrative Science Quarterly* 21 (1976), pp. 571–97; P. Y. Martin, "Size in Residential Service Organizations," *Sociological Quarterly* 20 (1979), pp. 569–79; and Gooding and Wagner, "A Meta-Analytic Review," p. 463.

9. Y. Criden and S. Gelb, *The Kibbutz Experience: Dialogue in Kfar Blum* (New York: Herzl, 1974); and J. Blasi, *The Communal Experience of the Kibbutz* (New Brunswick, NJ: Transaction Books, 1986).

10. C. C. Miller, W. H. Glick, Y. Wang, and G. P. Huber, "Understanding Technology-Structure Relationships: Theory Development and Meta-Analytic

Theory Testing," *Academy of Management Journal* 34 (1991), pp. 370–99; and D. Miller, "Environmental Fit versus Internal Fit," *Organization Science* 3 (1992), pp. 159–78.

11. C. Perrow, "A Framework for the Comparative Analysis of Organizations," *American Sociological Review* 32 (1967), pp. 194–208; and D. Rousseau, "Assessment of Technology in Organizations: Closed versus Open System Approaches," *Academy of Management Review* 4 (1979), pp. 531–42.

12. J. Woodward, *Management and Technology* (London: Her Majesty's Stationery Office, 1958); see also J. Woodward, *Industrial Organization: Theory and Practice* (London: Oxford University Press, 1975).

13. F. M. Hull and P. D. Collins, "High Technology Batch Production Systems: Woodward's Missing Type," *Academy of Management Journal* 30 (1987), pp. 786–97; and R. Parthasarthy and S. P. Sethi, "The Impact of Flexible Automation on Business Strategy and Organizational Structure," *Academy of Management Review* 17 (1992), pp. 86–111.

14. J. D. Thompson, *Organizations in Action* (New York: McGraw-Hill, 1967) pp. 15–18.

15. Perrow, "A Framework for the Comparative Analysis"; R. G. Hunt, "Technology and Organization," *Academy of Management Journal* 13 (1970), pp. 235–52; W. H. Starbuck, "Organizational Growth and Development," in *Handbook of Organizations*, J. G. March, ed. (New York: Rand McNally, 1965), pp. 241–297; and Courtright, Fairhurst, and Rogers, "Interaction Patterns."

16. A. C. Bluedorn, R. A. Johnson, D. K. Cartwright, and B. R. Barringer, "The Interface and Convergence of the Strategic Management and Organizational Environment Domains," *Journal of Management* 20 (1994), pp. 201–62.

17. Burns and Stalker, *The Management of Innovation*; C. R. Hinings, D. J. Hickson, J. M. Pennings, and R. E. Schneck, "Structural Conditions of Intraorganizational Power," *Administrative Science Quarterly* 19 (1974), pp. 22–44; and R. B. Duncan, "Multiple Decision-Making Structures in Adapting to Environmental Uncertainty: The Impact of Organizational Effectiveness," *Human Relations* 26 (1973), pp. 273–91.

18. R. B. Duncan, "Characteristics of Organizational Environments and Perceived Environmental Uncertainty," *Administrative Science Quarterly* 17 (1972), pp. 313–27; and J. R. Galbraith, *Designing Complex Organizations* (Reading, MA: Addison-Wesley, 1973), pp. 4–6.

19. J. Flint, "Volume Be Damned," *Forbes*, April 12, 1993, pp. 52–53.

20. Galbraith, *Designing Complex Organizations*, p. 4.

21. O. O. Sawyerr, "Environmental Uncertainty and Environmental Scanning Activities of Nigerian Manufacturing Executives: A Comparative Analysis," *Strategic Management Journal* 14 (1993), pp. 287–99.

22. J. S. Adams, "The Structure and Dynamics of Behavior in Organization Boundary Roles," in *Handbook of Industrial and Organizational Psychology*, M. D. Dunnette, ed. (Chicago: Rand McNally, 1976), pp. 1175–99.

23. H. Aldrich and D. Herker, "Boundary Spanning Roles and Organization Structure," *Academy of Management Review* 2 (1977), pp. 217–39; R. H. Miles, *Macro Organizational Behavior* (Santa Monica, CA: Goodyear, 1979), pp. 320–39; and R. L. Daft and R. M. Steers, *Organizations: A Micro/Macro Approach* (Glenview, IL: Scott, Foresman, 1986), p. 299.

24. G. J. Castrogiovanni, "Environmental Munificence: A Theoretical Assessment," *Academy of Management Review* 16 (1991), pp. 542–65.

25. D. Greising, L. Himelstein, J. Carey, and L. Bongiorno, "Does Tobacco Pay Its Way?" *Business Week*, February 19, 1996, pp. 89–90; J. Carey, L. Bongiorno, and M. France, "The Fire This Time," *Business Week*, August 12, 1996, pp. 66–68; C. Farrell, M. J. Mandel, T. Peterson, A. Borrus, R. W. King, and J. E. Ellis, "The Cold War's Grim Aftermath," *Business Week*, February 24, 1992, pp. 78–80.

26. H. Mintzberg, *Structuring of Organizations* (Englewood Cliffs, NJ: Prentice Hall, 1979), p. 281; M. Yasi-Ardekani, "Effects of Environmental Scarcity on the Relationship of Context to Organizational Structure," *Academy of Management Journal* 32 (1989), pp. 131–56; and S. Chandler, "How TWA Faced the Nightmare," *Business Week*, August 5, 1996, p. 30.

27. Thompson, *Organizations in Action*, pp. 25–38.

28. G. R. Carroll, "The Specialist Strategy," *California Management Review* 26 (1984), pp. 126–37.

29. R. L. Daft and A. Y. Lewin, "Where Are the Theories for the 'New' Organization Forms? An Editorial Essay," *Organization Science* 4 (1993), pp. i–vi.

30. F. E. Emery and E. Trist, "The Causal Texture of Organizational Environments," *Human Relations* 18 (1965), pp. 21–32.

31. R. D'Aveni, *Hypercompetition: Managing the Dynamics of Strategic Maneuvering* (New York: Free Press, 1994); and H. W. Volberda, "Toward the Flexible Form: How to Remain Vital in Hypercompetitive Environments," *Organization Science* 7 (1996), pp. 359–74

32. J. Pfeffer and G. R. Salancik, *The External Control of Organizations: A Resource Dependence Perspective* (New York, Harper & Row, 1978).

33. R. D. Hof, N. Gross, and I. Sager, "A Computer Maker's Power Move," *Business Week,* March 7, 1994, p. 48.

34. O. Williamson, *Markets and Hierarchies: Analysis and Antitrust Implications* (New York: Free Press, 1975). See also J. R. Commons, *Institutional Economics* (Madison: University of Wisconsin Press, 1934); R. H. Coase, "The Nature of the Firm," *Economica N. S.* 4 (1937), pp. 386–405; and A. A. Alchian and H. Demsetz, "Production, Information Costs, and Economic Organization," *American Economic Review* 62 (1972), pp. 777–95.

35. For related discussions, see P. S. Ring and A. H. Van de Ven, "Structuring Cooperative Relationships between Organizations," *Strategic Management Journal* 13 (1992), pp. 483–98; and J. T. Mahoney, "The Choice of Organizational Form: Vertical Financial Ownership versus Other Methods of Vertical Integration," *Strategic Management Journal* 13 (1992), pp. 559–84.

36. G. Rifkin, "Reengineering Aetna," *Forbes ASAP,* June 7, 1993, pp. 78–86; see also M. Hammer and J. Champy, *Reengineering the Corporation: A Manifesto for Business Revolution* (New York: Harper Business, 1993).

37. J. A. Byrne, "The Horizontal Corporation: It's about Managing Across, Not Up and Down," *Business Week,* December 20, 1993, pp. 76–81; and J. A. Byrne, R. Brandt, and O. Port, "The Virtual Corporation: The Company of the Future Will Be the Ultimate in Adaptability," *Business Week,* February 8, 1993, pp. 98–102.

38. D. H. Freedman, "Culture of Urgency," *Forbes ASAP,* September 13, 1993, pp. 25–28.

Chapter Thirteen

Culture, Change, and Organization Development

The "HP way." For years, Hewlett-Packard topped everybody's list of the best-run U.S. companies. HP was credited with developing the blend of high technology and enlightened management that defined corporate life in the Silicon Valley. It was an often-cited example of how to encourage innovation—by abolishing rigid chains of command, shunning fancy executive offices, and requiring all employees to associate on a first-name basis.

But by the late 1980s, Hewlett-Packard had become bogged down by sluggish management and bureaucratic procedure. The typical manager found it necessary to deal with as many as 38 different in-house committees, responsible for deciding everything from how to design new software to what to name a new product. Costs were climbing and product development was slowing down. "There was a lot of decision overhead," remarked CEO John A. Young in retrospect.

In fact, the same culture of egalitarianism and mutual respect that had powered Hewlett-Packard's initial success grew into a web of consensus management that placed too much emphasis on getting along and too little on getting things done. Young realized that things had gotten out of hand when, in the spring of 1990, a manager warned him that the company's most important project, the development of a series of new high-speed workstations, was slipping a year behind schedule because of bureaucratic burdens. "I think I may have come unglued that day," reported Young in a later conversation. "It was a pretty clear signal to me."

Young attacked the workstation problem by removing the 200 engineers working on the project from the Hewlett-Packard management structure, so that they could do their jobs without the intrusion of committee oversight. To deal with the broader problems plaguing the company, Young called in company founder and board chair David Packard to discuss redesigning the company's structure and redirecting its culture. Together the two men analyzed

Hewlett-Packard's successful laser printer business, which had remained flexible and competitive despite the troubles of the larger company. What they discovered led them to offer many of Hewlett-Packard's managers an early retirement program. Among the smaller staff of managers that remained afterward, committees were disbanded, and the management hierarchy was flattened. Also, HP's computer business was divided into two separate divisions, each with its own sales force. One handled personal computers and printers sold through dealers, and the other was put in charge of workstations and minicomputers sold directly to larger customers.

Assessing the change, general manager Bob Frankenberg remarked, "The results are incredible. We are doing more business and getting product out quicker with fewer people." Rather than dealing with 38 committees, HP managers now rarely find it necessary to consult more than 3. Instead of requiring up to six years, new-product development now requires as little as nine months. As a consequence, the company has introduced extremely successful lines of personal computers, workstations, and printers. Two of these products, a palm-size computer with the capabilities of a desktop and a portable inkjet printer that can print in color at near-laser quality for about a quarter of the price, have proven wildly successful. Breakthroughs in digital video and deals with Pacific Telesis, BellSouth, Southern New England Telephone, and the government of Singapore promise to keep HP at the forefront of the rapidly developing market for cable video-on-demand services. Comments general manager James D. Olson, "We've transformed ourselves from gearheads into gladiators." Structural and cultural changes have brought Hewlett-Packard back from the brink of bureaucratic obsolescence.[1]

---

[1] B. Buell, R. D. Hof, and G. McWilliams, "Hewlett-Packard Rethinks Itself," *Business Week,* April 1, 1991, pp. 76–79; and R. D. Hof, "Hewlett-Packard," *Business Week,* February 13, 1995, p. 67.

Managing the organization, as an organization, is an extremely complex task. As discussed in Chapters 10 through 12, the management of macro organizational behavior requires that managers deal with issues of power, conflict, structure, and organization design. In addition, as indicated by activities at Hewlett-Packard, managers must shape the culture of norms, values, and ways of thinking that influences behavior throughout their firm. In the process, they must solve problems originating in change, whether that change affects interpersonal, group, intergroup, or organizational relations. Thus, in this chapter we discuss the topics of organizational culture, change, and development. We begin by describing organizational culture and describing how a particular firm's culture affects and reflects issues of power, structure, and organization design. Next we discuss issues associated with change in organizations, and introduce organization development as a process of change management. We conclude by describing organization development interventions that managers can use to initiate change aimed at resolving many of the OB problems identified in previous chapters of this book.

Organization Culture

Within every *formal* organization of prescribed jobs and structural relationships lies an *informal* organization of unofficial rules, procedures, and interconnections. This informal organization arises as employees make spontaneous, unauthorized changes in the way things are done. In discussing emergent role characteristics (Chapter 7) and group development (Chapter 8), we have already begun to discuss how such day-to-day adjustments occur in organizations. As these adjustments shape and change the formal way of doing things, a culture of attitudes and understandings emerges that is shared among coworkers. This culture is a

> pattern of basic assumptions—invented, discovered, or developed [by a firm's members] to cope with problems of external adaptation and internal integration—that has worked well enough to be considered valid and, therefore, to be taught to new members as the correct way to perceive, think, and feel in relation to those problems.[1]

An organization's **culture** is thus an informal, shared way of perceiving life and membership in the organization that binds members together and influences what they think about themselves and their work.

In the process of helping to create a mutual understanding of organizational life, organizational culture fulfills four basic functions. First, it *gives members an organizational identity.* Sharing norms, values, and perceptions gives people a sense of togetherness that helps promote a feeling of common purpose. Second, it *facilitates collective commitment.* The common purpose that grows out of a shared culture tends to elicit strong commitment from all those who accept the culture as their own. Third, it *promotes organizational stability.* By nurturing a shared sense of identity and commitment, culture encourages lasting integration and cooperation among the members of an organization. Fourth, it *shapes behavior by helping members make sense of their surroundings.* An organization's culture serves as a source of shared meanings to explain why things occur the way they do.[2] By performing these four basic functions, the culture of an organization serves as a sort of social glue that helps reinforce persistent, coordinated behaviors at work.

Elements of Organization Culture

Deep within the culture of every organization is a collection of fundamental norms and values that shapes members' behaviors and helps them understand the surrounding organization. In some companies, such as Polaroid, 3M, and DuPont Chemical, cultural norms and values emphasize the importance of discovering new materials or technologies and developing them into new products. In other companies, such as AT&T and Maytag Appliances, cultural norms and values focus on high product quality.[3] Fundamental norms and values like these are the ultimate source of the shared perceptions, thoughts, and feelings constituting the culture of an organization.[4]

ELEMENT	DESCRIPTION
Table 13-1 ■ Surface Elements of Organization Cultures	
Ceremonies	Special events in which organization members celebrate the myths, heroes, and symbols of their firm
Rites	Ceremonial activities meant to communicate specific ideas or accomplish particular purposes
Rituals	Actions that are repeated regularly to reinforce cultural norms and values
Stories	Accounts of past events that illustrate and transmit deeper cultural norms and values
Myths	Fictional stories that help explain activities or events that might otherwise be puzzling
Heroes	Successful people who embody the values and character of the organization and its culture
Symbols	Objects, actions, or events that have special meanings and that enable organization members to exchange complex ideas and emotional messages
Language	A collection of verbal symbols that often reflects the organization's particular culture

How are these fundamental norms and values expressed? How are they passed from one person to another? Certain surface elements of the culture, overviewed in Table 13-1, help employees interpret everyday events in the organization and are the principal means by which cultural norms and values are communicated from one person to another.[5]

Ceremonies are special events in which the members of a company celebrate the myths, heroes, and symbols of their culture.[6] Ceremonies thus exemplify and reinforce important cultural norms and values. In sales organizations like Mary Kay or Amway, annual ceremonies are held to recognize and reward outstanding sales representatives. Part of the reason for holding these ceremonies is to inspire sales representatives who have been less effective to adopt the norms and values of their successful colleagues. Whether they personify the "Mary Kay approach" or the "Amway philosophy," the people who are recognized and rewarded in these ceremonies greatly enhance the attractiveness of their companies' cultural underpinnings.

Often, organizational ceremonies incorporate various **rites,** ceremonial activities meant to send particular messages or accomplish specific purposes.[7] For instance, *rites of passage* are used to initiate new members and can convey important aspects of the culture to them. In some businesses, new recruits are required to spend considerable time talking with veteran employees and learning about cultural norms and values by listening to these veterans' stories about their experiences at work. In other companies, the rite of passage is merely a brief talk about company rules and regulations delivered by a human resources staff member to newcomers during their first day at work. In the latter case, the rite is little more than a formal welcoming and does not really help newcomers learn much about the culture of the firm.

When employees are transferred, demoted, or fired because of low productivity, incompatible values, or other personal failings, *rites of degradation* may draw the attention of others to the limits of acceptable behavior. Today, rites of degradation are generally deemphasized, involving little more than quiet reassignment, but they have on occasion been quite dramatic. In the early days of NCR, executives would learn that they had lost their jobs by discovering their desks burning on the lawn in front of corporate headquarters.

Rites of enhancement also emphasize the limits of appropriate behavior, but in a positive way. They recognize increasing status or promotion to a new position in a firm and may range from simple promotion announcements to intricate recognition ceremonies, such as the Mary Kay and Amway ceremonies just described.

In *rites of integration,* members of an organization are given the opportunity to express and share the common feelings that bond them together. Often in rites of this sort, official titles and hierarchical differences are intentionally ignored so that members can get to know each other as people rather than as managers, staff specialists, clerks, or laborers. At Tandem Computer, for example, a "thank God it's Friday" (TGIF) party is held each week, giving employees the opportunity to chat informally over pizza and drinks. Company picnics, golf outings, softball games, and holiday parties can also serve as rites of integration.

A rite that is repeated on a regular basis becomes a **ritual,** a ceremonial event that continually reinforces key norms and values. The morning coffee break is a ritual that strengthens important workplace relationships. So, too, is the annual stockholder meeting held by management to convey cultural norms and values to company shareholders. Just as routine coffee breaks enable coworkers to gossip among themselves and reaffirm important interpersonal relationships, annual stockholder meetings give the company the opportunity to strengthen connections between itself and people who would otherwise have little more than a limited financial interest in its continued well-being.

Stories are accounts of past events that serve as reminders of cultural values.[8] Often, the stories are familiar to all employees. As organization members tell stories and think about the messages the stories convey, the concrete examples facilitate their later recall of the concepts presented. Stories also provide information about historical events in the development of a company that can improve employees' understanding of the present:

> In one organization, employees tell a story about how the company avoided a mass layoff when almost every other company in the industry . . . felt forced to lay off employees in large numbers. The company . . . managed to avoid a layoff of 10 percent of their employees by having everyone in the company take a 10 percent cut in salary and come to work only 9 out of 10 days. This company experience is thus called the "nine day fortnight."[9]

The story of the nine-day fortnight vividly captures the cultural value that looking after employees' well-being is the right thing to do. Present-day employees continue to tell the story among themselves as a reminder that their company will avoid layoffs as much as possible during economic downturns.

A **myth** is a special type of story that provides a fictional but likely explanation for an event or thing that might otherwise seem puzzling or mysterious. Ancient civilizations often created myths about gods and other supernatural forces to explain natural occurrences such as the rising and setting of the sun, the phases of the moon, and the formation of thunderstorms. Similarly, the members of an organization sometimes develop fictionalized accounts of the company's founders, origins, or historical development to provide a framework for explaining current activities in their firm. In many instances, organizational myths actually contain at least a grain of truth. For example, myths repeated throughout General Motors about the management prowess of Alfred P. Sloan, one of the company's earliest chief executives, are based in part on a study of GM's structure and procedures that Sloan performed in 1919 to 1920. It is this bit of truthful information that make myths sound completely true.

Heroes are people who embody the values of an organization and its culture:

> Richard A. Drew, a banjo-playing college dropout working in 3M's research lab during the 1920s, [helped] some colleagues solve a problem they had with masking tape. Soon thereafter, DuPont came out with cellophane. Drew decided he could go DuPont one better and coated the cellophane with a colorless adhesive to bind things together—and Scotch tape was born. In the 3M tradition, Drew carried the ball himself by managing the development and initial production of his invention. Moving up through the ranks, he went on to become technical director of the company and showed other employees just how they could succeed in similar fashion at 3M.[10]

Heroes such as 3M's Drew serve as role models, illustrating personal performance that is not only desirable but attainable. And, like stories, heroes provide concrete examples that make the guiding norms and values of a company readily apparent.

Symbols are objects, actions, or events to which people have assigned special meanings. Company logos, flags, and trade names are symbols that come readily to mind. Mercedes's three-point star logo is synonymous with quality in most people's minds, and even the youngest children know that the McDonald's golden arches mark the locations of fast-food restaurants. As is suggested by these examples, symbols represent a conscious or unconscious association with some wider, usually more abstract, concept or meaning.[11] In organizations, symbols may also include official titles, such as chief operating officer. Or, special eating facilities, official automobiles, or airplanes may be given symbolic status. Sometimes even the size of an employee's office, or its placement or furnishings have special symbolic value.[12]

Symbols mean more than might seem immediately apparent. For instance, despite the fact that a reserved parking space is just a few square feet of asphalt, it may symbolize its holder's superior hierarchical status or clout. It is the ability to convey a complex message in an efficient, economical manner that makes symbols so useful and important:

> When two people shake hands, the action symbolizes their coming together. The handshake may also be rich in other kinds of symbolic significance. Between free-masons it reaffirms a bond of brotherhood, and loyalty to the order to which they belong. Between politicians it is often used to symbolize an intention to cooperate and work together. To members of the counter-culture of the 1960s and early 1970s, their special hand clasp and a cry of "Right On!" affirmed a set of divergent values and opposition to the system. The handshake is more than just a shaking of hands. It symbolizes a particular kind of relationship between those involved.[13]

Clearly, symbols are absolutely necessary. They convey emotional messages that cannot easily be put into words. Without symbols, many of the fundamental norms and values of an organization's culture could not be communicated among the members.

Language, too, is a means for sharing cultural ideas and understandings. In many organizations, the language members use is itself a reflection of the organization's particular culture.[14] At Microsoft, for example, a language of "techspeak" has developed, largely because of the technical background of the firm's founder, Bill Gates, and the firm's workforce. *Hardcore* means serious about work. A confusing or illogical situation is called *random. Bandwidth* is a measure of personal intelligence, referring to the amount of information a person can absorb. Things that go right are labeled *radical* or *super cool.*[15] Whatever the source of a common vocabulary, the fact that such a vocabulary exists attests to the presence and acceptance of a shared set of norms and values.

Managing Organization Culture

Organizational culture grows out of informal, unofficial ways of doing things. It influences the formal organization by shaping the way employees perceive and react to formally defined jobs and structural arrangements. In turn, culture influences the attitudes employees hold and behaviors they engage in at work.[16] All this happens because cultural norms and values provide **social information,** and such information helps employees determine the meaning of their work and the organization around them.[17] For example, in a company that promotes the Protestant work ethic, the idea that working hard is the way to get ahead in life, employees are led to view their jobs as critical to personal success and therefore as important, interesting, challenging, and in other ways worthwhile. By encouraging employees to perceive success as something to be valued and pursued, these norms also encourage the development of a need for achievement (see Chapter 4) and motivate hard work and high productivity. As Figure 13-1 indicates, cultural norms and values convey social information that can influence the way people choose to behave on the job. They do

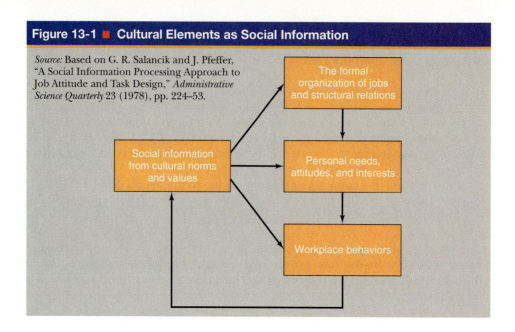

Figure 13-1 ■ Cultural Elements as Social Information

Source: Based on G. R. Salancik and J. Pfeffer, "A Social Information Processing Approach to Job Attitude and Task Design," *Administrative Science Quarterly* 23 (1978), pp. 224–53.

so by affecting the way employees perceive themselves, their work, and the organization (see box).

Can organizational culture be managed? It might seem that the answer to this question should be no, for any of the following reasons:

1. Cultures are so spontaneous, elusive, and hidden that they cannot be accurately diagnosed or intentionally changed.
2. Considerable experience and deep personal insight are required to truly understand an organization's culture, making management infeasible in most instances.
3. There may be several subcultures in a single organizational culture, complicating the task of managing organizational culture to the point where it becomes impossible.
4. Cultures provide organization members with continuity and stability. Therefore, members are likely to resist even modest efforts at cultural management or change because they fear discontinuity and instability.[18]

Many OB experts disagree with these arguments, however, and suggest that organizational cultures can be managed through the use of the two approaches discussed next.

In one approach, **symbolic management,** managers attempt to influence deep cultural norms and values by shaping the surface cultural elements, such as symbols, stories, and ceremonies, that people use to express and transmit cultural understandings.[19] Managers can accomplish shaping of this sort in a number of ways. They can issue public statements about their vision for the future of the company. They can recount stories about themselves and the company. They

Why Managing Organizational Culture Matters

Managers accustomed to dealing with the "hard facts" of financial performance and market share sometimes underestimate the competitive importance of organizational culture. Yet, managing this seemingly "softer" side of an organization can have tremendous effects on bottom-line performance and long-term survival. Just ask management at Flagstar Companies, parent of the Denny's chain of restaurants.

On April 1, 1993, the same day that Denny's settled a federal race discrimination suit filed on behalf of African-American customers in California, six African-American secret service agents at a Denny's restaurant in Annapolis, Maryland, waited for more than an hour for breakfast. While the agents were ignored, white customers ordered, were served, and finished their meals at nearby tables. Newspaper and television news accounts of this incident led to an immediate falloff in business throughout the chain, and calls for a protracted boycott.

The company responded by hiring Ron Petty, and later Jim Adamson, both former executives of Burger King U.S.A., to survey the situation and develop a corrective strategy. What the two found was an organizational culture of entrenched racial prejudice, manifested in practices ranging from denying minority clients service without prepayment to refusal to consider the franchise applications of minority applicants. Similar bigotry had previously put the Sambo's restaurant chain—a Denny's competitor—out of business, which led Petty and Adamson to pursue swift, sweeping change.

Managers at Denny's, Flagstar, and Flagstar's other chains—El Poco Loco, Quincy's, and Hardee's—were required to complete reeducation programs in cultural sensitivity and race relations. The percentage of minority officers at corporate headquarters was increased from 0 to 11 percent. The number of minority-owned Denny's franchises rose from 1 in 1993 to 27 in 1995, with a goal of 65 by the end of 1997. And Adamson made his personal feelings known by telling employees, "I will fire you if you discriminate."

Denny's is now considered a model example of how discrimination should be handled, but it has paid a total of $54 million to 295,000 aggrieved customers and their lawyers. The firm is also being supervised by an independent civil rights monitor for seven years. Clearly, an organizational culture that once abetted racial discrimination nearly cost Denny's its future and has left an indelible mark on its recent past.[1]

[1] K. H. Hammonds, "Making Amends at Denny's," *Business Week,* November 21, 1994, p. 47; N. Harris, "A New Denny's—Diner by Diner," *Business Week,* March 25, 1996, pp. 166–68; and F. Rice and A. Faircloth, "Denny's Changes Its Spots," *Fortune,* May 13, 1996, pp. 133–42.

can use and enrich the shared company language. In this way, managers not only communicate the company's central norms and key values but devise new ways of expressing them.

Managers who practice symbolic management realize that every managerial behavior broadcasts a message to employees about the norms and values of the organization. They consciously choose to do specific things that will symbolize and strengthen a desirable culture. For example, deciding to promote from within and avoid hiring people from outside the firm sends employees the message that strong performance is rewarded by career advancement. This message reinforces cultural norms and values that favor hard work. Filling positions by hiring from other organizations gives precisely the opposite message—that hard work may *not* be rewarded by promotion—and undermines cultural norms and values that suggest otherwise.

The fact that symbolic management involves the manipulation of symbols is apt to lead some managers to underestimate its importance. Telling stories, performing ceremonies, and anointing heroes might seem softheaded or a waste of time to managers who do not understand the importance of managing culture. However, playing down the importance of symbolic management can have disastrous consequences. Managers at companies ranging from Disney to DuPont agree that managing symbols is a critical part of their job.[20]

Another way of managing the culture of an organization is to use organization development (OD) interventions like those discussed next. OD interventions can contribute to cultural management by helping the members of an organization progress through the following steps:

1. *Identifying current norms and values.* OD interventions typically require people to list the norms and values that influence their attitudes and behaviors at work. This kind of list gives members insight into the organization culture.
2. *Plotting new directions.* OD interventions often make it possible for the members of an organization to evaluate present personal, group, and organization goals and consider whether these goals represent the objectives they really want to achieve. Evaluation of this sort often points out the need to plot new directions.
3. *Identifying new norms and values.* Those OD interventions that stimulate thinking about new directions also provide organization members with the opportunity to develop new norms and values that will promote a move toward new goals.
4. *Identifying culture gaps.* To the extent that current (step 1) and desired (step 3) norms and values are articulated, the OD process enables organization members to identify as culture gaps the differences between the current and desired situations.
5. *Closing culture gaps.* Organization development gives people the opportunity to forge agreements that new norms and values will replace old ones and that every employee will take responsibility for managing and reinforcing these changes.[21]

When people engage in behaviors that are consistent with the new norms and values developed in an OD intervention, they reduce culture gaps and, in effect, change the organization's culture.

Change and Organization Development

Besides being a way of stimulating and solidifying cultural change, **organization development** is more generally a process of planning, implementing, and stabilizing the results of any type of organizational change. Organization development is also a field of research that specializes in developing and assessing specific **interventions,** or change techniques.[22] As both a management process and a field of research, organization development is characterized by five important features:

1. *Organization development emphasizes planned change.* The field of organization development evolved out of the need for a systematic, planned approach to managing change in organizations. It is organization development's empha-

sis on planning that distinguishes it from other processes of change in organizations that are more spontaneous or less methodical.

2. *Organization development has a pronounced social-psychological orientation.* OD interventions can stimulate change at many different levels—interpersonal, group, intergroup, and organizational. The field of organization development is thus neither purely psychological (focused solely on individuals) nor purely sociological (focused solely on organizations), but instead incorporates a mixture of the two orientations.

3. *Organization development focuses primary attention on comprehensive change.* Although every OD intervention focuses on a specific organizational target, of equal importance are effects on the total system. No OD intervention is designed and implemented without consideration of its broader implications.

4. *Organization development is characterized by a long-range time orientation.* Change is a continuing process that can sometimes take months—or even years—to produce desired results. Although managers often face pressure for quick, short-term gains, the OD process is not intended to yield stopgap solutions.

5. *Organization development is guided by a change agent.* OD interventions are designed, implemented, and assessed with the help of a **change agent,** an individual who serves both as a catalyst for change and as a source of information about the OD process.[23]

Together, these five features suggest the following definition: Organization development is a planned approach to interpersonal, group, intergroup, and organizational change that is comprehensive, long-term, and under the guidance of a change agent.

Resistance to Change

Change is the act of varying or altering conventional ways of thinking or behaving. In organizations, it is both an important impetus and a primary product of OD efforts, reshaping the ways in which people and groups work together. Whenever managers attempt to set any change in motion, they can expect resistance, because people tend to resist what they perceive as a threat to the established way of doing things. The more intense the change, the more intense the resulting resistance is likely to be.

Setting change in motion requires identifying and overcoming sources of resistance, on the one hand, and encouraging and strengthening sources of support, on the other. **Force field analysis** is a diagnostic method that diagrams the array of forces for and against a particular change in a graphic manner. It is a useful tool for managers and change agents who are attempting to envision the situation surrounding a prospective change.

The diagram shown in Figure 13-2 is an example of a typical force field analysis. In the figure, two lines are drawn, one representing an organization's present situation, and the other the organization after the desired change has been implemented. Next, forces identified as supporting change are depicted as arrows pushing in the direction of the desired change, and forces resisting change are drawn as arrows pushing in the opposite direction.

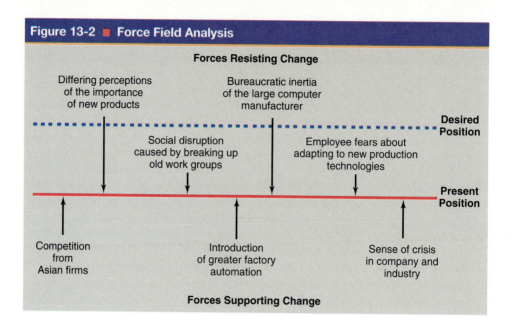

Figure 13-2 ■ Force Field Analysis

Forces Resisting Change

Differing perceptions of the importance of new products

Bureaucratic inertia of the large computer manufacturer

Desired Position

Social disruption caused by breaking up old work groups

Employee fears about adapting to new production technologies

Present Position

Competition from Asian firms

Introduction of greater factory automation

Sense of crisis in company and industry

Forces Supporting Change

The length of each arrow indicates the perceived strength of the force relative to that of the other forces in the force field.

The specific situation represented in the figure occurred during the early 1990s, when companies including Compaq, Zenith Data Systems, and NEC introduced small, portable computers intended to take the place of larger desktop personal computers in U.S. businesses. Forces resisting this change included (1) differing perceptions among the managers of U.S. companies about the need for new products (as opposed to continuing to use existing computers), (2) concerns of employees in the computer firms about the social disruption likely to occur as old work groups were disbanded to staff new production facilities, (3) bureaucratic inertia stemming from the rules and procedures used to coordinate existing ways of doing things, and (4) employee fears about not being able to cope with the demands of new production technologies.

Opposing these forces were others supporting change. The supporting forces included (1) the growing need among many U.S. users for greater computer portability, (2) a drive in computer firms to introduce simplified product designs and greater factory automation, in order to increase quality and control costs, and (3) a general sense of impending crisis throughout the worldwide computer industry. In the end, forces supporting change won out, with the introduction of notebook and "subnotebook" computers that proved to be quite successful in the marketplace.

There is no universal, fail-safe way to overcome the resistant factors identified in a force field analysis. Of the many available options, the six that are used most often are the following:

1. *Education and communication.* Information about the need and rationale for a prospective change can be disseminated through one-on-one discussions,

group meetings, and written memos or reports. This approach is best used when change is being undermined by a lack of information or when available information is inaccurate. Its strength is that once persuaded through education, people will often help with the implementation of change. Its primary weakness is that it can be quite time-consuming if many people must be involved.

2. *Participation and involvement.* Those who will be affected by an intervention should be involved in its design and implementation. Employees should meet as members of special committees or task forces to participate in the decision making. This option works well when information required to manage change is dispersed among many people and when employees who have considerable power are likely to resist change if not involved themselves. It facilitates information exchange among people and breeds commitment among the people involved, but it can slow down the process if participants design an inappropriate change or stray from the task at hand.

3. *Facilitation and support.* Needed job training and emotional support should be provided through instructional meetings and counseling sessions for employees to be affected by a change. This method is most useful when people are resisting change because of problems with personal adjustment. No other method works as well with adjustment problems, but it can consume significant amounts of time and money and still fail.

4. *Bargaining and negotiation.* Resistant employees should be worked with through bargaining and the proposal of trade-offs to provide them with incentives to change their minds. This technique is sometimes used if an individual or group with the power to block a change is likely to lose out if the change takes place. Negotiation can be a relatively easy way to avoid resistance in such situations, but it can prove costly if it alerts other individuals and groups to the fact that they might be able to negotiate additional gains for themselves.

5. *Hidden persuasion.* Covert efforts at providing information should be considered for use on a selective basis to get people to support desired changes. This approach is sometimes used when other tactics will not work or are too costly. It can be a quick and inexpensive way to dissolve resistance. However, it can lead to future problems if people feel unfairly treated, and may seem overly manipulative in retrospect even if suitable results are achieved.

6. *Explicit and implicit coercion.* Power and threats of negative consequences may be employed to change the minds of resistant individuals. Coercion tends to be used when speed is essential and when those initiating change possess considerable power. It can overcome virtually any kind of resistance. Its weakness is that it can be risky if it leaves people angry.[24]

Action Research

Organization development is a structured, multiple-step process. The **action research model** is a detailed variation of this process that promotes adherence to the scientific method (see Chapter 15) and places particular emphasis on

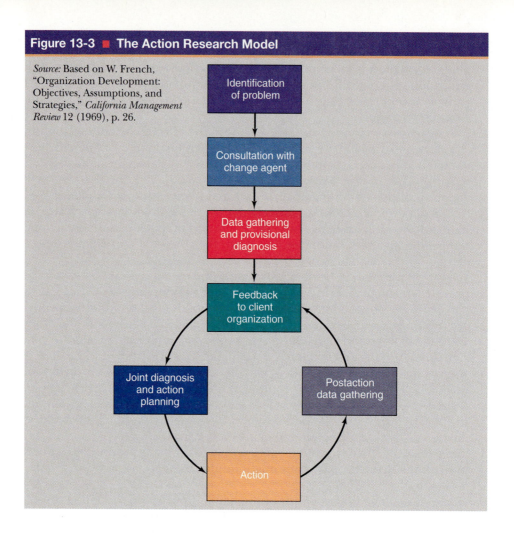

Figure 13-3 ■ **The Action Research Model**

Source: Based on W. French, "Organization Development: Objectives, Assumptions, and Strategies," *California Management Review* 12 (1969), p. 26.

Identification of problem

Consultation with change agent

Data gathering and provisional diagnosis

Feedback to client organization

Joint diagnosis and action planning

Postaction data gathering

Action

postchange evaluation.[25] As indicated in Figure 13-3, it consists of seven stages, the last four of which form a recurrent cycle.

In the initial stage of action research, *problem identification,* someone in an organization perceives problems that might be solved with the assistance of an organization development change agent. Specific problem statements can usually be formulated at this stage. Sometimes, however, problem identification cannot progress beyond an uneasy feeling that something is wrong. Consultation with a change agent may then be required to crystallize the problems.

In the second stage, *consultation,* the manager and a change agent clarify the perceived problems and consider ways of dealing with them. During this discussion, they assess the degree of fit between the organization's needs and the change agent's expertise. For example, if the organization is troubled by poor interpersonal relations, does the change agent know how to help people relate? Or if the organization is having problems with group performance, does the change agent have experience in team building? If the agent fits the situation, action research progresses to the next stage. If not, another change agent is called in and consultation begins anew.

In the third stage, that of *data gathering and provisional diagnosis,* the change agent initiates the diagnostic process by gathering data about the organization and its perceived problems. The agent observes and interviews employees and analyzes performance records. A member of the organization may assist during this process, facilitating the agent's entry into the firm and providing access to a significant amount of otherwise hidden or unavailable data. The change agent concludes this stage by examining the data and performing a provisional analysis and diagnosis of the situation.

Next, during the stage of *feedback to the client organization,* the data and provisional diagnosis are submitted to the client organization's top-management group. Informing top management early on of the OD process under way is absolutely necessary to secure the managerial support that any OD effort must have to succeed. The change agent is careful, during this presentation, to preserve the anonymity of people serving as sources of information. Identifying them could jeopardize their openness and willingness to cooperate later on, especially if they possess information that might be unflattering to management or portray the organization in negative terms.

During the fifth stage of action research, *joint diagnosis and action planning,* the change agent and the top-management group discuss the meaning of the data, their implications for organizational functioning, and any need for further data gathering and diagnosis. At this point, other people throughout the organization may also become involved in the diagnostic process. Sometimes employees meet in feedback groups and react to the results of top management's diagnostic activities. At other times, work groups elect representatives who then get together to exchange views and report back to their coworkers. If the firm is unionized, union representatives may also be consulted. No matter which members of the organization are specifically involved in the change process, however, the important point to remember is that in action research, the change agent does not impose interventions on the client organization. Instead, members of the organization deliberate jointly with the change agent and work together to develop wholly new interventions and plan specific action steps.

Next, the company puts the plan into motion and executes its action steps. In addition to the jointly designed intervention, the *action* stage may involve such activities as additional data gathering, further analysis of the problem situation, and supplementary action planning.

Because action research is a cyclical process, data are also gathered after actions have been taken, during the stage of *postaction data gathering and evaluation.* The purpose is to monitor and assess the effectiveness of an intervention. In evaluating the intervention, groups in the client organization review the data and decide whether they need to rediagnose the situation, perform further analyses of the situation, and develop new interventions. The change agent's role during this process is to serve as an expert on research methods as applied to the process of development and evaluation. In filling this role, the agent may perform data analyses, summarize the results of these analyses, guide subsequent rediagnoses, and position the organization for further intervention.

Table 13-2 ■ Organization Development Interventions

| TARGET | FOCAL PROBLEM | DEPTH | |
		SHALLOW	DEEP
Interpersonal relations	Problem fitting in with others	Role analysis technique	Sensitivity training
Group relations and leadership	Problem with working as a group	Process consultation	Team development
Intergroup relationships	Problem with relationships between groups	Third-party peacemaking	Intergroup team building
Organization-wide relationships	Problem with functioning effectively	Survey feedback	Open system planning

Organization Development Interventions

There are many, perhaps hundreds, of different OD interventions that can be selected on the basis of data gathered through action research and used to facilitate the stages of joint diagnosis and action planning, action, and postaction data gathering and evaluation just described. In this section, we overview eight of these interventions that, as indicated in Table 13-2, differ in terms of depth and target.

The **depth** of an OD intervention is the degree or intensity of change that the intervention is designed to stimulate.[26] A *shallow* intervention is intended mainly to provide people with information or to facilitate communication and minor change. In contrast, a *deep* intervention is intended to effect massive psychological and behavioral change. An intervention of this type attacks basic beliefs, values, and norms in an attempt to bring about fundamental changes in the way people think, feel, and behave.

The **target** is what an intervention focuses on. Interpersonal, group, intergroup, and organizational relations can all serve as targets of OD interventions. Associated with these different targets are different kinds of problems, as shown in Table 13-2 and indicated in earlier chapters of this book.

Interpersonal Interventions

Interpersonal interventions focus on solving problems with interpersonal relations such as those described in Chapter 7. Depending on the particular intervention, attempts may be made to define personal roles, clarify social expectations, or strengthen sensitivity to others' needs and interests.

Role Analysis Technique.   The **role analysis technique** (RAT), an interpersonal intervention of moderately shallow depth, is intended to help people form and maintain effective working relationships.[27] As we saw in Chapter 7, people at work fill specialized *roles* in which they are expected to engage in specific sorts

Figure 13-4 ■ Steps in the Role Analysis Technique

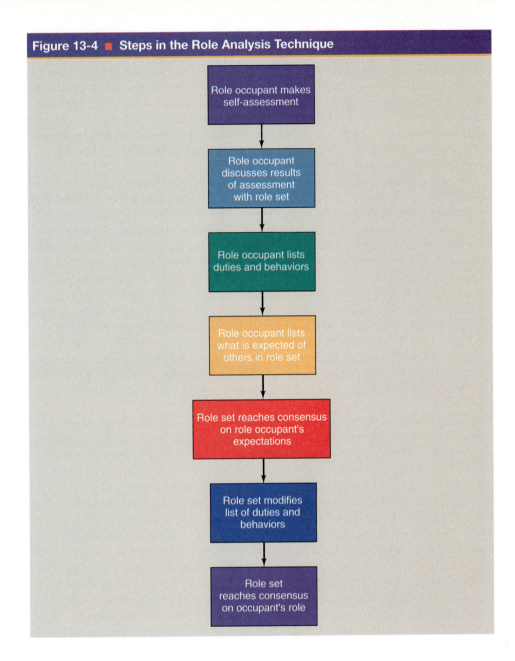

of behavior. Often, however, employees lack a clear idea of what their roles entail, or they are overburdened by role demands. RAT, outlined in Figure 13-4, is designed to help reduce role ambiguity and conflict by clarifying interpersonal expectations and responsibilities.

To initiate a RAT intervention, the occupant of a troublesome role contacts a change agent about the problem and receives instruction from the agent on the RAT procedure. Next, the role occupant works alone to analyze the rationale for the role, as well as its place in the organizational network of interpersonal relations. The role occupant tries to determine how to use the role in meeting personal, group, and organizational goals. Then the role occupant discusses the results of the analysis in a meeting attended by everyone whose work is directly affected by the role occupant's role. During this discussion, the change agent lists on a blackboard or flip chart the specific duties and behaviors of the role as identified by the role occupant. The rest of the group suggests corrections to this list. Behaviors are added or deleted until the role occupant is satisfied that the role as performed is defined accurately and completely.

Next the change agent directs attention to the role occupant's expectations of others. To begin this step, the role occupant lists what is expected of the roles that are connected with the role occupant's own. The group then discusses and modifies these expectations until everyone agrees on them. After this, all participants have the opportunity to modify their expectations about the role occupant's role, in response to that person's expectations of them. So, as you can see, RAT is a process of negotiation. The person who is the focus of the intervention can ask things of others, and others can ask the role occupant to do something for them.

In the final step of role analysis technique, the role occupant writes a summary, or profile, of the role as it has been defined. This profile specifies which behaviors are absolutely required and which are discretionary. It thereby constitutes a clearly defined listing of the role-related activities to be performed by the role occupant. The meeting continues, focusing on the roles of the other RAT participants, until all relevant interpersonal relationships have been clarified.

Sensitivity Training.   As a deep interpersonal intervention, **sensitivity training** focuses on developing greater sensitivity to oneself, to others, and to one's relations with others.[28] Designed to promote emotional growth and development, sensitivity training typically takes place in a closed session away from work. It may involve a collection of people who do not know each other, a group of people who are well acquainted, or a combination of both. A sensitivity training session may last for as little as half a day or go on for several days. It is begun by a change agent, who announces that the change agent's role is to serve solely as a nondirective resource. The change agent then lapses into silence, leaving the participants with neither a leader nor an agenda to guide interpersonal activities. The purpose of putting people in such an ambiguous situation is to force them to structure relationships among themselves and, in the process, question long-held assumptions about themselves, about each other, and about interpersonal relations.[29]

Sensitivity training participants take part in an intense exchange of ideas, opinions, beliefs, and personal philosophies as they struggle with the process of structuring interpersonal relations. Here is a description of one four-day session:

> The first evening discussion began with a rather neutral opening process which very soon led to strongly emotional expression of concern. . . . By the second day the participants had begun to express their feelings toward each other quite directly and frankly, something they had rarely done in their daily work. As the discussion progressed it became easier for them to accept criticism without becoming angry or wanting to strike back. As they began to express long-suppressed hostili-

ties and anxieties the "unfreezing" of old attitudes, old values, and old approaches began. From the second day onward the discussion was spontaneous and uninhibited. From early morning to long past midnight the process of self-examination and confrontation continued. They raised questions they had never felt free to ask before. Politeness and superficiality yielded to openness and emotional expression and then to more objective analysis of themselves and their relationships at work. They faced up to many conflicts and spoke of their differences. There were tense moments, as suspicion, distrust, and personal antagonisms were aired, but more issues were worked out without acrimony.[30]

By completing this process, people learn more about their own personal feelings, inclinations, and prejudices and about what other people think of them.

A word of warning: Sensitivity training is a deep intervention that can initiate profound psychological change. It is not uncommon for participants to engage in intensely critical assessments of themselves and others that can be both difficult and painful. Therefore, the change agent overseeing sensitivity training *must* be a trained professional who can help participants deal with criticism in a constructive manner. In the absence of expert help, participants could be at risk of serious psychological trauma.[31]

Group Interventions

Group interventions are designed to solve problems with group performance and leadership such as those identified in Chapters 8 and 9. In general, these interventions focus on helping the members of a group learn how to work together to fulfill the group's task and maintenance requirements.

Process Consultation. **Process consultation** is a relatively shallow group-level OD intervention. In a process consultation intervention, a change agent meets with a work group and helps its members examine group processes such as communication, leadership and followership, problem solving, and cooperation. The specific approach taken during this exploration varies from one situation to another, but may include the following steps:

1. The change agent asks stimulus questions that direct attention to relationships among group members. Ensuing discussions between group members may focus on ways to improve these relationships and on how such relationships can influence group productivity and effectiveness.
2. In a process analysis session, the change agent watches the group as it works. This session is followed by additional feedback sessions in which the change agent offers observations about how the group maintains itself and how it performs its task. There may also be supplementary feedback sessions to allow the change agent to clarify the events of earlier sessions for individual group members.
3. The change agent makes suggestions that may pertain to group membership, communication, interaction patterns, and the allocation of work duties, responsibilities, and authority.[32]

Whatever the change agent's approach in a given situation, the primary focus in process consultation is on making a group more effective by getting its members to pay more attention to important *process* issues. The change agent wants the members to focus on *how* things are done in the group rather than on the issues of *what* is to be done that normally dominate a group's attention. The ultimate goal of process consultation is to help the group improve its ability to solve its own problems by increasing the ability of members to identify and correct faulty group processes.[33]

Team Development.   **Team development** is a deep, group-level extension of interpersonal sensitivity training. In a team development intervention, a group of people who work together on a daily basis meet over an extended period of time to assess and modify group processes.[34] Throughout these meetings, participants focus their effort on achieving a balance of such basic components of teamwork as the following:

1. An understanding of, and commitment to, common goals
2. Involvement of as many group members as possible, in order to take advantage of the complete range of skills and abilities available to the group
3. Analysis and review of group processes on a regular basis to ensure that there are sufficient maintenance activities
4. Trust and openness in communication and relationships
5. A strong sense of belonging on the part of all members[35]

To begin team development, the group first engages in a lengthy diagnostic meeting in which a change agent helps members identify group problems and map out possible solutions. The change agent asks the members to observe interpersonal and group processes and to be prepared to comment on what they see. Thus the group works on two basic issues. They look for solutions to problems of everyday functioning that have come up in the group, and they observe the way group members interact with each other during the meeting.

Based on the results of these efforts, team development then proceeds in two specific different directions. First, the change agent and group implement the interventions chosen during diagnosis to solve the problems the group was able to identify. Second, the change agent initiates group sensitivity training to uncover additional problems that might otherwise resist detection:

> As the group fails to get [the change agent] to occupy the traditional roles of teacher, seminar leader, or therapist, it will redouble its efforts until in desperation it will disown him and seek other leaders. When they too fail, they too will be disowned, often brutally. The group will then use its own brutality to try to get the [change agent] to change his task by eliciting his sympathy and care for those it has handled so roughly. If this maneuver fails, and it never completely fails, the group will tend to throw up other leaders to express its concern for its members and project its brutality onto the consultant. As rival leaders emerge it is the job of the consultant, so far as he is able, to identify what the group is trying to do and explain it. His leadership is in task performance, and the task is to understand what the group is doing "now" and to explain why it is doing it.[36]

Group sensitivity training is really an interpersonal sensitivity training intervention conducted with an intact work group. It enables coworkers to critique and adjust to interpersonal relations problems that are inevitable during the workday. For this reason, the same cautions applicable to interpersonal sensitivity training are also relevant to group sensitivity training. Only a change agent trained to manage the rigors and consequences of a deep intervention should be allowed to take a leadership role.

Intergroup Interventions

Intergroup interventions focus on solving the types of intergroup problems identified in Chapter 10. In general, these problems concern conflict and associated breakdowns in intergroup coordination. Thus, OD interventions developed to manage intergroup relations involve various open communication techniques and conflict resolution methods.

Third-Party Peacemaking. **Third-party peacemaking** is a relatively shallow intervention in which a change agent seeks to resolve intergroup misunderstandings by encouraging communication between or among groups. The change agent, who is not a member of any of the groups and is referred to as a third party, guides a meeting between the groups. To be productive, the meeting must be characterized by the following attributes:

1. *Motivation.* All groups must be motivated to try to resolve their differences.
2. *Power.* A stable balance of power must be established between the groups.
3. *Timing.* Confrontations must be synchronized so that no one group can gain an information advantage over another.
4. *Emotional release.* People must be given the time to work through the negative thoughts and feelings that have built up between the groups. They need to recognize and express their positive feelings as well.
5. *Openness.* Conditions must favor openness in communication and mutual understanding.
6. *Stress.* There should be enough stress, enough pressure on group members, to motivate them to give serious attention to the problem, but not so much that the problem appears insoluble.[37]

The change agent facilitates communication between the groups both directly and indirectly. The change agent may interview group members before an intergroup meeting, help to put together a meeting agenda, monitor the pace of communication between groups during the meeting, or actually referee the interaction. Acting in a more subtle, indirect way, the change agent may schedule the meeting at a neutral site or establish time limits for intergroup interaction. The whole process can be as short as an afternoon but is more likely to be as long as several months of weekly sessions. As the result of meetings like these, the group members begin to learn things about each other and their relationships that can help them focus on common interests and begin to overcome conflictual tendencies.

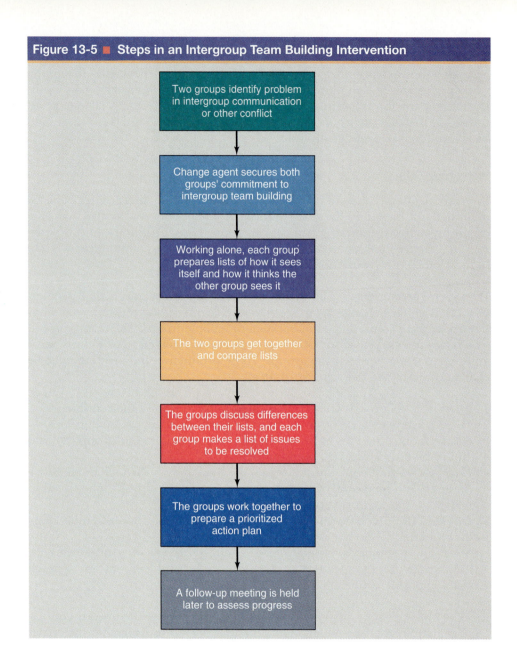

Figure 13-5 ■ Steps in an Intergroup Team Building Intervention

Two groups identify problem in intergroup communication or other conflict

Change agent secures both groups' commitment to intergroup team building

Working alone, each group prepares lists of how it sees itself and how it thinks the other group sees it

The two groups get together and compare lists

The groups discuss differences between their lists, and each group makes a list of issues to be resolved

The groups work together to prepare a prioritized action plan

A follow-up meeting is held later to assess progress

Intergroup Team Building. **Intergroup team building** is a deep intervention that has three primary aims. They are (1) to improve communication and interaction between work-related groups, (2) to decrease counterproductive competition between the groups, and (3) to replace group-centered perspectives with an orientation that recognizes the necessity for various groups to work together.[38]

As indicated in Figure 13-5, during the second step of intergroup team building, two groups (or their leaders) meet with an OD change agent and discuss whether relationships between the groups can be improved. If both groups agree that improvement is possible, the change agent asks the two groups to commit themselves to searching for ways of improving their relationship. Once they do so, they move to the third step. The two groups meet in separate rooms, and each makes two lists. The group's perceptions of, thoughts about, and attitudes toward the other group are on one list. Their thoughts about what the other group is likely to say about them are on the other. In the fourth step, the two groups reconvene and compare their lists. Each group can compare its view of the other group with the way the other group expects to be seen. Discrepancies uncovered during this comparison are discussed during the fifth step, when the groups meet separately. Each group reacts to what it has learned about itself and the other group. Then each group makes a list of important issues that need to be resolved between the two groups.

The two groups come back together during the sixth step and compare the lists of issues, setting priorities. Then they work together on a plan of action to resolve the issues in order of their priority. They assign individual responsibilities and target dates for completion. The final step is a follow-up meeting held later to assess progress. At that time, additional actions are planned as required to make sure that intergroup cooperation will continue over the long run.

Organizational Interventions

Organizational interventions are intended to deal with structural and cultural problems like those identified in Chapters 11 and 12, and the first part of this chapter. Some of these interventions are directed at improving communication and coordination within the organization. Others focus on diagnosing problems with relations between the organization and its external environment, and strengthening those relations.

Survey Feedback.   The main purpose of **survey feedback** is to stimulate information sharing throughout the entire organization. Planning and implementing change are of secondary importance. Thus it is a relatively shallow organization-level intervention.

The survey feedback procedure normally proceeds in four stages.[39] First, under the guidance of a trained change agent, top management engages in preliminary planning, deciding such issues as who should be surveyed and what questions should be asked. Other organization members may also participate in this first stage if their expertise or opinions are needed. Second, the change agent and the agent's staff administer the survey questionnaire to all organization members. Third, the change agent categorizes and summarizes the data. After presenting the data to management, the change agent holds group meetings to let everyone who responded to the questionnaire know the results. Fourth, the groups that received the feedback information hold meetings to discuss the survey. Group leaders take the groups through an interpretation of the data, helping them to evaluate the results and identify specific problems, make plans for constructive changes, and prepare to report on the data and proposed changes to groups at the next lower hierarchical level. The change agent usually

Figure 13-6 ■ Two Approaches to Data Collection by Questionnaire

	Traditional Approach	Survey Feedback, or OD Approach
Data collected from:	Workers and maybe foreman	Everyone in the system or subsystem
Data reported to:	Top management, departments heads, and perhaps to employees through newspaper	Everyone who participated
Implications of data worked on by:	Top management (maybe)	Everyone in work teams, with workshops starting at the top (all superiors with their subordinates)
Third-party intervention strategy:	Design and administration of questionnaire, development of report	Obtaining concurrence on total strategy, design, and administration of questionnaire, design of workshops, appropriate interventions in workshops
Action planning done by:	Top management only	Teams at all levels
Probable extent of change and improvement:	Low	High

Source: Reprinted with the publisher's permission from W. L. French and C. H. Bell Jr., *Organization Development: Behavioral Science Interventions for Organization Improvement,* 4th ed. (Englewood Cliffs, NJ: Prentice Hall, 1990), p. 170.

acts as a process consultant during these discussions to ensure that all group members get to contribute their opinions.

As shown in Figure 13-6, survey feedback is very different from the traditional questionnaire method of gathering information. In survey feedback, not only are data collected from everyone, from the highest to the lowest level of the hierarchy, but everyone in the organization participates in analyzing the data and in planning appropriate actions. These key characteristics of survey feedback reflect OD's basic values, which stress the critical importance of participation as a means of encouraging commitment to the organization's goals and stimulating personal growth and development.

Open System Planning. **Open system planning** is a fairly deep organization-level intervention. It is distinguished by its focus on the organization as a system open to its surrounding environment. That is, it sees the organization as a configuration of work processes that depend for their good function on external situations and events that impinge on them. The primary purpose of open system planning is to help the members of an organization devise ways to accomplish the mission of their firm in light of demands and constraints that originate with

Figure 13-7 ■ **Steps in an Open System Planning Intervention**

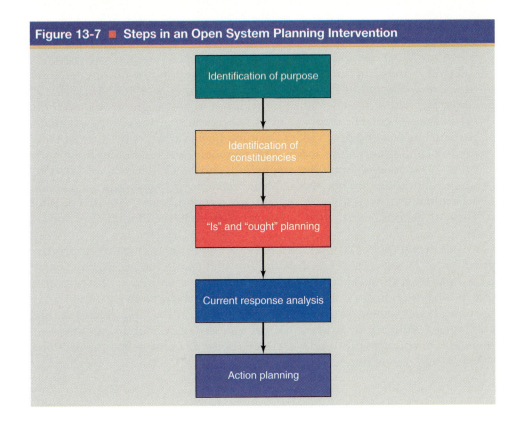

Identification of purpose

Identification of constituencies

"Is" and "ought" planning

Current response analysis

Action planning

constituency groups in the organization's environment. As indicated in Chapter 12, these groups may include raw-material suppliers, potential employees, customers, government regulators, and competitors.

As shown in Figure 13-7, the intervention consists of the following five steps:

1. *Identification of core mission, or purpose.* The members of the organization meet and, through open discussion, define the firm's basic purpose, and the goals required to accomplish this purpose.
2. *Identification of important constituency groups.* Then participants identify the environmental constituencies that can affect the firm's ability to accomplish its goals and purpose.
3. *"Is" and "ought" planning.* Next, participants describe current relations between the organization and its constituencies. They consider each constituency separately, focusing on the importance and duration of the relationship. Other relevant characteristics of the relationship are the frequency with which the parties are in contact and the organization's ability to sense and react to changes in the constituency group. Then participants determine how satisfactory the relationship *is* to both organization and constituency. If this assessment uncovers deficiencies, participants then specify what the relationship *ought* to be to be satisfactory to both sides.

4. *Analysis of current responses to constituency groups.* Participants then assess the organization's current response to each constituency group by answering these questions: What does this constituency want from us? What are we currently doing in response to this demand? Is our current response moving us closer to where we want to be in relation to our company's goals and purpose?

5. *Action planning.* If the current situation is not what it ought to be, and if the organization's current response to its constituency groups is not adequate, participants face the final task of deciding how to redirect the firm's behavior. In planning corrective action, firm members usually consider these questions: What actions should be taken, and who should take them? What resource allocations are necessary? What timetable? When should each action start and finish? Who will prepare a progress report, and when will it be due? How will actions be evaluated to ensure progress in the desired direction?[40]

Unlike most other OD interventions, open system planning directs primary attention to factors *outside* the organization that can influence organizational performance. It is especially useful in providing a structured yet participatory way to establish a firm's purpose and set the goals required to accomplish this purpose. Open system planning can also help identify critical environmental contingencies during the process of organization design. Identifying these contingencies encourages the development of a better fit between an organization's structure and its environment.

Evaluating Change and Development

No matter which organization development intervention is used, the concluding stage of the OD process always consists of an evaluation of effectiveness. Based on the results of this evaluation, efforts may be devoted to ensuring the permanence of newly developed attitudes, values, and behaviors. Alternatively, organization development may begin anew, and additional interventions may be initiated to stimulate further change. Table 13-3 contains a checklist of questions that can be useful in deciding what criteria to use and how to measure them when evaluating the effectiveness of organization development.

As suggested by the checklist, resources are expended to acquire the outcomes generated by the OD process. So organization development's effectiveness must be judged partly in terms of its outcomes. In addition, measuring its effectiveness requires remembering why it was undertaken to begin with and assessing what took place during each stage of the OD process. This procedure guarantees that an OD effort labeled "effective" not only accomplished its intended purpose but did so in a manner that left everyone more informed about the process of change and how to manage it. Finally, the effects of external and internal factors, whether positive or negative, on the OD process must be examined and cataloged for subsequent reference. That way, the factors that support change can be called into play when needed again in the future, and the ones that are resistant can be anticipated and neutralized.

Table 13-3 ■ Criteria for Evaluating Change Efforts

CRITERION	SUGGESTED QUESTIONS
Overall Results	
Desired outcomes	What were the intended outcomes of the intervention? How do they compare with the outcomes actually realized?
Guiding assumptions	How explicit were the assumptions that guided the intervention? Did experience prove them to be both valid and appropriate? Did everyone understand and agree with the intervention's purpose as a result?
Theory foundation	How consistent with current theories of organizational behavior and organization development were the guiding assumptions? Was everything that was currently known with regard to the intervention's focus and purpose incorporated in the intervention?
Phase of Intervention	
Identification phase	What was the reason for starting the intervention? Who was initially involved? Was the intervention initiated because of a broadly felt need or a narrow set of special interests?
Consultation phase	What activities were there at the start of the intervention process? Who was involved in them? Was the intervention implemented prematurely, without adequate diagnosis? Did unnecessary resistance arise as a result?
Data-gathering phase	What specific data collection and provisional diagnostic activities took place? Were they carried out fully and effectively?
Feedback and planning phase	What aspects of the organization were evaluated to determine the target and depth of the intervention that was to be implemented? How was the intervention planned, and who planned it? How were resources used in this effort? How explicit and detailed were the plans that resulted?
Action phase	What was actually done? When was it done? Who did it? How do the answers to these questions compare with the action plan as initially developed?
Postaction phase	Was postaction evaluation included from the outset as part of the intervention? Were deficiencies identified during evaluation corrected through a careful, planned modification to the intervention or its action plan?
External Factors	
Workforce traits	Were the results of the intervention affected, either positively or negatively, by workforce characteristics (e.g., age, gender, and education)?
Economy	What was the state of the economy and the firm's market at the time of the intervention? Did economic factors affect the success of the intervention?
Environment	How much did the organization's environment change over the course of the intervention? Are the intended results of the intervention still desirable given the organization's current environment?
Internal Factors	
Size	How large is the organization? Did its size permit access to the resources required for the intervention to succeed?
Technology	What is the organization's primary product, and what sort of technology is used to make it? Do the results of the intervention fit in or conflict with the requirements of this technology?
Structure	How mechanistic or organic is the organization's structure? Do the results of the intervention fit in or conflict with this structure?
Culture	What are the organization's prevailing norms and values concerning change? Concerning involvement in OD interventions?

Sources: Based on N. Tichy and J. N. Nisberg, "When Does Work Restructuring Work? Organizational Innovations at Volvo and GM," *Organizational Dynamics* 4 (1976), pp. 13–36; and W. L. French, "A Checklist for Organizing and Implementing an OD Effort," in *Organization Development: Theory, Practice, and Research,* W. L. French, C. H. Bell Jr., and R. A. Zawacki, eds., rev. ed. (Plano, TX: Business Publications, 1983), pp. 451–59.

SUMMARY

The *culture* of an organization consists of deep-seated norms and values, as well as surface expressions of these norms and values. The latter include *ceremonies, rites, rituals, stories, myths, heroes, symbols,* and *language.* Culture is a cohesive force that influences the way the firm's members perceive the formal organization, their behaviors, and themselves. *Symbolic management* and OD interventions can be used to manage the culture of an organization.

Organization development is both a field of research and a collection of *interventions* intended to stimulate planned change in organizations. Associated with organization development is a concern about managing resistance to change and strengthening forces that favor change. *Force field analysis* is a technique that can be used to aid in the pursuit of these complementary goals. The *action research model* describes how *change agents* often manage the OD process.

OD interventions differ from each other in the *depth* of change they are intended to stimulate and the types of organizational behavior that are their *target.* The *role analysis technique* and *sensitivity training* are interventions that target interpersonal problems; sensitivity training is the deeper of the two. *Process consultation* and *team development* are group interventions, the latter being deeper than the former. *Third-party peacemaking* and *intergroup team building* are intergroup interventions, intergroup team building being the deeper option. *Survey feedback* and *open system planning* are organization-level interventions; open system planning is the deeper of the two. No matter which intervention is used, all OD efforts should conclude with an evaluation of program effectiveness.

Review Questions

1. As a manager, you face the task of reversing cultural norms that favor low performance. What do you do to accomplish this task? What role do the surface elements of culture play in your plan?
2. How do cultural norms and values act as social information? What effects does this information have on organizational behavior? Why is it important for managers to take social information into account when designing jobs and structuring the organization?
3. What differences are there between organization development and other approaches that might be used to stimulate change in organizations? What is gained by understanding and using the action research model?
4. Suppose you were given the assignment of developing a new grading system for your OB class. Draw a force field analysis diagram showing the major forces for and against change that you would probably encounter while implementing your new grading system. What would you do to weaken the forces against change? How would you strengthen the forces for change? Is it likely that your change intervention would succeed?

5. Why is it important to avoid using an intervention that is deeper than needed to stimulate the required amount of change? How can you increase the likelihood that the intervention is focused on the appropriate target?
6. Which of the OD interventions described in this chapter would you choose for each of the following situations: individuals who understand their personal roles in a group but can't seem to get along with coworkers; a group of people who get along with each other but fail to be as productive as expected; an organization suffering from poor internal communication; and an organization unsure about its place in the broader business environment.
7. Why is it always important to evaluate the results of an OD intervention? What kinds of information should you collect and consider during an evaluation?

Implementation Guide

Managing organization culture requires knowledge about the norms and values that shape the informal side of organizational behavior. Organization development is one way of acquiring this knowledge, and it is also a general approach to the management of change that can help managers solve many of the other interpersonal, group, intergroup, and organizational problems identified in this book. The following questions offer practical guidance for such activities.

1. What cultural norms and values guide behaviors and understandings in the firm? Do surface elements reinforce these deeper elements? Do differences between surface elements and cultural norms and values suggest ongoing cultural change? Is this change desirable?
2. Does the culture help hold the organization together in a way that supports the formal organization? Does it provide social information that is consistent with the firm's purpose and general well-being?
3. Beyond cultural considerations, what sort of change is being contemplated? What sources of resistance to this change exist in the organization? What might you do to overcome this resistance? How successful are you likely to be?
4. Based on a force field analysis, what are the forces in the organization that favor the change? How can you strengthen them? How strong can they be made? What is the likely combined effect of the forces for and against change? Is it realistic to attempt to institute change, or should the status quo be accepted instead?
5. Do the depth and target of the OD intervention being implemented seem to match the problem? Note that the shallowest intervention likely to stimulate the required amount of change is the one that should be selected for implementation.
6. Is evaluation an integral part of the OD effort? As evaluation criteria and procedures are established, are serious attempts made to guard against bias and distortion?
7. How likely is it that positive change will persist after the OD effort has ended? What can be done to ensure lasting change?

1. E. H. Schein, *Organizational Culture and Leadership* (San Francisco: Jossey-Bass, 1985), p. 9.

2. L. Smircich, "Concepts of Culture and Organizational Analysis," *Administrative Science Quarterly* 28 (1983), pp. 339–58; and S. G. Harris, "Organizational Culture and Individual Sensemaking: A Schema-Based Perspective," *Organization Science* 5 (1994), pp. 309–21.

3. T. E. Deal and A. A. Kennedy, *Corporate Cultures: The Rites and Rituals of Corporate Life* (Reading, MA: Addison-Wesley, 1982), p. 15.

4. H. M. Trice and J. M. Beyer, *The Cultures of Work Organizations* (Englewood Cliffs, NJ: Prentice Hall, 1993), pp. 1–2.

5. M. J. Hatch, "The Dynamics of Organizational Culture," *Academy of Management Review* 18 (1993), pp. 657–93; and L. K. Gundry and D. M. Rousseau, "Critical Incidents in Communicating Culture to Newcomers: The Meaning Is the Message," *Human Relations* 47 (1994), pp. 1063–88.

6. Deal and Kennedy, *Corporate Cultures,* p. 63.

7. J. M. Beyer and H. M. Trice, "How an Organization's Rites Reveal Its Culture," *Organizational Dynamics* 15 (1987), pp. 3–21; and Trice and Beyer, *The Cultures of Work Organizations,* pp. 107–27.

8. J. Martin, "Stories and Scripts in Organizational Settings," in *Cognitive Social Psychology,* A. Hastorf and A. Isen, eds. (New York: Elsevier–North Holland, 1982), pp. 225–305; C. D. Hansen and W. M. Kahnweiler, "Storytelling: An Instrument for Understanding the Dynamics of Corporate Relationships," *Human Relations* 46 (1993), pp. 1391–1409; D. M. Boje, "The Storytelling Organization: A Study of Story Performance in an Office-Supply Firm," *Administrative Science Quarterly* 36 (1991), pp. 106–26; and D. M. Boje, "Stories of the Storytelling Organization: A Postmodern Analysis of Disney as 'Tamara-Land'," *Academy of Management Journal* 38 (1995), pp. 997–1035.

9. A. L. Wilkins, "Organizational Stories as Symbols Which Control the Organization," in *Organizational Symbolism,* L. R. Pondy, P. J. Frost, G. Morgan, and T. C. Dandridge, eds. (Greenwich, CT: JAI Press, 1983), pp. 81–92.

10. Deal and Kennedy, *Corporate Cultures,* pp. 40–41.

11. D. A. Gioia, "Symbols, Scripts, and Sensemaking," in *The Thinking Organization,* H. P. Sims, ed. (San Francisco: Jossey-Bass, 1986) pp. 48–112.

12. J. Pfeffer, *Power in Organizations* (Marshfield, MA: Pitman, 1981), p. 50.

13. G. Morgan, P. J. Frost, and L. R. Pondy, "Organizational Symbolism," in *Organizational Symbolism,* L. R. Pondy, P. J. Frost, G. Morgan, and T. C. Dandridge, eds. (Greenwich, CT: JAI Press, 1983), pp. 3–38.

14. Trice and Beyer, *The Cultures of Work Organizations,* p. 90.

15. R. Brandt, "The Billion-Dollar Whiz Kid," *Business Week,* April 13, 1987, pp. 68–76; and K. I. Rebello and E. I. Schwartz, "Microsoft: Bill Gates' Baby Is on Top of the World. Can It Stay There?" *Business Week,* February 24, 1992, pp. 60–64.

16. C. A. O'Reilly III, J. Chatman, and D. F. Caldwell, "People and Organizational Culture: A Profile Comparison Approach to Assessing Person-Organization Fit," *Academy of Management Journal* 34 (1991), pp. 487–516; and J. E. Sheridan, "Organizational Culture and Employee Retention," *Academy of Management Journal* 35 (1992), pp. 1036–56.

17. G. R. Salancik and J. Pfeffer, "A Social Information Processing Approach to Job Attitudes and Task Design," *Administrative Science Quarterly* 23 (1978), pp. 224–53; R. E. Rice and C. Aydin, "Attitudes toward New Organizational Technology: Network Proximity as a Mechanism for Social Information Processing," *Administrative Science Quarterly* 36 (1991), pp. 219–44; and H. Ibarra and S. B. Andrews, "Power, Social Influence, and Sense Making: Effects of Network Centrality and Proximity on Employee Perceptions," *Administrative Science Quarterly* 38 (1993), pp. 277–303.

18. J. B. Miner, *Organizational Behavior; Performance and Productivity* (New York: Random House, 1988), p. 571; and H. M. Trice and J. M. Beyer, "Using Six Organizational Rites to Change Culture," in *Gaining Control of the Corporate Culture,* R. H. Kilmann, M. J. Saxon, and R. Serpa, eds. (San Francisco: Jossey-Bass, 1985), pp. 370–99.

19. J. Pfeffer, "Management as Symbolic Action: The Creation and Maintenance of Organizational Paradigms," in *Research in Organizational Behavior,* L. L. Cummings and B. M. Staw, eds., vol. 3 (Greenwich, CT: JAI Press, 1981), pp. 1–52.

20. B. Dumaine, "Creating a New Company Culture," *Fortune,* January 15, 1990, pp. 127–31.

21. Miner, *Organizational Behavior,* pp. 574–75; and R. H. Kilmann, *Beyond the Quick Fix* (San Francisco: Jossey-Bass, 1984), pp. 105–23.

22. G. L. Lippitt, P. Longseth, and J. Mossop, *Implementing Organizational Change* (San Francisco: Jossey-Bass, 1985), p. 3; and E. Fagenson and W. W. Burke,

"The Current Activities and Skills of Organization Development Practitioners," *Academy of Management Proceedings,* August 13–16, 1989, p. 251.

23. A. C. Filley, R. J. House, and S. Kerr, *Managerial Process and Organizational Behavior,* 2d ed. (Glenview, IL: Scott, Foresman, 1976), pp. 488–90; and W. L. French and C. H. Bell Jr., *Organization Development: Behavioral Science Interventions for Organizational Improvement,* 4th ed. (Englewood Cliffs, NJ: Prentice Hall, 1990), pp. 21–22.

24. J. P. Kotter and L. A. Schlesinger, "Choosing Strategies for Change," *Harvard Business Review* 57 (1979), pp. 102–21; and J. M. Ivancevich and M. T. Matteson, *Organizational Behavior and Management,* 2d ed. (Homewood, IL: Irwin, 1990), pp. 621–22.

25. J. M. Bartunek, "Scholarly Dialogues and Participatory Action Research," *Human Relations* 46 (1993), pp. 1221–33; and F. Heller, "Another Look at Action Research," *Human Relations* 46 (1993), pp. 1235–42.

26. R. Harrison, "Choosing the Depth of Organizational Intervention," *Journal of Applied Behavioral Science* 6 (1970), pp. 181–202.

27. I. Dayal and J. M. Thomas, "Operation KPE: Developing a New Organization," *Journal of Applied Behavioral Science* 4 (1968), pp. 473–506.

28. J. P. Campbell and M. D. Dunnette, "Effectiveness of T-Group Experiences in Managerial Training and Development," *Psychological Bulletin* 65 (1968), pp. 73–104.

29. E. Aronson, "Communication in Sensitivity Training Groups," in *Organization Development: Theory, Practice, and Research,* W. L. French, C. H. Bell Jr., and R. A. Zawacki, eds. (Plano, TX: Business Publications, 1983), pp. 249–53.

30. G. David, "Building Cooperation and Trust," in *Management by Participation,* A. J. Marrow, D. G. Bowers, and S. E. Seashore, eds. (New York: Harper & Row, 1967), pp. 99–100.

31. C. A. Bramlette and J. H. Tucker, "Encounter Groups: Positive Change or Deterioration," *Human Relations* 34 (1981), pp. 303–14.

32. E. H. Schein, *Process Consultation* (Reading, MA: Addison-Wesley, 1968), pp. 102–3; and C. F. Paul and A. C. Gross, "Increasing Productivity and Morale in a Municipality: Effects of Organization Development," *Journal of Applied Behavioral Science* 17 (1981), pp. 59–78.

33. Schein, *Process Consultation,* p. 135.

34. R. T. Golembiewski, *Approaches to Planned Change, Part I: Orienting Perspectives and Micro-Level Interventions* (New York: Marcel Dekker, 1979), p. 301.

35. G. L. Lippitt, *Organization Renewal* (New York: Appleton-Century-Crofts, 1969), pp. 107–13.

36. A. K. Rice, *Learning for Leadership* (London: Tavistock Publications, 1965), pp. 65–66.

37. R. E. Walton, *Interpersonal Peacemaking: Confrontation and Third Party Consultation* (Reading, MA: Addison-Wesley, 1969), pp. 94–115.

38. R. R. Blake, H. A. Shepard, and J. S. Mouton, *Managing Intergroup Conflict in Industry* (Houston: Gulf, 1965), pp. 36–100; and R. Beckhard, *Organization Development: Strategies and Models* (Reading, MA: Addison-Wesley, 1969), pp. 33–35.

39. F. C. Mann, "Studying and Creating Change," in *The Planning of Change,* W. G. Bennis, K. D. Benne, and R. Chin, eds. (New York: Holt, Rinehart & Winston, 1961), pp. 605–13.

40. W. G. Dyer, *Strategies for Managing Change* (Reading, MA: Addison-Wesley, 1984), pp. 149–50.

Chapter Fourteen

International Organizational Behavior

In today's world economy, it is becoming increasingly difficult to find a company that does not conduct business across national boundaries. Indeed, "U.S." service firms like McDonald's, Time-Warner, Disney, and American Express do more than one-third of their business outside the United States, and dozens of "U.S." industrial companies, including IBM, Gillette, Xerox, Dow Chemical, and Hewlett-Packard, sell more of their products outside the United States than they do at home. These companies and others, for example "Japanese" companies like Sony, Mazda, and Mitsubishi, now do so much business outside their original homeland that they have become multinational enterprises, or **multinationals.**

A few multinationals have developed even further, growing into **global enterprises.** Also called *stateless corporations,* global enterprises are companies that span several countries, like multinationals, but go an additional step by customizing products to regional tastes and localizing business operations at each of the many sites they own. One such company, Syncordia, is a worldwide telecommunications outsourcing company owned jointly by MCI and British Telecom. Instead of being directed by either of its parent firms or managed from a central headquarters, Syncordia is run by teams of managers operating from diverse locations. Outside of a few standardized corporate guidelines, Syncordia's management teams are free to adapt business practices to regional conditions.[1] Logitech, maker of the ubiquitous computer mouse, is another global enterprise. Headquartered in the United States and Switzerland, Logitech has research and development facilities at both locations, as well as in Taiwan and Ireland. No single geographic center drives company operations. Rather, decision-making and management responsibilities are shared among the company's far-flung corporate offices.[2]

Global statelessness is a relatively new way to do business. Ford Motor Company is just now globalizing, having identified global outreach and restructuring as the preferred way to sustain growth in the face of the maturing North American automotive market. In a similar way, giant drugmaker Bristol-Myers Squibb Company, manufacturer of Bufferin, Excedrin, and the Clairol hair-care line, is struggling to remake itself in an effort to compete in the rapidly consolidating world market for health and beauty products.[3]

[1]M. W. Hordes, A. J. Clancy, and J. Baddaley, "A Primer for Global Start-Ups," *Academy of Management Executive* 9 (1995), pp. 7–11.

[2]B. M. Oviatt and P. P. McDougall, "Global Start-Ups: Entrepreneurs on a Worldwide Stage," *Academy of Management Executive* 9 (1995), pp. 30–44.

[3]J. A. Byrne, K. Kerwin, A. Cortese, and P. Dwyer, "Borderless Management: Companies Strive to Become Truly Stateless," *Business Week,* May 23, 1994, pp. 24–26.

Globalization can yield massive benefits. Honda Motor Company is now the number one exporter of North American–assembled automobiles, and is able to circumvent anti-Japanese trade barriers in Israel, Taiwan, and South Korea by shipping American-made Accords and Civics to these destinations. Unilever PLC controls major shares of the consumer products markets in North America and Europe, which provides it with the resources needed to expand aggressively into developing economies throughout Asia and Latin America. Statelessness is critical to the competitive success of these companies and others like them that are doing business in the international markets of today.[1]

However, with multinationalization and globalization come differences in nationality and culture that have major effects on micro, meso, and macro organizational behavior. These differences complicate the jobs of contemporary managers, because they require that management practices developed in one cultural region be modified for use in other national cultures. For this reason, today's managers *must* take international differences seriously if they expect to compete and succeed in global markets.

This chapter overviews several important international differences and examines how they can affect the management of organizational behavior. We begin by introducing a five-dimensional model that is useful in characterizing differences among national cultures. Next, we review key points of Chapters 4, 9, and 11 to summarize North American thinking on the OB topics of employee motivation, leadership, and organization structure. We then contrast this point of view with concepts and practices found in other national cultures, in a comparison of three extended examples. We conclude by discussing the managerial implications of international differences, focusing on developing a basic framework useful for fitting the management practices described in this book—practices that are overwhelmingly North American in origin and focus—to the job of managing people and organizations throughout the world.

International Dimensions

How do cultures differ from one region of the world to another? In what ways are the **national cultures** of different countries similar? What effects do these cultures have on people's attitudes and behaviors in organizations? In a pathbreaking study,

Dutch researcher Geert Hofstede set out to answer these questions by surveying employees of IBM offices located in 40 countries throughout the world. As he examined the data from 116,000 questionnaires, Hofstede discovered that most differences among national cultures could be described by four dimensions—uncertainty avoidance, masculinity-femininity, individualism-collectivism, and power distance.[2] In later research, Canadian researcher Michael Harris Bond questioned individuals in several other national cultures and uncovered a fifth dimension, short-term versus long-term orientation, which Hofstede added to his model.[3]

Uncertainty Avoidance

The degree to which people are comfortable with ambiguous situations and with the inability to predict future events with assurance is described by the dimension of **uncertainty avoidance.** At one extreme of this dimension, people with weak uncertainty avoidance feel comfortable even though they are unsure about current activities or future events. Their attitudes are expressed in the following statements:

- Life is inherently uncertain and is most easily dealt with if taken one day at a time.
- It is appropriate to take risks in life.
- Deviation from the norm is not threatening; tolerance of differences is essential.
- Conflict and competition can be managed and used constructively.
- There should be as few rules as possible, and rules that cannot be kept should be changed or eliminated.[4]

At the other extreme, people characterized by strong uncertainty avoidance are most comfortable when they feel a sense of certainty about the present and future. Their attitudes about uncertainty and associated issues can be stated as follows:

- The uncertainty inherent in life is threatening and must be fought continually.
- Having a stable, secure life is important.
- Deviant persons and ideas are dangerous and should not be tolerated.
- Conflict and competition can unleash aggression and must be avoided.
- There is a need for written rules and regulations; if people do not adhere to them it is because of human frailty, not defects in the rules and regulations themselves.[5]

In cultures characterized by high uncertainty avoidance, behavior is motivated at least partly by people's fear of the unknown and by attempts to cope with this fear. Often people in such cultures try to reduce or avoid uncertainty by establishing extensive formal rules. For instance, having extensive laws about marriage and divorce reduces uncertainty about the structure and longevity of family relationships. If uncertainty proves unavoidable, people with a cultural aversion to uncertainty may hire "experts" who seem to have the ability to apply knowledge, insight, or skill to the task of making something uncertain into something understandable. These experts need not actually accomplish anything so long as they are perceived as understanding what others do not. People with an uncertainty aversion may also engage in rituals intended to help them cope with the anxiety that uncertainty arouses. Such activities may include the development of extensive plans and forecasts designed to encourage speculation about the future and to make it seem more understandable and predictable. Plans and forecasts dispel anxiety, even if they prove largely invalid. For this reason, although people living in inconstant climates often joke about the inaccuracy of local weather forecasts, many still tune in to televised weather forecasts every night to plan what to wear and do the next day.

Masculinity-Femininity

Hofstede used the term *masculinity* to refer to the degree to which a culture is founded on values that emphasize independence, aggressiveness, dominance, and physical strength. According to Hofstede, people in a national culture that is extreme in its masculinity hold beliefs such as the following:

- Sex roles in society should be clearly differentiated; men are intended to lead and women to follow.
- Independent performance and visible accomplishments are what count in life.
- People live in order to work.
- Ambition and assertiveness provide the motivation behind behavior.
- People admire the successful achiever.[6]

Femininity, according to Hofstede, describes a society's tendency to favor such values as interdependence, compassion, empathy, and emotional openness. People in a national culture oriented toward extreme femininity hold such beliefs as the following:

- Sex roles in society should be fluid and flexible; sexual equality is desirable.
- The quality of life is more important than personal performance and visible accomplishments.
- People work in order to live.
- Helping others provides the motivation behind behavior.
- People sympathize with the unfortunate victim.[7]

The extremes of masculinity and femininity delineate the dimension of **masculinity-femininity** in Hofstede's model of cross-cultural differences. One important effect of the differences mapped by this dimension is the way in which a nation's work is divided into jobs and distributed among its citizens. In masculine national cultures, women are forced to work at lower-level jobs. Managerial work is seen as the province of men, who are portrayed as having the ambition and independence of thought required to succeed at decision making and problem solving. Women also receive less pay and recognition for their work than do their male counterparts. Only in "feminine" occupations such as teacher or nurse, or in supporting roles such as secretary or clerk, are women allowed to manage themselves. Even then, female supervisors are often required to imitate their male bosses in order to be accepted as managers.

In contrast, equality between the sexes is the norm in national cultures labeled as being feminine. In such cultures, neither men nor women are considered to be better managers, and no particular occupation is seen as masculine or feminine. Both sexes are equally recognized for their work, and neither is required to mimic the behavior of the other for the sake of acceptance in the workplace.

Individualism-Collectivism

According to Hofstede, **individualism-collectivism** is a dimension that traces cultural tendencies either to emphasize satisfying personal needs or to emphasize looking after the needs of the group. From the viewpoint of individualism, pursuing personal interests is more important, and succeeding in the pursuit of these interests is critical to both personal and societal well-being. If each person takes care of personal interests, then everyone will be well off. In keeping with this perspective, the members of individualistic national cultures espouse the following attitudes:

- "I" is more important than "we."
- People are identified by their personal traits.
- Success is a personal achievement. People function most productively when working alone.
- People should be free to seek autonomy, pleasure, and security through their own personal efforts.
- All members of society should take care of their personal well-being and the well-being of immediate family members.[8]

In contrast, the collectivist perspective emphasizes that group welfare is more important than personal interests. People who hold this viewpoint believe that only by belonging to a group and looking after its interests can they secure their own well-being and that of the broader society. The members of collectivistic national cultures are thus inclined to ignore personal needs for the sake of their groups, and believe in ensuring group well-being even if personal hardships must be endured. They agree on the following:

- "We" is more important than "I."
- People are identified by the characteristics of the groups they belong to.
- Success is a group achievement. People contribute to group performance, but groups alone function productively.
- People can achieve order and security and fulfill their duty to society only through group membership.
- Every member of society should belong to a group that will secure members' well-being in exchange for loyalty and attention to group interests.[9]

In national cultures located nearer the individualistic end of the dimension, membership in a group is something that can be initiated and terminated whenever convenient. Individualists do not necessarily have a strong feeling of commitment to any of the groups to which they belong. In more collectivistic national cultures, however, changes in membership status can be traumatic. Joining and leaving a group can be like finding and then losing one's sense of identity. The collectivist feels a very strong, enduring sense of commitment to the group.[10]

Power Distance

Power distance is a dimension that indicates the degree to which the members of a society accept differences in power and status among themselves. In national cultures that tolerate only a small degree of power distance, norms and values specify that differences in people's ability to influence others should be minimal, and that political equality should be encouraged instead. People in these cultures show a strong preference for participatory decision making and tend to distrust autocratic, hierarchical types of governance. They believe the following:

- Superiors should consider subordinates "people just like me," and subordinates should regard superiors in the same way.
- Superiors should be readily accessible to subordinates.
- Using power is neither inherently good nor inherently evil; whether power is good or evil depends on the purposes for, and consequences of, its use.
- Everyone in a society has equal rights, and these rights should be universally enforced.[11]

In contrast, national cultures characterized by a large degree of power distance are based on norms and values stipulating that power should be distributed hierarchically, instead of being shared more or less equally. People in these cultures favor using authority and direct supervision to coordinate people and jobs. They hold the following beliefs:

- Superiors and subordinates should consider each other to be different kinds of people.
- Superiors should be inaccessible to subordinates.
- Power is a basic fact of society; notions of good and evil are irrelevant.
- Power holders are entitled to special rights and privileges.[12]

Power distance influences attitudes and behaviors by affecting the way a society is held together. When the members of a national culture favor only a small degree of power distance, citizens have a strong, direct voice in determining national policy. In contrast, where societal norms and values favor larger power distance, government is less participatory. Authoritarian, autocratic government is the hallmark of larger power distance.

Short-Term versus Long-Term Orientation

The dimension of **short-term versus long-term orientation** reflects the extent to which the members of a national culture are oriented toward the recent past and the present versus being oriented toward the future. In national cultures characterized by a short-term orientation, individuals believe the following:

- It is important to respect traditions and to remember past accomplishments.

- To forget history is to risk repeating past mistakes.
- Failing activities should be halted immediately.
- Resources should be consumed now without concern for the future.[13]

The short-term orientation supports immediate consumption and opposes the deferral of pleasure and satisfaction. With this orientation, unpleasant tasks are avoided, even if they are necessary to ensure a pleasurable future. In contrast, in national cultures with a long-term orientation, people agree on the following:

- It is important to look ahead and to envision the future.
- History is only likely to repeat itself if looking to the past obscures visions of the future.
- Perseverance in the face of adversity can overcome failure.
- Resources should be saved to ensure a prosperous future.[14]

A longer-term orientation favors the opposite strategy, of doing what is necessary now, whether pleasant or not, for the sake of future well-being. Whether a culture has a short-term or a long-term orientation thus influences people's willingness to endure hardship in the present and defer pleasurable experiences into the future.

Three Cultural Examples

Hofstede's five-dimensional model is not without its critics. For instance, a study that used the original four dimensions to assess the societal values of American, Japanese, and Taiwanese managers in Taiwan revealed problems with measurement validity and reliability (see Chapter 15 for a discussion of these kinds of problems).[15] Nonetheless, the Hofstede model is the most comprehensive cross-cultural framework currently available, and it stimulates a variety of useful insights. Table 14-1 summarizes the average scores on the five dimensions for each of the 44 countries included in the studies by Hofstede and Bond. In the table, larger numbers signify greater amounts of uncertainty avoidance, masculinity, individualism, or power distance, or a longer-term orientation.

What effects do the differences quantified in Hofstede's model have on the management of organizational behavior? To get some idea, consider the ways in which two of Hofstede's dimensions—individualism-collectivism and power distance—work together to influence the management of three important aspects of organizational behavior discussed in this book: motivation, from the area of micro organizational behavior; leadership, from the area of meso organizational behavior; and structure, from the area of macro organizational behavior.

To establish a comparative baseline, think about the national culture of the United States and the way organizational behavior is managed in American organizations. The U.S. national culture is extremely individualistic. It is also oriented toward larger degrees of power distance than many of the other cultures

Table 14-1 ■ A Comparison of Cultural Characteristics

NATIONAL CULTURE	UNCERTAINTY AVOIDANCE	MASCULINITY-FEMININITY	INDIVIDUALISM-COLLECTIVISM	POWER DISTANCE	SHORT-TERM VERSUS LONG-TERM ORIENTATION
Argentina	86	56	46	49	—
Australia	51	61	90	36	—
Austria	70	79	55	11	—
Belgium	94	54	75	65	—
Brazil	76	49	38	69	—
Canada	48	52	80	39	—
Chile	86	28	23	63	—
China	60	50	20	80	118
Colombia	80	64	13	67	—
Denmark	23	16	74	18	—
Finland	59	26	63	33	—
France	86	43	71	68	—
Germany	65	66	67	35	—
Great Britain	35	66	89	35	—
Greece	112	57	35	60	—
Hong Kong	29	57	25	68	—
India	40	56	48	77	—
Indonesia	48	46	14	78	25
Iran	59	43	41	58	—
Ireland	35	68	70	28	—
Israel	81	47	54	13	—
Italy	75	70	76	50	—
Japan	92	95	46	54	—
Mexico	82	69	30	81	—

in Hofstede's study (see Table 14-1). Consequently, the models and practices described in this book—which are primarily American in origin and focus—are attuned to individualism and moderately large power distance. As indicated in Chapter 4, employee performance in American organizations is motivated by the receipt of rewards expected to satisfy personal needs, especially when those rewards are received in proportion to personal performance. Piece-rate wages or commission payments are often used to motivate the individual employee, reflecting the individualism of the U.S. national culture.

As described in Chapter 9, leadership in traditionally managed U.S. firms is largely a task of directing the behaviors and enhancing the motivation of individual employees. Individualism requires that leaders in U.S. firms use direct supervision to coordinate the work of their subordinates, so that success at personal jobs leads to fulfillment of group and organizational goals. The leader is the "glue" that keeps groups of coworkers from falling apart. Large power distance justifies the leader's use of the power necessary to accomplish this feat.

Table 14-1 ■ A Comparison of Cultural Characteristics *(continued)*

NATIONAL CULTURE	UNCERTAINTY AVOIDANCE	MASCULINITY-FEMININITY	INDIVIDUALISM-COLLECTIVISM	POWER DISTANCE	SHORT-TERM VERSUS LONG-TERM ORIENTATION
Netherlands	53	14	80	38	—
New Zealand	49	58	79	22	—
Norway	50	8	69	31	—
Pakistan	70	50	14	55	—
Peru	87	42	16	64	—
Philippines	44	64	32	94	—
Portugal	104	31	27	63	—
Russia	90	40	50	95	10
Singapore	8	48	20	74	—
South Africa	49	63	65	49	—
Spain	86	42	51	57	—
Sweden	29	5	71	31	—
Switzerland	58	70	68	34	—
Taiwan	69	45	17	58	—
Thailand	64	34	20	64	—
Turkey	85	45	37	66	—
United States	46	62	91	40	—
Venezuela	76	73	12	81	—
West Africa	54	46	20	77	16
Yugoslavia	88	21	27	76	—

Source: Based on G. Hofstede, "Motivation, Leadership, and Organization: Do American Theories Apply Abroad?" *Organizational Dynamics* 9 (1980), pp. 42–63; and G. Hofstede, "Cultural Constraints in Management Theories," *Academy of Management Executive* 7 (1993), pp. 81–94.

Finally, U.S. firms tend to be structured as relatively tall, pyramidal hierarchies in which rules and procedures govern most employee behaviors, in the manner discussed in Chapter 11. The type of direct supervision undertaken as part of the task of being a leader, just described, is implemented when rules and procedures fail to provide the necessary guidance. This kind of hierarchical structuring requires agreement with the belief that differences in power are a normal part of everyday life. It is made possible by the fact that the U.S. national culture favors norms supportive of large power distance.

How would the U.S. way of management—and the contents of this book—look if shaped instead by a national culture of individualism and small power distance? We can approximate an answer to this question by looking at how things are done in the Scandinavian countries of Norway and Sweden. As Table 14-1 shows, the cultures of both these countries are individualistic (though not to the same extreme as the U.S. culture) and oriented toward relatively small power distance.

How would the U.S. approach appear if attuned instead to collectivism and a large level of power distance? We can address this second question by analyzing the workings of Japanese organizations. As shown in Table 14-1, Japan's national culture is fairly similar to that of the United States in terms of power distance, but is noticeably more collectivistic.

How would the models and practices used in the United States look if formed instead in a culture of collectivism and small power distance—a culture exactly opposite to the U.S. national culture? We can approach this third question by looking at practices in Israeli kibbutz organizations. The Israeli national culture is characterized by collectivism and very small power distance, and kibbutz work organizations are even more collectivistic than the Israeli norm shown in Table 14-1.

Scandinavian Industrial Democracies

In Norway and Sweden, companies like Volvo, Saab, Hunsfos Paper, and Norsk Hydro include many participatory features in their management practices. Most Scandinavian firms are **industrial democracies,** organizations required by law to permit their members to govern themselves. In Norway, the first companies to become industrial democracies were government-owned firms. Their conversion to this form took place in the mid-1930s, after the formal establishment of national labor-management relationships. In the 1970s, many private firms followed suit and began to experiment with democratic management procedures.[16] The movement began even earlier in Sweden, where labor-management cooperation was mandated by the national government in 1928. Later laws led to the creation of works councils in many Swedish industrial firms. Those councils soon became participatory forums in which organizational policies related to working conditions, productivity, employee facilities, training, and corporate expansion programs could be developed through negotiations between labor and management representatives.

Various examples of shop floor participation grew out of the policies formulated by works councils. Prominent among these were **semiautonomous work groups,** or groups of coworkers charged with the task of managing themselves as they performed their jobs. To determine whom to hire, how to divide the group's work into jobs, whom to assign to each job, and whether to rotate assignments among jobs, group members talked with one another and made decisions by consensus. The democratic participation thus encouraged still serves as the basis of industrial democracies.[17]

Motivation.   In Scandinavian countries, national welfare programs provide for the basic necessities of food, clothing, shelter, and health care. For this reason, methods of motivating employees are aimed at satisfying personal needs for autonomy, growth, and development. The opportunity for shop floor participation afforded by semiautonomous groups fits in well with this approach to motivation, because it is the opportunity for the employees to control their own working lives—to manage themselves. Scandinavian managers consider granting employees the right to participate in decision making to be an important means of encouraging productivity as well as combating turnover and absenteeism.

In most Scandinavian firms, wages consist of a base payment designed to further ensure employees' basic welfare, an incentive payment based on the productivity of a group of employees with whom the recipient works, and a second incentive payment based on the number of job skills a worker has.[18] This system of payment reflects and reinforces the participatory, group-oriented structure of the Scandinavian industrial firm and also encourages continued personal development.

Leadership. Scandinavian managers often do not supervise employees directly, nor are they always required to issue direct orders to coordinate work activities. Managers function instead as boundary spanners who facilitate the flow of work between groups while allowing employees to handle intragroup coordination responsibilities themselves. They also resolve conflicts within groups and help members communicate with one another in the course of participatory decision making. In sum, managers are more active as facilitators or social catalysts than as direct supervisors.

Structure. Thanks to their emphasis on worker participation, Norwegian and Swedish industrial democracies are structured differently than the typical U.S. industrial firm. A U.S. organization is usually built around a single hierarchy. Scandinavian firms, on the other hand, often incorporate a **collateral structure**— a second hierarchy of groups and committees that parallels and sometimes takes the place of the primary managerial hierarchy.[19] This collateral structure, an example of which is shown in Figure 14-1, is made up of three types of groups— works councils, special-interest committees, and semiautonomous work groups.[20]

The **works council** is composed of worker representatives who are elected by their peers and management representatives who are appointed by top management. There is usually only one works council in an organization. It is the council's responsibility to develop overall organizational policies and procedures. Works councils have little or no direct decision-making power, but they provide

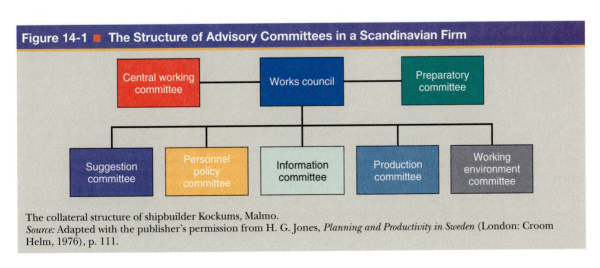

Figure 14-1 ■ The Structure of Advisory Committees in a Scandinavian Firm

The collateral structure of shipbuilder Kockums, Malmo.
Source: Adapted with the publisher's permission from H. G. Jones, *Planning and Productivity in Sweden* (London: Croom Helm, 1976), p. 111.

a forum in which worker representatives can express their opinions and thereby be instrumental in shaping the mission and strategic direction of the firm.

Special-interest committees, which are also composed of worker and manager representatives, provide the works council with advice on specific issues, such as job design, plant sanitation, personnel practices, and environmental safety. These committees combine with middle management to produce yearly reports that assist works councils with the task of formulating company policies. Such reports might include an analysis of water and air pollution caused by the company, a set of guidelines for curbing absenteeism, or a proposal on how to reduce the amount of costly inventory kept on hand.

As already indicated, *semiautonomous work groups* consist of groups of employees who are given the responsibility for completing a particular job. In each of these groups, members negotiate the breakdown of work responsibilities into individual tasks and decide who will perform these tasks. They may also have a say in hiring and firing decisions that affect group membership.

In addition to these three types of groups, there are typically several general advisory committees that support the works council and that are located lower in the organization hierarchy. These advisory groups may include suggestion committees, personnel policy committees, and information committees. Their purpose is to provide advice on general problems or issues lying outside the domains of the special-interest committees. As a whole, a collateral system such as the one shown in Figure 14-1 provides a structure in which employees and management can work together to influence company policies and procedures.

Large Japanese Corporations

Unlike Scandinavian industrial democracies, large Japanese corporations are based on strict, hierarchical management procedures. However, they also support and depend on close interpersonal relationships.[21] Every Japanese organization is the product of many influences. Most important is the legacy of feudal and kinship traditions that developed between 1634 and 1868. Japan's isolation during this period encouraged the development of a homogeneous culture based on feudal master-servant obligations that created a kind of permanent state of dependence within families, and between families and their feudal lords. Children were obligated to follow the wishes of their parents, who were required to obey their feudal master. The *zaibatsu*, large companies spanning many businesses and owned by wealthy, powerful clans, were built around these vertical chains of obligation.

The period of Allied occupation that followed World War II also had a profound influence on Japanese organizations. In an effort to westernize Japanese businesses, U.S. military commanders forcibly disbanded the *zaibatsu* and required companies to permit the formation of workers' unions. In addition, massive capital restoration programs enabled the Japanese to build modern, sophisticated production facilities. Japanese businesses reorganized into six *keiretsu* industrial conglomerates (Mitsui, Mitsubishi, Sumitomo, Fuyo, Sanwa, and Dai-Ichi Kangyo) and a number of independent firms, such as Nissan, Toyota, and Sony. The six *keiretsu* were essentially the original *zaibatsu*, now centered in banks rather than in feudal clans (see box). In addition, a collection of smaller satellite companies developed

U.S. Multinational–Japanese *Keiretsu* Partnerships

At a time when the costs of keeping up with technological change and global expansion are overwhelming even the richest companies, U.S. and Japanese companies are joining together in global alliances that build on the Japanese *keiretsu* partnerships that emerged following the end of World War II. Once considered a sign of weakness, international alliances between *keiretsu* and multinational firms are now seen by Japanese and U.S. managers alike as a way to pool valuable resources and thrive in the heated competition of international markets.

In one alliance, Toshiba and IBM did what was once unthinkable when they agreed to share long-guarded secrets about computer chip making. Just outside Nagoya, Japan, Toshiba launched a $1 billion manufacturing facility that incorporated IBM know-how in chemical mechanical polishing, needed to smooth the many surfaces of multilayered chips. IBM engineers then transferred the Nagoya plant's technology back to an IBM-Toshiba plant in Manassas, Virginia, gaining Toshiba's expertise in using ultraviolet light to etch circuits less than one micron wide.

In another alliance between a Japanese *keiretsu* and a U.S. multinational, Mitsubishi and Caterpillar joined together in a 50-50 venture to design a line of excavators and heavy equipment. Both were motivated by a keen desire to compete with Japanese equipment manufacturer Komatsu on its home turf, but neither had the resources to go it alone. Today, products manufactured in the venture's two Japanese factories are sold through Cat's network of 186 independent dealers in 197 countries.

The growing links between Japanese and U.S. firms complicate debates about U.S. trade deficits with Japan, and blur important differences between corporate and national interests—when Eastman Kodak convinced the U.S. government to back its bid to penetrate Japan's allegedly rigged photography market, few Americans realized that Kodak and Japanese archrival Fuji Photo Film Company had for years collaborated on joint research projects. Nonetheless, managers in both Japan and the United States look at alliances as important sources of financing for new projects and international expansion, and few predict that current trends will reverse. In fact, many experts expect U.S.-Japanese ventures to expand to include European partners, forming alliances that are truly global in location and reach.[1]

---

[1]B. Bremner, Z. Schiller, T. Smart, and W. J. Holstein, "*Keiretsu* Connections," *Business Week,* July 22, 1996, pp. 52–54.

---

to supply the large corporations with raw materials, parts, and supplementary labor. These companies often started out under the management of retirees from the large organizations.

Motivation. For the current managers of large Japanese corporations, managing motivation is primarily a matter of stimulating in each employee a sense of loyalty, obligation, and dependence on superiors and coworkers. The resulting feelings reinforce the collectivism that keeps Japanese organizations together. The practice in larger Japanese firms of offering lifetime employment (to age 56) to permanent employees goes a long way toward encouraging workers' loyalty. Japanese employees find it difficult to behave disloyally toward a firm that is willing to commit itself to them up to their retirement.[22]

Collectivistic loyalty is also encouraged in large Japanese firms by the *nenko system* of wage payment. Under the *nenko* system, the employee's pay is composed of a basic wage plus merit supplements and job-level allowances. The basic wage, which constitutes about 55 percent of total pay, consists of the employee's starting wage plus yearly increases. Those increases are determined by (in order of importance) seniority, or length of service with the company; age; and supervisory ratings on such qualities as seriousness, attendance, performance, and cooperativeness.[23]

Merit supplements make up an additional 15 percent of the employee's pay and are based on supervisory assessments of specific job behaviors. They are meant, in principle, to reward exemplary performance. In fact, however, merit supplements are heavily influenced by seniority because they are calculated as a percentage of the basic wage. Moreover, junior employees' performance is typically rated below senior employees' work regardless of real differences between the two.[24] Clearly, Japanese merit supplements reward loyalty and longevity with the company.

Job-level allowances, which account for about 30 percent of each worker's total pay, are based on the importance of each worker's job in relation to the other jobs in the organization. Job-level allowances may sound similar to the pay increments that result in the United States from job evaluation procedures. In Japan, however, each employee's position in the hierarchy of jobs—which affects the employee's job-level allowance—is more directly influenced by seniority than by skill.[25]

Thus, seniority is the single most important factor in determining a Japanese worker's compensation. It affects the basic wage, merit supplements, and job-level allowances. The large Japanese firm is like an idealized family in the sense that its employees spend their lives in a stable social setting and receive positions of increasing social importance as they grow older.[26] Along with the *nenko* method of financial compensation, this family-like system provides its members with social rewards for loyalty to the company over everything else. Employees' decisions to attend work and to perform productively grow out of their sense of loyalty and obligation to the family-like firm.

Leadership. The primary leadership task in large Japanese corporations is to guarantee the continued existence of vertical dependence—subordinates' acceptance of hierarchical relationships and obedience to superiors. At the lowest levels of management, shop floor foremen (Japanese managers at all levels are virtually all male) wear two hats. By day, they perform the same types of jobs as their subordinates. Indeed, to the casual observer, superior and subordinate seem almost indistinguishable at work. Away from work, however, foremen visit the homes of sick employees to inquire about their health and the welfare of their families. From time to time, they may also give subordinates small gifts and host social events for them and their families. In return, subordinates are led by their sense of obligation (*giri*) to perform as their supervisors direct. Subordinates cannot fully repay their obligations by simply returning visits, reciprocating in gift giving, helping sponsor social events, or even following orders. Among Japanese employees, feelings of continued obligation require unending obedience.

Lower-level management's primary leadership function, then, is to maintain subordinates' followership. The practices of foremen just described enable management in large Japanese firms to operate quite autocratically.[27] Employees feel obligated to put in long hours, work in unsafe conditions, and ignore responsibilities outside the company if requested by their manager to do so. Taken to the extreme, it is even considered acceptable for lower-level Japanese managers to arrange marriages among subordinates and then order the female spouse to leave the company. As indicated by this practice, besides directing employees' workplace behaviors, lower-level managers at large Japanese companies can also exert significant influence over what employees do and how they live away from work.

Manager-leaders higher in the organization ensure similar followership among their management subordinates first by immersing them in a program of intensive socialization upon their entry into the organization. Groups of new managers learn the history of the organization, its mission, and its values. These "entering classes" then spend several years together rotating among functional departments. In this manner, new managers develop horizontal ties and acquire a generalist's understanding of the organization. By the time they have completed the process of socialization, managerial employees have learned the importance of followership (*tsukiai*) and typically behave accordingly.[28]

Upper management also emphasizes followership and the importance of respecting vertical relationships by teaching and repeatedly encouraging the use of the *ringi* decision-making process. In this process, decision making is initiated by subordinates, and possible decisions are circulated upward for superiors' approval. Though seemingly participatory, this form of decision making is often, for the subordinates, little more than an exercise in anticipating superiors' wishes. Middle managers try to make only those suggestions that their management superiors will approve in order to avoid embarrassment.[29] Japanese aversion to standing out in a crowd and concerns about saving face would make such embarrassment intolerable.

Structure. Outwardly, the structures of most large Japanese corporations resemble the hierarchical, pyramidal structures of large U.S. companies. In fact, Japanese organization charts often display the same hierarchy of vertical relationships that characterize a U.S. firm's organization chart. In Japanese firms, however, these vertical relationships are often patterned after the parent-child (*oyabun-kobun*) relationship of traditional Japanese families. In the organizational version of this relationship, subordinates are encouraged to feel loyal and obligated to their superiors, and also dependent on them. This feeling of dependence in turn encourages—in fact, requires—acquiescence to the superior's demands.[30]

Another critical difference between U.S. and Japanese organizations has to do with communication patterns. In traditionally structured U.S. organizations, the vertical lines of command that appear on organization charts are meant to be the primary formal channels of communication. To communicate with a colleague in another department or division, an employee is expected to pass a message up the hierarchy to a superior, who then sends it downward to the final recipient. In Japanese corporations, however, certain formally designated *horizontal* relationships are accorded the same degree of importance as the vertical relationships depicted on the organization chart. These horizontal relationships, which allow communication to flow across the hierarchy rather than having to go up and down, connect managers who entered the company at the same time. They are encouraged by the group socialization that managers receive upon first entering the company—others in a manager's group become lifetime contacts throughout the company. They are also encouraged by the practice of rotating Japanese managers among the different functional areas of the firm—marketing, accounting, production, finance, and so forth. This causes each manager to become more of a generalist than a specialist, and to cultivate a collection of horizontal linkages that unites the manager with management peers across functional boundaries.[31]

Together, the kinds of dependence relations and communication patterns encouraged in Japanese organizations create a **latticework structure** of vertical and horizontal relationships among the company's managers. Continuing relations among management peers from different functional areas, such as marketing and manufacturing, help stimulate harmony and coordination between functional groups. Nonetheless, in large Japanese firms, decision-making authority remains highly centralized. This combination of central control and strong relationships among peers is unique to the latticework structure of large Japanese corporations.

Israeli Kibbutz Industries

Israeli kibbutzim combine the commitment of members found in large Japanese corporations with the participatory aspect of Scandinavian industrial democracies. The **kibbutz** (*kibbutzim* is the plural form) is a close-knit community of people organized on the principles of collective ownership and direct participation in self-governance. Kibbutzim, which range in size from about 40 to 2,000 members, were started early in the 20th century by young European Jews who moved to Palestine to escape anti-Semitic persecution. In keeping with the philosophies of the European youth movements of the day, the first kibbutz settlers favored Marxist economics and a rural, naturalistic lifestyle. These beliefs led them to establish a number of small agricultural communities in which they shared everything from food and clothing to child-rearing and civic obligations. Contemporary kibbutzniks (kibbutz dwellers) continue to embrace the same principles, and sharing work responsibilities and the material results is still the norm in modern kibbutzim.[32]

Motivation. Kibbutzniks are motivated by concerns about the security of their community and by values that encourage hard work. The founders of the first kibbutzim believed that people realize their true worth only by working hard, and motivation in the kibbutz has continued to derive from the notion that physical labor is an intrinsically important endeavor. In research on Israeli motivation, Simcha Ronen compared the job satisfaction of workers in a kibbutz industrial branch with the satisfaction of industrial employees in Israel's private sector. Ronen found that kibbutzniks' satisfaction was strongly influenced by the tasks they performed; that is, higher task performance was associated with stronger satisfaction. In contrast, private-sector workers in Ronen's study based job satisfaction on such things as power, prestige, and wealth. Their degree of satisfaction was strongly related to the wages and benefits they received, not to the tasks they performed.[33]

Kibbutznik motivation also grows out of concern for community well-being. Within the kibbutz, every member derives equal benefit from kibbutz resources. For example, everyone eats the same food (subject to health-related dietary restrictions), everyone wears the same clothing, and everyone lives in a similar kind of structure. The kibbutz system of compensation for work performed is wageless, based instead on egalitarian sharing—except for cash allowances for travel outside the kibbutz and small amounts of pocket money for miscellaneous purposes. The well-being of all kibbutz members is thus equally guaranteed.

Because members need not concern themselves with personal welfare, they are free to direct their full attention to improving the state of the kibbutz as a whole. Kibbutzniks identify this freedom from concern for personal security as a valuable reward of kibbutz membership. Desires to preserve it are an important motivational force underlying kibbutznik performance.[34]

Leadership.   Leadership is shared among the adult members of each kibbutz, being vested in the kibbutz's general assembly rather than in the hands of a small management group. The general assembly, which is the principal governing body of the kibbutz, meets once a week in most kibbutzim. Topics considered in assembly meetings may include the purchase, cleaning, and repair of kibbutznik clothing, since all clothing is collectively owned, or the practices used to raise and educate kibbutz children, since children are raised in communal quarters. Participation in assembly meetings is nearly universal, because all members who are kibbutz-born and 19 or older, or who have completed a one-year naturalization program have a vote.

The secretariat, an administrative board consisting of elected officials, is empowered only to implement policies approved by the kibbutz assembly. No official is permitted to act outside assembly mandates. Thus, in contrast to the managers in other kinds of organizations, kibbutz officials occupy positions *beneath* the general assembly. They are elected by the assembly, serve fixed terms of office, and cannot hold the same office for more than one consecutive term. As a result, the ability of any officeholder to amass the power needed to function as an autonomous leader is strictly limited. On occasion, a small number of members may rotate among the various kibbutz offices, allowing for the possible emergence of a dominant group. However, because officials are under the watchful eyes of every other member, it is virtually impossible for them to usurp the kibbutz's power without being caught.[35]

Structure.   Virtually all kibbutzim have a farm, organized as a branch with its own assembly and secretariat. Some also have industrial branches, added to supplement their agricultural activities. These branches are organized around industrial assemblies and internal governance processes that reflect those of the larger kibbutz. Each industrial branch's officials are elected by its workforce and are charged with implementing decisions reached by the branch's assembly. Decisions that might affect the larger kibbutz—major decisions about industrial operations, for example—are made by the full kibbutz assembly. Officials of the kibbutz secretariat oversee industrial operations to make sure they conform with kibbutz policies. Nevertheless, kibbutz industrial branches are the most decentralized, participatory form of industrial organization in the world.[36]

Cross-Cultural Comparison

How do the three kinds of organizations just described compare with one another and with the U.S. models and practices described in this book? What cultural effects are uncovered by such comparisons?

In response to these questions, we begin by pointing out that it is possible to isolate the effects of individualism by looking for similarities in the way things are done in U.S. business firms and Scandinavian industrial democracies, because both of these types of organization are located in individualistic national cultures. To examine some of the effects of collectivism on organizational behavior, one can look instead for similarities in the workings of large Japanese businesses and Israeli kibbutzim, both of which are found in collectivistic national cultures.

In both U.S. businesses and Scandinavian industrial democracies, people are motivated to do their jobs by the desire to satisfy personal needs. In addition, in both the United States and Scandinavia, achievement on the job is seen as attributable to individual effort. In contrast, in Japan and in Israeli kibbutzim, work motivation grows out of a sense of loyalty and a concern for the well-being of everyone in the organization. In addition, both Japanese and Israeli employees view job performance as something people can accomplish only by working together. In contrast to the way things work in U.S. and Scandinavian organizations, in large Japanese businesses and Israeli kibbutzim the focus is on groups, group tasks, and group performance. Personal needs, individualized work, and individual performance are not considered important.

Thus, it appears that the amount of individualism or collectivism in the national culture can have major effects on employee motivation. Cultural individualism focuses attention on the performance and satisfaction of the individual and therefore on the individualization of rewards. Cultural collectivism directs attention to the performance and satisfaction of the group. Sharing takes the place of individuation in the assignment of rewards. As suggested by Hofstede, among individualists, "I" is important, whereas among collectivists, "we" is more critical.

What about the effects of power distance? Consider first the workings of U.S. business organizations and large Japanese businesses, both of which are located in national cultures oriented toward large power distance. Structurally, both kinds of firms emphasize coordination processes that are based on a combination of rules, procedures, and direct orders issued by hierarchical superiors. They use direction rather than participation to integrate work activities. Leadership activities reflect this directive orientation, focusing on supervising subordinates and making sure that superiors' orders are carried out.

However, in Scandinavian industrial democracies and Israeli kibbutz industries, both of which are surrounded by national cultures with small power distance, successful structural relationships are far more participatory. People who occupy positions lower in the structural hierarchy are able to advise hierarchical superiors or even become directly involved in decision making. Leadership is more a process of facilitating communication and mutual adjustment than one of ensuring that subordinates follow the directives of superiors.

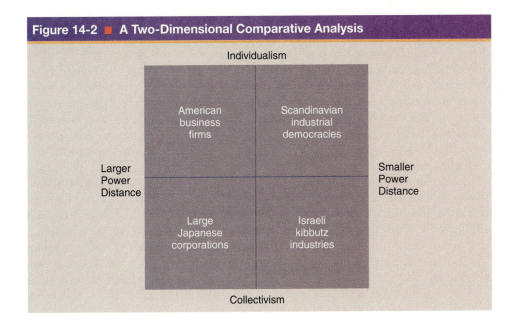

Figure 14-2 ■ A Two-Dimensional Comparative Analysis

Individualism

American business firms

Scandinavian industrial democracies

Larger Power Distance

Smaller Power Distance

Large Japanese corporations

Israeli kibbutz industries

Collectivism

From this pattern, it is possible to conclude that the power distance of the surrounding national culture has strong effects on organizational structure and leadership processes. Large power distance stimulates pronounced structuration and directive, supervisory leadership. Small power distance supports participation more than structural differentiation, and leadership that concentrates on facilitation.

The cross-cultural comparison depicted in Figure 14-2 suggests that features of the surrounding national culture can have significant effects on the characteristics of an organization and on the management of organizational behavior. The lesson it portrays is that organizations throughout the world differ, but in more or less predictable ways. Knowing about the general characteristics of a particular national culture increases the likelihood that you will be able to make accurate predictions about how to motivate employees, fulfill leadership expectations, structure organizational relationships, or adapt other familiar management procedures for use in different national cultures. With this in mind, consider next the process of cross-cultural adaptation.

Organizational Behavior in a Multicultural World

Although the cross-cultural differences just described are readily evident, it is sometimes suggested that management practices throughout the world are growing more alike.[37] Consistent with this suggestion is the fact that practices developed in one culture are occasionally borrowed for use in another. For instance, in the United States, teams of coworkers are being formed where employees once worked as individuals, in interventions patterned after Scandinavian programs. Quality circles resembling Japanese QC groups are becoming so prevalent that they are now considered part of the U.S. approach to job design. U.S. business organization structures are also becoming flatter and more participatory as downsizing reduces the size of management staffs and as reengineering breaks down barriers among different tasks and task groups. All of these changes are occurring as U.S. companies strive to become more flexible and customer oriented.

In contrast, throughout Scandinavia, the use of semiautonomous groups is being scaled back to streamline production processes and economize on production costs. In the process, participatory management practices are being deemphasized. Volvo's famous Kalmar plant, once a leader in the use of semiautonomous groups as a means of encouraging shop floor participation, is now closed. Other Scandinavian companies are considering similar closures in order to reduce costs and increase efficiency. At the same time, they are moving toward the traditional U.S. approach of individualizing tasks and managing through autocratic means.

In Japan, lifetime employment is not as assured as it once was because economic turmoil has reduced the ability of large Japanese businesses to offer such a costly benefit.[38] Collectivism in the surrounding national culture is also eroding as the Japanese adopt U.S. marketing practices that focus on taking care of one's own needs and interests. Japanese employees are becoming less willing to allow management to control their nonworking lives, asking instead for more leisure time and looking for ways to enrich their lives away from work. The sense of loyalty and obligation that once motivated performance in large Japanese corporations seems to be slowly giving way to the type of motivation through wage payments that is found in the United States.

Finally, in Israeli kibbutzim, an influx of gifts from the outside has put severe strains on kibbutzniks' tradition of sharing all possessions. Where the members of kibbutzim once ate together in communal dining facilities, members now complain that many no longer attend kibbutz meals because households have their own refrigerators. Parents are growing reluctant to cede responsibilities for child rearing to the kibbutz, instead desiring to raise their children themselves. Young kibbutzniks dream of having privacy and the freedom to make personal decisions without interference from the general assembly. Kibbutzim are growing less unique as collectivistic sharing and participatory decision making lose emphasis.

Trends like these seem to support the **convergence hypothesis,** which suggests that national cultures, organizations, and management practices throughout the world are growing more alike.[39] In a review of studies that have examined this hypothesis, John Child found evidence for convergence but also some evidence for divergence, or continued cross-cultural differences. Interestingly, Child found that the studies that supported convergence typically focused on organizational variables, such as structure and technology, whereas the studies that revealed divergence in practices usually concerned employee attitudes, beliefs, and behaviors.[40] He concluded that organizations themselves may be becoming more alike throughout the world but that people in these organizations are maintaining their cultural distinctiveness. Management in a multicultural world currently requires an understanding of cultural differences, and it appears that it will continue to do so for quite some time.

Understanding Behavior in Other Cultures

How can the information in this chapter help managers understand and recognize cultural differences? You can find out by putting yourself into the managerial role and applying the Hofstede model to evaluate several intercultural differences. In the following scenarios, try using the five dimensions of the model to explain the differences described.

1. *Feelings about progress.* Being modern and future oriented is highly valued in China. From the modernist perspective, something that has been around for awhile may seem oldfashioned or obsolete. In Russia, however, tradition, the status quo, and the past are more highly revered. To a traditionalist, familiar things are perceived as trustworthy, proven, and worthwhile. Which dimension explains this difference?

2. *Tendencies toward confrontation or consensus.* In Greece it is important to smooth over differences to preserve agreement. Emphasis is placed on building consensus among coworkers and avoiding personal confrontation. In Denmark, conflict and confrontation are accepted or even encouraged. Conflict is perceived to be a signal of the need for change. How can this difference be explained?

3. *Locus of control.* The national culture of Australia instills a sense of personal responsibility for the outcomes of individual behaviors. Rewarding people for personal performance is considered a logical consequence of the value Australians place on personal responsibility. In Pakistan, however, people focus instead on external social causes to explain similar outcomes. Giving people rewards for personal performance seems unwarranted in light of cultural beliefs that behaviors are caused by outside forces. How can you explain this difference?

4. *Status and social position.* In India, status is accorded on the basis of family, class, ethnicity, and even accent. High-status people are able to impose their will on people of lower status even when such people are as knowledgeable and competent as they. In New Zealand, where status is earned through personal achievement, shared governance by majority rule or participatory decision making is valued over personal fiat. Expertise outranks social position in determining who will be involved in decision-making procedures. What explains this difference?[41]

Were you able to explain the first scenario? Differing feelings about progress are produced by cross-cultural differences in short-term versus long-term orientation. Cultures such as Russia's, which have short-term orientations, honor tradition and feel threatened by new ways of doing things. Cultures such as China's, which have long-term orientations, more readily embrace modern ways.

The second scenario focuses on conflict avoidance, a cultural tendency that is closely associated with uncertainty avoidance. Conflict creates uncertainty, and cultures that cannot deal with uncertainty, such as the Greek culture, cannot handle the competition and aggression that conflict unleashes. In contrast, cultures like Denmark's that can tolerate uncertainty are also able to cope with conflict.

The third scenario concerns locus of control, and the difference seen here arises out of cross-cultural differences in individualism versus collectivism. On the one hand, the sense of personal responsibility stimulated by believing that the locus of control for personal behavior lies inside the individual is consistent with the norms and values of an individualistic national culture like that of Australia. On the other hand, the focus on social causes for behaviors that is prompted by an external locus of control is compatible with the cultural collectivism of countries such as Pakistan.

The fourth scenario shows how cultural differences in power distance can show up as differences in the way status and social position are accorded and perceived. Cultures such as India's, in which status and position are birthrights—the special-privilege approach—also tend to be oriented toward large power distance. In contrast, cultures in countries like New Zealand, in which status and position are awarded according to personal abilities—the equal opportunity approach—are more inclined toward smaller power distance.

Managing Multicultural Differences

The four scenarios illustrate how Hofstede's five-dimensional model can be used to recognize differences in national culture and understand the cultural roots of everyday customs and behaviors. Such recognition and understanding is critical to success in the management of international organizational behavior, because it is the first step toward determining whether familiar management practices must be reconfigured before being used abroad. Along this line, note that a glance back at Table 14-1 indicates that the national cultures of the United States and Canada are approximately equal in terms of power distance, uncertainty avoidance, masculinity, and individualism. Because of this similarity, U.S. managers can expect to succeed in Canada, and Canadian managers can anticipate working effectively in the United States, without making major adjustments to customary management practices.

According to Hofstede's findings, however, the level of uncertainty avoidance in Denmark is about half that of the United States and Canada. Therefore, North American managers are likely to find it necessary to tailor their normal way of doing things if required to work in Denmark. More generally, managers working in national cultures characterized by weaker uncertainty avoidance must learn to cope with higher levels of anxiety and stress while reducing their reliance on planning, rule making, and other familiar ways of absorbing uncertainty. On the other side of the coin are managers working in cultures with stronger uncertainty avoidance than they are accustomed to. They must learn not only to accept but also to participate in the development of rules that seem unnecessary and planning that appears meaningless in order to help other organization members cope with stressful uncertainty. Rituals that at first glance might seem useless or even irrational may serve the very important function of diminishing an otherwise intolerable level of uncertainty.

Consider next the dimension of masculinity-femininity. Female managers working in cultures with more cultural masculinity than their own, face the prospect of receiving less respect at work than they feel they deserve. To cope with gender discrimination of this sort, a female manager may want to seek out male mentors in senior management to secure her place in the organization. Conversely, male managers in national cultures with more cultural femininity than their own must control aggressive tendencies and learn to treat members of both sexes with equal dignity and respect. Acting as mentors, female managers can demonstrate that women are as adept at their jobs as men.

The next dimension is individualism-collectivism. Managers who must work in national cultures that are more individualistic than their own must first learn to cope with the sense of rootlessness that comes from the absence of close-knit group relationships. They must also learn not to be embarrassed by personal compliments, despite their belief that success stems from group effort. At work, they must develop an understanding of the importance of rewarding individuals equitably and must adjust to the idea that organizational membership is impermanent. Conversely, managers attempting to work in cultures that are more collectivistic than their own must learn to deal with demands for self-sacrifice in support of group well-being. They must also learn to accept equal sharing in lieu of equity and exchange at work. Consequently, they must refrain from paying individual employees compliments and instead praise group performance. Managers adjusting to collectivistic national cultures must also learn to understand that belonging to an organization in such cultures is more than just a temporary association. It is an important basis of each employee's personal identity.

Managers working in cultures that favor less power distance than do their native cultures may feel initial discomfort stemming from an unfamiliar decentralization of authority and a perceived loss of control. They must learn to be less autocratic and more participatory in their work with others. On the other hand, managers facing cultural tendencies toward more power distance must accept the role that centralization and tall hierarchies play in maintaining what is deemed to be an acceptable level of control in such cultures. They must also adopt a more authoritarian, autocratic style of management, and they may even find that subordinates, if asked to participate in decision making, will refuse on the grounds that decision making is management's rightful job.

Finally, the dimension of short-term versus long-term orientation may have its greatest effect during the planning activities that are an integral part of management. For managers used to a short-term orientation, working in a culture characterized by a long-term orientation will require paying less attention to past successes or failures and more attention to future possibilities as they set organizational objectives and define group and individual goals. In contrast, managers from cultures with long-term orientations must accept that colleagues with short-term orientations will spend considerable energy looking backward in time to decide what to do in the future. These colleagues are also likely to favor traditional approaches over innovation and creativity, and may pay much attention to avoiding the mistakes of history.

Grouped together, the five dimensions introduced in this chapter form a model that highlights important contrasts among different national cultures. As you use this model in the future, it will be important for you to remember that each dimension is a simplification of the kinds of differences that exist among the world's national cultures. Such simplification is the necessary consequence of the goal of researchers like Hofstede to create theories and models that can be readily understood and used in many situations.[42] It will also be important for you to realize that this simplification encourages stereotyping, that is, the perception that all of the members of a particular culture are alike in some specific way. Always keep in mind the fact that beneath societal similarities like those discussed in this chapter lie subtle differences among people that also vary along the lines identified in the Hofstede model. For example, although it is true that the U.S. and Canadian national cultures are highly individualistic, it is also true that a significant number of people in North America are collectivists.[43] For this reason, we suggest that you exercise caution when employing the five-dimensional model, lest you overlook relatively less conspicuous but nonetheless influential cultural complexities and dissimilarities.

SUMMARY

Whether comparisons are made within a single *national culture* or across different ones, no two organizations are exactly alike. And no two people in the world hold exactly the same beliefs and values. Thus, discussions in this chapter have necessarily involved generalization. Not every Japanese organization has a fully developed *latticework structure,* and not every kibbutznik is completely collectivistic. Nevertheless, firms in a particular national culture are more like each other than they are like organizations in other national cultures. Moreover, people in the same national culture tend to think and act more similarly than people from different cultures. Cross-cultural differences exist and can have significant effects on organizational behavior.

The most important of these cross-cultural differences are captured by five dimensions: *uncertainty avoidance, masculinity-femininity, individualism-collectivism, power distance,* and *short-term versus long-term orientation.* Differences in individualism-collectivism and power distance seem to explain many of the differences among U.S., Scandinavian, Japanese, and Israeli (kibbutz) management practices. Compared to U.S. firms, Scandinavian companies are more participatory, Japanese organizations encourage stronger feelings of obligation and dependence, and Israeli kibbutzim require greater member commitment to community well-being. Considered together, the five dimensions are helpful in understanding why people in a particular national culture behave the way they do and can be useful to managers as they strive to adapt familiar management practices for use in unfamiliar cultures.

Review Questions

1. As compared to the national culture of Sweden, how would you characterize the national culture of the United States in terms of the level of uncertainty avoidance? In which country would you expect to find greater evidence of ritualistic behavior? Why? How would your answers to these questions change if you were

asked to compare the United States with Greece?

2. Hofstede's findings indicate that the U.S. national culture at the time of his research was more masculine than many of the other national cultures he examined. In your opinion, is the U.S. culture still as masculine as Hofstede's research suggests? Why or why not?

3. According to Hofstede's research, the three most individualistic national cultures are found in the United States, Australia, and Great Britain. Can you think of a reason why these three countries would share this cultural characteristic? Does your answer also explain the relatively strong individualism of the Canadian national culture?

4. Would you expect the structures of organizations in Denmark to be taller or flatter than those of organizations in the United States? Why? How are organization structures in Mexico likely to compare to those in Denmark and the United States?

5. Comparing U.S. business firms with Scandinavian industrial democracies, large Japanese businesses, and Israeli kibbutz industries, in which are the wage payments of workers most likely to reflect differences in personal performance? In which are workers more likely to receive the same payment regardless of differences in personal performance? What explains this difference?

6. If you had to adapt the theories and models described in this book for use in China, what kinds of changes would you think about making? Explain your answer using Hofstede's five-dimensional model.

Implementation Guide

National cultures can have major effects on organizations and the behaviors of their members. Thus it is critical that managers be able to assess the characteristics of surrounding national cultures and understand the effects of those cultures on organizational behavior. The following questions may facilitate this process.

1. What are the characteristics of your own national culture? Is it more individualistic or collectivistic? Are its values consistent with more or less power distance? Is it characterized more by masculinity or femininity? Does it favor strong or weak uncertainty avoidance? Is it more consistent with a short-term or a long-term time orientation?

2. What are the characteristics of the national culture surrounding your organization? How do they compare with the characteristics of your own national culture?

3. Based on your evaluation of cultural differences, what adjustments should you make to familiar management practices to fit them to the current cultural situation?

4. Do you have colleagues in the organization that can help you with the necessary adaptation? Should others outside the organization also be asked to help?

5. Might other managers benefit in the future from what you learn as you cope with cultural adjustment in the present? Will informal mentoring provide enough guidance? Should a formal program be designed and implemented instead?

1. K. Naughton and A. Borrus, "America's No. 1 Car Exporter Is . . . Japan?" *Business Week,* February 26, 1996, p. 113; J. A. Byrne, K. Kerwin, A. Cortese, and P. Dwyer, "Borderless Management: Companies Strive to Become Truly Stateless," *Business Week,* May 23, 1994, pp. 24–26; and W. J. Holstein, S. Reed, J. Kapstein, T. Vogel, and J. Weber, "The Stateless Corporation: Forget Multinationals— Today's Giants Are Really Leaping Boundaries," *Business Week,* May 14, 1990, pp. 98–105.

2. G. Hofstede, "Motivation, Leadership, and Organization: Do American Theories Apply Abroad?" *Organizational Dynamics* 9 (1980), pp. 42–63; and G. Hofslede, *Culture's Consequences: International Differences in Work-Related Values* (Beverly Hills, CA: Sage, 1984), pp. 153–212.

3. G. Hofstede, "Cultural Constraints in Management Theories," *Academy of Management Executive* 7 (1993), pp. 81–94.

4. Hofstede, "Motivation, Leadership, and Organization," p. 47.

5. Ibid.

6. Hofstede, "Motivation, Leadership, and Organization," p. 49.

7. Ibid.

8. Hofstede, "Motivation, Leadership, and Organization," p. 48.

9. Ibid.

10. H. C. Triandis, *Individualism and Collectivism* (Boulder, CO: Westview Press, 1995); and M. Erez and P. C. Earley, *Culture, Self-Identity, and Work* (New York: Oxford Press, 1993).

11. Hofstede, "Motivation, Leadership, and Organization," p. 46.

12. Ibid.

13. Hofstede, "Cultural Constraints," p. 90.

14. Ibid.

15. R. Yeh, "Values of American, Japanese, and Taiwanese Managers in Taiwan: A Test of Hofstede's Framework," *Academy of Management Proceedings* 1988, pp. 106–10.

16. F. E. Emery and E. Thorsrud, *Form and Content in Industrial Democracy* (London: Tavistock, 1964), p. 24; F. E. Emery and E. Thorsrud, *Democracy at Work* (Leiden, The Netherlands: Kroese, 1976), p. 46; and B. Gustavson and G. Hunnius, *New Patterns of Work Reform: The Case of Norway* (Oslo: Universitetsforlaget, 1981), p. 37.

17. *Job Reform in Sweden* (Stockholm: Swedish Employers' Confederation, 1975), p. 6.

18. *Pay Reform in Sweden* (Stockholm: Swedish Employers' Confederation, 1977), p. 18; and H. Lindestadt and J. P. Norstedt, *Autonomous Groups and Payment by Result* (Stockholm: Swedish Employers' Confederation, 1973).

19. D. E. Zand, "Collateral Organization: A New Change Strategy," *Journal of Applied Behavioral Science* 10 (1974), pp. 63–89.

20. H. Lindestadt and G. Rosander, *The Scan Vast Report* (Stockholm: Swedish Employers' Confederation, 1977), pp. 3–12; Emery and Thorsrud, *Democracy at Work,* pp. 27–32; and J. F. Bolweg, *Job Design and Industrial Democracy: The Case of Norway* (Leiden, The Netherlands: Martinus Nijhoff, 1976), pp. 98–109.

21. P. B. Smith, "The Effectiveness of Japanese Styles of Management: A Review and Critique," *Journal of Occupational Psychology* 57 (1984), pp. 121–36.

22. R. E. Cole, *Japanese Blue Collar* (Berkeley: University of California Press, 1971), pp. 72–100; R. Dore, *British Factory—Japanese Factory* (Berkeley: University of California Press, 1973), pp. 74–113; and E. Fingleton, "Jobs for Life," *Fortune,* March 20, 1995, pp. 119–25. It is important to note that *nenko* employment occurs only in large firms and applies to no more than a third of Japan's labor force; for further information, see T. K. Oh, "Japanese Management: A Critical Review," *Academy of Management Review* 1 (1976), pp. 14–25.

23. Cole, *Japanese Blue Collar,* p. 75.

24. Dore, *British Factory—Japanese Factory,* p. 112.

25. Cole, *Japanese Blue Collar, p. 79;* and Dore, *British Factory—Japanese Factory,* p. 390.

26. R. Clark, *The Japanese Company* (New Haven, CT: Yale University Press, 1979), p. 38.

27. Dore, *British Factory—Japanese Factory,* p. 228.

28. R. Atsumi, "Tsukiai: Obligatory Personal Relationships of Japanese White-Collar Company Employees," *Human Organization* 38 (1979), pp. 63–70.

29. For further discussion on this topic, see S. P. Sethi, N. Namiki, and C. L. Swanson, *The False Promise of the Japanese Miracle: Illusions and Realities of the Japanese Management System* (Boston: Pitman, 1984), pp. 34–41.

30. Dore, *British Factory—Japanese Factory;* P. F. Drucker, *Management* (New York: Harper & Row, 1974); N. Hatvany and C.V. Pucik, "Japanese Management Practices and Productivity," *Organizational Dynamics* 9 (1981), pp. 5–21.

31. Cole, *Japanese Blue Collar;* and R. J. Samuels,

"Looking behind Japan Inc.," *Technology Review* 83 (1981), pp. 43–46.

32. H. Darin-Drabkin, *The Other Society* (New York: Harcourt, Brace, & World, 1963), pp. 66–70.

33. S. Ronen, "Personal Values: A Basis for Work Motivational Set and Work Attitudes," *Organizational Behavior and Human Performance* 21 (1978), pp. 80–107.

34. Y. Criden and S. Gelb, *The Kibbutz Experience: Dialog in Kfar Blum* (New York: Herzl, 1974), p. 33.

35. Criden and Gelb, *The Kibbutz Experience,* pp. 37–57; and J. Blasi, *The Communal Experience of the Kibbutz* (New Brunswick, NJ: Transaction Books, 1986), p. 112.

36. A. S. Tannenbaum, B. Kavcic, M. Rosner, M. Vianello, and G. Weiser, *Hierarchy in Organizations* (San Francisco: Jossey-Bass, 1974), p. 34.

37. C. Kerr, J. T. Dunlop, F. H. Harbison, and C. A. Meyers, *Industrialism and Industrial Man* (Cambridge, MA: Harvard University Press, 1960), pp. 282–88; J. K. Galbraith, *The New Industrial State* (Boston: Houghton Mifflin, 1967), pp. 11–21; and F. Harbison, "Management in Japan," in *Management in the Industrial World: An International Analysis,* F. Harbison and C. A. Meyers, eds. (New York: McGraw-Hill, 1959), pp. 249–64.

38. G. Koretz, "A Big Worry for Japan, Inc," *Business Week,* February 6, 1995, p. 28.

39. P. J. Dowling and R. S. Schuler, *International Dimensions of Human Resource Management* (Boston: PWS-Kent, 1990), pp. 163–64.

40. J. Child, "Culture, Contingency, and Capitalism in the Cross-National Study of Organizations," in *Research in Organizational Behavior,* L. L. Cummings and B. M. Staw, eds. (Greenwich, CT: JAI Press, 1981), pp. 303–56.

41. For additional examples, see L. Sayles, "A 'Primer' on Cultural Dimensions," *Issues and Observations of the Center for Creative Leadership* 9 (1989), pp. 8–9.

42. W. Thorngate, " 'In General' vs. 'It Depends': Some Comments on the Gergen—Schlenker Debate," *Personality and Social Psychology Bulletin* 2 (1976), pp. 404–10; and K. E. Weick, *The Social Psychology Of Organizing,* 2d ed. (Reading, MA: Addison-Wesley, 1979).

43. J. A. Wagner III and M. K. Moch, "Individualism-Collectivism: Concept and Measure," *Group and Organization Studies* 11 (1986), pp. 280–304.; and J. A. Wagner III, "Studies of Individualism-Collectivism: Effects on Cooperation in Groups," *Academy of Management Journal* 38 (1995), pp. 152–72.

Chapter Fifteen
Thinking Critically about Organizational Behavior

Many companies are recognizing that, in order to gain a competitive advantage in today's fast-changing world, they must strive for continuous improvement in all areas of operations. Continuous improvement demands a commitment to constantly learning new and better ways of getting work done, and organizations that have succeeded in fulfilling this commitment have come to be known as *knowledge-creating companies* or *learning organizations.*[1] Boeing, Corning Glass, General Electric, Xerox, Chaparral Steel, Allegheny Ludlum, and GTE are just a few of the organizations that have been recognized for their skill at acquiring and creating new knowledge, and then modifying their organizational policies to take advantage of the new information.[2]

Two primary features of learning organizations set them apart from their competitors. First, they critically analyze their experiences and the experiences of others in order to maximize their capacity to learn from past successes and failures. For example, Boeing's Project Homework was a three-year study that compared the development process for the lackluster 737 and 747 plane programs with the process associated with the 707 and 727 programs, which had produced the company's two most profitable planes. The project group generated a list of over 100 "lessons learned" and transferred these to the start-ups of the 757 and 767 plane programs. Guided by critically analyzed past experience, these launches proved to be the most error-free and successful in Boeing history. Other organizations strive to maximize what can be learned from the experience of others. For example, Xerox has extensive benchmarking programs that seek to identify the best practices of other organizations. Once identified, these practices are studied through site visits and interviews and then are analyzed for potential implementation at Xerox.

The second primary feature of learning organizations is their penchant for experimentation, and their use of the scientific method to promote innovation. For example, Corning Glass is continually experimenting with different raw materials and different processes to increase both the yield and the quality of its finished glass. Allegheny Ludlum, a specialty steelmaker, expects every manager to be engaged in at least one experimental program each year, and the result of this forward-looking philosophy has been a history of productivity improvement averaging close to 8 percent a year.

Although many readers of this book are business majors, one fact that should not be overlooked is that many of the most successful CEOs are not MBAs. Instead, people like General Electric's Jack Welch and Intel's Andy Grove were formally trained in the hard sciences. Although the specialized skills learned in an MBA program are useful for entry-level positions, those who rise to the top of the organization are often those who generate, test, and implement new ideas and discoveries.[3]

---

[1] I. Nonaka, "The Knowledge Creating Company," *Harvard Business Review* 79 (November-December 1991), pp. 97–109.

[2] D. A. Garvin, "Building a Learning Organization," *Harvard Business Review* 81 (July-August 1993), pp. 78–91.

[3] H. Mintzberg, "Ten Ideas Designed to Rile Everyone Who Cares about Management," *Harvard Business Review* (July-August 1996), pp. 61–67.

Learning organizations rely on critical thinking and rigorously analyzed hard data to provide a long-term sustainable competitive edge relative to others in their industry. Unfortunately, knowledge-creating organizations are still rare. Too many U.S. businesses instead "fall prey to every new management fad promising a painless solution, especially when it is presented in a neat, bright package."[1] Indeed, this tendency has created a veritable cottage industry of "pop" management books, which often substitute for serious thinking about the best way to manage in specific companies.[2] One commentator on these books has noted, "No advice is too lame to get a polite, respectful hearing from a business audience."[3] Sadly, it is true that the vague, "one best way" recommendations in these books rarely stand up to rigorous scientific scrutiny.[4]

To avoid this quick-fix mentality, managers need to keep current with the literature in the field of management and to pay particular attention to journal articles that translate research findings into practical guidelines. Second, managers need to be skeptical when simple solutions are offered, and to analyze such solutions (and their supposed evidence) thoroughly. Third, managers need to ensure that the concepts they apply are based on science rather than advocacy, and managers should experiment with new solutions themselves whenever possible— in other words, strive to make their organizations learning organizations.

The purpose of this last chapter in the book is to help promote the kind of philosophy embodied by knowledge-creating organizations. Whereas all of our previous chapters have focused on *content* and learning what is already known about management, this chapter will focus on the thinking *process* so that you yourself can learn new and innovative approaches to management that will stand the test of time. Being the first to discover and implement innovative management techniques will help give you a sustainable competitive advantage relative to those relying on ineffective and widely copied business fads.

We will begin this chapter by examining the nature of the scientific process in order to show you how to successfully conduct your own experiments. We will then discuss how to draw valid causal inferences so that you can maximize your ability to learn from your own experiences, as well as to critically evaluate the claims made by others. We will also show you how to generalize research results to determine whether the results found in one sample and setting are likely to be repeatable in a different sample and setting. Finally, we will describe some of the scientific sources you can turn to in seeking answers to your managerial questions.

Critical Thinking and the Scientific Process

Traditional Ways of Knowing

To form a learning organization, all employees, but especially managers, must become more disciplined in their thinking and pay more attention to detail. They must continually ask, "How do we know that's true?" and push beyond the symptom level to get at underlying causes.[5] But how do we come to know things? When we say we know that there are nine planets in our solar system, how do we know this is true? When we say we know that providing workers with specific and difficult goals leads them to perform better than just telling them to do their best, how do we know this is true? Finally, when we say we know that an effective organization's structure must match its technology and its environment, how do we know this is true?

Personal Experience.   Philosophers of science have explored many ways of arriving at knowledge.[6] The most common source of knowledge for most of us is *personal experience.* Most people tend to believe information they acquire through interacting with other people and the world at large and to conclude that their experience reflects truth. Our own personal experiences may not always be a reliable source of truth, however, for several reasons. First, different people may have different experiences that point to different truths. Second, as we saw in Chapter 3, people's perceptions and memories of their experiences are often biased, inaccurate, or distorted over time.[7] Finally, even if we disregard inaccuracies of perception or memory, the fact remains that any one person can experience only a tiny fraction of all possible situations, and thus the knowledge acquired by personal experience will necessarily be extremely limited.

Despite these shortcomings, a reflective and critical approach to one's past experience can lead to enhanced understanding. This is especially the case with "productive failures" that when critically analyzed lead to insight, understanding, and then future success. For example, IBM's 360 computer series, one of the most popular and profitable ever built, was based on the technology of the failed Stretch computer that preceded it.[8] Productive failures can be even more important to an organization's long-term viability than "unproductive successes," in which something goes well but nobody knows why. We will discuss some of the keys to critically analyzing past experiences in the section on causal inferences.

Scientific Method.   Earlier we noted the tendency of many managers to look for quick-fix remedies to their problems. Sustainable competitive advantage does not come from simple solutions to complex problems. Instead, what managers need is a method that will help them generate and test new ways of competing.[9] One such method is the **scientific method.**

The problems and pitfalls of simply using personal experience as a means of discerning what is true led to the development of the **scientific method.** As Charles Sanders Peirce has stated, "To satisfy our doubts . . . it is necessary that a method should be found by which our beliefs may be determined by nothing human, but by some external permanency. . . . The method must be such that the ultimate conclusion of every man shall be the same. Such is the method of science."[10]

Thus **objectivity,** that is, the degree to which scientific findings are independent of any one person's opinion about them, stands as the major difference between the scientific approach to knowledge and the other approaches described so far. Science as an enterprise is *public* in the sense that methods used and results obtained by one scientist are shared with others. It is also *self-correcting* in the sense that erroneous findings can be isolated through the replication of a scientist's work by that same scientist or by another scientist. It is *cumulative* in the sense that one scientist's experiment often builds on the work of another. These features of the scientific method make it ideal as a means of generating reliable knowledge, and it is no coincidence that the physical, natural, and social sciences receive so much emphasis in today's colleges and universities. For all these reasons, it will be useful for us in this chapter to explore the nature of the scientific process more closely. We will look first at the major goals, or purposes, of science and then at how the scientific method is structured to achieve these goals.

The Purposes of Science

The basic goal of science is to help us understand the world around us. Science defines the understanding it seeks as the ability to describe, predict, control, and explain the subjects of its inquiry. We will examine each of these objectives.

Description.   The purpose of some research is simply *description,* that is, drawing an accurate picture of a particular phenomenon or event. In Chapter 1, for example, we presented data from Mintzberg's study of managerial roles. The purpose of Mintzberg's research was simply to find out what managers actually do on the job on a daily basis.[11] In Chapter 2, we reviewed research that described the major dimensions of personality. In Chapter 6, we looked at descriptive research that sought to delineate the dimensions best suited to describing the nature of jobs. The development of scientific knowledge usually begins with descriptive work. The ultimate criterion for evaluating all descriptive research is the fidelity with which its results reflect the real world.

Prediction.   *Predicting,* or stating what will happen in the future, is the primary goal of many scientific studies. Prediction requires that we know the relationships between certain conditions and outcomes. For example, in Chapter 5, we looked at research that attempted to predict who would leave organizations and who would stay. In Chapter 9, we reviewed studies of leadership that predict when decisions are best made by groups and when they are best left to individuals. In Chapter 13, we discussed studies that predicted the effects of different kinds of organizational cultures on people's behavior. When we cannot accurately predict what will happen when a given situation is repeated, we have generally failed to understand the situation.

Control.   Studies that focus on prediction often lead to further research in which the goal is to *control* the situation. Predictive studies often uncover relationships between causes and effects, and if it is possible to manipulate the causes, it may be possible to affect some outcome in a desirable manner. In Chapter 4, for example, we reviewed studies that show that by manipulating pay practices, firms can also manipulate how hard individuals will work. In Chapter 8, we discussed research that shows how group performance can be controlled by the manipulation of patterns of communication. In Chapter 12, we showed how changing the characteristics of organizational design can improve the fit between the firm and its environment. It is in the area of control that the interests of scientists and practitioners most clearly converge.

As we have seen already, managers in organizations are responsible for controlling the behaviors of others. Thus, the more information a study provides on how control can be achieved, the more useful it is to practicing managers. Indeed, research guided by the other objectives is often perceived by managers as being academic and not worthwhile. However, studies dealing with control often are the by-products of earlier descriptive or predictive studies. Without good descriptive and predictive research, we would probably never do much successful research aimed at control.

Explanation.   The ultimate goal of science is *explanation*—stating why some relationship exists. Some might argue that as long as we can describe, predict, and control things, there is no reason to go any further. For example, if managers in the insurance business know that people with college degrees sell more life insurance than people with high school degrees, why do they need to know more? Why not just hire college graduates for all sales positions? Well, if researchers can uncover the reason for college graduates' greater success, managers may be able to bring about the desired outcome (selling more insurance) in a more efficient or cost-effective way.

For example, suppose that college-educated salespeople outperform those without higher education, not because they have more years of study per se, but because on average they are more self-confident. Perhaps this self-confidence increases persistence on sales calls, which causes higher sales volume. If this were the true explanation, a manager might be able to get the same high success rate by hiring—at lower salaries—high school graduates who are high in self-confidence. A manager might also hire high school graduates and then train them to be more self-confident and persistent. As suggested by this example, if we know the exact reason why something occurs, we can usually control it much more efficiently.

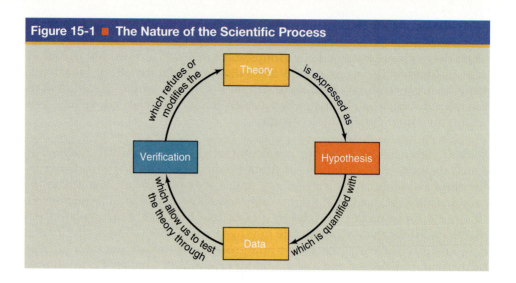

Figure 15-1 ■ The Nature of the Scientific Process

The Interplay of Theory and Data

Having discussed the different ways of arriving at knowledge and the goals, or purposes, of scientific inquiry, we now need to consider precisely what the scientific method entails. Figure 15-1 represents our conception of scientific inquiry and depicts science as a continuous process that links theory, which resides in the world of abstract ideas, with data, which reside in the world of concrete facts. A theory is translated into real-world terms by the process of creating hypotheses, and real-world data are translated back into the realm of ideas through the process of verification. These processes, then, form a chain, and any one scientific study is only as strong as its weakest link. If one link breaks apart (e.g., if the theory is not appropriately expressed in the hypotheses), then the whole process breaks down.

Kerlinger defines a **theory** as "a set of interrelated constructs, definitions, and propositions that presents a systematic view of a phenomenon by specifying relationships among variables."[12] With your understanding of the purposes of science and this definition of theory, can you see why theory plays such a central role in the scientific process? A good theory, through its constructs and definitions, should provide us with a clear description of a part of the real world. Moreover, by specifying relations among variables, a theory facilitates both prediction and control. Finally, a theory's systematic nature allows us to explain the relationships described. The preceding chapters of this book are filled with theories that can help you understand how to manage the behavior of people in organizations.

To have any practical utility, theories must prove themselves in the world of data. Through a process of deduction, **hypotheses,** or specific predictions about the relationships between certain conditions in the real world, are generated. These hypotheses are related to the theory in the sense that if the theory is correct, then what the hypotheses predict should be found in the real world.

This is where data enter the scientific process. Once hypotheses are formulated, we can collect data and compare the hypothesized results with the actual results. Then, through the process of **verification,** we use this comparison to check the accuracy of the theory and to judge the extent to which it is true. If there is very little correspondence between the hypothesized results and the actual findings, we must reject the theory. At this point, the process must begin all over again with the generation of a new theory. If there is some correspondence between the projected and actual findings, we may need to change the theory in some way so as to make it consistent with the data. If there is almost complete correspondence between the hypothesized results and the actual findings, we may be tempted to claim that we have proven that the theory is true. Such a conclusion would not be warranted, however, unless we could establish that all other possible explanations for the results not accounted for by the theory had been eliminated. Because this is almost never possible, we usually refer to data that correspond closely with a hypothesis as "supporting" rather than "proving" the theory.

Characteristics of Good Theories.   You do not have to be a scientist to have a theory. Indeed, in our daily lives, we all develop informal theories, or **implicit theories,** about the world around us. We arrive at these theories through our personal experience and are often unaware that they exist. Many of these implicit theories can be lumped together under the general heading of common sense. Thus, although some real-world managers claim to be skeptical of "theories," what many fail to realize is that they each carry around a large number of implicit theories of their own (one of which is the theory that theories are too academic and not practical).

Scientific theories are usually developed more formally. We will refer to these as **explicit theories** in order to distinguish them from implicit theories. As you have seen, the purpose of much of this book is to get managers to replace their implicit theories with explicit theories that have been supported by research. However, explicit theories are not always better than implicit theories. Moreover, there are often multiple explicit theories that deal with a given subject, and some may be better than others. How do we judge whether a theory is good or bad or decide which of two competing theories is best?

John B. Miner has offered several good criteria for judging the worth of theories in organizational behavior.[13] First and foremost, a theory should contribute to the objectives of science. That is, it should be useful in describing, predicting, controlling, or explaining important things. Most theories, whether implicit or explicit, meet this test.

Second, a theory must be logically consistent within itself. Here is where many implicit theories (and some explicit ones) fall short. For example, common sense tells us that "fortune favors the brave." On the other hand, common sense also tells us that "fools rush in where angels fear to tread," which has the opposite implication. Similarly, common sense tells us that "two heads are better than one," but it also tells us that "too many cooks spoil the broth." As you can see, common sense, and many of the implicit theories on which it is based, is not good theory at all because it contradicts itself.

Third, it is also important that a theory be consistent with known facts. For example, many people have an implicit theory that "a happy worker is a productive worker." In fact, a vast amount of research shows that satisfaction and performance are unrelated in nonservice jobs.[14] Any theory that stated directly or implied that these two variables were related would not be a good theory.

A fourth criterion by which to evaluate a theory is its consistency with respect to future events. The theory must not only predict, but it must also make *testable* predictions. A prediction is testable if it can be refuted by data. A theory that predicts all possible outcomes says nothing at all. For example, if a theory states that a particular leadership style can increase or decrease employee performance or leave it unchanged, it has really said nothing about the relationship between that leadership style and worker performance.

Finally, simplicity is a desirable characteristic of a theory. Highly complex and involved theories are not only more difficult to test but also more difficult to apply. A theory that uses only a few concepts to predict and explain some outcome is preferable to one that does the same thing with more concepts. Simplicity is hard to maintain, however. Theories are by their nature oversimplifications of the real world. Yet, for a theory to be consistent with real-world data, we must inevitably push it toward increasing complexity over time. A good theory is one that can walk the fine line between being too simple (when it will fail to predict events with any accuracy) and being too complex (when it is no longer testable or useful for any purpose).

Good Data.   Experienced managers have long known that "if you can't measure it, you can't manage it." Most data for testing theories are gathered through measurements of the theory's important concepts. Good data are just as important to scientists as good theory. Several characteristics make some measures, and therefore the data they generate, better than others.

First, the measures must possess **reliability;** that is, they must be free of random errors. Suppose, for example, that the person who was interviewing you for graduate school was interested in your scholastic aptitude because this was predictive of success in graduate school. Imagine, then, that to assess your aptitude the interviewer handed you two dice and asked you to toss them, at the same time suggesting that a high score would mean you had high aptitude and a low score would mean you had low aptitude. At this point, you would probably start wondering about the aptitude of the interviewer. The unreliability of dice tossing as a measure makes it virtually worthless.

This is an obvious case, but consider the following. It was once believed that interviewers, after talking to job applicants in an unstructured way for about 30 minutes, could provide ratings reflecting the applicants' suitability for many different jobs. Research showed, however, that these ratings were about as reliable as the dice tossing in the example just cited.[15] An interviewer would rate the same applicant high one day and low another day. In making important decisions like whether or not to admit an applicant to graduate school, most institutions rely heavily on test scores like those of the Graduate Record Examination (GRE), the Graduate Management Admission Test (GMAT), and the Law School Admission Test (LSAT). Although these tests are not perfectly reliable (students taking them repeatedly will not get the exact same score each time), they do exhibit a high degree of consistency.

Second, the measures of a theory's concepts must possess **validity;** that is, they must assess what they were meant to assess. To see whether the GMAT is valid, for example, we might want to test whether those who perform better on the test actually perform better in graduate school. This type of validity testing is called **criterion-related validation** because it tests whether the measure really predicts the criterion (e.g., grade point average) that it is supposed to be able to predict. Criterion-related validation is based upon an objective assessment of a measure's ability to predict future events. In contrast, we can also assess validity of a measure subjectively by having experts on the concept examine the measure. These experts can then assess the extent to which the content embodied in the measure actually reflects the theoretical concept being studied. This is called **content validation** because it tests whether the content of the test is appropriate according to experts on the subject.

Reliability and validity are closely related. Reliability is necessary for validity, but it is not sufficient because we could develop highly reliable measures that might not prove valid. For example, we could probably measure people's height reliably, but this measure would have little validity as a measure of scholastic aptitude (i.e., it could not predict who would do well in graduate school). Reliability is necessary for validity, however, because an unreliable measure cannot pass any of the tests necessary for establishing validity. An unreliable measure does not relate well even to itself.

A third desirable property of the measures of a theory's concepts is **standardization,** which means that everyone who measures the concepts uses the same instrument in the same way. Because it takes time and effort to develop measures that are reliable and valid, a great deal of *efficiency* can be achieved by using existing standardized measures.[16]

Standardized measures provide two other advantages. First, they are far more likely than other measures to achieve *objectivity.* Because everyone uses the same procedures, the results of measurement are much less likely to be affected by who happens to be doing the assessing. Second, standardized measures make it easy to *communicate* results and compare them across situations. You could construct a scale to measure job satisfaction in your own company, but even if you did succeed in developing a reliable and valid measure (a difficult task), you could not compare the satisfaction level in your company to that in other companies because other companies would not have used (and might not be willing to use) your measure. The Job Descriptive Index, or JDI, discussed in detail in Chapter 5, is a standardized measure of job satisfaction that has been used in hundreds of companies. For most standardized measures, a great deal of existing data allows you to compare your company to other companies that have all measured the same criteria in the same way.

For these and other reasons, managers should rarely try to develop their own measures for every situation. At worst, the measures would lack reliability and validity, and at best, those managers would be reinventing the wheel. It is possible, of course, that on some occasion you will need to test new concepts or develop measures that are unique to your situation. Such cases, however, will be the exception rather than the rule. For this reason, throughout this book we have provided you with either specific, standardized measures of various concepts or the sources from which such measures can be obtained.

Causal Inferences

We can use the scientific method to further our understanding of management, but to translate this enhanced understanding into more effective practice, we must be able to apply what we know. Knowledge is most applicable when it can be expressed in terms of cause-and-effect relationships. Once these relationships are identified, we can often manipulate the causes to bring about the specific effects we want (e.g., enhanced productivity or job satisfaction). Good theory and good measures take us a long way toward this objective, but they are not sufficient for identifying cause-and-effect relations (i.e., making causal inferences). As we will show later, making causal inferences depends not only on how the data are obtained but also on when the data are obtained and on what is done with the data once they are collected.

Moreover, even if one is not engaging in scientific experimentation, but is just trying to learn from one's daily experience, rigorously thinking about cause-and-effect relationships will help to ensure that one does not learn the wrong lesson from one's past experience. True learning can take place only when one seriously reflects upon one's past experience and analyzes it critically. For this reason, we will closely examine how to go about making the proper causal inferences.

Criteria for Inferring Cause

One of the foremost authorities on the philosophy of science, John Stuart Mill, argued that in order to establish that one thing causes another, we must be able to establish three things. First, we must establish temporal precedence; that is, the cause must come before, not after, the effect in time. Second, we need to be able to document covariation; that is, if the cause is varied (e.g., turned on or off), the effect must vary as well. Finally, we must also be able to eliminate alternative explanations for the observed results.

Temporal Precedence. The first step in establishing a cause-and-effect relationship is demonstrating **temporal precedence,** which simply means that the cause must precede the effect in time. One of the common mistakes made by people trying to learn from experience is that they often falsely infer a causal relationship between two variables just because those variables are observed to be related at one point in time. For example, imagine yourself touring a factory and observing that work groups with low absenteeism rates have supervisors who give team members a great deal of latitude and allow them to participate in decision making. In contrast, in the same factory tour you observe that the work groups with the highest absenteeism rates are closely monitored by their supervisors at all times and not allowed to participate in making decisions. It would be a mistake to jump to the conclusion that close supervision causes high absenteeism. It would be an even greater mistake to then act on this conclusion by demanding that all the managers of your company "loosen up" their supervision.

This would be a mistake because the causal order between these two variables may be in the opposite direction. That is, it might have been the case that all supervisors started out acting the same. However, high absenteeism in some groups caused their supervisors to tighten their control, and low absenteeism in other groups led their supervisors to provide them with more latitude. Failing to consider temporal precedence in this case would lead us to learn the wrong lesson from this factory tour. If we then acted on this misinformation and loosened up the supervision of the managers in our plant, we might find that absenteeism actually went up rather than down. Instead of solving a problem, we might actually have made the situation worse.

Covariation. The second criterion for inferring cause is **covariation,** which simply means that the cause and effect are related. For example, if we believe that providing day care for employees' children causes lower absenteeism, then there should be a relationship between company day care services and low employee absenteeism.

There are several ways to assess covariation, all of which rely on statistical methods. Because this is not a statistics book, we will limit our discussion here to two simple but widely applicable statistical techniques. Although not perfect for every situation, they are useful in a wide variety of contexts. The first, known as a *test of mean differences,* compares the average scores of two different groups on the outcome we wish to change. For example, Table 15-1 presents data on absenteeism for two groups of workers: Ten work at plant A, where there is an in-house day care center, and 10 work at plant B, where there are no on-site provisions for

Table 15-1 ■ Absence Data at Two Hypothetical Plants		
	Number of Absences	
EMPLOYEE	**PLANT A (WITH DAY CARE)**	**PLANT B (WITHOUT DAY CARE)**
1	10	12
2	11	11
3	8	13
4	11	8
5	3	16
6	4	14
7	3	10
8	2	4
9	1	2
10	5	3
Average	5.8	9.3

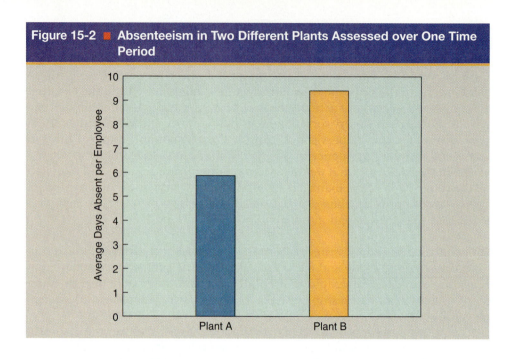

Figure 15-2 ■ **Absenteeism in Two Different Plants Assessed over One Time Period**

Table 15-2 ■ **Absence Data for One Hypothetical Plant at Two Different Times**

| | Number of Absences at Plant A | |
EMPLOYEE	BEFORE DAY CARE	AFTER DAY CARE
1	12	10
2	14	11
3	10	8
4	12	11
5	6	3
6	8	4
7	4	3
8	2	2
9	1	1
10	6	5
Average	7.5	5.8

day care. As you can see from Figure 15-2, the level of absenteeism is much higher for Plant B than for Plant A. This simple analysis of mean differences suggests that day care provision and absenteeism are in fact related. We might also test for mean differences between numbers of absences at Plant A before and after the establishment of the day care center and generate data like those displayed in Table 15-2 and graphed in Figure 15-3. If the average absenteeism rates were

Figure 15-3 ■ **Absenteeism at One Plant Assessed over Two Different Time Periods**

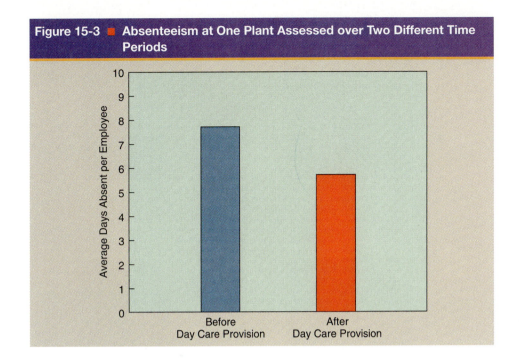

found to be higher before the day care center was put in than after it was in place, we might again conclude (before engaging in more rigorous analyses) that there was a relationship between provided day care and lower absenteeism. Both of these mean differences are easy to comprehend when presented in the form of a bar chart like those shown in Figures 15-2 and 15-3.

A second means of establishing covariation is through the use of the **correlation coefficient.** This statistic, a number that ranges from +1.0 to −1.0, is an expression of the relationship between two things. A +1.0 correlation means that there is a perfect positive relationship between the two measures in question (e.g., absenteeism rates and employee age). That is, as the value of one increases, the value of the other increases to the same relative degree. A correlation of −1.0 reflects a perfect negative relationship between the two measures. Here, as the value of one increases, the value of the other decreases, again to the same relative degree. Finally, a correlation of .00 indicates that there is no relationship whatever between the measures, so that as the value of one increases, the value of the other can be anything—high, medium, or low. To give you a feel for other values of the correlation coefficient, Figure 15-4 shows plots of points, where each point represents a person of a given age (specified on the x-axis) and that person's corresponding level of absenteeism (specified on the y-axis). This figure depicts four different correlation values, +1.0, +.50, +.20, .00 and −.50. As you can see, the sign of the correlation reveals whether the relationship is positive or negative, and the absolute value of the correlation reveals the magnitude of the relationship.

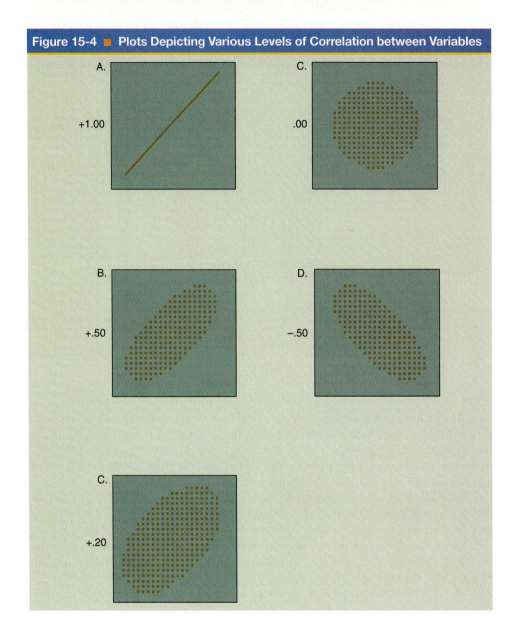

Figure 15-4 ■ Plots Depicting Various Levels of Correlation between Variables

A.

+1.00

C.

.00

B.

+.50

D.

−.50

C.

+.20

Let's go back to our employees at plants A and B. In Table 15-3, in addition to the data on day care and rates of absenteeism, we also show data on the ages of all the workers. We could use the correlation coefficient to find if there is a relationship between age and absenteeism. In fact, the correlation between age and absenteeism for these data is −.50, indicating that older workers are absent less often than younger ones. If we were to plot these data on a graph, where x was the horizontal axis and y the vertical axis, the graph would look just like the one shown in Figure 15-4D. Again, you can see that graphically depicting the

Table 15-3 ■ Absence and Age Data at Two Hypothetical Plants

EMPLOYEE	Plant A (Day Care) NUMBER OF ABSENCES	AGE	Plant B (No Day Care) NUMBER OF ABSENCES	AGE
1	10	27	12	27
2	11	31	11	34
3	8	30	13	31
4	11	26	8	25
5	3	40	16	33
6	4	61	14	35
7	3	52	10	25
8	2	47	4	40
9	1	46	2	52
10	5	41	3	46
Average	5.8	40.1	9.3	34.6

correlation in this fashion makes it easy to understand the strength and nature of the relationship between these two variables.

Eliminating Alternative Explanations. Once we have established both covariation and temporal precedence, we are only one step away from establishing that something actually caused something else. The *elimination of alternative explanations,* Mill's third criterion for establishing cause, is a big step, however. In our continuing example, if we are to infer that providing day care caused lower absenteeism, we must also show that there was not some other factor causing the low rates. Most real-world situations are so complex that it is very difficult to rule out all other possible explanations. Indeed, this problem, more than any other, is what makes it so difficult to conduct research in the social sciences.

In the physical sciences, experimenters can use physical means like lead shields and vacuum chambers to isolate variables and rule out alternative causes. This kind of tight control is harder to achieve in social science research and, in fact, some valid alternative explanations are so common that they are given special names.

The **selection threat** is the danger that the groups we selected for comparison were not the same to begin with.[17] If we had had only the data on absenteeism at the two plants (the data in Table 15-1), the lower mean rate of absenteeism at the plant with day care might have led us to conclude, based upon our past experience, that providing day care caused lower absenteeism. We have additional data, however, that show that age is negatively related to absenteeism, and it happens that workers at plant A are older than those at plant B. In fact, if we were to control for age by comparing only workers who were the same age, we would find no differences in absenteeism between the plants.

At this point you may be saying, "So what—what difference does it make?" It makes a huge difference if, based on your incorrect judgment as to what caused what, your company invested a lot of money in providing day care facilities on a corporation-wide basis. This large investment would be based on your conclusion that day care would pay for itself through lower absenteeism. But because day care was actually irrelevant to absenteeism, this investment would be completely lost, and many people would be left wondering what had happened. The selection threat is the most common threat to studies that compare two different groups at one point in time.

The **history threat** is the most common problem in studies in which one group is observed in a "before and after" situation. It comes into play when the real cause may have been, not the change you made, but something else that happened at the same time. In Figure 15-3, we compared the mean number of absences for plant A *before* day care with the mean number of absences *after* day care, and we found a lower average rate of absenteeism after than before. We might be tempted to infer that the day care center caused lower absenteeism. Suppose, however, that we obtained the "before" measure during the summer months and the "after" measure during the winter. It is possible that people find more reasons to be absent in the summer than in the winter. Thus, it could have been the weather rather than the day care center that caused the difference in absenteeism rates. If this were the case, and we were to extend the day care program throughout the corporation, we would find that it would not reduce absenteeism and we would be left wondering why.

Designing Observations to Infer Cause

The timing and the frequency of data collection affect our ability to make causal interpretations. Deciding on the timing of measurement is an important part of research design.

Faulty Designs.   Consider the two *faulty designs* shown in Figure 15-5. In the One Group Before-After design (Figure 15-5A), data are collected both before and after some event or treatment. If the after score (CD_2) is different from the before score (CD_1), it is assumed that the treatment (represented by Δ) caused the difference. The reason this is a faulty design is that the history threat leaves open the possibility of an alternative explanation for the results. If in our day care example, for instance, we collected data from only one plant, once in the summer and once in the winter, we would be using this type of faulty design.

In the After Only with Unequal Groups design (Figure 15-5B), data are collected from two different groups, one of which receives some experimental treatment whereas the other does not. The reason this design is faulty is that we do not know that the groups were equal before the treatment or during the treatment, and thus the selection threat leaves open the possibility of an alternative explanation for the results. In our day care example, we collected data from both plant A and plant B without making sure that the people at those plants were similar (e.g., were the same age on average), and thus we would have this kind of faulty design. These kinds of designs constitute the underlying structure of many of our day-to-day experiences and can lead us to learn the wrong lessons from our past experiences if we do not analyze them critically.

Figure 15-5 ■ Two Faulty Research Designs

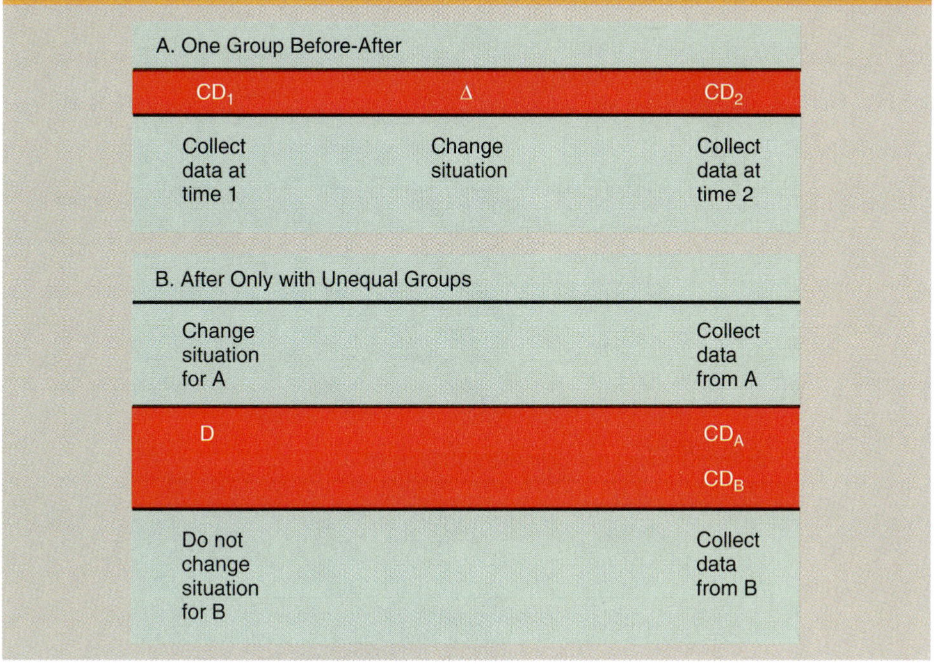

A. One Group Before-After

CD_1	Δ	CD_2
Collect data at time 1	Change situation	Collect data at time 2

B. After Only with Unequal Groups

Change situation for A	Collect data from A
D	CD_A
	CD_B
Do not change situation for B	Collect data from B

Improved Designs. There are several ways of designing situations that can help eliminate some of these threats. Let's take the One Group Before-After design, where the history threat is the major problem. We are somewhat better off in this situation if we add a control group (i.e, a group that does not receive the day care assistance), turning the design into the Two Groups Before-After design shown in Figure 15-6A. This design allows us to test whether the two groups were equal to begin with by comparing CD_{1A} with CD_{1B}. That is, in our day care example, was the rate of absenteeism at plants A and B similar before the treatment—the day care center—was put in place? This design also allows us to test whether some historical factor other than the day care center could have caused the results. That is, if the real cause was time of the year (summer versus winter), we could expect a decrease in absenteeism at plant B as we moved from time 1 to time 2, even though no day care center was established there.

The Two Groups After Only with Randomization model shown in Figure 15-6B is an even better design. It is just like the one shown in Figure 15-5B with one major exception: The people studied are randomly assigned to groups. **Random assignment** of people to conditions means that each person has an equal chance of being placed in either the experimental group or the control group. This random arrangement can be achieved by pulling names out of a hat, flipping coins, tossing dice, or using a random numbers table from a statistics book. In our day care study, if at the outset we could simply have assembled the twenty workers at the two

Figure 15-6 ■ Two Improved Research Designs

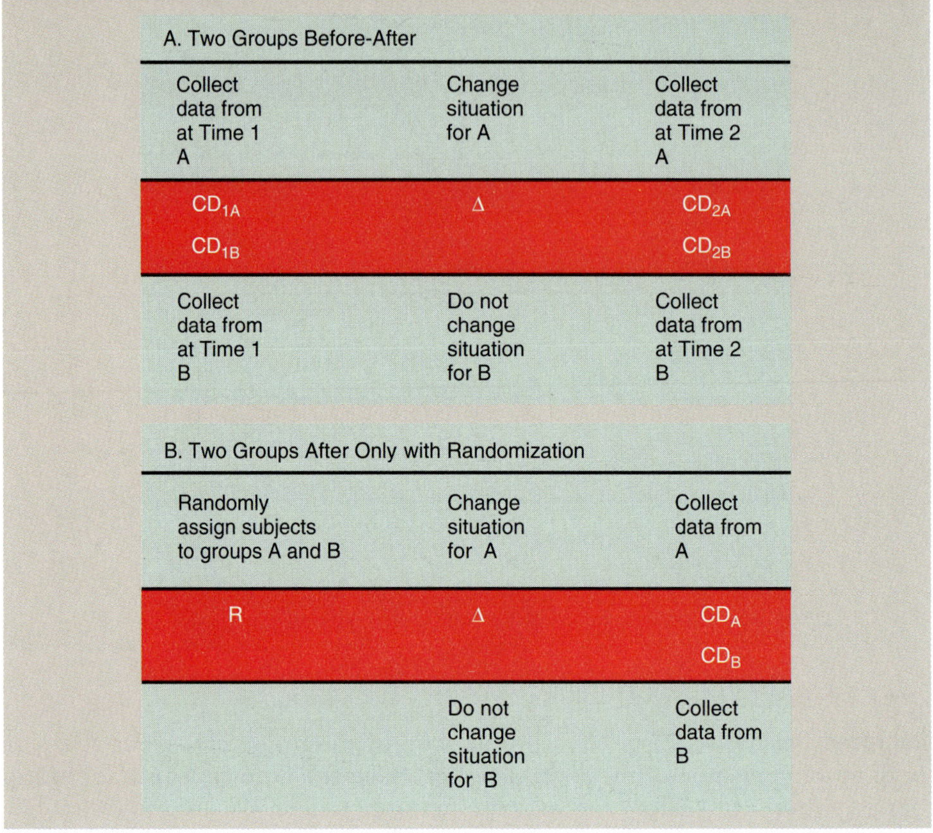

A. Two Groups Before-After

Collect data from at Time 1 A	Change situation for A	Collect data from at Time 2 A
CD_{1A}	Δ	CD_{2A}
CD_{1B}		CD_{2B}
Collect data from at Time 1 B	Do not change situation for B	Collect data from at Time 2 B

B. Two Groups After Only with Randomization

Randomly assign subjects to groups A and B	Change situation for A	Collect data from A
R	Δ	CD_A
		CD_B
	Do not change situation for B	Collect data from B

plants and then tossed a coin to see who would get day care and who would not, the odds are that when we were finished, the two resulting groups would have been equal in age. That is, each group would have had roughly the same number of people of a given age.

In fact, the real value of randomization is that it not only equalizes groups on factors (like age) that we would expect to influence our results, but it also equates groups on virtually all factors. Thus, in our day care study, if we randomized the groups at the outset, we could be fairly confident that they would be equated not only on age but on other things, such as height and weight. You might not think that a person's height or weight would relate to absenteeism, but some research has actually found a relationship between absenteeism and weight.[18] It is nice to know that, even if we were unaware of this relationship when we started the day care study, randomization would solve a potential problem for us by equalizing the groups on the factor of weight. Because of randomization's ability to rule out both anticipated and unanticipated selection threats, people conducting experiments should randomly assign subjects to treatments whenever possible.

Because randomization is not always possible, however, we often need other tools to rule out selection threats. For example, suppose that when we start our day care experiment, we know that workers at the two plants are not evenly distributed in terms of age, and we also know that age affects absenteeism. In the real world, we cannot randomly move people from plant to plant; we have to work with existing groups.

What, then, can we do to rule out age as the alternative explanation for our results? We have several choices. First, we could *use homogeneous groups,* that is, study groups that do not differ in age. For example, we might compare absenteeism at the two plants, but only among workers who are 25 to 35 years old. As you can see from Table 15-3, we would compare subjects 1, 2, 3, and 4 at plant A with subjects 1, 2, 3, 4, 5, 6, and 7 at plant B. With this sample, if we still found lower absenteeism at plant A than at plant B, we could not attribute the difference to age because all subjects would have been roughly the same age.

We could also equate groups by *matching subjects.* For example, we might use only the subjects at plant A for whom there are corresponding subjects at plant B, or subjects who are within two years of each other in age. Thus, looking again at Table 15-3, we could match subjects 1, 2, 5, 7, and 9 at plant A with subjects 1, 3, 8, 9, and 10 at plant B. Again, if we then found that absenteeism was lower in one plant than another, we could not attribute this result to age because we would have equated the groups on this factor.

Finally, we could also *build the threat into the design.* By this we mean that we could simply treat age as another possible factor affecting rate of absenteeism and examine its effect at the same time that we examine the effect of day care. One advantage of building alternative explanations into your design is that it allows you to test for **interactions.** An interaction exists when the relationship between the treatment (e.g., the day care center) and the outcome (e.g., absenteeism) depends upon some other variable (e.g., age). Figure 15-7 shows what we might find if we built the alternative explanation of age into our day care study. As you can see, among the younger group, providing day care does lower absenteeism, but among the older group it has no effect at all. Thus, the relationship between day care and absenteeism depends on the factor of age.

At this point you can see how many factors must be considered in designing studies that allow us to infer causality. Clearly, the more variables we can control, the tighter our research design and the more likely it is that we will be able to rule out alternative explanations for any relationships we discover.

Generalizing Research Results

Research is usually conducted with one sample, in one setting, across one time period. Often, however, we wish to know the **generalizability** of results, where **generalizability** is defined as the extent to which results obtained in one sample-setting-time configuration can be repeated in a different sample-setting-time configuration. This is sometimes of interest when we are conducting research,

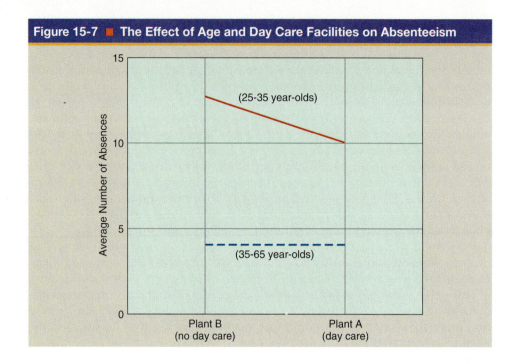

Figure 15-7 ■ The Effect of Age and Day Care Facilities on Absenteeism

(25-35 year-olds)

(35-65 year-olds)

Average Number of Absences

Plant B
(no day care)

Plant A
(day care)

but it is always of interest when we evaluate research findings to see whether what worked for the investigators can be applied in a real-world setting.

Sample, Setting, and Time

Our day care example provides a good illustration of how results might not generalize across different samples. Recall that the results of our study eventually showed that day care reduced absenteeism among workers who were 25 to 35 years old but not in the older group. Astute managers who studied our results would only want to apply these results in their company if they employed a large number of workers in the younger age category.

Suppose, however, that our design had homogenized our subjects on age (i.e., used only those in the 25-to-35 bracket). In this case, we would have reported simply that providing day care reduced absenteeism. A manager who read these results, but did not pay enough attention to the details on age, might institute a day care center in a company where most of the workers were between 35 and 65 years old. This person would soon discover that the results of our work did not generalize to this other organization. One of the major drawbacks of making groups homogeneous is that it limits our ability to generalize results across other types of samples.

We may also be concerned about generalizing research results across settings. For example, suppose that the plants in our original study were both located in rural settings. Assume further that it is more difficult to obtain high-quality day care in rural settings than in urban settings. Someone reading our study who manages a plant in an urban area might establish an in-plant day care center only to find that because child care is not a problem for workers in urban settings, the center has no effect on absenteeism. Here again, our results would not generalize to another setting.

Finally, we might also be concerned about whether our results would generalize across time. For example, suppose that we had conducted our study at a time when there was a huge labor shortage; many more jobs were available than there were people to fill them. At such a time, unemployment rates would have been low, both parents might well have been working, and many people who might in other circumstances have served as day care providers would very likely have been working at different and perhaps higher-paying jobs. Thus, when we conducted our study, there may have been a great demand for day care services but a small supply. By providing our own day care services, we solved a major problem for our workers with small children, and this ultimately led to lower absenteeism rates.

Now let's move forward 10 years, say, to a time when there is a labor surplus. Unemployment is high, there is a good chance that one parent is not working, and anyone capable of setting up a day care center is open for business. In this situation, because the demand for day care is small and the supply of day care services large, company-sponsored day care does not provide a needed service to employees, and so there is no relationship between providing day care and lowering absenteeism. Here our results do not generalize across time.

Facilitating Generalization

You may be wondering whether any findings are generalizable given the many factors that might differ from one unique sample-setting-time combination to another. From a researcher's perspective, can anything be done to increase the ability to generalize? The answer is yes. Technically, we can safely generalize from one sample to another if the original sample of people we study is *randomly selected* from the larger population of people to which we wish to generalize.

As an example of random selection, consider the following. You may have noticed that in presidential elections the television networks usually declare a winner when less than 10 percent of the actual results are available. Making the wrong call here might be very embarrassing, so why are the networks taking such a big risk? The key to their success is that when they poll people who have just finished voting, they do so randomly. In this way they ensure that the small percentage of people they poll are by all odds very similar to the larger group of voters. In fact, this is a case in which the researchers are so sure that their results will generalize that they have no fear whatsoever in publically declaring a winner way in advance of the final results. Just as the ability to generalize to other people can be assured only with random selection of subjects, generalizing from one setting or time to another can be assured only if we randomly sample settings and time periods.

Although random selection is the only way to ensure the ability to generalize, from a practical perspective it is often very difficult to achieve. Studies that employ random selection are usually huge in scale, requiring a large number of investigators and a great deal of money. More often, in the real world of research, the ability to generalize a finding is achieved not by one big experiment but by many small experiments, using the same measures, in which results are replicated over and over again in a host of different sample-setting-time configurations.[19] For example, in Chapter 4 we discussed research results that generalize very well, that is, the repeated finding that high performance is more likely to result from setting specific and difficult goals than from offering vague goals like "do your best." The generalizability of this finding comes not from one large study that randomly sampled people, settings, and times, but from many smaller studies, each of which used different samples, settings, and times, and yet got the same result.

As we have noted, although generalizing results is always of interest in evaluating research, it is not always interesting to the original researchers. Often, research is conducted strictly to test or build theories. Here investigators may be less interested in what *does* happen than in what *can* happen.[20] For example, in Chapter 5, when we discussed stress, we looked at research that shows that people can learn to control some of their own physiological processes, such as heart rate and blood pressure, when hooked up to special devices that give them feedback on these processes. You might think of few real-world situations that correspond to the one in which subjects in this kind of research find themselves. However, the point of this research was not to simulate what happens in the real world. The purpose of this research was to test a theory that states that human beings can voluntarily control supposedly involuntary physiological responses when provided with the right feedback. There is nothing inherent in this theory that suggests it would not be applicable to college sophomores in a laboratory setting at some specific time period. Thus, if the results fail to support the theory in this sample-setting-time configuration, the theory must be either rejected or modified and retested. The fact that neither subjects, settings, nor times were randomized is completely irrelevant. With this kind of research, the ultimate aim is not to make the laboratory setting more like the real world, but to make the real world more like the lab—that is, to change the real world in ways that benefit us all.

Linking OB Science and Practice

Employees in knowledge-creating companies, or learning organizations, are encouraged to experiment. As a practicing manager, you should know that there is a wealth of research conducted by others that is just waiting to be discovered. Table 15-4 provides a list of the major scientific journals that publish theory and research related to topics in this book. These journals are rank ordered by their influence in the field. A high ranking means that the findings reported in that journal tend to be more widely cited in the organizational sciences than those in lower-ranked journals.

A great deal of the research conducted in this area is performed by people working in university settings. Thus, you may also be able to uncover research on the topics that interest you by contacting university faculty who publish a good deal on topics related to organizational behavior. Many companies enlist

Table 15-4 ■ The 10 Most Influential Journals in Organizational Behavior

1. *Administrative Science Quarterly*
2. *Academy of Management Review*
3. *Academy of Management Journal*
4. *Personnel Psychology*
5. *Journal of Management*
6. *Journal of Applied Psychology*
7. *Journal of Vocational Behavior*
8. *Organizational Behavior and Human Decision Processes*
9. *Journal of Occupational Psychology*
10. *Human Relations*

Source: W. Starbuck and J. Mezias, "Journal Impact Ratings," *The Industrial Psychologist* (April 1996), pp. 101–5.

the help of faculty and students at local universities, and these people help bring fresh perspectives, unique skills, and diverse experiences to the organization. In addition, the internships, case studies, or field research provided by university personnel provide excellent learning opportunities that the company can use to promote organizational effectiveness. One company, Chaparral Steel, even sends its first-line supervisors on academic sabbaticals to develop an understanding of new work practices and technologies. They then bring what they have learned back to the company and apply it to daily operations. As the result of initiatives like this, Chaparral is one of the five lowest-cost steel producers in the world. Specialized expertise in certain areas of management can also be found in some consulting companies. However, as the Securing Competitive Advantage box illustrates, one should not count on gaining a great deal of sustainable competitive advantage from these types of outside sources.

People who teach organizational behavior and executive development often lament the fact that there is not enough dialogue between practicing managers and researchers. This kind of dialogue can develop only when managers and researchers understand each other's work and appreciate its value for their own efforts. Practicing managers need to know what organizational behavior researchers do and why they do it the way they do. Researchers need to know what practitioners' most pressing problems are so that they can study issues that managers view as significant. It is in large part because we feel that it is so important to create and encourage this kind of ongoing practitioner-researcher dialogue that we have included this chapter on research methods in our book.

Even though you may not actually conduct research yourself, you will find it invaluable to familiarize yourself with the wealth of scientific evidence available on topics that will be crucial to you, your employer, and your employees. Although this research may not provide you with all the answers, it will most assuredly give you something to think about, perhaps promoting the kind of spirit embodied in some of the learning organizations described at the outset of this chapter.

Utilizing Consultants: Buyer Beware

The only way for consultants at the partner level to make a lot of money is to suck money out of their clients as fast as they can . . . thus, consulting firms teach their young to cling tenaciously to every client, and that they'll be promoted on the basis of their ability to do that. When I was a consultant, I spent more time thinking about what I was going to sell the client next than the problem I was supposed to be fixing.[1]

In the quest to gain competitive advantage, it is often tempting for managers to bring in outside experts and consultants. Indeed, we opened this book's first chapter with the example of a hypothetical situation in which a manager had to weigh the opinions of four different outside consultants with respect to solving a problem with employee productivity levels. In many ways, the whole purpose of the book was to provide you with the types of skills you would need to solve these problems yourself, rather than by seeking outside help. If after reading this text, you

are still tempted to turn to outsiders for your solutions, hopefully the quote just provided will cause you to stop and reconsider. There are three primary reasons why it is difficult, if not impossible, to sustain long-term competitive advantage from this type of outside source.

First, as the quote implies, the financial interests of the consultant and the client are not always the same. The goal of the manager is to solve a specific problem, but the goal of the consultant is to generate "billable hours" and this becomes impossible once the problem is actually solved. Second, consultants are often more interested in finding a solution to the problem that matches the skills of their consulting company, as opposed to finding the best solution for your company. One ex-consultant notes, for example, "If I know I'm up against a boutique that doesn't have computer systems capability, you can be sure that my pitch will be that you have to have a new information system." Third, whatever a consultant is willing to sell to you

can also be sold to your competition. One consultant states, for example, "I know of one consulting organization that analyzed the cost structure of every steel company in Europe and then went and sold that research to every steel company in Europe. When consulting firms put their people to work that way, it hardly creates a competitor-crushing advantage for their clients."[2]

Sustainable competitive advantage comes about when people within the organization invent and successfully test their own unique ways to solve problems and then treat these solutions with the same type of security typically reserved for formulas like those for Coke or Kentucky Fried Chicken. If the employees of your organization cannot discover their own solutions to problems, get new employees—do not bring in temporary outside help. Moreover, if you, as the manager, start outsourcing the job of management, it will not be long before someone higher up starts questioning your own "value added" to the company.[3]

[1] Anonymous, "Confessions of an Ex-Consultant," *Fortune,* October 14, 1996, pp. 107–12.
[2] R. B. Lieber, "Controlling Your Consultants," *Fortune,* October 14, 1996, pp. 114–15.
[3] T. A. Stewart, "Think for Yourself, Boss," *Fortune,* October 2, 1995, p. 162.

SUMMARY

The traditional way of acquiring knowledge, personal experience, has many limitations. The advantage of science relative to these more traditional means is its *objectivity,* and science as an enterprise tends to be public, self-correcting, and cumulative. The major goals of science are the description, prediction, control, and explanation of various phenomena. These goals are achieved through an interplay of *theory* and *data,* whereby ideas contained in theories are expressed in testable *hypotheses,* which are then compared to actual data. The correspondence (or lack thereof) between the hypothesized results and the actual results is then used to verify, refute, or modify the theory.

Good theories are characterized by simplicity, self-consistency, and consistency with known facts, and they should contribute to the objectives of science. To be useful, data for testing theories should be *reliable* and *valid,* and there are many advantages to using established *standardized* measures.

At the core of many theories is the idea of establishing causes. Cause can be inferred only when we establish *temporal precedence* and *covariation* and when all *alternative explanations* have been eliminated. This last requirement is often the most troublesome aspect of research in the social sciences, and some kinds of threats like *selection* and *history threats* are especially problematic. These threats can be partially avoided through research designs that use control groups and make these comparable to experimental groups through *randomization, matching,* or *homogenization.*

To be able to *generalize* the findings from a study to another context, it is necessary to randomly select samples, settings, and time periods. This is rarely achieved in the social sciences. However, if, over time, experimental results have repeatedly been confirmed in different samples and settings and at different times, it may be possible to generalize such findings.

Review Questions

1. Many theories can be shown to follow a similar pattern. They start out simple, grow increasingly complex as empirical tests on the theory proliferate, and then die out or are replaced by new theories. Look back at the criteria for a good theory and discuss why this pattern is so common. In your discussion, specify possible conflicts or inconsistencies among the criteria for a good theory.

2. Objectivity is one of the hallmarks of scientific inquiry. Yet all scientists can be shown to have their own subjective beliefs and biases surrounding the phenomena they study. Indeed, some scientists are motivated to do their work by passionate beliefs about these phenomena. Discuss whether this kind of passion is an asset or a liability to the scientist. Discuss further how science can be an objective exercise when people who practice it can be shown to have biases. What prevents a passionate scientist from cheating or distorting results in favor of personal beliefs?

3. Experiments in organizations usually involve people other than the experimenters, that is, managers or employees. What are some of the ethical responsibilities of an experimenter with respect to these people? Is it ethical, for example, for an experimenter to use one group of employees as a control group when that experimenter strongly suspects that the treatment given to the experimental group will enhance their chances for success, promotion, or satisfaction? If the experimenter is afraid that explaining the nature of the experiment will cause people to act differently than they would otherwise (and hence ruin the experiment), is it ethical to deceive them about the study's true purpose?

4. Philosopher of science Murray S. Davis once remarked that "the truth of a theory has very little to do with its impact."[21] History, according to Davis, shows that the impact of a theory depends more on how interesting the theory is perceived to be by practitioners and scientists than on how much truth it holds. We listed criteria for good theories in this chapter; list what you think are criteria for "interesting" theories. Where do these two lists seem to conflict most, and what can be done by scientists and the practitioners they serve to generate theories that are both interesting and truthful?

ENDNOTES

1. I. I. Mitroff and S. A. Mohrman, "The Slack Is Gone: How the United States Lost Its Competitive Edge in the World Economy," *Academy of Management Executive* (1987), p. 69.

2. E. Shapiro, *Fad Surfing in the Boardroom: Reclaiming the Courage to Manage in the Age of Instant Answers* (Boston: Addison-Wesley, 1995) pp. 21–22.

3. A. Farnham, "In Search of Suckers," *Fortune,* October 14, 1996, pp. 119–26.

4. Ibid., p. 95.

5. Garvin, "Building a Learning Organization," p. 81.

6. See, for example, J. Buchler, *Philosophical Writings of Peirce* (New York: Dover, 1955); M. Cohen and E. Nagel, *An Introduction to Logic and the Scientific Method* (New York: Harcourt, 1954); M. Polyani, *Personal Knowledge* (Chicago: University of Chicago Press, 1958); and L. B. Christenson, *Experimental Methodology* (Boston: Allyn & Bacon, 1977).

7. E. F. Stone, *Research Methods in Organizational Behavior* (Santa Monica, CA: Goodyear, 1978), p. 13.

8. D. Nadler, "Even Failure Can Be Productive," *New York Times,* April 23, 1989, p. 3.

9. Mitroff and Mohrman, "The Slack Is Gone."

10. Buchler, *Philosophical Writings of Peirce,* p. 18.

11. H. A. Mintzberg, "Structured Observation as a Method to Study Managerial Work," *Journal of Management Studies* 7 (1970), pp. 87–104.

12. F. N. Kerlinger, *Foundations of Behavioral Research* (New York: Holt, Rinehart & Winston, 1986), p. 9.

13. J. B. Miner, *Theories of Organizational Behavior* (Hinsdale, IL: Dryden Press, 1980).

14. M. T. Iaffaldono and P. M. Muchinsky, "Job Satisfaction and Performance: A Meta-Analysis," *Psychological Bulletin* 97 (1985), pp. 251–73.

15. R. Arvey and M. Campion, "The Employment Interview: A Summary and Review of Recent Research," *Personnel Psychology* 34 (1982), pp. 281–322.

16. J. C. Nunnally, *Psychometric Theory* (New York: McGraw-Hill, 1978), p. 4.

17. T. D. Cook and D. T. Campbell, *Quasi-Experimentation: Design Analysis Issues for Field Settings* (Chicago: Rand McNally, 1979), p. 53.

18. K. R. Parkes, "Relative Weight, Smoking and Mental Health as Predictors of Sickness and Absence from Work," *Journal of Applied Psychology* 72 (1987), pp. 275–87.

19. Cook and Campbell, *Quasi-Experimentation.*

20. D. G. Mook, "In Defense of External Invalidity," *American Psychologist* 38 (1983), pp. 379–87.

21. M. S. Davis, "That's Interesting! Towards a Phenomenology of Sociology and a Sociology of Phenomenology," *Philosophy of the Social Sciences* 1 (1978), pp. 309–44.

Glossary

Action research model A model of the OD process that permits the development and assessment of original, innovative interventions.

Administrative principles perspective The management perspective in which management principles are proposed in order to streamline administrative procedures.

Agreeableness A class of traits that deals with the degree to which a person is likable, cooperative, and good natured.

Attention stage The stage in the information-processing cycle in which the individual decides what will be processed and what will be ignored.

Authoritarian A leader who makes almost all decisions independently, minimizing the input of subordinates.

Availability bias The tendency of decision makers to judge the likelihood that something will happen by the ease with which they can recall examples of it.

Bargaining A process in which offers, counteroffers, and concessions are exchanged as conflicting groups search for some mutually acceptable resolution.

Base rate bias The tendency of decision makers to ignore the underlying objective probability, or base rate, that a particular outcome will follow a particular course of action.

Basic coordination mechanism A mechanism that sustains structural interconnections in and among groups by helping to mesh interdependent task activities.

Biofeedback A technique that uses machines to monitor bodily functions once thought to be involuntary, such as heartbeat and blood pressure, so that a person can learn to regulate these functions.

Boundary spanner A member or unit of an organization that interacts with individuals or firms in the organization's environment.

Bounded discretion The limited area of acceptable alternatives that is offered to a decision maker, bounded by social, legal, moral, and organizational restrictions.

Buffering The action of certain positive factors in the person's environment to limit the capacity of other factors to create dissatisfaction and stress.

Bureaucracy An idealized description of an efficient organization based on clearly defined authority, formal record keeping, and standardized procedures.

Bureaucratic structures Structures used in large, complex organizations that involve significant standardization, formalization, and specialization.

Burnout A condition of emotional, physical, and mental exhaustion resulting from prolonged exposure to intense stress.

Centrality The position of a person or group within the flow of work in an organization.

Centralization The concentration of authority and decision making at the top of an organization; the opposite of decentralization.

Ceremonies Special events in which the members of an organization celebrate myths, heroes, and symbols of their culture.

Change The act of varying or altering; it is both an important impetus and a primary product of the process of organization development.

Change agent A person who manages the OD process, serving both as a catalyst for change and as a source of information about organizational development.

Charismatic leadership Creating a new vision of an organization and getting group members to commit themselves enthusiastically to the new mission, structure, and culture embodied in the vision; encouraging members to transcend self-interest on behalf of the organization as a whole.

Coercive power Interpersonal power based on the ability to control the distribution of undesirable outcomes.

Cohesiveness A measure of the interpersonal attraction among members of a group and their attraction to the group as a whole.

Collateral structure A second hierarchy of groups and committees that parallels and sometimes takes the place of the primary managerial hierarchy in Scandinavian industrial democracies.

Communication The exchange of information between people through a common set of symbols.

Communication structure The pattern of interactions by which group members share information.

Competitive group rewards Group rewards distributed in such a way that members receive equitable rewards in exchange for successful performance as individuals in a group.

Comprehensive interdependence A type of member interaction in which every group member depends on every other.

Comprehensive job enrichment A type of work design that combines both horizontal and vertical improvements to stimulate employee motivation and satisfaction.

Conflict A process of opposition and confrontation that can occur between either individuals or groups.

Conformity Loyal but uncreative adherence by group members to both pivotal and peripheral norms.

Conscientiousness A class of traits that deals with the degree of dependability, organization, conformity, and responsibility that a person possesses.

Consideration Leader behavior aimed at meeting the social and emotional needs of workers, such as helping workers, doing them favors, looking out for their best interests, and explaining decisions to them.

Constituency groups Groups such as employees, customers, and suppliers upon whom the organization depends for survival; constituency groups make demands that they expect will be fulfilled in return for their support of the organization.

Content validation Establishing validity by showing that, according to expert judges, the measure samples the appropriate material.

Convergence hypothesis A theoretical assertion that organizations and management practices throughout the world are growing more alike.

Cooperative group rewards Group rewards distributed in such a way that each member receives an equal reward in exchange for the successful performance of the group.

Core job characteristics Job characteristics identified in the Hackman-Oldham model that lead jobholders to experience certain critical psychological states.

Core technology The dominant technology used in performing work at the base of the organization.

Correlation coefficient A statistic that assesses the degree of relationship between two variables.

Covariation The degree to which two variables are associated with each other; the degree to which changes in one are related to changes in the other.

Creative individualism Acceptance by group members of pivotal norms but rejection of peripheral ones.

Criterion-related validation Establishing validity by showing that a measure predicts some variable that, based on theory, it should predict.

Critical contingencies Events, activities, or objects that are required by an organization and its various parts to accomplish organizational goals and to ensure continued survival.

Critical psychological states Mental conditions identified in the Hackman-Oldham model as being triggered by the presence of certain core job characteristics.

Culture The shared attitudes and perceptions in an organization that are based on a set of fundamental norms and values and that help members understand the organization.

Decentralization The dispersion of authority and decision making downward and outward through the hierarchy of an organization; the opposite of centralization.

Decoding The process by which a transmitted message is converted into an abstract idea in the mind of the person to which the communication is directed.

Decoupling mechanism A structural approach to managing conflict in which intergroup relations are eliminated, either by buffering or by self-containment.

Democratic leader A leader who works to ensure that all subordinates have a voice in making decisions.

Departmentation The process of clustering structural groups into larger units, called departments or divisions.

Depth The degree or intensity of change that an organization development intervention is designed to stimulate.

Differentiation The second stage of group development, characterized by conflicts that erupt as members seek agreement on the purpose, goals, and objectives of the group and the roles of its members.

Direct supervision A basic coordination mechanism in which one person takes responsibility for the work of a group of others and has the authority to determine which tasks need to be performed, who will perform them, and how they will be linked together to produce the desired end result.

Discretion An area of latitude wherein decision makers can use their own judgment in developing and deciding among alternative decisions.

Division of labor The process and result of breaking difficult work into smaller tasks.

Divisional structure The type of bureaucratic structure characterized by standardization, divisional departmentation, and moderate decentralization.

Economic rationality The belief, underlying the rational decision-making model, that people attempt to maximize their individual economic outcomes.

Efficiency perspective An approach to work design that focuses on the creation of jobs that economize on time, human energy, raw materials, and other productive resources.

Emergent task elements The components of work roles that are not formally recognized by the organization but arise out of expectations held by others for the role incumbent.

Emotional adjustment A class of personality variables that deals with the extent to which a person experiences affective distress or engages in socially unacceptable behaviors.

Employee-oriented behavior Leadership behavior designed to meet the social and emotional needs of group members.

Empowerment perspective An approach to work design that suggests that fitting the characteristics of jobs to the people who perform them increases personal growth and satisfaction at work.

Encoding The process by which a communicator's abstract idea is translated into the symbols of language for transmission to someone else.

Entity attraction Satisfaction with other persons in the workplace that comes about because these people share one's fundamental values, attitudes, or philosophy.

Environment The context surrounding an organization, consisting of economic, geographic, and political conditions that impinge on the firm.

Environmental change An environmental characteristic concerning the extent to which conditions in an organization's environment change unpredictably.

Environmental complexity An environmental characteristic defining the degree to which an organization's environment is complicated and therefore difficult to understand.

Environmental diversity The degree to which an organization's environment is varied or heterogeneous in nature.

Environmental domain A part, or segment, of the environment in which an organization does business.

Environmental receptivity The degree to which an organization's environment supports the organization's progress toward fulfilling its purpose.

Environmental turbulence A factor describing the speed and scope of change that occurs in the environment surrounding an organization.

Environmental uncertainty An environmental characteristic formed by the combination of change and complexity that reflects the absence of information about environmental factors, activities, and events.

Equity theory A theory of motivation that suggests that behavior is motivated by the desire to reduce guilt or anger associated with social exchanges that are perceived to be unfair.

Ergonomics Another name for human factors engineering, a type of methods engineering that focuses on designing machines to match human capacities and limitations.

Established task elements The components of work roles that are contained in written job descriptions and formally recognized in the organization.

Escalation of commitment Investing additional resources in failing courses of action that are not justified by any foreseeable payoff.

Eustress A particular kind of stress created when an individual is confronted with an opportunity.

Expectancy A person's beliefs regarding the link between efforts and performance.

Expectancy theory A broad, cognitive theory of motivation that explains behavior as a function of expectancies, instrumentalities, and valences.

Expert power Interpersonal power based on the possession of expertise, knowledge, and talent.

Explicit theories Internally consistent, formal theories that are subject to empirical test.

Extinction The gradual disappearance of a response that occurs after the cessation of positive reinforcement.

Extroversion A class of traits that deals with the degree to which a person is sociable, ambitious, talkative, and assertive.

Forcefield analysis A diagnostic method that depicts the array of forces for and against a particular change in a graphic manner; often used as a component of the OD process.

Formalization The process of planning the regulations that will control organizational behavior; also the written documentation produced by the planning process.

Functional attraction Satisfaction with other persons in the workplace that comes about because these other people help one attain valued work outcomes.

Functional grouping The grouping of people into units according to similarities in the functions they perform.

Functional structure The type of bureaucratic structure characterized by standardization, functional departmentation, and centralization.

General adaptation syndrome The theory developed by Hans Selye that the body's response to stress occurs in three distinct stages: alarm, resistance, and exhaustion.

General cognitive ability The totality of an individual's mental capacity, summing across specific mental abilities such as verbal comprehension, quantitative aptitude, reasoning ability, and deductive ability.

Generalizability The degree to which the result of a study conducted in one sample-setting-time configuration can be replicated in other sample-setting-time configurations.

Global enterprise A multinational business that customizes its products or services to regional tastes and localizes business operations at each of the different sites it owns.

Goal commitment A person's willingness to put forth effort in accomplishing goals and unwillingness to lower or abandon goals.

Goal-setting theory A theory of motivation originated by Locke that suggests that behavior is driven by goals and aspirations, such that specific and difficult goals lead to higher levels of achievement.

Group effectiveness An assessment of the extent to which a group is accomplishing its task in the most productive and satisfactory manner.

Group formation The process of grouping the members of an organization into work groups or units.

Group-maintenance roles Group roles that help ensure a group's continued existence by building and preserving strong interpersonal relations among its members.

Hedonism The belief that human beings generally behave so as to maximize pleasure and minimize pain.

Heroes People who embody the values of an organization's culture and serve as role models for other members in the organization.

Hierarchical sensitivity The average level of dyadic sensitivity that characterizes a team in its team decision making.

History threat A threat to validity that exists when some important variable other than the one manipulated experimentally might have changed during an experiment.

Horizontal job enlargement A type of work design based on the idea that increasing the number of tasks a jobholder performs will reduce the repetitive nature of the job and thus eliminate worker boredom.

Horizontal specialization The type of specialization in which the work performed at a given hierarchical level is divided into special jobs.

Human factors engineering A type of methods engineering which experts design machines, operations, and work environments so that they match human capacities and limitations.

Human relations perspective The management perspective that emphasizes increasing employee growth, development, and satisfaction.

Hygiene factors Characteristics of the job that, according to Frederick Herzberg, influence the amount of dissatisfaction experienced at work.

Hypothesis A specific, testable prediction, typically derived from a theory, about the relationship between two variables.

Implicit theories Loose, informal theories about phenomena that people rarely test in a rigorous, empirical fashion.

Incubation A stage in the creative decision-making process in which a person apparently stops attending to the problem at hand.

Individualism-collectivism A cross-cultural dimension that describes the degree to which a culture places emphasis on satisfying personal interests on the one hand, or on looking after group needs, on the other.

Industrial democracy An industrial organization that is required by law to permit its members to govern themselves.

Industrial engineering A branch of engineering that concerns itself with how to maximize the efficiency of the methods, facilities, and materials used to produce commercial products.

Industrial robots Machines that can be programmed to repeat the same sequence of work movements over and over again.

Information overload A condition in which people are presented with more information that they can possibly process.

Initiation The initial stage of group development, characterized by uncertainty and anxiety.

Initiating structure Leader behavior aimed at meeting the group's task requirements, such as getting workers to follow rules, monitoring performance standards, clarifying roles, and setting goals.

Inquisitiveness A class of traits that deals with the degree to which a person is imaginative, curious, open minded, and sensitive.

Insight A stage in the creative decision-making process in which the solution to a problem manifests itself in a flash of inspiration.

Instrumentality A person's subjective belief about the relationship between performing a behavior and receiving an outcome.

Integration The third stage of group development, which is focused on reestablishing the central purpose of the group in light of the structure of roles developed during differentiation.

Interaction An experimental outcome in which the relationship between two variables changes depending on the presence or absence of some third variable.

Intergroup team building A deep OD intervention intended to improve communication and interaction between work-related groups.

Intervention A particular organization development technique, such as counseling or team building, that is used to stimulate change in an organization.

Jargon Idiosyncratic use of language that is often helpful among specialists but that inhibits their ability to communicate with nonspecialists.

Job depth The amount of discretion a jobholder has in choosing job activities and outcomes.

Job extension A type of horizontal job enlargement in which several simplified jobs are combined to form a single new job.

Job range The number of tasks a jobholder performs to complete the job.

Job rotation A process whereby an individual is systematically moved from one job to another over the course of time.

Job satisfaction The perception that one's job enables one to fulfill important job values.

Job-oriented behavior Leadership behavior that focuses on careful supervision of employees' work methods and performance level.

Kibbutz A close-knit community of people located in Israel and organized on the principles of collective ownership and direct participation in self-governance.

Laissez-faire leader A leader who lets a group run itself, with minimal intervention from upper levels of the organizational hierarchy.

Language A system of shared symbols that the members of an organization use to communicate cultural ideas and understandings.

Latticework structure The structure of vertical and horizontal relationships found in many large Japanese corporations.

Leader-follower relations A component of Fielder's contingency theory that describes the level of trust and respect a follower has for a leader.

Leadership The use of noncoercive influence to direct and coordinate the activities of the members of an organized group toward the accomplishment of group objectives.

Leadership grid figure A two-dimensional representation of leadership behaviors in which concern for people and concern for production combine to produce five behavioral styles.

Legitimate power Interpersonal power based on holding a position of formal authority.

Loose coupling Managing interrelatedness across different functional areas by not allowing the actions or decisions of one functional unit to have an overly large or immediate impact on the actions or decisions of other functional units.

Loss aversion bias The tendency of most decision makers to weigh losses more heavily than gains, even when absolute values of the two are equal.

Macro organizational behavior The subfield of organizational behavior that focuses on understanding the structure and processes of entire organizations.

Masculinity-femininity A cross-cultural dimension that describes the degree to which a culture is founded on values that emphasize independence, aggressiveness, dominance, and physical strength, on the one hand, or interdependence, compassion, empathy, and emotional openness, on the other.

Maslow's need theory A theory of motivation that suggests that behavior is driven by the urge to fulfill five fundamental types of needs: physiological, safety, love, esteem, and self-actualization.

Matrix structure The type of bureaucratic organization structure that incorporates both functional and divisional departmentation, along with significant mutual adjustment at the top of the organization.

Maturation contingencies Structural contingency factors associated with an organization's level of maturity that determine whether prebureaucratic, bureaucratic, or postbureaucratic structures are more likely to produce effectiveness.

Maturity The fourth and final stage of group development, in which members begin to fulfill their prescribed roles and work toward attaining group goals.

Mechanistic structures Machinelike organization structures designed to enhance efficiency; characterized by large amounts of formalization, standardization, specialization, and centralization.

Memomotion analysis A type of work measurement in which industrial engineers examine longer activity sequences by using slow speed to film or videotape a person at work and then playing back the resulting film or tape at normal speed.

Meso organizational behavior The subfield of organizational behavior that bridges the other two subfields, focusing on understanding the behaviors of people working together in teams and groups.

Methods engineering An area of industrial engineering that attempts to improve the methods used to perform work.

Micro organizational behavior The subfield of organizational behavior concerned with understanding the behaviors of individuals working alone.

Micromotion analysis A type of work measurement in which industrial engineers analyze the hand and body movements required to do a job.

Motivation The factors that initiate, direct, and sustain human behavior over time.

Motivator factors Characteristics of the job that, according to Frederick Herzberg, influence the amount of satisfaction experienced at work.

Multinational A company that does a significant percentage of its business in a country or countries outside of its original home country.

Multiunit structure The type of postbureaucratic structure consisting of two or more autonomous business units, which themselves may contain autonomous groups of employees joined together by a computer network.

Mutual adjustment A basic coordination mechanism in which coordination is accomplished via communications among coworkers who occupy positions of similar hierarchical authority.

Myth A story that provides a fictional but plausible explanation for something that might otherwise seem puzzling.

National culture The collection of societal norms and values in the environment surrounding an organization.

Negative affectivity A person's tendency to often experience feelings of subjective distress such as anger, contempt, disgust, guilt, fear, and nervousness.

Negative reinforcement The experience of obtaining the removal of an aversive stimulus that results from engaging in a response and that leads to an increase in that response.

Negotiation A process in which groups with conflicting interests decide what each will give and take in exchange between them.

Nenko system A Japanese system of payment in which the pay an employee receives is composed of a basic wage plus merit supplements and job-level allowances.

Noise A collective term for the number of factors that can distort a message as it is transmitted from one person to another.

Norms A strong set of expectations that members of a role set have for the role occupant.

Objectivity In science, the degree to which a set of scientific findings are independent of any one person's opinion about them.

Open revolution Rejection by group members of both pivotal and peripheral norms.

Open system planning A deep organization-level intervention that helps the members of an organization devise ways to accomplish the mission of their firm in light of the demands of environmental constituency groups.

Open systems perspective The management perspective that characterizes every organization as a system that is open to the influence of the surrounding environment.

Organic structures Organism-like organization structures designed to enhance flexibility and innovation; characterized by large amounts of mutual adjustment and decentralization.

Organization design The process of diagnosing the situation that confronts a particular organization and selecting and putting in place the organization structure most appropriate for that situation.

Organization development A planned approach to interpersonal, group, intergroup, and organization-wide change that is comprehensive and long-term and under guidance of a change agent.

Organization size The number of members in an organization; its volume sales, clients, or profits; its physical capacity (e.g., a hospital's number of beds or a hotel's number of rooms); or the total financial assets that it controls.

Organization stage The stage in the information-processing cycle in which many discrete bits of information are chunked into higher-level, abstract concepts.

Organization structure The relatively stable network of interconnections or interdependencies among the people and tasks that make up an organization.

Organizational behavior A field of study aimed at predicting, explaining, understanding, and changing human behavior as it occurs in organizations.

Organizational commitment Identification with one's employer that includes the willingness to work hard on behalf of the organization and the intention to remain with the organization for an extended period of time.

Organizational effectiveness The degree to which an organization is successful in achieving its goals and objectives while at the same time ensuring its continued survival by satisfying the demands of interested parties, such as suppliers and customers.

Organizational efficiency The ratio of inputs consumed to units of output produced; minimizing the raw materials and energy consumed by the production of goods and services.

Organizational power Types of interpersonal power (reward, coercive, and legitimate power) that often derive from company policies and procedures.

Organizational productivity The amount of goods or services produced by an organization; higher productivity means that more goods and services are produced.

Ownership norms Norms in a society's culture that support or reject the private ownership of organizations and property.

Peripheral norms Group norms for which adherence is desirable but not essential.

Personal power Types of interpersonal power (expert and referent power) that are based on the possession of certain personal traits or characteristics.

Physical ability The ability to perform a task involving body movement, strength, endurance, dexterity, force, or speed.

Pivotal norms Group norms for which adherence is an absolute requirement for continued group membership.

Pooled interdependence A type of interaction in which individuals draw off of a common resource pool but do not interact with each other in any other way.

Position power A component of Fielder's contingency theory that describes the degree to which a leader can administer significant rewards and punishments to followers.

Positive reinforcement The experience of obtaining a pleasurable stimulus that results from engaging in a response and that leads to an increase in that response.

Postbureaucratic structures Extremely flexible structures that substitute various information-processing mechanisms for hierarchy and incorporate significant mutual adjustment, decentralization, and either functional or divisional departmentation among different autonomous units or allied organizations.

Power The ability to influence the conduct of others and resist unwanted influence in return.

Power distance A cross-cultural dimension that describes the degree to which the members of a society accept differences in power and status among themselves.

Prebureaucratic structures Structures used in small, simple organizations, lacking standardization, formalization, and a large amount of specialization.

Preparation A stage in the creative decision-making process in which a person accumulates information needed to solve a problem.

Prepotency The notion, arising from Maslow's theory, that higher-order needs can influence motivation only if lower-order needs are largely satisfied.

Privacy The freedom to work unobserved by others and without undue interruption.

Process consultation A shallow group-level OD intervention in which a change agent meets with a work group and helps its members examine group processes such as communication, leadership and followership, problem solving, and cooperation.

Process engineering A type of methods engineering in which specialists study the sequence of tasks required to produce a particular good or service and examine how these tasks fit together into an integrated job.

Process loss The difference between what is actually produced by a group of individuals and what the group could be expected to produce on the basis of the knowledge, skills, and abilities of its members.

Production blocking The negative effect on productivity caused by people getting in each other's way as they try to perform a group task.

Prototype One type of schema that involves a unified configuration of personal characteristics that is used to classify persons into types.

Punishment Receiving an aversive stimulus as the result of engaging in a response, which leads to a decrease in response.

Quality circles Small groups of employees who meet on company time to identify and resolve job-related problems.

Quality perspective An approach to work design in which elements of the efficiency and empowerment perspectives are combined to improve the quality of goods or services produced.

Quantitative ability A specific form of cognitive ability that deals with the understanding and application of mathematical rules and operations.

Random assignment A method of increasing the validity of a study by ensuring that each subject has an equal probability of being assigned to any one experimental condition; eliminates the selection threat.

Reasoning ability An individual's capacity to invent solutions to many different types of problems.

Reciprocal interdependence A type of interaction in which there are two-way links among individuals.

Referent power Interpersonal power based on the possession of attractive personal characteristics.

Reinforcement theory A theory of motivation that suggests that people are motivated to engage in or avoid certain behaviors because of past rewards and punishments associated with those behaviors.

Reliability The degree to which a measure of an individual, group, organizational, or environmental attribute is free from random error and thus replicable.

Reward power Interpersonal power based on the ability to control how desirable outcomes are distributed.

Rite A ceremonial activity meant to communicate particular messages or accomplish specific purposes.

Ritual A ceremonial event that occurs repeatedly and continues to reinforce key norms and values.

Role The typical and expected behaviors that characterize an individual's position in some social context.

Role ambiguity Lack of clarity surrounding expectations about a person's role in an organization.

Role analysis technique An interpersonal OD intervention of moderate depth intended to help people form and maintain effective working relationships by clarifying role expectations.

Role conflict Conflict arising from incompatible or contradictory demands facing a person who occupies a particular role.

Role custodianship A product of socialization in which a new group member adopts the means and ends associated with the role unquestioningly.

Role innovation A product of socialization in which a new group member is expected to improve on both the goals for the job and the means of achieving them.

Role occupant The current incumbent of an existing role.

Role scope The total number of expectations that exist for the person occupying a particular role.

Role set The entire group of individuals who have an interest in and expectations about the way role occupants perform their jobs.

Satisficing Settling for a decision alternative that meets some minimum standard of acceptability, as opposed to trying to maximize utility by considering all possible alternatives.

Schema Cognitive structures that group discrete bits of perceptual information in an organized fashion.

Scientific management perspective The management perspective that focuses on increasing the efficiency of production processes through scientific study.

Scientific method An objective method of expanding knowledge characterized by an endless cycle of theory building, hypothesis formation, data collection, empirical hypothesis testing, and theoretical modification.

Script A schema that involves well-known sequences of action.

Selection The process of choosing some job applicants and rejecting others based on individual differences.

Selection threat A threat to validity that exists when experimental and control groups might have differed from each other before an experimental manipulation.

Self-efficacy The judgments people make about their ability to execute courses of action required to deal with prospective situations.

Self-inventory A measure of personality characteristics that asks individuals to describe themselves by means of standardized responses to questionnaire items.

Self-managing teams Teams of employees empowered with the opportunity to determine job procedures, work assignments, membership, and so forth.

Semiautonomous work groups Groups that are subject to the management direction needed to ensure adherence to organizational policies but are otherwise responsible for managing themselves.

Sensitivity training A deep interpersonal OD intervention that focuses on developing greater sensitivity to oneself, to others, and to one's relations with others through an intense, leaderless group experience.

Sequential interdependence A type of interaction in which individuals are arrayed in a chain of one-way links.

Shaping Bringing about a desired behavior by rewarding successive approximations to that behavior.

Short-term versus long-term orientation A cross-cultural dimension that reflects the degree to which people emphasize tradition and the present, on the one hand, or innovation and the future, on the other.

Simple differentiated structure The type of prebureaucratic structure in which coordination is achieved by means of direct supervision.

Simple undifferentiated structure The type of prebureaucratic structure in which coordination is achieved solely by means of mutual adjustment.

Social density An index of crowding, typically calculated as the number of people occupying an area divided by the number of square feet in that area.

Social desirability bias The tendency for individuals responding to self-inventories to describe themselves in socially flattering ways.

Social information Information growing out of cultural norms, values, and shared opinions that shapes the way people perceive themselves, their jobs, and their organization.

Social learning theory A theory of motivation originated by Bandura that suggests that behavior is often driven by the desire of an observer to model the behavior of some other person.

Social loafing The result of the choice made by some group members to take advantage of others by doing less work, working more slowly, or in other ways contributing less to group productivity.

Social support The active provision of sympathy and caring by people in the surrounding environment.

Socialization The process by which a person acquires the social knowledge and skills necessary to assume a role.

Sociotechnical enrichment A type of work design that recognizes the importance of satisfying the needs of employees within the technical requirements of an organization's production system.

Solution verification A stage in the creative decision-making process wherein a person tests the efficacy of a proposed novel solution.

Spatial visualization An individual's capacity to mentally manipulate objects in space and time.

Special-interest committees Committees in Scandinavian industrial democracies composed of worker and manager representatives; they combine with middle management to produce yearly reports that assist works councils with the task of formulating company policies.

Specialization The division of an organization's work into jobs of reduced scope and limited variability.

Staff validity The average level of correctness of the individual-level decision recommendations made by members of a team.

Standard time analysis A time study technique in which an analyst matches the results of micromotion analysis with standard time charts to determine the average time that should be required to perform a job.

Standardization In the context of scientific measurement, the practice of ensuring that all people measure the same variables with the same instruments applied in the same manner.

Stopwatch time analysis A time study technique in which an analyst uses a stopwatch to time the sequence of motions needed to complete a job.

Story An account of past events that serves as a reminder of cultural understandings.

Stress An unpleasant emotional state resulting from the perception that a situational demand exceeds one's capacity and that it is very important to meet the demand.

Structural contingency factors Characteristics of an organization and its surrounding circumstances that influence whether its structure will contribute to organizational effectiveness.

Substitutability The extent to which other people or groups can grant access to the same critical contingencies provided by the focal person or group.

Subversive rebellion Acceptance by group members of peripheral norms but rejection of pivotal ones.

Survey feedback A shallow organization-level OD intervention intended to stimulate information sharing throughout the entire organization.

Symbol An object, action, or event to which people have assigned special meaning.

Symbolic management A process in which managers attempt to influence deep cultural norms and values by shaping the surface cultural elements that organization members use to express and transmit cultural understandings.

Target The specific focus of an OD intervention's change efforts.

Task structure A component of Fielder's contingency theory that describes the clarity of goals and means-end relationships in a group's task.

Team A type of group characterized by tight interdependence, cross-functional expertise, and differential distribution of information among members.

Team development A deep group-level extension of interpersonal sensitivity training in which a group of people who work together on a daily basis meet over an extended period to assess and modify group processes.

Team informity The average level of decision informity for a given team across many decisions.

Technology The knowledge, procedures, and equipment used in an organization to transform unprocessed resources into finished goods or services.

Temporal precedence The fact that a measured cause actually precedes a given effect in time.

Theory A set of interrelated constructs, definitions, and propositions that present a systematic view of a phenomenon by specifying relations among variables.

Theory X A managerial point of view that assumes nonmanagerial employees have little interest in attaining organizational goals and must therefore be motivated to work toward meeting the needs of the organization.

Theory Y A managerial point of view that assumes that nonmanagerial employees will readily direct behavior toward organizational goals if given the opportunity.

Third-party peacemaking A shallow OD intervention in which a change agent seeks to resolve intergroup misunderstandings by encouraging communication between or among groups.

Transaction costs Costs incurred while initiating and conducting business transactions, either within or between organizations.

Uncertainty avoidance A cross-cultural dimension that describes the degree to which people are comfortable with ambiguous situations and with the inability to predict future events with assurance.

Uncertainty reduction The lessening or eliminating of doubt about the continued availability of critical contingencies.

Unit-linking mechanism A structural approach to managing conflict and coordinating intergroup relations that works by encouraging communication among interdependent groups.

Utility maximization A process by which a decision maker selects the one alternative that leads to the highest possible payoff.

Valence The amount of satisfaction an individual anticipates receiving from a particular outcome.

Validity The degree to which a measure of an individual, group, organizational, or environmental attribute does what it is intended to do.

Verbal ability A specific type of cognitive ability that deals with the comprehension and use of language.

Verification A stage in the scientific process in which scientists assess the degree to which hypotheses based on theories match empirical data.

Vertical dyad Two persons who are related hierarchically, such as a supervisor-subordinate pair.

Vertical job enrichment A type of work design based on the idea that giving jobholders the discretion to choose job activities and outcomes will improve their satisfaction.

Vertical specialization The type of specialization in which the management of work is separated from the performance of that work, establishing a number of levels of hierarchy in the organization.

Virtual structure The type of postbureaucratic structure consisting of multiple companies specializing in different functional tasks and joined together by a computer network.

Voice The formal opportunity to complain to the organization about one's work situation.

Work design The process of deciding what specific tasks each jobholder should perform in the context of the overall work that an organization must accomplish.

Work flow grouping The grouping of people into units according to similarities in the products they make or markets they serve.

Work measurement An area of industrial engineering concerned with measuring the amount of work accomplished and developing standards for performing work of an acceptable quantity and quality.

Works council A committee of worker representatives who are elected by their peers and management representatives who are appointed by top management; this committee oversees policy formulation in Scandinavian industrial democracies.

■ Index

Name Index

Company Index

A

Adolph Coors, 26
Aetna Institute for Corporate
    Education, The, 26
Aetna Life and Casualty
    Corporation, 26, 139, 327
Alco Standard, 295
Allegheny Ludlum, 395–96
Allstate, 132
All-Weather Safety Whistle Co., 71
American Civil Liberties
    Union, 74
American Cyanamid, 35
American Express, 246, 367
American Express Financial
    Advisors (AEFA), 301–2
American Federation of Labor
    and Congress of Industrial
    Organizations (AFL-CIO), 112
American International Group
    (AIG) Insurance, 223
American Motors, 16
American Multi Cinema
    (AMC), 35
Ameritech, 42
Amoco Oil, 61
Amway, 338–39
Apple Computer, 246, 308, 326
Astra USA, 248–49
AT&T, 140, 150, 272, 337
Atlas Industrial Door, 297
Automatic Data Processing, 328
Avon, 43

B

Bell Atlantic, 49–50, 58
BellSouth, 336
Bethlehem Steel Company, 6–7
Boeing, 23, 395
Boeing Company, 110, 271–72
Bridgestone-Firestone, 257
British Telecom, 367
Burger King, 280, 310, 343

C

C. R. England, 78
California Institute of
    Technology, 70
Campbell's Soup, 112
Cannondale Corporation, 237
Career Blazers, 166
Caterpillar, 237, 257, 379
Catholic Church, 6, 10
Ceridian Corporation, 42
Chaparral Steel, 395, 417
Charles Schwab and
    Company, 317
Chase Manhattan Bank, 173, 293
Chemical Bank, 27, 173
Chicago Bulls, 250
Chrysler Corporation, 16, 112,
    131, 139, 151, 153, 205, 310,
    318–19

Chunking, 69
Clorox Company, 187
Coca-Cola, 308, 418
Colgate-Palmolive, 164, 177, 265
Comambault, 8
Commentry-Fourchambault-
    Decazeville, 8
Compaq, 177, 346
Corning Glass, 42–43, 395
CTI, 124
Cummins Engine, 150

D

Dai-Ichi Kangyo, 378
Dallas Cowboys, 77, 228
DEC, 177
Delta Airlines, 57, 272
Denny's, 343
Detroit Lions, 250
Disney, 344, 367
Doctors Hospital, 121–22
Dow Chemical, 42, 367
DuPont Chemical, 41, 57, 99, 337,
    340, 344

E

Eastman Kodak, 151, 379
Eddie Bauer, 113
Eli Lilly, 101, 246
El Poco Loco, 343
Equal Employment Opportunity
    Commission (EEOC), 249
Equitable Life Insurance, 125
Exxon, 26

F

Flagstar Companies, 343
Food Lion, 120
Ford Motor Company, 16, 131,
    140, 151, 153, 206, 263, 276,
    286, 295, 310, 312, 321, 367
French Foreign Legion, 180
Freudenberg-NOX, 152–53
Fuji Photo Film Company, 379
Fuyo, 378

G

Gaines Pet Food, 284
Gannett News, 41
Gap, The, 228
Gaylord Container
    Corporation, 41
General Dynamics
    Corporation, 29
General Electric, 2, 87, 97, 150,
    188, 191, 321, 324, 326,
    395–96
General Motors Corporation, 2,
    11, 16, 35, 131, 146, 151, 246,
    286, 310, 327–28, 340, 361
Gillette, 367
Grace Logistics Services, 245

GTE, 26, 97, 395
GVO, 328

H

Harcourt General, 166
Hardee's, 343
Harley-Davidson, 1, 3
Hewlett-Packard (HP), 111, 188,
    226, 281, 297, 335–36, 367
Home Shopping Network
    (HSN), 44
Honda, 1, 206
Honeywell, 101
HSC Security, 36
Hunsfos Paper, 376

I

I/N Tek, 208
IBM, 2, 41, 150, 177, 272, 306, 321,
    326, 328, 367, 369, 379, 397
Inland Steel, 208
Intel, 396
Internal Revenue Service
    (IRS), 57
International Business Machines.
    See IBM
International Management
    Institute, 11
Israeli Army, 53

J

J. C. Penney, 35
John Deere and Company,
    145–46
Johnson and Johnson, 73, 271–72

K

Kawasaki, 1
Kentucky Fried Chicken, 418
Kockums, Malmo, 377
Kodak, 112

L

L. L. Bean, 71, 113
L. M. Ericsson, 274
Land's End, 113
Lantech, 98
Levi Strauss, 169, 297, 317
Lockheed, 73, 151, 266
Logitech, 367

M

McDonald's Corporation, 36,
    43–44, 310, 320, 340, 367
McDonnel Douglas, 23
McNeil, 271
Malden Mills, 113
Management Recruiters, 57
Marriott Hotels, 34
Mary Kay, 338–39
MasterCard, 77

Subject Index

Personal power, 251
PERT, 8
Physical ability, 28–29
Physical conditioning, 124
Piecework plan, 97
Pivotal norm, 168–69
Placid clustered environments, 16
Placid random environments, 16
Planned change, 344
Planning, 8
Political science, 5
Pooled interdependence, 163
Position power, 232
Positive reinforcement, 85
Postbureaucratic structures, 295–97
Power
    charismatic, 249
    coercive, 248
    critical contingencies model of, 253–54
    defined, 246
    ethics of, 248
    expert, 250
    interpersonal sources of, 247–50
    legitimate, 248
    organizational, 251
    personal, 251
    politics and, 246–56
    referent, 249
    reward, 247
    structural sources of, 253–55
    third-party peacemaking and, 355
Power distance, 371–72, 389
Power imbalance, 173
Praise, supervisors' and subordinates' views of, 52
Prebureaucratic structures, 288, 308
Precedent, 168
Preparation, 70
Prepotency, 82
Privacy, 114–15
Procedural justice, 181
Process consultation, 353–54
Process engineering, 132–36
Process loss, 165, 194
Production, flexible cell, 313
Production
    blocking, 194
    continuous process, 312
    mass, 312
    small-batch, 311
Productivity
    group, 189, 193–203. *See also* Group productivity
    norms, cohesiveness and, 198–201
    organizational, 304
    technology and, 77
Professional, 281
Professional development seminars, 73

Professionalization, 280
Profit-sharing plans, 99
Prototype, 55
Psychology
    clinical, 4
    experimental, 4
    industrial, 4
    social, 5
Punishment, 86

Q

Quality
    as "job one," 276
    perspective, 154–55
Quality circles (QCs), 151–52, 386
Quantitative ability, 30

R

Random assignment, 411–12
Random socialization, 178
RAT. *See* Role analysis technique
Rational decision-making model, 60–64
Realistic job previews (RJPs), 125
Reasoning ability, 31
Recall, 56–57
Reciprocal interdependence, 164
Reengineering, 27–28
Referent power, 249
Relaxation techniques, 124
Reliability, 402
Repetitive stress injuries RSIs), 138
Representative groups, 265
Resource(s)
    allocation, conflict and, 258–59
    control, 254
    critical, 262–63
Restructuring, negotiation and, 260–66
Retention rates, employee and customer, 105
Return on investment (ROI), 19
Reward power, 247
Rites, 338–39
Ritual, 339, 388
Robotics, 153–54
Role(s)
    defined, 165
    elements of work, 166
    group-maintenance, 194
    organization, 119–20
    perceptual accuracy of, 90–93
    socialization and, 165–79
Role ambiguity, 119–20
Role analysis technique (RAT), 350–52
Role conflict, 119–20, 170
Role custodianship, 176–77
Role episode, 170–71
Role innovation, 177
Role occupant, 170
Role overload, 120
Role scope, 119–20

Role-sending message, 170
Role set, 170
Role underload, 120
Rules, 280

S

Sabotage, 138
Sales value of production (SVP), 100
Satisfaction, workplace, 105–29
Satisficing, 67
Scalar chain, 9
Scalar principle, 11
Scanlon Plan, 100
Schema, 55, 58
Scholastic Aptitude Test (SAT), 32
Science, purposes of, 398–400
Scientific management, 6–7, 132
Scientific method, 347, 398
Scientific process, critical thinking and, 397–404
Script, 55
Selection
    employee, 25–26
    threat, 409
Self-contained tasks, 264
Self-efficacy
    behavior and, 89
    theory, 80
Self-managing teams, 152–53
Self-reinforcement, 88
Semiautonomous work groups, 147–48, 376, 378
Sensitivity training, 44, 352–53
Sent role, 170
Sequential interdependence, 163
Sequential socialization, 177
Serial socialization, 178
Service technologies, Thompson's, 313–15
Shaping, 87
Shared mental model, 208–9
Shared norms, 276
Short-term vs. long-term orientation, 372–73, 389
Sick-building syndrome, 114
Simple differentiated structure, 289
Simple undifferentiated structure, 288
Simultaneous structures, 293
Skill(s)
    standardization, 275, 281
    professional, 281
    training, 122
Slack resources, 264
Small-batch production, 311
Social density, 114
Social information, 341–42
Social information processing, 150
Socialization, 174–79, 281
    in foreign legion, 180
    roles, 165–79
    strategies, 177
Social justice, 248